Historical Dictionary of INDONESIA

by

ROBERT CRIBB

Asian Historical Dictionaries, No. 9

The Scarecrow Press, Inc.
Metuchen, N.J., & London
1992

ASIAN HISTORICAL DICTIONARIES
Edited by Jon Woronoff

1. *Vietnam,* by William J. Duiker. 1989
2. *Bangladesh,* by Craig Baxter and Syedur Rahman. 1989
3. *Pakistan,* by Shahid Javed Burki. 1991
4. *Jordan,* by Peter Gubser. 1991
5. *Afghanistan,* by Ludwig W. Adamec. 1991
6. *Laos,* by Martin Stuart-Fox and Mary Kooyman. 1992
7. *Singapore,* by K. Mulliner and Lian-The Mulliner. 1991
8. *Israel,* by Bernard Reich. 1992
9. *Indonesia,* by Robert Cribb. 1992

British Cataloguing-in-Publication data available

Library of Congress Cataloging-in-Publication Data

Cribb, R. B.
Historical dictionary of Indonesia / Robert Cribb.
p. cm. — (Asian historical dictionaries ; no. 9)
Includes bibliographical references.
ISBN 0-8108-2542-2 (alk. paper)
1. Indonesia—History—Dictionaries. I. Title. II. Series.
DS633.C75 1992
959.8′003—dc20 92-19210

Manufactured in the United States of America

Printed on acid-free paper

CONTENTS

EDITOR'S FOREWORD

Indonesia is Asia's third largest country in both population and area, a sprawling tropical archipelago of some 180 million people from hundreds of ethnic groups with a complex and turbulent history. One of Asia's newly industrializing countries, it is poised to become a major economic powerhouse of the region. The twin language barriers of Indonesian and Dutch (the language of Indonesia's former colonial rulers), however, make reliable information on the country's past and present often difficult to find.

The *Historical Dictionary of Indonesia* is an essential reference work for all who need to find their way through the archipelago's tangled history, both beginners looking for an introduction to this fascinating and important country and specialists wanting a convenient compendium of information. The *Dictionary* covers people, places, and organizations, as well as economics, culture, and political thought from Indonesia's ancient history up until the recent past in over 800 clear and succinct entries. Many of the entries direct the reader to further sources of information listed in the unusually comprehensive Bibliography.

Robert Cribb is a specialist on Indonesia and has written widely about its history and politics on the basis of both archival research and fieldwork in the country itself. His enthusiasm for Indonesia and its people and his pleasure in writing about them are clear from these pages. Dr. Cribb presently teaches Southeast Asian history at the University of Queensland in St. Lucia, Australia.

Jon Woronoff
Series Editor

ACKNOWLEDGMENTS

A work such as this is indebted more than any other to the community of scholars, past and present, who write and speak on Indonesia. During the years it has taken to write the *Historical Dictionary of Indonesia,* numerous colleagues have helped me in countless ways, with ideas and information, encouragement, and warning. In particular, however, I would like to thank my colleagues, the staff and students of the Department of Pacific and Southeast Asian History in the Research School of Pacific Studies at the Australian National University for their cheery help and friendly advice. It was they who provided the first critical assessments of this *Dictionary* as it began to take shape, and they formed a model for part of the audience for whom I was trying to write. I also benefited immensely from the scholarly collegiality of a year at the Netherlands Institute for Advanced Study in Wassenaar and the efficiency of Mrs. Young and the library staff. I benefited from the collegial support of the History Department at Queensland University. I also visited Indonesia twice during the preparation of the volume and I owe a further debt to the many people there who pointed out and filled in gaps in my knowledge and coverage. A number of people have made a special contribution by reading and commenting on parts of the manuscript. Colin Brown, Jane Drakard, Tony Reid and Susan Cribb, as well as Krishna Sen and Gerrit Knaap, helped with the long task of balancing the selection of topics, streamlining the prose, and ironing out errors. My mother, Joan Cribb, checked the scientific nomenclature. And throughout all of this, my wife Susan remained tolerant and encouraging. To her, my deepest thanks.

PREFACE AND GUIDE TO USE

The *Historical Dictionary of Indonesia* is intended primarily as a convenient reference tool for those whose studies or professional activities demand ready access to reliable information on Indonesia's history up to the recent past. Such users, I have assumed, will be better served by a wide range of brief entries on places, organizations, terms, people, and products than by longer entries on fewer topics. It is important to point out that this *Dictionary* is not a standard history of Indonesia consumed, as it were, by its index; the inclusion of entries and the space devoted to them is intended to reflect the probable reference needs of readers rather than to imply any judgment about the relative importance of topics. The proper place for such judgments is a standard narrative history, and readers will find a number of such works listed in the Bibliography.

This *Historical Dictionary* covers the entire area now included in the Republic of Indonesia; it thus deals with some areas, such as Irian Jaya (West New Guinea) and East, formerly Portuguese, Timor, whose historical connections with the rest of the archipelago were weak for long periods, and excludes other areas, such as the Malay peninsula and Mindanao, whose connections have from time to time been strong but which are covered by the forthcoming volumes in this series on Malaysia and the Philippines. Because the focus is Indonesia, and not simply the archipelago, I have given greatest attention to historical information about the present, especially as it concerns the institutions of the modern Indonesian state. The emphasis thus is on political and economic history and on the period since 1800; no attempt has been made to deal comprehensively with the many traditional social institutions and cultural forms of the archipelago or to insert new data which became available in the later stages of production except where this shed especial light on existing entries.

Since entries are not organized chronologically, a basic chronology, with cross references, has been provided at the start of the volume. As well as providing convenient reference, however, this *Dictionary* is intended to guide those unfamiliar with Indonesia through the country's history by means of cross-references. I have chosen to use these cross-references to order Indonesian history in two ways not generally well served by standard histories. First, I have endeavored to chart as carefully as possible the evolving form of, and changing relationships between, major institutions, both public and private. While Indonesian institutions have often been judged to be weak, there is a growing recognition of the role they have played in transforming Indonesian society and a corresponding need has thus arisen to pinpoint structural continuities and discontinuities between them.

Second, I have attempted to outline the structure of ideas which have been voiced on the nature of Indonesian society. There has never been a consensus, either amongst Indonesians or amongst foreign scholars, on the appropriate intellectual tools to be used in analyzing Indonesia, and a consequence of this is that a wide variety of terms and concepts remains in circulation. I believe that this *Dictionary* will perform a valuable function for students if it can locate such terms and concepts in relation to each other and within their respective broader theoretical frameworks. A consequence of attention to these themes is a rather selective approach to the inclusion of individuals in a single-volume dictionary. I have chosen to deal with many political figures in context, that is under the rubric of the organization in which they were active. Readers will here find their dates of birth and death (where known) and other details of their careers. In general only those individuals of unusual interest or importance, those whose careers straddled a number of organizations and historical periods, and those important for their ideas (in a broad sense) are treated separately.

In the course of Indonesian history, both Indonesians and Dutch have made extensive use of both abbreviations and acronyms, words formed by a combination of initials and/or word fragments which are then used and pronounced as a single word (see also ETYMOLOGY). The Muslim political party Masyumi was formally the Majelis Syuro Muslimin Indonesia, but was known almost invariably by its acronymic title. Such words present an especial problem in a volume of this kind. In general I have followed the following rule: where the acronymic origin of a word has become obscure, as with Masyumi or Fretilin, the word is spelled, as here, in capitals and lower case and the main entry will be found under this name. Where an acronym is more clearly an abbreviation, such as BAPPENAS or KOPKAMTIB, it is spelled in capitals and its primary entry is under the full name. Where cross-reference is made from other entries to such organizations using (q.v.), the reader not familiar with the organization's full title will find it in the List of Abbreviations and Acronyms.

A final problem is the use of contentious terms. Not all people agree, for instance, that the territory immediately to the west of Papua New Guinea should be called Irian. In selecting the term under which entries should be made, I have endeavored in general to follow the best established usage, and no particular political judgment is intended by this.

This *Historical Dictionary* concludes with a substantial Bibliography, classified by subject and intended as a guide to further reading. A list of this size cannot include more than a fraction of what has been written on Indonesia. Works selected, therefore, are mainly in English and have been chosen either as up-to-date sources in their own right, or as useful points-of-entry to a broader literature, or as classics. As a further guide to readers, numbers in square brackets [ ] within or following entries in the *Dictionary* section refer to relevant items in the Bibliography.

Spelling: All works on Indonesian history require an explanation of spelling. I have preferred on the whole to enter proper names and terms in their modern Indonesian spelling (*ejaan yang disempurnakan,* EYD, see INDONESIAN LANGUAGE), and to use the contemporary Indonesian terminology and spelling for place names, thus Kalimantan and Sulawesi, not Borneo and Celebes. For Java and Sumatra, however, I have used the common English spellings rather than Jawa and Sumatera.

Personal names, however, present a vexed problem for which there is no simple solution. Throughout the colonial era, Indonesian names were rendered into Roman script using Dutch spelling conventions, most notable of which are the use of *tj* for English *ch, j* for *y, oe* for *u, dj* for *j,* and *sj* for *sh*. The Indonesian spelling reform of 1973, which brought most of these spellings closer to English language usage, was intended to apply to personal names as well as to the language in general. In practice, however, many people have preferred to retain or even adopt the old style spelling for their personal names. This has led to the unusual situation in Indonesia today where the name of a figure such as Tjokroaminoto, who knew nothing but the old spelling, is commonly spelled Cokroaminoto, while contemporary political figures, such as Benny Moerdani, use old style names. Western scholarship, if anything, prefers to reverse this convention, preserving pre-1973 names in old form and rigorously insisting on new spelling for contemporary figures. The situation, however, is in flux, with some elements of the old spelling (such as *ch* rather than the modern *kh*) prevailing in most circumstances while others have virtually disappeared (*j,* for instance, being almost universally replaced by *y*). No spelling convention, it is clear, can be consistent and satisfactory to all.

I have adopted a compromise position. In general all names are spelled using the modern conventions. I have, however, retained the use of *tj* and *ch,* since it is these more than any other which continue to have a sentimental attraction for Indonesians and for scholars working on Indonesia. The names of Indonesian Chinese are given in their usual unmodernized form; since there was no standard rendering of Chinese characters into Indonesian or Dutch spelling, conversion of Chinese names into EYD or into their Pinyin equivalent would make them unrecognizable in many cases.

The spelling of Dutch also underwent several reforms shortly after World War II but since most Dutch influence was felt before 1942, I have preferred the older convention for formal institutions, thus Nederlandsch, not Nederlands, Regeering not Regering, and Indisch, not Indies, though here this has occasionally meant imposing the conventions of the late nineteenth century on the far less regulated language of the seventeenth and eighteenth centuries. The spelling of Dutch proper names has, however, not been altered. In this lexicographical jungle, I wish the reader well.

Dr. Robert Cribb
Department of History
University of Queensland
St. Lucia, Australia

INTRODUCTION TO INDONESIA

Indonesia is an archipelagic nation lying between the Asian and Australian continents and between the Indian and Pacific Oceans. It straddles the Equator, lying between 6°08′ N and 11°15′ S and between 94°45′ W and 141°05′ E, and shares land borders with Papua New Guinea on the island of New Guinea (Irian) and with Malaysia on the island of Borneo (Kalimantan), and sea borders with India, Thailand, Malaysia, Singapore, Vietnam, the Philippines, the republic of Belau (Palau), Papua New Guinea and Australia. Its annexation of the Portuguese overseas territory of East Timor has not received full international recognition. There are three official time zones, seven-to-nine hours ahead of Greenwich mean time.

The country is 2,027,087 km^2 in area, plus 3,166,163 million km^2 in territorial waters and is 5100 km long on its east-west axis and 1888 km broad on its north-south axis. It consists of approximately 13,669 islands the size of a tennis court or larger; the exact number changes frequently due to siltation and volcanic eruptions. About 6,000 islands are named and 1,000 are inhabited. The islands are customarily grouped into four regions: the Greater Sundas (Sumatra, Java, Kalimantan, and Sulawesi); the Lesser Sundas or Nusatenggara (the chain of islands running from Bali eastwards to Timor); the Moluccas, or Maluku, between Sulawesi and Irian; and Irian. Over 80% of Indonesia's land area is accounted for by its five largest islands, Kalimantan, Sumatra, Irian, Sulawesi, and Java.

The Greater Sunda Islands and part of the Nusatenggara sit on the Sunda shelf, a southeastern extension of the Asian continental plate partly covered by shallow seas. A zone of volcanic activity along the southern rim of this shelf has created a chain of volcanoes which forms the spine of Sumatra and Java. Irian sits on the Sahul shelf, a geologically stable extension of the Australian continental plate. Between these two shelves, Maluku is an area of extreme geological instability, with volcanic mountains and deep sea trenches. Australia is still moving north and the mountains of Irian rise 4 to 5 cm per century. The highest is the snowcapped Puncak Jaya in Irian at 5,030 meters.

As Indonesia lies in the tropics, temperatures are determined primarily by the time of day and by elevation. The maximum recorded temperature range in Jakarta is 18°-to-36°C. There are permanent, but receding, snowfields in the Maoke mountains of Irian. Rainfall is generally heavy, with all of Kalimantan, most of Sumatra and Java, eastern and southern Sulawesi, Maluku, and Irian receiving an average annual rainfall of 200 cm or more. Timor and Sumba, which lie in Australia's rain shadow, receive 100-to-150 cm per year. In recent times it has been recognized that the El Niño Southern Oscillation regularly changes rainfall patterns to produce a pronounced dry season in much of the archipelago.

High temperatures and heavy rainfall generally work to encourage chemical weathering which impoverishes tropical soils. In much of Indonesia, especially Kalimantan, this process was sidestepped by the growth of tropical rain forest, rooted in a shallow layer of topsoil from which nutrients are rapidly recirculated. Where this rain forest layer is lost, soil degradation has been rapid except where replenished by volcanic eruption. Basic andesitic volcanic materials ejected from volcanoes in Java and West Sumatra are responsible for the high levels of fertility in those regions. There are approximately 829 active volcanoes in Indonesia today. Except in Kalimantan and Irian, there are few long rivers.

Indonesia's population is predominantly mixed Austronesian-Austromelanesian in origin, with the Austromelanesian component becoming stronger in the east. There has been considerable admixture of Chinese and Arab elements over the centuries and there is a large Chinese minority. The population is estimated at 186,000,000, of whom the majority live on Java. Islam is the principal religion, but there are significant Christian (Protestant and Catholic), Hindu, and Buddhist minorities.

Since independence in 1945, Indonesia has been a Republic. The country's first constitution envisaged a strong executive presidency, but this was replaced after a few weeks with a system of parliamentary democracy. The 1945 Constitution was restored in 1957. Under the terms of Indonesia's peace settlement with the colonial Dutch in 1949, a federal system was briefly introduced, but since 1950 the country has been a unitary state, divided (now) into 27 provinces, including three 'special territories', Aceh, Yogyakarta, and the capital Jakarta. The official language is Indonesian (*Bahasa Indonesia*). The national flag is two horizontal bars, red over white.

At independence Indonesia was primarily a producer of raw materials, including oil, tin, and other mining products as well as rubber, coffee, tea, and other plantation products. Many efforts have been made since then to diversify the economy, with some success. In 1986 it was estimated that 68% of the population worked in the agricultural sector, 23% in industry and commerce, and 10% in services. Japan is Indonesia's largest trading partner, followed by the United States and Singapore. The United States and Japan are also major investors in the country, but there is also a large government-owned sector of the economy. Average per capita income is US$500. The currency is the rupiah.

Although the first human settlement in the archipelago has been dated from 1.9 million years ago, the ancestors of most modern Indonesians arrived from the north from about 3000 B.C. Hindu and Buddhist kingdoms emerged in many parts of the western archipelago from the 5th Century A.D. From the 14th to 17th Centuries many regions converted to Islam. The wealth of the spice islands (Maluku) drew European traders to the archipelago from the 16th Century and amongst these the Dutch gradually established preeminence, though it was not until the 19th Century that the colonial rule was firmly established in most of the region. A nationalist movement emerged in the 20th Century and one of its leaders, Sukarno, declared independence in 1945 at the end of a 3-½ year interregnum of Japanese occupation. Four-and-a-half years of war and negotiation followed before the Dutch finally transferred sovereignty to the Indonesian Republic. The parliamentary governments of the 1950s were plagued by regional dissent, administrative breakdown, and rising political tensions, and in 1957 Sukarno began to introduce a more authoritarian system known as Guided Democracy. Tensions, however, continued to mount, especially between the Communist party on the one hand and the army and Muslim groups on the other. In 1965 an ambiguous coup in Jakarta precipitated a massacre of Communists, the overthrow of Sukarno, and the installation of military rule under Suharto. The so-called New Order has presided over a dramatic improvement in most economic indicators, but an apparently increasing gap between rich and poor.

ABBREVIATIONS AND ACRONYMS

ABRI, Angkatan Bersenjata Republik Indonesia (q.v.), Armed Forces of the Republic of Indonesia.

AD, Angkatan Darat, Army (q.v.).

ADITLA, Associação Democrática para Integração Timor-Leste con Australia (q.v.), Democratic Association for the Integration of East Timor and Australia.

AH, anno hijrae, Muslim year. See CALENDARS.

AJ, anno Javanicae, Javanese year. See CALENDARS.

ALRI, Angkatan Laut Republik Indonesia, Navy (q.v.) of the Republic of Indonesia.

AMS, Algemene Middelbare School, General Secondary School. See EDUCATION.

ANETA, Algemene Nieuws en Telegraaf Agentschap, General News and Telegraph Agency. See NEWS AGENCIES.

ANP, Acção Nacional Populár (q.v.), National People's Action.

APODETI, Associação Populár Democrática Timorense (q.v.), Timorese Popular Democratic Association.

APRIS, Angkatan Perang Republik Indonesia Serikat, Armed Forces of the Federal Republic of Indonesia. See ARMY.

ASDT, Associação Social Democrática Timorense, Timorese Social Democratic Association. See FRETILIN.

ASEAN, Association of Southeast Asian Nations (q.v.).

ASPRI, Asisten Presiden Republik Indonesia. Assistants to the President of the Republic of Indonesia. See MALARI.

AURI, Angkatan Udara Republik Indonesia, Air Force (q.v.) of the Republic of Indonesia.

BABINSA, Bintara Pembina Desa, NCOs (noncommissioned officers) for Village Development. See DWIFUNGSI.

BAKIN, Badan Koordinasi Intelijen Negara (q.v.), State Intelligence Coordinating Agency.

BAKORSTANAS, Badan Koordinasi Bantuan Pemantapan Stabilitas Nasional (q.v.), Coordinating Body to Assist in Maintaining National Security.

BAPERKI, Badan Permusyawaratan Kewarganegaraan Indonesia (q.v.), Consultative Body on Indonesian Citizenship.

BAPPENAS, Badan Perencanaan Pembangunan Nasional (q.v.), National Development Planning Board.

BB, Binnenlandsch Bestuur (q.v.), lit. administration of the interior, the European bureaucracy of the Netherlands Indies.

BBI, Barisan Buruh Indonesia, Indonesian Labor Front. See LABOR UNIONS.

BFO, Bijeenkomst voor Federale Overleg, Meeting for Federal Consultation. See FEDERALISM.

BIMAS, Bimbingan Massal, mass guidance. See GREEN REVOLUTION.

BKKBN, Badan Koordinasi Keluarga Berencana Nasional, National Family Planning Coordinating Body. See FAMILY PLANNING.

BKR, Badan Keamanan Rakyat, People's Security Organization. See ARMY.

BKS, Badan Kerja Sama (q.v.), Cooperative Bodies.

BNI, Bank Negara Indonesia, Indonesian National Bank. See BANKING.

BPK, Badan Pemeriksa Keuangan, State Audit Board. See CONSTITUTIONS.

BPM, Bataafsche Petroleum Maatschappij, Batave Petroleum Company (now Shell Petroleum, N.V.). See 'KONINKLIJKE'; OIL.

BPS, Badan Pendukung Sukarnoisme (q.v.), Body to Support Sukarnoism.

BPS, Biro Pusat Statistik, Central Statistical Bureau. See STATISTICS.

BPUPKI, Badan Penyelidik Usaha Persiapan Kemerdekaan Indonesia (q.v.), Investigatory Body for Preparatory Work for Indonesian Independence.

BTC, Banking and Trading Corporation. See STATE ENTERPRISES.

BTI, Barisan Tani Indonesia (q.v.), Indonesian Peasants' Front.

BULOG, Badan Urusan Logistik Nasional (q.v.), National Logistical Supply Organization.

CCP, Chinese Communist Party. See CHINA, Relations with.

CONEFO, Conference of the New Emerging Forces. See NEKOLIM.

CSIS, Centre for Strategic and International Studies (q.v.).

DEKON, Deklarasi Ekonomi, Economic Declaration. See GUIDED ECONOMY.

DEPLU, Departemen Luar Negeri, Department of Foreign Affairs. See FOREIGN POLICY.

DGI, Dewan Gereja Indonesia, Indonesian Council of Churches. See PROTESTANTISM.

DI, Darul Islam (q.v.), 'House of Islam'.

DIY, Daerah Istimewa Yogyakarta, Special Territory of Yogyakarta. See YOGYAKARTA.

DKI, Daerah Khusus Ibukota, Special Capital Territory. See JAKARTA.

DPA, Dewan Pertimbangan Agung (q.v.), Supreme Advisory Council.

DPN, Dewan Pertahanan Negara (q.v.), State Defence Council.

DPR, Dewan Perwakilan Rakyat (q.v.), People's Representative Council;-D, Daerah, Regional; -GR, Gotong Royong, Mutual Self-help; -S, Sementara, Provisional.

DRET, Democratic Republic of East Timor (q.v.).

Drs, Doctorandus. See TITLES.

DVG, Dienst voor Volksgezondheid, Public Health Service. See HEALTH.

EB, Europeesch Bestuur, European Administration. See BINNENLANDSCH BESTUUR.

ELS, Europeesche Lagere School, European Lower School. See EDUCATION.

EYD, Ejaan Yang Disempurnakan, Perfected Spelling. See INDONESIAN LANGUAGE.

FALINTIL, Forças Armadas de Libertação Nacional de Timor, Armed Forces for the National Liberation of Timor. See FRETILIN.

FBSI, Federasi Buruh Seluruh Indonesia, All-Indonesia Federation of Labor. See LABOR UNIONS.

FDR, Front Demokrasi Rakyat (q.v.), People's Democratic Front.

FOSKO, Forum Studi dan Komunikasi. See PETITION OF FIFTY.

FRETILIN (q.v.), Frente Revolucionária do Timor Leste Independente, Revolutionary Front for an Independent East Timor.

G-30-S, Gerakan Tiga Puluh September, September 30th Movement. See GERAKAN SEPTEMBER TIGA PULUH.

GANEFO, Games of the New Emerging Forces. See NEKOLIM.

GAPI, Gabungan Politik Indonesia (q.v.), Indonesian Political Federation.

GBHN, Garis Besar Haluan Negara, Broad Outlines of State Policy. See MAJELIS PERMUSYAWARATAN RAKYAT.

GERINDO, Gerakan Rakyat Indonesia (q.v.), Indonesian People's Movement.

GERWANI, Gerakan Wanita Indonesia (q.v.), Indonesian Women's Movement.

GESTAPU, Gerakan September Tiga Puluh (q.v.), September 30th Movement.

GHS, Geneeskundige Hogeschool, Medical School. See EDUCATION.

GIKI, Gabungan Indo Untuk Kesatuan Indonesia, Indo Association for Indonesian Unity. See INDO-EUROPEANS.

GOLKAR (q.v.), Golongan Karya, Functional Groups.

HANKAM, (Departemen) Pertahanan dan Keamanan, (Department of) Defence and Security. See ANGKATAN BERSENJATA REPUBLIK INDONESIA.

HANSIP, Pertahanan Sipil, Civil Defence or village guards. See ANGKATAN BERSENJATA REPUBLIK INDONESIA.

HBS, Hogere Burger Scholen, Higher Civil Schools. See EDUCATION.

HCS, Hollandsch-Chineesche Scholen, Dutch Chinese Schools. See EDUCATION.

HIR, Herziene Inlandsch Reglement, Revised Native Regulations. See LAW.

HIS, Hollandsch-Inlandsche School, Dutch Native School. See EDUCATION.

HKTI, Himpunan Kerukunan Tani Indonesia, Association of Indonesian Peasant Leagues. See LABOR UNIONS.

HMI, Himpunan Mahasiswa Islam (q.v.), Muslim Students Association.

HNSI, Himpunan Nelayan Seluruh Indonesia, All-Indonesia Fishermen's Association. See LABOR UNIONS.

HVK, Hoge Vertegenwoordiger van de Kroon, High Representative of the Crown. See GOVERNOR-GENERAL

IAIN, Institut Agama Islam Negeri, State Islamic Religious Institute. See EDUCATION.

IEV, Indo-Europeesch Verbond, Indo-European Union. See INDO-EUROPEANS.

IGGI, Inter-Governmental Group on Indonesia (q.v.).

INGI, International Non-Governmental Group on Indonesia. See INTER-GOVERNMENTAL GROUP ON INDONESIA.

IPEDA, Iuran Pembangunan Daerah, Regional Development Tax. See LAND RENT and TAXATION.

IPKI, Ikatan Pendukung Kemerdekaan Indonesia (q.v.), League of the Supporters of Indonesian Independence.

IPTN, Industri Pesawat Terbang Nurtanio [now Nusantara] Aircraft Industry. See AIR SERVICES.

Ir, Ingenieur. See TITLES.

ISDV, Indische Sociaal-Democratische Vereeniging (q.v.), Indies Social Democratic Association

JABOTABEK, Jakarta-Bogor-Tanggerang-Bekasi. See JAKARTA.

Kabir, kapitalis birokrat, bureaucratic capitalist. See CLASS ANALYSIS.

KAMI, Kesatuan Aksi Mahasiswa Indonesia (q.v.), Indonesian Students' Action Front.

KAPPI, Kesatuan Aksi Pemuda dan Pelajar Indonesia, Indonesian Youth and School Students Action Front. See KESATUAN AKSI MAHASISWA INDONESIA.

KASI, Kesatuan Aksi Sarjana Indonesia, Indonesian Graduates' Action Front. See KOMANDO AKSI SARJANA INDONESIA.

KNI, Komite Nasional Indonesia (q.v.), Indonesian National Committee.

KNIL, Koninklijk Nederlands-Indisch Leger (q.v.), Royal Netherlands Indies Army

KNILM, Koninklijk Nederlands-Indische Luchtzaartmaatschappij, Royal Netherlands Indies Air Company. See AIR SERVICES.

KNIP, Komite Nasional Indonesia Pusat (q.v.), Central Indonesian National Committee.

KNPI, Komite Nasional Pemuda Indonesia (q.v.), Indonesian National Youth Committee.

KODAM, Komando Daerah Militer, Regional Military Command. See DEFENCE POLICY; DWIFUNGSI.

KOGA, Komando Siaga, Readiness Command. See KOMANDO OPERASI TERTINGGI.

KOGAM, Komando Ganyang Malaysia, Crush Malaysia Command. See KOMANDO OPERASI TERTINGGI.

KOKAR, Korps Karyawan, Employees' Corps. See KORPS PEGAWAI REPUBLIK INDONESIA.

KOPASSANDHA, Komando Pasukan Sandi Yudha, Secret Warfare Commando Unit. See KOMANDO PASUKAN KHUSUS.

KOPASSUS, Komando Pasukan Khusus (q.v.), Special Commando Unit.

KOPKAMTIB, Komando Operasi Pemulihan Keamanan dan Ketertiban (q.v.), Operational Command for the Restoration of Security and Order.

KORPRI, Korps Pegawai Republik Indonesia (q.v.), Corp of Civil Servants of the Republic of Indonesia.

KOSGORO (q.v.), Koperasi Serba Guna Gotong Royong, All-Purpose Cooperative for Gotong Royong.

KOSTRAD (q.v.), Komando Cadangan Strategis Angkatan Darat, Army Strategic Reserve.

KOTA, Klibur Oan Timur Aswain (q.v.), Popular Association of Monarchists of Timor.

KOTI, Komando Operasi Tertinggi (q.v.), Supreme Operational Command

KOTOE, Komando Tertinggi Operasi Ekonomi, Supreme Operational Command for the Economy. See DWIFUNGSI.

KOWILHAN, Komando Wilayah Pertahanan, Regional Defence Commands. See DEFENCE POLICY.

KPM, Koninklijke Paketvaart Maatschappij (q.v.), Royal Packetship Company.

KRIS, Kesatuan Raayat Indonesia Semenanjung, Union of Indonesian People of the Peninsula.

KUHAP, Kitab Undang-undang Acara Pidana, Procedural Code for Criminal Law. See LAW.

KUHP, Kitab Undang-undang Hukum Pidana, Criminal Code. See LAW.

LBH, Lembaga Bantuan Hukum, Legal Aid Bureau. See LEGAL AID.

LEKRA, Lembaga Kebudayaan Rakyat (q.v.), Institute of People's Culture.

LKB, Lembaga Kesadaran Berkonstitusi, Institute for Constitutional Awareness. See PETITION OF FIFTY.

LKBN, Lembaga Kantor Berita Nasional, National News Agency Institute. See ANTARA.

LKBN, Lembaga Keluarga Berencana Nasional, National Family Planning Institute. See FAMILY PLANNING.

LKMD, Lembaga Ketahanan Masyarakat Desa, Institute for Village Community Resilience. See DESA.

LMD, Lembaga Musyawarah Desa, Village Consultative Council. See DESA.

MAHMILLUB, Mahkamah Militer Luar Biasa (q.v.), Extraordinary Military Tribunal.

MALARI (q.v.), Malapetaka 15 Januari, Disaster of 15 January.

MANIKEBU, Manifes Kebudayaan (q.v.), Cultural Manifesto.

MANIPOL, Manifesto Politik (q.v.), Political Manifesto.

MAPHILINDO (q.v.), Malaya, Philippines, Indonesia.

MASYUMI (q.v.), Majelis Syuro Muslimin Indonesia, Consultative Council of Indonesian Muslims.

MIAI, Majelis Islam A'laa Indonesia (q.v.), Supreme Islamic Council of Indonesia.

MKGR, Musyawarah Kekeluargaan Gotong Royong, Council for Familial Self-Help. See GOLKAR.

MONAS, Monumen Nasional, National Monument. See JAKARTA.

MPR (S), Majelis Permusyawaratan Rakyat (q.v.) (Sementara), (Provisional) People's Deliberative Assembly.

Mr, Meester in de Rechten. See TITLES.

MULO, Meer Uitgebreide Lagere Onderwijs, Broader Lower Education. See EDUCATION.

NASAKOM (q.v.), Nasionalisme, Agama, Komunisme, Nationalism, Religion, Communism

NEFIS, Netherlands Forces Intelligence Service. See POLITIEK INLICHTINGEN DIENST.

NEFO, New Emerging Forces. See NEKOLIM.

NEKOLIM (q.v.), Neo-Kolonialis, Kolonialis dan Imperialis, Neocolonialists, Colonialists, and Imperialists.

NHM, Nederlandsche Handel Maatschappij (q.v.), Netherlands Trading Company.

NIAS, Nederlandsch-Indische Artsenschool, Netherlands Indies Physicians' School. See HEALTH.

NICA, Netherlands Indies Civil Administration (q.v.).

NII, Negara Islam Indonesia. See DARUL ISLAM.

NIROM, Nederlandsch-Indische Radio Omroep Maatschappij, Netherlands Indies Radio Broadcasting Company. See RADIO.

NIT, Negara Indonesia Timur (q.v.), State of East Indonesia.

NSB, Nationaal-Socialistische Beweging, (Dutch) National Socialist Movement.

NTB, Nusatenggara Barat, Western Lesser Sundas.

NTT, Nusatenggara Timur, Eastern Lesser Sundas.

NU, Nahdatul Ulama (q.v.), Revival of the Religious Scholars.

OLDEFO, Old Established Forces. See NEKOLIM.

OPM, Organisasi Papua Merdeka (q.v.), Free Papua Movement.

OPSUS, Operasi Khusus (q.v.), Special Operations.

ORBA, Orde Baru, New Order (q.v.).

ORI, Oeang [i.e. Uang] Republik Indonesia, Currency (q.v.) of the Indonesian Republic.

ORMAS, Organisasi Massa (q.v.), mass organizations.

OSVIA, Opleidingsschool voor Inlandsche Ambtenaren, Training School for Native Civil Servants. See EDUCATION.

PAI, Persatuan Arab Indonesia, Indonesian Arab Union. See ARABS.

PANGESTU (q.v.), Paguyuban Ngèsti Tunggal, Association for Striving towards Harmony with God.

PARAS, Partai Rakyat Sosialis, Socialist People's Party. See PARTAI SOSIALIS.

PARI, Partai Republik Indonesia, Party of the Indonesian Republic. See TAN MALAKA.

PARINDRA, Partai Indonesia Raya (q.v.), Greater Indonesia Party.

PARKINDO, Partai Kristen Indonesia (q.v.), Indonesian Christian Party.

PARMUSI, Partai Muslimin Indonesia (q.v.), Indonesian Muslims' Party.

PARSI, Partai Sosialis Indonesia, Indonesian Socialist Party. See PARTAI SOSIALIS.

PARTINDO, Partai Indonesia (q.v.), Indonesia Party.

PBI, Partai Buruh Indonesia (q.v.), Indonesian Labor Party.

PBI, Persatuan Bangsa Indonesia (q.v.), Association of the Indonesian People.

PDHB, Parisada Dharma Hindu Bali, now Parisada Hindu Dharma. See HINDUISM.

PDI, Partai Demokrasi Indonesia (q.v.), Indonesian Democratic Party.

PELNI, Perusahaan Pelayaran Nasional Indonesia, Indonesian National Shipping Company. See SHIPPING.

PEPUSKA, Pemilikan Pusat Kapal-Kapal, Central Shipowning Authority. See SHIPPING.

PERADIN, Persatuan Advokat Indonesia, Indonesian Advocate's Union. See LEGAL AID.

PERMESTA (q.v.), Piagam Perjuangan Semesta Alam, Universal Struggle Charter.

PERTAMINA (q.v.), Perusahaan Tambang Minyak dan Gas Bumi Nasional, National Oil and Gas Mining Corporation

PERTI, Persatuan Tarbiyah Islamiyah (q.v.), Islamic Education Association.

PESINDO, Pemuda Sosialis Indonesia (q.v.), Indonesian Socialist Youth.

PETA, Pembela Tanah Air (q.v.), Defenders of the Fatherland.

PETRUS, Penembakan misterius, mysterious (extra-judicial) shootings. See BANDITRY.

PGRS, Pasukan Gerilya Rakyat Serawak, Serawak People's Guerrilla Movement. See PONTIANAK.

PI, Perhimpunan Indonesia (q.v.), Indonesian Association.

PID, Politiek Inlichtingen Dienst (q.v.), Political Intelligence Service.

PIR, Persatuan Indonesia Raya (q.v.), Greater Indonesian Association.

PKI, Partai Komunis Indonesia (q.v.), Indonesian Communist Party.

PKK, Pembinaan Kesejahteraan Keluarga, Family Welfare Development. See DESA.

PKN, Pakempalan Kawula Ngayogyakarta (q.v.), Yogyakarta People's Party.

PKRI, Persatuan Katolik Republik Indonesia, Catholic Union of the Republic of Indonesia. See PARTAI KATOLIK.

PMP, Pendidikan Moral Pancasila, Pancasila Moral Education. See PANCASILA.

PN, Perusahaan Nasional, State Enterprise (q.v.).

PNG, Papua New Guinea. See PAPUA NEW GUINEA.

PNI, Partai Nasional Indonesia (q.v.), Indonesian Nationalist Party.

PNI-Baru, New PNI. See PENDIDIKAN NASIONAL INDONESIA.

PP, Persatuan Perjuangan (q.v.), Struggle Union.

PPKI, Panitia Persiapan Kemerdekaan Indonesia, Committee for the Preparation of Indonesian Independence. See BADAN PENYELIDIK USAHA PERSIAPAN KEMERDEKAAN INDONESIA.

PPKI, Persatuan Politik Katolik Indonesia, Indonesian Catholic Political Union. See PARTAI KATOLIK.

PPKJ, Pakempalan Politik Katolik Jawi, Political Association of Javanese Catholics. See PARTAI KATOLIK.

PPP, Partai Persatuan Pembangunan (q.v.), Unity Development Party.

PPPKI, Permufakatan Perhimpunan Politik Kebangsaan Indonesia (q.v.), Confederation of Indonesian Political Organizations.

PRC, People's Republic of China. See CHINA, Relations with.

PRRI, Pemerintah Revolusioner Republik Indonesia (q.v.), Revolutionary Government of the Republic of Indonesia.

PSI, Partai Sosialis Indonesia (q.v.), Indonesian Socialist Party.

PSII, Partai Sarekat Islam Indonesia (q.v.), Indonesian Islamic Association Party.

PT, Perusahaan Terbatas, Limited Liability Company.

PUSA, Persatuan Ulama Seluruh Aceh, All-Aceh Ulama Association. See ACEH.

PUSKESMAS, Pusat Kesehatan Masyarakat, Center for Society's Health. See HEALTH.

PUTERA, Pusat Tenaga Rakyat (q.v.), Center of the People's Power.

PWI, Persatuan Wartawan Indonesia, Indonesian Reporters Association. See JOURNALISM.

R., Raden, R.A., Raden Ajeng. See TITLES

REPELITA, Rencana Pembangunan Lima Tahun (q.v.), Five-Year Development Plan.

RHS, Rechtshogeschool, Law School. See EDUCATION.

RIS, Republik Indonesia Serikat (q.v.), Republic of the United States of Indonesia.

RMS, Republik Maluku Selatan (q.v.), Republic of the South Moluccas.

RPKAD, Resimen Para Komando Angkatan Darat (q.v.), Army Paracommando Regiment.

RR, Regeeringsreglement, Government Regulating Act. See CONSTITUTIONS.

RRI, Radio Republik Indonesia, Radio of the Republic of Indonesia. See RADIO.

RUSI, Republic of the United States of Indonesia. See REPUBLIK INDONESIA SERIKAT.

SARBUPRI, Sarikat Buruh Perkebunan Republik Indonesia, Union of Plantation Workers of the Republic of Indonesia. See SENTRAL ORGANISASI BURUH SELURUH INDONESIA.

SBG, Serikat Buruh Gula, Sugar Workers' Union. See SENTRAL ORGANISASI BURUH SELURUH INDONESIA.

SESKOAD, Sekolah Staf dan Komando Angkatan Darat, Army Staff and Command School. See ARMY.

SH, Sarjana Hukum. See TITLES.

SI, Sarekat Islam (q.v.), Islamic Association.

SIT, Surat Ijin Terbit, Publication Licence. See CENSORSHIP.

SIUPP, Surat Ijin Usaha Penerbitan Pers, Permit to Operate a Press Company. See CENSORSHIP.

SOBSI, Sentral Organisasi Buruh Seluruh Indonesia (q.v.), All-Indonesia Federation of Labor Organizations.

SOKSI, Sentral Organisasi Karyawan Seluruh Indonesia (q.v.), All-Indonesia Federation of Employee Organizations.

SPSI, Serikat Pekerja Seluruh Indonesia, All-Indonesia Workers Union. See LABOR UNIONS.

St, Sutan. See TITLES.

STICUSA, Stichting voor Culturele Samenwerking, Institute for Cultural Cooperation. See LEMBAGA KEBUDAYAAN RAKYAT.

STOVIA, School tot Opleiding van Inlandsche Artsen, School for the Training of Native Physicians. See EDUCATION; HEALTH.

SUPERSEMAR (q.v.), Surat Perintah Sebelas Maret, Executive Order of 11 March 1966.

TABANAS, Tabungan Pembangunan Nasional, National Development Savings Scheme. See BANKING.

TAPOL, Tahanan politik (q.v.), political prisoners.

THS, Technische Hogeschool, Institute of Technology. See EDUCATION.

TKR, Tentara Keamanan Rakyat, People's Security Army. See ARMY.

TNI, Tentara Nasional Indonesia, Indonesian National Army. See ARMY.

TRI, Tentara Republic Indonesia, Army of the Republic of Indonesia. See ARMY.

TRIP, Tentara Republik Indonesia Pelajar, Student Army of the Indonesian Republic.

TRITURA, Tri Tuntutan Rakyat, Three Demands of the People. See KESATUAN AKSI MAHASISWA INDONESIA; MALARI.

TVRI, Televisi Republik Indonesia, Television of the Republic of Indonesia. See TELEVISION.

UDT, Unio Democrática Timorense (q.v.), Timorese Democratic Union.

USDEK. See MANIFESTO POLITIK.

UUD, Undang-Undang Dasar, Constitution. See CONSTITUTIONS.

VFR, Voorlopige Federale Regeering, Provisional Federal Government. See SUCCESSION.

VOC, Vereenigde Oost-Indische Compagnie, United East Indies Company. See DUTCH EAST INDIES COMPANY.

VSTP, Vereeniging van Spoor- en Tramweg Personeel, Union of Rail and Tramway Personnel. See LABOR UNIONS.

ZOPFAN, Zone of Peace, Freedom, and Neutrality. See ASSOCIATION OF SOUTHEAST ASIAN NATIONS.

CHRONOLOGY

1.9 million years ago	Hominids *Pithecanthropus* and *Meganthropus* lived in Java (see PREHISTORY)
40,000 years ago	Wajak Man (*Homo sapiens*) lived in Java
15,000–8,000 years ago	Sea levels rise, separating Java, Sumatra and Kalimantan from the Asian mainland and New Guinea from Australia
ca 3000 B.C.	Austronesian peoples begin moving into Indonesia from the Philippines (see MIGRATIONS)
ca 1000 B.C.	Kerbau (q.v., water buffalo) introduced to Indonesia
ca 400 A.D.	Hindu kingdoms of Tarumanegara and Kutai (qq.v.) emerge in West Java and East Kalimantan
ca 675	Rise of Srivijaya (q.v.) in Sumatra
ca 732	Emergence of Mataram (q.v.) under Sanjaya
ca 760	Construction of Sivaitic temples at Dieng

ca 824	Construction of Borobudur (q.v.) begins
ca 840	Construction of Prambanan (q.v.) begins
860–ca 1000	Golden age of Srivijaya
ca 910	Political center of Java moves to East Java; rise of Hindu kingdoms on Bali (q.v.)
914–1080	First known Hindu kingdom on Bali (q.v.)
1006	Srivijaya attacks Java
1019–1041	Airlangga (q.v.) rules Java
1023–1068	Chola raids on Sumatra
1042	Airlangga divides his kingdom into Kediri and Janggala
1222	Ken Angrok founds Singosari (q.v.)
1292	Civil war in Singosari; Jayakatwang kills Kertanegara; Mongol invasion joins Wijaya against Jayakatwang
1293	Wijaya founds kingdom of Majapahit (q.v.) and rules (1293–1309) as Kertarajasa
ca 1297	Sultan Malek Saleh of Pasai (q.v.), first known Muslim ruler in the archipelago

ca 1330–1350	Adityavarman rules Minangkabau (q.v.)
1331–1364	Gajah Mada prime minister of Majapahit
1387	Founding of Banjarmasin (q.v.)
1402	Kingdom of Melaka (q.v.) founded
1406, 1408, 1410, 1414, 1418	Expeditions by Zheng He (Cheng Ho) to Southeast Asia
ca 1478	Demak (q.v.) becomes first Muslim state on Java
1511	Portuguese seize Melaka
1522	Portuguese build fort in Ternate (q.v.)
1527	Sultanate of Demak defeats Majapahit
1552–1570	Banten (q.v.) rises as independent state under Sultan Hasanuddin
1570	Revolt against the Portuguese in Ternate
1575–1601	Senopati rules Mataram (q.v.)
1596	First Dutch ships under de Houtman (q.v.) arrive in Banten

1605	Dutch seize Ambon (q.v.)
1607–1645	Rise of Aceh (q.v.) under Sultan Iskandar Muda
1613–1645	Sultan Agung (q.v.) rules Mataram
1619	Dutch establish base in Jayakarta (later Batavia, q.v.)
1621	Dutch seize control of Banda (q.v.) Islands
1623	'Amboyna Massacre' (q.v.) Mataram subjugates Gresik and Surabaya (q.v.)
1629	Sultan Agung unsuccessfully attacks Batavia
1641	Dutch capture Melaka from Portuguese
1641–1675	Aceh ruled by Queen Taj al-Alam
1663	Treaty of Painan establishes Dutch influence in Minangkabau (q.v.)
1667	Makassar (q.v.) falls to Dutch and Bugis forces; Treaty of Bungaya; VOC wins control of north coast of Java
1671–1679	Revolt of Trunojoyo (q.v.) on Java
1704–1708	First Javanese War of Succession

1719–1723	Second Javanese War of Succession
1723	Forced delivery of coffee (q.v.) to Dutch by regents of Priangan (q.v.) begins
1740	Revolt of the Chinese in Batavia
1746–1755	Third Javanese War of Succession
1755	Treaty of Giyanti (q.v.)
1778	Bataviaasch Genootschap van Kunsten en Wetenschappen founded
1790–1820	Gold (q.v.) rush in West Kalimantan (see KONGSI WARS)
1795	Batavian Republic (q.v.) founded; first census (q.v.) conducted on Java
1799	VOC bankrupt
1 January 1800	VOC Charter allowed to lapse; Company properties taken over by the Dutch state
1803–1837	Paderi Wars in Minangkabau (q.v.), West Sumatra
1808–1811	Daendels (q.v.) governs the Dutch Indies
August–September 1811	British conquest of Java

1811–1816	Raffles (q.v.) lieutenant-governor of Java
1812	British seize Bangka and Belitung (qq.v.) from Palembang
1813	First land rent (q.v.) introduced; Sultanate of Banten abolished
1815	Eruption of Tambora (q.v.)
1816	Dutch restored to their Indonesian possessions
1817	Botanical gardens (q.v.) at Bogor founded; revolt by Pattimura in Ambon
1821	Cholera (q.v.) reaches Indonesia
1824	Anglo-Dutch Treaty (q.v.); founding of Nederlandsche Handel Maatschappij
1825–1830	Java War (q.v.)
1828	Dutch settlement at Lobo in Irian (q.v.)
1830	Cultivation System (q.v.) introduced
1846	Commercial coal (q.v.) mining begins in South Kalimantan
1854	Revised Regeeringsreglement (Constitution, q.v.) of the

	Netherlands Indies promulgated
1859–1863	War of Succession in Banjarmasin (q.v.)
1863	Tobacco (q.v.) cultivation begins in East Sumatra (q.v.)
1864	First railway (q.v.) established
1870	Agrarian Law (q.v.); start of Liberal Policy (q.v.)
1871	Undersea telegraph cable laid between Java and Australia
1873–1904	Aceh War
1877	End of *batig slot* (q.v.) transfers to Dutch treasury
1878	Coffee plantations devastated by disease
1880	Coolie Ordinance (q.v.) introduced
1883	Eruption of Krakatau (q.v.)
1886	First oil (q.v.) discovery at Pangkalan Brandan
1888	Anticolonial uprising in Banten (q.v.)
1891	Tooth of Java Man (q.v.) discovered in East Java
1894	Dutch conquest of Lombok (q.v.)

1901	Start of Ethical Policy (q.v.)
1902	Transmigration (q.v.) begins
1905	Dutch occupy Tapanuli, North Sumatra; decentralization (q.v.) measures introduced in Dutch territories
1905–1906	Dutch conquest of Bone (q.v.)
1908	Budi Utomo (q.v.) founded
1908	Dutch conquer southern Bali (q.v.)
1910	Outbreak of bubonic plague (q.v.) on Java; Sarekat Islam and Indische Partij (qq.v.) founded
1912	Muhammadiyah (q.v.) founded
1914	Indische Sociaal-Democratische Vereniging (q.v.) founded
1916	Volksraad (q.v.) installed
1917	Rebellion in Toraja (q.v.) land
1918	Influenza (q.v.) pandemic
1920	Partai Komunis Indonesia (q.v.) founded
1923	Communists expelled from Sarekat Islam

November 1925	Algemeene Studieclub (q.v.) founded
November 1926	Communist uprising in Banten; internment camp established at Boven Digul (q.v.)
31 December 1926	Nahdatul Ulama (q.v.) founded
January 1927	Communist uprising in West Sumatra
4 July 1927	Partai Nasional Indonesia (q.v.) founded
28 October 1928	Youth Pledge (q.v.)
December 1929	Sukarno (q.v.) jailed
April 1931	PNI dissolves itself
1931	New PNI and PARTINDO (Partai Indonesia, q.v.) founded
5 February 1933	Mutiny on the *Zeven Provinciën* (q.v.)
December 1935	PARINDRA (Partai Indonesia Raya, q.v.) founded
July 1936	Sutarjo Petition (q.v.)
1936	Becak (q.v.) appear as a means of public transport in Batavia
24 May 1937	GERINDO (Gerakan Rakyat Indonesia, q.v.) founded

1937	Antara (q.v.) news agency founded
July 1941	Netherlands Indies stops exports of oil, tin, and rubber to Japan (q.v.)
27–28 February 1942	Battle of the Java Sea (q.v.)
9 March 1942	Dutch forces capitulate to Japan at Kalijati, West Java
7 September 1944	Japanese Prime Minister Koiso promises independence
1 June 1945	Sukarno (q.v.) formulates the Pancasila (q.v.)
15 August 1945[1]	Surrender of Japan
17 August 1945	Declaration of Independence
18 August 1945	Promulgation of Constitution (q.v.) and formation of Republic of Indonesia
29 September 1945	First Allied landings in Jakarta
5 October 1945	Formation of Indonesian army (q.v.)
1 November 1945	Manifesto Politik (q.v.) of the Indonesian Republic issued
10 November 1945	Battle of Surabaya (q.v.)

1. Here and elsewhere, local Indonesian dates are used. When the Japanese surrender at the end of World War II was announced it was still 14 August 1945 in North America.

14 November 1945	First parliamentary cabinet under Sutan Syahrir (q.v.)
April 1946	First formal negotiations begin between Indonesian and Dutch
15 November 1946	Linggajati Agreement (q.v.) initialled
24 December 1946	Negara Indonesia Timur (q.v.) founded
June 1947	Egypt and Syria recognize the Indonesian Republic
21 July 1947	Dutch First 'Police Action' (q.v.)
17 January 1948	Renville Agreement (q.v.)
September 1948	Madiun Affair (q.v.)
19 December 1948	Second Dutch 'Police Action'
1 March 1949	General attack on Yogyakarta led by Suharto (q.v.)
7 May 1949	Rum-van Roijen Agreement
6 July 1949	Republican government returns to Yogyakarta
7 August 1949	Darul Islam (q.v.) movement declares an Islamic state
23 August 1949	Round Table Conference (q.v.) begins in The Hague
27 December 1949	Transfer of sovereignty (excluding Irian, q.v.)

23 January 1950	Attempted coup by R.P.P. Westerling (q.v.) in Bandung
April 1950	Benteng Program (q.v.) launched
5 April 1950	Andi Aziz (q.v.) Affair
25 April 1950	Declaration of Republik Maluku Selatan (q.v.)
17 August 1950	Reestablishment of unitary state (see FEDERALISM)
26–29 September 1950	Indonesia joins United Nations (q.v.)
17 October 1952	Army (q.v.) campaigns for dissolution of parliament and holding of elections (q.v.)
1953	Java Bank nationalized (see BANKING)
September 1953	Aceh revolt begins
April 1954	Ali Sastroamijoyo (q.v.) attends Asian Prime Ministers' meeting in Colombo
18–24 April 1955	Asia-Africa Conference (q.v.) held in Bandung
29 September 1955	General elections
8 May 1956	Indonesia unilaterally abrogates Netherlands Indonesian Union

4 August 1956	Indonesia repudiates international debt (q.v.) to the Netherlands
December 1956	Regional rebellions begin in Sumatra and Sulawesi
9 April 1957	Sukarno commissions first Business Cabinet (Kabinet Karya)
May 1957	Dewan Nasional (q.v.) founded
3 December 1957	PNI and PKI unions begin seizure of Dutch businesses in Indonesia (see NATIONALIZATION)
5 December 1957	Justice Ministry orders expulsion of 46,000 Dutch citizens
13 December 1957	Nasution announces that army will manage seized enterprises
December 1957	Muhammad Natsir (q.v.) and other Masyumi leaders flee Jakarta
15 February 1958	Pemerintah Revolusioner Republik Indonesia (q.v.) declared in Bukit Tinggi, West Sumatra
April–June 1959	PRRI-Permesta rebellion suppressed
14 May 1959	Alien Chinese banned from trading in rural areas
5 July 1959	Restoration of 1945 Constitution

I / Chronology

17 August 1959	Sukarno outlines the Manifesto Politik (q.v.) (see GUIDED DEMOCRACY)
5 March 1960	Sukarno dissolves parliament
1961	First postindependence census (q.v.)
19 December 1961	Sukarno announces military campaign against Dutch in Irian
15 August 1962	Dutch hand authority in Irian to United Nations
March 1963	Sukarno's *Deklarasi Ekonomi* (see GUIDED ECONOMY)
1 May 1963	United Nations hands Irian to Indonesia
23 September 1963	Sukarno announces plans to crush Malaysia (see CONFRONTATION)
October 1963	Manifesto Kebudayaan (q.v.)
17 August 1964	Sukarno's 'Year of Living Dangerously' speech
30 September 1965	Coup attempt by Gerakan September Tiga Puluh (q.v.)
2 October 1965	General Suharto (q.v.) given responsibility for restoring 'security and order'
Late 1965–1966	Mass killings of PKI members and associates
13 December 1965	Rp 1,000 devalued to Rp 1 (see CURRENCY)

13 February 1966	First post-GESTAPU MAHMILLUB (q.v.) trial begins
11 March 1966	Sukarno issues Supersemar (q.v.) order, transferring full executive authority to Suharto
12 March 1966	PKI and associated organizations banned
11 August 1966	Relations with Malaysia (q.v.) normalized, end of Confrontation
September 1966	Indonesia rejoins United Nations
12 March 1967	MPR-S strips Sukarno of presidency and appoints Suharto Acting President
April 1967	Indonesia rejoins World Bank
8 August 1967	Formation of ASEAN (q.v.)
20 February 1968	PARMUSI (q.v.) founded
27 March 1968	MPR appoints Suharto President
6 June 1968	Suharto forms first Development Cabinet
1 April 1969	Launch of first Five-Year Plan (REPELITA, q.v.)
15 July–2 August 1969	Kabupaten councils in Irian opt for integration with Indonesia in ‘Act of Free Choice’
2 October 1969	Attorney-General Sugiharto announces plans to settle alleged Communist detainees on Buru (q.v.)

2 February 1970	'Committee of Four' on corruption established
17 March 1971	Treaty of Friendship with Malaysia (q.v.)
3 July 1971	Second general elections
23 August 1971	Indonesia and Malaysia claim territorial rights over the Strait of Melaka
5 January 1973	Partai Persatuan Pembangunan (q.v.) formed
10 January 1973	Partai Demokrasi Indonesia (q.v.) formed
12 February 1973	Indonesia signs border agreement with Papua New Guinea (q.v.)
August 1973	Indonesian-Malaysian Language Agreement (see INDONESIAN LANGUAGE)
15 January 1974	Malari (q.v.) Affair
8 August 1974	Indonesia signs marine border agreement with India (q.v.)
February–March 1975	State oil company Pertamina (q.v.) in financial difficulties
11 March 1975	Indonesia reaches border agreement with Philippines
29 July 1975	Indonesia recognizes Provisional Revolutionary Government of South Vietnam

26 August 1975	Portuguese colonial government abandons East Timor (q.v.)
November 1975	Indonesia joins International Bauxite Association
28 November 1975	Fretilin (q.v.) declares Democratic Republic of East Timor (q.v.)
7 December 1975	Indonesian forces invade Dili, capital of East Timor
3 March 1976	Ibnu Sutowo, director of Pertamina, dismissed
31 May 1976	Indonesian-sponsored People's Assembly of East Timor declares integration with Indonesia
26 June 1976	Major earthquake in Irian
22 September 1976	Government authorities claim to have uncovered coup plot by Sawito Kartowibowo (q.v.)
14 January 1977	Further seabed agreement with India
2 May 1977	Third general election
May 1977	Paratroops dropped in the central valley of Irian to crush rebellion by OPM (q.v.)
16 January 1978	Bandung students issue 'White Book' (q.v.) criticizing New Order performance

22 March 1978	MPR reelects Suharto as President
29 March 1978	Third Development Cabinet formed
15 November 1978	Rupiah devalued (see CURRENCY)
July–December 1979	Ten thousand political prisoners released
18 December 1979	Border agreement with Papua New Guinea
February 1980	ABRI Masuk Desa program introduced (see DWIFUNGSI)
5 May 1980	Petition of Fifty (q.v.)
October–December 1980	Anti-Chinese riots in Aceh and Central Java
11 March 1981	Radical Muslims attack police station at Cicendo in West Java
28 March 1981	Radical Muslims hijack Garuda DC-9 en route from Palembang to Medan
25 February 1982	Malaysia recognizes Indonesia's 'Archipelagic Concept' (q.v.)
18 March 1982	Lapangan Banteng riot
4 May 1982	Fourth general election
September 1982	DPR passes legislation to codify Dwifungsi (q.v.)

December 1982	Law of the Sea Convention at Jamaica effectively recognizes Indonesia's 'Archipelagic Concept' (q.v.)
1982–1983	Serious drought through much of Indonesia
1983	Forest fire in Kalimantan (q.v.)
30 March 1983	Rupiah devalued
April 1983	'Mysterious killings' of criminals begins (see BANDITRY)
October 1983	Sudharmono and Sarwono Kusumaatmaja take over leadership of Golkar; Golkar restructuring begins
20–22 August 1984	First national congress of PPP (q.v.) accepts Pancasila as its sole basic principle
12 September 1984	Tanjung Priok Affair: security forces kill unknown number of demonstrators in Jakarta (see WHITE PAPER)
29 October 1984	Massive explosions at Marines (KKO) base in Cilandak, south Jakarta
5 November 1984	Transmigration goals officially shifted from food production to export crop production
Early December 1984	Muhammadiyah (q.v.) adopts Pancasila as its sole basic principle

Mid December 1984	NU (q.v.) adopts Pancasila (q.v.) as its sole basic principle, but withdraws from PPP
1 January 1985	Export of unprocessed logs banned (see FORESTRY)
21 January 1985	Bomb explosion on Borobudur (q.v.)
1 February 1985	Fire guts royal palace in Solo
1 April 1985	Value Added Tax introduced
1 May 1985	Most of the functions of the customs service transferred to a Swiss firm, Société Générale de Surveillance
May 1985	Legislation requires all mass organizations to accept the Pancasila (q.v.) as their sole basic principle
5 July 1985	Resumption of direct trade with China (q.v.)
18 August 1985	H.R. Dharsono placed on trial for subversion (see WHITE PAPER)
August–November 1985	1,600 people dismissed, mainly from the oil industry, for alleged links with the PKI
August 1985	First of a series of executions of PKI members detained after the 1965 Gestapu (q.v.) affair

29 October 1985	Indonesia signs economic protocol with Soviet Union
December 1985–August 1986	International oil price drops from US$25 to $12 per barrel
8 January 1986	H.R. Dharsono sentenced to ten years jail for subversion
10 April 1986	Critical article in *Sydney Morning Herald* precipitates crisis in Indonesia-Australia relations
May 1986	Legislation passed requiring mass organizations (q.v.) to adopt the Pancasila (q.v.) as their sole basic principle
6 May 1986	Fiscal and monetary reforms, including a liberalization of foreign investment regulations
12 September 1986	Rupiah devalued by 31%
October 1986	Treaty of Mutual Respect, Friendship and Cooperation with Papua New Guinea (q.v.)
October 1986	World Bank issues report critical of management of transmigration (q.v.)
9 October 1986	Newspaper *Sinar Harapan* banned

4 February 1987	Plans announced to privatize some of Indonesia's state enterprises (q.v.)
23 April 1987	Fifth general election
September 1987	Indonesia sends high level trade mission to Fiji, following the military coups there
December 1987	Indonesia and Malaysia agree to cooperate in marketing palm oil, rubber, and other products
14 December 1987	Suharto calls for nuclear weapons free zone in Southeast Asia
24 December 1987	Major reduction announced in government regulation of imports, exports, foreign investment, and tourism
5 January 1988	1988/89 budget allocates 36% of predicted foreign income to service international debt (q.v.)
10 March 1988	Suharto reelected as president
1 July 1988	Indonesia bans export of semiprocessed rattan (q.v.)
5 September 1988	Indonesia and Australia (q.v.) fight over maritime jurisdiction in the so-called 'Timor Gap'
22 September 1988	KOPKAMTIB (q.v.) abolished

September 1988	Indonesia closes Sunda and Lombok straits for three days for a naval exercise
20–25 October 1988	Golkar (q.v.) national conference; Sudharmono replaced as chairman by Wahono
27 October 1988	Deregulation of the banking sector (see BANKING)
21 November 1988	Further loosening of import regulations announced
November 1988	Indonesia recognizes state of Palestine
28 November 1988	Indonesia heavily restricts foreign missionary activity
1 January 1989	Indonesia bans export of some categories of raw rubber (q.v.) to stimulate local processing
6–8 February 1989	Violent clashes in Lampung between troops and local settlers facing eviction from their lands
24 February 1989	Indonesia and China (q.v.) agree to restore diplomatic relations
March 1989	Commercial television introduced to Jakarta
April 1989	Golkar members protest over 25% increase in electricity prices

April 1989	Student protests over dispossession of small farmers for development projects
24 May 1989	Australia-Indonesia Institute founded
8 June 1989	Suharto receives United Nations Population award for Indonesia's family planning program
16 June 1989	Private stock exchange opened in Surabaya
28–30 August 1989	Second national congress of PPP (q.v.) removes Jaelani Naro as leader
September 1989	Suharto visits Soviet Union
October 1989	Pope John Paul visits Indonesia
13 October 1989	New patent law passed to protect intellectual property rights (see COPYRIGHT).
11 December 1989	Indonesia signs Timor Gap agreement with Australia
4 January 1990	Suharto calls on private companies to offer 25% of their shares to employees' cooperatives

MAPS

MAP 1: INDONESIA: ISLANDS AND SEAS

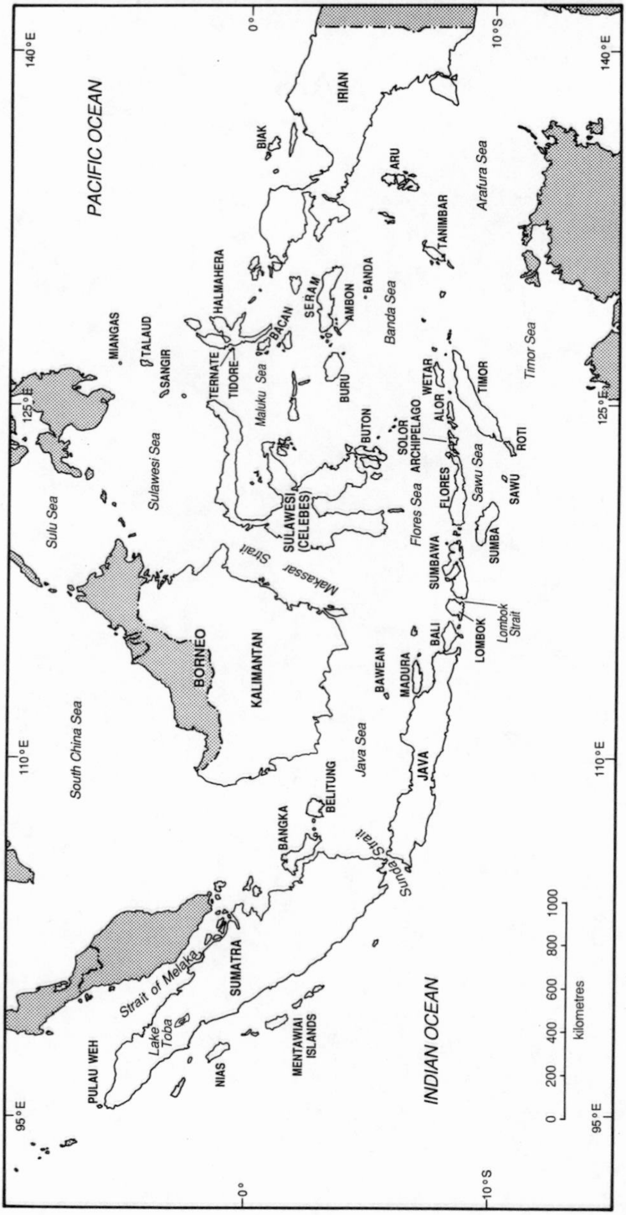

MAP 2: INDONESIA: CITIES AND PLACES MENTIONED IN THE TEXT

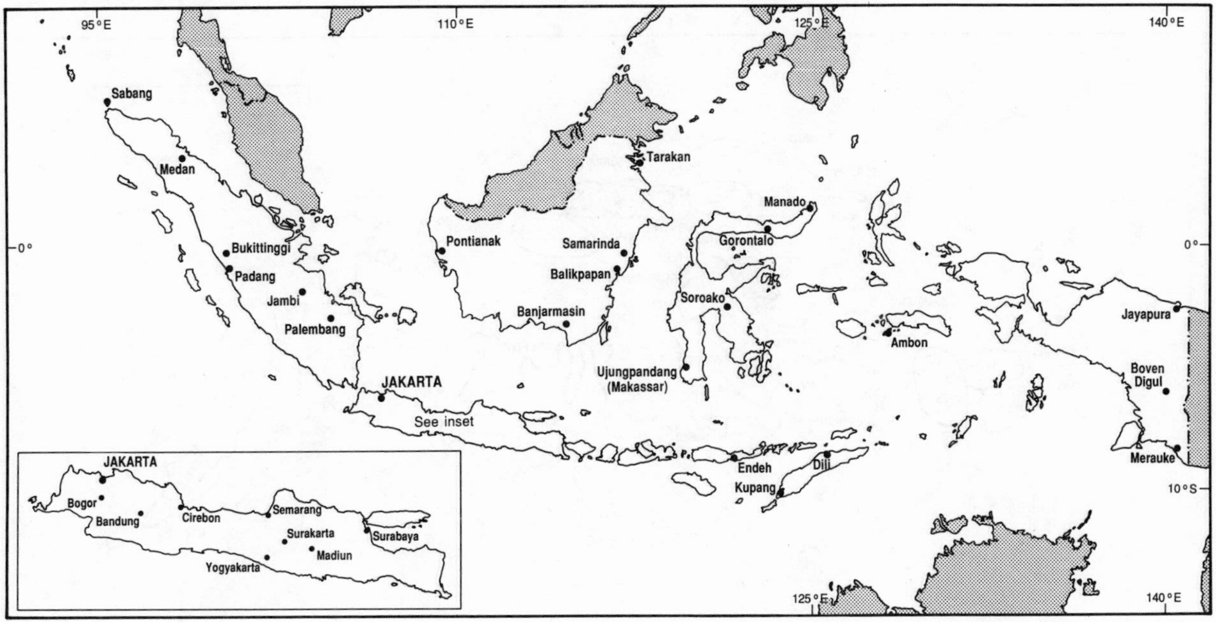

MAP 3: INDONESIA: TRADITIONAL DISTRIBUTION OF ETHNIC GROUPS
NOTE: ALL BOUNDARIES ARE APPROXIMATE AND REFLECT POPULATION CIRCA 1800.

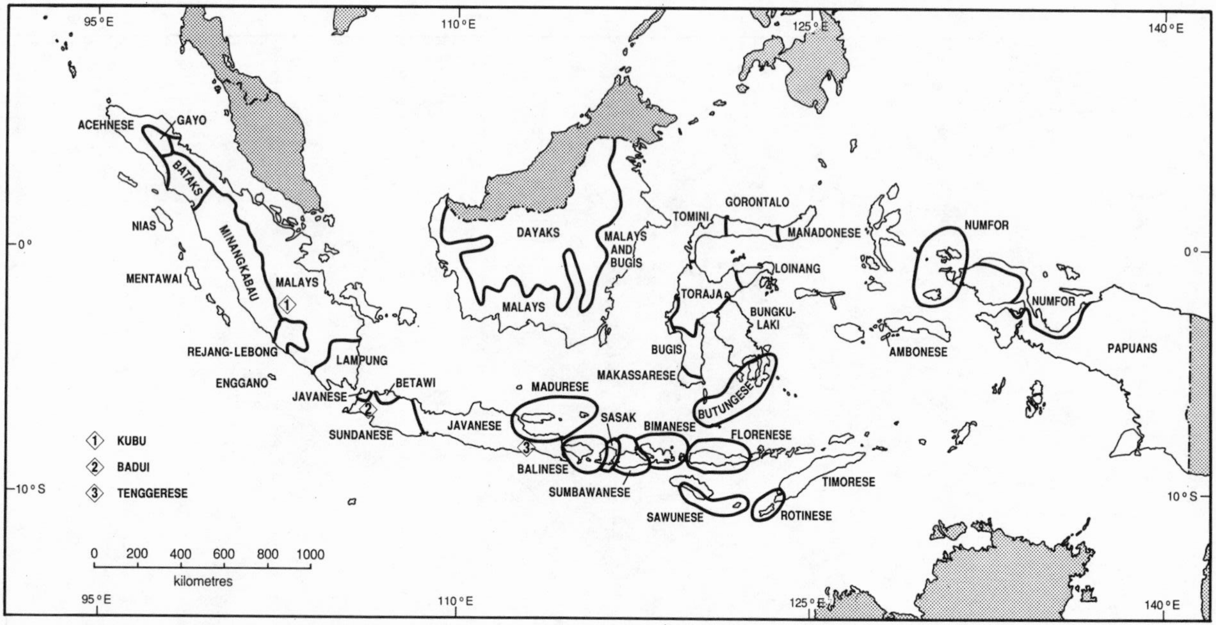

MAP 4: INDONESIA: AREAS OF SUBSTANTIAL MINORITY SETTLEMENT

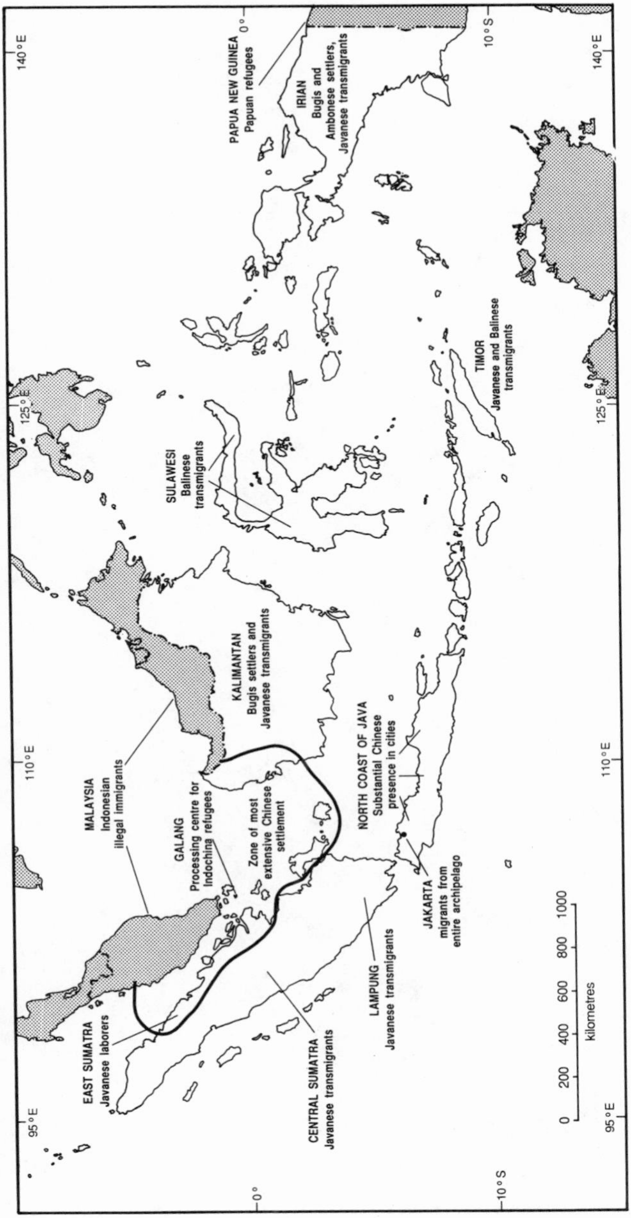
95°E
110°E
125°E
140°E
0°
10°S
EAST SUMATRA
Javanese laborers
CENTRAL SUMATRA
Javanese transmigrants
LAMPUNG
Javanese transmigrants
MALAYSIA
Indonesian
illegal immigrants
GALANG
Processing centre for
Indochina refugees
Zone of most
extensive Chinese
settlement
JAKARTA
migrants from
entire archipelago
NORTH COAST OF JAVA
Substantial Chinese
presence in cities
KALIMANTAN
Bugis settlers and
Javanese transmigrants
SULAWESI
Balinese
transmigrants
TIMOR
Javanese and Balinese
transmigrants
IRIAN
Bugis and
Ambonese settlers,
Javanese transmigrants
PAPUA NEW GUINEA
Papuan refugees
0
200
400
600
800
1000
kilometres

MAP 5: WESTERN INDONESIA: EARLY STATES
NOTE: THE STATES MARKED ON THIS MAP WERE NOT NECESSARILY CONTEMPORANEOUS.

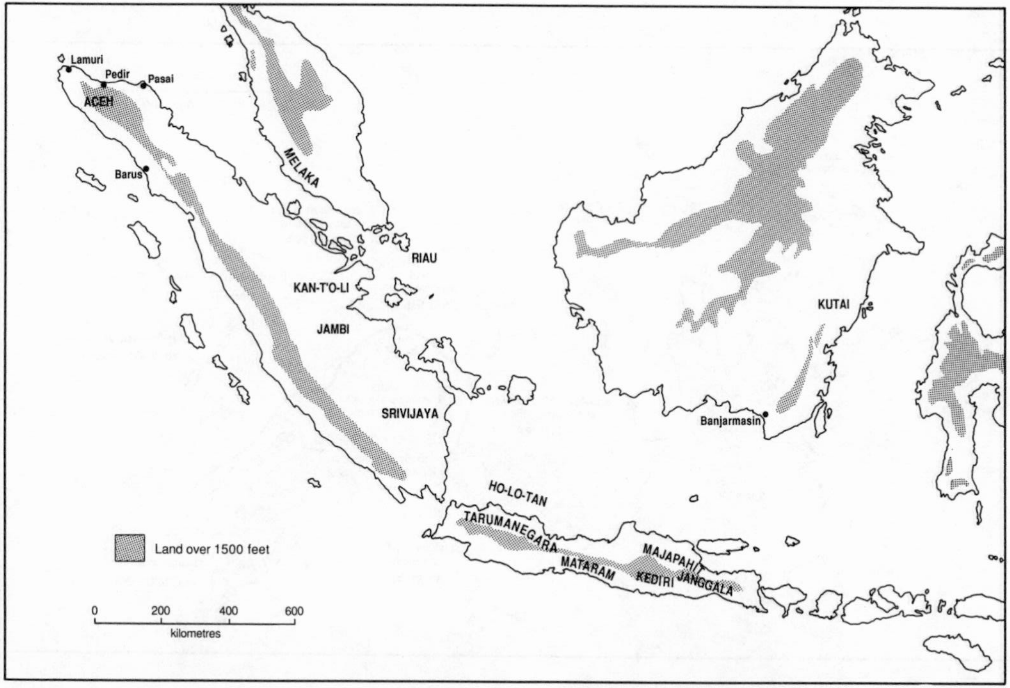

MAP 6: JAVA IN THE 16TH AND 17TH CENTURIES: THE EXPANSION OF MATARAM

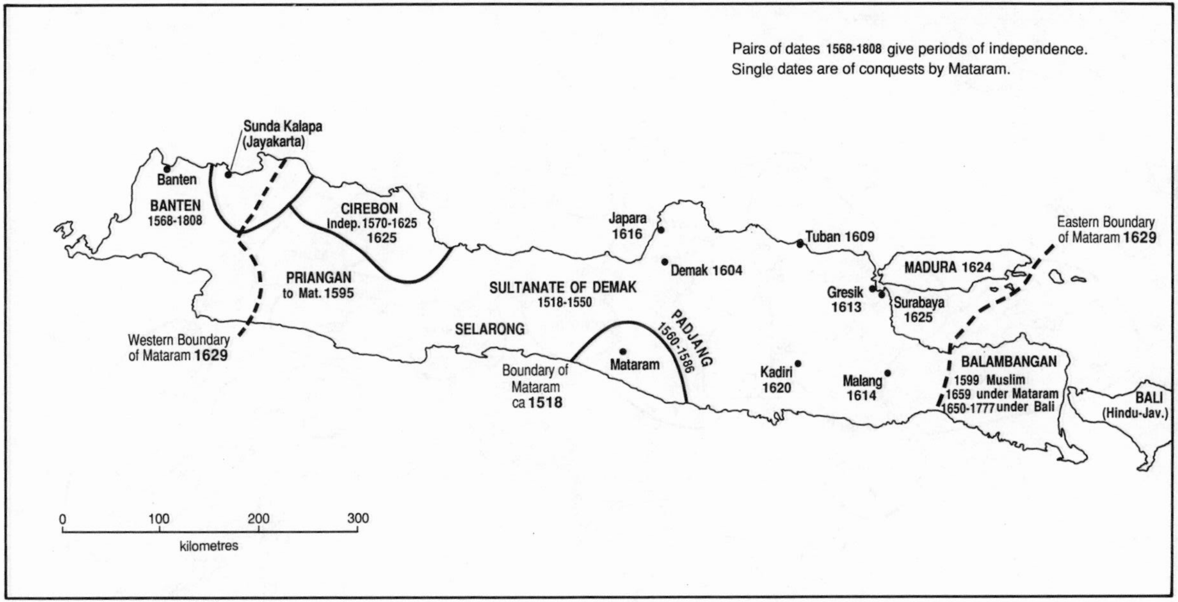

MAP 7: INDONESIA IN THE 17TH CENTURY: MAJOR STATES
NOTE: ALL THESE STATES CONTROLLED FLUCTUATING AND ILL-DEFINED TERRITORIES, AND THE BORDERS MARKED ARE APPROXIMATE ONLY.

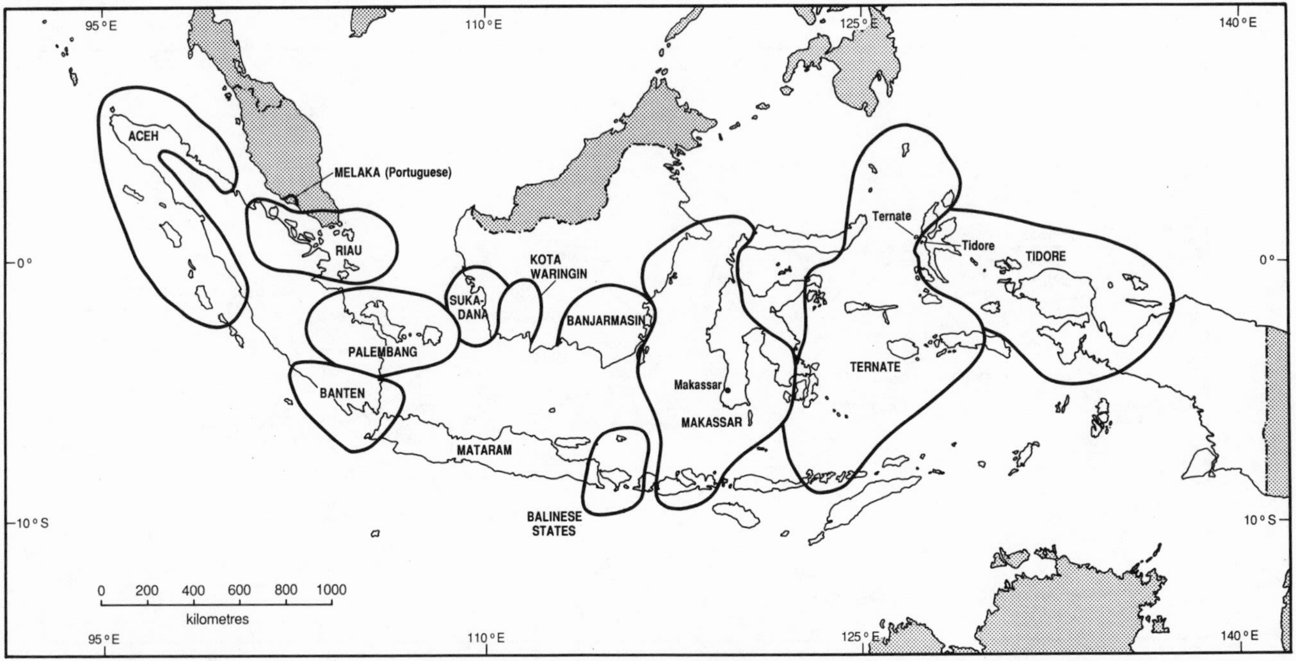

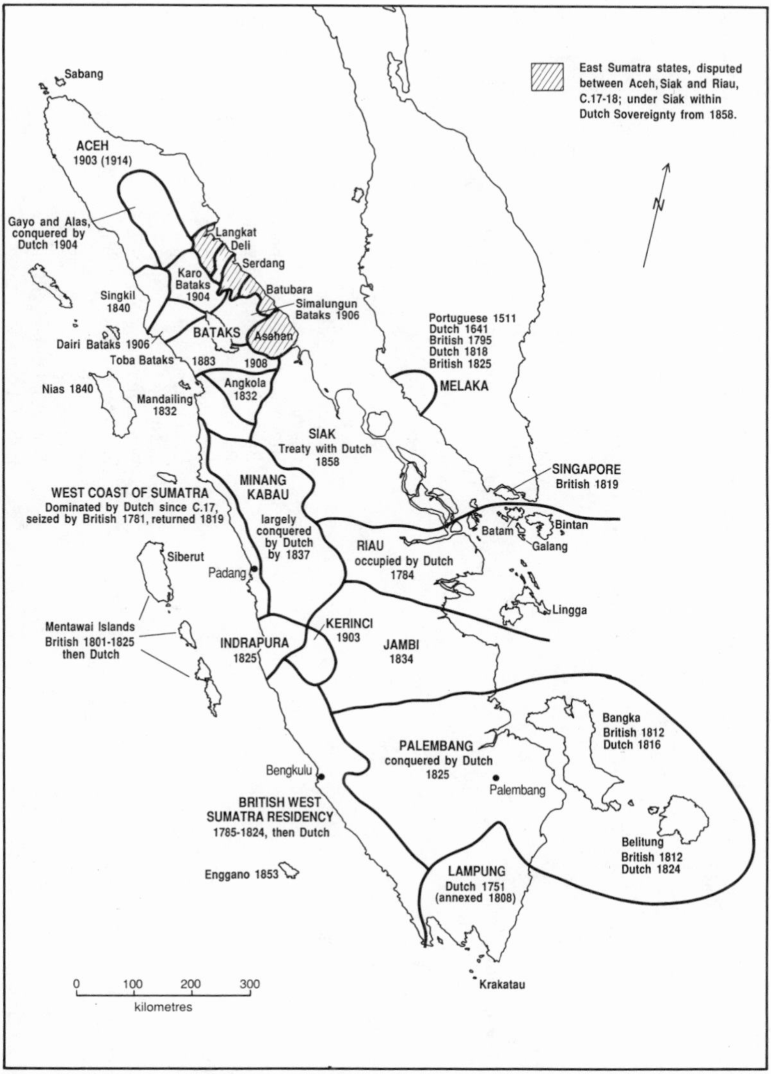

MAP 8: SUMATRA IN THE 19TH CENTURY: THE EXPANSION OF DUTCH POWER
SINGLE DATES ARE THOSE FOR CONQUEST OR ANNEXATION BY THE DUTCH

MAP 9: NETHERLANDS EAST INDIES: ADMINISTRATIVE DIVISIONS IN 1940

Note: Maritime boundaries are drawn to include offshore islands in their respective jurisdictions, but do not imply actual marine jurisdiction. A three-mile territorial waters limit was in force at the time.

Status of divisions:

REGIONS	GEWESTEN
Provinces	**Provinciën**
West Java	West-Java (Pasoendan)
Central Java	Midden-Java
East Java	Oost-Java
Governments (with residencies)	**Gouvernementen (met residenties)**
Yogyakarta	Djockakarta
Surakarta	Soerakarta
Sumatra	Sumatra
Aceh	At jeh en Onderhoorigheden
East Coast of Sumatra	Oostkust van Sumatra
Tapanuli	Tapanoeli
West Coast of Sumatra	Sumatra's Westkust
Jambi	Djambi
Riau	Riouw en Onderhoorigheden
Bangka	Bangka en Onderhoorigheden
Palembang	Palembang
Bengkulu	Benkoelen
Lampung	Lampongsche Districten
Borneo	Borneo
West Borneo	Westerafdeeling van Borneo
South and East Borneo	Zuider-en OOsterafdeeling van Borneo
Great East	Groote Oost
Moluccas	Molukken
Timor	Timor en Onderhoorigheden
Bali and Lombok	Bali en Lombok
Manado	Manado
Celebes	Celebes en Onderhoorigheden

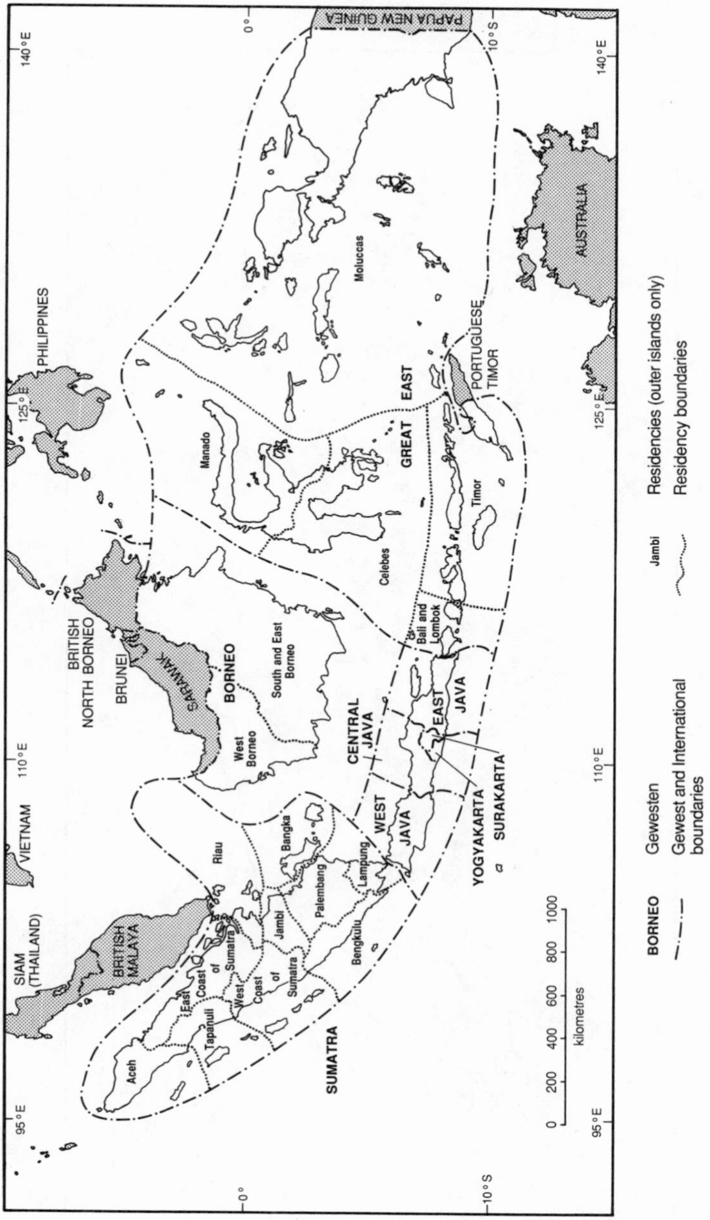
PHILIPPINES
VIETNAM
SIAM (THAILAND)
BRITISH MALAYA
BRITISH NORTH BORNEO
BRUNEI
SARAWAK
PAPUA NEW GUINEA
AUSTRALIA
PORTUGUESE TIMOR
SUMATRA
Aceh
Tapanuli
East Coast of Sumatra
West Coast of Sumatra
Riau
Jambi
Palembang
Bengkulu
Lampung
Bangka
BORNEO
West Borneo
South and East Borneo
WEST JAVA
CENTRAL JAVA
EAST JAVA
YOGYAKARTA
SURAKARTA
Bali and Lombok
GREAT EAST
Celebes
Manado
Timor
Moluccas
95°E
110°E
125°E
140°E
0°
10°S
0 200 400 600 800 1000
kilometres
BORNEO Gewesten
Gewest and International boundaries
Jambi Residencies (outer islands only)
Residency boundaries

MAP 10: NETHERLANDS INDIES: ZELFBESTUREN (NATIVE STATES UNDER INDIRECT RULE)

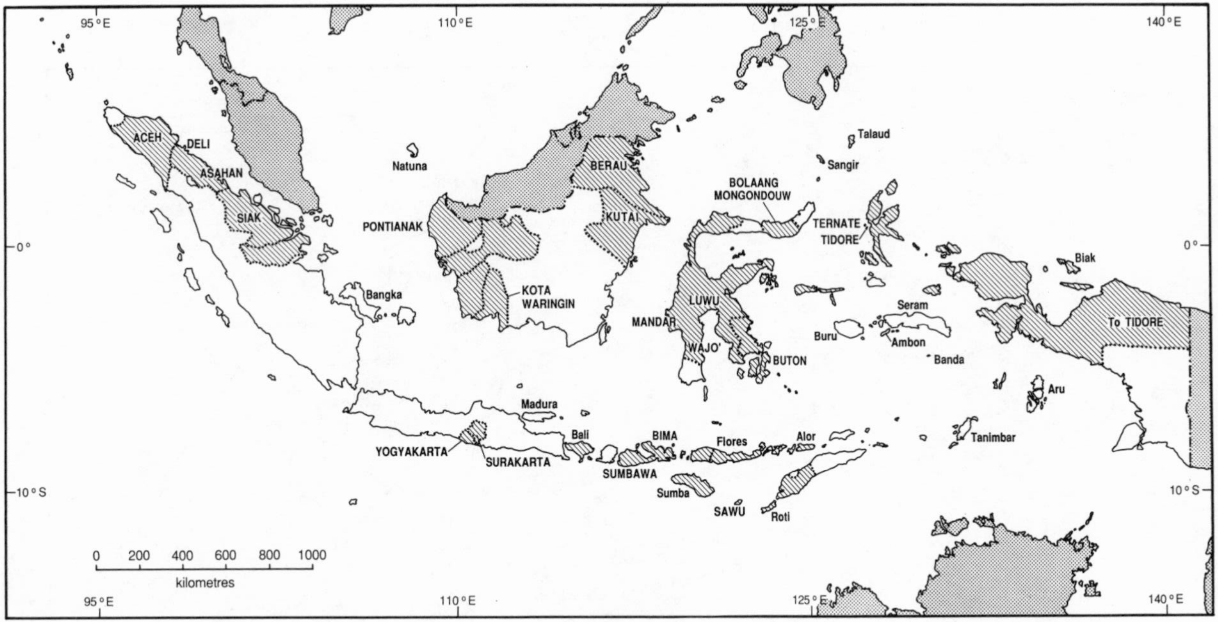

MAP 11: INDONESIA ON THE EVE OF THE SECOND MILITARY ACTION, DECEMBER 1948

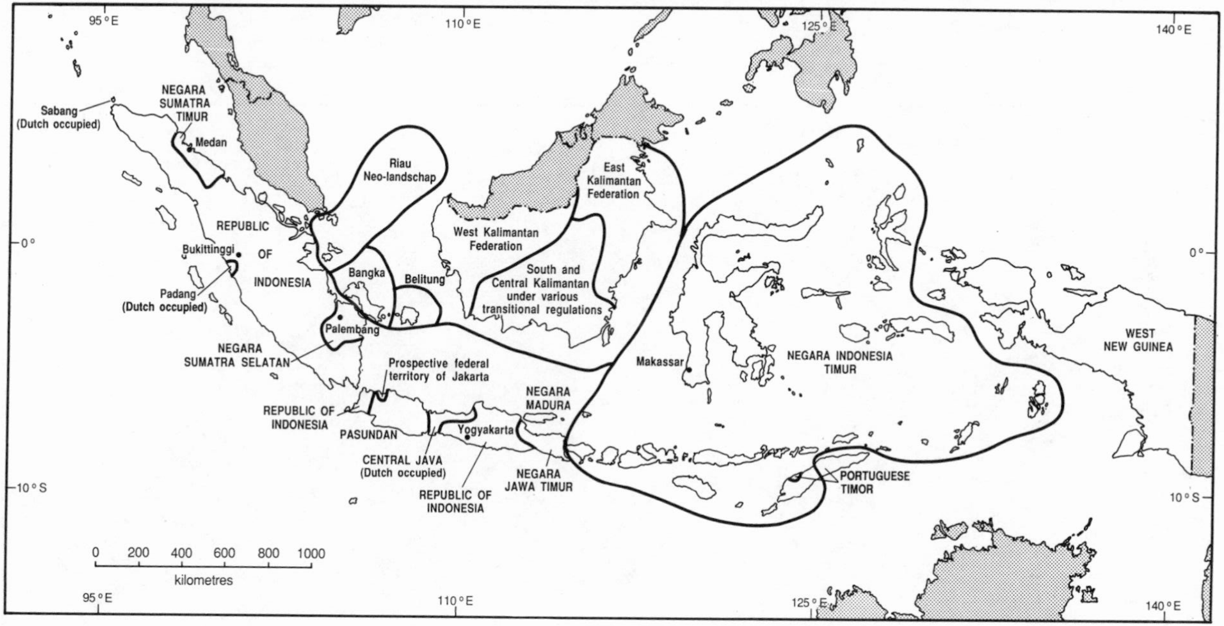

MAP 12: CONTEMPORARY INDONESIA: PROVINCES AND INTERNATIONAL BORDERS

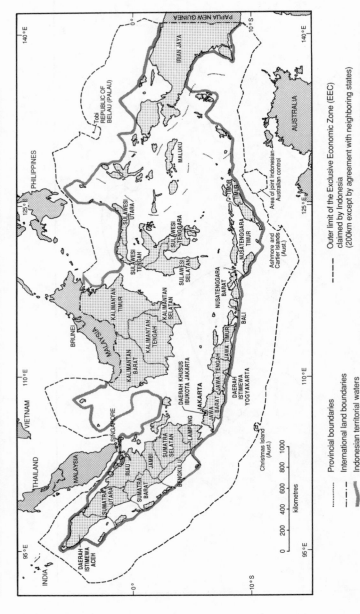

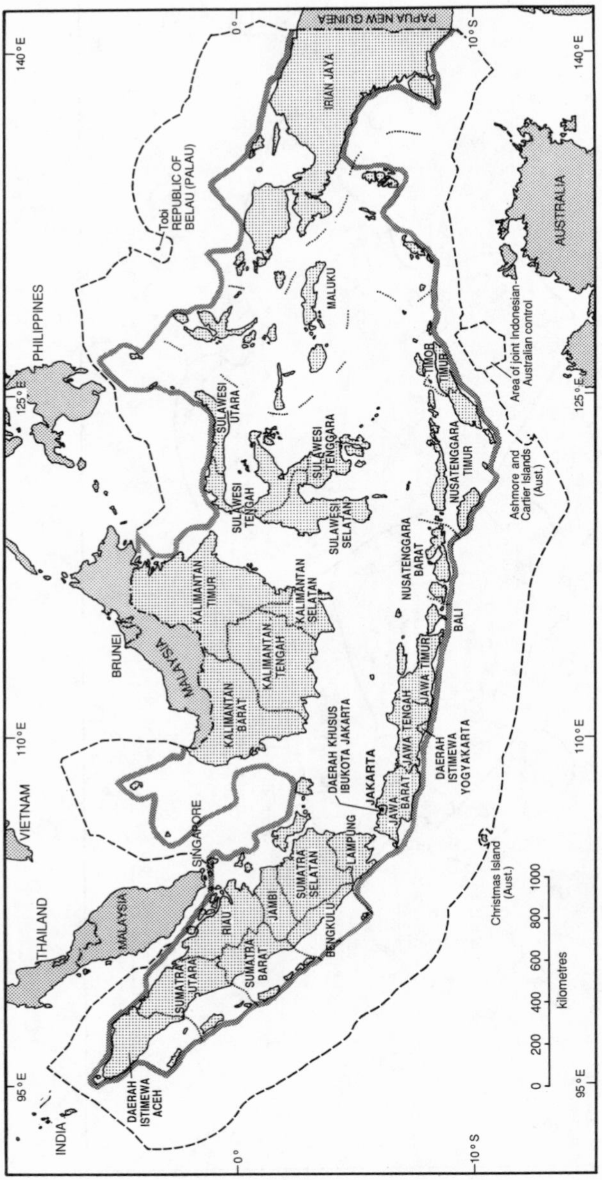

Provincial boundaries
International land boundaries
Indonesian territorial waters
Outer limit of the Exclusive Economic Zone (EEC) claimed by Indonesia (200km except by agreement with neighboring states)

THE DICTIONARY

A

ABANGAN (from Jav. *abang,* red), term popularized by Geertz in East Java to describe Javanese Muslims whose religion, sometimes called *kejawen* or 'Javanism', encompasses many non-Islamic elements, especially mysticism and respect for local spirits. Followers of kejawen insist that their religious commitment is different from, not less than, that of orthodox santri (q.v.) Muslims. See also ALIRAN; ISLAM; KEBATINAN. [1005, 1018, 1030, 1127]

ACÇÃO NACIONAL POPULÁR (ANP, National Popular Action), founded by António Salazar in 1930 as the União Naçional, was the sole legal political party in Portugal and its overseas provinces, including East Timor (q.v.). It was predominantly a party of bureaucrats, many of whom were more or less obliged to join it, and its main task was the promotion of Salazar's corporatist ideology. Under Salazar's successor, Marcello Caetano, it expanded its popular base slightly but was abolished in 1974 after the armed forces coup in Portugal. Many of its former members in East Timor later joined the conservative União Democrática Timorense (q.v.). [0905]

ACEH, Muslim state in the northernmost part of Sumatra (q.v.), founded in C.15 by rulers of the state of Lamuri after their expulsion by Pedir (q.v.). Sultan Ali Mughayat Syah (r.1514–30) was able to draw many

Muslim traders to his port of Banda Aceh (Kutaraja) after the fall of Melaka (q.v.) to the Portuguese in 1511, transforming it into a major emporium for trade in pepper (q.v.) and Indian cloth. With European weapons purchased from the profits of this trade, he conquered much of northern Sumatra, including Pasai (q.v.) and Pedir. Under Sultans Alauddin Riayat Syah al-Kahar (r. 1537–71) and Iskandar Muda (q.v. r. 1607–36), Aceh fought a protracted war with the Portuguese and with the sultanate of Riau-Johor (see RIAU). Sultan Alauddin sought with partial success to concentrate the pepper trade in Kutaraja and turned his court into a major regional center of Islamic law and learning. He was patron to the writers Hamzah Fansuri (q.v.) and Syamsuddin of Pasai. Iskandar Muda used revenue from taxation and his own personal trade to build a strong centralized state which was able to subdue the Acehnese commercial nobility (*orang kaya*) as well as the feudal rulers of the interior (*uleëbalang*). He pushed Acehnese rule southwards along both coasts of Sumatra as far as Padang and Nias (qq.v.) in the west and Aru (q.v.) in the east, as well as dominating Pahang, Kedah and Perak on the Malay peninsula. He launched major but unsuccessful attacks on Riau-Johor in 1613 and 1623 and on Melaka in 1614 and 1629, losing most of his navy in the latter campaign.

After the fall of Melaka to the Dutch and the shift of trading activity to Batavia (q.v.) and the Sunda Strait, Aceh was ruled by a succession of four queens, beginning with Taj al-Alam (1641–75), in coalition with the orang kaya, but state power declined under Dutch military pressure and the rise of uleëbalang power based on the growing rice trade. At the same time, Islam (q.v.) became more and more firmly established, leading to the rise of powerful Islamic scholars, or *ulama,* whose influence ended the tradition of female rule. The

Anglo-Dutch treaty of 1824 (q.v.) guaranteed Aceh's independence, but in 1871 the British authorized the Dutch to invade to avoid possible French annexation. The Dutch annexed Aceh in 1874, but the ferocious Aceh War lasted from 1873 to 1903 and the Dutch won thanks only to the advice of Snouck Hurgronje (q.v.) to support the uleëbalangs against the sultanate and by vigorous military action under the generalship of van Heutsz (q.v.). According to official estimates, 100,000 Acehnese and 12,000 Dutch were killed in the operations. Guerrilla warfare continued until 1914, led mainly by ulama and a revolt broke out in the region in 1942 just prior to the Japanese invasion, partly directed by the ulama organization PUSA (Persatuan Ulama Seluruh Aceh, All-Aceh Union of Ulama).

In 1945, after the Japanese surrender, the ulama declared for the Indonesian Republic and launched a social revolution in which most uleëbalang were killed or deposed. Except for the island of Pulo Weh (Sabang), the region was never invaded by the Dutch during the Revolution. Aceh was briefly made a province by the Emergency Republican Government of Syafruddin Prawiranegara (q.v.) in 1949, but in 1950 was united with the province of North Sumatra. Resentment over the setting aside of local leaders and over the secularist policies of the central government led to the outbreak of a revolt in September 1953, led by Muhammad Daud Beureu'eh (q.v.), which was affiliated with the more general Darul Islam (q.v.) uprising. The designation of Aceh as a province in 1957 and as a *daerah istimewa* (special territory) with greater autonomy in religious and educational matters in 1959 largely ended the revolt, though an *Aceh Merdeka* (Free Aceh) movement under Hasan Tiro has continued to wage a low level guerrilla war against the central authorities. See also GAMBLING; TJIK DI TIRO; UMAR, Teuku. For a list of the rulers of Aceh, see the Appendix. [0416, 0468, 0528, 0535, 0645, 0659, 1043, 1047]

'ACT OF FREE CHOICE'. See IRIAN; OPERASI KHUSUS.

ADAT, Arabic term literally meaning 'custom', as distinct from law laid down in the Qur'an and other texts. *Adat* has come to denote all indigenous customary law in Indonesia, as opposed to the codified civil and criminal law of the colonial and Republican governments, as well as, more narrowly, the body of customary law as recorded in late C.19 and C.20 by Dutch scholars, notably van Vollenhoven, Snouck Hurgronje (qq.v.) and G.A. Wilken and given the name *adatrecht* ('adat law'). The compilers identified 19 *adatrechtskringen* or adat law zones of similar legal tradition. This codification was undertaken to allow the partial application of 'traditional' law to the indigenous peoples of the regions as part of a more general policy of indirect rule. Adat law, as codified, has tended to emphasize the collectivist aspects of traditional practice, in which crimes committed by an individual against another are seen as committed by and against the whole community. See also ISLAM; LAW; ZELFBESTUREN. [0366, 0870, 0872, 0875, 0877, 0878, 1123]

ADONARA. See SOLOR ARCHIPELAGO.

AFFANDI (1910–1990), painter with a vigorous style described as impressionist and reminiscent of van Gogh. He was a founder of Pelukis Rakyat (People's Painters) and a member of LEKRA (q.v.), but later in life became less sympathetic to the notion that art should have a social purpose. In 1955 he was elected to the Constituent Assembly (q.v.) under PKI (q.v.) sponsorship but sat in the Assembly in sessions as a non-party member. See also CULTURE, Debate on the role of. [0116]

AFRICA, Historical links with. Although Austronesians probably touched the east coast of Africa en route to Madagascar (q.v., see MIGRATIONS) and although that coast was raided by Southeast Asian pirates, perhaps Indonesian, in C.10, Indonesia has had little influence on the African continent, except perhaps in the field of music (q.v.). Jones has argued that several features of African traditional music have an Indonesian origin. The principal trade route which took Indonesian cinnamon, cloves, and other spices to the Mediterranean in classical times probably ran via East Africa, and Africa was also the source of an important number of cultivated plants used in the archipelago, especially kapok and oil palm (q.v.).

The Dutch settlements in South Africa were formally under the VOC, though independent of Batavia for most practical purposes, and an important 'Malay' community exists in South Africa, the descendants of slaves and political exiles from the VOC's East Indies possessions. The first of these arrived in 1667 and there was a substantial import of slaves from 1715 to 1767 when the trade was banned by the Raad van Indië. Troops were recruited in Dutch settlements on the coast of Guinea in West Africa for service in the colonial army (KNIL, q.v.) until the loss of those colonies in 1872.

Some intellectual links existed between the liberation movements in Portugal's African colonies and Fretilin (q.v.) in East Timor (see also EXILE), and those former colonies, along with Portugal, have led international resistance to Indonesia's annexation of the colony in 1976. From December 1962 to April 1963 an Indonesian unit, the Pasukan Garuda, served in the Congo as part of the UN forces there. [0118, 0751, 0764]

AGAVE. See SISAL.

AGRARIAN LAW of 1870 (more correctly the Agrarian article of the Regeeringsreglement or Constitution, q.v.) marked a major change in colonial agrarian policy. Under the Cultivation System (q.v.), villages had been the owners of land but acquired with ownership the obligation to provide land and labor (qq.v.) for government purposes, while Europeans were largely prohibited from acquiring land. Under the 1870 law, Western companies were at last allowed long-term leases over land, though the ban on freehold sale of land to non-Indonesians was strengthened. The law provided that leases should be for no longer than 75 years on 'unused' land and 21 years on village land, and that leases could not infringe upon traditional rights of indigenes. It also declared all 'unclaimed' land to be government property, though it recognized indigenous usufruct rights on such lands. The law removed the right of nonresident noncitizens to lease land. Except for the provision on unclaimed land, it applied only to Java and Madura (qq.v.). Although the Law had the beneficial effect of preventing alienation of peasant land to foreigners, it also worked in the interests of the Western plantations, allowing them to adjust their holdings from year to year and keeping the peasant landowners tied to their villages. See also BESCHIKKINGSRECHT; INDO-EUROPEANS; LAND; LIBERAL POLICY; RACE. [0371, 0601]

AGRICULTURAL INVOLUTION, term coined by Clifford Geertz (q.v.) for the process, beginning under the Cultivation System (q.v.), by which land tenure arrangements on Java allegedly became steadily more complex and intertwined with systems of credit, lease, and usufruct as population grew. It was allegedly able to emerge because the cultivation of rice (q.v.) permitted steadily greater labor inputs with only slightly diminished productivity per capita. A consequence of agricultural involution, in Geertz' view, was the absence of a clearly defined landlord class and a set of social obligations on both rich and poor which hindered capital formation. This hampered the development of a vibrant entrepreneurial economy such as that of Japan. Presented originally as a hypothesis rather than a fully elaborated theory, the idea of agricultural involution generated abundant research, much of which tended to disprove its conclusions. In particular, research has shown enormous regional variation and numerous examples of capital and class formation in rural Java. See also BESCHIKKINGSRECHT; CLASS ANALYSIS; DESA; SHARED POVERTY. [0244, 0272]

AGUNG, Gunung. See HINDUISM; VOLCANOES.

AGUNG, Sultan (r.1613–46), ruler of Mataram (q.v.), came to the throne amid a sustained campaign by his father Seda ing Krapyak to defeat the port cities of Java's north coast, especially Surabaya (q.v.) and Tuban. Agung conquered Sukadana (q.v.) in Kalimantan in 1622 and Madura (q.v.) in 1624, and finally starved Surabaya into submission in 1625. His campaigns devastated much of the countryside, causing severe food shortages and badly damaging Java's overseas trade, but established, for the first time since Majapahit (q.v.) a single city, around Agung's court at Karta near modern Yogyakarta, as a center of Javanese culture. In 1629 he attempted unsuccessfully to capture the Dutch fortress of Batavia, but was able to conquer most of East Java in a series of campaigns from 1635 to 1640, in honor of which he took the Islamic title Sultan in 1641. [0456]

AIR FORCE (Angkatan Udara Republik Indonesia, AURI). Founded in 1945 with a few former Japanese trainer aircraft, the air force contributed to the revolution mainly by using its planes to import war materials. Its operations were plagued by crashes, in one of which its first commander Halim Perdanakusuma was killed. Air commodore Suryadi Suryadarma (1912–75) became chief of staff in 1946. Especially dependent on modern technology, the air force received extensive supplies from the Soviet Union in the 1960s and was the most left wing of the armed forces, especially from January 1962 under air vice-marshal Omar Dhani (b. 1924). Some of the events of the GESTAPU (q.v.) coup took place at Halim air force base, and Dhani was later executed for his part in the affair; the force itself was heavily purged. Under the New Order the separate identity of the air force has gradually been submerged in that of ABRI (q.v.). [0663, 0669]

AIR SERVICES. Although the KLM was established in 1919 partly to provide air links with the Indies, regular services did not begin until the founding of the Koninklijk Nederlands-Indische Luchtzaartmaatschappij (KNILM) in 1927, with a subsidy from the colonial government. Since 1950, international air services have been provided by Garuda (q.v.). In 1976, B.J. Habibie (b.1936), later minister for research and technology, founded the Industri Pesawat Terbang Nurtanio (IPTN, Nurtanio [now Nusantara] Aircraft Industry) in Bandung which produces aircraft under license from Western corporations, but recently also developed the CN-235 light aircraft in a joint venture with Construcciones Aeronaúticas of Spain. Until 1988 Nusantara enjoyed a monopoly of light aircraft sales to Indonesia's 55 domestic airlines.

AIRLANGGA or Erlangga (991–1046), king of east and central Java. Of Javanese and Balinese royal descent, Airlangga was at the court of the king of Java in 1006 to be married to the king's daughter Dharmawangsa when the court was abruptly attacked by forces from Srivijaya (q.v.). Alone amongst the royal family, Airlangga escaped and established his rule over an attenuated kingdom in East Java and Bali (q.v.). After the fall of Srivijaya in 1024–25, he expanded his power on Java, creating a network of alliances and vassalages centered on the Brantas river valley. Although regional chiefs (bupati, q.v.) remained powerful, Airlangga's kingdom was more centralized than any to that time. Airlangga built irrigation works in the Brantas delta which controlled flooding and enabled a major expansion in the cultivation of rice (q.v.) which was exported through the new deepened harbor of Surabaya (q.v.) to other parts of the archipelago. He is also credited with increasing the Javanese content of court culture and diminishing Indian elements. In 1045, Airlangga abdicated to become an ascetic and is said to have divided his kingdom between his two sons to form the kingdoms of Kediri and Janggala. See also JAVA. [0116, 0392, 0396, 0413]

AKSI SEPIHAK (direct action). See LAND REFORM.

ALANG-ALANG (*Imperata cylindrica* Poaceae), a hardy grass which is an early colonizer in cleared rain forest areas. Its matted root system makes it difficult to eradicate and its spread is traditionally one of the factors prompting shifting cultivators to move. It is intolerant of shade, and so gradually gives way to tree species, but where repeated fires hamper the growth of broad-leafed plants it may form extensive fields resistant to forest succession, leading to the so-called 'Green Desert', something of a misnomer, since many communities do return alang-alang fields to cultivation. Shifting cultivators are commonly blamed for the spread of the grass, but it seems that some of the largest areas of infestation were caused by extensive cultivation of pepper and gambier (qq.v.) in C.19. [0242, 0267, 0936]

ALCOHOL. In pre-Muslim times alcohol, often called *tuak* or toddy, was brewed for consumption from various palm sugars (aren, lontar qq.v.), and from honey (q.v.). It continues to be popular in non-Muslim regions. *Arak* (arrack) is distilled from cane sugar factory syrup. In C.20, the colonial government regarded import restrictions and a heavy excise duty on alcohol as an important means of discouraging overconsumption. The spread of Islam diminished consumption of alcohol, but seldom eradicated it. From 1912 Sarekat Islam (q.v.) launched a series of campaigns against alcohol use. See also OPIUM; TOBACCO.

ALFURS (Arafuras, Alifuru, from North Moluccan, 'wilderness'), common derogatory term in eastern Indonesia from C.17 for 'uncivilized', that is, neither Christian nor Muslim, highland peoples, especially on Seram (q.v.), regardless of race or language. [0445]

ALGEMENE RECHERCHE. See POLITIEK INLICHTINGEN DIENST.

ALGEMENE STUDIECLUB (General Study Club), was founded in November 1925 on the model of study clubs organized by Dr Sutomo (q.v.) to bring together young Indonesian intellectuals to discuss politics and philosophy. The Algemene Studieclub in Bandung included Sukarno (q.v.) and was openly political. After the banning of the PKI (q.v.) in 1927, the club became the core around which the PNI (q.v.) was formed. See also NATIONALISM. [0719]

ALI-BABA FIRMS arose from efforts to circumvent 1950s legislation encouraging *pribumi* (q.v.) business at the expense of Chinese. In practice firms were still run by a Chinese ('Baba'), with an Indonesian ('Ali') as nominal head, sometimes providing political protection. See also

CHINESE IN INDONESIA; CUKONG; INDONESIANIZATION. [0280, 0920]

ALI HAJI IBN AHMAD, Raja (ca 1809–ca 1870), descendant of the Bugis dynasty which had held the office of Yang di Pertuan Muda in Riau (q.v.) but was deprived of office and influence by the imposition of Dutch rule in 1824. He was an accomplished writer and prepared works on language, religion, and politics. He is best known for his *Tuhfat al-Nafis* (Gift of the Prophet), which he expanded from a shorter draft by his father, Raja Ahmad. The Tuhfat described the history of the Bugis in the Malay world, concluding that strict adherence to Islamic law is the only basis on which a kingdom can be prosperous and happy. [0384]

ALI SASTROAMIJOYO (1903–75), nationalist politician, prominent in the Perhimpunan Indonesia (q.v.) in Holland and after independence leader of the left wing of the PNI (q.v.). As prime minister from July 1953 to July 1955, he sponsored the Asia-Africa Conference and abrogated the Netherlands Indonesian Union, but also overloaded the bureaucracy with party appointees and oversaw a substantial growth in corruption and smuggling. This cabinet fell after the army (q.v.) refused to accept its nomination of Bambang Utoyo as chief of staff. Ali formed a second cabinet in March 1956 which was also dogged by scandals and regional rebellions. Its resignation on 14 March 1957 marked the end of parliamentary democracy. He remained party leader during Guided Democracy, but was purged in 1966. [0634, 0647, 0691]

ALIRAN (lit. 'stream' or 'current'). 1. In Indonesian usage, any group characterized by adherence to similar ideas or ideals, e.g., *aliran sosialis*. 2. In Western social science, following the work of Geertz (q.v.), the two major cultural-religious traditions in Muslim Javanese society, the syncretist *abangan* and the orthodox *santri* (qq.v.). A third aliran identified by Geertz, the *priyayi* (q.v.), is now commonly regarded as a class category, referring to the aristocratic aspect of the abangan aliran (and sometimes extended to part of the santri elite). Aliran structure has been said to resemble the *verzuiling* ('pillarization') of Dutch society, most people belonging in the 1950s and 1960s to aliran-specific (rather than national, regional, or class-based) political, social, and other organizations. Organizational life in Java, however, has always been far more fragmented than this would imply. The 1955 election results, for instance, suggest the existence of four or more aliran. In many regions, the classification is subethnic, santri coming from the pasisir (q.v.) and abangan from the interior of Java. The classification is made more problematic by the fact that some santri Muslims, especially of the Nahdatul Ulama (q.v.), draw a good deal of their thought from non-Islamic Javanese traditions. See ISLAM; KEBATINAN. [0640, 0644, 0649, 1005, 1018, 1030, 1121]

ALISYAHBANA, Sutan Takdir (b. 1908), novelist and philosopher. Born in North Sumatra, Alisyahbana studied law in Batavia and worked as editor for the Balai Pustaka (q.v.) before founding the journal *Poedjangga Baru* (q.v.) with Armijn Pané (q.v.) and Amir Hamzah. He played a major role in developing the Indonesian language (q.v.) as a tool for sophisticated intellectual and technical usage, especially through his editing of the journal *Pembina Bahasa Indonesia*. [0141, 0158, 0597, 0769]

ALOE-WOOD (*kayu gaharu, tarum*), aromatic product from partly decomposed wood of the tree *Aquilaria agallocha* (Thymelaeaceae), used in classical times for incense, perfumes, cosmetics, and medicines. For these purposes it was traded in C.5 and later from Bangka, Belitung, Sumatra, and Java (qq.v.) to India and Africa, and from C.13 to China, though aloe-wood from mainland Southeast Asia was generally thought superior to the product from Indonesia. The trade was seized by the Portuguese (q.v.) in C.16. [0751, 0939]

ALOR, island and archipelago in Nusatenggara. The mainly animist population still produces cast bronze drums whose cultural origin is uncertain. See also GAMELAN. [1008]

AMANGKURAT I (r. 1646–77), son and successor to Sultan Agung (q.v.). He sought to consolidate his father's empire by gathering all authority in the land to himself, but in doing so he alienated both court officials and regional lords. He responded to their resistance and opposition with a reign of terror which left thousands dead. Not daring to leave his court in Plered for fear of a coup in his absence, he was unable to tend to the military affairs of the kingdom. In 1647 he lost control of the Balambangan (q.v.) region; most of Mataram's former vassals in Sumatra and Kalimantan also fell away. Agung's devastation of the north coast had already badly damaged Javanese external trade, but Amangkurat went further. He forbade his subjects from leaving the island and in 1652 banned the export of rice and timber, though his aim seems to have been to gain control of the trade, especially with the VOC (q.v.), for himself. His authoritarian rule precipitated the revolt of the Madurese prince Trunojoyo (q.v.) in 1671, in the course of which Amangkurat was driven from his capital in 1677 to die in exile. [0371, 0456]

AMBON (Amboina), island and city in Maluku (q.v.), originally a part of the sparsely populated hinterland of Ternate and Tidore (qq.v.). The Portuguese established a fort in 1574, but in 1605 the VOC seized the island, made it the center of their operations in the east of the archipelago under Cornelis de Houtman (q.v.), and planted extensive clove (q.v.) orchards. For most of the century, the Dutch struggled to exclude other foreigners (see 'AMBOYNA MASSACRE'; ENGLISH EAST INDIA COMPANY) and to establish a monopoly on the spice trade (see HONGI RAIDS). The island was seized by British forces during the Napoleonic Wars (1796–1802, 1810–17) and the restoration of Dutch rule was followed by a revolt on the nearby island of Saparua in 1817, led by Thomas Matulesia (1783–1817), also known as Pattimura.

In the latter part of the colonial period, the Ambonese gained a reputation for strong loyalty to Dutch rule. This was partly because service in the colonial army or KNIL (q.v.) was one of the few employment opportunities available to Ambonese and they were posted widely through the archipelago (though the military category 'Ambonezen' also included many from the Minahasa and Timor [qq.v.]). Christian Ambonese had European legal status (see LAW; RACE), though seldom enjoyed practical legal equality. Christians formed around half the Ambon population.

Ambon was the scene of heavy fighting between Japanese and Australian troops in 1942 and was bombed by the Allies in 1945. It became part of the NIT (q.v.) in 1946 and after the transfer of sovereignty in 1949, became a base of the separatist Republik Maluku Selatan (q.v.). [0019, 0060, 0375, 0445, 0457, 0506, 1108]

'AMBOYNA MASSACRE'. In 1623 Dutch authorities on Ambon (q.v.) executed ten English merchants and ten Javanese alleged accomplices on charges of conspiring to seize the local Dutch fort. Dutch writers have cited the affair as an example of English perfidy while British writers, in turn, have complained that the governor of

Ambon had reneged on his promise to protect the merchants. The massacres hastened the withdrawal of British interests from the archipelago to India. See also ENGLISH EAST INDIA COMPANY. [0375, 0437]

AMERICAS, Historical links with the. Tropical America was a major source of plants cultivated in the Indonesian archipelago from C.17. These included chilli, cinchona, pepper, rubber, sisal, soursop, vanilla (qq.v.), papaw, and pineapple. The disease syphilis (q.v.) probably also derives from the Americas.

AMIR SYARIFUDDIN (1907–48) nationalist politician. While training in law in Batavia, he became involved in the nationalist movement, secretly joining the PKI (q.v.) in 1927. In 1937, he helped to establish the GERINDO (q.v.) and argued strongly that Japanese fascism was an even greater danger to Indonesia than Dutch colonialism. When Japan (q.v.) attacked, he received £25,000 from the Dutch to set up an underground resistance, but was arrested in January 1943, condemned to death and spared only by the intercession of Sukarno (q.v.). After independence, he joined Syahrir in the Partai Sosialis (qq.v.), becoming deputy prime minister and defence minister in the Syahrir cabinets. He cooperated closely with A.H. Nasution and with the PESINDO (qq.v.) and was one of the architects of the Indonesian conventional army. He deposed Syahrir as prime minister in June 1947, but continued Syahrir's policy of negotiating with the Dutch (see DIPLOMASI AND PERJUANGAN), signing the Renville Agreement (q.v.) in January 1948. Opposition to Renville led him to resign tactically on 23 January 1948, apparently expecting to be reappointed on the basis of his supporters' strong position in parliament. Sukarno, however, chose Hatta (q.v.) as prime minister and Amir went into opposition, forming a People's

Democratic Front (FDR, q.v.) in February and denouncing the Renville Agreement. The power of the left, however, gradually eroded as the government demobilized leftist army units. In August 1948 Amir announced that he had been a Communist since before the war (a claim then widely doubted) and accepted the authority of the PKI (q.v.) leader Musso who had just returned from Moscow. In September he joined the unsuccessful Madiun (q.v.) rising and was captured in late October. He was summarily shot by government troops at the start of the second Dutch 'Police Action' on 19/20 December 1948. [0656, 0703]

AMOMUM (*Amomum* sp., Zingiberaceae), spice of the ginger family, often confused with the related cardamom. It was extensively traded to China during the Sung dynasty (960–1279). [0424, 0751, 0938]

AMORPHOPHALLUS sp. (Araceae), jungle plant producing a huge inflorescence (flowering body) which in the case of *A. titanum* can reach 2 meters in height. Unlike *Rafflesia* (q.v.), with which it is sometimes confused, its inflorescence is not a single flower, but it shares with *Rafflesia* a strong smell of decaying flesh attractive to the flies which spread its pollen. [0936, 0938]

AMUK, temporary derangement which leads an individual (normally male) to wild and directionless violence, usually against other people. It is not clear whether *amuk* has any strictly clinical causes; most observers attribute it to a reaction against the extreme suppression of personal feelings allegedly demanded in many Indonesian societies, but it may have developed, like the Viking *berserk,* as a technique for inspiring terror in enemies during battle and could apparently be encouraged by use of cannabis or opium (qq.v.). See also LATAH; WARFARE. [0484, 1169]

ANAK BUAH, lit. 'fruit child', protégé, client. See BAPAK.

ANDALAS. Older term for Sumatra (q.v.). See also PERCA, Pulau.

ANGKATAN BERSENJATA REPUBLIK INDONESIA (ABRI, Armed Forces of the Republic of Indonesia) encompasses the army (Angkatan Darat), navy (Angkatan Laut), air force (Angkatan Udara), and police (Polisi Negara or Angkatan Kepolisian)(qq.v.). In 1962, Sukarno created ABRI as a central body over the previously separate individual forces, mainly as a device to remove Nasution (q.v.) from command posts. Until the advent of the New Order, therefore, the central armed forces command had little power over the separate services; Sukarno in particular preferred to balance the services against each other. Since the abolition of separate service ministries in 1967, however, the armed forces, except the police, have gradually been integrated within a single command structure under the Ministry of Defence and Security (HANKAM, Departemen Pertahanan dan Keamanan). From 1967 to 1983, the posts of defence minister and ABRI commander were always held by the same man. In 1988, the armed forces consisted officially of 284,000 personnel, with a further 800,000 in 'reserves', which include the village guards (HANSIP, Pertahanan Sipil). Armed Forces Day is celebrated on 5 October. For a list of Armed Forces Commanders, see the Appendix. See also DWIFUNGSI; 'FIFTH FORCE'. [0033, 0663, 0863]

ANGKATAN '45; ANGKATAN '66. See GENERATIONS.

ANGLO-DUTCH TREATY, signed 17 March 1824, revising British and Dutch colonial holdings in western

Indonesia. The British, ceding Bengkulu (q.v.) to the Dutch and receiving Melaka (q.v.) in exchange, confined themselves to and were given exclusive rights on the Malay peninsula, where they immediately established the port of Singapore (q.v.). The Dutch were given a free hand on Sumatra, but agreed to guarantee the independence of Aceh (q.v.). The treaty permanently split the territories of the sultanate of Riau-Johor. The treaty explicitly permitted the British to retain their interests in northern Borneo and to trade in areas not annexed by the Dutch, and fear that trade might become a cover for further British expansion, encouraged the Dutch to consolidate their holdings in the archipelago in following years. See also BELITUNG; NETHERLANDS INDIES, Expansion of; RAFFLES, Thomas Stamford; RIAU. [0538]

ANSOR (from Arabic *al-ansar,* followers of the Prophet), youth organization founded in 1934 and affiliated with the Nahdatul Ulama (q.v.), known for its participation in massacres of Communists, especially in East Java, in 1965–66. See also MASSACRES OF 1965–66.

ANTARA ('Between'), founded on 17 December 1937 by R.M. Sumanang and A.M. Sipatuhar and developed by Adam Malik (q.v.) and others as a private, nationalist news agency. During the occupation it was merged with the Japanese agency Domei but became Indonesia's official news agency in 1945. Several agencies were merged with Antara in 1963 to form the Lembaga Kantor Berita Nasional (LKBN, National News Agency Institute), but the name Antara is retained for daily use. See also NEWS AGENCIES. [0342, 0354]

ANTASARI. See BANJARMASIN.

ARAB WORLD, Historical links with. Trade in spices linked Indonesia and the Arab world even before the emergence of Islam, but it is the *haj* (q.v.), or pilgrimage to Mecca, and the study of Islam in general, which has taken the largest number of Indonesians to the Middle East. Arabs (q.v) were prominent in the archipelago as traders and mercenaries. Ten thousand Indonesians (so-called *mukim,* lived semi-permanently in Arabia in late C.19. From early C.20, many Indonesians studied at Al-Azhar University in Cairo.

In November 1946, the Arab League recommended recognition of the Indonesian Republic, and this was done by Egypt and Syria in June 1947, the first states to do so. In the 1950s Indonesia joined Arab states in the Non-Aligned Movement (see ASIA-AFRICA CONFERENCE). In the 1970s and 1980s, relations were somewhat cooler, Arab countries often seeing Indonesia as insufficiently Islamic, and Indonesia seeing especially Libya and Iran as possible promoters of Muslim unrest. Since 1987, the number of Indonesians working in the Middle East has increased substantially. Indonesia has no diplomatic relations with Israel but recognized the state of Palestine only in November 1988. See also ISLAM. See also TURKEY, Historical links with. [0065, 0430, 0722, 0750, 0759, 1128, 1140, 1141]

ARABS, especially from Hadramaut, settled in Indonesia in small impermanent trading communities from perhaps C.5, and Arab adventurers founded the kingdom of Pontianak (q.v.); other dynasties also had an Arabic ancestry. As with the Chinese (q.v.), Arab communities absorbed much local culture, some disappearing altogether, others forming distinctive *peranakan* (q.v.) communities, which tended to harden under the Dutch system of racial classification and to form a class of wealthy traders and money lenders (despite Islam's ban on usury). Greatest immigration took place in the second half of C.19, when large communities settled especially on the north coast of Java. Sharing Islam with most Indonesians, the Arabs were often better able than the Chinese to be accepted as part of the nationalist movement. In 1934, A.R.A. Baswedan founded the Persatuan Arab Indonesia (PAI, Indonesian Arab Association) in Semarang to encourage the allegiance of peranakan Arabs to Indonesia. The PAI joined GAPI (q.v.) in 1939–40. An Indo-Arabische Beweging (Indo-Arab Movement) founded in 1939, on the other hand, argued for continued separate status. [0367, 0932]

ARAFURAS. See ALFURS.

ARCHEOLOGY. The earliest serious archeological work in the archipelago was conducted by the Bataviaasch Genootschap van Kunsten en Wetenschappen (q.v.), while in early C.19 Raffles (q.v.) did some work on the antiquities of Java, such as the excavation and partial reconstruction of Borobudur (q.v.). Extensive archeological work, however, did not begin until the foundation of the Commissie in Nederlandsch-Indië voor Oudheidkundig Onderzoek op Java en Madoera (Netherlands Indies Commission for Investigation of Antiquities on Java and Madura) in 1901 under J.L.A. Brandes. Headed successively by N.J. Krom (1910–16), F.D.K. Bosch (1916–36), and W.F. Stutterheim (1936–42), and becoming the Oudheidkundige Dienst (Archeological Service) in 1913, it was active in investigating and protecting the archipelago's antiquities, though it paid greatest attention to the Hindu-Buddhist relics of Java. The postindependence Dinas Purbakala dan Peninggalan Nasional (National Archeological and Remains Service, now Pusat Penelitian Arkeologi Nasional, National Center for Archeological Research) under H.R. van Heekeren (to 1956) and then Sukmono continued this work while giving greater attention to the archeology and prehistory of the other islands. [0087, 0089, 0391]

ARCHIPELAGIC CONCEPT (*Wawasan Nusantara*). Upon achieving independence, Indonesia inherited a 3-mile territorial-waters limit around each of its (then) 13,677 islands. Largely for security reasons, this was expanded by a declaration of 13 December 1957 and an Act of 18 February 1960 to 12 miles, measured from a straight baseline drawn from the outermost points of each island, thus covering the entire archipelago. The 1973 Act on Indonesia's Continental Shelf claimed seabed resources, but required the reaching of seabed agreements with Malaysia (1969, 1971, 1981); Thailand (1971, 1975, 1977); Australia (then including Papua New Guinea) (1971, 1972, 1973); India (1974, 1977); Singapore (1973, 1978); and Papua New Guinea (1980). A further treaty was signed with Australia in 1988, establishing a marine border in the so-called Timor Gap, covering the territorial waters of former Portuguese Timor. Overlapping claims with Vietnam and China in the South China Sea remain unresolved and Indonesia has not yet signed agreements with the Philippines or Palau. The principle, argued by Indonesia since the 1958 Convention on the Law of the Sea, that an archipelagic nation is entitled to claim all waters between its islands as internal waters was upheld by the United Nations International Convention on the Law of the Sea in 1982, though the Sunda and Lombok straits are recognized as international waterways. On 21 March 1980, Indonesia claimed a 200 km Exclusive Economic Zone around its outer perimeter, and this was formalized by law in 1983. See also CONTINENTAL DRIFT; MALAYSIA, Relations with; PIRACY. [0729, 0732]

ARCHITECTURE. Austronesian migrants to Indonesia in ca 3000 B.C. apparently brought with them techniques for building thatched communal dwellings (see MIGRATIONS), of a kind still seen amongst the Dayaks (q.v.). In later times, however, smaller dwellings for individual (extended) families became more common, and the typical house throughout much of the archipelago was a light, impermanent structure built of palm and bamboo materials, with a steep roof against tropical rains and constructed on poles as a protection against flooding. Royal palaces adopted the same style on a grander scale. In Java, the characteristic structure of royal palaces is the *pendopo,* consisting of a steep roof with decorated ceiling supported on pillars over a raised floor, with no walls.

Foreign influences may have registered first in religious architecture: Hindu and Buddhist temples were often of stone and brick and many examples still survive especially on Java (see ARCHEOLOGY; BOROBUDUR; KRATON). The Indonesian style of mosque is also distinctive, being square, with four supporting pillars and a veranda (*serambi*) facing east. European trading companies used brick and stone extensively for their trading posts, partly for defensive reasons, and their early dwelling houses were closely modelled on European styles. A distinctive Dutch colonial architecture emerged in early C.19, with high ceilings, marble or tiled floors, deep verandas, neoclassical pillars, living areas opening directly onto the garden, and separate pavilions for cooking, bathing etc. This style declined in C.20 with a return to European urban models. Since independence, many Indonesian architects have endeavored to incorporate traditional forms and motifs in their work. While the government is often suspicious of manifestations of regional ethnic identity in matters such as language, it has expressly encouraged the preservation of the strikingly different characteristic architectural styles of Indonesia's many ethnic groups; this official sanctioning is seen perhaps most clearly in Jakarta's Taman Mini Indonesia Indah (Beautiful Indonesia in Miniature theme park). [0091–0101, 0421]

ARECA. See BETEL.

AREN (*Arenga saccarifera, A. pinnata* Arecaceae), sugar palm. The young male inflorescence is bruised, left for a few days and then cut, allowing the collection of a sugary liquid which is concentrated by boiling, producing cakes of palm sugar, or *gula jawa*. A single inflorescence can produce 7 liters of liquid a day for 2-½ months. Because *gula jawa* ferments readily, it has been generally displaced by cane sugar (see SUGAR CANE), except where valued for its distinctive flavor. The poisonous fruits of the aren are said to have been used by besiegers to poison the water supply of Surabaya (q.v.) in 1545. Other palms such as the coconut, *lontar* (qq.v.) and *gebang* (*Corypha utan*) are also tapped for sugar. See also ALCOHOL; HONEY. [0938, 0958]

ARISAN. A rotating credit association, typically of 10 to 20 persons, common on Java. Members meet regularly to pay fixed contributions, the entire kitty at each meeting being taken by one member, chosen by lot or prior agreement. The arisan ends when all members have drawn from it. See also PAWNSHOPS. [0305]

ARMED FORCES. See ANGKATAN BERSENJATA REPUBLIK INDONESIA and individual services.

ARMY (Angkatan Darat, AD). The Indonesian army dates its founding to 5 October 1945, when the new national government announced the creation of a Tentara Keamanan Rakyat (TKR, People's Security Army) and gave a mandate for the actual formation of an army to Urip Sumoharjo, a retired major from the Dutch colonial army, or KNIL. The government had previously on 22 August created a quasimilitary Badan Keamanan Rakyat (People's Security Organization), responsibility for which was largely devolved to regional national committees (Komite Nasional Indonesia, q.v.); BKR units in general formed the basis of the TKR.

The new army drew its officer corps principally from former soldiers and officers of the KNIL (q.v.) and the Japanese-sponsored Pembela Tanah Air (q.v.), or PETA. Many units consisted initially of PETA soldiers, but enthusiastic recruitment soon diluted the Japanese-trained element. The TKR was an army of young men (see PEMUDA) and it remained for about forty years under the domination of the so-called generation of '45 (see GENERATIONS) who first made their mark and obtained command posts during the National Revolution. The ranks of this generation were thinned in later years by the exclusion and self-exclusion of many fundamentalist Muslims and leftists, so that the social base of the officer corps could increasingly be described as conservative, *abangan* (q.v.) and from the small town elites of Java. In the 1980s, however, the generation of 1945 steadily retreated to the upper levels of military command and with the appointment of Try Sutrisno (b.1935) as armed forces commander in 1988 the army is now entirely in the hands of officers without revolutionary experience who received training at the military academy at Magelang.

Since 1945, a gradual centralization of military authority has taken place. Initially most army units depended financially and logistically on local civilian governments, and regional commanders enjoyed extensive autonomy from the center. Notions of popular sovereignty were widespread during this time and many commanders came to power through election by their own troops. Senior officers met in Yogyakarta on 12 November 1945 and elected Sudirman (q.v.) as army commander, relegating the government's choice, Urip, to the post of chief of staff. The navy and air force (qq.v.) were separate organizations under the ministry of defence. Hierarchy was further weakened by the existence of numerous armed organizations outside the army (see BADAN PERJUANGAN; HIZBULLAH; LASYKAR). Gradually, however, military authority was concentrated in the general staff, dominated by former KNIL officers. With the help of the ministry of defence under Amir Syarifuddin (q.v.), irregular armed units were disbanded or incorporated, Sudirman's authority was gradually diminished, and 'reliable' officers were gradually placed in key positions. In this process the TKR changed its name to Tentara Keselamatan Rakyat (TKR, 1 January 1946), Tentara Republik Indonesia (TRI, 24 January 1946), and Tentara Nasional Indonesia (TNI, June 1947). In 1949 the Republic's armed forces were merged with the KNIL (q.v.) to form the APRIS (Angkatan Perang Republik Indonesia Serikat, Armed Forces of the RIS, q.v.), becoming APRI in August 1950.

The post-revolutionary army was over-large (perhaps 500,000 in late 1949) and deeply segmented. Divisional commanders, especially of the Siliwangi, Diponegoro, and Brawijaya divisions in West, Central, and East Java respectively, enjoyed great autonomy, while the regional commanders in East Sumatra and Minahasa (qq.v.) maintained major smuggling operations. The High Command was unable to meet army financial needs and the following decades saw a gradual movement towards reduction of size and centralization of authority, promoted particularly by A.H. Nasution (q.v.) as minister of defence. This process included the creation of elite commando-style units (KOSTRAD, RPKAD, qq.v., Banteng Raiders) directly under central command, and an expansion of formal military training both at the Army Staff and Command School (SESKOAD, Sekolah Staf dan Komando Angkatan Darat, Army Staff and Command School) in Bandung and at Fort Leavenworth in Texas. In 1952, Nasution began a program of transferring regional commanders away from their power bases. When the officers mobilized parliamentary support against the transfers and demobilizations, Nasution and others organized demonstrations in Jakarta on 17 October, calling for the dissolution of parliament. Sukarno refused and Nasution was suspended from duty for three years, leaving the High Command much weakened.

In 1954, reconciliation began within the army and in February 1955 an officers' conference at Yogyakarta adopted a charter of unity. Nasution was reinstalled as Chief of Staff in November and resumed his transfer program. When these sparked the regional military coups which preceded the PRRI and Permesta (qq.v.) uprising, Nasution proposed the declaration of Martial Law to defuse the insubordination by legalizing it. Martial Law, however, allowed army commanders to exercise greater powers throughout the country, banning parties (q.v.), suspending newspapers, removing Chinese (q.v.) from rural trade, and organizing direct political links with other social groups through Badan Kerja Sama (q.v.). From 1960, army officers were appointed as provincial governors (see DWIFUNGSI). Dismissals after the PRRI-Permesta affair and an expansion of the army to 330,000 for the Irian (q.v.) campaign increased the power of the high command, headed from 1962 by Ahmad Yani (q.v.). During Guided Democracy, President Sukarno, suspicious of army power, promoted the distinctive identities of the navy, air force, and police, but in 1967–70, the four separate ministries were reabsorbed into the Defence Ministry. In 1988, army personnel officially numbered 215,000. For a list of Army Commanders, see the Appendix. See also ANGKATAN BERSENJATA REPUBLIK INDONESIA; DEFENCE POLICY; DWIFUNGSI; MILITARY BUSINESS OPERA-

TIONS; WARFARE. [0652, 0663, 0669, 0675, 0714, 0805, 0812, 0835]

ARU, Malay-Batak kingdom on the east coast of Sumatra, near modern Deli. Seldom fully independent, it was occupied by Javanese forces from Majapahit (q.v.) in 1350, became briefly independent around 1460, and was later contested by the Muslim rulers of Aceh and Riau (qq.v.). It fell to Aceh in ca 1600, but during C.17 reemerged as the independent sultanate of Deli (q.v.). [0528]

ARU Islands, archipelago in southeastern Indonesia with a largely Melanesian population. The islands were formally annexed by the VOC (q.v.) in 1623 as a source of pearls and birds-of-paradise (qq.v.), but there was little active Dutch presence and they were effectively under Bugis (q.v.) and Makassarese domination until Dutch administration was established in 1882. Commercial pearl fishing expanded in early C.20. [0026]

ARUNG PALAKKA (1634–96), prince of the Bugis (q.v.) state of Soppeng in southern Sulawesi. After rebelling against Sultan Hasanuddin of Makassar (q.v.) in 1660, he took refuge with his followers on Butung (q.v.) before serving as mercenaries for the VOC (q.v.) in Batavia in 1663. He joined the VOC attack on Makassar in 1666–67 and in reward was made commander in chief and later (1672) Arumpone, or king, of Bone (q.v.). He assisted the VOC against Trunojoyo (q.v.) on Java in 1678. His autocratic rule in South Sulawesi prompted an exodus of Bugis to other parts of the archipelago. [0433]

ASAHAN. Malay-Batak and Acehnese sultanate on the east coast of Sumatra, founded 1695 and formerly subordinate to Siak (q.v.). It was annexed by the Dutch in 1865 and the Sultan exiled to Riau, but in 1885 he was returned with reduced powers to provide a legal and political basis for the expansion of European tobacco cultivation, which was later replaced by rubber. In 1932, Dutch firms involved in the mining of bauxite (q.v.) on Bintan made plans for an alumina plant powered by hydroelectricity from the Asahan river, which flows out of Lake Toba. War and other concerns, however, delayed plans and not until July 1979 did work actually begin on the so-called Asahan project. This was a joint venture with Japanese investors which opened in February 1982, involving the construction of a hydroelectric dam on the Asahan river to supply power for aluminium smelter at Kuala Tanjung. Since that time, however, the water level in Lake Toba has dropped two meters due to declining rainfall in the catchment area and consequently the factory at times has had to cease production. [0528]

ASIA-AFRICA CONFERENCE (aka the Bandung Conference). Held in April 1955 on the initiative of the Ali Sastroamijoyo (q.v.) cabinet, this Conference was attended by the leaders of 29 Asian and African states, including Zhou Enlai, Nehru, Sihanouk, and Nasser. The Conference endorsed Indonesia's claim to Irian (q.v.) and helped to establish Sukarno's credentials as a major Non-Aligned Bloc leader. See also FOREIGN POLICY. [0634, 0721, 0740]

ASLI ('original'). 1. Term widely used to describe cultural elements and traditions believed to predate Muslim, Christian, and often Hindu-Buddhist influence. Several small tribal groups, the Badui (West Java), Tenggerese (East Java), Bali Aga (Bali) (qq.v.), Buda (Lombok) and Donggo (Sumbawa) are believed to preserve the traditional culture of their respective regions. See also SAMIN MOVEMENT. [0373]

2. Ambiguous term for non-foreigners, often used in the context of some form of discrimination against foreigners. Asli may mean 'born in Indonesia'—the 1945 Constitution prescribes that the president (q.v.) shall be 'asli' and seems to be based on the article of the U.S. Constitution which required the president to be native-born—or it may refer more narrowly to ethnicity, thus excluding descendants of Chinese, Arabs, and Europeans. See also PRIBUMI.

ASMAT, Papuan ethnic group inhabiting the swampy lowlands of southeastern Irian (q.v.). They had little contact with the outside world before early C.20 and their society was disrupted by intensive intervillage warfare between 1942 and 1958. In 1964 the Indonesian administration attempted to eliminate headhunting by banning man-houses, the residences of unmarried males. Since the 1970s Asmat society has been further disrupted by labor recruitment for the timber industry and by relocation of communities for this purpose. [0899, 0901, 1020]

ASSOCIAÇÃO DEMOCRÁTICA PARA INTEGRAÇÃO TIMOR-LESTE CON AUSTRALIA (ADITLA, Democratic Association for the Integration of East Timor and Australia). A tiny political organization which emerged in some urban areas of Portuguese Timor after the military coup of 1974 to press for the absorption of the colony by Australia (q.v.). It withered and disappeared once it became clear that Australia had no interest in this proposition. [0905]

ASSOCIAÇÃO POPULÁR DEMOCRÁTICA TIMORENSE (APODETI, Timorese Popular Democratic Association) was formed in Portuguese Timor in 1974 by Arnoldo dos Reis Araujo to press for the colony's integration into Indonesia as an autonomous province. APODETI drew its rather meager support from the small Muslim community and from people in border areas, but received substantial financial help from BAKIN (q.v.) and the Indonesian consulate in Dili. It allied with UDT (q.v.) in July 1975, just before the UDT (q.v.) coup and many of its leaders were jailed by Fretilin (q.v.) in the subsequent civil war. It disappeared as a party after the Indonesian invasion of December 1975, but many of its followers were appointed to posts in the new provincial government after 1976. [0905]

ASSOCIATION OF SOUTHEAST ASIAN NATIONS (ASEAN). ASEAN was founded on 8 August 1967 and comprised Indonesia, Malaysia, The Philippines, Singapore (qq.v.), and Thailand. The ASEAN secretariat is in Jakarta and H.R. Dharsono (b.1925) was first secretary-general. Its members saw their principal security threats as internal and aimed to avert these by promoting economic development through regional cooperation. ASEAN formally aims to create a Zone of Peace, Freedom, and Neutrality (ZOPFAN) in Southeast Asia, but its members have commonly disagreed on the extent to which great powers should be a part of this goal. Little economic integration has been achieved, but ASEAN has successfully operated as a unit in international affairs, especially in the continuing discussions over Kampuchea (Cambodia). See also FOREIGN POLICY. [0002, 0728]

ASSOCIATION PRINCIPLE. A doctrine, linked with the Ethical Policy and especially Snouck Hurgronje (qq.v.), which argued that colonial rule should aim to assimilate the Indonesian elite to modern Western secular culture by means of education and the opening of government positions to qualified Indonesians. It was opposed both by conservatives who saw in it an end to colonial rule and by the proponents of *adat* (q.v.), who believed it would rob Indonesians of their own culture. See also DJAJADININGRAT, Ahmad; MUIS, Abdul.

AUSTRALIA, Historical links with. Up to about 3000 B.C., much of Australia and the Indonesian archipelago seems to have formed a single cultural region inhabited by Austro-Melanesian (Australoid) people who reached the area 50,000–100,000 years ago, perhaps earlier. This continuity was broken by the arrival of Austronesians in the archipelago (see MIGRATIONS); although the Austronesians certainly reached the Australian coast from time to time, there is no trace of permanent settlement.

In C.17 Dutch authorities in Batavia sent expeditions to the south to look for trading opportunities, but these explorers reported nothing of commercial advantage there. The Dutch technique of sailing to Indonesia by heading directly east from the Cape of Good Hope led a number of vessels to sight, and run against, the western Australian coast. In C.18, the exhaustion of trepang (bêche de mer) fields in the archipelago brought Indonesian fishing fleets of up to 2,000 vessels, mainly from Makassar, to the northern coast of Australia, where some cultural influences on Aborigines are still visible.

During the first years of British settlement in eastern Australia in late C.18, the Dutch settlements in Indonesia were the nearest point of European civilization, and during C.19 Australian produce found something of market there. There were also important scientific connections between the two colonies in the field of tropical agriculture. A telegraph (q.v.) link between Banyuwangi on Java and Darwin was laid in 1871. Australian tourism (q.v.) to Indonesia began in early C.20 and Australian commercial interests became involved in eastern Indonesia, especially in the pearl industry of the Aru Islands (q.v.).

During C.19, the Dutch colonial authorities became increasingly worried by the possibility of Australian imperialist expansion in the eastern archipelago, and well-founded Dutch suspicion of Australia's intentions hampered cooperation in the defence of the Indies against Japan, although the two countries were joined with Britain and the United States in the so-called ABDA (American-British-Dutch-Australian) command. During the Japanese occupation of Indonesia (q.v.), the colonial rulers formed a government-in-exile in Australia and attempted to stave off Australian ambitions to establish some form of hegemony in Irian and Timor (qq.v.). [0365, 0407, 0734]

AUSTRALIA, Relations with. At the close of World War II, Australian forces accepted the Japanese surrender and restored Dutch rule in eastern Indonesia, despite Australian ambitions in the region. The Indonesian struggle, however, quickly attracted the sympathy of the left in Australia, where dock workers organized strikes against Dutch shipping, the first tangible sign of international support for the Republic. Australian policy makers, historically unsympathetic to the Dutch and keen to cultivate good relations with prospective neighbors, increasingly sided with Indonesia in international fora, and Australia was Indonesia's nominee on the UN (q.v.) Good Offices Committee in 1947–48.

Relations with Indonesia deteriorated in the late 1950s over Indonesia's continued claim to Irian (q.v.), seen in Australia as expansionist, and in the early 1960s Australian troops fought Indonesians in northern Borneo during the so-called Confrontation (q.v.) campaign. Relations were good during the first decade of the New Order, as Australia increasingly sought friends in Asia while Indonesia looked for Western aid, but the Indonesian invasion of East Timor in 1975, including the killing of five journalists from Australia, and later what Indonesia has seen as persistently hostile press reporting have soured relations, which reached a nadir in 1986 after a report in the *Sydney Morning Herald* (10 April) on the Suharto family's wealth. [0366, 0724, 0733, 0734, 0737]

AUSTRONESIANS. See LANGUAGES; MIGRATION; RICE; TARO.

AZAS TUNGGAL ('sole principle'). See PANCASILA.

AZIZ, Andi Abdul, KNIL (q.v.) captain who seized control of Makassar in a limited coup on 5 April 1950, partly to prevent the landing of Republican troops who, he feared, might begin to dismantle the Negara Indonesia Timur (q.v.), partly out of frustration at the slow progress made in integrating former KNIL troops into the RIS (q.v.) armed forces. The Aziz affair ended when the NIT government failed to back him and he was arrested in Jakarta on 18 April. The resemblance of the affair to the abortive coup by Westerling (q.v.) in Bandung was an important element in discrediting the NIT.

B

BABAD, Javanese verse chronicles commonly written to describe and glorify the rise or rule of a particular king, though some deal exclusively with mythical tales. The term 'babad' also means 'to clear forest', suggesting that these chronicles were associated with the founding of kingdoms; they appear to be an indigenous development, though all known babad were written after the conversion of Java to Islam. [0380, 0384, 0387]

BABAD TANAH JAWI, babad (q.v.) celebrating the power of C.17 Mataram (q.v.), probably composed in the court of Sultan Agung, though all known manuscripts date from C.18 and 19.

BACAN, island in northern Maluku. Its people probably came originally from Halmahera (q.v.), but now include a sizeable Christian community of part-Portuguese descent. The Portuguese founded a fort there in 1558 which fell in 1609 to the Dutch, who placed Bacan under the sovereignty of Ternate (q.v.) [0020, 0026]

BADAN KEAMANAN RAKYAT. See ARMY.

BADAN KERJA SAMA (BKS, Cooperative Bodies) were formed in 1957–58 to allow coordination between the army (q.v.) and party mass organizations (*organisasi massa,* q.v.) under the general idea, which was strongest in the army, that the military should play a guiding role in directing national energies. The largest of these bodies, the BKS Bumil (*Buruh-Militer,* Labor-Military) and the BKS Tamil (*Tani-Militer,* Peasant-Military) were formed in October 1957 and September 1958 respectively. PKI mass organizations, though initially involved in the BKS, soon withdrew and the BKS then evolved into clearly anticommunist coordinating bodies. In December 1962, they were dissolved and absorbed into SOKSI (q.v.). See also DWIFUNGSI. [0663]

BADAN KOORDINASI BANTUAN PEMANTAPAN STABILITAS NASIONAL (BAKORSTANAS, Coordinating Body to Assist in Maintaining National Security), security organization formed 5 September 1988 to replace KOPKAMTIB (q.v.). Its responsibilities are vague, but include monitoring security matters and giving advice to the government. President Suharto is formal head of the organization (unlike KOPKAMTIB, which was in a technical sense independent of the presidency), and General Try Sutrisno effective commander, but BAKORSTANAS (q.v.) boards at each level include civilian as well as military officials. At the time of writing, the nature of BAKORSTANAS operations is not yet clear.

BADAN KOORDINASI INTELIJEN NEGARA (BAKIN, State Intelligence Coordinating Body), nominally civilian intelligence organization, separate from military intelligence structures and reporting directly to the president. Its functions overlap substantially with those of KOPKAMTIB (q.v.) and include surveillance of civilian dissent. BAKIN was headed from January 1974 to late 1989 by Lt-Gen. Yoga Sugama (b.1925).

BADAN PENDUKUNG SUKARNOISME (BPS, Body to Support Sukarnoism) was founded in September 1964 by a group of journalists, including Adam Malik (q.v.), opposed to the PKI (q.v.) in an attempt to distinguish publicly between Sukarnoism and Communism, and to separate Sukarno from the PKI. It was banned by Sukarno as an alleged CIA plot on 17 December 1964. [0669]

BADAN PENYELIDIK USAHA PERSIAPAN KEMERDEKAAN INDONESIA (BPUPKI, Investigatory Body for Preparatory Work for Indonesian Independence). In March 1945 the Japanese occupation (q.v.) authorities on Java set up the BPUPKI following Prime Minister Koiso's promise of eventual independence for the region. Membership included most of the better-known prewar nationalists and represented most streams of thought. The Body met in Jakarta from 28 May 1945 and was the forum to which Sukarno (q.v.) presented his speech outlining the Pancasila (q.v.) on 1 June. It also drafted a constitution for independent Indonesia (10–17 July) and decided that Indonesia should include the Malay peninsula (q.v.), northern

Borneo and East Timor (q.v.), though this was later rejected by the Japanese. On 7 August the BPUPKI was replaced by a 21-member Panitia Persiapan Kemerdekaan Indonesia (PPKI, Preparatory Committee for Independence) as a kind of proto-parliament for the impending state. After the declaration of independence (q.v.), the committee formally adopted the constitution, elected Sukarno and Hatta (q.v.) president and vice-president, and on 29 August transformed itself into the KNIP (q.v.). See also ISLAMIC STATE, Demands for an; SUCCESSION. [0606, 0615]

BADAN PERENCANAAN PEMBANGUNAN NASIONAL (BAPPENAS, National Development Planning Board), Indonesia's principal economic planning body, founded in 1963 by Sukarno but later the stronghold of the group of New Order (q.v.) economic policymakers known as the 'technocrats' or 'Berkeley Mafia' (many of them studied at the University of California at Berkeley). The group included Wijoyo Nitisastro, Ali Wardhana, Emil Salim, Mohamad Sadli, and Barli Halim; it had the patronage of Sumitro Joyohadikusumo (q.v.) and was initially strongly influenced by the International Monetary Fund view that the economic difficulties faced by the country under Sukarno's Guided Economy (q.v.) could be remedied by sober financial policies, looser economic controls, and an opening of the country to foreign investment. See also CENTRE FOR STRATEGIC AND INTERNATIONAL STUDIES; DEVELOPMENT IDEOLOGY; RENCANA PEMBANGUNAN LIMA TAHUN. [0277, 0758]

BADAN PERJUANGAN (struggle organizations) sprang up widely in 1945 as an expression of popular will to defend the Indonesian Republic from the returning Dutch. Often untrained and armed only with bamboo spears, they were rarely effective in battle and by early 1946 had generally consolidated into better-organized *lasykar* (q.v.), joined the army (q.v.), or disbanded. See also DIPLOMASI AND PERJUANGAN; SURABAYA. [0628, 0656, 0660]

BADAN PERMUSYAWARATAN KEWARGANEGARAAN INDONESIA (BAPERKI, Consultative Body on Indonesian Citizenship), a political organization of Indonesian Chinese, founded by Siauw Giok Tjhan (1914–80) on 13 March 1954 to succeed the Partai Demokrat Tionghoa (Party of Democratic Chinese). It encouraged Chinese to accept Indonesian citizenship, but defended the right of Chinese to retain their own culture as citizens. This attitude was opposed by the pro-assimilation Lembaga Pembinaan Kesatuan Bangsa (Institute for Developing National Unity). BAPERKI was politically close to the PKI (q.v.) and was banned in 1966. [0920]

BADAN URUSAN LOGISTIK NASIONAL (BULOG, National Logistic Supply Organization). Established in 1967 as a government purchase agency, BULOG expanded its role in the 1970s to supervise and stabilize the distribution and price of basic commodities such as rice, sugar, and flour, partly as an aid to political stability. It was sharply criticized for corruption (q.v.) in the allocation of distributorships by the Commission of Four.

BADUI, tribe of southern Banten, widely believed to be descendants of pre-Muslim Sundanese who refused to convert to Islam, but probably of much greater antiquity. They worship *lelembut,* ancestral spirits who dwell near the source of the rivers Ciujung and Cisemet. Only forty Badui families, the 'Inner Badui', are permitted by custom to inhabit this sacred area and these are forbidden all contact with the outside world. The remainder, the Outer Badui, are permitted some contact but are forbidden to make use of introduced technology such as horses, writing (q.v.), vehicles, and beds. See also ASLI.

BAHASA INDONESIA. See INDONESIAN LANGUAGE.

BAJAU, also known as Sea People (*orang laut*) or Sea Gypsies, a seafaring Malay people of eastern Indonesia and the southern Philippines, typically living aboard boats or in small settlements of temporary houses on stilts over the sea. Their dispersal from a presumed home in southern Sulawesi may date from the fall of Makassar (q.v.) to Dutch and Bugis (q.v.) forces in 1667 or to the commercial opportunities offered by trepang (bêche de mer) collection. During C.18–19, Bajau fleets ranged as far as Australia (q.v.) in search of trepang for the China trade. [0433, 0481, 1046]

BALAI PUSTAKA, the government commission for literacy and popular publication, founded in 1917 as the Comite (later Kantoor) voor de Volkslectuur (Committee, Office for Popular Literature). It published cheap reading material in Malay, Sundanese, and Javanese (both original works and translations from Dutch, including the letters of Kartini [q.v.] in 1921), maintained libraries, and provided court interpreters. [0159]

BALAMBANGAN, the last Hindu kingdom on Java, controlling the eastern end of the island (Besuki and Probolinggo) after the fall of Majapahit (q.v.). It was fought over by Mataram (q.v.) and the Balinese state of Gelgel in early C.17, but flourished as in independent kingdom from 1670 to 1690. In 1697 it was attacked once more by Mataram and the Balinese rulers of Buleleng.

Mataram transferred its claim over the region to the Dutch East Indies Company (q.v.) in 1734 and the Company subdued it in a major campaign in 1771–72. Constant warfare and the piratical raids of Madurese severely depopulated the region and further destruction was caused by an eruption of Mt. Ijen in 1817. In C.19, the area was extensively settled by Madurese. The name now refers to the forested peninsula on Java's southeast corner, rather than to the former territory of the kingdom. [0384, 0467, 0485]

BALI. Although the culture and society of Bali have been studied extensively, relatively little has been written on the island's history. Probably Hindu from C.8 or 9 (the first Hindu inscriptions record a king Warmadewa in C.9), Bali was ruled at least in part by the Javanese king Airlangga (q.v.) in early C.11 and was conquered by Majapahit (q.v.) in 1334. A period of intensive Javanization followed, and contemporary Balinese sometimes refer to themselves as *wong Majapahit* (people of Majapahit). There is said, too, to have been considerable migration of Javanese Hindus to Bali following the fall of Majapahit to the Pasisir (q.v.) states in 1527. The unified kingdom of Gelgel in the south broke up during C.17 into nine warring states of Klungkung, Karangasem, Mengwi, Badung, Bangli, Tabanan, Gianyar, Buleleng, and Jembrana, though the rulers of Klungkung, whose territory included the temple of Besakih on Mt. (Gunung) Agung and who were known as the Dewa Agung, were sometimes regarded as overlords. Slaves were a major export in C.17 and 18, the average annual export being one to two thousand. This trade was in the hands of the rajas. Balinese formed an important element in the Betawi (q.v.) communities around Batavia. Balinese mercenaries also fought in various wars in Java and the island was a major producer of rifles in C.18.

Dutch political interest in the island began in C.19. To exclude other Europeans, the Dutch obtained acknowledgments of sovereignty from Badung, Klungkung, Karangasem, and Buleleng in 1841 and launched a series of military operations on the island in 1846, 1848, and 1849. The Dutch were also keen to stop Balinese piracy (q.v.) and plunder of shipwrecks and attempted to intervene to control practices such as slavery (common) and widow-burning (very uncommon). Buleleng and Jembrana were brought under closer control in 1853 and Karangasem and Gianyar were conquered in 1882. The plunder of a Dutch shipwreck in 1904 provided the pretext for full military operations on the island against Badung in 1906 and Klungkung in 1908. In the final battles of each campaign the respective royal families committed collective suicide (*puputan*), walking into the guns of the Dutch forces.

After a period of direct rule by the Dutch, during which Singaraja on the north coast was the island's capital, the former kingdoms were restored in 1929 to their former rulers as *zelfbesturen* (q.v., 'self-governing territories' under Dutch authority) in a massive ceremony at Besakih, partly as a result of the Dutch policy of *ontvoogding* or detutelization and partly out of a respect for traditional Balinese culture which they sought to protect and preserve. An Indonesian nationalist rising on the island in 1945–46 was suppressed and Bali was incorporated into the Dutch-sponsored federal state of East Indonesia (see FEDERALISM; NEGARA INDONESIA TIMUR) in 1946. After the NIT was dissolved in 1950, much of the old power arrangements remained more or less intact, the kingdoms being converted into kabupaten and the rajas, or members of their families, generally taking the office of bupati. Head of the region (*kepala daerah*) and from 1958 governor of the province was Anak Agung Bagus Suteja (?-1965), who played an important role in increasing the representation of the PKI (q.v.) and other leftists in the island's administration and legislative bodies. Social tensions mounted during the early 1960s, partly as a result of a land reform (q.v.) campaign by the PKI and apprehension mounted especially after several thousand people died in an eruption of Mt. Agung in 1963. Perhaps 60,000 people were slaughtered as alleged Communists or leftists in 1965–66. See also HINDUISM; LANGE, Mads Johansen; MASSACRES OF 1965–66. [0068, 0146, 0398, 0533, 0915, 0918, 1003, 1004]

BAMBOO (Poaceae, *buluh, aur*), grasses with exceptionally light, strong stems, widely used for construction and household purposes. Abundant and easily grown, they were never a major item of trade, though in C.17 they were amongst the products demanded by the VOC. See also RATTAN. [0938]

BANANA (*Musa* sp., Musaceae), characteristic fruit 'tree' of the archipelago. It was probably domesticated by the Austronesians (see MIGRATIONS) and forms an important part of the diet in many regions. See also SCANDINAVIA, Historical links with. [0938]

BANDA Islands, small archipelago in Maluku, known especially for the cultivation of nutmeg (q.v.). Dependent on Java for rice, Banda came under the rule of Majapahit (q.v.) in C.14 and attracted a Portuguese fleet under d'Abreu in 1511. Dutch trade in the islands began in 1599, and the Dutch East Indies Company (VOC) under Coen (q.v.) annexed them in a bloody campaign from ca 1609 which left the islands largely depopulated, with perhaps 15,000 Bandanese being killed. The islands were divided into nutmeg 'groves' or *perken,* with each perk being under a VOC *perkenier* with slaves to work for him. Perkeniers were obliged to deliver their produce to the company and later the colonial government at fixed prices. With abolition of the monopoly in 1864, the perkeniers became immensely wealthy until the depression of 1894. [0375, 0459]

BANDITRY. Crime is presumably as old as human society in Indonesia, but the earliest known form of organized crime in the archipelago is rural banditry, along with its marine counterpart, piracy (q.v.). The plundering of travellers and the raiding of outlying settlements is often difficult to distinguish from early state building and a number of rulers of parts of Java, notably Ken Angrok (q.v.) began their careers as rural criminals. Criminal gangs generally formed around a single leader and did not survive his death or loss of prestige. Leaders commanded not only martial arts (*pencak silat*), but also magical powers such as the ability to confer invulnerability, invisibility, or inaudibility on their followers. The extent of rural banditry is always difficult to estimate, since there are ample reasons for both exaggeration and under-reporting, but many areas of Java had a reputation as 'unsafe' throughout the colonial period.

Bandit gangs frequently took part in peasant uprisings against the colonial power and in C.20 came into contact with nationalist groups. Sarekat Islam and the PKI (qq.v.) in particular valued the bandits both as a source of potential armed strength and as a representation of the strength of the mass of the people. Gangs provided some of the armed support for the PKI's uprising in the Jakarta region in 1926, but were generally ineffective against colonial police.

During the Revolution (q.v.), gangsters in the Jakarta region and elsewhere joined nationalists in armed resistance organizations (*lasykar,* q.v.), but they were generally unsuccessful in holding back the Dutch and most were suppressed by the Republic's own army in the course of the Revolution. In the chaotic years which followed the transfer of sovereignty, rural banditry was rife in many regions, though it was often associated with political dissent. Under the New Order greatly increased social control in the countryside has diminished the incidence of banditry there, though urban crime remains rampant. In the 1982 elections, in particular, figures associated with the government were said to be employing urban criminals both to intimidate the other parties and as agents provocateurs. The elections were followed by a dramatic upsurge in violent crime, perhaps encouraged by this rumor of approval. However much criminal activity was suppressed by the government's program of extra-judicial killings known as *petrus* (*penembakan misterius*) beginning in early 1983, which claimed several thousand victims. [0372, 0678, 0887, 0888, 1021, 1040]

BANDUNG, major city in the Priangan (q.v.), developed by the Dutch after 1810 as a center for the region's plantation industry. It was capital of the Priangan from 1864 and grew rapidly after the arrival of the railway in 1880. The colonial Department of War transferred there in 1916 and the city was proposed as an eventual capital of the Netherlands Indies. In 1946 the southern part of the city was burnt by Indonesian nationalists forced to evacuate by the Allies. [0458, 0660]

BANDUNG CONFERENCE. See ASIA-AFRICA CONFERENCE.

BANGKA, large island between Sumatra and Kalimantan and site of major tin (q.v.) mines since 1710. The island was operated at first by the sultan of Palembang (q.v.), who began to introduce laborers from China, Siam, and Vietnam (qq.v.). British forces seized Bangka in 1806 and abolished the sultanate in 1816, but the island was restored to the Dutch, who continued tin mining as a government enterprise. The island also became a major exporter of white pepper in C.19, producing 90% of world supply. After falling to the Japanese in World War II, Bangka was reoccupied by the Dutch in early 1946. [0515]

BANGSA INDONESIA ('Indonesian nation'), ambiguous ethnic term which may refer simply to those born in Indonesia; more commonly, however, it describes ethnicity and excludes citizens of European, Chinese, Indian, Arab, and other exogenous ancestry. See also ASLI; PRIBUMI.

BANJARMASIN, kingdom on the Barito river in southern Kalimantan, reputedly founded by Empu Jamatka in 1387. It quickly became an important source of diamonds, bezoar stones, and dragon's blood (qq.v.), but was dependent on Java for the supply of rice and was tributary in succession to the Javanese states of Majapahit, Demak, and Mataram (qq.v.). Its ruler converted to Islam in ca 1520 and the sultanate received many refugees from the north coast of Java after the fall of Surabaya (q.v.) to Mataram in 1625. In C.17 pepper, gambier, gold, and rattan (qq.v.) became major trading commodities, attracting Chinese traders as well as the Dutch and English East Indies Companies (qq.v.). Large areas of alang-alang (q.v.) grassland in the region today are a legacy of the indiscriminate clearing of forest for pepper and gambier cultivation in this period. Both the Dutch and the British attempted to enforce monopolies in the port, but successive agreements with sultans were unenforceable as economic and political power collected in the hands of powerful pepper planters. The sultan of Banjarmasin formally ceded sovereignty to the Dutch in 1786–7, though he retained his throne and continued to rule with little interference.

Governor-General Daendels (q.v.) abandoned Dutch holdings in Banjarmasin in 1809, but in 1857 the Dutch reasserted their right to appoint the deceased sultan's successor and imposed a half-Chinese son of the previous sultan on the unwilling aristocracy. A full scale war of succession ensued (1859–63), with the anti-Dutch party, strongly Islamic, being led by a junior prince Pangeran Antasari (1797–1862) and a peasant leader Sultan Kuning. The Dutch formally abolished the sultanate in 1860. Sporadic fighting continued beyond the formal end of major hostilities until 1905.

The area was a site of tough resistance to the Dutch by guerrillas under Hasan Basry in the period 1945–49 and much of the hinterland remained in Republican hands, though, to the indignation of local leaders it was not recognized formally as Republican territory in the Linggajati or Renville Agreements (qq.v.). In January 1948, the Dutch established a federal state, the Daerah Banjar, to be a constituent of the Indonesian Federal Republic (see FEDERALISM), but this was dissolved in March 1950. Resentment against central government policies led to a local uprising under Ibnu Hajar which became associated with the Darul Islam (q.v.) and lasted until 1963. [0052, 0415, 0521, 0632]

BANKING. The Dutch East Indies Company (q.v.) initially drew its capital from the Netherlands and, having a monopoly of trade in the archipelago, had no wish to allow local credit facilities for others. In 1746, however, Governor-General van Imhoff established a Bank van Leening (Lending Bank) in Batavia for the support of trade enterprises. This minor retreat of Dutch capital from direct investment to the financing of others was continued in C.19 by the Nederlandsche Handel Maatschappij (q.v.), which began as a trading company and ended as a largely banking operation. Other major banks in the Netherlands Indies were the Nederlandsch-

Indische Handelsbank (estab. 1863), the Nederlandsch-Indische Escompto-Maatschappij (estab. 1857), and the Koloniale Bank. The Java Bank (Javasche Bank) was established in 1828 as a semiprivate, semigovernmental bank of circulation (issuing currency), while the Algemeene Volkscredietbank (founded 1934) undertook small scale loans to and from the public.

During the Japanese occupation, commercial banking was taken over by the Yokohama Specie Bank while the Syomin Ginko replaced the Volkscredietbank, becoming Bank Rakyat after independence. The Bank Negara Indonesia (BNI) was founded in 1946 as the Republic's state bank. When the Indonesian Republic nationalized the Java Bank in 1953, turning it into the Bank Indonesia, BNI was given the responsibility for financing general development; the Bank Industri Negara (originally the Bureau Herstel Financiering, established by the Dutch in 1948) was made responsible for financing industrial development. Other Dutch banks were nationalized in 1958, Escompto becoming the Bank Dagang Negara (State Trading Bank), which now especially finances mining and the NHM (q.v.) becoming the Bank Koperasi Tani dan Nelayan. In 1965, the various state banks were merged into the BNI, but they separated again in December 1968. A National Development Savings Scheme (TABANAS, Tabungan Pembangunan Nasional) was introduced in 1971. On 27 October, 1988 Indonesia announced a major deregulation of the banking sector, including easier availability of foreign exchange licenses and permission for state enterprises (q.v.) to deposit funds with private banks. See also CURRENCY; PAWNSHOPS. [0039, 0211, 0213, 0228, 0292, 0298, 0366]

BANTEN (Bantam), town on the northern coast of West Java, seized by Muslims of the sultanate of Demak (q.v.) in 1527. It rapidly expanded during C.16, and under Fatahillah conquered the Pajajaran (q.v.) port of Sunda Kalapa in the early 1520s. After Banten defeated a Portuguese fleet in Sunda Kalapa harbor in 1527 the city was renamed Jayakarta. Banten emerged as the dominant entrepôt and outlet for pepper (q.v.) from West Java and South Sumatra. It was in continual conflict with Mataram (q.v.) over control of the Priangan. In 1601, ships of the Dutch East Indies Company (q.v.) defeated a Spanish-Portuguese fleet in Banten harbor. The city began to decline after the foundation of Batavia (q.v.) in 1619. Raffles (q.v.) abolished the Banten sultanate in 1813. In 1888 a major anticolonial uprising took place in Banten and in 1926 the PKI (q.v.) organized a rising there. [0532, 0603, 0645]

BANTENG (*Bos javanicus*), bovine similar to cattle (q.v.), occurring wild or feral on many islands and elsewhere in SE Asia, recognizable by a white disc on the buttocks. First known to have been domesticated in Thailand before 3500 B.C., it is valued for its agility, its easy trainability and more recently, its low-fat meat. Most 'cattle' on Bali and Timor are in fact banteng, while the cattle of Madura (q.v.) appear to be a stable banteng-zebu cross-developed ca 500 A.D. A banteng's horned head represents national unity on the Indonesian coat of arms and was adopted as symbol by PNI (4) and PDI (qq.v.). It is sometimes confused by Westerners with the buffalo (*kerbau,* q.v.), to which, however, it is not closely related. [0943]

BAPAK. ('father'). 1. common term of deferential address for superiors, believed to promote a collectivist, familial attitude to society. Often abbreviated to 'Pak'. In 1981 Suharto accepted the title *Bapak Pembangunan*. See also 'BUNG'. 2. a patron who protects, sponsors, and otherwise assists protégés (*anak buah*). See also PATRIMONIALISM.

BARISAN PELOPOR (Vanguard Corps, from Dutch *voorloper,* pioneer), youth wing of the Jawa Hokokai (q.v.), formed August 1944, initially to conduct propaganda, but in May 1945 becoming a paramilitary brigade of about 80,000, though training was limited. At the outset of the Revolution, with the dissolution of the PETA (q.v.), it took the name Barisan Banteng (Banteng, q.v., Corps) and was the only quasimilitary force at the disposal of Republican leaders. It was not incorporated into the army (q.v.) and became one of the more important lasykar (q.v.) units. [0628]

BARISAN TANI INDONESIA (BTI, Indonesian Peasants' Front), founded November 1945 and affiliated soon after with the PKI (q.v.). The BTI aimed initially at improving conditions on state-owned lands and in forest areas, but from the mid-1950s began to work more widely in rural areas, organizing peasants and using its party contacts to remedy injustices. Despite a shortage of cadres, it reached a claimed membership of 16 million by 1965. It was the main agent by which the PKI promoted land reform and conducted direct action (*aksi sepihak*) in the villages and it aroused great hostility amongst landowners. It was banned in 1966. [0822, 0823, 0827]

BATAKS, ethnic group in northern Sumatra, consisting of the Toba, Simalungun, Karo, Dairi, Angkola, and Mandailing (though the latter two groups, predominantly Muslim, often reject the term Batak). The Bataks were traditionally organized in villages (*huta*) which were frequently at war with one another, with no higher state organization, though larger clan groups (*marga*) such as the Nasution and Lubis were strong and a line of priest kings called Sisingamangaraja (q.v.) played a unifying spiritual role. Ancestor worship was at the center of traditional religion, though there was some recognition of a creator god, Mulajadi na Bolon. Contacts with the outside world were limited at first to trade in benzoin and camphor (qq.v.) through Baros on the west coast; Batak legend also acknowledged some allegiance to Aceh, Minangkabau (qq.v.), and Ayudhya (Siam, q.v.). In 1825 Paderis from Minangkabau overran southern Tapanuli, killing Sisingamangaraja X. German missionaries became active in North Tapanuli from 1857, while South Tapanuli converted to Islam (q.v.) in the same period. Dutch rule was gradually established in the period up to 1907, when Dutch troops shot Sisingamangaraja XII. Under Dutch rule the position of traditional leaders steadily weakened, though the colonial authorities made some attempt to bolster them by forming a Tapanuli Council in 1938 (see DECENTRALIZATION). [0203, 0416, 0452, 0550, 0645, 1029, 1045]

BATAM, island in the Riau (q.v.) archipelago opposite Singapore, site of a plan by Pertamina (q.v.) to construct a major port in direct competition with Singapore. The project was suspended in 1976 after Pertamina's bankruptcy.

BATAVIA, capital city of the Netherlands Indies, site of a VOC post from 1610, and founded in 1619 by J.P. Coen (q.v.), as regional headquarters for the Dutch East Indies Company (q.v.), on the site of the Banten (q.v.) port of Jayakarta. It was first constructed as a Dutch city, complete with canals and walls to resist attack from Mataram (q.v.), and much of the surrounding countryside was cleared of its inhabitants to create a kind of cordon sanitaire around the city. Batavia became a major center of settlement by Chinese (q.v.), who lived within the city under their own laws. Tension between the Dutch and the Chinese led to a massacre of Chinese in 1740. The social composition of the city was also influenced by a large slave community, much of it Balinese in origin (see SLAVERY), who formed the basis for a constantly evolving mestizo culture in the city. By C.19 observers identified the *Betawi* (q.v.) as a distinct ethnic group. See also PARTICULIERE LANDERIJEN.

Chronic health problems as a result of waterborne diseases, especially malaria (q.v.), led the colonial authorities in 1810 to shift the center of administration to Weltevreden (the area around the Koningsplein, the present Medan Merdeka). Further government offices shifted to Bogor and Bandung (qq.v.). A modern harbor was completed at Tanjung Priok in 1886. In 1905, as part of more general administrative reforms, the city was made a *gemeente* (municipality), with limited autonomy (see DECENTRALIZATION). The city's population in the 1930 census was 435,000. In 1942, Batavia was occupied by Japanese forces and its name was changed the following year to Jakarta (q.v.). See also HEALTH. [0375, 0491, 0495, 0514, 0542, 0593]

BATAVIAASCH GENOOTSCHAP VAN KUNSTEN EN WETENSCHAPPEN (Batavian Society of the Arts and Sciences) was founded in 1778 by J.C.M. Radermacher (1741–83) to conduct linguistic, geographical, and anthropological research in the archipelago. Its library forms the nucleus of the National Library of Indonesia collection. See also ARCHEOLOGY. [0991]

BATAVIAN REPUBLIC (Bataafsche Republiek). In 1794–95 French revolutionary troops joined 'patriots' (*patriotten*) in overthrowing the conservative Dutch Republic, founding the Batavian Republic, which survived until its incorporation into the French Empire in 1806. Among the various reforms undertaken by the new state was to replace the VOC's Heeren XVII in 1795 with a Comite tot de Zaken van de Oost-Indische Handel en Bezittingen (Committee for the Affairs of the East Indies Trade and Possessions) and to take possession of the VOC on 17 March 1798. When the VOC charter, which governed Indies affairs, lapsed at the end of 1799, the Republic set up a Raad van Aziatischen Bezittingen en Etablissementen (Council for Asian Possessions and Establishments) and in 1803 promulgated a colonial Charter, preserving most of the existing system by making the colonial government responsible for the first time to the metropolitan government. In 1806, the Charter was replaced by a more liberal 'Reglement op het Beleid der Regeering enz'. The effect of these measures was limited, however, by the Napoleonic Wars and the occupation of the Indies colonies by Britain (q.v.). The Republic ceased to exist when the Netherlands was occupied by France in 1811. See also DAENDELS; NETHERLANDS, Constitutional relationship with Indonesia. [0491]

BATIG SLOT (budgetary surplus). From 1799 to 1903, the treasury of the Netherlands Indies was part of that of the Netherlands. From the inception of the Cultivation System (q.v.) in 1831 until 1877, regular *batig slot* transfers were made to the Dutch treasury from the Indies, totalling ▪823 million over the four decades. See also 'EERESCHULD, Een'; INDIË VERLOREN, RAMPSPOED GEBOREN. [0510]

BATIK. Method of cloth dyeing by wax-resist, first reliably reported from Java in C.17. Traditionally, beeswax (q.v.) is applied with a metal pen (*canting*), but in late C.19 metal stamps (*cap*) were introduced widely, as were German aniline dyes to replace the traditional vegetable pigments. Since the 1970s, silk screen prints of fine batik motifs have become widespread. Batik motifs have symbolic significance, specific designs formerly being reserved for particular social groups and occasions. In the early C.20, Pekalongan became the center for a batik style incorporating European motifs. Batik 'painting' (smaller batiks for display rather than wearing) emerged in the 1960s. Batik has generally been seen as socially conservative, though after independence Sukarno promoted a bright pattern called 'batik Indonesia'. The Solo designer Mohamad Hadi incorporated left-wing motifs in cloths in the early 1960s.

The time-consuming work of fine batik production is commonly the work of women (q.v.), both in villages and in the courts. Village producers were generally dependent on *bakul* (suppliers of cloth and materials) and much batik trading came into Chinese hands in the early C.20, prompting a struggle between indigenous and Chinese merchants which contributed to the emergence of nationalism (see SAREKAT ISLAM). A number of successful trade cooperatives emerged in the 1920s and 1930s to keep the industry in indigenous hands. Recent dramatic price rises for high quality batik have allowed the reemergence of indigenous batik entrepreneurs. See also CLOTH. [0111, 0125, 1171]

BAUXITE has been mined on Bintan island in Riau (q.v.) since the 1920s, mainly for export to Japan. Operations are now under the state firm, PT Aneka Tambang. See also ASAHAN. [0321]

BAWEAN, volcanic island in the Java Sea. Settled by Madurese in C.14, it was at first an independent state and was later ruled by Mataram (q.v.), until it was conquered by the VOC in 1743 and was administered from Surabaya. The population is predominantly Muslim with a strong tradition of *merantau* (q.v.). Baweanese formed an important trading minority on Java in C.19. [0006, 1054]

BECAK, Three-wheeled pedicab, mostly with driver at rear, introduced in 1936 but becoming a common form of urban and rural public transport especially on Java only during and after World War II. In 1971 becaks were banned from some main roads in Jakarta, partly to reduce congestion and partly because they were considered demeaning to the drivers. Since then the ban has been extended to other roads and cities, and becaks have been replaced partly by three-wheeled motorized *bajaj*. [0355, 0357, 0359, 0495]

BEESWAX was traded to China from southern Sumatra from at least C.13, but the main market is now the batik (q.v.) industry of Java. See also HONEY. [0938]

BELITUNG (Billiton), large island between Sumatra and Kalimantan. It was formerly under the sultanate of Palembang (q.v.), but in 1812 was seized by the British along with Bangka (q.v.) as reparations for the so-called massacre of Palembang. It was disputed by Britain and the Netherlands until 1824 and remained barely occupied until 1851, when the Billiton Maatschappij began mining tin (q.v.) there. Extensive immigration of Chinese laborers began in 1852.

BENGKULU (Bencoolen), town and region on the western coast of Sumatra, formerly subject successively to Minangkabau, Banten, and the Dutch East Indies Company. The English East India Company (q.v.) founded a settlement there, Fort Marlborough, in 1685 after the Dutch had forced them out of Banten (q.v.). Bengkulu was the only major region of British influence in the archipelago until their expansion during the Napoleonic wars. Pepper (q.v.) was the principal trade good, but the colony was seldom more than marginally profitable, being hampered especially by a poor harbor. After a brief period under the energetic rule of Raffles (q.v.), who tried to expand the production of nutmeg, cloves (qq.v.), and cassia, Bengkulu was ceded to the

Dutch in the Anglo-Dutch Treaty of 1824 (q.v.). Effective Dutch control was not established there until 1868. [0375]

BENTENG PROGRAM, measures introduced in 1950 to provide *pribumi* (q.v.) entrepreneurs with import licences in order to hasten the development of an indigenous business class. In 1956, however, the program's formal discrimination against Chinese was ended and it was abolished by Juanda (q.v.) in 1957. See also ALI-BABA FIRMS; INDONESIANIZATION; SYAFRUDDIN PRAWIRANEGARA. [0280]

BENZOIN (*Styrax benzoin,* Styracaceae; from Arabic *luban al-Jawi,* 'frankincense of Java'), aromatic gum used in incense, medicines and perfumery. It was extensively traded from Sumatra to the Roman Empire (0–400 A.D.), to China in the Sung dynasty (960–1279), and to the Arab world (q.v.). [0430, 0751, 0938]

BERAU, state in east Kalimantan, founded in C.17. It was initially subject to Banjarmasin (q.v.), but became independent in ca 1750 under Sultan Hasanuddin and dominated the neighboring states of Bulungan and Sumbaliung. Some authorities believe that it was the model for Patusan in *Lord Jim* (Joseph Conrad, q.v.). A Dutch protectorate was established there in 1906.

BERI-BERI, disease caused by lack of vitamin B1 (thiamine). In the 1870s it became a major health problem in the plantation regions of North Sumatra, where workers were fed with mechanically husked rice. The idea of deficiency disease was then unknown and many medical researchers attributed the disease to fungal contamination. In the 1880s, C. Eijkman in Batavia showed that beri-beri was a consequence of eating hulled rice, but not until 1909 did G. Grijns develop the specific idea that a substance was lost in the milling process.

'BERKELEY MAFIA'. See BADAN PERENCANAAN PEMBANGUNAN NASIONAL.

BESCHIKKINGSRECHT (right of disposal or allocation). With the strengthening of village (*desa* q.v.) structure on Java in C.19, the colonial government acknowledged the collective right of villages to allocate land to their own members or to other purposes, such as *tanah bengkok* (q.v.) according to circumstances. Under the Liberal Policy (q.v.), this right enabled village elites to allocate rice land to sugar companies on rotating leases. As part of his Agricultural Involution (q.v.) argument, Geertz suggested that sugar and rice, demanding similar ecological conditions, enhanced each other's productivity, thus keeping Javanese villages tied to a subsistence economy. Closer investigation has shown, however, that the different growing cycles and irrigation methods of the two crops work against rice production. The term beschikkingsrecht also applied to the right of the colonial government to allocate *woeste* or waste land—that is, areas not under active cultivation—to European companies for sugar production, as forest reserve, or for other purposes, though van Vollenhoven (q.v.) argued in the 1920s that this should not permit villages to be deprived of their usufruct rights over nonagricultural land. See also AGRARIAN LAW OF 1870.

BETAWI ('Batavians'), an ethnic group which emerged in Batavia from amongst the many Indonesian residents of the city and the surrounding countryside (*ommelanden*). In a broad sense the term applied to all the many Indonesian mestizo cultures which emerged there, but it applies most strictly to a group which first became apparent in C.19. The Betawi proper spoke Malay with heavy Balinese and Chinese influence and considered themselves strongly Islamic (though they were less than orthodox in practice). Because of the dominating presence of the colonial establishment and Indonesian immigrant communities and the influence of the *particuliere landerijen* (q.v.), Betawi seldom flourished in their own city: they had an unusually high illiteracy rate and played little role in the administrative or political life of the capital. Muhammad Husni Thamrin (1894–1941) founded a political organization called *Kaum Betawi* in 1923. See also MARDIJKERS. [0495, 1154]

BETEL. The seed or 'nut' of the palm *Areca catechu* (Arecaceae), *jambe* or *pinang,* native to the region. It has been reported chewed as early as C.7, generally in combination with other substances: commonly lime, pepper leaf (*sirih*), and gambier (q.v.) and occasionally opium, amomum, cloves, camphor, nutmeg, and/or tobacco (qq.v.). Seeds were exported to China in C.13. Betel chewing is addictive and leads to loss of appetite, excessive salivation, and general deterioration. It was gradually displaced by tobacco smoking from C.16. [0483, 0938]

BEUREU'EH, Teungku Muhammad Daud (ca 1900–1987), Acehnese Muslim scholar and leader, one of the founders of the anticolonial PUSA (Persatuan Ulama Seluruh Aceh, All-Aceh Union of Ulama) in 1939. In August 1947 he became military governor of Aceh (q.v.) and was governor of the short-lived Aceh province from January to August 1950. Hostile to the inclusion of Aceh in North Sumatra province along with the Christian Bataks, disappointed at the failure of the central government to adopt Islam as the basic principle of the state, and alarmed by the arrest of PUSA activists in August 1951 (at a time when Communists were being arrested elsewhere in Indonesia), he joined the Darul Islam (q.v.) in ca September 1953, declaring Aceh to be part of the Islamic State of Indonesia and launching a general revolt throughout the region. The rebels never controlled more than half the province and failed to capture the capital, Banda Aceh, but they were well entrenched in the countryside, especially in the north. Beureu'eh headed both civil and military commands for the Islamic state in Aceh and in January 1955 was appointed vice-president next to Kartosuwiryo (q.v.), but there was little effective coordination with the rebellion elsewhere. As the rebellion dragged on, many on both sides began feeling their way towards a compromise, but it was only after Beureu'eh's followers deposed him in a bloodless coup in March 1959 that a settlement was reached, Aceh receiving the status of a Daerah Istimewa (Special Territory). Beureu'eh then briefly formed an alliance with remnants of the PRRI (q.v.) rebellion, but ceased resistance in May 1962.

BEZOAR STONES. Stone-like bodies found in the stomachs of many animals, consisting of a deposit of ellagitannin on a nucleus of wood or bark. Highly valued as an antidote to poison, Kalimantan bezoar stones from porcupines and monkeys were traded to India until at least C.19. See also BANJARMASIN; RHINOCEROS. [0938]

BHARATAYUDDHA ('War of the Bharatas'). Old Javanese *kakawin* (poem) based on the Mahabharata (q.v.) and composed in 1157 by Mpu Sedah and Mpu Panuluh under patronage of Joyoboyo (q.v.) of Kediri. It describes the 18-day battle which ends the war between the Kurawa and Pandawa. [0116]

BHINNEKA TUNGGAL IKA (Old Javanese 'They are many, they are one', usually translated as 'Unity in diversity'). Phrase reputedly coined by Empu Tantalar in C.15, and adopted on 17 August 1950 as Indonesia's national motto. See also GARUDA.

'BIG FIVE', the five major Dutch trading houses in late colonial Indonesia, which also held a dominant place in the export economy until they were nationalized in 1957. They were the Internationale Crediet en Handelsvereeniging Rotterdam (Internatio), Jacobson van den Bergh, Borneo Sumatra Maatschappij (Borsumij), Lindetevis Stokvis, and Geo. Wehry. See NATIONALIZATION. [0228]

BILLITON. See BELITUNG.

BIMA, kingdom on the island of Sumbawa (q.v.), founded perhaps C.11 when there are signs of Hindu influence. It was a vassal of Makassar in early C.17 and converted to Islam in ca 1640. The VOC (q.v.) assumed suzerainty in 1667, though effective control was not established until late C.19. [0477]

BIMBO, popular music group best known for their song 'Tante Sun' ('Auntie Kiss') which satirized the alleged high-living, wheeling, and dealing of wives of New Order powerholders. See also MUSIC.

BINNENLANDSCH BESTUUR (BB, internal administration), the generalized administrative corps of the Netherlands Indies. Until C.19, the term meant little more than the body of Dutch East Indies Company officials in the colony, especially those posted to represent the governor-general outside the capital, Batavia (q.v.). The BB emerged as a distinct structure on Java in early C.19 under Daendels (q.v.), who divided the island into prefectures and created a relatively ordered bureaucratic hierarchy. This structure was somewhat modified by

Raffles (q.v.), who replaced the prefects with *residents,* and by the decentralization (q.v.) program of early C.20.

Administrative dualism was a central principle of the BB. The organization was divided into the *Europeesch Bestuur (EB),* or European administration, and the *Inlandsch Bestuur* (q.v.) or native administration, the latter supervising the former, so that, according to the aims of the system, all contacts by the Indonesian masses with their rulers would be through fellow Indonesians. In 1865, the Europeesch Bestuur on Java numbered only 175 men, backed of course by the colonial army. On Java, the rank of *controleur* was paired with that of *bupati* in the Inlandsch Bestuur (qq.v.), as a putative advisory 'elder brother' to the Indonesian ruler. In time the Europeesch Bestuur developed an extended hierarchy running (from below) *adspirant controleur, controleur, assistent resident, resident,* and *gouverneur,* and holders of senior posts were generally recruited from lower ranks in the hierarchy.

In C.19 and 20 the role of the BB was diminished by the emergence of distinct specialist branches of government, beginning with finances in 1854. By the end of the colonial era, departments of justice, finances, education and religion, economic affairs, transport and water affairs, and war and naval affairs had emerged alongside the BB, all of them open at all levels, unlike the EB, to Indonesians. [0366]

BIRDS' NESTS. Nests of the swiftlet *Collocalia* species are constructed as cups against the walls of caves from salivary secretions of the birds. Valued by the Chinese as a delicacy, they have been a minor export crop from Java, Kalimantan, and Sumatra for several centuries. [0058, 0458, 0983]

BIRDS OF PARADISE (*cenderawasih*), birds of the family Paradisaeidae, found principally on the island of New

Guinea and adjacent regions. The males are often spectacularly plumed and have been used by people of the island for adornment since early times. The first pelts to reach Europe were sewn so as to conceal the feet so that the belief grew that these birds never rested, but always flew as if in paradise. Trade in bird of paradise pelts was under way in C.16 and is probably much older. China was the principal market at first, but it was displaced by Europe in C.19. In 1911 43,000 pelts were exported from Ternate. Concern over the effect of this trade helped to prompt the first nature conservation measures in the Netherlands Indies. See also CONSERVATION, Nature. [0944]

BOEKE, Julius Herman (1884–1944), prominent economic advisor to the colonial government and professor at Leiden University. Influenced by the writings of M.K. Gandhi, he proposed the notion of dualism (q.v.), rejecting the application of Western economic theory to the Asian village and urged a dualistic economic policy which would protect and even restore what he saw as traditional communal village life while providing general welfare for the Westernized sections of society. He was interned in Buchenwald 1941–44 for anti-Nazi activities. See also DESA; DEVELOPMENT IDEOLOGY. [0212]

BOGOR, formerly Buitenzorg, city in the foothills of Mt. Salak, south of Jakarta. Governor-General van Imhoff established a private house there in 1745 and the official residence of the governor-general was gradually transferred there. The city was the site of an agricultural research station which became the basis of the Landbouwkundige Faculteit, subsequently the Bogor Agricultural Institute (Institut Pertanian Bogor) (see EDUCATION) and of a botanical gardens (q.v.).

BONE, Bugis (q.v.) state in southern Sulawesi, founded in C.14 and the main rival of Makassar (q.v.), which conquered and converted it to Islam in 1611, though it was left autonomous. Bone was awarded by the Dutch to Arung Palakka (q.v.) under the Treaty of Bungaya in 1667. The rulers of Bone took advantage of the opportunity offered by the British interregnum in the Indies during the Napoleonic Wars to repudiate the treaty of Bungaya and in 1824 they launched a war on local Dutch garrisons. Though defeated by Dutch and Makassarese forces from Gowa in 1825, Bone continued to resist the Dutch during the Java War (q.v.) and accepted the renewed treaty only in 1838. Bone resistance to Dutch power revived under Queen Basse Kajuara and in 1859 the Dutch sent another expedition, which deposed her and formally made the kingdom a subject rather than an ally of the Dutch. A further expedition in 1905 captured the capital, Watampone, and deposed the ruler, who was not replaced until 1931. See also MAKASSAR. [0384, 0416, 0433]

BOROBUDUR. Buddhist monument in Central Java, constructed ca 800 under the Sailendras (q.v.). It is in the form of a massive stupa, with seven terraces. The quadrangular four lower galleries of reliefs tell the life story of the Buddha and other Buddhist teachings such as the Jatakas. One gallery of lower reliefs was later covered with earth to prevent collapse of the structure. Three circular upper terraces are bare but for 72 small stupas containing statues of the Buddha. A single larger stupa is at the center. The overall form of the monument is also a representation of Buddhist philosophy, with the crowded lower terraces symbolizing the distractions of daily life and the bare upper terraces representing the achievement of detachment. The reliefs are carved in the Indian style and show a mixture of Indian and

Javanese motifs—elephants (q.v.) for instance, which are not native to Java (though formerly they were imported from Sumatra), and a cockatoo, which is not found in India.

Borobudur was damaged by earthquakes and buried by volcanic ash some time after its construction and was first reexcavated by Raffles in 1814. A full-scale reconstruction was undertaken by the colonial archeological service under Theodor van Erp in 1907–12 and a further restoration under the auspices of UNESCO from 1973 to 1983, costing US$60 million. In 1985 an explosion of uncertain origin damaged the upper part of the monument though this was subsequently repaired. See also ARCHEOLOGY; BUDDHISM. [0086–0088, 0091]

BOTANICAL GARDENS ('sLands Plantentuin, Kebun Raya), founded in Bogor (Buitenzorg) in 1817 by Reinwardt (q.v.) and directed successively by Carl Ludwig Blume (1796–1862), Melchior Treub (1851–1910) and others, the gardens became one of the finest tropical plant collections in the world. In 1860 a branch was established in Cibodas. Until the establishment of a separate conservation section in the Department of Agriculture in 1951 the gardens had primary responsibility for conservation (q.v.) of nature in the Netherlands Indies and Indonesia. [0984, 0986, 0987, 0989]

BOTH, Pieter (?-1615), first governor-general (q.v.) of the Netherlands Indies. He expelled the Spaniards from Tidore and the Portuguese from Fort Henricus on Solor, opened VOC offices in Java at Sunda Kelapa (later Batavia, q.v.) and Japara, and sent the first Dutch mission to the court of Mataram (q.v.). [0375, 0530]

BOVEN DIGUL (Tanah Merah), detention center on the upper Digul river in West New Guinea (Irian, q.v.), established in 1926 primarily for those accused of involvement in the 1926–27 PKI uprisings. 1,308 alleged Communists and nationalists, including figures such as Hatta and Syahrir (qq.v.), were detained there under the so-called *exorbitante rechten* of the governor-general (see EXILE). In 1943, detainees from Boven Digul were removed to Australia (q.v.), where they were later released under pressure from Australian labor unions. See also TAHANAN POLITIK. [0573]

BRITAIN, Historical links with. The English East India Company (q.v.) was the main agent for British involvement in the archipelago during C.17 and 18. In 1800, after the Dutch colonial administration had recognized the pro-French Batavian Republic (q.v.), British forces occupied Melaka, West Sumatra, and Dutch possessions in Maluku. A British fleet appeared before Batavia (q.v.), but lacked forces to take the city. The colonies were restored under the Treaty of Amiens in March 1802.

In August and September 1811, after French forces had occupied the Netherlands in 1810, Company forces from British India conquered Java and other Dutch possessions in the archipelago (Ambon, Minahasa, qq.v.) in order to remove French influence, and established an interim administration on Java under Raffles (q.v.) as lieutenant-governor, with an advisory council of Dutch and British. Hoping to retain the island for Britain, Raffles undertook major reforms there, but he was unable to convince the Company's directors that the colony would be worthwhile, and it was restored to the Dutch in August 1816 under the terms of an Anglo-Dutch Convention signed in 1814. British policy was also that the Kingdom of the Netherlands in Europe (then including Belgium) should be bolstered as a powerful bulwark against possible French expansion and

Britain saw the revenues from Indonesia as playing some role in this. Britain retained its existing settlements in Bengkulu (q.v.) until 1824.

From this time on, however, Dutch rule in the colony remained to some extent at British sufferance. The Anglo-Dutch Treaty of 1824 (q.v.) allowed the Dutch extensive holdings in the archipelago, but Britain acquiesced in this partly because the Netherlands had ceased to be a major European power and thus played a useful role for Britain in keeping French and later German political influence out of the region. The Singapore (q.v.) naval base, established in 1921, became the keystone of Dutch defence policy in the colony. At the same time, the Dutch felt constrained to allow considerable British commercial investment in the colony as a further guarantee of their tenure. British investments in the Netherlands Indies in 1929 were valued at *f*277.9 million, second only after those of the Netherlands. Only in a few cases, such as the shipping (q.v.) industry, did the Dutch discriminate actively against British interests (see also TELEGRAPH).

British and Dutch forces cooperated with those of the United States and Australia (qq.v.) in the defence of the region against the Japanese in 1941–42 and after the Allied counterattack began, Sumatra was included in the predominantly British South East Asia Command under Lord Louis Mountbatten. On 16 August 1945, this command was extended to cover the entire Netherlands Indies, thus giving the British primary responsibility for accepting the Japanese surrender, evacuating Allied prisoners-of-war and internees, and restoring the colonial government. The Netherlands Indies was, however, low on the British list of priorities and by the time British forces arrived in Jakarta in late September, the Indonesian Republic was relatively firmly established. Unwilling to fight a major colonial war to restore Dutch control (especially since Britain was in the process of withdrawing from India), the British attempted to play a mediating role between the Dutch and the Republic, sponsoring first informal contacts and then negotiations which ultimately led to the Linggajati Agreement (q.v.). Britain's formal post-surrender responsibilities ended on 30 November 1946. During the 1950s, Indonesia became suspicious of British intentions in retaining the Singapore naval base and relations declined sharply as Britain planned a formula for granting independence to its Southeast Asian possession without giving up its base (see CONFRONTATION). In May 1965, Sukarno claimed on the basis of a letter said to be from the British ambassador Sir Anthony Gilchrist, that Britain was plotting with army (q.v.) groups to overthrow him. See also INDIA, Relations with. [0048, 0063, 0064, 0528, 0538, 0563]

BROAD OUTLINES OF STATE POLICY. See MAJELIS PERMUSYAWARATAN RAKYAT.

BUBONIC PLAGUE (*Pasteurella pestis*). It is possible that parts of Indonesia were affected by the plague pandemics of C.6 and 14, but evidence suggesting this is slender. The disease is first known definitely to have reached Java in 1910 aboard a rice ship from Burma, and outbreaks continued on the island until the 1940s. The death toll from the disease in the period 1911–39 is officially given as 215,000, but was almost certainly many more. Fears of the virulence of the disease led the colonial government, through its Dienst der pestbestrijding (Plague control service), founded in 1915, to undertake a massive control program, which included extensive quarantine, the destruction and fumigation of property, the reconstruction of 1-¼ million houses to rat-proof designs and, from 1934, an extensive vaccination program in which seven million people were vaccinated or revaccinated. The common method of diagnosing plague deaths, by puncturing the spleen of the deceased, was strongly resisted by Muslims, who saw it as a violation of the dead. See also ETHICAL POLICY; HEALTH. [0483, 0981]

BUDDHISM. Theravada Buddhism was probably established briefly in southern Sumatra in C.5, but was soon replaced by Mahayana. Srivijaya (q.v.) became a major center of Buddhist studies in C.7 having close ties with Nalanda in Bihar. In later centuries strong influences from Tantrism were felt. The massive stupa of Borobudur (q.v.) was succeeded by Hindu rather than Buddhist temples, but Buddhism seems to have survived as an aspect of Hinduism, rather than being displaced. The religion of Majapahit (q.v.) was Hindu and Buddhist, but formal adherence to Buddhism largely ceased amongst indigenous Indonesians with the conversion to Islam in C.13–16, though Buddhism remains an important element in Hindu religious practice on Bali.

In colonial times, Buddhism was largely a religion of the Chinese in Indonesia (q.v.), but in the 1930s, under influences from theosophy, Buddhism underwent a revival amongst Europeans in the colony. After independence, Buddhist leaders made determined efforts to recruit indigenous Indonesian members, forming the Perbuddhi (Perhimpunan Buddhis Indonesia, Indonesian Buddhist Association) in 1958. Buddhists now constitute approximately 4-½% of the population. Under the New Order the insistence of the Pancasila (q.v.) on 'Belief in God' has led some Buddhists to revise their philosophy to include a single supreme deity, Sang Hyang Adi Buddha. Vesak Day has been a national holiday in Indonesia since 1983. See also RELIGION AND POLITICS. [0373, 1112, 1123]

BUDI UTOMO ('Noble Endeavour'), society founded 20 May 1908 by Dr Wahidin Sudiro Husodo (1857–1917),

Dr Sutomo (q.v.), and Gunawan Mangunkusumo and regarded as the start of Indonesia's national awakening (*kebangkitan nasional*). It aimed at first to promote the study of Javanese culture and to improve access to Western education, but slowly became more political, arguing in 1914, for instance, for an Indies militia. Dominated by the lesser priyayi of the colonial civil service, it was always conservative and was viewed with approval by the colonial government as a positive result of the Ethical Policy (q.v.). As a result it was somewhat distrusted by other nationalist parties. In 1935 it dissolved itself into the PARINDRA. See also ASSOCIATION PRINCIPLE; NATIONALISM. [0574]

BUFFALO. See KERBAU.

BUGIS, ethnic group in southern Sulawesi (q.v.). Like the neighboring Makassarese, the Bugis were traditionally divided into many small states, but Bone (q.v.) became increasingly powerful in C.16 until it was conquered by Makassar (q.v.) and converted to Islam in early C.17. Led by Arung Palakka (q.v.), many Bugis joined the VOC against Makassar in the campaigns of 1660, 1666–67, and 1668–69, but in late C.17, following the defeat of Makassar, many Bugis fled Arung Palakka's authoritarian rule and settled widely on Sumatra, Kalimantan, and the Malay peninsula, founding the last dynasty of the sultans of Aceh (q.v.). Such communities are featured in several works by Joseph Conrad (q.v.). Bugis troops were often used as mercenaries. Bugis are the major interisland trading community of eastern Indonesia. See also RIAU. [0433]

BUITENGEWESTEN. See OUTER ISLANDS.

BUITENZORG. See BOGOR.

'BUNG', common term of address (for males) during the revolution, derived from Javanese *abang* ('brother') and implying revolutionary equality; it is now seldom used except to refer to leaders of the revolution, especially Bung Karno (Sukarno, q.v.). The Sundanese equivalent, 'Bang', is routinely adopted by governors of Jakarta as a populist gesture. See also BAPAK.

BUPATI. In pre-colonial Java, the bupati was a local chief generally in a vassal relationship with a nearby king or senior chief. His authority was over households, or *cacah,* (and thus men-at-arms) rather than over territory and was likely to fluctuate widely with the vagaries of war and economic change. The most powerful bupati were regional warlords, the weakest headed bands of a couple of dozen men. There was a natural tendency, however, for the domain of a bupati (*kabupaten*) to coincide with economic and geographical boundaries, so that although the political geography of Java was always in flux the boundaries of kabupaten remained historically relatively stable.

Under Dutch rule, the fealty of the bupati was shifted from the royal courts to the Dutch East Indies Company (q.v.), or VOC, and they were tied increasingly to specific areas of land rather than to scattered households, though they retained something of the character of allies, rather than officials, of the Company. They were obliged only to organize the delivery of crops demanded by the VOC and were left in full control of internal administration of their territories. Under Daendels and Raffles (qq.v.), however, the bupati became unambiguously officials of the colonial administration (Binnenlandsch Bestuur, q.v.), with the title *regent*. The Dutch also reduced the number of bupati dramatically in some regions, placing each bupati at the head of a native hierarchy within his *kabupaten* or regency (see INLANDSCH BESTUUR). Restraining, and at times reversing, this trend towards bureaucratization was the need of the colonial government to employ the traditional authority of the bupati as a key to the control of the Javanese peasantry. Under Daendels, and later under the Cultivation System (q.v.), the bupati were primarily responsible for mobilizing labor in service of production for the colonial state, and colonial authorities were not only reluctant to tamper with this system but sought from time to time to bolster the position of the bupati as small-time kings or princes, especially by making the office hereditary. In 1913, a conservative Regentenbond (Regents Society) was formed.

The bupati were largely retained in office during the Japanese occupation (q.v.) as *ken-cho*. On independence, the Indonesian Republic retained the kabupaten, headed by a bupati, as a major administrative unit, and it has now been extended throughout Indonesia as the principal administrative division below province, known formally as Daerah Tingkat II (Second Level Region). Between 1957 and 1959, bupati were elected to office. See also DECENTRALIZATION; DESA; PRIYAYI. [0366, 0455, 0575, 0596]

BURU, mountainous island in Maluku, originally inhabited by Alfurs (q.v.). From ca 1520 it was under the rule of Ternate, which converted the coastal areas to Islam, and was an important clove producing area until VOC hongi raids (q.v.) in 1652 destroyed the plantations. Local resistance to the Dutch in 1657 gave the VOC the excuse to move the indigenous population to the area around Kaleji Bay. In early C.19 the island became a major center for the production of kayuputih (q.v.) oil. After the GESTAPU (q.v.) affair of 1965, many thousands of political prisoners (*tahanan politik* q.v.) were detained in prison camps on the island from 1969. [0019, 0166, 0680, 0983]

BUTON (Butung), Muslim sultanate established in 1540, based on the earlier kingdom of Wolio and covering the islands off the southeast arm of Sulawesi (q.v.). It was conquered by Ternate (q.v.) in 1580 and successive sultans thereafter tried to play off Ternate, Makassar and the VOC (qq.v.). With the fall of Makassar, the kingdom came definitely within the Dutch sphere of influence. They weakened the political base of the kingdom, however, by exporting slaves on a large scale. After a Dutch military expedition in 1906, the sultan signed the Korte Verklaring in 1912. The sultanate was abolished in 1960. Asphalt has been mined on Buton since 1926. See also ZELFBESTUREN. [0489]

C

CACAO (*Theobroma cacao* Sterculiaceae). Mexican shrub, seeds of which are used to make cocoa. It was planted widely on Java after the destruction of coffee (q.v.) plantations by disease in 1878. It is now produced most extensively on the island of Bacan in Maluku (q.v.). [0938]

CAJUPUT. See KAYUPUTIH.

CALENDARS. Numerous traditional calendars have been employed in the archipelago at various times. The Muslim calendar is lunar, with a year of 354 or 355 days divided into 12 months. The counting of years commenced in 622 A.D. with Muhammad's flight (*hijrah*) to Medina and Muslim dates are commonly denoted in English by AH (*anno hijrae*), in Indonesian by H (years according to the Christian calendar being marked with M for *Masehi*). The year 1410 AH commenced on 3 August 1989 A.D. The Javanese calendar, also lunar with 354–355 days per year, was adopted by Sultan

Agung of Mataram (q.v.), using much Muslim terminology, but with a somewhat different division of months and arrangement of leap years and a base year of 78 A.D., the putative start of the Hindu-Javanese era. Years are now commonly denoted with the initials AJ (*anno Javanicae*). For agricultural purposes, the Javanese also used sun-years (*mangsa*), but these were not counted. The year 1922 AJ commenced on 3 August 1989 A.D.

During the Japanese occupation (q.v.), the traditional Japanese system of counting years from the founding of the imperial dynasty was used; 1942 thus became 2602. See also TIME. [0026]

CAMPHOR (from Mal. *kapur*), an aromatic crystalline substance collected from cavities in the trunks of felled *Dryobalanops aromatica* (Dipterocarpaceae) trees, especially in northern Sumatra. It was used in incense and medicines and for the preservation of corpses and was traded extensively since C.6 from Kalimantan and from north Sumatra through the west coast port of Barus to China, India, the Arab world, and the Mediterranean. Collection was done in great secrecy and collectors developed a secret language to conceal their activities. Trade with China declined after techniques were developed to extract camphor from the East Asian tree *Cinnamomum camphora*. *Dryobalanops* is now more important as a timber tree. [0430, 0452, 0751, 0938]

CANNABIS (*Cannabis sativa* Cannabaceae, *ganja*). Native to the area around the Caspian Sea, but reported from Java in C.10, cannabis was used both for its fibre and as an intoxicant, though its use never approached that of betel, opium, or tobacco (qq.v.). Its use was banned in 1927, but it is still found wild in northern Sumatra and has been the subject of a government antinarcotic campaign since the late 1970s. See also COCA. [0245, 0246, 0938]

CARDAMOM. See AMOMUM.

CASSAVA (*Manihot esculenta* Euphorbiaceae, *ubi kayu*), root crop from tropical America. The first varieties introduced to Indonesia, probably in C.17, were relatively unproductive and only with the arrival of better strains in 1851 did cultivation spread. Production was expanded during World War I to cover rice (q.v.) shortages. Dried cassava (*gaplek*) is a major source of cheap calories in time of hardship. [0245, 0246, 0938]

CASTOR (*Ricinus communis* Euphorbiaceae), introduced from Africa probably in early times. The oil was used medicinally and for lighting until it was displaced by kerosene in C.19. Production expanded briefly during the Japanese occupation. [0245, 0246, 0938]

CATHOLICISM. Although the Franciscan Odoric of Pordonone preached in Java, Sumatra, and Kalimantan in ca 1324, formal Catholic missionary activity in Indonesia began only after the Portuguese captured Melaka (q.v.) in 1511 and established outposts in Maluku (q.v.). Francis Xavier worked in Ternate and Ambon (1546–47) and significant conversions were made in Ambon, Ternate, Flores, Timor (qq.v.), and the north coast of Java. Militarized Dominican friars claimed much of the islands of Flores and Timor (q.v.) for Portugal in mid C.16 and were the principal agents of Portuguese domination there until early C.19. They were expelled by the Portuguese government in 1834.

The Dutch East Indies Company banned the promotion of Catholicism, and though formal freedom of religion was allowed with the fall of the Company in 1800, many practical restrictions remained. The Catholic Church continued to be banned from certain regions, notably the Batak (q.v.) regions of northern Sumatra and the Toraja (q.v.) areas of Sulawesi, but in mid C.19

was allocated Flores and Timor as mission area as part of an agreement with the Portuguese over jurisdictions in east Nusatenggara. The present Catholic population, ca 5 million, is concentrated on Flores and Timor and to a lesser extent in Central Java, where it has been adopted by many Chinese Indonesians. Albert Sugiyopranoto (1896–1963) was the first Indonesian to be appointed bishop. See also CHRISTIANITY; PARTAI KATOLIK; RELIGION. [0919, 1123]

CATTLE (*Bos taurus* and *B. indicus*) were abundant on Java from C.10 and dried meat was exported to China in C.19. There was little traditional use of milk in the archipelago except in parts of Sumatra and for ritual purposes. Dairies, however, were established by the VOC in Ambon and the Batavia region in C.17 and milk became a luxury especially associated with European ways of life. From 1880 condensed milk was imported from Europe and Australia (q.v.) and use of milk began to spread increasingly to Indonesians. The colonial agriculture department began systematic improvement of cattle strains in 1904. The first hygiene regulations for milk were issued in 1920. Under the New Order, attempts have been made to develop the cattle industry as consumer demand for meat and milk grows. See also BANTENG; KERBAU; PASTEUR INSTITUTE. [0250]

CELEBES. See SULAWESI.

CEMPEDAK. See JACKFRUIT.

CENDANA GROUP. General term for those business interests associated with the presidential palace, notably the holdings of the President's wife Siti Hartinah (Tien) Suharto (especially the charitable organization Yayasan Harapan Kita); her brother-in-law Probosutejo (especially the Mercu Buana group); her sons Tommy (Hutomo), Sigit, and Bambang; and with President Suharto's banker, Liem Sioe Liong (q.v.). See also CLOVES; SUHARTO. [0280, 0287]

CENSORSHIP (Print). Until 1815 the governor-general (q.v.) had absolute right to restrict or ban circulation of publications in the Indies, though this right was exercised mainly in the centers of European settlement. Although the free circulation of Netherlands publications was guaranteed by the Regeeringsreglement (Constitution, q.v.) of the Netherlands Indies in 1815, local and foreign publications were subject to censorship. The 1856 Reglement op de Drukwerken (Regulation on Publications) provided for prepublication censorship and the governor-general had the right, in consultation with the Raad van Indië, to ban local periodicals on grounds of agitation or the undermining of state authority. Like the exorbitante rechten (see EXILE), this power was not subject to judicial appeal or review. In 1906 postpublication censorship was introduced: all publications had to be submitted to the censor within 24 hours and could be suspended. From 1914, prosecution was also possible under the so-called *haatzaai* articles (see SUBVERSION). Revised regulations for press muzzling (*persbreidel*) were introduced in 1931 and in the following five years 27 nationalist newspapers were restricted. Prepublication censorship was restored under the Japanese.

In the first years of independence, there was virtually no censorship, but control was restored in 1957 with the imposition of martial law. Publications were censored by pre-publication government instructions (similar to the British D-Notice), by bans on distribution, by the blacking out of offending articles (especially in the case of foreign publications), and by withdrawal of a publication's Surat Ijin Terbit (SIT, Publication Licence), introduced in 1958. Heavy press restrictions were introduced in 1965–66, when 46 newspapers were banned and the Indonesian Journalists' Association (Persatuan Wartawan Indonesia) was purged. Restrictions were formalized in a new Press Law of December 1966, intended officially to ensure that the press would be 'free but responsible'. Another Press Law in September 1982 replaced the SIT with a Surat Ijin Usaha Penerbitan Pers (SIUPP, Permit to Operate a Press Company), withdrawal of which can stop publication not just of the offending publication, but also of all other business operations associated with it. See also NEWSPAPERS. [0354, 0356, 0891]

CENSUSES. Most rulers in Indonesia have required some form of population count for taxation (q.v.) purposes, and Wallace describes an ingenious method of counting attributed to the ruler of Lombok (q.v.). Most commonly, however, households rather than individuals were counted and the association with taxation makes early figures, which are not common in any case, highly unreliable. S.C. Nederburgh conducted the first census of Java in 1795 and the Dutch conducted a partial count of the population of the Indies in 1905, a more extensive count in 1920 and a full census in 1930. A further census planned for 1940 was cancelled because of the war. The first census in independent Indonesia was held in 1961 but was incomplete and many of the detailed results have since been lost. Full censuses were held in 1971, 1980 and 1990. See also POPULATION. [0044, 0045, 0075]

CENTRE FOR STRATEGIC AND INTERNATIONAL STUDIES, CSIS, research center associated with Lt-Gen. Ali Murtopo (1924–84) and Operasi Khusus (q.v.). CSIS played a major role in developing a political format for New Order Indonesia, especially a number of important tools for political control such as the principle of *monoloyalitas* (q.v.) for civil servants, and the notion of the 'floating mass' (q.v.). In economic policymaking it has taken a somewhat similar corporatist view, generally arguing against the 'internationalist' views of the BAPPENAS (q.v.), and for close coordination between government and business as in Japan, with the state setting investment priorities and encouraging import-substitution industrialization. CSIS was close to the head of Pertamina (q.v.), Ibnu Sutowo, and oil revenues provided Indonesia with a degree of financial independence which made some of the CSIS policies possible. Major figures in CSIS have been the conservative Catholic Chinese Liem Bian Kie (Jusuf Wanandi), Jusuf Panglaykim, and Harry Tjan Silalahi. See also KOMITE NASIONAL PEMUDA INDONESIA. [0280, 0675]

CERAM. See SERAM.

CERAMICS were introduced to the archipelago probably by Austronesian immigrants ca 3000 B.C., and some local traditions continue to exist. The region, however, has been a major importer of ceramics from China (C.10–16) and later Thailand and Vietnam (qq.v.). [0152]

CHAERUL SALEH (1916–67). One of the youth leaders who pressed Sukarno and Hatta (qq.v.) to declare independence in August 1945, Chaerul Saleh later moved close to the radical position of Tan Malaka (q.v.) and briefly joined a lasykar (q.v.) unit in West Java in 1949 to press for a less accommodating settlement with the Dutch. Twice arrested by the army, he was exiled to Holland in 1952, but returned in 1955. He was close to, but not a member of, the Murba (q.v.), and soon came close to Sukarno, entering the first *kabinet karya* in 1957. In 1963, after the death of Juanda (q.v.), he became one of three deputy prime ministers (with Subandrio and Leimena, qq.v.), and was increasingly seen as a possible leftist successor to Sukarno, though he was popular with neither the army nor the PKI (qq.v.), which tried to have him 'retooled' (*i.e.,* removed) in 1964 after he had promoted the Badan Pendukung Sukarnoisme (q.v.). He was jailed in 1966 and died soon after. [0628, 0634]

CHAIRIL ANWAR (1922–49), poet. Though his total output was tiny, Chairil Anwar is credited with enormously widening the scope of Indonesian poetry from the formal style of the kakawin and pantun (qq.v.) to a terse, personal style. See also GENERATIONS; JASSIN, H.B. [0152, 0155, 0156, 0160, 0175]

CHENG HO. See ZHENG HE.

CHERIBON. See CIREBON.

CHILLI (*Capsicum* sp. Solanaceae). Native to central America, the chilli had reached Indonesia by late C.16, rapidly taking over many of the functions of pepper (q.v.) in local cuisine. [0483, 0938]

CHINA, Historical links with. Trade created the earliest links between China and the Indonesian archipelago. The Strait of Melaka was also an important staging post on trade routes between India and China (see SRIVIJAYA). This early trade was the basis for a political relationship between China and Indonesian states which is still not clear. Until C.10, trade seems to have been largely in the hands of Indonesian traders whose large vessels took spices and forest products to the ports of South China and carried Chinese goods, especially ceramics and silk (qq.v.), back to Southeast Asia for local consumption and onward trade. These traders were permitted to operate in Chinese courts only if their rulers acknowledged Chinese suzerainty and paid tribute to China. Much trade, in fact, was conducted within this framework, goods from Southeast Asia being delivered as 'tribute' with Chinese goods being returned as imperial 'largess.' Imperial sale of goods obtained in this fashion was an important source of state revenue, especially during the Sung period, and in 1381 an Imperial edict forbade Southeast Asian 'envoys' from using their 'diplomatic' status to trade privately. The permission to trade in southern China was economically important to Indonesian rulers, and they may have acquiesced simply in order to continue trading. Some rulers, on the other hand, seem to have courted Chinese imperial favor to mark their seniority over neighboring kingdoms, and a few requested diplomatic and military assistance against enemies in a way which suggests true vassal status (see 'HO-LO-TAN'). No practical Chinese assistance, however, ever appears to have reached the archipelago.

Between C.10 and C.12, the tributary trade was gradually displaced by so-called 'private trade', in which Chinese traders themselves came for the first time to Southeast Asia. The manufacture of ceramics for the Southeast Asian market was a major industry in southern China during the Southern Sung (1127–79) and Yuan (1279–1368) dynasties. In C.13, the Mongol rulers of China clearly misinterpreted the China-Indonesia relationship to assume a much closer vassalage. Their effort to assert this authority on Java in 1292, however, was a failure (see MAJAPAHIT). Under the first Ming emperor, the tributary trade was restored and Chinese exports dramatically declined. With the rise of the VOC, relations were dominated by the question of China's responsibility for and to the local Chinese community, and policy varied from outright rejection to enthusiastic espousal of local Chinese interests. See also

CHINESE IN INDONESIA; ZHENG HE. [0409, 0430, 0432, 0752, 0753]

CHINA, Relations with. Relations between Indonesia and China since 1945 have been dominated by the question of China's relationship with the Chinese resident in Indonesia (see following entry). Indonesia recognized the PRC in June 1950, but sought to keep relations at a low level to minimize official Chinese contact with local Chinese. Relations improved after Sukarno visited China in 1956, and China granted Indonesia credits of US$11.2 million for rice and textiles in 1958. They cooled again when China opposed the 1959 law expelling Chinese traders from the countryside (see CHINESE IN INDONESIA). China's global antiimperialist policy, however, fitted well with Sukarno's militant foreign policy and in 1961 they signed a treaty of friendship and cooperation. By 1964 there was talk of a Jakarta-Peking antiimperialist axis. Initially the PKI kept some distance from the CCP in order to avoid appearing to take sides in the Sino-Soviet dispute, but by 1964 most observers saw the PKI as pro-Beijing rather than pro-Moscow. After the 1965 coup, however, China was accused of having abetted the PKI, especially by allegedly importing 100,000 small arms for use by the 'Fifth Force' (q.v.) under PKI control. Demonstrations attacked the Chinese embassy and in October 1967 Indonesia officially cut relations. Diplomatic contacts resumed in 1973 and direct trade in 1985, but it was not until 1989 that the two countries announced their intention to normalize relations. A 1980 citizenship law in China has removed all recognition of dual nationality. Indonesia and China have disputed claims to areas of the South China Sea. [0742, 0748]

CHINESE IN INDONESIA. The earliest known Chinese residents of the archipelago were the Buddhist pilgrims,

Fa Xien (414) and I Jing (689–692), who spent time studying in Srivijaya (q.v.) on their way to or from major monasteries in India. Chinese traders arrived from approximately C.10, forming enclave settlements in the coastal ports. The initial position of these Chinese was in many ways analogous to that of Hindu-Buddhist and later Islamic traders. They represented an advanced culture from which local rulers found it useful to borrow culturally and politically, though the political influence of Chinese thought in Indonesia was never more than superficial. A few traders thus entered court life, reaching high rank as ministers if they were especially able, while the majority remained as temporary residents, living in Chinese quarters similar to those of the Indonesian trading groups. The number involved was never large, and in adopting local culture and customs they lost their Chinese identity. Many married local women and their descendants merged with the indigenous population. Muslims from the Chinese empire (especially Yunnan) formed a significant community in northern Java in C.15, but claims that one or more of the nine walis credited with converting the island to Islam (q.v.) were Chinese remain controversial.

Under the Dutch East Indies Company (q.v.), or VOC, the Chinese first began to emerge as a distinct intermediary class in Indonesia. With the decline of the indigenous courts, upwardly mobile Chinese sought their fortunes in the VOC sphere. They found the VOC, however, racially and culturally more exclusive and bureaucratically more rigid. Chinese could rise far less in the Company world than in the courts of Java and Sumatra, and they found the most profitable employment on the fringes of VOC activity, as farmers (see PACHT) for the collection of tolls and market taxes and the sale of salt and opium. In C.19, Chinese were important in the operation of pawnshop, opium, and gambling farms. There thus emerged a Chinese community which was economically powerful but excluded from access to political power in the colony, a state of affairs which has applied ever since. Chinese communities were typically organized as semiautonomous corporations under Chinese 'officers', with ranks such as captain and major, who were responsible for taxation and for maintaining order in their communities. In C.19 the separation of the Chinese from the remainder of society was formalized with the creation of the legal category of Foreign Oriental (see RACE). Resident Chinese continued to adopt local ways at the expense of their Chinese customs and a distinct local Chinese culture, called Baba or *peranakan* emerged, mainly on Java. Peranakan Chinese in general retained Chinese names and religion but spoke Malay and adopted many other elements of Malay culture such as the use of batik.

During C.19, however, peranakans were joined by large numbers of new arrivals, generally called *totoks* or *singkeh,* often impoverished men from the southern provinces of Guangdong, Fujien, and Guangxi (ethnically described as Hokkien, Hakka, Tiuchiu, Cantonese etc.). Many of these came initially as laborers, first in the gold mines of West Kalimantan (where there were 50,000 Chinese miners in the middle of the century, see PONTIANAK) and in the tin mines of Bangka and Belitung (qq.v.), and later as indentured laborers on the plantations in East Sumatra (q.v.). The Chinese population of Indonesia in 1860 is estimated to have been 222,000. In Kalimantan many later settled down as peasants. More, however, moved into trade and with family connections in other parts of Southeast Asia were able to build up powerful regional trading networks. Singkeh tended to dominate big capital and small trade, while peranakan were most often found in credit, agricultural production, and the professions.

The economic power of the Chinese communities led the Dutch to see them from time to time as dangerous.

In 1740 Dutch fears of a Chinese coup led to a massacre of the Chinese in Batavia and to restrictions on Chinese residence. Later, Chinese were seen as pitiless exploiters, a danger to the welfare of indigenous Indonesians (and the profits of the Dutch). Until 1904 they were banned from residence and travel (q.v.) in rural areas. During the Ethical Policy (q.v.), they were excluded from the revenue farms which had previously been their mainstay and they moved into retail trade and credit, especially in rural areas. In early C.20, Chinese interests began to move into the manufacture of batik and kretek (qq.v.). Chinese business operations were generally organized on a family basis, with the founder and family head remaining in general charge of most operations. While Chinese in general remained dominant in these areas, therefore, individual families rose and fell.

The status of Chinese in Indonesian nationalism was always vague. Because they were legally distinct and to some extent privileged, they tended to be excluded (and to exclude themselves) from Indonesian nationalism. Unlike local Arabs (q.v.), they did not generally share Islam with the local population, and their role in the sale of opium and alcohol and in gambling and prostitution gave them an unsavory reputation. Even before the emergence of Indonesian nationalism, the political resurgence of nationalism in China drew strong support from the totok community in Indonesia and the Guomindang (Kuomintang, Nationalist Party) was active in the colony.

At independence, therefore, the status of the Chinese was uncertain. In 1946, all resident Chinese were offered citizenship retrospective to 17 August 1945 unless they specifically repudiated it and a similar provision was made under the transfer of sovereignty in 1949. Under Chinese law, however, all such Chinese retained dual nationality. In 1954 the foreign ministers of both countries, Sunaryo and Zhou Enlai, signed a treaty (ratified in 1958) requiring all with dual nationality to choose one or the other by December 1962. Indonesia repudiated this treaty unilaterally in April 1969, thus voiding citizenships taken out under it and leaving about 80,000 Chinese stateless. There are presently some five million people in Indonesia identified as 'Chinese', of whom about two thirds are Indonesian citizens and one million citizens of the PRC. Procedures for resident Chinese to obtain citizenship were simplified in 1980, but corruption and obstruction by officials and reluctance on the part of Chinese have slowed the acceptance rate.

In August 1958, the Guomindang was banned and the army took over the property of pro-Taiwan Chinese. Then, on 14 May 1959, a government order revoked the licenses for alien Chinese to operate in retail trade in rural areas, affecting an estimated 83,783 out of 86,690 traders. This led to an exodus to the cities. One hundred nineteen thousand Chinese left Indonesia for the PRC and 17,000 for Taiwan. Other restrictions on Chinese Indonesians since 1965 have included the abolition of the Chinese language press, except for the government-controlled bilingual *Warta Indonesia,* a ban on the import of Chinese language materials, encouragement for Chinese to take 'Indonesian' (commonly Sanskritic or Muslim) names, and a 2% limit on the proportion of Chinese enrollments at most state tertiary educational institutions (and a 30% limit in private institutions). Still, however, Chinese are widely perceived as being privileged, especially because of the position of *cukong* (q.v.) and anti-Chinese violence has broken out on many occasions. Much anti-Chinese violence accompanied the anticommunist massacres of 1965–66 (q.v.), and particularly extensive riots took place in Central Java in November 1980. See also CONFUCIANISM. [0018, 0032, 0440, 0595, 0920, 0922–0929, 0933–0935]

CHOLERA, bacterial disease (*Vibrio cholerae*) of the intestine, native to Bengal. It reached Indonesia in 1821, and has been endemic ever since, though the death rate diminished considerably after the development of a vaccine by Nijland in 1909. [0483, 0981]

CHRISTIANITY. Scattered, evanescent communities of foreign-born Christians, mostly Armenian and Persian Nestorians, existed in the archipelago from perhaps C.5, but there was no significant conversion to Christianity in the archipelago until the arrival of Catholic priests with the Portuguese. See also CATHOLICISM; JUDAISM; PROTESTANTISM; RELIGION, Political significance of. [1165]

CHUO SANGI-IN (Central Advisory Council), consultative body established by the Japanese military authorities on Java in October 1944. Its membership drew on the Indonesian nationalist establishment, but it had none of the powers and freedoms of the prewar Volksraad (q.v.), being limited to offering advice and suggestions in response to questions from the Japanese. Regional councils (Shu Sangi-kai) set up in September 1944, seem to have played a similar, limited role. [0563, 0615]

CINCHONA spp. (Rubiaceae), tree from Andes regions of South America, the bark of which is processed to produce quinine, the major medicine for preventing and treating malaria. In 1852 the colonial government sent J.K. Hasskarl to South America to collect seeds and plants. These were brought to Java in 1854 and after some experiments were planted successfully at Cibodas in West Java. Under the vigorous direction of Junghuhn (q.v.), the strain was improved and commercial plantations laid out. In 1930, Java produced 11,900 tons of kina (cinchona bark), most of the world's supply. [0245, 0246, 0269]

CINNAMON (from Mal. *kayu manis,* 'sweet wood'), the bark of *Cinnamomum macrophyllum* and related species (Lauraceae), was exported to ancient Egypt and the Roman world via East Africa, for use in food, medicine, and the embalming of bodies. [0751, 0938]

CIPTO MANGUNKUSUMO. See TJIPTO MANGUNKUSUMO.

CIREBON (Cheribon), port city on Java's north coast, founded in C.16 by Sunan Gunung Jati (d.1570) (see ISLAM IN INDONESIA). From 1640 to 1677 it was vassal to Mataram (q.v.) and came in 1681 under VOC rule, but it remained a major center of Pasisir (q.v.) culture. From 1662 sovereignty was shared and the territory of the state divided between three royal families, Kanoman, Kesepuhan, and Cirebonan. See also PRIANGAN. [0375, 0550]

CITIES. In contrast with the great European cities, many of which have been major centers for millennia, the location of Indonesian cities has tended to change with time, and most of the large cities of the modern archipelago were not important centers five hundred years ago. This was partly due to the custom of traditional rulers to shift their capitals, partly due perhaps to the impermanence of much traditional architecture, and partly due to the fact that ritual, rather than monument, was the essential feature of royal display. See also PORTS.

Modern urban growth began in the 1870s with the expansion of Batavia, Surabaya, Bandung, Surabaya, Yogyakarta, Surakarta (qq.v.), and Semarang on Java and Medan and Palembang (qq.v.) on Sumatra. The term city was first given administrative meaning with the creation of municipalities under the decentralization (q.v.) of 1903. Urbanization was 3.8% in 1930, 14.8% in

1961. In 1930, half the indigenous population of the cities of Batavia, Bandung, and Surabaya were born outside the cities, though all census figures are inaccurate to the extent that the administrative divisions used for counting fail to reflect the actual extent of urbanization. The 49 municipalities formed by the Dutch (see DECENTRALIZATION) have been retained by the Republic as Kotamadya, with a status analogous to that of the kabupaten (Daerah Tingkat II). Newly important towns requiring some form of distinct administration are now designated *kota administratif* (administrative towns) within kabupaten; there were 29 of these in 1987. [0425, 0484, 1162, 1163, 1172]

CIVET, glandular secretion of the civet 'cat', *Viverra* sp. (*V. tangalunga* in Southeast Asia), used mainly in medicine and perfumery. Though traded in the archipelago, its importance was limited due to the wide availability of civet from Africa and India and the easy domesticability of the animals. [0943, 0983]

CLASS ANALYSIS of Indonesian society was uncommon even amongst Marxists before 1925, many believing that the Indonesia-Dutch conflict (itself perhaps a class conflict) transcended class divisions within Indonesian society (see also NATIONALISM). Most class analysts have acknowledged the existence of an aristocratic class or classes. Debate has focused rather on the existence and nature of the commercial bourgeoisie (middle class) and the identification of potential allies of the proletariat.

Since early times, extensive commerce has taken place in the coastal regions of Indonesia but no indigenous capitalist bourgeoisie emerged to seize state power. This has been attributed variously to culture (see DUALISM; SHARED POVERTY), religion, and the fact that taxation (q.v.) in various forms prevented traders from accumulating investment capital. Colonial policies in turn inhibited the rise of an Indonesian bourgeoisie which would compete with Dutch interests and allowed middle levels of the economy to be dominated by Chinese (see CHINESE IN INDONESIA). Although the Chinese constituted a bourgeoisie in some senses, they were precluded from gaining political power by their failure to assimilate culturally. In independent Indonesia, the state itself seized Dutch investments (see NATIONALIZATION), restricted Chinese business, and sought to foster an Indonesian middle class. The PKI described those who administered state enterprises and profited from government patronage as 'bureaucratic capitalists' (*kapitalis birokrat, kabir*), but few of these seem to have been able to accumulate significant investment capital. Under the New Order, however, the scale of capital accumulation by groups close to or within the government and the extent of their investments within Indonesia suggests that they may be developing the commercial economic power independent of state patronage which is the hallmark of a bourgeoisie. See also CENDANA GROUP; INDONESIANIZATION.

A separate but related issue has been the relative absence of a class of large landowners, especially in the countryside of Java. Most observers have noted that, although there are clear differentiations of wealth and power within Javanese villages, control of land (q.v.) is not concentrated in a small number of wealthy families as, say, in the Philippines. This has been attributed both to cultural features of Javanese rural society (see AGRICULTURAL INVOLUTION; DESA; DUALISM; SHARED POVERTY) and to policies of the Dutch, which limited the opportunities for capital accumulation in the countryside (see INDIË VERLOREN, RAMPSPOED GEBOREN) and encouraged the traditional aristocracy of Java to remain or become primarily agents of the state rather than landowners in their own right (see CULTIVATION SYSTEM; LIBERAL POLICY). There is some evidence that under the impact of the Green Revolution (q.v.) a class of wealthy agricultural businessmen is developing in many parts of Java.

The Indonesian proletariat (working class), whether strictly or loosely defined, has always been small and revolutionaries have consequently sought class allies for it. From the 1920s, debate focussed on whether the so-called bourgeois nationalists were appropriate allies. This debate, which reflected similar discussion in Marxist circles elsewhere, was never resolved satisfactorily. Until the 1950s peasants were seldom considered, partly because of romantic ideas of village life (see DESA) and partly because of Marx's Asiatic Mode of Production model. The PKI (q.v.) under Aidit suggested that peasants as a class were oppressed by feudalism and (neo)colonialism and thus could also be revolutionary, but the party was seldom able in practice to identify clear class divisions in rural areas. More recently some observers have noted a widening gap between rich and poor as a result of the Green Revolution (q.v.) and have suggested that a rural bourgeoisie and proletariat are emerging. See also MARHAEN; PATRIMONIALISM. [0280, 0281, 0287, 0383, 0672, 0776, 0788, 0853]

CLOTH. The earliest cloth in the archipelago was made of felted bark, in a style still found in parts of Kalimantan, Sulawesi, Seram, and Irian (qq.v.). With the arrival, however, of cotton (q.v.), weaving became a major activity, symbolic of creation and preeminently the work of women (q.v.), as metal-working (q.v.) was the work of men. Many traditional cultures of the archipelago use ritual cloths, such as the celebrated ship cloths of Lampung (q.v.), to celebrate rites of passage. Indonesian cloth manufacture is best known for its dyeing techniques, especially *ikat,* in which the threads are tie-dyed before weaving, and *batik* (q.v.). Traditional dyes were indigo (q.v.), *soga* (a brown dye from plant roots), and the red *mengkudu*. The complexity of the production process made cloth a rare commodity and until C.14 most people continued to wear clothes of bark and plaited vegetable fiber. Large quantities of Indian cotton cloth and smaller amounts of Chinese silk (q.v.) began to arrive in C.14, partly to pay for spices purchased in the archipelago, and the *sarung* became the common item of clothing, though local weaving continued in many areas and the finest of cloth, such as the *songket* of Islamic Sumatra with its gold and silver thread, continued to be made in the archipelago.

In C.20, Japanese cloth strongly penetrated the Indonesian market, leading the colonial government to apply quotas in the 1930s. This encouraged an expansion of domestic production dominated by indigenous entrepreneurs such as A.M. Dasaad (q.v.). Within a few years, however, the industry was largely in the hands of Chinese businessmen. Automated weaving began in the 1960s and 1970s, and Japanese industrial cloth production has expanded since 1965. [0119, 0129, 0132, 0307, 0311, 0317]

CLOVES (*cengkeh*), the dried immature flower-buds of *Syzygium aromaticum* (Myrtaceae), used widely in food, medicine, and perfume. Originally found only on Ternate, Tidore (qq.v.), and adjacent islets, cloves were traded to China from ca 500 B.C., to India from ca 200 B.C. and perhaps to Africa. Until C.16, Javanese merchants were prominent in the trade, but they were partly displaced by the Portuguese (q.v.), who expanded production on Ambon (q.v.) and surrounding islands. On gaining hegemony in Maluku, the Dutch restricted production outside Ambon and destroyed trees in order to keep the price high (see HONGI RAIDS). In 1789, however, a tree was smuggled to Mauritius in French territory and from there spread to Penang and Zanzibar, breaking the Dutch monopoly.

Cloves form an important ingredient in Indonesian *kretek* cigarettes (see TOBACCO), and were imported from Zanzibar for this purpose until 1987, when domestic production rose dramatically. In 1968, a lucrative monopoly of clove imports was granted to P.T. Mercu Buana (owned by President Suharto's half-brother Probosutejo) and P.T. Mega, owned by the president's banker, Liem Sioe Liong (q.v., see also CENDANA GROUP). Culinary clove production for export is now well established on Java and other islands and annual production is ca 50,000 tonnes. [0245, 0246, 0751]

COAL. With the development of steamships, the coal deposits of the archipelago became important as a source of fuel. The first commercial field was opened in 1846 near Martapura (South Kalimantan) and was exploited by private enterprise as were later fields near Kutai (q.v.) and in Sumatra. The Ombilin mine at Sawahlunto in West Sumatra began production in 1892 as a state enterprise (q.v.), reaching a peak production in 1930 of 1,870,823 tonnes. Although Indonesia is currently a net importer of coal, with production in 1988 only 4.5 million tonnes, proven reserves of 1,730 million tonnes exist. Since 1988 open cut production in East Kalimantan has been expanded for export and is due to reach full production in 1993/94, as availability of oil (q.v.) for export diminishes. [0321]

COCA (*Erythroxylum coca* Erythroxylaceae), bush from the Andes region of South America, widely distributed throughout the tropics by the Royal Botanical Gardens, Kew. The leaves can be chewed as a narcotic and significant amounts were exported from Javanese plantations after 1879 and in early C.20 until antinarcotics campaigns led to restrictions on production and use in 1927.

COCOA. See CACAO.

COCONUT (*Cocos nucifera* Arecaceae), widespread and versatile palm tree which supplies food, clothing, and building materials in tropical coastal regions. There is much debate about its origins, but most evidence suggests that it originated and was domesticated in the western Pacific. It is closely related to human settlement and most commonly spreads by planting. Coconuts became a commercial crop only in mid C.19 with a rise in demand for copra for soap-making. Extensive plantations were established in this period, but smallholders accounted for 95% of production especially in Minahasa (q.v.). With 112 million trees in 1918, Indonesia was the world's largest prewar producer. Production declined in the 1970s and 1980s due to disease and the need to remove old trees for replanting. For some producers, sugar production from coconut flowers is now more lucrative than copra. See also AREN. [0245, 0246, 0390, 0392]

COEN, Jan Pieterszoon (1587–1629), founder of Dutch power in the Indies. As fourth governor-general from 1619 (though he was appointed in 1617), he established a trading post at Sunda Kelapa (q.v.) in 1610 and a fort there in 1618 which later became Batavia (q.v.), which he turned into the headquarters of the Dutch East Indies Company (q.v.) operations in the east. In 1621, he brutally conquered the Banda (q.v.) islands. His term of office ended in 1623, but he was persuaded by the Heeren XVII to resume it in 1627 and defended Batavia against two unsuccessful attacks by Mataram (q.v.). [0375]

COFFEE (*Coffea* spp. Rubiaceae). Native to the Middle East, coffee plants were brought to Indonesia by the Dutch East Indies Company (q.v.), or VOC, in 1696. The Company encouraged planting by the bupatis in Priangan (q.v.) in early C.18 and it was soon taken up as a cash crop by the local population. The first Java coffee was sold in Amsterdam in 1712 and in 1725 production exceeded that of the previous market leader, Yemen; after 1726, the VOC controlled 50–75% of the world's coffee trade. Cultivation was initially free, but in 1725 came under a VOC monopoly and became one of the major crops of the West Java Preangerstelsel. Production of *C. arabica* in central and eastern Java expanded greatly, especially under Daendels (q.v.), so that Java coffee dominated world markets by 1811. Coffee then became one of the principal crops of the Cultivation System (q.v.) and a government monopoly of production on Java was maintained until 1915. Estate production of coffee began in East Java in 1870. In 1878, the coffee leaf disease *Hemileia vastatrix* devastated plantations on Java, leading to a shift to *C. robusta* in late C.19 and an expansion of cultivation in southern Sumatra, Bali, Timor, and Sulawesi, but coffee's share of the total value of Indies exports never recovered, standing at 2.27% in 1938 and declining further after World War II. Production in 1950 was 12% of that before the war, but expansion of cultivation, especially by transmigrants in Lampung (q.v.), has made Indonesia the world's third largest producer, with 7% of global production and export. [0245, 0246, 0258, 0454, 0938]

COKROAMINOTO, Haji Umar Said. See TJOKROAMINOTO, Haji Umar Said.

COLA (*Cola* spp. Sterculiaceae), fruits of which are the basis of cola drinks. Originally from West Africa, cola trees were first reported from Java in 1852 and spread towards the end of C.19 as a subsidiary crop on cacao (q.v.) plantations in Central Java. [0245, 0246, 0938]

COLIJN, Hendrikus (1869–1944), Dutch prime minister. Colijn joined the colonial army (KNIL, q.v.) as a young man and took part both in the conquest of Lombok (q.v.) and, as adjutant to van Heutsz (q.v.) in the Aceh (q.v.) War from 1895 to 1904. On his return to the Netherlands he entered politics and business, becoming director of the Bataafsche Petroleum Maatschappij (see OIL) and, in 1923, minister of finance. He was prime minister 1925–26 and from 1933 until 1939. During the Depression he was a major spokesman for free trade. He died in German internment during World War II. [0578]

COLONIES, Netherlands Ministry of. With the dissolution of the Dutch East Indies Company (q.v.), the Netherlands government established its formal authority over the Indonesian possessions through a colonial department which went through various names until finally becoming the Ministry of Colonies (Ministerie van Koloniën) in 1848. The ministry's task was preparing general policy lines and handling relations between the colony and the Netherlands, rather than direct administration, and no minister of colonies visited the Indies until 1941. In C.20, however, ministers were generally technical specialists with Indies experience; nine of the 25 held the post of governor-general before or after. In February 1945, the ministry's title was changed to Overseas Territories (Overzeese Gebiedsdelen). For successive names of the ministry and a list of ministers, see the Appendix. See also NETHERLANDS, Constitutional relationship with Indonesia.

COMMISSIONER-GENERAL. Under the Dutch East Indies Company (q.v.), commissioners (*commissaris-*

sen-generaal) were occasionally appointed as representatives of the Netherlands government in the East. From 1814 to 1819, three commissioners-general, C.T. Elout, G.A.G.P. van der Capellan, and A.A. Buyskes governed the Indies with the tasks of resuming control of the colony from Britain (q.v.) and establishing a new colonial administration, a complex constitutional and technical task after the fall of the VOC and the interregna under French and British rule. Van der Capellan was also governor-general, that is executive head of the government, and continued in this post as sole commissioner-general until 1826. His successors du Bus de Gisignies and van den Bosch also held the post briefly alongside the governor-generalship to 1834. In 1946–48, Willem Schermerhorn, Max van Poll, and Feike de Boer were commissioners-general for the purpose of negotiating a settlement with the Indonesian Republic. [0614]

COMMUNICATIONS. See POSTAL SERVICE; RAILWAYS; ROADS; SHIPPING; TELEGRAPHS.

COMMUNISM. See MARXISM; PARTAI KOMUNIS INDONESIA.

CONFRONTATION (Konfrontasi). Indonesia's opposition to the creation of Malaysia (q.v.) as a federation of Malaya, Singapore, and British colonies in northern Borneo was first expressed as 'confrontation' by Subandrio (q.v.) in January 1963, but a full campaign against the new federation did not begin until 23 September, when Sukarno (q.v.) announced that Indonesia would *ganyang* (lit. 'gobble raw', but generally translated as 'crush') Malaysia. Aside from their objections to Malaysia itself, Indonesian political forces had their own reasons for Confrontation: the army wished to retain its privileged position and access to funds after the recovery of Irian (q.v.); the PKI (q.v.) wished to engage key army units away from the centers of power of Java and to keep at arm's length the United States and the IMF, which had offered extensive aid in exchange for budget cuts, price increases, and other measures; and Sukarno wished to maintain the momentum of popular mobilization he had begun during the Irian campaign. To increase pressure on Malaysia, the army's KOTI (q.v.) command was reorganized and border incursions began into Sarawak, where Indonesian troops were largely unsuccessful against British Commonwealth forces. In August and September 1964 small scale landings took place on the Malay peninsula. Army enthusiasm for the conflict, however, soon diminished, partly because they did not want to deploy capable forces away from the centers of power on Java and partly because Confrontation was one of the grounds for leftwing arguments in favor of a worker-peasant 'Fifth Force' (q.v.). Confrontation also won Indonesia little sympathy in the rest of the world, which saw it as unacceptable bullying of a smaller neighbor. From mid 1965, even before the rise to power of Suharto (q.v.), the intelligence officers Benny Murdani and Ali Murtopo were maintaining contacts with Malaysia, and in May 1966, shortly after the Supersemar (q.v.) order gave Suharto executive power, negotiations with Kuala Lumpur began. Relations were normalized on 11 August 1966. [0742, 0746]

CONFUCIANISM (*Konghucu*), the general term given to traditional Chinese religion in the archipelago, though what is practised is an eclectic blend of Confucianism with Buddhism and Taoism rather than Confucianism proper, despite a Confucian revival in late C.19. Like other recognized religions, Confucianism in Indonesia has been under pressure to conform to official notions of what constitutes a religion, and has tended increasingly to treat Tien (Heaven) as a deity and Confucius as a prophet and to identify Confucian classics as holy scripture. [1115, 1147]

CONRAD, Joseph (1857–1924), visited the archipelago as a sailor between 1883 and 1888, and set several of his novels there, especially *Almayer's Folly* (1895), *An Outcast of the Islands* (1896) and *Lord Jim* (1899–1900). Much of his writing describes the venality of European activity in the region. [0158, 0168, 0529]

CONSERVATION, Nature. The director of the Bogor Botanical Gardens, Melchior Treub suggested creation of a nature reserve on Mt Gede, near Bogor in 1889. Ordinances to protect the bird-of-paradise were first issued in 1905 and were revised in 1909 to include rhinoceros, elephant, and orangutan (qq.v.). The first nature reserves (*natuurmonumenten*) were gazetted in 1916 at the urging of the Nederlandsch-Indische Vereeniging tot Natuurbescherming (Netherlands Indies Society for Nature Preservation), founded in 1912 by S.H. Koorders and K.W. Dammerman. By 1942 natural monuments and game reserves covered 130,000 ha (55 reserves) on Java, ca 500,000 ha on Sumatra, and over a million ha on Borneo. Andries Hoogerwerf was appointed Nature Protection Officer in 1935. In 1951 Kusnadi was appointed head of the Nature Protection Division of the Agriculture Department. In the mid1970s, Indonesia cooperated with the World Wildlife Fund in developing a national conservation strategy which resulted in the declaration of the country's first five national parks in 1980 and a further 11 in 1982. National parks and reserves now cover ca 6% of the country. See also DEPOK; ENVIRONMENTAL PROTECTION; KOMODO; UJUNG KULON. [0010, 0792, 0943]

CONSTITUENT ASSEMBLY (Konstituante), elected in December 1955 to draft a constitution (q.v.) to replace

Indonesia's provisional 1950 Constitution. The composition of the Assembly largely followed that of the 1955 parliament, though there were more independent members. The Assembly convened in November 1956, but was unable to reach agreement on the question of whether Islam or Pancasila (qq.v.) should be the foundation of the state. This deadlock was amongst the factors leading Sukarno (q.v.) to dissolve the Assembly and restore the 1945 Constitution by decree on 5 July 1959. [0634]

CONSTITUTIONS. Until the establishment of crown rule in 1815, the charter of the Dutch East Indies Company (q.v.) and the various treaty arrangements with individual states in the archipelago were all that passed for a constitution. In 1815, the Dutch government promulgated a *Regeeringsreglement* (RR, Government Regulating Act), which functioned as the constitutional basis for the state of the Netherlands Indies. Reissued in various forms up to 1854, the RR of that year, though modified in 1925 and renamed the *Wet op de Staatsinrichting van Nederlandsch-Indië,* remained in force until the end of Dutch rule. (See also GOVERNOR-GENERAL, Office of the; NETHERLANDS, Constitutional relationship with Indonesia; SUCCESSION.)

The first constitution (*Undang-Undang Dasar,* UUD) of the Republic of Indonesia was adopted on 18 August 1945 and was based on a draft prepared by the BPUPKI (q.v.), established by the Japanese in March 1945. The preamble (*pembukaan*) established the Pancasila (q.v.) as Indonesia's national philosophy but omitted the Jakarta Charter (q.v.). The constitution put sovereignty in the hands of the people, to be exercised by the Majelis Permusyawaratan Rakyat (q.v., People's Deliberative Assembly), and provides for four independent branches of government, the President, the Dewan Perwakilan Rakyat (qq.v.), Audit Board (Badan Pemeriksa Keuangan, BPK), and the Supreme Court (Mahkamah Agung). These prescriptions were largely ignored during the Indonesian Revolution (1945–49), when the country was ruled for the most part by prime ministers responsible to the Komite Nasional Indonesia Pusat (q.v.).

A second constitution, federal in structure, was drafted at the Round Table Conference (q.v.) and came into force with the creation of the Republik Indonesia Serikat (q.v.) on 27 December 1949. This constitution provided for a prime ministerial system and gave extensive constitutional protection to the federal states (see FEDERALISM) but with the dissolution of the states in 1950 was replaced on 14 August by a provisional third constitution, unitary in structure but retaining the prime ministerial system. After elections in 1955, a Constituent Assembly (q.v.) attempted unsuccessfully to agree on a new constitution. On 5 July 1959, Sukarno (q.v.) restored the 1945 Constitution by presidential decree. The 1945 Constitution authorizes changes to itself by a two-thirds majority of the MPR (q.v.), but in 1983 the sitting MPR renounced this right and prescribed that any change must be referred to the people by referendum and must be approved by at least 90% of the voters in a turnout of at least 90%. This resolution, however, is probably not constitutionally binding on future MPRs. [0628, 0656]

CONTINENTAL DRIFT. The present general topography of Indonesia is largely a result of the breaking up of the former great southern continent Gondwana and the separate northward movement of several of its parts into the southern flank of the old Laurasian landmass. One section of Gondwana, bearing what is now Nusatenggara, parts of Maluku, western Sulawesi, Java, Kalimantan, Sumatra, the Malay peninsula, Thailand and Burma, seems to have begun to move north around

200 million years ago. Initially, this landmass formed an east-west belt bulging northwards over the Tropic of Capricorn, but the northward movement of the Indian plate during the Cretaceous period (after 136 million years ago) pushed its western end northwards, creating the present oblique northwest-southeast alignment of Sumatra and Malaya. Australia, New Guinea, and eastern Sulawesi broke from Gondwana about 90 million years ago, pushed northwards at about 10 cm per year and collided violently with the rest of what is now Southeast Asia about 19–13 million years ago. The mountains of New Guinea were thrust up, the Nusatenggara island chain was twisted north to create much of Maluku, and eastern Sulawesi and the island of Sula were thrust into western Sulawesi, opening the gulf of Bone and twisting the northern arm around to form the gulf of Tomini. See also PREHISTORY; SUNDA SHELF; WALLACE'S LINE. [0964, 0972, 0974]

CONTROLEUR. Lower level Dutch administrative official, abolished on Java in 1922. See also BINNENLANDSCH BESTUUR.

COOLIE ORDINANCE (*Koelieordonnantie*). Until 1880, contract laborers brought from South China and later from Java to work in the plantations of East Sumatra (q.v.) could be held to their contracts only by indirect social controls (see GAMBLING; OPIUM) and by civil legal process, which was often ineffective. From 1880, the Coolie Ordinance gave government sanction to the contracts, allowing imprisonment of laborers who broke their contracts, under the so-called *poenale sanctie* (penal sanction). Employers, in turn, were required to provide defined levels of wages, accommodation, health care, general treatment and repatriation, but conditions were very bad. *De millioenen uit Deli* (1902), a report by J. van den Brand, increased pressure for change under the Ethical Policy (q.v.), leading to the formation of a Labor (q.v.) Inspectorate in 1907 and legislation from 1911 to phase out the penal sanction. The coolie ordinance was strongly criticized in the United States (q.v.) as a form of disguised slavery enabling Sumatra tobacco to compete unfairly with that of America and the threat of import bans hastened the sanction's disappearance. By this time, however, labor was abundant and employers had little need to use the sanction. During the Depression, many laborers hired under contract were released and reemployed at lesser rates. The sanction was largely abolished in 1936. See also LABOR. [0237, 0263, 0536]

COOPERATIVES. Form of social and economic organization based ideologically on notions of traditional village collectivism (see DESA) and promoted especially by Hatta (q.v.) as an alternative to both colonialism and indigenous capitalism. Hatta favored a restructuring of the economy by the creation of production, consumption, and credit cooperatives, but most cooperatives have been racked by inefficiency and corruption and the history has generally been depressing. [0215]

COPAL, resin of the tree *Agathis alba* (Coniferae), occurring widely in Sulawesi and Maluku and sporadically elsewhere. Used for the commercial manufacture of Manila copal for varnish, it is often mixed and sometimes confused with damar (q.v.). [0025, 0938]

COPPER, found in West Sumatra, West Java, and Timor, was mined since early times for the production of bronze, often with a high lead content (see also TIN). Production was never extensive and declined with the large scale import of Chinese copper cash from C.15 and Dutch copper doit in C.18. A huge mine in the Carstensz Mountains of Irian (q.v.) was opened by Freeport

Minerals Inc. in April 1967. The enormous capital investment involved was seen as a major sign of Western business confidence in the New Order (q.v.). See also CURRENCY. [0321, 0399]

COPRA. See COCONUT.

COPYRIGHT. Indonesia has not signed the Berne Convention on copyright protection and until recently gave formal protection only to material published or recorded first in Indonesia. This resulted in a thriving trade in so-called 'pirate tapes', audiocassette recordings of classical and modern music. An estimated 70-to-85 million such tapes were produced annually, of which 35 million were exported to the Middle East. In September 1987, however, following negotiations with European recording companies, Indonesia passed a law protecting most European material; this was followed in August 1988 by a similar law protecting U.S. material, and in August 1989 by a law protecting computer software copyright. See also MUSIC.

CORN. See MAIZE.

'CORNELL REPORT', an analysis of the origins and details of the GESTAPU (q.v.) coup of 30 September 1965 prepared soon after the event by Benedict Anderson and Ruth McVey at Cornell University. The report cast doubt on the then generally accepted view that the coup was the work of the PKI, arguing that it was most probably the work of junior army officers and was used as an excuse to do away with the PKI. The report was circulated confidentially to a small number of scholars but was soon leaked to the wider world, where its then-unorthodox view and its apparent secretiveness earned it some notoriety. [0629]

CORNELL UNIVERSITY, especially its Modern Indonesia Project, founded 1955, is a major U.S. center for study of Indonesia, emphasizing the study of culture as a key to understanding history and politics. It has often taken an activist, generally liberal view of political events and its journal *Indonesia* is the premier journal of Indonesian studies. See also 'CORNELL REPORT'.

CORRUPTION is a phenomenon most easily recognizable in bureaucratic structures, where employees are expected to carry out their duties efficiently and dispassionately for a fixed, regular salary paid by the employer. It makes little sense to talk of corruption in Indonesia before the arrival of the bureaucratically-organized European trading companies, since there were no general, formal standards laying down how much and under what circumstances officials might obtain money or other benefits from the positions.

Under the Portuguese and the Dutch East Indies Company (q.v.) or VOC, 'corruption' consisted largely of infringing official monopolies of trade, though the fact that salaries of VOC officials were ludicrously low gave employees little alternative but to engage in illicit activities of one sort or other. Senior VOC officials deplored corruption for its effects both on Company profits and for the fact that money-making activities distracted lower officials from their administrative tasks; the later Governor-General G.W. van Imhoff went as far as suggesting in 1746 that the VOC trading monopoly be abolished in order to eliminate corruption. This was not done, and it is widely accepted that corruption made a major contribution to the VOC's insolvency and collapse at the end of the century.

Only under Daendels (q.v.) and his successors was the notion of bureaucratic propriety taken seriously and attempts made to control the outside activities of officials. Considerable attention was given to the question of whether the demands of the bupatis (q.v.) on their subjects could and should be limited. The polemic novel *Max Havelaar* argued that the bupatis' exactions were corrupt and unjust, and this view gradually became orthodox, though the colonial government remained extremely reluctant to discipline bupatis on these grounds except in the most extreme cases.

Corruption increased dramatically during the Japanese occupation (1942–45), partly because salary payments to officials became increasingly inadequate as the occupation currency depreciated in value, partly because Japanese attempts to regulate the economy (requiring permits, for instance, for the transport of food from one kabupaten to another) increased the number of opportunities for officials to demand illicit payment. During the Indonesian Revolution (1945–49), it became difficult once more to speak unambiguously of corruption: bureaucratic salaries were paid with such irregularity and at such a depreciated rate that many officials, and especially sections of the armed forces, were forced to levy the population for their own survival. Though there were a number of cases in which officials and military personnel enriched themselves unduly, the significance of 'corruption' in this period was the habits and contacts it formed, rather than its direct effect on public welfare.

During the 1950s and 1960s, corruption became part of an administrative vicious circle, in which lack of revenue led to inadequate salaries for officials, in turn diminishing government performance and reducing both the contribution of the state to general economic welfare and the state's capacity to collect revenue. These problems remained acute under the New Order. In 1970, a presidential inquiry, known as the Commission of Four, investigated corruption in BULOG, Pertamina, the Department of Forestry, and the state tin company, P.N. Timah. Such investigations typically caught a number of small offenders while leaving the most corrupt unscathed. The oil boom of the 1970s led to even more extravagant instances of corruption in upper levels of the government (see BIMBO; PERTAMINA).

In the 1980s a trend towards administrative deregulation has diminished some of the opportunities formerly available for corruption. In 1985, for instance, the government contracted the Swiss firm Société Générale de Surveillance to undertake customs inspections on its behalf, thus bypassing the notoriously corrupt state customs service. Customs officials were suspended on full pay, but with dramatically diminished income (see also SHIPPING). [0583, 0789, 0800, 1056]

COTTON (*Gossypium* spp. Malvaceae). Introduced to Indonesia around 300 B.C. from India, cotton was extensively grown in Java, Bali, and Nusatenggara for the local cloth (q.v.) industry, though never in sufficient quantity or quality to supplant imported cloth (see DUTCH EAST INDIES COMPANY; INDIA, Historical links with). In late C.18, production contracted under pressure from Indian imports. Palembang and Semarang (qq.v.) were the main areas of production. From 1858 the colonial government attempted to extend production, especially for the Dutch cotton mills in Twente, but largely without success. [0245, 0246]

COUNCIL OF THE INDIES. See RAAD VAN INDIË.

COUPERUS, Louis (1863–1932), Dutch author, raised on Java. His novel *De stille kracht* (*The silent force,* 1900) was a psychological exploration of Dutch society in the Indies, stressing the exoticism of the Indies environment and the impossibility of Dutch assimilation to it. See also DUTCH IN INDONESIA. [0147, 0173]

COWRY SHELLS. With the Maldives and East Africa, eastern Indonesia was a major source of cowries

(*Cypraea* spp, especially *C. moneta* and *C. annulus*) used as currency in central Asia before 300 B.C. Because of their local abundance, they had no use as currency (q.v.) in the region. Export of cowries continued until C.18. [0941, 0942, 0946]

CREDIT. See ARISAN; BANKING.

CUKONG, a Chinese businessman who receives protection and privilege from a powerful, often military, patron in exchange for business assistance and/or a share of the profits. The largest cukong are Liem Sioe Liong (q.v.) and William Suryajaya (Tjia Kian Liong, b. 1922). Liem's commercial activities began in supplying sections of the army in Central Java in the revolution, during which time he first became associated with Suharto (q.v.). His capital base derives especially from a monopoly over clove (q.v.) imports granted in 1968 and later from automobile distributorships, but he is now heavily represented in manufacture (especially cement and flour) and banking (q.v.), with extensive offshore interests (see also CENDANA GROUP). Suryajaya's P.T. Astra has major interests in automobile distributorships, property, road construction, banking, agribusiness, and trade.

Although Chinese businessmen once made their way primarily on the basis of their business acumen, it is now the case that significant economic success is not possible without some degree of patronage from within the state. All or most successful Chinese businessmen are thus cukong to some degree and this appearance of favor has led to much resentment. Cukong were a major target of hostility in the so-called Malari (q.v.) riots of 1974. The riots led the government to apply some formal restrictions to cukong activities, but these have seldom been enforced. See also ALI-BABA FIRMS; CHINESE IN INDONESIA. [0280, 0287, 0920]

CULTIVATION SYSTEM (*Cultuurstelsel,* once commonly but inaccurately translated as Culture System). In 1830 the state finances of the Netherlands (which included those of the Netherlands Indies) were in crisis following the Belgian secession and the Java War (q.v.). To save the budget, Governor-General Johannes van den Bosch (1780–1844) introduced a system of agricultural deliveries which operated in theory as follows: the villages of Java were invited to use one-fifth of their lands and approximately 66 days or one-fifth of a year's work to grow crops designated by the government—principally sugar cane and indigo, but also coffee, tobacco, and tea (qq.v.)—in exchange for exemption from land tax, then levied at 40% of the market value of the rice crop. Villages taking part in the Cultivation System were also to be freed from other tax-like obligations, such as corvée labor service (*herendiensten,* q.v.), were to be paid the difference in value between the land rent and the value of produce they had delivered, and were indemnified against crop failures beyond their control. By 1836 the direct connection between land rent and product delivery was broken; land rent was levied in full and suppliers received payment in full for produce delivered. The system brought unprecedented amounts of money into Javanese villages, reflected in the fact that steadily increasing land taxes took unprecedented amounts of money back out of them. In 1847 it was estimated that 60-to-70% of crop payments returned to the colonial government as tax.

For the Dutch, the system thus was a great success. Valuable tropical crops were produced in abundance and not only were the costs of governing the colony readily paid but, under the unified budget system, a substantial budget surplus (*batig slot,* q.v.) was transferred to the Netherlands each year, paying off the country's international debt and financing the national railway system. In the 1850s these transfers comprised

31% of the Dutch national income (see INDIË VERLOREN, RAMPSPOED GEBOREN). Private investors in Java, including the later minister of colonies I.D. Fransen van de Putte, made huge profits, especially from the sugar factories which processed government cane. The Dutch royal family profited handsomely through the Nederlandsche Handel Maatschappij (q.v.).

The effect of the system on the Javanese is less clear. Undisputed are the following: villages close to factories were often required to plant far more than one-fifth of their land with the designated crops; peasants were never indemnified against crop losses; *bupati* (q.v.) and other indigenous officials continued to demand extensive labor services; and full payment for the value of the crops was seldom received by the peasants entitled to it. The system was blamed for widespread epidemics and famines on the island in the 1840s. There is a good deal of evidence, however, that the sheer volume of money flowing through the villages stimulated social change and the rise of indigenous rural entrepreneurs. The system also certainly strengthened the position of the *priyayi* (q.v.) on Java, since they received until 1868 a percentage of production under the system and their quasi-royal status was enhanced as a matter of Dutch policy. Some scholars have argued that the lucrative income to be had from acting as agents of the state discouraged the priyayi from moving into land ownership and agricultural production themselves and therefore averted the formation of a powerful class of rural landowners (see CLASS ANALYSIS).

The system began to be dismantled in ca 1850, initially because of a hostility in the Netherlands, under the new more democratic constitution of 1848, to the favored position of the sugar contractors and the NHM, and later because of growing interest in larger scale private interest in the Indies and because of political indignation over the oppressive practices linked with the cultivation system, especially as described in the novel *Max Havelaar* (q.v.). The Agrarian Law of 1870 (q.v.), which formally abolished forced cultivation, is generally regarded as the end of the Cultivation System, though some forced cultivation continued to 1890 and vestiges of the System lingered on into C.20 in the form of the coffee monopoly, which was not abolished until 1915. [0331, 0507, 0509, 0510, 0525]

CULTURE, Debate on the role of. A long running debate (*Polemik Kebudayaan,* polemic on culture) has taken place in Indonesia on the nature of modern Indonesian culture and its relation to society. It was instituted in 1935 by S. Takdir Alisyahbana (q.v.) with the argument, echoing the beliefs of Tjipto Mangunkusumo (q.v.), that modern Indonesian culture should incorporate in some essential way the best of Western culture and should accept the need to move beyond traditional culture in the process of becoming part of a universalist world culture. This view was challenged by Ki Hajar Dewantoro (Suwardi Suryaningrat, q.v.) and Sanusi Pané and many others, who argued that Western culture was characteristically materialist, intellectual, and individualist and thus essentially both undesirable and hostile to indigenous Indonesian culture (see also POLITICAL CULTURE). The latter position was formally ratified in 1959 with the promulgation of Sukarno's Manipol-USDEK (q.v.) doctrine of which the final principle, *Kepribadian Nasional* or National Identity, asserted the cultural autonomy of Indonesia. It proved nonetheless difficult to specify the nature of a modern Indonesian culture which contained no Western influences. Artists of the 'internationalist' Seni Rupa school of Bandung, for instance argued that painters of the ostensibly 'nationalist' Yogya school were influence by impressionism and other Western schools.

In the 1950s, the terms of the debate shifted somewhat. The universalists, led by H.B. Jassin (q.v.) and allegedly exemplified by the (then deceased) poet Chairil Anwar (q.v.) were attacked not by traditionalists but by the left, especially members of LEKRA (q.v.), who, in rejecting universalist culture, argued that art should reflect local social conditions and should serve to promote social consciousness. Art should be 'for the People' and should resist portraying individualist or bourgeois values. See also MANIFESTO KEBUDAYAAN. [0116, 0150, 0154]

CULTURE SYSTEM. See CULTIVATION SYSTEM.

CURRENCY. The use of gold and silver coinage in West Sumatra and Central and East Java dates from at least C.8, the earliest coins being gold *masa* of 2.42g stamped with a simple sesame seed design and silver coins of a similar weight stamped with a stylized sandalwood flower. The source of the metal is not certain, but early accounts speak of gold and silver production on both islands and it is reasonable to assume that some of this went into coinage (see GOLD; METALWORKING). These relatively high value coins were probably not in day-to-day circulation but were used for storing wealth and for ritual purposes. Although there is some evidence of an iron bar currency called *iket wsi* in use in late C.8, the general use of coins in daily life did not apparently begin until C.11, with the appearance of a number of smaller denominations (*kupang* = 1/4 *masa*) in port areas, presumably in response to a greater marketization of the economy. By C.13, gold coins were used extensively for the payment of salaries, debts, and fines. In Butung (q.v.) in southeast Sulawesi, small squares of cloth were reportedly used as currency.

Large quantities of low denomination Chinese copper and copper-lead cash, or *picis,* began to appear on Java in late C.12, prompting local imitations in tin, copper, and silver and displacing the older currency for most purposes by 1300. Picis became the standard currency of Majapahit (q.v.) and their use spread to Sulawesi, Kalimantan, and Sumatra, though from C.14 several Islamic states on Sumatra minted their own gold and tin coins. Picis were carried about in strings of fixed numbers from 200 to 100,000. Leaden and tin-lead picis, worth much less than copper, were fragile and often broke or disintegrated after a few years' use; copper coins, by contrast, were often taken from circulation for ceremonial purposes. So great was the flow of copper coins to Indonesia that the Chinese government banned their export for many years. The widely available picis led to a greater monetarization of the economy than before, allowing traders, often Chinese, to deal directly, for instance, with the hill people who provided pepper to Banten (q.v.) and encouraging the use of credit facilities. Blussé argues that the perishable nature of the picis also encouraged people to spend them quickly, thus promoting the circulation of money.

From ca 1580 silver coinage in the form of Spanish reals, minted from Peruvian and Mexican silver, became increasingly abundant, especially as extensive imports of lead by the Dutch and other Europeans in C.17 drove down the value of the picis. The VOC also produced silver rijksdaalders and, from 1733, copper *doit,* though picis remained in circulation in many places into C.18. In C.19, locally minted tin currency was the dominant currency in much of Sumatra.

From 1782 the VOC in Maluku issued promissory notes in denominations of 25 to 1,000 rijksdaalders; though bearing interest at 6%, these also acted in some respects as paper currency and continued in circulation into early C.19, as did bonds issued in 1810 by the Dutch authorities in East Java on security of 1 million rijksdaalders due in silver over ten years from a Chinese *pacht* (q.v.) holder in Probolinggo. This confused currency situation was somewhat regularized by the issue in 1815 of Netherlands Indies guilder (*gulden*) currency notes with handwritten serial number and signature. In 1851, the Java Bank took on the production of bank notes (backed by gold reserves), though the colonial government continued to issue low-value currency notes. Later in the century, plantations companies, especially in East Sumatra (q.v.) often issued their own currency notes (*muntbiljetten*) for the payment of workers.

During the Japanese occupation, the military authorities initially provided currency notes, but in March 1943 bank notes were issued by the Nanpo Kaihatsu Kinko (Southern Regions Development Bank). This currency rapidly depreciated in value, but it was retained in circulation by both the Allies and the Indonesian Republic after the Japanese surrender. Postwar Netherlands Indies currency notes were not issued on Java until March 1946 and Republican *rupiah* (ORI, *Oeang*, i.e., *Uang Republik Indonesia*) was first issued only in November. Separate local emergency Republican currencies were later issued in several parts of Sumatra and Java. In 1950 a new federal rupiah was issued and previous Dutch and Republican currencies were exchanged for it at various rates. Dutch colonial authorities in West New Guinea (Irian, q.v.) issued separate New Guinea notes from 1950, while various rebel governments such as the PRRI (q.v.) overprinted Republican currency for internal circulation.

In January 1950, US$1.00 purchased Rp 3.80. A devaluation on 13 March 1950 took this to Rp 7.60; a system of multiple exchange rates complicated the picture, but most observers argue that the rupiah was overvalued in this period, thus encouraging imports and discouraging exports. After a period of sustained inflation in the late 1950s, the currency was drastically reformed on 28 August 1959, with the freezing (i.e. demonetization) of notes of Rp 25,000 and above and the reduction of other currency to one-tenth of its nominal value (i.e. Rp 1,000 became Rp 100). Further depreciation of the currency under Guided Democracy (q.v.) led to a similar measure on 13 December 1965, Rp 1,000 becoming Rp 1. In the early 1970s, the exchange rate stabilized at US$1.00 = Rp 415, but this jumped to Rp 625 in late 1978, to Rp 970 in 1982, and to Rp 1,700 in the late 1980s. See also BANKING; COWRY SHELLS; SYAFRUDDIN PRAWIRANEGARA. [0039, 0295, 0299, 0297, 0304, 0366, 0427, 0440]

D

DAENDELS, Herman Willem (1762–1818), Dutch general, lawyer, and administrator. After gaining military experience in the forces of the Dutch 'Patriotten' who established the Batavian Republic (q.v.) in the Netherlands in late C.18, Daendels was sent to Indonesia in 1807 by the king Louis Napoleon of the Netherlands as governor-general (1808–11) with the task of organizing the defence of Java against the British. In addition to constructing defensive works on the north Java coast, including the first road along the entire length of the island (see ROADS), he introduced many internal reforms, especially to combat corruption (q.v.) amongst European officials and to reform the army. He also reduced the power of the bupatis (q.v.) on Java, placing them under nine regional prefects or *landrost*. He was recalled in 1811 when the Netherlands was incorporated into the French Empire and died as governor of Dutch possessions on the Gold Coast (now Ghana). [0375]

DAMAR. Resin, mostly from dipterocarps (q.v.), used locally for torches and the caulking of boats and in

Europe for varnish. It was often mixed, and sometimes confused, with copal (q.v.). [0938]

DAMAR WULAN STORIES, Javanese legend of Majapahit (q.v.). Damar Wulan, a nephew of the prime minister of Majapahit, is imprisoned by the prime minister for secretly marrying his daughter. He is released, however, on the orders of the Maiden Queen, Prabu Kenya, so that he can defeat the kingdom's enemy Menak Jingga, king of Balambangan (q.v.). With the help of a pair of smitten princesses, he overcomes Menak Jingga's invulnerability, kills him, and returns to Majapahit to marry the Queen, retaining also the prime minister's daughter, but not the smitten princesses. The story was performed traditionally using the *wayang (q.v.) klitik* and *wayang gedog* but is now a part of the *ketoprak* repertoire. [0116]

DANGDUT, style of modern popular music employing electric guitars, drums, and voices with a sinuous melody line and a heavy irregular beat. Dangdut first emerged in about 1972 as a blend of Western, Middle Eastern and *kroncong* (q.v.) elements. Its chief exponent is Rhoma (Oma) Irama (b. 1947), who has employed it for both political comment and the promotion of Islam. See also GAMELAN; MUSIC. [0112]

DANI, ethnic group in Irian (q.v.), inhabiting the Baliem valley of the interior highlands, 'discovered' only in the 1930s. They construct terraced, irrigated fields.

DANISH EAST INDIA COMPANY. See SCANDINAVIA, Historical links with.

DARTS, propelled from blowpipes and often smeared with poisons such as upas (q.v.) were the classic weapon of hunting in Indonesian jungles, especially Kalimantan, where room to move was limited and projectiles were not often deflected by winds. See also WEAPONS.

DARUL ISLAM (DI, House of Islam), general name for the Muslim revolutionary movement launched in West Java in 1948 by S.M. Kartosuwiryo (q.v.) with the twin aims of establishing an Islamic state and vigorously prosecuting the war of independence against the Dutch. The movement arose immediately after the Indonesian Republic had agreed, under the January 1948 Renville Agreement (q.v.), to withdraw its armed forces from West Java. In March 1948, it decided to establish its own administration in West Java, but stopped short of a total break with the Republic. The Darul Islam formally repudiated the Republic on 7 August 1949, after the final ceasefire between Dutch and Republican forces, by declaring an Islamic state, the Negara Islam Indonesia (NII).

The movement attracted not just those who wanted the implementation of Islamic law in independent Indonesia but many who opposed the strength of Dutch influence in the new Republik Indonesia Serikat (q.v.), and the movement spread to varying degrees to most Muslim parts of the archipelago, encompassing the rebellion in Aceh (q.v.) under Daud Beureu'eh, the rebellion of Kahar Muzakkar (q.v.) in South Sulawesi, and that of Ibnu Hajar in Banjarmasin (q.v.). From the start, the Masyumi (q.v.) was always ambivalent towards it, approving of its aims but rejecting its methods. West Java was always the core of the movement and there fighting was especially fierce, DI forces occasionally reaching the outskirts of Jakarta, but it crumbled after Kartosuwiryo was killed in 1962. See also KOMANDO KIHAD. [0632, 0641, 0657, 1132]

DASAAD, Agus Musin (1905–?), Indonesian businessman from southern Sumatra, where he began his operations trading produce from smallholder farmers of rubber, tea, coffee, and pepper. In the 1930s, he combined with other traders to import raw cotton to feed a local textile industry, and textiles became one of the major interests of his principal firm, Kancil Mas, a former German firm confiscated in 1940. Quasi-smuggling trade during the Revolution increased his fortune and he benefited both from the Benteng Program (q.v.) in the 1950s and from sole import licences during Guided Democracy (q.v.). His firms declined after 1966 with the loss of political patronage and the rise of Japanese competition. [0280, 0287]

DATUK. See TITLES.

DAYAKS, collective term for the indigenous peoples of Kalimantan (q.v.), comprising at least twenty different ethnic groups. They are generally divided into three groupings: the Dusun and Murut in the north, the Ngaju in the south and the Kenyah, Kayan, Kayang, and Iban in the center. Dayaks traditionally practice shifting agriculture (swidden) and hunting, and live in multifamily longhouses, up to 180 meters long. Political leadership is ephemeral as power relationships change within family groups. In precolonial times, head-hunting was said to be common, as a means of accumulating 'life force.' Tension between Dayaks and the Muslims of Banjarmasin (q.v.) led in 1958 to the creation of the province of Central Kalimantan. Governments have traditionally been uneasy over the way of life of the Dayaks, seeing it as unsettled, destabilizing and, in recent times, ecologically destructive (see ALANG-ALANG), and there have been many attempts to encourage Dayaks to establish permanent settlements, take up commercial crops such as cloves and pepper (qq.v.), and to convert to a major religion. Many Dayaks have converted over the years to Islam, the religion of the Malay inhabitants of the island's coastal regions and in doing so are said to *masuk Melayu,* 'become a Malay', religious change thus implying a change in ethnicity. In 1980, however, the traditional Dayak religion was recognized under the name Kaharingan as a branch of Hinduism. [0061, 1007, 1034, 1144]

DEBT OF HONOR. See 'EERESCHULD, Een'.

DECENTRALIZATION. Until 1903, all government officials and organizations in the Indies were formally agents of the governor-general for the administration of the colony and were entirely dependent on the central administration for their budgets. A Decentralization Law in 1903, however, established a limited degree of financial and administrative autonomy in thirty-two municipalities (*gemeenten*), mainly on Java, and fifteen territories (*gewesten*) throughout the colony. This was followed in 1922 by a so-called *bestuurshervorming* (administrative reform), under which the gemeenten became *stadsgemeenten* ('city municipalities') and the island of Java was divided into three provinces—West, Central, and East in 1926, 1930, and 1927 respectively. The Vorstenlanden (q.v.) on Java continued to be administratively separate as *gouvernementen*.

The situation in the Outer Islands (q.v.) remained complicated. Dutch rule was based on treaty relations with local rulers (*zelfbesturen,* q.v.). In 1922 Dutch authority was represented by three governors (Aceh, East Sumatra, and Celebes [Sulawesi]), 15 residents, and one assistant resident. The 1922 reform provided for the creation of gouvernementen of Sumatra, Borneo, and the 'Great East' (*Grote Oost*), though for financial reasons these were not implemented until July 1938, except for a proto-gouvernement of the Great East, covering Maluku and Irian formed in 1926. As a further measure, the Dutch established so-called adat-law communities (*adatrecht gemeenschappen*) in Minangkabau and Banjarmasin in 1938 and Palembang (qq.v.) in 1941.

The distinctive feature of all these new units was the presence of representative councils which played some role in the formulation of regulations and the allocation of budgets. They generally consisted of members elected (under a restricted franchise) and appointed by the governor-general from the three racial groups. Europeans were invariably overrepresented in relation to Indonesians, but the representation of each group varied to some extent in proportion to its share of the population. From 1924 all regency councils on Java had an Indonesian majority. The head of the local administration was both chairperson of the council and chair of its College van Gecommitteerden or Gedeputeerden (College van Burgemeester en Wethouders in the case of stadsgemeenten), the executive body for daily administrative matters of the council. It was these local councils which chose the elected members of the Volksraad (q.v.). The Indonesian Republic's Law no. 22 of 1948 established provinces (q.v., *daerah tingkat I*), *kabupaten* (*daerah tingkat II*) and villages as the key levels of government. Law no. 1 of 1957 gave local assemblies (Dewan Perwakilan Rakyat Daerah) the power to elect regional heads (bupati and governors), but this law was rescinded by Sukarno in September 1959. See also FEDERALISM. [0363, 0546, 0601, 0909, 0910]

DEFENCE POLICY. For most of C.19, after Britain (q.v.) restored the Indies to the Dutch in 1816, the principal task of the colonial army, or KNIL, was extending colonial power throughout the archipelago and guarding against rebellion in areas already controlled. External threats were few and were met by diplomatic rather than military precautions. In late C.19, the rise of German,

Japanese, and Russian sea power aroused Dutch alarm, but colonial defence policy focused on the defence of Java by land forces. During World War I, extensive debate took place over the desirability of an Indies militia, and in 1923 military service was made compulsory for Dutch citizens (thus excluding the majority of Indonesians). Possible expansion of the colony's naval defences was also much discussed, but not until 1936 did naval expenditure significantly increase.

Army officers of the Republic after 1945 initially disagreed sharply on questions of military strategy. In general, former KNIL officers favored construction of a compact, Western style, disciplined army, which might defeat the Dutch on their own terms, while former PETA (q.v.) officers advocated a larger armed force whose strength would lie in its confidence and commitment to an independent Indonesia. Both, however, believed in frontal warfare. Only after a long series of setbacks—beginning with the battle of Surabaya in November 1945—in which Indonesian forces offered heavy resistance to arriving Allied troops at great cost, did ideas of guerrilla warfare gradually spread among the military. Military thinkers, especially A.H. Nasution (q.v.), developed the idea of total people's war (now known as HANKAMRATA, Pertahanan Keamanan Rakyat Semesta, Total People's Defence and Security), central to which was the principle that national defence depended on close cooperation between a guerrilla army and the people. Though this strategy was never fully implemented during the Revolution (q.v.), it became the basis for the army's territorial defence structure in which considerable operational autonomy is given to regional military commanders. The names and scope of these regional military commands has varied from time to time. During the Revolution, the term Wehrkreis (pl. Wehrkreise) was used on a fairly ad hoc basis within a separate Java Command. In 1950 these were replaced by seven Teritorium dan Tentara (T & T, Territory and Army) commands, covering the entire country. T & T commanders developed deep local roots, often at the expense of subordination to the High Command. Between 1957 and 1959 these were gradually replaced by 16 (17 with Irian, q.v.) military regions (KODAM, Komando Daerah Militer), along with three overarching Inter-Regional Commands (Komando Antar Daerah, KOANDA), covering Sumatra, Kalimantan, and Eastern Indonesia. In 1963 the KODAM were replaced by PEPELRADA (Penguasa Pelaksana Dwikora Daerah, Regional Authorities for the Implementation of Dwikora). KODAM were restored in 1967, but in 1969 they lost their operational (but not territorial) functions to six new KOWILHAN (Komando Wilayah Pertahanan, Regional Defence Commands) with command of air, naval, and army units. In 1985 the KOWILHAN were abolished and their authority was restored to ten reorganized KODAM. From the late 1950s, this territorial strategy was reinforced with the notion of *dwifungsi* (q.v.) which asserts amongst other things that the military role in administration contributes to national resilience. In practice, however, there has been some retreat from this broad defence strategy, greater emphasis being placed on the one hand on technically sophisticated strike forces, such as KOPASSUS (q.v.), and on domestic intelligence functions. A Defence Law formalizing the dual strategy was passed in 1982. Defence expenditure is officially stated to be 3-to-3-½% of GNP, though some observers believe concealed expenditure to be a good deal higher. For a list of Defence Ministers, see the Appendix. [0652, 0663, 0791, 0804]

DELI, sultanate in East Sumatra (q.v.), successor state to the kingdom of Aru (q.v.), emerging in C.16 as an object of struggle between Riau and Aceh (qq.v.), which finally won suzerainty only to lose it to Siak (q.v.) in a long contest for power beginning in 1710. Deli was included in the Siak territories which submitted to the Dutch in 1858 but was acquired by the Dutch from Siak in 1884. [0528]

DEMAK, the first Muslim state on Java, founded probably by a Chinese Muslim trader in late C.15. This trader's grandson, Sultan Trenggana (ca 1504–46) conquered Majapahit (q.v.) in ca 1527 and extended his influence to south Sumatra and Banjarmasin (q.v), attacking Melaka (q.v.) in 1512. The kingdom was exhausted, however, in a major campaign in Balambangan (q.v.) in 1546 and after Trenggana's death, was rapidly eclipsed by Pajang and Mataram (qq.v.). See also PASISIR; WALI SONGO. [0456]

DEMANG. See INLANDSCH BESTUUR.

DEMOCRATIC REPUBLIC OF EAST TIMOR (DRET) was proclaimed in Dili on 28 November 1975, while Indonesian forces were invading the Portuguese colony from the West, with Francisco Xavier do Amaral as president and Nicolau Lobato as prime minister. The DRET was recognized only by Mozambique, and was never in a position to exercise unhampered administration over the country. The international position of the DRET has been weakened, moreover, by the fact that Portugal's insistence that it retains sovereignty over East Timor (q.v.) seems to represent one of the few diplomatic levers against the Indonesian presence. Do Amaral, dismissed as president in September over his willingness to negotiate with the Indonesians, surrendered to Indonesian forces in 1978 and was succeeded by Lobato, who was killed in battle later the same year. See also FRETILIN. [0898, 0905]

DEPOK, village south of Batavia (q.v.). In 1714 the *particuliere landerij* (q.v.) here was bequeathed by Cornelis Chastelein to his liberated Christian slaves and their descendants in perpetuity, and for around two centuries the 'Depokkers' formed a distinct indigenous Christian community on the outskirts of Batavia. Chastelein also instructed that part of the land never be cleared, and this area was handed over in 1913 as a nature reserve to the Netherlands Indies Society for Nature Protection. See also CONSERVATION, Nature.

DEPRESSION of the 1930s. The Great Depression struck the Netherlands Indies severely, halving the colony's exports and forcing dramatic cuts in the budget. Austerity measures effectively ended the Ethical Policy's program of government expenditure, leading on the one hand to the mutiny on the vessel *Zeven Provinciën* (q.v.) and on the other to the formation of the *Stuw* group of progressive colonial officials. Unemployment rose and taxes increased. In an effort to preserve the Western-dominated large rubber plantations, the government placed heavy restrictions on smallholder production in Sumatra. [0578, 0589]

DESA, village. According to common belief, the desa was the main unit of social organization in rural Java in pre-colonial times. Villages are said to have been geographically distinct entities comprising rice fields (*sawah*), orchards and dwellings, often in a single cluster, sometimes distributed among two or more hamlets (*kampung*). Village life, under an elected head, or *lurah,* was said to be a model of Indonesian democracy, decisions being taken by a process of exhaustive deliberation, (*musyawarah,* q.v.) producing a consensus (*mufakat*) articulated by the lurah. A sense of common destiny gave the villagers collective responsibility so that while the interests of an individual would always be subordinate to those of the desa, the community as a whole took an active interest in the welfare of all its members. This led to the habit of *gotong royong* (q.v.) or mutual self-help and, according to Geertz (q.v.), ultimately to 'shared poverty' (see AGRICULTURAL INVOLUTION). This view of village life influenced leaders searching for Indonesian forms of democracy; Guided Democracy (q.v.) was explicitly an attempt to implement village democratic forms at national level.

Recent research has cast doubt on this view of the precolonial village and suggests that rural society was organized in much smaller households (*cacah*) which were not geographically clustered and which were in patron-client (q.v.) relationships with local officials who acted as intermediaries between rulers, especially bupati (q.v.) and households. The collectivist enclosed village seems to have become an article of government faith first under Raffles (q.v.), who saw the village as an alternative unit of administration to the bupati. Villages were convenient administrative units for the levying of taxes and the mobilization of corvée labor, and British and Dutch policies on land rent and labor (qq.v.) did much to create a communal village life. The process was reinforced by romantic views of traditional village life, which helped to crystallize notions of a village culture and philosophy distinct from that of the courts or the trading cities (see ALIRAN; DUALISM). Whether original or constructed, however, the collectivist nature of the village has been breached by the penetration of the money economy, especially through taxation (q.v.) and the commercialization of agriculture. See GREEN REVOLUTION.

Since the time of Raffles, the desa has been one of the main administrative units on Java, headed by a *desahoofd* or *lurah* (now *kepala desa*). Since independence, as part of administrative standardization, the *kelurahan* has become the major local administrative unit throughout the country. In 1979 new regulations on village government replaced the former village councils (*dewan desa*) with Village Consultative Councils (LMD, Lembaga Musyawarah Desa) chosen within the village by 'consensus.' Each village also has a Lembaga Ketahanan Masyarakat Desa (LKMD, Institute for Village Community Resilience), headed by the lurah, as an agency for promoting development, inculcating the Pancasila (q.v.), and seeing to matters such as family planning and local security and order. The PKK (Pembinaan Kesejahteraan Keluarga, Family Welfare Development) is an officially sponsored women's organization promoting basic health care and education. In 1987 there were 61,439 desa, plus 4,952 urban kelurahan without LMDs. [0254, 0503, 0689, 0802, 0810, 0816, 0818, 0837, 0841]

DEVELOPMENT IDEOLOGY. The notion of macroeconomic development as a manageable process bringing eventual greater prosperity for all emerged in Germany in the second half of C.19 and influenced Dutch colonial thinking by the end of the century. Most thinkers tied the possibility of self-sustaining growth to the viability of capitalism. Followers of Boeke (q.v., see also DUALISM), believing that the indigenous economy would remain permanently precapitalist, saw Western enterprise as an essential part of such development, while others sought to use quasi-traditional institutions such as cooperatives (q.v.) to bring the indigenous economy into the capitalist world.

At the Declaration of Independence, many Indonesians felt strongly that colonial economic policies and the ravages of war had left the country economically backward and that a major program of development (*pembangunan*) was necessary, but it was only under the New Order (q.v.) that Pembangunan, conceived as a long-term process of perhaps twenty-five years, was elevated to become a central pillar of government policy. The precise nature of this program was always under debate, especially between the advocates of a more free-market economy and proponents of import-substitution industrialization, and more quietly over the extent to which true national prosperity (*kemakmuran*) could be divorced from justice (*keadilan*). Nonetheless, in conventional terms, the economic policies of the New Order have been responsible for massive economic growth, and in 1983 President Suharto (q.v.) felt justified in taking the title *Bapak Pembangunan* ('Father of Development'). See also BADAN PERENCANAAN PEMBANGUNAN NASIONAL; CLASS ANALYSIS. [0211, 0216, 0227, 0279, 0683, 0846, 0862]

DEWAN NASIONAL (National Council), formed by Sukarno in May 1957 as an assembly of 41 functional group representatives to advise cabinet after the fall of the Ali Sastroamijoyo cabinet. It was dissolved in June 1959 with the return to the 1945 Constitution. See also GUIDED DEMOCRACY. [0647, 0705]

DEWAN PERTAHANAN NEGARA (DPN, State Defence Council). Established 6 July 1946 under State of Emergency regulations, and comprising the prime minister, senior cabinet ministers, the army commander and lasykar (q.v.) leaders, the DPN became a central decision-making body of the Indonesian Republic during the Revolution (q.v.).

DEWAN PERTIMBANGAN AGUNG (DPA, Supreme Advisory Council), a respected but powerless council of senior and retired government figures which can offer proposals to the government on matters of national importance as well as opinions on matters raised by the president (q.v.). The Republic's first DPA, formed in

1945, was merged with other bodies into the parliament of the RIS (q.v.). The council was reestablished in July 1959 just before the return to the 1945 Constitution. See also DEWAN PERWAKILAN RAKYAT. [0808]

DEWAN PERWAKILAN RAKYAT (DPR, People's Representative Council), Indonesia's principal legislative body, constitutionally subordinate to the MPR (q.v.), to which all DPR members automatically belong. Though prescribed by the 1945 Constitution, its role was taken during the Revolution by the KNIP (q.v.). The unicameral parliament of the RIS (q.v.) was called the DPR and consisted of members of the two chambers of the RIS (q.v.) parliament, together with the members of the 1945 Republic's Dewan Pertimbangan Agung and the Working Committee of the KNIP (q.v.). Members of parliament elected in 1955 took their seats in March 1956. In 1959, members of this elected parliament became, with a few exceptions, members of a provisional DPR under the restored 1945 Constitution. Sukarno (q.v.), however, suspended this DPR in 1960 after it refused to pass his budget, and instead installed the DPR-Gotong Royong, whose members were appointed by him and which could be dissolved at his will. The DPR-GR was purged of its PKI and other left wing members in October and November 1965. Elections in 1971 reconstituted the DPR, then numbering 460, of whom 360 were elected and 100 appointed, 75 from the armed forces and 25 from other groups. In 1987 membership was increased to 500, with 100 appointed from the armed forces. [0634, 0808]

DHARMA WANITA (The Duty of Women), official association of the wives of government employees. (There is no such association for husbands.) Membership is strongly encouraged and the organization's hierarchy closely follows that of the bureaucracy, that is, the wife of a section head is automatically head of the section's Dharma Wanita. The function of Dharma Wanita is to separate the bureaucratic corps socially from other parts of the community in the interests of detaching the bureaucracy from supposedly extraneous interests. Dharma Pertiwi is the equivalent organization for wives of military personnel. See also KORPS PEGAWAI REPUBLIK INDONESIA; MONOLOYALITAS; WOMEN AND MEN.

DIAMONDS are found especially in West and Southeast Kalimantan and have been traded extensively since the second half of C.18, providing the original basis for the Amsterdam diamond trade, though they are mostly small (less than one carat). [0321, 0329]

DIEMEN, Anthony van (1593–1645), VOC director-general of trade under J.P. Coen (q.v.) from 1627 to 1629 and Coen's successor as governor-general 1636–45. He presided over the period of the Company's greatest expansion, when it seized Melaka (q.v.), Formosa, and Ceylon and ordered the drafting of the Bataviaasche Statuten which formed the basic law (q.v.) of the colony until 1848. [0375]

DIGUL. See BOVEN DIGUL.

DIPLOMASI AND PERJUANGAN ('diplomacy' and 'struggle'), alternative strategies for winning the Indonesian Revolution (1945–49, see REVOLUTION), as described by opposition parties at the time. The proponents of *perjuangan* denied that there was any need for the Republic to make concessions to the Dutch in order to obtain international recognition and that armed force alone could secure independence; the proponents of *diplomasi* argued that negotiations were necessary to remove the Dutch from the Outer Island regions they had occupied and that negotiations could remove the Dutch with fewer sacrifices. An important part of *diplomasi,* alongside maintaining an army which would give their negotiations credibility, was making the Republic agreeable to the Western Powers by guaranteeing foreign investments. Supporters of *perjuangan,* on the other hand, argued that the Republic could only win the commitment of the mass of people necessary for armed struggle by also introducing social-justice measures which would involve, amongst other things, restricting foreign investment. The ideological character of the conflict, however, was diminished by the fact that all governments of the period, of whatever political persuasion, supported *diplomasi* while opposition parties typically supported *perjuangan* until they entered government. See also DEFENCE POLICY; NASUTION, Abdul Haris; REVOLUTION. [0628, 0656]

DIPONEGORO, Pangeran (ca 1785–1855), Javanese prince, son of Sultan Hamengkubuwono III of Yogyakarta (q.v.). After being passed over for the succession to his father, Diponegoro withdrew to his estates and cultivated his reputation as a spiritual leader. He led the Java War (q.v.), 1825–30, against the Dutch, but was captured by the Dutch General de Kock while under guarantee of safe conduct for negotiations and was exiled to Makassar, where he died. [0504]

DIPTEROCARPS (Dipterocarpaceae, *meranti, kruing* and other local names), common rain forest trees in Western Indonesia, characteristic of the flora inherited from the ancient super-continent of Laurasia (see CONTINENTAL DRIFT) including *Dipterocarpus, Shorea* and *Dryobalanops.* Valued for their tall, straight trunks, they have been felled extensively for timber since 1966. Since many species flower and fruit for the first time up to sixty years after germination, long after they reach marketable girth, the regeneration of some dipterocarp forests is in doubt. See also FORESTRY; WALLACE'S LINE. [0936, 0938, 0948]

DIVORCE. See MARRIAGE, Political significance of.

DJAJADININGRAT, Pangeran Aria Ahmad (1877–1943), son of a bupati (q.v.) family and was one of the first of the Javanese elite to receive a Western education under the Association Principle (q.v.). The novelty of this idea is indicated by the fact that when he enrolled at a Dutch primary school in Batavia he used the name Willem van Banten, implying that he was an illegitimate Indo-European (q.v.), rather than his own, aristocratic Javanese name (see also NAMES, Personal). He became a protégé of Snouck Hurgronje (q.v.) and after completing secondary school succeeded his father as bupati of Serang. As later bupati of Batavia (q.v.), member of the Volksraad (q.v.), technical adviser to the Dutch delegation at the League of Nations and member of various government commissions, he was one of the most senior Indonesians in the colonial government. [1071]

DOUWES DEKKER, Eduard (Multatuli) (1820–87). Author of the celebrated novel *Max Havelaar* (1860, q.v.) based on his own experiences as assistant resident in Lebak in West Java. There, having accused the local bupati (q.v.) of extortion and corruption, he was himself dismissed in March 1856. [0523]

DOUWES DEKKER. E.F.E. (Setiabudi). See INDISCHE PARTIJ.

DRAGON'S BLOOD. Deep red kino from the canes *Daemonorops* spp. (Arecaceae), traded from Sumatra and Kalimantan (qq.v.) to the west by Arabs in C.16 for use as medicine and as lacquer for violins. [0938]

DUALISM. 1. Concept formulated by the Dutch economist J.H. Boeke (q.v.) to describe the existence within a single political order of a Western capitalist sector and an indigenous precapitalist one. Accepting much of the prevailing colonial view of the communal village (see DESA), Boeke argued that the indigenous economy was not driven by wages, prices, and capital but by mutual social obligations. He saw this precapitalist economy as an unchanging feature of the society (see GOTONG ROYONG, SHARED POVERTY), partly because modern capitalism was too advanced to offer the indigenous economy a point of entry. Boeke's ideas were criticized in the volume *Indonesian economics*. [0212, 0216, 0218, 0365, 1161]

2. Characteristic of traditional Indonesian religions identified by Dutch structural anthropology and described as the symbolic union of opposites, such as man-woman, earth-sky and left-right, within a whole, or in Hinduism and Buddhism (qq.v.) as dual aspects of a single truth. [0015, 0367, 1012, 1025, 1144, 1165]

3. Dualism was also used to refer to the division of the Binnenlandsch Bestuur (BB, q.v.) into European and native services. [0366]

DURIAN (*Durio zibethinus,* Bombacaceae), massive thorny fruit, probably native to Kalimantan. The specific epithet means civet-like, and refers to the fruit's strong smell, described by Wallace as that of custard passed through a sewer. Devotees, however, regard it as the world's finest fruit. [0075, 0936, 0938, 0983]

DUTCH EAST INDIES COMPANY (VOC, Vereenigde Oost-Indische Compagnie, lit. United East Indies Company), formed in 1602 by merger of several separate companies founded in the 1590s for trade in the Indian Ocean (see also van LINSCHOTEN). It was a joint stock company, that is, the separate holdings of the shareholders were not distinguished in the operations of the company; profit and loss were shared equally according to stock holdings. Under its charter from the States-General, the company had an official monopoly of all Dutch trade east of the Cape of Good Hope and west of the Magellan Straits and the right to exercise sovereignty in that region on behalf of the Dutch state. General company policy was set by the *Heeren XVII* (Seventeen Gentlemen), who met in turn in the different provincial cities of the Netherlands and appointed a governor-general (q.v.) to govern the company in Asia. From 1619, the company's headquarters in Asia was at Batavia (q.v.) (see also COEN, Jan Pieterszoon).

The VOC aimed from the start to gain a monopoly of the spice trade in Maluku (q.v.), using military force to impose restrictive treaties on indigenous states, to exclude foreign competitors, and to destroy spice trees outside Dutch territories (see 'AMBOYNA MASSACRE'; ENGLISH EAST INDIA COMPANY; HONGI RAIDS). In 1641 the company seized Melaka (q.v.) from the Portuguese and in 1666–69 conquered Makassar (q.v.) to deny it as a base for competitors, while in 1682 it successfully excluded foreign traders from Banten (q.v.). The VOC also sought to control the so-called interAsiatic trade, especially between the archipelago and India (q.v.); they established major interests in Bengal and on the Coromandel coast for the purchase of cotton (q.v.) cloth to be exchanged for spices. Java became important for the supply of rice (q.v.) and wood.

Throughout C.17 and 18, the VOC expanded its territorial holdings in the archipelago, making use of wars of succession, especially on Java, to extend its control. In C.18, however, the spice trade declined and with it the company. The increased costs of administering a land-based empire, together with rampant inefficiency and corruption, led the company to bankruptcy, and the States-General allowed its charter to lapse on 31 December 1799. All debts (some *f*140 million) and possessions were taken over by the Dutch government. See also BATAVIAN REPUBLIC. [0375, 0435, 0440, 0441, 0454, 0455, 0464, 0471, 0473, 0492, 0557]

DUTCH IN INDONESIA. Dutch traders arrived in Indonesia first as temporary visitors, but the growing scope of the operations of the Dutch East Indies Company (q.v.), or VOC, soon led Dutch men to settle in the archipelago for extended periods. In addition to serving as employees of the company, as officials, sailors, and soldiers, some entered the service of indigenous rulers. Although attempts were made in C.17 to establish settler colonies in Ambon and Banda (qq.v.), these were soon abandoned. Until C.19, therefore, Indies Dutch society was predominantly one of VOC employees, the elite made up of senior officials in Batavia (q.v.), the mass consisting especially of European soldiers and sailors sharing the universal culture of bars and barracks.

Because few Dutch women migrated to the colony before C.19, most Dutch men had permanent or semipermanent liaisons with Indonesian or other Asian women, and gave European status to their children (see RACE) even if not to their consorts. Dutch colonial society, therefore, especially in Batavia, was mestizo in character, and visitors frequently commented on the apparent readiness with which the Europeans had adopted Indonesian dress, food, and customs such as betel (q.v.) chewing. With the opening of the Suez canal in 1869, more Europeans reached the colony, staying there for briefer periods, and more European women arrived as semipermanent residents. A sharper social distinction began to emerge between Europeans and Indo-Europeans (q.v.), as well as between *trekkers,* who planned to return to the Netherlands at the end of their period of service, and *blijvers,* who planned to retire in the Indies. Colonial society was governed by a strict social hierarchy, with government officials at the top, followed then by military officers, businessmen, and churchmen. In 1930, the European population of Indonesia was about 240,000, of whom 70% were Indo-European. Half the European population was concentrated in 9 cities (37,200 in the Batavia-Mr Cornelis conurbation). In the sociëteiten (clubs) a strong jazz tradition developed and the Europeans of the colony produced an extensive literature. Political activity, such as it was, was focussed on the Netherlands, rather than on the colony, and a branch of the Nederlandsche Vereeniging voor Vrouwenkiesrecht (Netherlands Association for Female Suffrage) was founded in 1908. Only with the rise of Indonesian nationalism, did serious local politicking begin, especially through the Vaderlandse Club, formed in 1929. During the Depression, the Dutch Nazi NSB (Nationaal-Socialistische Beweging, National Socialist Movement), won considerable support in the colony and some NSB members were interned after the fall of Holland in 1940.

As the Japanese approached, the governor-general instructed the European population of Indonesia to stay put and share the fate of the Indonesians, and ca 100,000 were interned for the latter part of the Japanese occupation (q.v.). Approximately one in six died in the substandard conditions and many were detained by Indonesian revolutionary groups after 1945 as hostages for Dutch good behavior; some were not released until 1947. Dutch citizens were permitted to stay in Indonesia under liberal conditions after the transfer of sovereignty, but many chose to leave and on 5 December 1957 the remaining

45,000 were expelled over the Netherlands' retention of Irian (q.v.). See also COUPERUS, Louis. [0094, 0167, 0173, 0375, 0493, 0557, 0614, 1089]

DWIFUNGSI, ('dual function'), the official doctrine which authorizes the armed forces' extensive participation in politics and government. The army's territorial structure, a military hierarchy distinct from the combat commands and running parallel to the civilian bureaucracy from provincial (KODAM, Komando Daerah Militer, Regional Military Command) to village (Babinsa, Bintara Pembina Desa, NCOs for Village Development) level, provides military personnel with day-to-day involvement in the running of the country. The typical career pattern of an officer is alternating stints in the territorial and combat commands followed by 'retirement' into a post in the civil bureaucracy. The president and vice-president and many holders of the most powerful political and administrative posts are retired officers, while many lower civilian posts are routinely staffed with retired junior officers.

Military involvement in administration began during the Revolution, with the creation of the part-military Dewan Pertahanan Negara (q.v.). In 1948 several military governors (some of them civilians) were appointed in various parts of the Republic, and Nasution (q.v.) developed his theory of 'Total People's Defence' (see GERILYA), under which the civilian administration was, as it were, put at the disposal of the armed forces for the purpose of fighting the Dutch. In the early 1950s, civilian politicians attempted to restrict the army's political involvement; in 1954 armed forces were forbidden to campaign in uniform and senior officers were banned from election. In March 1957, following a seizure by military officers of the administation in several provinces, martial law was declared, formalizing the army's political intervention. In 1960, five army officers were appointed as provincial governors. Since 1960, the armed forces has also been represented formally in parliament by means of a bloc of reserved seats (on the basis of which serving military personnel are not permitted to vote in elections). In February 1980, the government announced a program called *ABRI masuk desa* (ABRI, q.v., enters the villages), in which armed forces personnel were posted into the villages both to familiarize themselves with village life and problems and to improve their public profile by helping village development. Dwifungsi, however, was first enshrined in legislation only in September 1982. In early 1962, several civilian officials, including Subandrio (q.v.) received titular military rank within the Komando Tertinggi Operasi Ekonomi (KOTOE, Supreme Operational Command for the Economy), in order to have authority over military officers serving within government departments and state enterprises (q.v.).

Dwifungsi is based on both historical and practical arguments. First, it is said that the army has saved the nation on several crucial occasions when civilian authorities proved lacking, in 1945, 1948–49, 1957–59, and 1965–66 and therefore has a kind of moral ascendancy over civilian institutions (see GERILYA; POLICE ACTIONS; GERAKAN SEPTEMBER 30). Second, it is argued that only the armed forces have the expertise and internal discipline needed to run the country, and the military participation is not only desirable for public well-being but also is a necessary part of the national defence strategy (see DEFENCE POLICY). What is not clear is whether Dwifungsi is to be a permanent or temporary state of affairs. Official statements by military figures have shown a strong disinclination to give up power or to believe that the country can manage without them. On the other hand, there has been a steady reduction in the number of officers and former officers in cabinet, and poor military performance by the armed forces in East Timor (q.v.) together with significant budget constraints since the collapse of oil prices have produced increased pressure for a smaller, leaner armed forces which would have correspondingly fewer resources to devote to politics and government. There are signs, thus, of a military retreat to the commanding heights of Indonesian politics, bolstered especially by an expanded intelligence apparatus.

Army units were initially highly dependent on logistic and financial support from the local and central governments, and the right to call upon the entire resources of society, especially of the civil authorities, for military purposes fairly soon became an article of faith for military planners. At the same time, however, because these resources did not flow down through a single regulated system of distribution, a myth of military self-sufficiency arose, particularly after the civilian cabinet allowed itself to be captured by the Dutch in Yogyakarta in the second 'Police Action' (q.v.). During the 1950s, therefore, the army came increasingly to see itself as having a special role in the polity. See also 'MIDDLE WAY' FOR THE ARMED FORCES. [0663, 0669, 0675, 0680, 0709, 0805, 0811]

E

EAST INDONESIA. See NEGARA INDONESIA TIMUR.

EAST SUMATRA (*Sumatra's Oostkust*), a lowland area around the modern city of Medan. In early times it was occupied by Batak (q.v.) communities, who were later conquered and partly displaced by Malay kingdoms and sultanates. Disputed by Aceh, Siak, and Riau (qq.v.), it finally emerged as a distinct region through the phenomenal development of its plantation sector in late C.19

and early C.20. Tobacco (q.v.) was introduced there in 1863, coffee, coconuts, rubber, sisal, and palm oil (qq.v.) somewhat later. The region was the site of the first major expansion of private investment in the Indies after the government controls of the Cultivation System (q.v.) were lifted. The Deli Maatschappij was formed in 1869 and by the end of the century it dominated the region along with three other companies: Senembah, the Deli-Batavia Maatschappij, and the Tabak Maatschappij Arendsburg. Labor was obtained from southern China (to 1931) and later from Java (see COOLIE ORDINANCE). There was also much immigration by Bataks (q.v.) from the interior and by 1930 the Malays comprised only 20% of the population. As the power of Western enterprises grew, that of the original rulers of the region, the sultans of Deli, Langkat, and Serdang (qq.v.), as well as Asahan, Batubara and others, was steadily eroded, though they were compensated by vast incomes from rents. Politically, the East Sumatra planters were influential in colonial circles, J.T. Cremer of the Deli Mij becoming minister of colonies for a time. Administratively, however, the region was always rather independent of Batavia, partly because of its close economic ties with Penang, partly because the large companies carried out many administrative tasks themselves, including even sometimes the issue of currency (q.v.). See also DELI.

In March 1946 a social revolution broke out against the sultans and rajas who had leased land to Western enterprises, who were seen as agents of Dutch colonial rule and exploiters in their own right; many were killed or driven out. Although the area was formally part of the Republic, Medan was soon occupied by Allied forces and the remainder of the region was carved up between warlords of various allegiances. The lawlessness of the Republican period led many to applaud Dutch conquest in July 1947 and the formation of the federal Negara Sumatra Timur (State of East Sumatra) on 25 December 1947 though this was dissolved in August 1950. Resentment in the region grew during the 1950s, partly over government insistence on removing squatters from foreign-controlled plantation lands occupied during the revolution, partly because of the new self-confidence of labor unions (q.v.), and partly because East Sumatra seemed to be generating most of Indonesia's wealth while getting little in return (a perception which did not take into account the widespread rubber smuggling from the region). A military revolt broke out in 1956, precipitating the national declaration of martial law in 1957, and the area was briefly held by the PRRI (q.v.) rebels. [0263, 0270, 0528, 0536, 0578, 0582, 0655, 0661]

EAST TIMOR (including the enclave of Oécusse) became clearly defined as a Portuguese colony only in 1859, though the Portuguese presence dated from C.16 (see TIMOR). Until 1896 the colony was ruled directly from Macau, but even after gaining a separate administration it remained a neglected corner of the Portuguese empire, exporting little more than coffee and horses (qq.v.). An indigenous uprising by Dom Boaventura was crushed in 1910–12, but by 1928 only 200 civilian officials and 300 troops were sufficient to maintain Portuguese rule. Business and government in the capital, Dili, was dominated by a mestizo and Chinese elite, while in the countryside local chiefs, or *liurai,* acted as deputies for the colonial rulers. A third of the population was Catholic, the rest animist, with the most widespread language being Tetum.

At the outbreak of World War II, Portugal declared its neutrality. Portuguese Timor, however, was briefly occupied in December 1941 by a joint Dutch-Australian force, with the idea of keeping it out of Japanese hands. Japanese troops occupied the territory from February

1942, and until 1945 the colony was under Japanese army rule (unlike eastern Indonesia which was under the Japanese navy) although Japan also formally recognized Portuguese neutrality. Australian troops fought a guerrilla war against the Japanese in the hinterland from March to December 1942. During the war, approximately 40,000 Timorese died of famine. At the end of the war Australia had ambitions to establish a sphere of influence over both parts of the island but was soon forced to accede in a return by the prewar administrations. Some Indonesians, too, made a general claim to Timor at this time, on the grounds that it had allegedly once been part of Majapahit (q.v.), but this vague assertion was eclipsed by the Indonesian claim to Irian (q.v.) which depended on the inviolability of colonial borders. Under the 1953 Organic Law on Overseas Territories, East Timor formally became a province of Portugal, divided into 13 districts called Conçelhos (Councils) under Portuguese administrators. Below these were 58 postos, of which 60% were headed by Timorese. An anti-Portuguese uprising, which apparently had some Indonesian backing, was suppressed in 1959.

After the Armed Forces coup in Portugal in April 1974, the new authorities announced three possibilities for the future of East Timor: independence, continued association with Portugal, and integration with Indonesia, and three political groups, UDT, Fretilin, and APODETI (qq.v.) formed to promote these possibilities respectively. A tiny group, ADITLA (q.v.), advocated integration with Australia. In January 1975 UDT and Fretilin formed a coalition to deal jointly with the Portuguese, but this broke down in May, partly because UDT became worried by Fretilin's proposals for radical agrarian and educational reforms, partly, it is said, because Indonesian authorities warned UDT leaders that Indonesia would not permit a government containing Fretilin to come to power in the colony. In June 1975, the Portuguese government announced firm plans for a three-year transitional period to full independence for the territory, including general election in October 1976.

Popular support for Fretilin was now such that it was likely to win a full majority in elections, and UDT sought to forestall this by staging a coup in Dili on 11 August with the help of the police force. Fretilin, supported by Timorese sections of the colonial army, resisted the UDT move and full civil war quickly broke out. The Portuguese governor withdrew to the offshore island of Atauro on 26 August. Fretilin forces soon seized power in the major centers, but UDT and APODETI supporters fled across the border into Indonesian Timor, where they regrouped, along with Indonesian 'volunteers', in what was called 'Operasi Komodo' and began a gradual invasion of East Timor, in the course of which five journalists from Australia were killed. On 11 October Fretilin formed a 'transitional' government and on 28 November declared the independence of the Democratic Republic of East Timor (q.v.). On 30 November Portugal requested United Nations (q.v.) help in regaining control of the territory. Indonesian armed forces mounted a full scale attack on Dili on 7 December 1975 and soon extended their control to all major population centers at the cost of extensive casualties amongst the civilian population. UDT, APODETI, and other anti-Fretilin groups formed a provisional government under Indonesian auspices and on 31 May 1976 an Indonesian-sponsored 'People's Representative Council' requested integration with Indonesia as the 27th province; this took place on 15 July. Indonesia's aim in conquering the territory seems to have been primarily to deny it as a base to foreign powers and to prevent the emergence of a probably left-wing government on her borders, but it seems certain that Suharto believed that the operation had the approval of the United States and Australian governments.

Fierce resistance by Fretilin continued. Widely reported atrocities carried out by Indonesian forces in the attack on Dili and continued systematic violence by the occupation forces alienated much of the population and relative security in the territory was only established after major military operations from September 1977 to March 1979 and by means of resettling parts of the population into strategic hamlets. The disruption of agriculture as a result of the war and the resettlements led to a major famine in which perhaps 100,000 people (of an original population of 650,000) died. Since 1979 fighting has continued, though on a much subdued scale, in the east of the territory. Although an East Timorese has always held the post of governor, the army is in close control of the province and military business operations (q.v.) dominate the coffee and sandalwood (q.v.) industries. Indonesia lifted formal restrictions on visiting the province on 1 January 1989. [0062, 0898, 0902, 0905, 0906, 0913]

EDUCATION. This entry is concerned mainly with formal, Western-style training, but what follows should be read with the understanding that traditional, home-based education has traditionally played an important role in Indonesia and was probably responsible, for instance, for a high level of literacy in precolonial times (see WRITING SYSTEMS). The classic traditional educational institution in Indonesia, derived from Indian models, was the *asrama,* a residential school where pupils gathered to receive largely religious instruction from a *guru* or teacher. This model of instruction was retained after the arrival of Islam (q.v.) in the form of the *pesantren* (q.v.) or *surau*. As in the West, this relatively formal education helped to define for both sexes a period of youth between childhood and adulthood.

European-style education in the archipelago initially followed a similar pattern. Schools were small, locally based, and mostly religiously-oriented. The VOC (q.v.) distrusted the effects of education on its indigenous subjects and gave schools little encouragement, and from 1648 to 1778 the giving of any kind of lessons required a government licence. Only after the Company's fall did extensive, government-sponsored education begin. A Dutch language primary school was set up in Batavia in 1816 followed by a three-year public elementary school in 1849 and a teacher training school in 1852. From 1864, the colonial state maintained so-called Europeesche Lagere Scholen (ELS, European Lower Schools), offering a seven-year Dutch language course, though it was not until 1867 that a department of education was established. Western education at this time was intended primarily for Europeans and it was expected that the children of Dutch residents would return to the Netherlands for more advanced studies if desired. The ELS, however, were opened to 'qualified' Indonesians and some 1,870 were enrolled by 1900. From 1860 the colonial government began to establish Hogere Burger Scholen (HBS, Higher Civil Schools), rigorous secondary schools following the Dutch metropolitan curriculum and so qualifying graduates for admission to Dutch universities.

General education for Indonesians was taken up on a large scale first by the Nederlandsch Zendelinggenootschap (see PROTESTANTISM) from 1830. In 1848, the state set up twenty 'regentschapscholen' (regency schools) to teach the children of the priyayi, but general education for Indonesians was not provided until 1907, when van Heutsz (q.v.) established Volksscholen (*dessascholen*) offering a three-year course in local languages with indigenous teachers. In 1940 ca 45% of children received some education at this level, though graduation rates were low. In 1908 Hollandsch-

Chineesche Scholen (HCS) and in 1914 Hollandsch-Inlandsche Scholen (HIS) were established to provide more advanced primary education to Chinese and Indonesians. The curriculum was much the same as that of the ELS, but the first years were taught in Chinese or Malay/Indonesian. From 1914, a kind of lower secondary education was provided by the MULO (Meer Uitgebreide Lagere Onderwijs, Broader Lower Education), which in turn fed into the Algemene Middelbare Scholen (AMS, General Secondary Schools) from 1919, intended to prepare MULO graduates for tertiary education. The interlinking of the lower education system was completed in 1921 with the creation of so-called *schakelscholen* (bridging schools) to prepare Volksschool graduates for the MULO. The rise of nationalism (q.v.), however, led to Dutch complaints that over-education was producing a kind of intellectual proletariat that was ripe for disruptive ideas and therefore from the mid 1920s the provision of Dutch language education was reduced. See also ASSOCIATION PRINCIPLE.

The emerging Indonesian nationalist movement also realized the importance of education in inculcating values and increasing national self-confidence and from the 1920s, members of the Pergerakan (q.v.) founded large numbers of so-called *wilde scholen* (wild schools), whose diplomas were not recognized by the colonial government. Best known of these were the *sekolah rakyat* (people's schools) of the Sarekat Islam, and the Taman Siswa and Kartini (qq.v.) schools. In September 1932 the colonial government attempted to restrict the operation of wild schools by issuing a 'wild schools ordinance' which required private schools to have government permission, although finance for government schools was being reduced during the Depression (q.v.). A national campaign against the ordinance, led by Ki Hajar Dewantoro of Taman Siswa, succeeded in having the ordinance withdrawn. Wild school numbers reached 2,200 by the late 1930s and an estimated 142,000 pupils were enrolled. In 1904, Dewi Sartika (1884–1947) established Sekolah Isteri (Women's Schools) in West Java to provide education for women.

University-level education began much later in the Netherlands Indies than in British India or French Indochina; Indonesians and Chinese as well as Europeans commonly went to the Netherlands for tertiary education. Quasitertiary education was offered by the Opleidingschool voor Inlandsche Ambtenaren (OSVIA, Training School for Native Civil Servants) and the School tot Opleiding van Inlandsche Artsen (STOVIA, School for the Training of Native Physicians), both founded in 1900. A veterinary school offering advanced secondary training was founded in Bogor in 1907 and a secondary law school in Batavia in 1909. Resident Europeans formed an Indische Universiteitsbeweeging (Indies University Movement) in 1910, but the authorities argued that there were too few high school graduates to support a full university. Instead, a series of tertiary colleges was established, beginning with the Technische Hogeschool (THS, Institute of Technology) in Bandung in 1920, and followed by the Rechtshogeschool (RHS, Law School) in 1924, the Geneeskundige Hogeschool (GHS, Medical School) in 1927, and a Literaire Faculteit (Faculty of Letters) in 1940, all in Batavia. A Landbouwkundige Faculteit (Agricultural Faculty) was founded in Bogor in 1941. A few days before the Japanese landed on Java, the Volksraad (q.v.) passed a resolution merging these faculties into a single university. An estimated 230 Indonesians possessed tertiary education qualifications by 1942. All tertiary institutions were closed by the Japanese at the start of the occupation, but in April 1943 a medical school, the Ika Daigaku, was reestablished (see also HEALTH).

From about January 1946, Republicans conducted limited tertiary education in Jakarta at various Perguruan Tinggi (tertiary colleges); in December 1949 these were merged into Gadjah Mada University in Yogyakarta. The Dutch opened a 'Nooduniversiteit' (emergency university) in Jakarta in January 1946, with faculties of medicine, arts, law, and agriculture, merging these with the other prewar faculties in 1947 to create the Universiteit van Indonesië. In 1950 national literacy was estimated at 10% and a massive expansion of education at all levels took place, with the expansion of both public and private education. Foreign language schools for Indonesians were banned in 1958. Since May 1984 five years of primary education has been compulsory for all Indonesian children.

State support for Muslim education began only in 1937, when the colonial government subsidized the establishment of a Muhammadiyah (q.v.) MULO in Yogyakarta, but after independence, the government allowed the emergence of a full Muslim educational system, run by the Department of Religion, alongside the national secular system under the Department of Education. Primary and secondary schools are classified as *madrasah,* providing 70% secular and 30% religious education and whose diplomas are considered equivalent to those of secular schools, *diniyah,* in which the proportions are reversed and which qualify students mainly for religious and quasireligious careers, and Pendidikan Guru Islam (Islamic teachers colleges), teaching 50% secular and 50% religious material. Muslim tertiary education is provided at 11 Institut Agama Islam Negeri (IAIN, State Islamic Religious Institutes). Religious education is also compulsory in secular schools. See also ISLAM; RELIGION AND POLITICS. [0366, 0483, 0576, 1061–1076]

'EERESCHULD, Een' ('a debt of honor'), title of an August 1899 article by the Dutch lawyer Conrad Theodor van Deventer (1857–1915) in *De Gids,* arguing that the millions of guilders received by the Netherlands state under the Cultivation System (q.v.) and by Dutch companies since 1870 had left the Dutch with a 'debt of honor' to Indonesia, an obligation to raise living standards and bring about economic development. The article contributed to the emergence of the Ethical Policy (q.v.), but only two capital transfers from the Netherlands took place. In 1905, *f*40 million was transferred on condition that it was used for the economic improvement of the Javanese and Madurese, while in 1936, *f*25 million was transferred as compensation to the Indies for reserving part of their market for the Netherlands during the Depression (q.v.). See also BATIG SLOT.

EGYPT, Relations with. See ARAB WORLD, Relations with.

ELECTIONS were first held in the Netherlands Indies in 1903 for members of municipal councils. The franchise was highly restricted and the councils were dominated by Europeans, but with reserved seats for each racial group, these elections provided Indonesia with its first experience of electoral competition (see DECENTRALIZATION). Members of the Volksraad (q.v.) were elected by members of these councils.

Independent Indonesia's first general elections, planned for the late 1940s, were not held until 1955. Voter turnout was 91%. Using proportional representation with effectively a single electoral district for the entire country, they produced what many see as an inconclusive result, the PNI (q.v.) gaining 57 seats with 22.3% of the vote, Masyumi (q.v.) 57 seats (20.9%), NU (q.v.) 45 seats (18.4%), and PKI (q.v.) 39 seats (16.4%) in a parliament of 257. Twenty-four other parties, including independents, were represented. General elections due for 1959 were never held, partly because a substantial gain in PKI votes seemed likely.

Elections have been held approximately every five years under the New Order (q.v.), in 1971, 1977, 1982 and 1987 (for detailed results, see Appendix). Campaigning was restricted to a period 60 days before polling day. Only the government electoral organization Golkar (q.v.) and the two officially sponsored political parties, PDI and PPP (qq.v.), are permitted to contest elections and all have to submit their candidates and campaign slogans to the security authorities for approval. Challenging the Pancasila or the Broad Outlines of State Policy (qq.v.) and attacking racial, social, or religious groups are not permitted, but contestants are permitted to discuss the implementation of the national development program. Voting is not compulsory, but all voters receive an invitation specifying when and where they should vote. A voter selects the party of his/her choice by using a nail to poke a hole through that party's symbol on the ballot paper and then places the ballot in one of three boxes according to party. Results are generally announced within a day or so.

Civil servants normally vote at their offices and are expected, under the doctrine of *monoloyalitas* (q.v.) to vote for Golkar. In the villages, too, Golkar has traditionally drawn extensively on support from the army and the bureaucracy. It has been common, for instance, for local authorities to declare villages *bebas parpol* (free of political parties) and to ban campaigning by nongovernment groups on the grounds that the residents had already decided to vote Golkar. New Order elections are strongly ritual in style. It is not possible that any party but Golkar will win overall and government rhetoric portrays the occasion as one of danger, when the social antagonisms of the 1950s and 1960s risk being revived.

Since 1971, elections have used proportional representation by province, the provincial allocation of seats being weighted to ensure that the provinces on Java, with two thirds of the voters, nonetheless elect only half the members of parliament. [0634, 0684, 0835–0841, 1165]

ELEPHANT (*Elephas maximus*). Native to Sumatra, where they were widely used in warfare and a symbol of royalty, especially in Aceh (q.v.). Although export was periodically banned for these reasons, at other times elephants were extensively traded to other parts of Western Indonesia, especially Java, and to India (q.v.). The wild elephants of Kalimantan are probably feral introductions. See also BOROBUDUR. [0390, 0483, 0945]

ENGLISH EAST INDIA COMPANY, chartered by Queen Elizabeth I in 1600 and, like the Dutch East Indies Company (q.v.), a joint stock company enjoying a national monopoly of trade in the region. The company's first expedition to Java in 1601 brought back so much pepper that the market was glutted and the company began to diversify. It established bases in Banten, Aceh, Makassar, Maluku (qq.v.), and Masulipatam (southern India) in the first decades of C.17, but by the end of the century had been driven out of the archipelago by the Dutch, except for the West Sumatra colony of Bengkulu (q.v.) (see also 'AMBOYNA MASSACRE'). The company was taken over by the British crown in 1858 after the Indian Mutiny. See also BRITAIN, Historical links with. [0375, 0438, 0439, 0448, 0450, 0455]

ENVIRONMENTAL PROTECTION. Three issues have dominated environmental concerns in the Indonesian archipelago since late C.19: (1) the preservation of unique animal and plant species (for which see CON-

SERVATION, Nature); (2) the maintenance of a stable water regime by maintaining forest cover and preventing erosion; and (3) the control of pollution. Current government legislation in these areas is based especially on the 1982 Basic Law on the Environment.

Forest protection for environmental reasons (rather than from illicit collectors of forest products) became an element of Dutch colonial policy only late in C.19, though in the middle of the century Junghuhn (q.v.) had suggested that areas above 500 meters should not be cleared. It was realized already that rainfall and runoff were more regular on forested slopes and that the agricultural prosperity of Java depended in part on leaving a part of the island with its forest cover intact, though the preservation of forests for timber production was also a major consideration. After several years of largely indiscriminate clearing in the 1970s, increasing government attention is now being paid to protection of forests, reforestation (*reboisasi*), and afforestation (*penghijauan*). See also FORESTRY.

Systematic regulations to control pollution (called AMDAL, Analisa Mengenai Dampak Lingkungan, Environmental Impact) were only introduced in 1987 and were enforced first in 1990 after government offices, private firms, and the public had familiarized themselves with its provisions. See also WERENG. [0792–0794, 0954, 0961]

ETHICAL POLICY. Common name given to Dutch colonial policy in the first decades of C.20, following a speech from the throne by Queen Wilhelmina in 1901 announcing: 'As a Christian power, the Netherlands is obliged to carry out government policy in the Indies in the consciousness that the Netherlands has a moral duty to the people of these regions.' This new policy was expressed in a new willingness of government to involve itself in economic and social affairs in the archipelago in the name of rational efficiency. It was a time of improved health care, extended education (q.v.), expansion of communications facilities, irrigation, and other infrastructure, and the commencement of transmigration (q.v.), measures which brought benefits to Western commercial interests as much as to the Indonesians themselves. The Depression of the 1930s (q.v.) led to budget cuts in most of these areas, effectively ending the Ethical Policy. The policy has been criticized most sharply for its paternalist approach, and the sharp contrast between the growing indigenous Indonesian capacity to manage a modern state and economy and the persistent Dutch supervision was one of the factors which strengthened the nationalist movement. See also 'EERESCHULD, Een'; NATIONALISM; *STUW De.* [0556, 0569, 0584]

ETYMOLOGY. Vocabulary in the Indonesian language (q.v.) changes rapidly and the derivation of words has taken on some political significance from time to time. The reforming role of the brief British occupation of Java, for instance, has been emphasized at the expense of the Dutch by folk legend which attributes many Indonesian words to Raffles (q.v.). Since independence there has been some attempt to reduce the number of words in Indonesian which are derived from Dutch, while a growth in the number of formerly Javanese words has been seen as a sign of Javanization (q.v.). *Anda* was introduced as a neutral form of the pronoun 'you' in 1957. The Komisi Bahasa Indonesia coined about 7,000 new words by during World War II, and its successor, the Komisi Istilah (Terminological Commission) had coined or ratified 321,710 new terms by 1970, seeking words first from Malay, second from other Indonesian languages, third from Arabic and Sanskrit, and fourth from European languages. Since the 1970s, however, the press has played a dominant role in the coining of words.

Many new words emerge from acronyms; *raker,* for instance, from *rapat kerja,* means working meeting. Sukarno (q.v.) was especially well known for such coinages, one of his best known being *berdikari,* from *berdiri di atas kaki sendiri,* 'to stand on one's own feet'. Derivations may also be used politically. Opponents of Sutan Syahrir (q.v.) claimed that his name stood for *Saya yang akan hancurkan Republik Indonesia Raya,* 'I am the one who will destroy the great Indonesian Republic'.

EURASIANS. See INDO-EUROPEANS.

EXILE, a common technique in both the Netherlands Indies and Indonesia for the removal of politically troublesome people. From 1854, under the so-called *exorbitante rechten,* in the interests of peace and order, the governor-general could expel from the colony anyone with European or Foreign Oriental status and could exile any Indonesian within the colony. This was an administrative right, not subject to judicial appeal or review, and was employed 1,150 times in the period 1855–1920. Diponegoro (q.v.) was exiled to Manado; E.F.E. Douwes Dekker (q.v.) to Surinam; Sukarno (q.v.) to Flores and Bengkulu; and Hatta and Syahrir (q.v.) and many others to Boven Digul (q.v.) in West New Guinea. For others, going on the *haj* (q.v.) to Mecca was a means of voluntary exile. After independence, figures such as Chaerul Saleh (q.v.) were informally exiled abroad on study tours, while under the New Order many senior army officers have been *didubeskan* ('ambassadored off'). In 1961, Sukarno (q.v.) resumed the right to place citizens under internal exile, and this right was reaffirmed in 1969. Though the inherited provisions of the exorbitante rechten have not been used in New Order Indonesia, the enforced residence of former political prisoners (*tahanan politik,* q.v.) on Buru (q.v.) amounts to much the same thing. The Portuguese practice of exiling dissidents from their African colonies to East Timor contributed to the radicalization of political opinion there. [0573]

EXORBITANTE RECHTEN. See CENSORSHIP; EXILE; GOVERNOR-GENERAL, Office of the.

F

FAMILY PLANNING. In colonial times, the publication of information on birth control techniques was a criminal offense. Sukarno's view that a large population was a sign of national power helped ensure that this remained so after independence, though limited promotion of family planning was carried out from 1952 by the Yayasan Kesejahteraan Keluarga (Foundation for Family Prosperity). The first family planning clinic was established in Jakarta in 1956, followed by the Perkumpulan Keluarga Berencana Indonesia (Indonesian Family Planning Association) in 1957, though both were limited by the technical illegality of their work. Indonesia's population policy was primarily one of transmigration (q.v.) from more to less densely settled areas. Only after the advent of the New Order did family planning become a part of public policy; in 1966 Ali Sadikin, governor of Jakarta (qq.v.), made the city available for a pilot project by the PKBI. In 1967, however, the Suharto government signed the United Nations Declaration on Population and in 1970 established the Badan Koordinasi Keluarga Berencana Nasional (BKKBN, National Family Planning Coordinating Body) which began an extensive program on Java and Bali to spread information on family planning and to provide free contraceptive services. Much of the earliest family planning work was done, however, by the semigovernmental Lembaga Keluarga Berencana Nasional (LKBN, National Family Planning Institute), founded in 1968. From 1974, the campaign was extended from Java and Bali to other islands. The program concentrated on providing information and free contraceptives and was conducted largely without coercion but with a good deal of community pressure and resulted in high acceptor rates (24% by 1977), which have in turn contributed to falling birth rates. See also POPULATION; WOMEN AND MEN. [0184, 0816, 0817]

FEDERALISM. The notion that Indonesia's many ethnic groups might coexist more happily in a relatively decentralized federal state than in a centralized unitary one was a matter of relatively uncontentious discussion by Indonesian nationalists before the World War II. Figures such as Hatta (q.v.) could then be proponents of a federal system for independent Indonesia without in any way compromising their nationalism. The Dutch *bestuurshervorming* law of 1922 (see DECENTRALIZATION) might have encouraged this trend if it had been earlier and more extensively implemented.

In 1946, however, in the midst of the national Revolution, Dutch authorities proposed a federal system as part of their political alternative to the independent Indonesian Republic. Conceived originally as a means of easing the reunification of the country, which had been administratively divided since 1942, federalism soon became a part of Dutch plans to isolate and ultimately to suppress what they saw as the radicalism of the Indonesian Republic. By playing on outer island fears of communism and of Javanese domination, and establishing a series of federal states (*negara*) in the territories they controlled, they hoped to entrench a conservative coalition of bureaucrats, aristocrats, Hindus, and Christians in the constitution of independent Indonesia and so to ensure continuing Dutch political and economic influence. Thus the first of the federal states, the Negara Indonesia Timur (q.v.), NIT, or East Indonesia, covered the entire, ethnically diverse eastern end of the archipelago (except West New Guinea), and was intended as a powerful counterweight to the Indonesian Republic.

As time went on, however, federalism became less a vehicle for political conservatism and more a format for ethnic separatism. Plans were abandoned for a *negara* in Kalimantan because of the island's ethnic diversity and the Negara Pasundan (q.v.), formed in 1948, was explicitly a state of the Sundanese people of West Java. Within the NIT itself, several semiautonomous ethnically-based regions were established from 1947. From July 1948 the federal states and protostates were assembled in a permanent Bijeenkomst voor Federale Overleg (Meeting for Federal Consultation) and it was the BFO with which the Republic of Indonesia fused to form the RIS (q.v.), which gained independence in 1949. The official recognition of ethnic subnationalism, however, later encouraged the revolt of the Republik Maluku Selatan (q.v.) and provided a basis for the Dutch to retain control of West New Guinea (see IRIAN) after the transfer of sovereignty in 1949.

This Dutch experiment with federalism wholly compromised the idea for nationalists and the federal negara were quickly dissolved after the transfer of sovereignty, the last disappearing on 17 August 1950. Since then, the topic has been off the political agenda. See also NATIVE TROOPS; PROVINCES; SUCCESSION. [0634, 0656, 0767, 0916]

FEDERASI BURUH SELURUH INDONESIA. See LABOR.

'FIFTH FORCE' (Angkatan Kelima). During Indonesia's Confrontation (q.v.) with Malaysia, Sukarno called at one point for 21 million volunteers to fight Malaysia. This idea was taken up in a smaller way by the leaders of the PRC who in November 1964 offered Indonesia 100,000 small arms for the new force, and by the PKI (q.v.), which pointed to Article 30 of the Constitution ('Every citizen shall have the right and duty to participate in the defence of the state') and argued that victory in the struggle demanded the arming of the workers and peasants. In May 1965, Sukarno described such a body as a 'fifth force' alongside the four existing armed forces (army, navy, air force, and police, qq.v.) and ordered the existing armed forces to prepare plans for it. Zhou Enlai repeated China's offer of arms in April 1965 and in July the air force began training some 2,000 PKI civilians at Halim air force base. The army saw this as a PKI attempt to gain weapons for an insurrection and resisted the proposal strenuously. In the weeks before the GESTAPU (q.v.) coup of September, extensive rumors circulated of a clandestine shipment of arms from the People's Republic of China to equip the force, though the truth of these rumors has never been proven. [0663, 0705]

FILM. Indonesia's film industry began before World War II, with several local studios, especially Tan Brothers, producing a range of films, mainly on romantic and adventure themes. Under the Filmordonnantie of 1925, the colonial government could ban films on moral or social grounds (including political) and film was little used by the nationalist movement, although the GERINDO leader A.K. Gani (q.v.) starred in some productions. The Japanese sponsored much film work on Java during World War II, partly for propaganda reasons and partly because of the absence of foreign entertainment films. United States (q.v.) films were widely shown during the 1950s, though Chinese and Indian films also held an important share of the market. This sparked a hostile reaction which criticized both the effect of foreign films on the domestic industry and the allegedly corrupting effect of displaying Western lifestyles. During the early 1960s, the campaign against Western film was spearheaded by the left-wing cultural organization LEKRA (q.v.) while local filmmakers produced a number of left-oriented films. After the GESTAPU (q.v.) coup of 1965, the Indonesian film industry was thoroughly purged and many films of the early 1960s were destroyed. Contemporary filmmaking tends to concentrate on romantic and historical topics, the most notable recent production being *Pengkhianatan G30s/PKI* ('The Treason of GESTAPU/PKI', 1984). [0138, 0139]

FISHERIES. Fishing has been a major industry in the archipelago since early times and salt fish were always a major trade item between the coast and inland regions, controlled by Chinese middlemen rather than by the fishermen themselves. Fish still provide over 60% of the protein intake of most Indonesians and the industry employs approximately 1.3 million, though fishermen are traditionally one of the poorest groups and PKI (q.v.) fishermen's organizations were strong before 1965. Major technological change took place after 1965 with the introduction of trawlers and later purse seines by Chinese entrepreneurs. This modern sector which in 1980 accounted for 23% of the catch but only 2% of the fishing fleet aroused much resentment amongst traditional fishermen, leading to violence in many areas. Trawling was banned by the government off Java and Sumatra in 1980 and elsewhere except the Arafura Sea in 1983. [0319, 0324, 0803]

FLAG. The national flag of red over white was formally adopted by the nationalist movement at the second Youth Congress in 1928. See also YOUTH PLEDGE.

'FLOATING MASS', policy formulated in the 1975 Law on Political Parties and Golkar, separating the populace, especially in rural areas, from political activity except at elections (q.v.). It is intended to ensure that the masses remain fully responsive to government direction for the sake of national development. See also DEVELOPMENT IDEOLOGY; MONOLOYALITAS. [0680]

FLORES (from Portuguese *labo de flores,* cape of flowers), island in Nusatenggara. In C.13, the kingdom of Larantuka came under rule of Majapahit (q.v.), but a century later Makassar (q.v.) was the dominant power. Portuguese missionaries arrived in 1613 though extensive conversion to Catholicism did not take place until C.19. In C.17, the island was dominated by the Topasses (see SOLOR ARCHIPELAGO; TIMOR). After Makassar submitted to the VOC in 1660 and 1667, the Dutch regarded Flores as within their domains, and in 1838 and 1856 they sent military expeditions to suppress slavery and the plundering of shipwrecks. The island was not fully conquered until 1907–08. [0508]

FOREIGN INVESTMENT denotes primarily the employment of foreign capital in productive operations such as plantations and factories. Direct foreign capital investment remained at a low level for much of the colonial period. The colony was opened to European private enterprise in the 1870s under the so-called Liberal Policy (q.v.), but most capital was generated locally by the reinvestment of profits, rather than by import. Only after the sugar crisis of 1884 and during the 1890s and 1900s, when many estates contracted debenture loans, did significant capital transfer take place (see also

BATIG SLOT). Few restrictions, however, were placed on foreign investment in colonial times, partly because the Netherlands wished to involve the great powers, especially Britain and the United States (qq.v.) in the defence of the colony.

During the Japanese occupation, existing enterprises were first taken over by the occupation authorities and then parcelled out both to government departments in lieu of taxation revenue and to Japanese private companies (see SUGAR), but there was no significant introduction of capital. At the start of the Indonesian Revolution, the Republic issued a Political Manifesto guaranteeing the security of foreign investments, partly to facilitate an agreement with the Dutch, partly to reassure the United States and Britain (see also DIPLOMASI AND PERJUANGAN). The final settlement between the Republic and the Dutch in 1949 provided for protection of foreign investments against nationalization (q.v.) and excessive taxation, but many foreign firms, such as the Koninklijke Paketvaart Maatschappij, KPM (q.v.), found their economic room to maneuver heavily constricted by foreign exchange and labor regulations, and began to disinvest. The nationalization of Dutch investments in 1957 further discouraged foreign investment, as did the seizure of some British and American interests in 1963. Under Guided Democracy (q.v.) a number of production-sharing agreements were concluded, especially with Japanese companies, for production of oil, tin, and timber.

Restoration of a favorable climate for foreign investment was a major part of New Order economic policies from 1966 (see BADAN PERENCANAAN PEMBANGUNAN NASIONAL) and a law on Foreign Investment Capital (*Penanaman Modal Asing*) was passed in January 1967, giving a renewed guarantee against nationalization, a three-year tax holiday, freedom to repatriate profits, full authority to select management, and some exemption from import duties to foreign firms willing to invest in the country. Foreign investment reached a value of US$4.72 billion in 1989. See also FORESTRY. [0275, 0281, 0285, 0286, 0325, 0738, 0768]

FOREIGN POLICY. Indonesia's foreign policy was originally formulated as an adjunct to the struggle for independence in the 1940s (see DIPLOMASI AND PERJUANGAN). This period established two persistent principles in Indonesian foreign policymaking. First was a deep suspicion of foreign intentions towards Indonesia. Indonesian policymakers see their country as wealthy and strategically located but politically and economically vulnerable to foreign adventurers. The chief focus of these suspicions has varied: in the 1950s and early 1960s it was the United States and the Netherlands (qq.v.); later it was China and to a lesser extent Vietnam (qq.v.) for political reasons and Japan (q.v.) for economic ones. Australia and the Arab world (qq.v.) have also come under suspicion. Second, while eschewing formal military alliances as incompatible with an 'active and independent' foreign policy, Indonesia has sought international friends in a variety of forums: the South East Asia League (q.v.) in 1948, the Non-Aligned Movement in the 1950s and early 1960s, the CONEFO and the brief Jakarta-Hanoi-Peking axis (see NEKOLIM) of the mid-sixties and since 1967 the Association of Southeast Asian Nations (q.v.).

The best-remembered elements of Indonesian foreign policy, however, have been less to do with these general principles than with questions of national security. Indonesia's long-running conflict with the Netherlands over the province of Irian (q.v.) was an attempt to recover what it saw as part of the national territory; Confrontation (q.v.) with Britain and Malaysia (qq.v.) was partly over the presence of British bases close to

Indonesian territory and over the right of Indonesia, as the largest regional power, to be consulted on matters of regional political development; the messy annexation of East Timor (q.v.) was an attempt to forestall the emergence of a left-wing government on Indonesia's borders; and Indonesia's often tactless handling of Papua New Guinea (q.v.) is related to the threat it sees from OPM (q.v.) guerrillas in Irian. Because of these security dimensions, foreign policy is often effectively negotiated between the Departments of Foreign Affairs (DEPLU) and Defence (HANKAM). For a list of foreign ministers, see the Appendix. See also ARCHIPELAGIC CONCEPT and entries on relations with the Arab World, Australia, China, Japan, the Netherlands, the Philippines, the Soviet Union, the United Nations, the United States, and Vietnam. [0721, 0728, 0730, 0742, 0745, 0766]

FORESTRY. From early times, forest products were major items of trade in the archipelago, while the teak (q.v.) forests of Java were an important economic resource for the rulers of Java for housing, shipbuilding, and firewood. A government forestry service (Dienst van het Boschwezen) was established on Java under Daendels (q.v.) and with it emerged a category of forest villages exempt from other forms of taxation in exchange for carrying out the often difficult and onerous tasks of forest management. The colonial government introduced German experts to give training and advice from 1849 and laid down comprehensive forest laws in 1865. Patrols of the state forests began in 1880. During the Japanese occupation, large areas of forest were cleared both for firewood and construction and to release land for the planting of other crops, and a shortage of fuel during the Revolution led to further cutting. In the early 1960s, the PKI (q.v.) often took the side of peasants in the vicinity of state forests in claiming land or the right to collect firewood.

Logging was a major area of foreign investment from the start of the New Order, since the allocation of logging permits and the clearing of tropical forests required relatively little economic infrastructure. Typically concessions were granted to joint operations between large Western firms such as Weyerhaeuser and Indonesian sleeping partners who contributed no capital to the venture and were members or friends of the ruling elite. Timber became the country's second largest export after oil and in 1973 Indonesia exported 18 million cubic meters of tropical timber.

In 1975, the Indonesian government began to encourage loggers to process timber in Indonesia rather than exporting raw logs. In 1980, each company's export of raw logs was limited to 32% of its total output, and on 1 January 1985 all export of unprocessed logs was banned. This policy led many Western firms such as Weyerhaeuser to withdraw from Indonesia, but their place has been taken by Japanese and Korean firms and a dramatic expansion of plywood production has taken place. Indonesia is now the world's largest exporter of plywood, with annual exports totalling $1000 million in value, and 29% of the country's landmass is under logging concessions. Reafforestation has now become a major part of government policy, especially in order to diminish problems of erosion and desiccation, and a number of concessionaires who failed to meet their reforestation obligations have not been renewed. See also ENVIRONMENTAL PROTECTION; CONSERVATION, Nature. [0235, 0264]

FOWL (*Gallus gallus*), probably native to the archipelago; undomesticated jungle fowl are still common in some areas, though there is evidence that the Austronesians also brought fowl with them (see MIGRATIONS). Cockfighting was a common pastime in villages in most parts of Indonesia in early times and can still be seen widely in Bali (q.v.). It probably began as a ritual blood offering at village religious ceremonies, but became important as a source of entertainment and an opportunity for gambling (q.v.). Puritanical rulers have attempted to ban it, but with limited success. [0483, 0943, 1016]

FRETILIN (Frente Revolucionária do Timor Leste Independente, Revolutionary Front for an Independent East Timor). Founded 22 August 1974 as the ASDT (Associação Social Democrática Timorense, Timorese Social Democratic Association), Fretilin was a grouping of young East Timor (q.v.) intellectuals and civil servants, many of them Portuguese-Timorese, who pressed for the territory's immediate independence after the Portuguese coup of 1974. Liberation movements in Africa (q.v.) influenced not only the choice of the name Fretilin but also the party's program, which included literacy classes, the establishment of cooperatives, and the creation of a multitude of affiliated mass organizations for women, farmers, students, etc.

Fretilin defeated a coup in Dili by the conservative UDT in August 1975 and began to establish an administration, but did not declare independence, in the form of the Democratic Republic of East Timor (q.v.) until November 1975, when the Indonesian invasion from the west was already under way. Driven from Dili and other centers in December 1975, Fretilin retained control of most of the countryside until September 1977 to 1979 when a series of Indonesian operations shattered both its political leadership and its army, the FALINTIL (Forças Armadas de Libertação Nacional de Timor, Armed Forces for the National Liberation of Timor). Its area of operation has been restricted largely to rugged country in the east of the territory. Its leader since 1981 has been Kay Rala Xanana Gusmão. [0898, 0902, 0905, 0913]

FRONT DEMOKRASI RAKYAT (FDR, People's Democratic Front), coalition of leftwing parties (PKI, Partai Buruh, Partai Sosialis and PESINDO [qq.v.]) formed in January 1948 following the fall of the Amir Syarifuddin (q.v.) government. Until 1948 the leftwing parties had been in government and generally pursued a line of negotiation with the Dutch and accommodation, in the short term, with Western business interests, but the formation of the FDR marked a radicalization of their policy and shift to promotion of armed struggle and rejection of foreign investment. The FDR dissolved on 1 September 1948 when the parties merged into the PKI. See also DIPLOMASI AND PERJUANGAN; MADIUN AFFAIR. [0563, 0656, 0662, 0749]

G

GABUNGAN POLITIK INDONESIA (GAPI, Indonesian Political Federation), assembly of Indonesian nationalist organizations formed in May 1939 on the initiative especially of M.H. Thamrin of the PARINDRA (q.v.) and including GERINDO and PSII (qq.v.). It called for Indonesian self-determination and an elected parliament, using the slogan 'Indonesia berparlemen' (Indonesia with a parliament). In December 1939 it sponsored a Kongres Rakyat Indonesia (Indonesian People's Congress), which called unsuccessfully for cooperation between Indonesians and Dutch in the face of the deteriorating world situation. See also SUTARJO PETITION. [0543]

GAJAH MADA, prime minister of Majapahit from 1330 to 1364. As a young man he helped defeat rebels against King Jayanegara, but later had Jayanegara killed after he had stolen Gajah Mada's wife. Under Queen Tribuwana he rose to become prime minister and was effective ruler of the kingdom until his death. He resumed the expansionist military program of King Kertanegara and is said to have sworn not to consume *palapa* (q.v.) until the Outer Islands (*Nusantara,* q.v.) had been conquered. Majapahit maintained a powerful fleet, but it is not certain that it had any real control beyond the shores of Java. Gajah Mada's palapa oath was widely publicized by Muhammad Yamin (q.v.) as an early manifestation of nationalism. [0395]

GALANGA (*lengkuas, laos*), the dried aromatic rhizome of *Alpinia galanga* (Zingiberaceae), traded to China during the Wei and Sui dynasties (385–618 A.D.) and to Europe. [0751, 0938]

GAMBIER (*Uncaria gambier* Rubiaceae, *gambir*), woody vine of unknown origin, generally grown in conjunction with pepper. Its leaves are used in tanning and are boiled to produce an extract which is chewed with betel (q.v.). Commercial plantation production began in Riau (q.v.) in the 1730s, but gave way by 1900 to rubber production. [0245, 0246, 0938]

GAMBLING existed in Indonesia in many forms from early times on contests such as boat races and cockfights (see FOWL) and was soon recognized as a useful source of state revenue. Raffles (q.v.) organized a lottery to help pay for the postal road along the northern coast of Java. Gambling farms were allocated on the *pacht* (q.v.) system and were commonly operated by Chinese. On the plantations in East Sumatra (q.v.) gambling became an important means for planters to keep their workforce tied by bonds of indebtedness. The Netherlands Indies government ran a state lottery which was taxed at 21% (20% for the government, 1% for the poor). Although the Sarekat Islam (q.v.) and other religious and nationalist parties campaigned strongly against government promotion of gambling, governments after independence have found the sponsoring of lotteries and casinos a convenient and lucrative source of finance. Religious and social organizations have consistently objected, especially on the grounds of its effects on the poor. Gambling was formally banned throughout the country in 1981, but in 1985 the government introduced soccer pools, called *porkas* ('forecast'), to finance sport. Tickets purchased in the porkas are formally designated as donations to social projects, with prizes, though even this is banned in Aceh (q.v.). The net revenue from the porkas in 1988 was ca Rp 962,400 million. See also SADIKIN, Ali. [0293, 0483]

GAMELAN. Traditional gong-chime music of Indonesia. Neolithic lithophones (stone slabs tuned to a seven-note scale) have been found in Vietnam and these may have been part of a general Southeast Asian musical tradition represented in Indonesia by (wooden) xylophones which have not survived. The first reliable traces of music in the archipelago, however, are cast bronze gongs resembling kettle drums which reached Indonesia in about 300 B.C. with the spread of Dongson culture from Vietnam (q.v.). They were probably used first for signalling in battle, but soon took on a ceremonial significance. The so-called 'Moon' of Pejeng in Bali is one such 'drum'. The first gongs in Indonesia were produced soon after on Java and were probably cast and hammered, rather than directly cast like the Dongson instruments (see METALWORKING). By C.2 or 1 B.C., these gongs, large kettle-like objects with a raised boss suspended horizontally on cords, were made with specific pitches in three-note gamelan ensembles. See also ALOR.

From this basis, the Javanese gamelan elaborated into a great variety of form and more complex instrumentation. A five-tone scale (*slendro*) was in use probably by C.6 or 7, and the seven-tone *pelog* by C.12. The *gong agung,* a larger, flatter, vertically suspended gong with a deep pitch and resonant voice appeared in C.10. The *saron,* or metallophone, was added in C.6 or 7 and may have been based on traditional xylophones. These instruments create interlocking strata of rhythms, said by some to derive from the rhythm of mortars used to husk rice. Bamboo flutes (*suling*) and spike fiddles (*gending* or *rebab*) were in use by C.8, the plucked zither (*celempung* or *kecapi*) by C.14, and the oboe (*serunai,* q.v.) perhaps a century later; all these instruments, and later the voice, added a melodic line of a kind not possible on the basic gamelan. This complexity turned the drum (*kendang*) into the pivotal instrument of the ensemble as rhythm-giver. Nonetheless, no true solo tradition has developed; the basic instruments of a gamelan cannot be tuned and are manufactured as a single entity, rather than a fortuitous assembly of instruments. Most players are expected to be able to shift easily from one instrument to another.

Bronze gamelan ensembles reached Bali (q.v.) around C.10, generally displacing traditional wind and string instruments. Around 22 distinct gamelan types are still in use on Bali. During the Majapahit (q.v.) era (C.13–16), gongs and gamelan ensembles were apparently exported extensively from Java and Bali to other parts of the archipelago and to the Southeast Asian mainland, though development of distinctive local styles was rapid.

Gamelan on Java has become 'high' art associated with the courts and with ritual (one scholar has described it as 'music not to listen to'), but it is nonetheless played on a great number of occasions, though increasingly the use of cassettes is reducing demand for musicians. On Bali, gamelan remains much more popular, partly because of the importance of musical offering in Hindu ceremonies and partly because musicians have consciously developed brighter rhythms and more exciting forms. *Kebyar* style on Bali now recognizes individual musicians, composers, and dancers as artists. See also DANGDUT; KRONCONG; MUSIC.

Gamelan has attracted considerable attention amongst Western musicians. Claude Debussy was inspired by gamelan performances at the Paris Exposition of 1896 to include gamelan motifs in his composition, while Olivier Messiaen has also made extensive use of gamelan themes. [0068, 0103, 0115–117, 0121, 0126, 0127, 0130, 0131, 0134]

GANGSTERS. See BANDITRY.

GANI, Adnan Kapau (1905–58), Indonesian nationalist and businessman from South Sumatra, trained as a physician. In the prewar period, he starred in various quasinationalist romantic films, such as *Asmara Murni* (Pure Passion, 1940). During the Indonesian Revolution, he was military governor of South Sumatra and later Minister of Economic Affairs of the Republic and built up a fortune trading rubber and pepper (qq.v.) from South Sumatra. See also FILM; PALEMBANG. [0563]

GARIS BESAR HALUAN NEGARA. See MAJELIS PERMUSYAWARATAN RAKYAT.

GARUDA. 1. Mythological eagle, the vehicle of the god Vishnu and the conqueror of serpents in Hindu mythology. In 1951, it was chosen as the Republic's official coat of arms, with a symbolic representation of the Pancasila (q.v.) on a shield around its neck and the motto *Bhinneka tunggal ika* (q.v.). 2. Indonesia's international airline, formed on 31 March 1950. Initially a joint venture with KLM, it became wholly Indonesian in 1954. After a period of declining standards and profitability in the late 1950s and early 1960s, and the loss of many staff in the purges of 1965–66, Garuda improved its position under Wiweko Suparno (president 1968–84), who expanded the fleet of wide-bodied jets as well as its domestic routes, though at the cost of a considerable accumulation of debt. Merpati Nusantara Airlines, founded in 1962, operates domestic flights only and now is a Garuda subsidiary. See also AIR SERVICES; INDONESIAN AIRWAYS.

GAYO, ethnic group in the highland areas of southern Aceh (q.v.), culturally intermediate between the Acehnese and Batak (q.v.) peoples. Muslim since C.17, they were incorporated into the Acehnese kingdom by Iskandar Muda and were annexed to the Netherlands Indies in 1904. Strong local resistance continued until 1913. There is a strong tradition of *merantau* (q.v.).

GEERTZ, Clifford (b.1926), American anthropologist who formulated a number of important concepts for the understanding of Indonesian society, especially agricultural involution and shared poverty (qq.v.). His major work, however, is anthropological and emphasizes the cultural meaning of human actions. See also 'MOJOKUTO' PROJECT. [1013–1016, 1017–1019, 1039, 1118, 1119, 1157]

GELIJKSTELLING. See RACE.

GENEESKUNDIGE HOGESCHOOL. See EDUCATION; HEALTH.

GENERATIONS. Because of the succession of dramatic political changes in C.20 Indonesia, the notion of generational groups has been a strong one in Indonesian historiography. The term *Angkatan '45* (Generation of '45) was originally applied by Jassin (q.v.) in 1951 to writers active immediately after the Declaration of

Independence, notably Chairil Anwar and Idrus (qq.v.), who transformed the literary use of the Indonesian language, but the expression soon became general for the former *pemuda* (q.v.), that is, the young people who had fought for independence after 1945. *Angkatan '45* remains the name of the official organization of veterans of the Revolution (q.v.). The students who helped to topple Sukarno after 1965 referred to themselves as *Angkatan '66,* while later student activists have sometimes identified themselves as *Angkatan* '74, '78, and so on. Some historians have identified 'generations' of '08, '26/'27 or '28 which are associated with Budi Utomo, the Youth Pledge (qq.v.), or the uprisings of the PKI (q.v.). It is in the Indonesian army that the notion of 'generation' is perhaps most apt, since senior positions were occupied from the 1940s to the 1980s by men who were young during the Revolution (see NASUTION; SUHARTO). The term *angkatan* also means 'force' as in Angkatan Kelima, or Fifth Force (q.v.).

GERAKAN RAKYAT INDONESIA (GERINDO, Indonesian People's Movement), left wing nationalist party formed 24 May 1937—its leaders including A.K. Gani, Amir Syarifuddin, and Muhammad Yamin (qq.v.)—to succeed the Sukarnoist PARTINDO (q.v.) and to oppose the conservative PARINDRA (q.v.). More strongly antifascist than anticolonialist, it attempted to cooperate with the colonial government against the Japanese threat but received little attention. Yamin left the party in mid 1939 and its activities were curtailed severely from May 1940 by the declaration of a State of War and Siege. [0543]

GERAKAN SEPTEMBER TIGA PULUH (G-30-S, GESTAPU, September 30th Movement). Late on the evening of 30 September 1965, army units led by Lt. Col. Untung launched a limited coup in Jakarta ostensibly to remove a Council of Generals (Dewan Jendral) said to be plotting against Sukarno (q.v.) with United States (q.v.) and British help. They killed six leading generals (Ahmad Yani [q.v.], Suprapto, S. Parman, Haryono, Sutoyo Siswomiharjo, and D.I. Panjaitan), seized state radio and telecommunications facilities and declared a revolutionary council (Dewan Revolusi). General A.H. Nasution (q.v.) escaped the plotters, though his daughter was killed in the melee. A lesser coup took place in Central Java involving units of the Diponegoro Division. The coup was crushed within 24 hours by KOSTRAD (q.v.) forces under General Suharto (q.v.) and Siliwangi Division units. These events (most of them on 1 October rather than 30 September) laid the basis for a gradual seizure of power by Suharto and the installation of the so-called New Order (q.v.). The security organization KOPKAMTIB (q.v.) was put in place to suppress remnants of the coup; the PKI (q.v.) was banned for its alleged role, and left wing elements were purged from the bureaucracy, the armed forces and society in general by imprisonment and massacre (see MASSACRES OF 1965/66). Untung, other direct participants in the coup and senior left wing figures were put on trial in the special tribunal MAHMILLUB (q.v.). For many years, from November 1973, KOPKAMTIB required citizens to obtain a certificate of noninvolvement in the coup (*Surat Bebas G-30-S*) in order to travel or to obtain certain kinds of work. This has now been substituted by a general requirement that those holding sensitive posts (including in the education system and the oil industry) come from a clean (*bersih*) social environment.

Conservative forces and public opinion in general seem to have attributed the coup immediately to the PKI and this remains the official view; G-30-S/PKI is now the common official term for both the coup and the party. This conclusion is supported by some circumstantial evidence, such as the apparent enthusiastic response to the coup by the party newspaper, *Harian Rakjat,* and the general difficulty of the PKI's political position which might have made a coup seem attractive. Evidence of direct PKI involvement in planning the coup, however, is slender and is mainly based on dubious confessions and on testimony concerning a so-called *Biro Khusus* (Special Bureau) of the PKI formed to recruit military officers for the party. Those arguing that the party is unlikely to have planned the coup point to its failure to follow up on the actions of the 30 September Movement in Jakarta. Outside Indonesia, observers have suggested that the coup was the work of a group of middle-ranking army and senior air force officers patriotically concerned over their superiors' hostility to Sukarno (q.v.) and that Sukarno himself may have inspired them. Some have speculated that Suharto planned or contributed to the affair in a Machiavellian plot to remove Sukarno, the army's commanding officers, and the PKI. That no orthodox scholarly interpretation has yet emerged is due partly to the formidable problems of evidence and plausibility, partly to the writings of Crouch and others which emphasize the extent to which military power was already firmly entrenched in government and hence the relative unimportance of the events which precipitated the transition to formal military rule. See also ARMY; 'CORNELL REPORT'; GUIDED DEMOCRACY; SUPERSEMAR. [0627, 0629, 0631, 0642, 0646, 0653, 0663, 0665, 0761]

GERAKAN WANITA INDONESIA (GERWANI, Indonesian Women's Movement), left wing women's movement, founded on 4 June 1950 as GERWIS (Gerakan Wanita Indonesia Sedar, Movement of Aware Indonesian Women), primarily to lobby for women's interests in the government. In March 1954, it took the name GERWANI, becoming increasingly close to, though never formally affiliated with, the PKI (q.v.). It worked for equal rights of women and men in marriage (q.v.) and greater penalties for rape and abduction, as well as establishing kindergartens and midwifery and literacy courses. In 1961 it claimed 9 million members. In the suppression of the left in Indonesia after 1965, special attention was given to the destruction of GERWANI, on the grounds that it allegedly encouraged women to abandon their duties within the family and promoted sexual promiscuity. See also SEX, Political significance of; WOMEN AND MEN. [0822]

GERILYA (guerrilla warfare), the period following the Second 'Police Action' (q.v.) during which the Indonesian Republic outside Aceh (q.v.) existed only as a network of civilian and military personnel who refused to submit to the Dutch. It came to an end with the restoration of Yogyakarta (q.v.) to the Republic in July 1949. See also DEFENCE POLICY. [0652, 0663, 0714]

GERMANY, Historical links with. In C.17 and 18, Germans were prominent amongst the European inhabitants of the Indies. The scientists Junghuhn, Reinwardt (qq.v.), and Blume conducted important research, many Germans served in the colonial army, and German Protestant missions were active in the region. German industrialization in C.19 made Germany a major market for Netherlands Indies products and major German commercial penetration began under the Liberal Policy (q.v.), with the shipping and trading interests of Norddeutscher Lloyd becoming most important. The Straits-und-Sunda-Syndikat, founded 1911, took major interests in trade, plantations, and mining, and by 1912 German investment had reached 120–180 million marks, ranking fourth after Dutch, British, and Franco-Belgian capital. Germany's late unification (1871) left it little chance for annexation of indigenous states in the region and ambitions to seize Portuguese Timor and/or part or all of the Netherlands Indies were repeatedly thwarted by British naval power. German business thus aimed at greater access to the colony through commercial penetration of the Netherlands. Germany's respect for Dutch neutrality in World War I aimed partly at preserving its investments and coaling facilities in the Indies from seizure by Britain. German citizens in the Netherlands Indies, including the painter Walter Spies (1895–1942), were interned after the German occupation of the Netherlands in 1940, partly to forestall a Vichy-style claim to the colony, but many were released under the Japanese. [0750, 0762]

GINGER (*Zingiber officinale* Zingiberaceae), prized for the hot flavor of its rhizome, which has been used extensively for culinary and medicinal purposes. It is perhaps native to East Java, but has been cultivated widely since early times. Potted ginger plants were often carried aboard ships travelling in and from the archipelago for consumption as a protection against scurvy. [0751, 0938]

GIYANTI, Treaty of, signed in 1755 by the Dutch East Indies Company (q.v.) and the rebel prince Mangkubumi, partitioned the rump of the kingdom of Mataram (q.v.) into the Sunanate of Surakarta (q.v.) under Pakubuwono III and the Sultanate of Yogyakarta (q.v.) under Mangkubumi, who took the name Hamengkubuwono I. [0485]

GIYUGUN. See PEMBELA TANAH AIR.

GOA. See MAKASSAR.

GOLD. Ancient Indian texts vaguely refer to Southeast Asia as Suvarnadwipa ('Land of Gold') and in his *Guide to Geography,* Claudius Ptolemy (ca 90–168) described a

'Golden Chersonese' or peninsula in the Southeast Asian region, which many scholars have identified as Sumatra and/or the Malay peninsula. It seems, however, that major exports of gold from the archipelago did not begin until C.1, after the emperor Vespasian banned the export of gold from the Roman empire. At various times, Banjarmasin and Minangkabau (qq.v.) were major centers of the gold trade. Gold coins were minted in the region from C.8 (see CURRENCY). Major gold extraction began in western Kalimantan in the 1740s, largely in the hands of Chinese (see KALIMANTAN; KONGSI WARS), and in mid C.19 the same area was covered with concessions to around 150 European mining companies, most of which failed within a few years. In 1987 a further gold rush began in the interior of East Kalimantan. [0424, 0426, 0451, 0518]

GOLKAR (Golongan Karya, Functional Groups, formerly Sekber, *i.e.,* Sekretariat Bersama [Joint Secretariat], Golkar), formed in October 1964 by army leaders to succeed the Badan Kerja Sama (q.v.) as a coordinating body for and later a federation of anticommunist social organizations (a number of which were themselves federations, especially SOKSI, KOSGORO [qq.v.], and MKGR [Musyawarah Kekeluargaan Gotong Royong]). Golkar was of relatively little importance until about 1971, when it became a vehicle for New Order plans to reshape the electoral system. The organization itself remained a federation of social groups, but the name Golkar became a rubric under which people could vote for the government in successive elections. The strength of Golkar as a vote winner came from the military and civil service backing it received at election time, not from its own cadres, and indeed it had no individual members at all and little organizational life between elections.

In October 1983, Golkar's appearance changed dramatically with the appointment of the state secretary Sudharmono as president and Sarwono Kusumaatmaja as secretary-general and with the decision to open Golkar to individual membership. A crash recruitment campaign was announced and by 1988, when Sudharmano resigned in favor of Lt. Gen. Wahono, Golkar had nine million members on its books. Opinions differ of whether this change is significant; many new members have presumably joined for career or social reasons, rather than out of political commitment and there is no doubt that Golkar's electoral support would plummet without military and bureaucratic backing. On the other hand, the organization's opening to individual membership raises the possibility that it will develop its own cadre and that it may become more responsive to interests of the growing middle class. See also ELECTIONS; MONOLOYALITAS. [0590, 0676, 0680, 0829]

GORONTALO, city and kingdom in northern Sulawesi. The Suwawa kingdom was founded here in C.8, but its links with the C.14 trading kingdom of Gorontalo are unknown. The area was dominated by Ternate (q.v.) in C.15 and 16 and the vassal King Matolodulakiki declared Islam (q.v.) the state religion in C.16. A federated kingdom of Lima Pohalaa emerged in 1673.

GOTONG ROYONG, mutual self-help, was said to be the principle inspiring village life throughout Indonesia, especially on Java (see DESA). While the existence of social differentiation in the village was acknowledged, under gotong royong all members of the village had a right and a duty to participate in the economic activities of other villagers. Thus, for instance, if a house were to be built all would join in the construction, or if a field were to be harvested, all had a right to take part and to receive a share of the crop as their reward. The share a harvester received was intended to be in proportion to the amount she or he had collected, but as the number of harvesters grew with the village population, the share of the crop received by the harvesters en masse tended to grow, in accord with the principles of gotong royong. Landlords, however, have often tried to restrict access to the harvest to smaller groups of privileged workers, sometimes entirely from outside the village, in order to increase their own crop share and to ensure a more docile workforce. See also LAND REFORM; RICE. [0590, 0842]

GOVERNOR-GENERAL, Office of the, post created in 1610 by the directors of the Dutch East Indies Company (q.v.) to centralize control over the Company's trade operations in the East and to organize its military operations. The governor-general was also in charge of the administration of law (q.v.) in the colony. Headquarters of the governor-general were first on Ambon (q.v.), but shifted under J.P. Coen to Batavia (qq.v.). From 1815 to 1848 he was appointed personally by the Dutch king, thereafter by the Crown on the advice of cabinet. From 1815–36 and 1854–1925 the governor-general (also known as the *Landvoogd*) ruled jointly with the Raad van Indië (q.v.), but he remained the sole official point of contact between the colonial government and the metropolitan power: all instructions and requests from The Hague passed formally through the governor-general. A lieutenant governor-general was occasionally appointed, and under H.J. van Mook (q.v.), when no governor-general was appointed, this was the highest administrative post in the colony. In November 1948, the post of governor-general was abolished and replaced by that of *Hoge Vertegenwoordiger van de Kroon* (HVK, High Representative of the Crown). For list of governors-general, see the Appendix. See also COMMISSIONER-GENERAL; EXORBITANTE RECHTEN; NETHERLANDS, Constitutional relationship with Indonesia. [0375, 0601]

GOWA. See MAKASSAR.

GRASS, major but little recognized crop grown as fodder for horses and cattle (qq.v.). Until early C.20, grass was also imported from Australia (q.v.). [0936, 0938]

GREATER SUNDAS. See JAVA; KALIMANTAN; SULAWESI; SUMATRA.

GREEN DESERT. See ALANG-ALANG.

GREEN REVOLUTION, general term for the dramatic increase in agricultural production, especially of rice (q.v.) begun in the mid 1960s. The program started as an agricultural extension program in the Karawang area of West Java in 1963 and from 1964 was extended to the rest of the island under the name BIMAS (Bimbingan Massal, Mass Guidance), covering 462,000 ha by 1966 and over 2 million ha by 1969. The program includes the introduction of new high-yielding varieties (HYV) of rice, new cultivation techniques, especially with machinery, extended irrigation, and the use of pesticides and fertilizer and allows up to five crops in two years, and is said to have increased production on Java from an average 2.58 tonne/ha in 1968 to 4.76 in 1985. It was supported by the international chemical producers CIBA and Hoechst. Problems with the program have included the vulnerability of HYVs to disease and weather variation, the high cost and unreliability of seed and chemical supplies, poisoning of fishponds and rivers by pesticides and fertilizers, corruption, and the fact that the continual cultivation of rice fails to break the life cycle of insect pests such as the wereng (q.v.). [0240, 0247, 0248, 0259, 0260]

GUIDED DEMOCRACY (*Demokrasi Terpimpin*), general term for the years 1959–65, in which Indonesia was dominated politically by Sukarno (q.v.) and during which enormous political tension arose between the army and the PKI (qq.v.). Guided Democracy was initially a reaction to the apparent mendacity and divisiveness of parliamentary governments in the 1950s, and to the fact that the parties were unable to agree on a cabinet after the fall of the second Ali Sastroamijoyo (q.v.) cabinet in 1957 or on a constitution (q.v.) to replace the provisional 1950 Constitution. Parliamentary democracy was further discredited by the inability of the central government to maintain control in the provinces and by the participation of members of the Masyumi and PSI (qq.v.) in the PRRI and Permesta (qq.v.) rebellions. The transition to Guided Democracy began with a declaration of martial law and Sukarno's appointment of himself as prime minister and ended with Sukarno's restoration of the country's original 1945 Constitution on 5 July 1959.

The rhetoric of Guided Democracy was both radical and conservative; on the one hand Sukarno dedicated the nation to completing the unfinished Revolution (q.v.) and incorporated Marxist ideas extensively in his numerous ideological statements, especially Nasakom (q.v.). He praised the PKI (q.v.), protected it from army hostility, and promoted its participation in the institutions of the state. On the other hand, Sukarno consistently eschewed class conflict, promoting instead a corporatist view of the state in which there were no fundamental conflicts of interest between different social groups. He argued especially against what he described as the Western notion of 50% + 1 democracy, which enabled a tyranny by the majority. See also MANIFESTO POLITIK.

Institutionally, too, the picture was confused: the PKI made use of Sukarno's protection and the favorable ideological climate to expand its membership dramatically, while, as a result of martial law and the nationalization (q.v.) of Dutch property, the armed forces became firmly established in government and the economy. It became common to speak of a political triangle consisting of Sukarno, the army, and the PKI, but the strengths of each were very different and uncertainty over where Guided Democracy was leading the country contributed to growing tension in the 1960s which culminated in the GESTAPU (q.v.) coup attempt of 30 September 1965. See also GUIDED ECONOMY. [0170, 0635, 0647, 0650, 0664, 0700, 0705, 0730, 0854]

GUIDED ECONOMY (*Ekonomi Terpimpin*). Sukarno's vision of a political reconstruction of Indonesia under Guided Democracy (q.v.) was paired with plans for a thorough-going restructuring of the country's economy. Whereas parliamentary governments in the 1950s had generally aimed at Indonesianization (q.v.) of the economy by encouraging indigenous entrepreneurs, Sukarno proposed massive state direction of and intervention in the economy by means of regulation and direct state involvement. In Sukarno's view, much of Indonesia's economic difficulty stemmed from its subordination to economic imperialism and he aimed by means of state investment both to do without foreign capital investment and to create an industrial base which would lessen Indonesia's import of manufactured goods. These plans were laid down in an Eight-Year Plan announced in August 1960 and were restated in the Economic Declaration (*Deklarasi Ekonomi,* DEKON) of March 1963.

The nationalization (q.v.) of Dutch enterprises in

1957–58 provided the state with control of major parts of the economy and government controls on other sectors tightened considerably. The money for reinvestment, however, was not there. Nationalized businesses, many of them in military hands, were milked for funds both corruptly and to cover shortfalls in the government budget. Plantations in particular, already badly neglected in the 1940s and short of funds in the 1950s, were starved of reinvestment capital needed for replanting. Production declined steadily, leaving the budget steadily less able to meet government commitments. Inflation reached 500% p.a. by late 1965 as the government covered expenditure by printing money and the balance of payments steadily declined. [0220, 0223, 0295, 0365, 0664]

GUTTA PERCHA (*getah perca,* Sumatra latex), coagulated latex, especially of *Palaquium* spp. (Sapotaceae). From 1849 until the development of techniques to vulcanize rubber (q.v.) in early C.20, gutta percha had wide use for coating wires in telegraphy (see TELEGRAPHS). Collection of the latex involved felling the entire tree, making this a particularly destructive industry. See also JELUTUNG. [0938]

H

HAATZAAI ARTIKELEN. See SUBVERSION.

HAJ, the Muslim pilgrimage to Mecca, one of the five pillars of Islam. The steady stream of Indonesian pilgrims was and remains one of the important channels of political and cultural contact between Indonesia and the Arab world (q.v.). Already itself a sign of faith, the haj tended to increase the conviction of those who undertook it and for this reason it was feared by the Dutch as a potential source of political unrest. From 1825, therefore, they tried to discourage pilgrims by requiring them to obtain a passport and to pay a tax of *f*110. They also encouraged the local tradition that seven pilgrimages to Demak (q.v.), site of the first Muslim state on Java, were equivalent to one to Mecca. The tax, however, was abolished in 1852, and the number of pilgrimages began to increase. Until early C.20, most pilgrimages were arranged by so-called 'pilgrim sheikhs', who organized tickets, accommodation, and often finance for the journey. From 1922, however, the haj came under state control under the so-called Pelgrimsordonnantie, which regulated shipping, passports, vaccination, quarantine, and the welfare of Dutch subjects in Arabia. In 1926–27 52,412 pilgrims travelled from the NI to Arabia, the largest group of any country. Tight control has continued since independence, for similar reasons, to preserve Indonesia's foreign exchange, and to prevent people selling rice lands to finance the pilgrimage. It is not possible for Indonesians to make the haj except on government-organized programs. In 1989 the number of pilgrims was 57,903. [0573, 0577, 0813, 1150]

HALMAHERA (Gilolo, Jailolo), large island facing Ternate and Tidore (qq.v.). The coastal people are largely Malay, with aboriginal tribes ('Alfurs', q.v.) in the interior. A sultanate of Jailolo briefly emerged in C.17, but was conquered by Ternate. [0020, 0472]

HAMENGKUBUWONO IX (1912–88), sultan of Yogyakarta (q.v.). After studying Indology in Leiden, he became sultan on 18 March 1940, steering the sultanate to slightly greater autonomy under the Japanese from 1942. He is best remembered, however, for siding immediately with the Indonesian Revolution in 1945 and for putting his domains at the disposal of the Republic. Yogyakarta became first de facto and then formal capital of the Republic and the sultan, as minister of state and general in the Republican army, took part in the senior counsels of the Republic especially in 1948–49. His refusal to cooperate with the Dutch after the fall of Yogyakarta helped to force the Dutch to restore Republican government in July 1949. Hamengkubuwono held the defence ministry 1949–50 and 1952–53 and was governor of the Yogyakarta Special Territory until his death. He reentered the cabinet in 1963 as head of the State Audit Board (Badan Pemeriksa Keuangan) and emerged with Suharto and Adam Malik (qq.v.) as a prominent figure in the early New Order, becoming deputy prime minister for Economics, Finance and Development in March 1966 and vice-president (q.v.) 1973–78. [0628, 0634]

HAMKA (Haji Abdul Malik bin Abdulkarim Amrullah, 1908–81), Muslim writer and journalist. He founded his first magazine at age 18, composed numerous novels, was active in the Muhammadiyah (q.v.), and became one of Indonesia's foremost Islamic men of letters. In the 1960s he became the subject of a virulent attack by LEKRA (q.v.) on the basis of alleged plagiarism. [0160, 0456, 0707]

HAMZAH FANSURI (fl. late C.16?), poet born in the west Sumatran camphor (q.v.) port of Barus (also called Fansur). He lived for a time in Ayudhya in Siam (q.v.) and may have joined the mystic Islamic Wujudiyyah sect there. He also spent time in Baghdad. His poems, especially 'Sharab al-ashiqin' ('The lovers' beverage'), were highly regarded in the court of Iskandar Muda (q.v.) but were later strongly criticized by Nuruddin Raniri (q.v.) as heretical.

HARAHAP, Burhanuddin (b.1917), Masyumi (q.v.) leader and from August 1955 to March 1956 prime minister in a Masyumi-PSI coalition. His government oversaw the first general elections (q.v.) in September 1955 in which the Masyumi did poorly and the PSI was devastated. Although Harahap prepared legislation for the dissolution of the Netherlands Indonesian Union in May 1956, he was deeply suspicious of the trend to radicalism in Indonesian politics and joined the PRRI (q.v.) rebellion in February 1958, for which he was jailed 1962–65. [0634]

HATTA, Mohammad (1902–80), political leader, born in West Sumatra, where he came early under the influence of modernist Islamic teachers. He studied economics in Rotterdam 1923–32 and was active as chair of the Perhimpunan Indonesia (q.v.). In 1927 he was arrested and tried with three others on charges of promoting resistance to Dutch rule in Indonesia on the basis of article he wrote for the PI journal *Indonesia Merdeka* but was acquitted for lack of evidence. On his return to Indonesia he quickly became prominent amongst the noncooperating nationalists. He was struck by the ease with which the Dutch had been able to break up Sukarno's PNI (q.v.) by arresting its leaders and he founded with Sutan Syahrir (q.v.) the Pendidikan Nasional Indonesia (q.v.) as part of a long-term plan to build a cadre for the nationalist movement. In 1934, however, he was sent into internal exile (q.v.) in Boven Digul (q.v.) and later Banda and Sukabumi. He was released by the Japanese and agreed to work for them as political adviser, along with Sukarno. Though the two leaders were kept from direct organizational contact with the masses in this period, their public prominence confirmed them as the two dominant nationalist leaders. Hatta was involved in negotiations with the Japanese over independence for Indonesia and after the Japanese surrender declared independence with Sukarno on 17 August 1945. He became the country's first vice-president (q.v.) on 18 August. See also NATIONALISM.

Though the vice-presidency held no executive power, Hatta was prominent in economic and administrative policymaking in the early revolution and was a consistent advocate of negotiation with the Dutch (see DIPLOMASI AND PERJUANGAN). Sukarno appointed him prime minister on 31 January 1948 after the fall of the Amir Syarifuddin (q.v.) cabinet and he then set out systematically to dismantle the power of the left, especially after the Madiun Affair (q.v.) of September-October 1948. He was captured by the Dutch in the Second 'Police Action' (q.v.), but headed the Republican delegation at the Round Table Conference (q.v.) and signed the transfer of sovereignty in December 1949 on behalf of the Republic. He resigned as prime minister in September 1950.

Hatta's influence shrank sharply in the 1950s. He differed with Sukarno over the relative emphasis to be given to economic reconstruction and to political goals, such as the recovery of Irian (q.v.), and on 26 July 1956 he resigned as vice-president (from 1 December). Many saw him as a possible focus for opposition to Sukarno and to Guided Democracy but he lacked the charisma of Sukarno and was in any case always reluctant to break the unity of the Republic. Under the New Order he became personal adviser to Suharto but his plans to create a Partai Demokrasi Islam Indonesia were thwarted. Hatta's ideology was complex. Though strongly influenced by both Islam and Marxism, he was suspicious of Islamic radicalism and of communism. He wished to promote a moral capitalist economy in which prosperity could be achieved without exploitation and he saw cooperatives (q.v.) as a path to this goal. He was willing to accept extensive foreign investment in the advanced sectors of the economy but was especially hostile to smaller Chinese businesses, which he saw as exploitative. [0560, 0561, 0563, 0628, 0699, 0713]

HAYAM WURUK. See MAJAPAHIT.

HEALTH. The early history of health and disease in the Indonesian archipelago is difficult to reconstruct because of generally vague descriptions of ailments. It seems likely that diseases such as malaria (q.v.), dysentery, and hookworm have long been established in the region, while bubonic plague, cholera, influenza, smallpox and syphilis (qq.v.) are more recent introductions. Beri-beri (q.v.) is a product of recent technological change. During C.18, Batavia (q.v.) especially had a reputation for unhealthiness and during the Napoleonic Wars governor-general van Overstraten suggested that in the event of attack Dutch forces should weaken the enemy by letting them capture Batavia and thus contract the diseases occurring there. See also PIG.

Epidemic diseases which struck the workforce and the armed forces first drew the attention of colonial authorities, and the earliest public health care was in the form of smallpox vaccination and the treatment to sufferers of syphilis. Batavia became a major center for research into tropical diseases. In 1910 a Civil Medical Service was established separate from that of the military and from 1925 the Dienst voor Volksgezondheid (DVG, Public Health Service) conducted major campaigns emphasizing public hygiene (drainage, sanitation etc.). Nonetheless, in 1938 the colonial government provided only 116 hospitals, with 17,976 beds, for the entire colony. A further 38,122 beds were provided by private, often mission-based, hospitals, which created unease in Muslim communities who, often correctly, saw provision of medical care as an attempt at conversion.

The earliest official medical training was of smallpox vaccinators and midwives from ca 1817. In 1857 midwifery training was abandoned, but from 1849 a school for paramedical *dokter Djawa* (Javanese doctors) was attached to the hospital in Batavia. A full European-style medical course was offered from 1875 and in 1898 the School tot Opleiding van Inlandsche Artsen (STOVIA, School for the Training of Native Physicians) was founded. The Nederlandsch-Indische Artsenschool (NIAS, Netherlands Indies Physicians' School) was established in Surabaya in 1913 and a medical college (Geneeskundige Hogeschool) in Batavia in 1927. See also EDUCATION.

The need for an extensive system of health care for village Indonesia was realized from the time of independence and a public health education program was launched in 1954. These early efforts, however, were hampered by lack of personnel and by poor coordination between government departments. In 1968, a new plan was developed for village health centers or PUSKESMAS (Pusat Kesehatan Masyarakat, Centers for Society's Health) and since the 1970s these have played a central role in bringing health care to most Indonesians. [0054, 0483, 0978–0981, 0984]

HEEREN XVII. See DUTCH EAST INDIES COMPANY.

HEIHO, Indonesian paramilitary units recruited for auxiliary service by the Japanese forces in Indonesia from mid 1943. Some saw action against the Allies in eastern Indonesia and their experience was later welcome in the Republican army. Unlike the PETA (q.v.), the Heiho trained no Indonesian officers, but they numbered 25,000 by the end of the war and provided many troops of the postwar Republican army (q.v.). [0563, 0615, 0622]

HERENDIENSTEN (services to the lord). Alongside the allocation of revenue farm rights (see PACHT), corvée, or compulsory labor, was a major 'income' source for traditional rulers in the archipelago, and was the means by which many tasks of the state, such as road maintenance, were carried out. The demand for labor went under a wide variety of names, but herendiensten was probably the most common and important. Tension arose over the issue of herendiensten in C.19 when the colonial government sought to channel taxation as far as possible to itself. In 1882, several categories of herendiensten on Java were replaced with an annual poll tax (*hoofdgeld*) of *f*1, but the institution remained in place in some *zelfbesturen* (q.v.) until 1942. A form of compulsory labor service remains in force today as *kerja bakti,* 'voluntary labor' required for development works and community services. See also LABOR; SLAVERY; TAXATION.

HEUTSZ, Joannes Benedictus van (1851–1924), professional soldier, from 1898 civil and military governor of Aceh (q.v.) and from 1904–09 governor-general. His extensive military campaigns, especially in Aceh and eastern Indonesia, marked the final stage of Dutch territorial consolidation. [0535]

HIKAYAT (Arabic *hikaya,* tale, story). Malay prose narrative dealing with history, law, biography, and/or folklore.

HIMPUNAN MAHASISWA ISLAM (HMI, Muslim Students Association), large Muslim student organization, formed 1947. It was close to the modernist Muslim party Masyumi, but survived Masyumi's banning in 1960 to become one of the most vocal opponents of the PKI under Guided Democracy (q.v.). It was a major element in the so-called New Order coalition of military, students, and Muslims and initially it favored the program-oriented policies of the New Order. In the early 1970s was dominated by the so-called 'renewal group', especially Nurcholis Majid, which argued in favor of secularization. In 1983 it resisted government attempts to impose the Pancasila (q.v.) as its sole basic principle. [0845, 0861, 1148]

HINDERORDONNANTIE, regulation issued in 1926 requiring permission from the local authorities for the establishment of any factory or enterprise which might cause damage or danger in the immediate environment. See also ENVIRONMENTAL PROTECTION. [0028]

HINDUISM arrived in Indonesia along with Buddhism (q.v.) in ca C.4–5 A.D. (see INDIA, Historical links with), and merged with traditional beliefs to become the folk religion of much of Java and the coastal regions of the western archipelago. Saivism was the dominant form of Hinduism, though Buddhism often also became an aspect of Hinduism in Indonesian practice. A class of priests (*pedanda*) conducted rituals, and local belief emphasized the importance of *dharma* (destiny, duty) but the Indian class and caste system was only weakly transferred. With the penetration of Islam (q.v.), however, Hindu belief was restricted to Bali (q.v.) and isolated pockets elsewhere such as Tengger in the mountains south of Pasuruan in East Java, though much of Balinese 'Hinduism' pays attention to pre-Hindu local deities rather than to the philosophical principles derived from India. Balinese Hinduism was studied and to some extent protected by Dutch colonial officials, and after independence Sukarno (q.v.), who was half-Balinese, played a similar role. The Muslim-dominated Ministry of Religion, however, was reluctant to recognize it since it was not monotheist, and had no sacred book and no prophet, these being regarded as the characteristics of true religions, and classified Hinduism with animism, thus opening Bali officially to Muslim and Christian missionary activity. In response Balinese

Hindus formed the Parisada Dharma Hindu Bali in 1959 both to lobby in favor of Hinduism in government circles and to standardize, define, and democratize Hindu doctrine and practice on Bali. Arguments that Hinduism recognized a single supreme god in the form of Sang Hyang Widi resulted in the religion's formal recognition by the ministry in 1962. In 1964 the PDHB changed its name to Parisada Hindu Dharma.

In 1963 Hindu authorities celebrated the ritual of Eka Dasa Rudra, a two-month-long cleansing ceremony needed once a century but previously held probably in C.18. On 18 February 1963, three weeks before the climax of the ritual, the volcanic Mt. Agung erupted, causing extensive destruction and loss of life on the island. The eruption was taken by many Balinese as a sign that much was wrong on the earth, and some scholars have argued that the mass killing of PKI (q.v.) members on Bali in 1965–66 was seen by many Balinese as a necessary cleansing operation (see MASSACRES OF 1965–66). The ceremony was repeated without volcanic intervention in 1979.

Since 1965, Hinduism has grown dramatically outside Bali. Growth took place first on Java, where from 1967 many abangan (q.v.) Muslims, appalled by the santri (q.v.) role in the massacres there and by the prospect of stricter enforcement of Islamic religious law, and driven also by the government insistence that all citizens adhere to a religion, turned instead to Hinduism as the religion of Majapahit (q.v.). In other parts of Indonesia, moreover, Hinduism provided a convenient rubric for government recognition of the traditional beliefs of communities such as the Toraja and the Dayaks (qq.v.). See also RELIGION AND POLITICS. [0317, 1022, 1122, 1123, 1149]

HIZBULLAH ('Army of God'), paramilitary force founded by the Japanese in West Java in December 1944 affiliated to the Masyumi (q.v.), as a Muslim counterpart to the Pembela Tanah Air (q.v.). At the end of the occupation, it had around 500 members and was in no way strong enough to press for an Islamic state (see ISLAMIC STATE, Demands for an). During the revolution, however, the name Hizbullah was taken up by many armed groups affiliated with local Muslim leaders and with the Muslim political party Masyumi (q.v.). After 1948, many joined the Darul Islam (q.v.), partly because of belief in an Islamic state, partly because of fear of demobilization. See also ARMY; LASYKAR; SABILILLAH. [0563, 0632]

HOAKIAO, respectful term for the Chinese (q.v.) minority in Indonesia.

HOGENDORP, Dirk van (1761–1882), VOC (q.v.) official on Java 1791–98. He sharply criticized VOC rule on Java for its 'feudal' exactions from the population and he proposed extensive changes to the structure of government and finance on Java, including property rights for the Javanese, transforming the *bupati* (q.v.) into a salaried bureaucracy, and reforming the taxation system, many of which foreshadowed the ideas of Daendels and Raffles (qq.v.). In 1798 he was jailed for these views by the conservative commissioner-general S.C. Nederburgh but in 1799 escaped to the Netherlands where he continued his campaigns in a series of polemic brochures. [0375]

'HO-LO-TAN', Chinese transcription of the name of an otherwise unknown kingdom on the north coast of West Java. It sent seven tributary missions to China from 430 to 552, including one in 436 from King Vishamvarman requesting diplomatic and military assistance against internal and external enemies. The kingdom may have been conquered by Tarumanegara (q.v.) soon after 552.

See also CHINA, Historical links with; 'KAN-T'O-LI'. [0409, 0430]

HONEY produced by tropical bees, *Apis cerana,* was an important traditional source of sugar in the archipelago (see also ALCOHOL; AREN; LONTAR), though on Java the production of low-acid wax for batik (q.v.) was at least as important a reason for bee-keeping. Modern hive techniques were introduced in the 1920s. Since the 1970s, the state forestry corporation Perhutani (q.v.) has encouraged bee-keeping in forest areas to promote pollination and raise local standards of living, thereby to reduce the economic pressure for illegal timber cutting. [0938]

HONGI ('fleet') RAIDS, named for the war canoes, or *kora-kora,* of eastern Indonesia but referring generally to Dutch naval operations in C.17 to destroy spice plantations in Maluku (q.v.) outside their areas of control in order to ensure their own monopoly of the lucrative trade. See also DUTCH EAST INDIES COMPANY; PIRACY. [0375, 0464]

HORSES (*Equus caballus*) were probably introduced to the archipelago from India around C.1 and later from China and Arabia. Many distinctive local breeds, mostly small, were developed on Java and the Lesser Sundas (especially Sumba and Sumbawa), as well as in Aceh, Tapanuli, Minangkabau and South Sulawesi. Generally valued for their agility and docility, they were widely traded within and beyond the archipelago and were used for transport and in warfare, but rarely in agriculture. Larger breeds from Australia (q.v.) were introduced for the colonial army in C.19. There were 630,000 horses in the archipelago in 1934, but there are many fewer now. See also GRASS. [0483]

HORSFIELD, Thomas (1773–1859), American naturalist. He was first appointed by Governor-General Siberg to investigate the medicinal properties of Indonesian plants, but remained in Indonesia from 1801 to 1819 under the patronage of successive governments to study the botany and zoology of the archipelago. He published *Zoological researches in Java and the neighboring islands* in 1824 and *Plantae Javanicae rariores* in 1838–52 (with Bennet and Brown). [0982]

HOUTMAN, Cornelis de (ca 1565–99) commanded the first Dutch commercial expedition to Indonesia in 1595–97, which demonstrated the possibility of direct trade with the Indies. He was, however, authoritarian and tactless and was murdered on orders of the sultan of Aceh (q.v.) on his second voyage to the Indies. His brother Frederik (1571–1627) was imprisoned in Aceh for two years and made important early linguistic and astronomical studies there. He later became the first governor of Ambon (1605–11) and governor of Maluku (1621–23) and is commemorated by Houtman's Abrolhos off the West Australian coast. [0375]

HUNTING was an important source of food for many peoples of the archipelago, though vegetables, both cultivated and collected, were always a more important source of protein and starch. In areas of intensive rice cultivation the purpose of hunting was principally to protect crops and human and animal lives, rather than for food. Tigers (q.v.) were hunted for use in public fights, elephants (q.v.) for ivory, and rhinoceros (q.v.) for their horns and bezoar stones (q.v.). Hunting was also a popular sport of the European community in the late colonial period. See also CONSERVATION, Nature.

I

IDRUS (1921–79), author known especially for his 'Surabaya' (1947) and other short stories of the Japanese occupation and Indonesian Revolution, many of which dwell on the brutal and grubby aspects of the events described. His terse style is reminiscent of the poetry of Chairil Anwar (q.v.). [0160, 0163–164]

IKATAN PENDUKUNG KEMERDEKAAN INDONESIA (IPKI, League of the Supporters of Indonesian Independence), political party formed in May 1954 by supporters of A.H. Nasution (q.v.) who attributed the country's postindependence malaise to selfish politicians. They called themselves a movement, rather than a party, and were strongest in West Java, where Nasution's old Siliwangi (q.v.) Division was based, though they obtained only 1.4% in the 1955 elections. Initially in favor of Guided Democracy (q.v.) which they saw as a way of ending party politics, they turned against it when it appeared that Sukarno intended to leave them out of his DPR-GR (q.v.). Some branches joined the PRRI (q.v.) rebellion and were banned, but the party survived Guided Democracy to be merged in 1973 into the PDI (q.v.). [0634, 0663, 0709]

IMAM BONJOL, Tuanku (1772–1864), a religious leader (*tuanku*) of the Paderi movement which spread reformist Islam though the Minangkabau (q.v.) region. After remnants of the anti-Paderi aristocracy asked for Dutch help and transferred the region to Dutch sovereignty in exchange, Imam Bonjol became one of the major military leaders of resistance to the Dutch in the so-called Paderi War (1803–37). He was captured by the Dutch in 1834, shortly after the fall of his stronghold at Bonjol in the Alahan Panjang valley and was exiled first to West Java and Ambon and finally (1841) to Manado. [0451]

INDEPENDENCE, Declaration of. Indonesia's Declaration of Independence was made by Sukarno and Hatta (qq.v.) in the grounds of Sukarno's house, Pegangsaan Timur 56 in Jakarta, on the morning of 17 August 1945. The text read: 'We the Indonesian people hereby proclaim the independence of Indonesia. All matters concerning the transfer of power etc. will be carried out in an orderly manner and in the shortest possible time. In the name of the Indonesian people, Sukarno-Hatta.' Since 1945, 17 August, or a date close to it, has been the occasion for a major speech by the president (q.v.). See also SUCCESSION. [0114, 0563, 0628]

INDIA, Historical links with. Indian civilization fused with indigenous cultural traditions to produce a distinctive Southeast Asian Hindu-Buddhist civilization which in various forms dominated the archipelago as far east as the coast of New Guinea from C.5 until the arrival of Islam (q.v.). The principal historical sources for studying this process of 'Indianization' or 'Hinduization' are Sanskritic inscriptions found in various parts of the archipelago (see TARUMANEGARA), archeological discoveries of Indian trade goods (see TRADE), and the accounts of Chinese (q.v.) travellers, none of which have been adequate to demonstrate the nature or extent of the process. Although it is no longer believed that Indian culture was introduced by the wholesale migration of Indians to the region or through its conquest by Indian princes, historians have been unable to agree on whether the primary initiative for the spread of Indian culture came from Indians or Indonesians, whether it was Indonesian rulers who sent traders to the ports of India and summoned Hindu priests to their courts to provide details of Hindu ritual for royal glorification, or whether missionary, commercial, and imperial motives brought Indians themselves to the archipelago. It now appears likely that all these processes played a role, though the movement was more one of ideas than of people. Trade between the archipelago and India began in C.1 or 2 A.D., but there is no evidence of major Indian settlement in the region and the C.11 raids of the Cholas on Srivijaya (q.v.) were the only significant military excursions across the Bay of Bengal.

It is clear, nonetheless, that most influence was exercised by Brahmans (most Sanskrit vocabulary in Indonesian languages is religious and there is no sign of an Indian-influenced traders' pidgin), while the courts of local rulers were the major channel for Indian influence. The growth of trade (q.v.) with India and China from early in the Christian era must have significantly changed that distribution of power and wealth in local societies. If local rulers did not themselves profit from trade, they were probably displaced by those who did, and the new economic order demanded a redefinition of the political order. Rulers saw in Hindu-Buddhist cosmology a means of exalting their own positions (see KEDIRI; MATARAM; SAILENDRA). As adopted in Indonesia, Hinduism and Buddhism argued for an analogy between the state and the cosmos, the ruler analogous to the supreme god, and often a temporary incarnation (*avatar*) of a Hindu deity. From this followed the construction of palaces (*kraton,* q.v.) which physically resembled the cosmos and the entrenchment of the ruler's right to demand corvée labor (see LABOR) from his subjects. Scholars have differed over the extent to which Indian cultural influence reached beyond the court. Van Leur argued that it was never more than a 'thin and flaking glaze' over powerful indigenous traditions, but more recent scholars have held that influence went rather deeper and that 'culturally Southeast Asia became nearly as "Indian" as parts of India' (Mabbett). See also MEGALITHS.

Hindu-Buddhist Indonesia maintained close cultural contact with India, especially through the Buddhist monastery at Nalanda in Bihar, where a Sailendra ruler of Java helped to endow a monastery and which received many pilgrims from Srivijaya. The use of the zero, though an Indian invention, is recorded earlier in Java (732) than in India itself (870).

Th early Indonesian nationalist movement was inspired to some extent by the successes of the older Indian movement. PARTINDO (q.v.) in particular adopted the principle of *swadeshi* (use of local made products) at its foundation in 1931 and a few figures were impressed by Gandhi's philosophy of nonviolence, but on the whole direct influence was sparse. See also BUDDHISM; HINDUISM; MAHABHARATA; RAMAYANA; WRITING SYSTEMS. [0307, 0401, 0403–0405, 0425, 0426, 0430]

INDIA, Relations with. When Indonesia declared independence in 1945, India was still a British colony, but large areas of government had been devolved to Indians and full independence was in the offing. Nehru's insistence that the Indian troops, who were heavily present amongst the British forces sent to accept the Japanese surrender, should not be used to suppress an Asian nationalist movement was one of the factors leading Britain to attempt to balance Dutch and Indonesian interests in 1945 and 1946, and India later assisted Indonesia with supplies of cloth (in exchange for rice) and with diplomatic support. In 1948–49, after the so-called Second 'Police Action', India and other Asian states hampered the Dutch military effort by denying them overflight rights and in March-April 1949 India invited Indonesians delegated to the Asian Relations Conference in New Delhi. The two countries signed a treaty of 'perpetual peace and unalterable friendship' on 3 March 1951, and Sukarno (q.v.) was, with Nehru, a prominent figure in the Non-Aligned Movement, but the two countries drifted apart as Indonesia grew closer to China (q.v.) in the early 1960s. See also FOREIGN POLICY. [0563, 0723]

'INDIË VERLOREN, RAMPSPOED GEBOREN' ('The Indies lost, disaster follows'), title of a 1914 pamphlet by C.G.S. Sandberg, deploring the gradual constitutional separation of the Netherlands Indies from the Netherlands (see NETHERLANDS, Constitutional relationship with Indonesia), but taken up later as a slogan, especially during the Indonesian Revolution, by those in the Netherlands who believed that Dutch prosperity depended on continuing colonial rule of Indonesia. They pointed especially to the return on Dutch investments in Indonesia, to Dutch markets there, and to the supply of materials for Dutch industry, as well as to the calculations of 1938 that the colonies contributed 13.7% of Dutch national income, arguments which reinforced the nationalist view that Dutch rule was the source of Indonesia's major problems. The example of the Cultivation System (q.v.), which had rescued the Dutch economy after 1830, was certainly influential here. A subsidiary argument was that possession of Indonesia gave the Netherlands world power status and that without it they would be reduced to 'the rank of Denmark'. Recent scholars have shown, however, that Dutch investment in Indonesia at the close of the colonial period (40% of the country's external investment) was lower in proportion than that of Britain in her empire (50%), and that returns on that investment were modest (3.9% in 1938). After 1945, a powerful counter-argument to the *rampspoed geboren* proposition was the likely enormous cost of postwar reconstruction, though this argument was not widely made. See also BATIG SLOT; 'EERESCHULD, Een'. [0526, 0725]

INDIGO (*Indigofera* spp., Fabaceae), dye plant introduced to Indonesia from the Middle East and widely found in the archipelago by C.17. It was traded from Java to China in C.18. Production declined after late C.19 with the development of German aniline dyes. [0245, 0246, 0938]

INDISCHE PARTIJ (Indies Party), founded in 1911 by the Eurasian E.F.E. Douwes Dekker (1880–1950). The party initially reflected a growing feeling in parts of the Indo-European (q.v.) community that their primary ties were with Indonesia rather than the Netherlands, but it was soon joined by the Javanese intellectuals Suwardi Suryaningrat and Tjipto Mangunkusumo (qq.v.) and became one of the first political organizations explicitly to transcend ethnic, religious, and regional divisions within the colony and to call for the independence of the Indies ('Indië los van Holland') from Dutch rule. The party collapsed in 1913 after the government refused it official recognition and sent its leaders into exile though a few members continued party activities, first in the Nationale Indische Partij (1918) and from 1937 under the name Insulinde (q.v.). Douwes Dekker was interned by the Indies government in 1941 and exiled to Surinam. He returned to Indonesia in 1946, joining the Republic and taking the name Danudirja Setyabuddhi. See also NATIONALISM. [0701, 0718]

INDISCHE SOCIAAL-DEMOCRATISCHE VEREENIGING (ISDV, Indies Social Democratic Association), founded in May 1914 by Henk Sneevliet (1883–1942) and others as the first Marxist organization in Indonesia. Initially European in its membership and orientation, it soon began recruiting Indonesians, including Semaun, Tan Malaka (q.v.), and Alimin. Sneevliet was sent into exile (q.v.) in December 1918 and on 27 May 1920 the association transformed itself into the Perserikatan Komunis di Hindia (Communist Association of the Indies), later PKI (q.v.). [0571, 0831]

INDO-EUROPEANS. During the first two centuries of the Dutch presence in Indonesia, few European women reached the colony and through concubinage and casual liaisons between European men and Indonesian women there emerged a large community of people of mixed descent, many with official European status (see RACE). The extent to which such people were socially accepted as equal to other Europeans varied from time to time (see DUTCH IN INDONESIA), but with the arrival of large numbers of European women in C.20, the mixed race group became increasingly sharply demarcated as a distinct social group, called Indo-Europeans (with the derogatory abbreviation 'Indo'), occupying subaltern positions in society as clerks, petty officials, and NCOs. Their European status excluded them from purchase of land (see AGRARIAN LAW OF 1870), though in 1904 the government began to lease small plots to individuals for gardens. This separation, accompanied by increasing racial discrimination, led to two divergent tendencies: on the one hand, Indo-Europeans came to see Indonesia as their primary home and to downplay the connection with the Netherlands; the Indische Partij (q.v.) was at first a strong sign of this. On the other hand, especially with the growth of Indonesian nationalism, many Indo-Europeans became worried by the threat to their still privileged position in relation to Indonesians, and became strong supporters of the colonial order. The Indo-Europeesch Verbond (IEV, Indo-European Union), founded in 1919 sought to defend Indo-European interests in the Volksraad (q.v.) and argued for economic assistance and social emancipation. Amongst the Dutch motives for retaining the province of Irian (q.v.) after 1949 was as a possible place of settlement for displaced Indo-Europeans, and about 6,000 went there in a largely unsuccessful settlement scheme. About 100,000 Indo-Europeans left Indonesia for Holland shortly after independence, only a little over 10% taking Indonesian citizenship at once, partly because they were subject to similar restrictive regulations as Chinese (q.v.) Indonesian citizens. In 1951, the IEV became the Gabungan Indo Untuk Kesatuan Indonesia (GIKI, Indo Association for Indonesian Unity) and restricted its membership to citizens. [0367, 0602, 0930, 0931]

INDONESIA (from Greek *indos,* India, and *nesos,* island). The fixing of a clear terminology for the region now called Indonesia has been bedeviled by changing political realities and changing understandings of the cultural and biological character of the region. Southeast Asia (itself a relatively recent term) was once referred to commonly as Further India, the East Indies (*Oost Indië* in Dutch), the Indian or Malay Archipelago, or simply the Indies, in recognition of the Indian cultural influences there. The Dutch possessions were thus simply called Netherlands India, the Netherlands Indies, or occasionally Tropical Netherlands. Attempts, mainly by anthropologists, to differentiate the predominantly Malay, Muslim world of island Southeast Asia from the Buddhist realms of the mainland led to the coining of the words Malesia, Insulinde, Nusantara (qq.v.), Malaysia, and Indonesia, the latter being first used by a British anthropologist, J.R. Logan, in 1850, in analogy with Polynesia, and popularized by the German anthropologist Adolf Bastian in his book *Indonesien* (1884). The Malay term for the region was at first simply *Hindia Timur* (East India), but in 1917 Indonesians in the Netherlands formed the Indonesisch Verbond van Studeerenden (Indonesian Students Society) and in 1922 the Indische Vereeniging (Indies Association) in the Netherlands adopted the name Indonesische Vereeniging, or Perhimpunan Indonesia (q.v.). In 1928 the nationalist movement formally adopted the name Indonesia to designate the future nation, its citizens, and language.

This was long rejected by the Dutch as implying a false unity of the colony's ethnic groups, but in their 1948 Constitution, the Dutch formally adopted the term Indonesië for the colony. [0562, 0575]

'INDONESIA RAYA', Indonesia's national anthem, composed in 1928 by Wage Rudolf Supratman (1903–1938) for the All-Indonesia Youth Congress. See also MUSIC; YOUTH PLEDGE.

INDONESIAN AIRWAYS, commercial airline established in Burma in late 1948 to obtain funds for Republican representatives abroad during the latter part of the Revolution. It operated first with a single Dakota and flew primarily under contract for the government of Burma. Wiweko Suparno was managing director. See also GARUDA.

INDONESIAN LANGUAGE (*Bahasa Indonesia*), the national language, derived from Malay, the language of the coastal regions of eastern Sumatra, the Riau archipelago, and the Malay peninsula (see also LANGUAGES). From C.17, Malay became increasingly the lingua franca of the archipelago and it was adopted by the Dutch East Indies Company (which called it *Maleis,* Malay) in its dealings with indigenous authorities. The Balai Pustaka (q.v.) was influential in promoting Malay as a literary language. Malay was preferred by nationalists over the numerically more important Javanese especially because it was not associated with any major ethnic group and because it has no formal levels of speech as does Javanese, which was thus considered to be a 'feudal' language. On 28 October 1928 a nationalist youth congress adopted it as the national language (see YOUTH PLEDGE). Use of Indonesia for administrative purposes increased during the Japanese occupation when the use of Dutch was banned. Although authorities have tried to reduce the influence of European languages on Indonesian vocabulary (see ETYMOLOGY), European influence on Indonesian syntax has been strong, for instance in the use of prefixes such as *pra-* (pre-) and *tuna-* (without) and use of *dari* (Dutch, *van*) to mean 'of'.

A spelling system for Indonesian was formalized by Ch.A. van Ophuijsen in 1901, but this was altered after independence, first by the substitution of *u* for *oe* (introduced by Suwandi in 1947) and then by a more extensive set of changes under an Indonesian-Malaysian Language Agreement signed in August 1973 providing for harmonization of the two countries' versions of Malay. Vocabulary and grammatical change in Indonesian is rapid and the two remain distinct. An earlier agreement to harmonize the two languages, Melindo, reached in 1959, was never implemented because of Confrontation (q.v.). The new spelling, known as *ejaan yang disempurnakan* (EYD, perfected spelling) changed *tj* to *c, dj* to *j, j* to *y,* and *ch* to *kh,* and removed the distinction between *e* and *é*. [0185, 0191, 0193, 0202, 0205]

INDONESIANIZATION, general term applied to programs of Indonesian governments in the 1950s to place a greater share of the economy in the hands of Indonesian (by which was generally meant *pribumi,* q.v.) businessmen. It was in many ways a continuation of the philosophy of the colonial Liberal and Ethical Policies (qq.v.), under which government sought to create a conducive environment for economic activity without being a major entrepreneur itself. The Benteng (Fortress) program (q.v.), begun in 1950, aimed to help indigenous businessmen accumulate capital by giving them privileged access to lucrative import licences. In practice, however, much of the money and most of the licences went to political and bureaucratic associates of the government or to Ali-Baba firms (q.v.). In 1951, an Economic Urgency Program, formulated by Sumitro Joyohadikusumo (q.v.), aimed at using state funds to set up viable enterprises for later transfer to cooperatives (q.v.) or private ownership. From 1956 these programs were abandoned and Indonesianization began to be replaced by a program of direct state intervention in the economy and regulation of indigenous business. See GUIDED ECONOMY; NATIONALIZATION; STATE ENTERPRISES. [0228, 0273, 0280]

INDRAPURA emerged as a sultanate on the southern edge of the Minangkabau realm in early C.16, after the fall of Melaka (q.v.) to the Portuguese diverted Muslim traders to the western coast of Sumatra. It was a major exporter of pepper (q.v.) and was conquered by the Acehnese forces of Iskandar Muda (q.v.) in 1633. With the decline of Acehnese power, Indrapura rose again but was wracked by disputes between the sultans and regional lords, in which the Dutch and British East Indies Companies became heavily involved. Sultan Muhammad Syah was forced to abdicate in 1696 and thereafter the kingdom was under Dutch domination. [0462]

INDUSTRIALIZATION. For most of the colonial period, Indonesia was for the Netherlands primarily a market and a source of raw materials, and local industrialization was not encouraged. This policy was reversed during World War I when it was realized how vulnerable dependence on manufactured imports had made the colony; under the Ethical Policy (q.v.), too, the colonial government wished to provide more employment opportunities for the growing population. In 1915 a Commissie tot Ontwikkeling van de Fabrieksnijverheid in Nederlandsch-Indië (Commission for the Development of Industry in the Netherlands Indies) was formed to encourage industrial development; its major but modest achievement was a paper factory in Bandung established in 1923. After independence import substitution industrialization became a strong element in economic policy. See also BADAN PERENCANAAN PEMBANGUNAN NASIONAL; IRON; RENCANA PEMBANGUNAN LIMA TAHUN. [0041, 0213, 0325, 0327, 0366]

INFLUENZA. The influenza pandemic of 1918, which developed on the battlefields of Western Europe at the end of the First World War, killed probably 1.5 million people in Indonesia. [0981]

'INLANDER' ('native'), the legal category into which all indigenous subjects of the Netherlands Indies were placed. Though this was a subordinate category, with distinctly fewer privileges than the Europeans, the shared status it gave contributed to the development of an Indonesian identity. See also LAW; NATIONALISM; RACE.

INLANDSCH BESTUUR ('native administration'). In the directly ruled territories of Java and Madura, the colonial administration (Binnenlandsch Bestuur, q.v.) was divided into distinct European and native (*inlandsch*) corps. This situation arose out of the manner of Dutch expansion on Java, in which the VOC (q.v.) took over the fealty of *bupati* (q.v.) from the rulers of Mataram (q.v.), but the system was preserved after the reforms of Daendels and Raffles (qq.v.) so that colonial officials dealing directly with the Indonesian population would as far as possible be drawn from the traditional elites and would thus enjoy greater authority. The Inlandsch Bestuur, accordingly, was not subject to the same demands for expertise and competence as the Europeesch (European) Bestuur. The precise role expected of it in successive eras, however, varied considerably. Both Daendels and Raffles (qq.v.) introduced administrative reforms to bypass the Inlandsch Bestuur for the sake of more efficient government. In early C.19, on the other hand, the Dutch reemphasized the traditional authority, especially of the bupati, encouraging them to assume the status of minor royalty (the correspondence of Kartini [q.v.], daughter of a bupati, was published as *Letters of a Javanese princess*) and generally ignored their abuses of power (see *MAX HAVELAAR*). From 1870 the Dutch placed greater emphasis on developing the administrative and technical expertise of the Inlandsch Bestuur. The most senior rank in the Inlandsch Bestuur was the bupati. His deputy was normally the *patih* and he presided over a hierarchy of regional officials, the *wedana, camat,* and at the head of the village or *desa* (q.v.) the *lurah*.

In the directly ruled territories outside Java and Madura, no uniform system was in force, though in general the colonial government sought to preserve the so-called *Inlandsche gemeenten* (native communities) as the basic unit of government. In many parts of Sumatra, the colonial government installed *demang* and assistent-demang as regional links between the European and traditional governments. In Java and elsewhere, the participation of the Inlandsch Bestuur in Dutch rule was often resented and there were violent social revolutions against it in many areas at the start of the Revolution. See also PAMONG PRAJA; PRIYAYI; TIGA DAERAH. [0366, 0596, 0601]

INSULINDE (Latin *insula,* island, *Inde,* India), poetic term for the Indonesian archipelago, coined by Multatuli in *Max Havelaar* (q.v.) in 1860. The name was adopted in 1913 for remnants of the Indische Partij (q.v.) and was displaced in poetic usage (except in French) by Nusantara (q.v.). See also INDONESIA. [0718]

INSULTING THE HEAD OF STATE. See PRESIDENT, Position of; SUBVERSION.

INTER-GOVERNMENTAL GROUP ON INDONESIA (IGGI), established in 1967 as a forum for discussion of the socioeconomic conditions in Indonesia and the coordination of foreign economic aid. The Netherlands (q.v.) chairs the organization, which also includes Australia, Britain, France, Japan, the United States (qq.v.), Austria, Belgium, Canada, West Germany, Italy, New Zealand, Spain, and Switzerland, along with the World Bank, the International Monetary Fund, the Asian Development Bank, and the United Nations Development Program. In the early years of the New Order, the IGGI had great influence on Indonesia's economic policies, emphasizing the rehabilitation of infrastructure, currency stabilization, guarantees for foreign investment, and limits on the role of the state in the economy. The IGGI provided 60% of Indonesia's development budget under the first Five-Year Plan. In 1989, Indonesia received US$4,000 million in aid via the IGGI, of which $1,400 million was provided by Japan. An International Non-Governmental Group on Indonesia (INGI, also Inter-NGO Conference on IGGI Matters) was formed in Amsterdam in 1985 to discuss issues raised at the annual IGGI meeting and to marshal alternative information to influence IGGI decision making. See also BADAN PERENCANAAN PEMBANGUNAN NASIONAL; RENCANA PEMBANGUNAN LIMA TAHUN. [0213, 0757, 0777]

INTERNATIONAL DEBT. In the colonial period, large amounts of money were transferred annually to the Netherlands (q.v.) as the so-called budgetary surplus (*batig slot,* q.v.), though this did not constitute a true international debt. Following World War II, the Netherlands laid a claim for *f*25,000 million in reparations against Japan (q.v.) for losses and destruction during the occupation; of this, however, only *f*130 million was received, most of it by the expropriation of Japanese property in Indonesia itself. After independence, Japan paid a further $223 million in reparations to Indonesia. Under the terms of the Round Table Agreement of 1949, Indonesia took over a debt of *f*4,300 million from the former Netherlands Indies; this was a source of considerable resentment, since it was believed to include some of the costs of the colonial war against the Republic and since it represented a drain on independent Indonesia's program of economic development. The Ali Sastroamijoyo (q.v.) government repudiated 85% of this debt on 4 August 1956. Under Sukarno, Indonesia acquired a debt of US$2,358 million (of which $990 million was to the USSR and its allies) and the task of managing this debt first brought the Inter-Governmental Group on Indonesia (q.v.) together. Indonesia's international debt in 1989 was $51.8 billion (the largest in Asia), requiring ca $5.5 billion annually in servicing and consuming ca 40% of export revenues. [0301, 0303]

IRIAN. The word Irian, derived from a Biak phrase meaning 'shimmering land', can be used for the whole of the island of New Guinea or, as here, for its western, Indonesian portion, covering the province of Irian Jaya ('Victorious Irian'), the former Dutch territory of West New Guinea. Indonesians formerly called the territory Irian Barat (West Irian), but this was abandoned in 1972 as implying possibly territorial claims on the eastern part of the island. Indigenous separatists on the island prefer the term Papua, or West Papua, derived from the Portuguese *papuas,* said to be from a local word meaning 'curly hair'. The indigenous population today numbers about one million and speaks 200 distinct languages (q.v.).

The island was settled by Melanesians around perhaps 20,000 B.C. Archeological evidence of increased erosion and charcoal deposits suggests that extensive agriculture began in 7,000 B.C. Domestic pigs (q.v.), which are not native to the island, were present from 6,000 B.C. and by 4,000 B.C. a strong economy based on tropical tubers such as taro (q.v.) was in place, enabling the Melanesians to resist the later Austronesians, though some Papuan tribes came to speak Austronesian languages (see MIGRATIONS). Bronze tools were in use by 1,000 B.C. and irrigation ditches in the highlands date from at least C.1 A.D.

The island had little contact with western Indonesia until C.20, though there is evidence of trade with Majapahit (q.v., see also PANATARAN). In early C.17 the Portuguese Luis Vaez de Torres discovered accidentally that the island was separate from Australia. Offshore islands and some coastal regions were claimed by the sultan of Tidore (q.v.), and the Dutch claim rested on their conquest of Tidore. During C.19 repeated European expeditions mapped the coastline and investigated the natural history of the island, but a Dutch settlement at Lobo in 1828 was abandoned in 1836 because of cost overruns and debilitating disease, and permanent occupation was not restored until 1896 when the Netherlands feared expansionism by Australia (q.v.) on the island. The border between Dutch, Australian, and German holdings was fixed at 141°E in 1875. An official enquiry was commissioned in 1912 to investigate why Australia seemed so much more successful in its part of the island. Much of the coastal region was 'explored' in the 1920s, and a penal settlement for Indonesian nationalists and those involved in the uprising of the PKI (q.v.) was established at Boven Digul (q.v.) in the southeast in 1926. The densely populated Baliem valley of the interior was 'discovered' only in 1938. Merauke, in the far southeastern corner, remained under Dutch rule throughout World War II and the rest of the island was reconquered by Allied (United States and Australian) troops in 1944, before the Japanese surrender.

When the Netherlands transferred sovereignty to the Indonesian Republic in 1949, it retained provisional control over Irian, arguing that the indigenous inhabitants were ethnically and culturally dissimilar to other Indonesians and would become victims of 'Javanese imperialism'. Some Dutch also wished to provide a place of settlement for displaced Indo-Europeans (q.v.), saw retention of the region as a way of maintaining their status as a world power and were impressed by the mining potential of the province. Since, however, the region had never been constitutionally distinguished from the rest of Indonesia in the colonial era, Indonesians regarded this separation as uncalled for, an attack on national sovereignty and an attempt to preserve colonialism in the region. The status of the territory was left unresolved by the Round Table Conference (q.v.) in 1949 and the issue quickly became a running sore in relations between Indonesia and the Netherlands. Dutch actions to bring the Papuans to a separate independence included the establishment of a semirepresentative Nieuw-Guinea Raad (New Guinea Council) in 1961. Under Guided Democracy (q.v.), Sukarno stepped up pressure on the Dutch, announcing a military campaign on 19 December 1961. Military infiltration began in early 1962. After protracted negotiations in which the United States (q.v.) put heavy pressure on the Dutch to capitulate, the Dutch administration handed the territory over to the United Nations (q.v.) on 15 August 1962; the UN in turn handed it to Indonesia on 1 May 1963, with the proviso that an 'Act of Free Choice' be held in five years to determine the wishes of the people of the territory. No details of this Act were specified and Ali Murtopo's Operasi Khusus (q.v.) carried it out in July-August 1969 by inviting the opinions of 1,025 selected tribal leaders, assembled especially for the occasion, who agreed without a vote to confirm integration with the Republic.

Since 1972, the economy of the province has been transformed by the growth of forestry (q.v.), by a massive Freeport copper (q.v.) mine, by the arrival of Javanese settlers under the transmigration (q.v.) program, and by the immigration of Bugis smallholders. Christian and to a lesser extent Muslim missionary activity have been extensive and Indonesian officials have encouraged tribespeople to abandon their traditional dress and customs. Official policy is that traditional culture should not be preserved as if in a museum but should give way to 'modern' lifestyles.

Resentment over government cultural and economic policies and over the domination of government posts by non-Papuans led in 1965 to the founding of the OPM (q.v., Free Papua Movement) which continues to conduct a sporadic guerrilla war against government forces. Indonesian military operations along the border with Papua New Guinea (q.v.) have been a source of friction between the two countries, especially as Papuan refugees from Irian continue to cross the border into PNG. See also ASMAT; DANI. [0004, 0276, 0502, 0726, 0743, 0912, 0914]

IRON, traditionally imported from China and the Ryukyus and mined and locally smelted in West Sumatra, West Kalimantan, Bangka, Belitung, and central Sulawesi, was used for the manufacture of agricultural and fishing tools, household goods, and weapons. Iron exports may have been the basis of the economy of Luwu (q.v.) in Sulawesi. Iron was exported from Kalimantan and Sulawesi to Majapahit in C.14, but from late C.18 imports from outside the archipelago dominated the market. Dutch plans for a steel industry in central

Sulawesi in 1917 were abandoned, though a small scale industry was established in the Banjarmasin area in the 1920s. See also INDUSTRIALIZATION. [0327, 0399, 0483, 1059]

ISKANDAR MUDA (ca 1581–1636) came to power as sultan of Aceh (q.v.) in ca 1607 and, like his contemporary Sultan Agung (q.v.) on Java launched a campaign of military expansion, using a navy of heavy galleys and an army which included corps of elephants (q.v.) and Persian horses as well as artillery. He briefly conquered Riau (q.v.) in 1613 and pushed Acehnese control far down the east and west coasts of Sumatra. His only major defeat was the destruction of several hundred ships in an abortive attempt to seize Melaka (q.v.) from the Portuguese in 1629. Iskandar Muda's military power was based on his success in controlling the pepper trade, which he centralized in the capital Kutaraja (now Banda Aceh), but he always had difficulty controlling the hinterland, where his rule was based on an uncertain alliance with regional war leaders or *uleëbalang*. He seems to have kept his courtiers in a state of fear through frequent purges—he had his own son killed—but his court became a center of learning, patronizing for instance the poetry of Hamzah Fansuri (q.v.). The experience of Iskandar Muda's rule, however, led the Acehnese elite after his death to prefer a line of more pliable queens as rulers. [0371]

ISLAM IN INDONESIA. Unassimilated communities of Muslims probably existed in the trading ports of the Indonesian archipelago from soon after the emergence of Islam, but extensive conversion to Islam did not begin until C.14, when the Sumatran port city of Pasai (q.v.) converted, followed by Melaka (q.v.) in C.15, Aceh, Banten, and the Java Pasisir (qq.v.) in C.16 and Makassar, Minangkabau (qq.v.), and central Java in

C.17. The reasons for conversion are complex, varied, and not wholly clear. Muslim authorities stress the missionary element, especially the role of the so-called Nine Saints on Java (see also CHINESE IN INDONESIA; WALI SONGO). Islam first attracted sizeable numbers of Indonesians in the form of Sufism, whose mystical elements fitted easily with the existing blend of Hinduism, Buddhism, and traditional religion on Java. Political and economic factors, however, also seem to have been important. The fall of the sultanate of Melaka (q.v.) dispersed Muslims to other parts of the archipelago. Especially under threat from the Portuguese (q.v.), rulers found that conversion to Islam brought valuable alliances; there is no evidence of Islamic revolutions from below playing any role in the conversion of states. Several kingdoms, such as Pontianak (q.v.), were founded as Muslim states; in others, such as Aceh and Minangkabau (qq.v.), Muslim hegemony was established or strengthened at various times by civil war. Perhaps more important, Islamic commercial law provided a sounder framework for conducting trade than did traditional and Hinduistic law, while individual traders found that conversion made them part of an extensive trading diaspora within which they could more easily obtain credit, information, and other facilities and perhaps also that it released them from otherwise costly community responsibilities which made capital accumulation difficult. Those who had made the *haj* (q.v.) to Mecca were often well placed to use contacts made there to commercial advantage and in parts of Java the word *haji* became more or less synonymous with 'wealthy trader'.

There are no strict denominational divisions within Indonesian Islam, but scholars have found it useful to see a number of broad categories of adherence to Islam. The Islam of parts of Java, whose adherents are sometimes called *abangan* (q.v.), is a strong blend of

Islam with pre-Islamic practices, especially the recognition of spirits and emphasis on ascetic practice and meditation and a corresponding disregard for the pillars of Islam, such as fasting and making the pilgrimage to Mecca. Abangan religion on the whole is not publicly practised but is a matter of personal devotion, and in C.20 at least this category has also tended to encompass nominal Muslims as well as pious adherents of the abangan religion.

The term Islamic traditionalism is generally applied to followers of the four traditional schools of Sunni jurisprudence. Although sultans were the protectors of religion, religious authority lay with Islamic scholars, called *ulama* and *kyai,* who devoted their lives to studying not just the Qur'an and Hadiths but the enormous body of supplementary literature, and to teaching in Islamic schools, called *pesantren* (q.v.) or *surau*. Indigenous traditional law (*adat,* q.v.) in many cases became entwined with this corpus of religious and legal doctrine, so that pious Islamic observance was often combined with acceptance of customs not recognized in the Islam of the Middle East, such as the matriliny of the Minangkabau. Within this category are various groups influenced by successive waves of Islamic reformism, especially Wahhabism. On Java one finds many abangan elements in the belief and practice of Islamic traditionalists, but adherents share a much stronger sense of being Muslim and of being part of a religious community. Clifford Geertz employed the term *santri* (q.v.) for this group, but its usage has become imprecise, referring sometimes to traditionalists, sometimes to modernists (see below), and sometimes to both.

From early C.20, Islamic traditionalism was challenged by the rise of Islamic modernism. In religion, modernism asserted the primacy of the Qur'an and Hadiths and the need for direct individual study of these texts. They emphasized the importance of the community (*ummat*) of believers and discounted the religious authority of the ulama and kyai, at least as far as it was based on the exhaustive study of other texts. In much Western writing, the term Islamic modernism is used primarily for a variety of Islam which shares many features of Western Christian humanism, such as tolerance of religious diversity, compassion for the socially disadvantaged, enthusiasm for democracy and for technological developments, and moral conservatism. Historically, this stream of modernism saw the heavy weight of traditionalist learning as a barrier to mastery of modern science and the development of a democratic society; they have often been compared to European Christian democrats and are sometimes described as 'Islamic socialists'. This comparison is somewhat misleading, since it ignores the modernist commitment to an Islamic state (q.v.) as prescribed by the Qur'an and Hadiths. Where modernists differ is over the appropriate strategy for achieving this goal. The Islamic socialists accept the Indonesian Republic as an appropriate framework within which to promote Islam into the foreseeable future; radicals (often vaguely called 'fundamentalists') argue for a more rapid transition to an Islamic state, and in some cases seek to promote this by armed struggle. Many Islamic traditionalists have also taken part in armed struggle for an Islam state and 'fundamentalism' is thus a political rather than a doctrinal category in Indonesian Islam.

Formal Muslim organizations date only from C.20. The modernist Muhammadiyah (q.v.), founded in 1912, and the traditionalist Nahdatul Ulama (q.v.), founded in 1926 are the most important social organizations of Indonesian Islam. Muslim political organizations have been more ephemeral. Sarekat Islam (q.v.), founded in 1909 as an extended traders' cooperative, was for a time the main vehicle for Indonesian nationalism but suffered badly from internal division and Dutch restriction. Masyumi (q.v.), created by the Japanese, was for a time the only significant Muslim political party, but it too split over internal differences. Nahdatul Ulama has moved in and out of politics as component of other parties and as a party in its own right. The current Partai Persatuan Pembangunan (q.v.) is a Muslim party in only a limited sense: Islam forms no part of its platform or its symbolism and it is open to non-Muslim members, but it is dominated (insofar as it is not controlled by the government) by Muslim organizations. Since soon after independence, extra-legal Muslim organizations have fought unsuccessfully for an Islamic state in place of the Indonesian Republic. From 1948 to 1965 these organizations were generally, if not always accurately, called Darul Islam (q.v.); since the early 1980s, a Holy War Command (Komando Jihad, q.v.) is reported to be actively seeking to overthrow the Republic by armed force. After the massacres of 1965–66, there was some conversion on Java from Islam to Hinduism and Christianity, but on the whole state sponsorship of religious activity through the Ministry of Religion has increased adherence to orthodox Islam. See also ARAB WORLD, Historical links with; KEBATINAN; MARRIAGE, Political Significance of; NATIONALISM; RELIGION AND POLITICS. [0001, 0365, 0451, 0577, 0608, 0674, 0845, 0852, 0922, 0992, 1118, 1121, 1123–1143]

ISLAMIC STATE, Demands for. The creation of an Islamic state, which will administer and enforce Islamic law, is one of the central political demands of Islam (see previous entry). This demand was satisfied in many parts of precolonial Indonesia by sultanates, states in which the sultan acted as protector of Islam and appointed officials to enforce Islamic law. The extent to which Islamic law was actually enforced varied considerably from place to place, but the imposition of colonial rule was a major step backwards in Muslim eyes from the ideal state of affairs. A number of anticolonial revolts attempted to restore Islamic rule by (re)establishing sultanates, but especially in C.20 many Muslims were reluctant to return to this autocratic form and proposed instead an Indonesian Islamic state, probably in the form of a republic.

Closer definition of what a modern Islamic state might mean was hampered by division within the Islamic community over such matters as the proper role of Islamic scholars and by the fact that Indonesia, wherever its borders might be drawn, was bound to contain substantial non-Muslim minorities as well as Muslims to whom Islamic law was uncongenial. An Islamic state, therefore, was never part of the platform of the nationalist movement and arguments for an Islamic state were rejected during the drafting of the 1945 Constitution by the BPUPKI (q.v.) on grounds that this would discriminate against non-Muslim minorities. A compromise requiring Muslims alone to follow Islamic law (the Jakarta Charter, Piagam Jakarta) was agreed for the preamble, but was omitted from the final version. After Sukarno in 1953 publicly rejected the possibility of an Islamic state, the Islamic case was argued again in the 1957–59 Constituent Assembly (q.v.) but foundered once more on the problem of the non-Muslim minorities, though the reluctance of *abangan* (q.v.) Muslims was probably a more important barrier. Since 1948, several groups have pursued an Islamic state by armed means, notably the Darul Islam and the Komando Jihad (qq.v.). The New Order argues that the constitution's recognition of both religion and 'belief' precludes a religious state. See also KEBATINAN; PANCASILA. [0632, 0880, 1107, 1111]

J

JACKFRUIT (*Artocarpus heterophyllus* Moraceae, *nangka*), tree with massive edible fruits borne on the trunk, introduced from India probably by C.15. The similar *cempedak* (*A. chempeden*) is native to the archipelago and appears on friezes on Borobudur (q.v.). [0938]

JAKARTA, known until 1943 as Batavia (q.v.), became Indonesia's capital with the Declaration of Independence in 1945. The city was occupied by British forces in October 1945, and most Republican offices shifted to Yogyakarta (q.v.), but until July 1947 local administration was shared uneasily by a Republican city hall (Balai Agung) and a Dutch municipal administration. With the signing of the Renville Agreement (q.v.), Jakarta ceased formally to be the Republic's capital but was given special status by the Dutch as future capital of the projected federal republic. The special federal territory of Jakarta was abolished along with federalism (q.v.), and in the mid 1950s many proposals were made to shift the capital elsewhere, partly for climatic reasons, partly because of resentment over corruption and government expenditure in the city; in a celebrated article, Takdir Alisyahbana (q.v.) described the city as a leech on the country's head. In 1957, however, these proposals were abandoned and the expanded city was given a status equivalent to province as the Daerah Khusus Ibukota (DKI, Special Capital Territory). A master plan for urban development was accepted in 1967 and from 1977 expanded to encompass the so-called JABOTABEK (Jakarta-Bogor-Tanggerang-Bekasi) region, extending beyond the boundaries of the DKI.

The city's southward expansion, begun in colonial times, has continued. In 1948 Kebayoran Baru was created in the southwest as an elite residential suburb and new elite areas have since developed still further south. In recent years penetration of sea water into the water table for several kilometers inland has made coastal areas less liveable, though it is precisely in these areas that the greatest number of *kampung* are found. Ringroads and a freeway to Bogor, the so-called Jagorawi highway, have been built. Food shortages reduced Jakarta's population during the Japanese occupation, but since 1945 the population has increased steadily as people seek work in the growing service and administrative sectors. The city was closed to further immigration in 1970. In 1989 the population was officially estimated at 7 million but is probably one or two million greater. Successive governments have been keen to make the city a showcase of Indonesian development. Sukarno (q.v.) installed numerous monuments especially the National Monument (Monas) in Medan Merdeka. Ali Sadikin (q.v.) as governor promoted the development of the Jalan Sudirman artery while his successors have attempted to shift *kampung* residents to the fringes of the city by repossessing land and restricting a number of economic activities followed by the poor such as street-selling and becak (q.v.) riding. Under the New Order, Jakarta has been a center of political dissent, erupting into violence in the Malari (q.v.) riots of 1974 and the Tanjung Priok Affair in 1984 (see WHITE PAPER), and registering strong votes for the PPP (q.v.), especially in 1977. [0495, 0542, 0645, 0859, 1154, 1159]

JAKARTA CHARTER (Piagam Jakarta). See ISLAMIC STATE, Demands for.

JAMBI. Along with Srivijaya (q.v.), Jambi emerged as a minor trading and raiding state on the Strait of Melaka in C.5 and after (see PIRACY). It became subordinate to Srivijaya in 683, but after the fall of Srivijaya in early

C.11, Jambi briefly rose to replace it as the dominant power on the strait. It was never able to establish the same degree of hegemony and was raided in ca 1275 by King Kertanegara of Singosari (q.v.), thereafter remaining under Javanese suzerainty until it was incorporated into the Minangkabau (q.v.) kingdom of Adityavarman, though it was later also subject to Palembang (q.v.).

In C.17, an independent sultanate rose once again, based on the pepper trade, over which it fought a protracted war with Riau-Johor (see RIAU). Sultan Muhammad Fahruddin recognized Dutch sovereignty in 1834, but the rebellion of a later sultan, Ratu Taha Saifuddin, lasted until 1904. The post of sultan was left empty after 1901. From late C.19 Jambi became an important area of Dutch rubber (q.v.) estates and is today Indonesia's largest rubber producer. [0430, 0434]

JAPAN, Historical links with. Although Austronesian languages may have contributed slightly to the vocabulary of modern Japanese, and some Japanese musical traditions, especially the drum music of the south, may owe something to the traditions which led to gamelan (q.v.), historical contact between Indonesia and Japan is a relatively recent phenomenon. Nagasaki was one of the trading posts of the Dutch East Indies Company (q.v.) and from 1612 Japanese served as soldiers and occasionally officials of the Company in Southeast Asia. After Japan closed its doors in 1640, the small Japanese communities abroad soon assimilated with local populations.

Contact resumed with the opening of Japan in 1854. Japan was first known for providing prostitutes for the region, but Japan's rapid industrialization quickly made it a model to which burgeoning Asian nationalist movements looked, especially after its victory in the Russo-Japanese War (1904–5). The assimilation of Japanese to European status (see RACE) under the

'Japannerwet' of 1899 also provided a model. From ca 1914 Japanese trade with the archipelago began to expand rapidly, Japan providing cheap manufactured articles and cloth and receiving oil and sugar from the Indies. Between 1913 and 1932, Japan's share of Indies imports rose from 1% to 32% (though it took only 5% of Indies exports). In 1933, the so-called 'Crisis Act' provided for discriminatory tariffs against imports from Japan. Several Japanese political leaders had interests in companies trading in the region and from the 1930s Japanese shipping carried a major part of the cargoes in eastern Indonesia. Japanese firms were involved in fishing and silk industries in Minahasa (q.v.) in C.20.

In July 1941, with the consolidation of Japanese power in China, the Netherlands Indies followed the U.S. in banning exports of oil, tin, rubber, and other strategic materials to Japan. Japan had previous tried to pressure the colonial government to guarantee these supplies by threatening to 'liberate' the colony. The Netherlands declared war on Japan on 8 December 1941, after Pearl Harbor, and Japanese forces began landing in Borneo in January 1942. The fall of the British naval base in Singapore (q.v.) and the Allied defeat in the battle of the Java Sea (q.v.) was followed by Japanese landings on Java on 1 March 1942 and the surrender of Dutch forces on 9 March. See also JAPANESE OCCUPATION OF INDONESIA. [0601, 0722]

JAPAN, Relations with. Japan's attitude to the Indonesian Declaration of Independence on 17 August 1945 was ambiguous. The Declaration took place with the active cooperation of a Japanese admiral, Tadashi Maeda, and many in the military were both more sympathetic to Indonesian nationalism than to the Allies and afraid of a popular uprising if they suppressed the Republic. They were required, on the other hand, by the terms of the surrender to maintain the political status quo, and they attempted thus a middle way, neither assisting the Republic nor suppressing it, though some local commanders handed weapons over to Republican armed units (see also PEMBELA TANAH AIR).

Formal diplomatic relations between Indonesia and Japan, however, were not established until 1957, following exhaustive discussions over Japan's reparations debt to Indonesia, which was finally agreed at US$223 million, plus $400 million in aid and cancellation of a $177 million trade debt. An expansion in Japanese investment followed, especially resource exploitation (oil, the Asahan aluminium project, rubber, and later forestry and fisheries, qq.v.) and textiles. Japan maintained relatively good ties with Indonesia during Guided Democracy (q.v.), providing credits of $49 million in 1963–65. In return Japan received 46% of Indonesia's total oil exports between 1960 and 1970. Resentment over Japanese economic power was amongst the factors leading to the Malari (q.v.) Affair in 1974. Since that time, Japan has expanded its foreign aid to Indonesia, especially through the Inter-Governmental Group on Indonesia (q.v), becoming the largest single donor in 1989, with $1,400 million. Japan's economic power, however, continues to cause friction. Since 1987 Indonesia has been in a protracted dispute with Japan over the allocation of production from the Asahan (q.v.) aluminum refinery. Indonesia raised its stake in the venture from 25% to 41% in June 1987, but was not permitted by its Japanese partner to increase the proportion of production available for domestic consumption. See also MARRIAGE, Political significance of. [0680, 0696, 0738, 0754, 0760, 0768]

JAPANESE OCCUPATION OF INDONESIA. Under Japanese rule, Indonesia was divided administratively, Java coming under the 16th Army, Sumatra and the

Malay peninsula under the 25th Army, and Kalimantan and eastern Indonesia under the 2nd southern squadron of the Japanese navy (Kaigun). In 1943 New Guinea was separated and placed under the 4th southern squadron, and Malaya was separated from Sumatra.

The Japanese authorities began by restricting the nationalist movement to a greater extent than the Dutch. All political parties were banned, tertiary educational institutions were closed, and the Kenpeitai (q.v.) closely monitored political activity. On Java the military administration (Gunseikanbu) allowed Indonesians to participate only in Japanese sponsored mass organizations (Tiga A Movement, PUTERA, and Jawa Hokokai, qq.v.), whose main aim was to mobilize support for the war effort. The occupation also dislocated the economy. Cut off from their traditional markets in the West, the plantations of Java and Sumatra were forced to close or to change crops; machines, equipment, and wealth were shipped to Japan; and Indonesian laborers (*rōmusha,* q.v.) were recruited, often with coercion, for work of defence projects in Indonesia and elsewhere in the Japanese empire, where they were treated harshly and fell victim to disease and malnutrition. In the final year of the war, Allied submarine raids in the South China Sea prevented virtually all import of manufactured goods from Japan, leaving the country desperately short of cloth, medicines, etc.

Japanese rule, however, prepared Indonesia for independence in a number of ways. The Japanese victory shattered the prestige of Dutch colonial rule and irreparably damaged the administrative capacity of the colonial state. A greater number of Indonesians, moreover, were appointed to higher administrative positions during the occupation than they had ever held under the Dutch. The military training of Indonesians in the Heiho and PETA (qq.v.) provided a core of experience valuable in the later War of Independence. And the prominence of Sukarno and Hatta (qq.v.) within the PUTERA and Jawa Hokokai helped to confirm their political preeminence in the postwar period.

Japan's long-term political intentions for Indonesia were not clear. There is evidence that they intended to retain the archipelago as a colony and to promote cultural Japanization there (in contrast to China, Burma, and the Philippines where they established puppet states). On 7 September 1944, however, with Japanese forces in retreat, the Japanese prime minister Kuniaki Koiso announced vague plans for granting independence to the region. As the war progressed, these plans became steadily more concrete, a Committee to Prepare for Indonesian Independence (BPUPKI, q.v.) being established in March 1945, but nothing had been carried out when Japan surrendered on 15 August. See also JAPAN, Relations with; SUCCESSION. [0563, 0593, 0606–0625, 0696]

JASSIN, Hans Baguë (b. 1917), critic, essayist, and editor with the Balai Pustaka (q.v.) and *Poedjangga Baru* and of many postwar literary and cultural magazines. He played a major role in placing figures such as Chairil Anwar (q.v.) in the canon of national literature and established an important documentation center for Indonesian literature. He strongly opposed LEKRA (q.v.) emphasis on the social engagement of writers and artists and in 1963 signed the Manifesto Kebudayaan (q.v.). See also GENERATIONS. [0160]

JAVA (Jawa) is the most densely populated of the major Indonesian islands and has been politically and economically central to the archipelago since C.13. For statistical purposes it is generally combined with Madura (q.v.), but historically it is useful to distinguish from the Javanese lands of the central and eastern part of the island not just Madura, but also the Sundanese regions of West Java (see SUNDA).

The epigraphic evidence is meager, but it appears that Hindu and Buddhist states began to emerge in Central Java in C.8. The earliest of these to achieve any prominence was the Buddhist kingdom of the Sailendras (q.v.) and the Hindu kingdom of Mataram (q.v.) under King Sanjaya and his successors. The former was responsible for the construction of Borobudur (q.v.) and Mendut temples; the latter was responsible for Prambanan (q.v.) and Candi Sewu. The precise sequence of and relationship between these kingdoms is unclear. In C.10, for reasons also unclear, the center of Javanese power moved to the valley of the Brantas river in East Java, which became the base of a succession of major Hindu kingdoms: Janggala (C.11), Kediri (ca 1059–1222), Singosari (1222–92), and Majapahit (1294-ca 1527) (qq.v.). Trade with other parts of the archipelago and beyond grew in this period, strengthening the position of the port towns on the north coast (see PASISIR), which converted to Islam between C.14 and C.16 (see ISLAM IN INDONESIA). In ca 1527 Muslim armies led by the sultanate of Demak (q.v.) defeated Majapahit, leading to a period of disorder in the interior. A state called Pajang (q.v.) briefly emerged, but was displaced in the 1570s by a second, Muslim, state of Mataram in Central Java. The Dutch East Indies Company (q.v.), or VOC, established itself on the coastal regions in early C.17 and began military intervention in Mataram's affairs in late C.17, finally breaking the power of the sultanate with the Treaty of Giyanti in 1755, which partitioned it between the successor courts of Surakarta (Solo) and Yogyakarta (qq.v.).

Approaching its eventual bankruptcy, the VOC did little to change the social or economic order in Java, but in early C.19 the Napoleonic-Dutch rule of Daendels (q.v.) from 1808 to 1811, a British interregnum under

Raffles (q.v.), 1811–16, and Dutch rule under the crown from 1816, saw increasing intervention in the island. The Java War (q.v.) of 1825–30 was the last major attempt by the old aristocracy to assert its power on the island and under the Cultivation System (q.v.) Javanese felt the full force of Dutch colonialism, though scholars are still not agreed on its effects. From 1870, with the onset of the Liberal Policy (q.v.), Java ceased to be the main producer of Indies wealth for the Dutch; population increased and the share of the Outer Islands (q.v.) in export production increased. The Ethical Policy (q.v.), introduced in 1901, was in part an attempt to deal with the increasing social problems on the island. Nationalism (q.v.) began to emerge on Java first in the form of organizations for cultural preservation and renewal, but soon took a political dimension. Many of the leaders of the movement came from outside Java, but it was the nationalist influence on the Javanese masses which most worried the colonial authorities. By 1930 70% of the population of the Netherlands Indies lived on Java.

Java-Madura was administratively separated from the rest of the archipelago at the start of the Japanese occupation in 1942 and as the war progressed it became increasingly isolated economically. With both exports and imports severely hampered, the people of the island suffered greatly. During the national revolution, Java formed, with Sumatra, the heartland of the Indonesian Republic and although the Dutch had occupied the entire island by the end of 1948, widespread guerrilla resistance made their position untenable. From the 1950s, Java became even more the center of politics and fears of Javanization (q.v.) were amongst the factors leading to regional rebellions such as the PRRI (q.v.), though part of Outer Island hostility was reserved for the non-Javanese capital, Jakarta (q.v.). [0057, 0266, 0389, 0408, 0417, 0479, 1021, 1030]

JAVA BANK. See BANKING.

JAVA MAN. A skull cap and wisdom tooth about 500,000 years old, found in Trinil (East Java) by Eugène Dubois in 1891, has been identified as of *Pithecanthropus* (now *Homo*) *erectus*. This was the first human fossil find outside Europe and led to speculation that Java had been the 'Garden of Eden'. It is now believed, however, that humans (*H. erectus*) arrived a million years or more earlier, thus predating Peking Man. These early inhabitants appear to have been displaced by later migrations (q.v.). See also PREHISTORY. [0365, 0390, 0418]

JAVA SEA, Battle of the. On 27–28 February 1942, a Japanese fleet under T. Takagi defeated an Allied fleet under Karel Doorman in the Java Sea. Although numerically about equal to the Allies, the Japanese were superior in air power and sank all but a few of the Allied vessels either in the battle or soon after. The defeat left Java open to the landing of Japanese land forces. See also JAPANESE OCCUPATION; NAVY. [0614, 0623]

JAVA WAR (1825–30), a major uprising against Dutch domination of central Java, led by Pangeran Diponegoro (q.v.) and drawing together several strands of discontent in the central Javanese kingdoms of Yogyakarta and Surakarta (qq.v.). Increasing taxation and harvest failures in the early 1820s had unsettled the peasants, while both Islamic leaders and younger members of the Yogyakarta aristocracy were disturbed by the rise of Dutch power and what was seen as the moral decay of the courts. Javanese messianic expectations focussed on Diponegoro as a potential *ratu adil* (just prince) who would establish an era of justice and prosperity. Although the widespread uprising was only loosely coordinated by Diponegoro, it was able to shake Dutch power in the region until Diponegoro's defeat at Gowok near Surakarta in October 1826. Thereafter Dutch counterguerrilla strategies of dividing the Javanese forces and keeping them short of food wore the rebels down. Disunity arose between Diponegoro and his main religious adviser Kyai Maja and in 1827 Diponegoro's nephew and chief lieutenant Sentot deserted. Diponegoro's capture at Magelang in 1830 ended the war, in which perhaps 250,000 Javanese died. See also JOYOBOYO. [0447, 0504]

JAVANESE ABROAD. See AFRICA, Historical links with; SURINAM, Javanese in.

JAVANESE LANGUAGE. Although numerically the largest of the Indonesian languages, Javanese became neither a lingua franca nor the national language. This was partly because the grammatical complexity and distinct script of Javanese led the Dutch to choose Malay as their language of administration, partly because other ethnic groups (and a good many Javanese) rejected it as feudal in structure. In common with many languages, Javanese speech varies according to the respective ranks of the speaker and the addressee thus, in the view of many, preserving social inequalities. In 1917 an organization called Djawa Dipa was founded in Surabaya with the aim of abolishing high (*kromo*) Javanese and making low (*ngoko*) Javanese standard. See also TJIPTO MANGUNKUSUMO; INDONESIAN LANGUAGE; JAVANIZATION; LANGUAGES. [0192, 0196, 0204, 0209]

JAVANIZATION. It is often said that a process of 'Javanization' is under way in Indonesia. By this is meant two phenomena. First is the control by Javanese of important political and administrative posts apparently out of proportion to their admittedly large numbers. While no statistical data is available to test this proposition, it is commonly believed that Javanese are more often posted to the other islands than other Indonesians are posted to Java. President Suharto (q.v.), however, has placed non-Javanese in senior government positions partly, it is said, because their ethnicity would prevent them from succeeding to the presidency. Second is a process by which Javanese cultural norms are made national norms. This can be seen in the spread of Javanese words into Indonesian and the portrayal of, for instance, wayang kulit as a part of national culture. While there is no doubt that this process is taking place, it is not certain that it is of such an extent to imply real Javanization rather than simple enrichment of a culture which has already drawn much from the outside. See also ETYMOLOGY; TRANSMIGRATION. [1044]

JAWA HOKOKAI (Java Service Association), founded January 1944 to mobilize the Javanese population (over 14 years) for the Japanese war effort. Sukarno (q.v.) and Hasyim Asyari were senior advisers, Mohammed Hatta (q.v.) and Mas Mansur managers. The organization was run at each level by regional Indonesian officials and thus provided a means of government control outside the normal channels. The structure of the Hokokai was repeated to some extent in the PNI-Staatspartij and in Golkar (qq.v.). See also BARISAN PELOPOR. [0563, 0606, 0609]

JAYADININGRAT, Ahmad. See DJAJADININGRAT, Pangeran Aria Ahmad.

JELUTUNG, like gutta percha (q.v.), a rubbery latex briefly used industrially before the vulcanization of rubber (q.v.). It had fallen out of use by the 1920s but underwent a minor revival during the U.S. Prohibition era, when it was used in chewing gum as a substitute for chicle. It was tapped in southern Kalimantan from trees of the genus *Dyera* (Apocynaceae). [0938]

JOURNALISM. The Persatuan Jurnalis Indonesia (Indonesian Journalists' Association) was formed in 1933 under Moh. Tabrani. It was replaced in February 1946 by the Persatuan Wartawan Indonesia (PWI, Indonesian Reporters' Association). See also CENSORSHIP; NEWSPAPERS. [0347]

JOYOBOYO (r.1137–57), ruler of Kediri (q.v.), chiefly remembered for his prophecies of Java's future, which foretold alternating periods of prosperity (*jaman raharja*) and suffering (*jaman edan*). After a period of unprecedented suffering, he foretold, this cycle would be broken by the appearance of a just prince (*Ratu Adil*) who would found a golden age of prosperity and justice. New versions of the prophecies have appeared regularly, often as part of growing peasant discontent with colonial rule. The most celebrated version was current during the Japanese occupation (q.v.), which asserted that the Javanese would be ruled by white men for three centuries and by yellow dwarfs for the life time of a maize (q.v.) plant, prior to the achievement of a golden age. See also JAVA WAR; SAMA RASA SAMA RATA. [0116, 0447, 1131]

JOYOHADIKUSUMO, Sumitro (b. 1917), son of the founder of the Bank Negara Indonesia, Margono Joyohadikusumo (1894–1978). During the Indonesian Revolution, Sumitro negotiated a number of trading agreements in the United States (q.v.) intended to draw U.S. business interests to the side of the Republic. A member of the PSI (q.v.), Sumitro held economic portfolios in several cabinets in the 1950s, arguing in favor of foreign investment as a key to development. Also head of the

Economics Faculty at the University of Indonesia, he cooperated with the Ford Foundation in training a cadre of economists later prominent in BAPPENAS (q.v.). Sumitro joined the PRRI (q.v.) rebellion in 1957 and after its collapse went into exile in Singapore until the New Order came to power. He was appointed minister for trade and commerce in 1968, but retreated to the portfolio of state research in 1973 after widespread accusations that PSI figures were too influential. In 1983, his son Prabowo Subianto married Siti Hediati Haryadi, daughter of President Suharto (q.v.). [0315, 0758]

JUANDA KARTAWIJAYA (1911–63) trained as an engineer at the technical college in Bandung before World War II. Though never linked to a political party, he served in many Republican cabinets after 1945 in economic portfolios and in 1957 was appointed by Sukarno (q.v.) as non-party prime minister following the inability of the parties to form a government. In 1959 Sukarno appointed himself prime minister but retained Juanda as First Minister with much the same duties as before. Juanda's death in office in 1963 contributed to the absence of economic policy in the later years of Guided Democracy (q.v.). [0635, 0647, 0664]

JUDAISM. In contrast to India and China, Indonesia never became the home of settled, partly acculturated Jewish communities. Jews entered the archipelago as part either of the European colonial elite or of the general Middle Eastern trading diaspora (see ARABS IN INDONESIA). The Jewish community in Surabaya maintains a synagogue. Indonesia has no diplomatic relations with Israel. See also ARAB WORLD, Historical links with. [0921]

JUNGHUHN, Franz Wilhelm (1809–64). German-born scientist, responsible for the first detailed geographical survey of Java's interior. He measured and climbed most of Java's peaks and studied the pattern of vegetation changes with altitude. He was the first scientist to warn against the ecological consequences of deforestation and he suggested a ban on forest clearing above 500 m. He also published a major study of the Bataks (q.v.) in Sumatra. See also CINCHONA; ENVIRONMENTAL PROTECTION. [0762]

JUTE (*Corchorus capsularis* Tiliaceae). Bengal jute fiber is much used in the packing of sugar, rice, and other Indonesian produce, but attempts by the Dutch to grow it commercially in the colony were always unsuccessful, leading to experiments with other coarse fibers such as rami and rosella (qq.v.). [0245, 0246, 0938]

K

KAHAR MUZAKKAR (1921–65) led a force of south Sulawesi emigrés in Java during the national revolution and returned to south Sulawesi in April 1950 to resist the Dutch. Though strongly opposed to the Negara Indonesia Timur (q.v.), he resented the abrupt dismantling of the NIT by central forces which, he said, acted like an army of occupation. In August 1951 he launched a rebellion against the central government and affiliated broadly with the Darul Islam (q.v.) in August 1952. Kahar attempted to establish Islamic rule in the region, limiting private property, establishing schools and hospitals and banning titles, lipstick, and jewelry, and controlled much of the hinterland of Makassar (q.v) until the early 1960s. He was finally shot by government forces in 1965. [0634, 0639, 0657]

KAHARINGAN. See DAYAKS.

KAKAWIN, classic Javanese poetic form, mostly long and divided into four-line verses with a fixed number of letter groups per line.

KALIMANTAN is used to denote both the island of Borneo and, as here, its southern, Indonesian portion, which constitutes approximately 73% of its area with a population of about 5.5 million. The name derives perhaps from Kali Intan, 'River of Diamonds', *i.e.,* the Barito in southeast Kalimantan. Kalimantan has no active volcanoes and its topography is dominated by a low central mountain spine running roughly NE-SW from which a number of rivers—the Kapuas, Sambas, Barito, and Mahakam—flow, often through swampy coastal plains, to the sea. Most of the island is below 200 m in elevation. The indigenous inhabitants, generally called Dayaks (q.v.) were pushed from the coastal regions in early times by Malay peoples, who established a series of small states such as Kutai (q.v.) at or near the mouths of rivers. Although these states sometimes provided reprovisioning facilities for interregional trade, acted as outlets for produce from the interior (rattan, dragon's blood, birds' nests, gold [qq.v.], and resins), and generally engaged in piracy (q.v.), as did states on the strait of Melaka (see SRIVIJAYA), none grew to any great significance and the coasts of the island are usually described as being subordinate to one or other dominant regional power (Srivijaya, Kediri, Majapahit, Melaka, Banten qq.v.). The coastal states converted to Islam (q.v.) around C.16. During C.18 there was extensive settlement by Bugis (q.v.) from southern Sulawesi in coastal regions.

Through Banten, the Dutch inherited a nominal interest in western Kalimantan and put trading posts at Sambas and Sukadana (q.v.) in early C.17. These, however, were soon evacuated. In late C.18 and early

C.19, the Dutch established greater control in Pontianak (q.v.), Sambas, and Mempawah to forestall possible British annexation and to restrict what they saw as piracy (q.v.). From 1790 to 1820, large numbers of Chinese came to gold fields between the Kapuas and Sambas rivers, where some later settled as farmers (see CHINESE IN INDONESIA; KONGSI WARS). Dutch control in Banjarmasin (q.v.) was not established until C.19. From 1938 the Dutch portion of the island was ruled as a *gouvernement* (province, see DECENTRALIZATION). Oil (q.v.), discovered on the east coast in late C.19, transformed that region economically, making it a major target of the Japanese invasion in 1942. During the national revolution, the Dutch briefly toyed with creating a federal state of Borneo on the island, but eventually declared a number of smaller states (see FEDERALISM).

During Indonesia's Confrontation (q.v.) with Malaysia, Indonesian troops fought British Commonwealth forces along the border with Sarawak. After 1965 the PKI (q.v.) briefly organized guerrilla resistance in West Kalimantan. Many local Chinese communities, suspected of involvement with the rebels, were expelled by the government. After 1967 East Kalimantan became a major logging region (see FORESTRY) and the island has been an important transmigration (q.v.) settlement site. In 1983 an enormous bushfire in East Kalimantan destroyed ca 3.1 million ha of forest. [0061, 0186, 0517, 0966]

'KAN-T'O-LI', Chinese transcription of the name of an otherwise unknown kingdom on the southeastern coast of Sumatra. It sent tribute to China (q.v.) from 441 and traded with China, India (q.v.), and other parts of the archipelago. It was superseded by Srivijaya (q.v.) in late C.7. See also 'HO-LO-TAN'. [0409, 0429, 0430]

KAPOK (*Ceiba pentandra* Bombacaceae). Probably African in origin, but depicted in Javanese carvings of C.10, kapok is valued primarily for the floss surrounding its seeds which can be used for pillows, lifebelts, etc. Export began in 1850, production being largely in the hands of indigenous smallholders in Java and South Sulawesi. Kapok was one of the few products relatively unaffected by the Depression (q.v.). [0245, 0246, 0938]

KARAWITAN, term coined in the 1950s by Ki Sindosawarno, first director of the conservatorium at Solo, to describe all drama and artistic forms incorporating gamelan (q.v.). [0103]

KARTASURA. See MATARAM.

KARTINI, Raden Ajeng (1879–1905), Javanese feminist writer and activist. The daughter of a progressive bupati (q.v.), she received some Western education but at puberty was secluded in preparation for marriage. She nonetheless opened a school in her father's residence at Japara in 1903 and, after marrying in November of that year, maintained the school in her husband's residence at Rembang. She died in childbirth in 1905. She is known largely for her memorandum to the colonial government, 'Educate the Javanese!' (1903) and her letters, published posthumously as *Door duisternis tot licht: gedachten over en voor het Javaanse volk* (*From darkness to light, thoughts about and on behalf of the Javanese people,* 1911), edited by J.H. Abendanon, with a foreword by Couperus (q.v.), and in English translated as *Letters of a Javanese princess* (1964). Her correspondence is important for its assertion of women's right to education and freedom from polygamy and child marriage. Royalties from the publication of her letters in the Netherlands helped to found a number of 'Kartini schools' giving education to girls. See also EDUCATION; WOMEN AND MEN. [0564, 0717, 1064, 1071]

KARTOSUWIRYO, Sekarmaji Marijan (1905–62), foster son of H.U.S. Tjokroaminoto (q.v.) and activist in the Partai Sarekat Islam Indonesia (q.v.) until his expulsion in 1939 over policy differences. In 1940 he established a school, the Suffah Institute, in Garut (West Java) to give religious and general education to young Muslims; this was closed by the Japanese in 1942, but Kartosuwiryo used contacts made then to form a branch of the Hizbullah (q.v.) in 1945. He joined Masyumi (q.v.), but felt betrayed by the party's agreement to implement the Renville Agreement (q.v.) and by the Siliwangi (q.v.) Division's abandonment of West Java in early 1948. In May he established an Islamic administration in the Garut region with the name Darul Islam (q.v.) and with himself as *imam* or religious leader. He remained the central figure in the West Java DI until he was captured by government forces in April 1962 and executed in September. [0632]

KARYAWAN (from *karya,* task, and *-wan,* person), term coined in the 1960s to describe all employees of a firm or office, including management. It was used as an alternative to the word *buruh* (worker, labor) to avoid the implication that workers might have interests separate from those of management. See also LABOR; LABOR UNIONS. [0333]

KAYUPUTIH (cajuput), medicinal oil obtained from leaves of *Melaleuca cajuputi* (Myrtaceae). Buru (q.v.) became a major center of commercial production in early C.20. [0245, 0246, 0938]

KEBATINAN (also called *kejawen, agama Jawa,* or 'Javanism'), Javanese mysticism, incorporating animist,

Hindu-Buddhist, and Islamic (esp. Sufi) mystical elements but often denying adherence to Islam. Officially legitimized by Article 29 of the 1945 Constitution (q.v.) which distinguishes and acknowledges both religion (*agama*) and belief (*kepercayaan*), it is organized in hundreds of separate associations (*e.g.*, Pangestu, q.v.) and is administered by the Ministry of Education and Culture rather than Religious Affairs. President Suharto, while officially Muslim, is personally associated with kebatinan. See also ABANGAN; ISLAMIC STATE, Demands for. [1035, 1135, 1146]

KEDIRI, kingdom in East Java created by the decision of Airlangga (q.v.) to divide his kingdom in 1049. Kediri sponsored a major flowering of Javanese culture, but was overthrown by Ken Angrok, founder of Singosari (qq.v.) in 1221–22. See also JOYOBOYO.

KEIBODAN, civil guard formed during the Japanese occupation to undertake routine security tasks such as evening village patrols. Though Keibodan units were generally armed only with bamboo stakes, the quasi-military experience they provided laid a basis for the formation of badan perjuangan (q.v.) during the revolution. [0563, 0615, 0617]

KEJAWEN. See KEBATINAN.

KEMPEITAI. See KENPEITAI.

KEN ANGROK. According to both the *Nagarakrtagama* and the *Pararaton* (qq.v.), the former brigand Ken Angrok first came to prominence when he murdered the regent of Tumapel with a kris he had specially commissioned from the master smith Mpu Gandring, whom he also killed. Having implicated the dead regent's bodyguards in the murder, Ken Angrok seized power, married the regent's widow Ken Dedes, and launched a revolt against the king of Kediri (q.v.), whom he defeated at the battle of Genter (1221). He founded the kingdom of Singosari (q.v.) at Tumapel in 1222 and reigned as Rangga Rajasa until his death in 1227.

KENPEITAI, Japanese military police force, founded in 1881, whose role was extended in occupied Indonesia and elsewhere to surveillance of the civilian population, censorship, and the collection of intelligence. The Kenpeitai gained a reputation for gratuitous cruelty and of 538 staff on Java at the end of the war, 199 were later committed for trial on war crimes charges. See also POLITIEK INLICHTINGEN DIENST. [0615, 0616, 0619]

KEPERCAYAAN. See KEBATINAN.

KERBAU or water buffalo *Bubalis bubalis* (not to be confused with the banteng, q.v.) were introduced to Indonesia after 1000 B.C., probably from India via Thailand. They quickly took on great importance as draft animals and sources of milk, becoming a measure of wealth and, by extension, a symbol of power. Buffalo and tiger (q.v.) fights were a common entertainment on Java, and buffalo fights occasionally replaced battles; according to legend, the Minangkabau (q.v.) averted certain defeat in battle with Javanese by proposing a buffalo fight. Against the Javanese buffalo they sent a thirsty calf with knives tied to its head which gored the Javanese beast while the calf nuzzled for milk. Individual buffalo can be identified by distinctive hair whorls, which are sometimes believed also to reflect individual character. [0943]

KERINCI, isolated upland valley in southern central Sumatra, culturally and politically on the fringes of the Minangkabau (q.v.) region and the sultanate of Jambi (q.v.). Gold (q.v.) production was important in C.17, but was gradually overshadowed by rice and by cinnamon (q.v.) produced for trade with the British in Bengkulu (q.v.). [0540]

KESATUAN AKSI MAHASISWA INDONESIA (KAMI, Indonesian Students' Action Front), founded on 25 October 1965 to spearhead the suppression of the PKI and the left in general following the GESTAPU (q.v.) coup of 30 September. It staged street marches and launched a campaign of pamphleteering, and was sponsored by and worked closely with the anticommunist Brig. Gen. Kemal Idris and Colonel Sarwo Edhie. From January 1966 it expressed its demands as the TRITURA (Tri-Tuntutan Hatinurani Rakyat, Three Demands from the Bottom of the People's Hearts): abolish the PKI (q.v.), purge the cabinet, and reduce prices. In much of its action, it cooperated closely with the Kesatuan Aksi Pemuda dan Pelajar Indonesia (KAPPI) representing school children and the Kesatuan Aksi Sarjana Indonesia (KASI) representing graduates. In the early 1970s, KAMI split between those who were absorbed into the government establishment and those who became increasingly critical of New Order (q.v.) policies. In 1973, the progovernment group became the core of the new KNPI (q.v.). [0669, 0681]

KIDUNG SUNDA, semihistorical Javanese poem. Hayam Wuruk, king of Majapahit (q.v.), obtained the hand of the daughter of the king of Pajajaran (q.v.), but on the arrival of the Sundanese wedding party at Bubat in East Java, the Majapahit courtiers insisted that the marriage meant Pajajaran would accept Javanese overlordship and, in some versions, that the princess would be Hayam Wuruk's concubine, not his queen. The Sundanese king refused to accept this insult, fought the Javanese and was slaughtered along with his men, while his daughter committed suicide. [0116]

KLIBUR OAN TIMUR ASWAIN (KOTA, Popular Association of Monarchists of Timor), founded 20 November 1974 by Tetum chiefs in East Timor (q.v.) keen to preserve their position in the changing situation. They traced their spiritual roots to the Camenassa Pact of 1719 between chiefs who opposed the Portuguese, but their greater fear in 1974 was the radicalism of the ASDT (later Fretilin, q.v.) and they soon came close to the Indonesian-sponsored APODETI (q.v.). [0905]

KOELIEORDONNANTIE. See COOLIE ORDINANCE.

KOMANDO JIHAD (Holy War Command), shadowy Islamic organization first reported in the early 1980s to be fighting for an Islamic state in Indonesia, much as the Darul Islam (q.v.) did in earlier years. Actions attributed to or associated with it include the hijacking of a Garuda DC-9 aircraft and an attack on the Cicendo police station near Bandung in 1981 and a supposedly Islamic rising in Lampung in 1989. The term Komando Jihad, however, is perhaps better understood as a general government label for militant Islam than as an actual organization. Imran Muhammad Zein was executed in February 1985 for his part in the 1981 events. [0880]

KOMANDO OPERASI PEMULIHAN KEAMANAN DAN KETERTIBAN (KOPKAMTIB, Operational Command for the Restoration of Security and Order). Extraconstitutional body created on 10 October 1965 to suppress the so-called GESTAPU (q.v.). Its tasks were defined on 6 December 1965 as being 'to restore security and order as a result of the abortive PKI 30 September coup d'etat attempt and to restore the authority and integrity of the government through physical military and non-military operations'. With the establishment of the New Order, KOPKAMTIB retreated in importance but was revitalized in 1969 as the central security apparatus of the state, its terms of reference being expanded to include defence of the Pancasila and the 1945 Constitution (qq.v.). Operating outside regular legal channels, it had extensive authority to arrest, interrogate, and detain. It screened election candidates, censored the press, and closely controlled popular organizations. It was a command within the Indonesian armed forces, giving the KOPKAMTIB commander direct authority over troops independent of the formal military hierarchy, rather than a distinct institution such as BAKIN (q.v.) and was thus a form of permanent martial law command. Its commander was theoretically able to act without reference to the President, as Suharto (q.v.) did in 1965–66. On 22 September 1988, it was replaced by BAKORSTANAS (q.v.). For a list of Commanders of KOPKAMTIB, see the Appendix. [0889, 0890]

KOMANDO OPERASI TERTINGGI (KOTI, Supreme Operations Command), military command formed in December 1961 for the liberation of Irian (q.v.), with Sukarno, Nasution, and Yani (qq.v.) as commander, deputy, and chief of staff; actual fighting was under the Mandala Command, headed by Suharto (q.v.). In January 1962, Indonesian forces were defeated and a deputy navy commander, Yos Sudarso, killed, but military pressure was amongst the factors removing the Dutch later that year. The command was reorganized in July 1963 to take charge of Confrontation (q.v.). An operational Komando Siaga (KOGA, 'Readiness Command') under air force commander Omar Dhani was created in May 1964, but in October its authority was limited to Kalimantan and Sumatra with the title Komando Mandala Siaga (KOLAGA). Army units formerly assigned to KOGA for a projected invasion of the Malay Peninsula were assigned to KOSTRAD (q.v.)

and posted to Java. In February 1966, KOTI was renamed KOGAM (Komando Ganyang Malaysia, Crush Malaysia Command), but it was abolished in July 1967. See also DEFENCE POLICY. [0663]

KOMANDO PASUKAN KHUSUS (KOPASSUS), Special Unit Command, formerly KOPASSANDHA, formerly RPKAD (q.v.), elite paracommando unit employed against pro-PKI regions in Java and Bali in 1966 and later in East Timor and Irian (qq.v.). See also MASSACRES OF 1965–66. See also ARMY. [0663, 0669]

KOMANDO TERTINGGI OPERASI EKONOMI. See DWIFUNGSI.

KOMITE NASIONAL INDONESIA (KNI, Indonesian National Committee), local committees established at every level of government shortly after the proclamation of the Indonesian republic in 1945. In the absence of direction from the KNIP (q.v.), local KNIs were initially responsible for most areas of government activity, including formation of the army (q.v.). In many cases, the authority of the KNI was exercised mainly through a small Working Committee (Badan Pekerja). Though put together in a very ad hoc manner, KNIs generally represented most political streams in their regions and, depending on the capacity of their members, were often key political decision-making bodies during the first year of the Revolution until their role was somewhat taken over by the regional defence councils (Dewan Pertahanan Daerah). See also DEWAN PERTAHANAN NASIONAL. [0563, 0628, 0656, 0660]

KOMITE NASIONAL INDONESIA PUSAT (KNIP, Central Indonesian National Committee), representative body which grew originally out of the Japanese-sponsored Committee for the Preparation of Independence (see BADAN PENYELIDIK USAHA PERSIAPAN KEMERDEKAAN INDONESIA). Having provisionally assumed the powers of the MPR and DPR (qq.v.) at its first session on 16–17 October 1945, it became the acting parliament of the Republic of Indonesia during the Revolution (q.v.). The Republic's prime minister was responsible to the KNIP, although the constitution prescribed a presidential system of government. Membership, however, was effectively by presidential nomination and Sukarno greatly expanded its size in order to have the 1947 Linggajati Agreement (q.v.) ratified. While the full KNIP generally exercised only legislative powers, closer supervision over the government and cabinet was exercised by a Working Committee (Badan Pekerja). [0563, 0628, 0656]

KOMITE NASIONAL PEMUDA INDONESIA (KNPI, Indonesian National Youth Committee), founded 23 July 1973 and led by a former KAMI (q.v.) leader David Napitupulu. Affiliated with Golkar and close to the CSIS (qq.v.) and Ali Murtopo, the KNPI was intended as a youth equivalent of the FBSI and HKTI (see LABOR UNIONS), having the sole right to represent Indonesian youth in political and social affairs so that their energies might be directed exclusively to the benefit of the New Order. Its control over student life, however, has always been sharply limited by independent student unions.

KOMODO, with a few neighboring islets, the only habitat of the Komodo 'dragon' or monitor, *Varanus komodoensis*. A nature reserve was declared in 1966 and a national park in 1980. [0049, 1053]

KONFRONTASI. See CONFRONTATION.

KONGSI WARS. The term *kongsi* refers commonly to a firm commercial partnership, often of several people, cemented by a sense of loyalty as well as self-interest. It was a characteristic organizational form of Chinese (q.v.) in Indonesia. On the goldfields of West Kalimantan, local kongsi became so powerful as to resemble ministates, with their own territory, government, justice system, currency, taxation, and schools entirely independent of the sultanates of Sambas and Pontianak (q.v.). Their independence and involvement in trading salt, opium (qq.v.), and gunpowder led the Dutch to suppress them in the so-called Kongsi Wars of 1850–54. [0518]

KONINKLIJK NEDERLANDSCH INDISCH LEGER (KNIL, Royal Netherlands Indies Army). The three decades following the fall of the Dutch East Indies Company (q.v.) in 1800 were militarily disastrous for the colonial government in Indonesia. Not only did Dutch possessions fall into British hands, but several major uprisings, notably the Java War (q.v.) took place as well. In 1830, therefore, Governor-General van den Bosch founded the KNIL to provide the colonial government with its own reliable military forces. The governor-general was commander-in-chief and from 1867 the KNIL was supported by a department of war, whose head was the KNIL commander. Dutch naval forces in the archipelago, operating from a large base in Surabaya, remained formally a part of the metropolitan navy. An air wing of the KNIL was formed in 1914.

The officer corps of the KNIL was always predominantly Dutch, though towards the end of the colonial period a small number of Indonesians received officer training at the Military Academy in Breda. In addition, the Sunan of Surakarta (q.v.) was a titular major-general in the KNIL and many other Javanese aristocrats held courtesy ranks. Troops were diverse in origin.

In 1861, 54% were 'native' and 46% 'European'. The European category included not only a great many Germans but also a number of Africans, the so-called *blanda hitam* (black Dutchmen) from Guinea. Like the British in India, the Dutch favored specific indigenous ethnic groups for recruitment. Ambonese and Menadonese were regarded as especially reliable, though Javanese always formed the largest bloc; in 1936, there were 4,000 Ambonese in the KNIL to 13,000 Javanese (see also NATIVE TROOPS).

The KNIL carried out the conquest of indigenous states in the Outer Islands in C.19 and early C.20, but its primary role was the maintenance of internal security and order (*rust en orde*) (see also van HEUTSZ). KNIL troops thus were most heavily concentrated on Java and in Aceh and north Sumatra. From 1917 male European residents of the colony were subject to conscription for service in the militia and *landstorm* (home guard) for the defence of the colony, but in C.20 the authorities relied increasingly on the British naval base in Singapore (q.v.) for their defence. The KNIL capitulated to Japanese forces at Kalijati in West Java on 9 March 1942 and much of the European component of the army spent the rest of the war in prisoner-of-war camps. KNIL troops which had escaped to Australia played a small role in the reconquest of eastern Indonesia in 1944–45.

The postwar KNIL under General S.H. Spoor (1902–49) recovered rapidly and took part with the Dutch army (Koninklijke Landmacht, KL) in the so-called Police Actions (q.v.) to crush the Indonesian Republic. In 1948, the KNIL comprised 15,500 Europeans and 50,500 non-Europeans. It was formally abolished on 26 July 1950, its troops being transferred to the KL or to the Indonesian army (APRIS) or demobilized. Troops to be demobilized were entitled to be discharged at a place of their own choosing and around 4,000 Ambonese requested demobilization in Ambon, where they would have been able to join the uprising of the Republik Maluku Selatan (q.v.) against the Republic. To avoid this, they were unilaterally transferred to the KL and 'repatriated' with their families to the Netherlands in 1951 for demobilization. See also ARMY. [0366, 0599, 0605, 1086]

'KONINKLIJKE' (the 'Royal'), common name for a group of companies involved in the extraction and sale of oil (q.v.) from Indonesia. The Koninklijke Nederlandsche Maatschappij tot Exploitatie van Petroleumbronnen in Nederlandsch-Indië was formed in 1890 to extract oil from concessions in Langkat in East Sumatra (q.v.) and began refining oil at Pangkalan Brandan in 1892. Under J.B.A. Kessler and (from 1901) Henri Deterding the firm moved into the sale and distribution of oil in Asia. Cooperation with the Nederlandsch-Indische Industrie-en Handel-Maatschappij, a subsidiary of the Shell Transport and Trading Company, led in 1903 to creation of the Asiatic Petroleum Co. In 1907 the parent companies merged their remaining holdings into the Bataafsche Petroleum Maatschappij (now Shell Petroleum NV) and the Anglo-Saxon Petroleum Co (now Shell Petroleum Co.), each owned respectively 60% and 40% by the Dutch and British partners. The Koninklijke sold most of its Indonesian holdings in 1966 after experiencing great difficulties under Guided Democracy (q.v.). In 1970, the group took over the Billiton tin (q.v.) companies. [0310]

KONINKLIJKE PAKETVAART MAATSCHAPPIJ (KPM, Royal Packetship Company), formed in 1888 to take over interisland mail routes in the colony. By use of preferential rates for loyal customers, provision of credit and managerial expertise, denial of facilities to rivals, and cross-subsidization of uneconomic routes, the KPM was able to establish an extensive network and a virtual monopoly of interisland trade in C.20, as well as a reputation for high quality, expensive service. The company was a major target for economic nationalism after independence and from 1952 began to disengage from Indonesia, moving its resources into deep-sea shipping and steadily running down its Indonesian operations. On 3 December 1957, its offices in Indonesia were seized by workers, and on the same day the company transferred its management to Amsterdam and ordered all its ships to leave Indonesian territorial waters. Those ships seized in port were later restored to the company after Lloyds insurance agents pressured the Indonesian government to release them. See also SHIPPING. [0680, 0686, 0781]

KONSTITUANTE. See CONSTITUENT ASSEMBLY.

KORPS PEGAWAI REPUBLIK INDONESIA (KORPRI, Corps of Civil Servants of the Indonesian Republic), the compulsory official association of Indonesian government officials, formed in November 1971 by the merger of various Korps Karyawan (KOKAR, Employees' Corps) of government departments. It is the sole social organization to which civil servants are ordinarily permitted to belong, ostensibly to prevent civil servants from becoming associated with sectional social interests. KORPRI is affiliated to Golkar (q.v.) and plays an important role in marshalling civil servant support for the government at election time (see MONOLOYALITAS). Its hierarchy (like that of the parallel wives' organization Dharma Wanita, q.v.) closely mirrors that of the departments in which its members work.

KORTE VERKLARING. See NETHERLANDS INDIES, Expansion of.

KOSGORO (Koperasi Serba Guna Gotong Royong, All-Purpose Gotong Royong Cooperative), large cooperative formed on the basis of the East Java student army of the revolutionary period, TRIP, and led by Mas Isman (1924–84), one of the major constituent bodies within Golkar (q.v.).

KOSTRAD (Komando Cadangan Strategis Angkatan Darat, Army Strategic Reserve, called Cadangan Umum Angkatan Darat, Army General Reserve until 1963), formed in March 1961 as a crack unit under direct control of the General Staff, thus independent of the army's powerful regional commanders. It drew on the existing paracommando unit RPKAD (q.v.) and selected units from the three Java commands and formed the military power base of General Suharto (q.v.) in his crushing of the GESTAPU (q.v.) coup. See also ARMY. [0663, 0669]

KRAKATAU (Krakatoa, Rakata), island in the Sunda Strait between Java and Sumatra, site of major eruptions on 20 May and 26–28 August 1883. Most of the volcano collapsed into an immense caldera, causing tsunamis 20 meters high which flooded neighboring coastlines, killing perhaps 36,000 people. Approximately 18 cubic kilometers of ash was thrown into the atmosphere, causing bright red sunsets for two years after. The sound of the explosion was audible over a quarter of the earth's surface. Further eruptions resulted in the appearance of a new island, Anak Krakatau (Child of Krakatau) in January 1928. It was included in the Ujung Kulon (q.v.) national park in 1980. See also VOLCANOES. [0970]

KRATON, the palace of an Indonesian, especially Javanese, ruler, typically constructed on a north-south alignment with numerous pavilions (*pendopo*) and enclosed courtyards. Traditionally the kraton was regarded as the physical center of the kingdom and the point from which royal power radiated. See also ARCHITECTURE. [0095, 0401]

KRETEK. The mixing of addictive drugs, such as betel and opium (qq.v.), with other substances was already widespread in the archipelago before the arrival of tobacco (q.v.), but by the 1930s tobacco and clove cigarettes known as *kretek* (perhaps onomatopoeic from the crackling sound they make as they burn) had become especially common. Initially a cottage industry, production of kretek came largely into Chinese hands in the 1950s and expanded greatly at the expense of conventional cigarettes (*rokok putih*) after 1968, partly with the help of a differential tariff which disadvantaged non-kretek brands. Despite their exceptionally high tar and nicotine content, kretek are smoked by approximately 60% of Indonesian men and 4% of women. Retail sales are estimated in 1989 at US$2.3 billion, of which $1.6 billion went to the government in excise duties. [0322, 0330]

KRIS. See METALWORKING; WEAPONS.

KRONCONG, music of the port cities of eastern Indonesia, introduced by the Portuguese (q.v.) in C.16 but rapidly assimilated, especially before the arrival of cassette decks, as the music for *pasar malam* (night markets). It reached Java in late C.19 but is now closely associated with the Betawi (q.v.) ethnic group. Kroncong typically features a simple melody line, generally sung by a woman, guitar accompaniment, and sentimental lyrics. In C.20, its form was influenced by Hawaiian styles. Far more than gamelan (q.v.), kroncong became a vehicle for nationalist music, typified by the works of Ismail Marzuki (1914–58). Since the 1970s, the popularity of kroncong has been somewhat diminished by the rise of dangdut (q.v.). See also MUSIC. [0104, 0122]

KUBU, primitive tribe in south Sumatra, once thought to be of mixed Veddoid and Negrito origin, and thus probably descendants of pre-Austro-Melanesian inhabitants of the archipelago (see MIGRATIONS), but now believed to be of mixed Austro-Melanesian and Austronesian origin. They are or were seminomadic forest dwellers, whose main contact with the outside world was by so-called 'silent barter', in which goods for trade were left at an agreed spot, without the Kubu and traders ever meeting.

KUTAI, region around the lower Mahakam river in east Kalimantan. Known only from epigraphic evidence, a Hindu or Buddhist state perhaps a couple of generations old existed there in early C.5, followed by the state of Martapura ruled by King Mulavarman. In ca 1280, refugees from Singosari (q.v.) on Java settling near the river mouth founded the kingdom of Kertanegara which converted to Islam in 1565 and later conquered the upstream remnants of Martapura. The sultanate was subject to Banjarmasin (q.v.) from time to time. The Dutch signed a monopoly treaty with the Sultan in 1635 and annexed the region in 1699, but warriors from Wajo' (q.v.) in Sulawesi conquered the area in 1726 and a prolonged period of Bugis (q.v.) settlement followed. In 1844 a Scottish adventurer, Erskine Murray, attempted to set himself up as a White Raja (q.v.). The Sultan signed a further treaty with the Dutch in 1873, and coal and oil (qq.v.) extraction began in 1882. The oil wells in particular were a target of the Japanese invasion in 1942 and an Australian counterinvasion in July 1945. The sultanate of Kutai was abolished in 1960. [0047, 0052, 0501, 0527]

KYAI. Javanese title of respect for learned men, now confined to specialists in Islamic learning. See also ISLAM. [1116, 1139, 1157]

L

LABOR. No clear picture of population (q.v.) patterns in the archipelago before C.19 has yet been drawn, but it seems that while land (q.v.) was relatively abundant labor was often scarce, and that control of labor thus was a major key to political and economic power. The adoption of Hinduism (q.v.) and the resulting exaltation of the king seem to have enabled rulers to shift beyond carefully negotiated patron-client relations with a small number of followers to the large-scale raising of corvée labor from the community (see STATE-FORMATION). The mobilization of labor on this large scale enabled the construction of monuments such as Borobudur and Prambanan (qq.v.) and underpinned the Dutch decision to retain the services of traditional elites for the recruitment of labor, especially under the Cultivation System (q.v., see also HERENDIENSTEN). Slavery (q.v.) also existed as a means of labor control, mostly at household level.

Immigration of laborers from China began on a small scale in C.17, but continued in waves until the 1930s, successive colonial authorities finding Chinese (q.v.) politically and socially more amenable than Indonesians. In early C.19, labor was still scarce enough for the colonial authorities to introduce strict regulations on travel (q.v.) and residence by Indonesians and even in 1880 the plantations of East Sumatra still needed the state-enforced Coolie Ordinance (q.v.) to keep workers in place. In early C.20, a scarcity of skilled labor enabled the emergence of labor unions (q.v.), especially on Java, while after independence unions drew strength from their association with political parties. In 1921, the Dutch established a Kantoor van de Arbeid (Labor Office), which collected information on labor conditions and drafted labor laws. On the whole, however, the steadily growing abundance of labor has weakened the bargaining position of workers. Unemployment was officially put at 2.2% in 1987, but most observers believe the figure to be much higher than this, perhaps 11 million out of a workforce of 67.5 million, though no official figures are published and extensive underemployment makes reliable estimates impossible.

The implications of rising population for agricultural labor have been discussed extensively. The Agricultural Involution (q.v.) thesis of Geertz suggested that there was little true unemployment of labor in the Javanese countryside; rather, that a complex system of lease, lease-back, sale, and share-cropping ensured that all had some right to land and that income was based on that right rather than on a strict calculation of wage-for-service. Fields were thus planted, tended, and harvested in a cooperative way designed to ensure the welfare of all members of the community. More recent research has cast doubt on whether this system was ever as extensive as Geertz seemed to imply, and most observers now see in any case a trend away from diffuse land rights and towards a distinct class of wage-earning agricultural laborers, whose bargaining position is severely weakened by the abundance of rural labor. [0211, 0213, 0237, 0249, 0253, 0331–0340, 0347, 0550]

LABOR UNIONS. Rising demand for skilled and semiskilled labor in the growing cities and in the colonial sugar (q.v.) industry dramatically strengthened the position of workers in the colony in early C.20, leading first to a large number of small-scale strikes in the first decade of the century and then to the formation of labor unions. European government employees were unionized earliest (1905), followed by railway workers in the Vereeniging van Spoor- en Tramweg Personeel (VSTP, Union of Rail and Tramway Personnel) in 1908 and the European postal and pawnshop workers in 1912 and 1913. Since the program of these unions often included preservation of the favorable treatment of European employees over Indonesians, indigenous workers soon began to form their own unions, especially in the pawnshop service and the railways, where the VSTP had come under Indonesian domination by 1918. There were few unions amongst ethnic Chinese or amongst the employees of smaller private firms. The Sarekat Islam and the PKI (qq.v.) were both active in organizing unions, though their organizers often found themselves torn between promoting the specific interests of the workers and supporting the broader program of the political movement.

By 1920 there was no longer a critical shortage of skilled labor; employees became less tolerant of what they regarded as agitation and they began resisting union claims and, in some cases, dismissing union leaders. Major strikes broke out in the railway service in 1920 and 1923, in the pawnshops in 1921, and in the ports in 1925, all of them unsuccessful. Although unions claimed large memberships, union discipline including the payment of membership fees was hard to enforce. By 1932, there were 132 unions registered in the colony with a total of 82,860 members.

Banned during the Japanese occupation, labor unions emerged in their hundreds during the Revolution, often completely taking over the management of factories and plantations. Many were affiliated through the labor federations BBI and SOBSI with the PKI (qq.v.) and in 1948 when the Hatta (q.v.) government began attempting to reassert managerial control in order to gain control of agricultural and industrial produce, political and class antagonisms coincided. A bitter strike in a state textile factory at Delanggu in Central Java in May, in particular, contributed to the tensions which produced the Madiun Affair (q.v.). During the 1950s and 1960s, left-wing control of trade unions diminished with the establishment of conservative trade union federations, such as SOKSI (q.v.). From 1957, great limits were placed on right to strike, strikes being prohibited in essential industries (including communications, development projects, the tourist industry, and government corporations) in 1963, and unions in general became vehicles for the mobilization of support for political parties, rather than purely industrial organizations.

Under the New Order (q.v.), the government has rejected the idea that unions are institutions for defending worker interests against management and government, and has argued instead that they are corporatist bodies for coordinating the workers' role in an essentially cooperative venture with management. The Basic Manpower Law of 1969 acknowledged the right of workers to form unions and to strike, but the principle of Pancasila Industrial Relations (*Hubungan Industri Pancasila*) laid down in 1974 specifically denies that workers may have interests distinct from those of the business and industry as a whole. Organizationally, too, unions have been brought under close control. On 20 February 1973, all unions except KORPRI (q.v.) were required to join the Federasi Buruh Seluruh Indonesia (FBSI, All-Indonesian Workers' Federation). Peasant organizations followed on 26 April with the formation of the Himpunan Kerukunan Tani Indonesia (HKTI, Association of Indonesian Peasant Leagues) and the Himpunan Nelayan Seluruh Indonesia (HNSI, All-Indonesia Fishermen's Association) in September 1973. Each of these organizations became in turn a member of Golkar (q.v.). Since then, there has been a major restructuring of unions into 21 largely industry-based ('vertical') organizations with appointed officials, replacing the former occupation-based ('horizontal') associations. In November 1985, this process was completed with the transformation of the FBSI into the Serikat Pekerja Seluruh Indonesia (SPSI, All-Indonesia Workers Union). Nationwide membership of unions is small (about

3 million in 1983), partly because much of the workforce is employed in small businesses, partly because of extensive female employment, and partly because of the relatively slender achievements of labor organization in the past. See also LEGAL AID. [0333, 0336, 0338, 0559]

LADANG, swidden (slash-and-burn) agriculture, assumed to be the earliest form of farming in the archipelago and still practised especially in parts of Kalimantan (q.v.). Typically, swiddeners clear and burn an area of upland rain forest, plant crops for a year or more and then, as soil fertility diminishes or weed growth becomes insurmountable, move on to a new area, returning perhaps a generation later, once the forest has regrown. Over the last century, swidden agriculture has aroused strong hostility amongst ecologists and agricultural scientists, who have argued, amongst other things, that it irreparably damages the rain forest, causing erosion, disrupting rainfall patterns, and promoting the spread of the grass *alang-alang* (q.v.), and that it needlessly wastes the precious genetic and timber resources of the forest. More recent research, however, has suggested that swidden agriculture, while contributing some erosion in the short term, seldom leads to alang-alang infestation or to permanent damage to the forest, that much of the ecological change attributed to swidden has been a consequence of commercial exploitation of rain forest areas, and that it is more productive in some respects than intensive wet rice cultivation. [0241, 0242, 1007]

LAKAWOOD (*kayu laka*), blood-red heartwood of a large liana, *Dalbergia parviflora* (Fabaceae), valued for its strong fragrance. It was extensively exported to China (q.v.) for use as incense. [0751, 0938]

LAMPUNG, southernmost province of Sumatra, settled according to tradition by three tribes, the Abung,

Publian and Peminggir probably in C.14. The region became an important pepper (q.v.) producing area in C.16 and came under the rule of Banten (q.v.) in ca 1530. The Dutch East Indies Company (q.v.) founded a fort at Menggala in 1668 and took general control of the region in 1751, Daendels (q.v.) formally annexing it in 1808. A long war of resistance led by Muslim communities followed (1817–56). In 1883 coastal regions were devastated by flooding following the eruption of Krakatau (q.v.). Lampung was the site of the first attempts at transmigration (q.v.) and in the 1970s became an important area of settlement, but was closed to further settlement in 1984. Much settlement, however, is already too dense and the clearing of forests for agriculture has created major hydrological problems. Lampung is now Indonesia's major coffee (q.v.) producing area.

LAMTORO (*Leucaena leucocephala* Mimosaceae), shrub introduced into Indonesia in C.19 and extensively used since 1966 for rapid revegetation of cleared areas, as a source of firewood and animal fodder and, thanks to its nitrogen-fixing capacity, as a soil rejuvenator. It is used most widely in the drier areas of eastern Indonesia where it has to some extent displaced *Lantana* as a favored ground cover.

LAND. For much of human history, land was relatively abundant in the archipelago. Although the effort involved in clearing it for agriculture inevitably gave it value, and religious beliefs may have invested it with spiritual significance, land scarcity was not a major problem and control of labor and trade (qq.v.) seem to have been more important sources of political power. Land may have been held collectively within communities, but individual rights also seem to have been respected. Forest lands, and land not in active cultivation, seem to have been more freely at the disposal of rulers, and the VOC (q.v.) allocated to private individuals large tracts of freehold land on the northern coast of Java (see PARTICULIERE LANDERIJEN). The growth of population and the rise of commercial production of crops, however, put an end to this abundance and from at least 1800, control of land was one of the major issues in politics, first on Java and later on other islands.

During the brief British interregnum, Raffles (q.v.) deemed all land on Java to be government property and on this basis began to charge peasant farmers a land rent (q.v.). Under the Cultivation System (q.v.), however, collective control of land was emphasized, the village receiving the right (*beschikkingsrecht*) to allocate and reallocate land to its members, villagers being required in turn to devote one-fifth of their land to crops for the government. Land rights, thus, were something of a burden, and the complicated land tenure arrangements described, amongst others, by Geertz as an aspect of an 'agricultural involution' (q.v.) were at least in part an attempt by landowners to shed the taxation burden. Correspondingly, Europeans were expected not to have land rights, and even leasehold of land by Europeans was banned from 1836 to 1853; even after a slight liberalization of regulations in 1856, little land came into European hands.

Major changes took place with the introduction of the so-called Liberal Policy (q.v.) in 1870. In that year, a colonial government *Domeinverklaring* declared all 'waste' land, that is land that was not actively and permanently cultivated, on Java and Madura to be government property. Traditional activities such as wood collecting were deemed to represent usufruct rights but not ownership, though the extent to which the state could override traditional use was a topic of continued debate. Also in 1870, the Agrarian Law (q.v.) allowed a form of lease called *erfpacht* for up to 75 years, while continuing to ban the sale of land by indigenes to non-indigenes. Regulations on the sugar (q.v.) industry specified that no more than one-third of village land might be leased out, fixed a minimum rent, and required that land be returned to the village for cultivation at least every three years, though these regulations were often not enforced. In 1885 regulations were introduced to permit so-called *conversierechten* (conversion rights), under which village land might be converted from collective ownership (subject to periodic redistributions) to private ownership, but these were little used, partly because an estimated 75% of land was already under individual hereditary title. Colonial land laws remained in force until 1960, when a new basic Agrarian Law (UU Pokok Agraria) simplified landholding by distinguishing between *hak milik* (ownership and disposal, restricted to Indonesian citizens), and *hak guna bangunan* (usufruct). A 1963 law on land reform (q.v.) was only weakly implemented. The registration of land ownership, however, still presents major problems in densely populated rural areas where complicated tenure relationships cannot easily be summed up in a title deed; in urban areas where large numbers of people have been resident for years on what is technically government or private land and are thus subject to expulsion at short notice and with meager compensation; and in outlying regions where indigenous rights over land for purposes such as hunting and gathering have been disregarded in the acquisition of land for transmigration (q.v.) sites. See also LEGAL AID.

The relationship between land and political power in Indonesia is still a topic of much discussion. On the whole, however, control of land seems seldom to have been a direct route to national political power, state power being a means to obtain control of land, rather than vice versa. The Javanese priyayi (q.v.), offered land grants in 1830 as part-payment for their participation in the Cultivation System (q.v.), rejected this in favor of salaries, a share of production, and continuing tributary rights. The dominance of large foreign companies in plantation production after 1870 also hindered the growth of an indigenous plantation-controlling elite. The colonial identification of the village (see DESA) as the holder of communal land rights in Java also inhibited the accumulation of land, so that despite clear inequalities in control of land, Indonesia did not develop a class of large landholders such as emerged in India or the Philippines. At the local level, on the other hand, there is often a clear link between land and power, wealthy farming families holding village headships and monopolizing contacts with the outside world. Even at the end of the colonial era, 82% of the land in West Java was said to be owned by 12% of families. Since independence, particularly under the influence of the Green Revolution (q.v.), village land holdings have tended to concentrate still more in the hands of a small number of local families, though purchase of land by outsiders has also greatly increased. [0253, 0254, 0550]

LAND REFORM. While many government measures have attempted to modify the pattern of landholding in Indonesia (see LAND), the term land reform refers most commonly to measures for the redistribution of land provided for by the 1960 Basic Law on Agriculture (Undang-Undang Pokok Agraria), which applied mainly to Java. The law, passed at the urging of the PKI (q.v.), provided for the breaking up of larger concentrations of land in the Javanese countryside. Although there was no class of large landholders in Java, there were clear social differences in access to land, as well as a general trend towards concentration of landholdings. The land reform law did not so much envisage the arbitrary distribution of land to the poor—there was clearly nowhere near enough land to go around—but rather aimed to assist those smallholders who had recently lost or were in danger of losing their land as a result of indebtedness. The PKI turned the issue into one of popular concern by linking it to the attempts of landlords to restrict participation of the population in production, especially at harvest time (see GOTONG ROYONG).

Only in rare instances was the land reform law implemented. Landowners commonly reduced the size of their holdings by distributing them amongst relatives or by donating them to religious institutions, especially mosques and *pesantren* (q.v.), or relied on delaying tactics by the land reform committees. In late 1963 the PKI announced *aksi sepihak* (unilateral or direct action) to implement land reform measures, accompanied by a campaign against the so-called 'seven village devils'. In several areas land was seized and commonly restored to former owners, but the party was accused of choosing its victims more for their hostility to the PKI than for their class, and most of the landlords targeted were *santri* (q.v.) Muslim supporters of the NU (q.v.). The actions aroused enormous tensions in the countryside of Java and contributed to the motives for the massacres of 1965–66 (q.v.). [0252, 0798]

LAND RENT (*landrente*). From late C.18 a number of reformers, such as van Hogendorp (q.v.) and Muntinghe sought ways of streamlining Dutch rule of Java by bypassing the entrenched position of the *bupati* (q.v.) as prime agents of the colonial government and bringing peasants into the money economy as a market for European manufactured goods. They proposed to achieve this by creating, amongst other things, a direct taxation relationship with the peasantry, and to do so suggested recognizing peasants' land rights, which could then be taxed. Raffles (q.v.) first introduced land rent in Kedu and Banten in 1812 and it was gradually extended, but, because of the need to obtain surveys of landholding, the whole of Java (excluding the Vorstenlanden and particuliere landerijen, qq.v.) was not covered until 1872, while a unified system of assessment based on fairly accurate surveys was established only between 1907 and 1921. Land rent was also levied in Bali, Lombok (qq.v.), and south Sulawesi. Land rent provided nearly half the revenue of the colonial government in 1867, but this proportion had sunk to 10% by 1928. After independence, land rent was formally abolished, though it seems still to have been collected in many regions. In 1959 it was replaced with an agricultural produce tax (*pajak hasil bumi*) and the proceeds were allotted to local (kabupaten) authorities. In 1965 it was renamed *Iuran Pembangunan Daerah* (IPEDA, Regional Development Tax). See also TAXATION. [0291, 0299, 0498, 0525]

LANGE, Mads Johansen (1806–56), Danish trader and adventurer, one of a number of Europeans who were able to prosper as intermediaries between the indigenous courts and Western traders. After operating in the Balinese court on Lombok (q.v.) from 1834, Lange settled at Kuta on the south coast of Bali (q.v.) in 1839, where he worked closely with the raja of Badung, who was also the chief trader of his kingdom. Both became immensely wealthy from the trade in slaves and other goods, but war and an outbreak of smallpox (q.v.) in Bali in mid-century undermined their position. After the sultan's death, Lange was unable to find a suitable new patron and died, probably of poison, in 1856. See also WHITE RAJAS. [0534]

LANGKAT, sultanate in East Sumatra (q.v.), acquired by the Dutch from Siak (q.v.) in 1858. Like the rest of East Sumatra it became a major area of Dutch tobacco plantations and in 1892 was the site of the colony's first commercial oil (q.v.) well at Telaga. The sultan was deposed in the social revolution of 1946. [0528, 0655]

LANGUAGES. Though it is often difficult to distinguish languages and dialects, it is commonly said that around 200 indigenous languages are spoken in the Indonesian archipelago. Most of the languages of western and central Indonesia are of the Western Austronesian division, formerly known as the Indonesian branch of the Malayo-Polynesian family, which includes also Malagasy (see MADAGASCAR, Historical links with) and the indigenous languages of Taiwan. Languages of the Pacific islands belong to the Eastern Austronesian division. Linguistic and archeological evidence suggests that the Austronesian languages first reached the eastern archipelago and had begun to disperse by at least 3000 B.C. (see MIGRATIONS). Features of these languages are a relatively simple morphology for nouns and verbs, use of roots which can become nouns or verbs, reduplication of words, and distinct forms for the second person including and excluding the listener.

Within the Western Austronesian division, the Sumatran languages Malay, Minangkabau, Acehnese, Rejang and Kerinci, together with Madurese, form one sub-group, with Gayo and Batak somewhat more distant relatives. Malay expanded from a relatively small base in east and south Sumatra and the Malay peninsula in C.13 to become a major lingua franca in the archipelago by C.16 and became the basis of modern Indonesian (see INDONESIAN LANGUAGE). Javanese (q.v.) and Sundanese, numerically the largest and second largest language groups (excluding Indonesian) form a distinct subgroup strongly influenced by Sanskrit. A large number of indigenous languages exist in Kalimantan, but Ngaju, a language of the southeast, acts as a lingua franca for much of the southern part of the island. In eastern Indonesia, approximately one hundred Austronesian languages are spoken but these are usually classified into Bima-Sumba, Ambon-Timor, Sula-Bacan, south Halmahera-western Irian, and several Sulawesi groups. Buginese is the most widely spoken of the Sulawesi languages. A number of Eastern Austronesian languages are spoken in the province of Irian Jaya, mainly along the north coast. All Western Austronesian languages show successive vocabulary influences from Sanskrit, Arabic, and/or European languages, depending on the history of their speakers.

Entirely distinct from the Austronesian family is the Papuan, or Indo-Pacific, group of languages, whose speakers occupy three-quarters of the island of New Guinea, with communities on Halmahera, Timor, and Alor (qq.v.). Insufficient research has been done to say that all languages classified as Papuan are related, but it seems probable that this is the case. Most are spoken by relatively few people and are highly complex grammatically. Verbs, for instance, vary enormously depending on the number and other characteristics of both subject and objects. Many are tonal; that is, variations in the pitch of a vowel or syllable change its meaning.

Of the European languages, Portuguese was an important lingua franca in the archipelago in C.16 and 17, and Portuguese-speaking communities survived in some regions until late C.19. The Dutch generally did not promote the use of their own language by Indonesians, developing Malay instead as the principal language of administration.

A number of Malay words have entered English: amok (from *amuk,* q.v.), compound (from *kampung*), kapok, mandarin (via Portuguese from *menteri,* itself derived from a Sanskrit word), paddy, and sarong. Gong derives from Javanese. See also ETYMOLOGY. [0185–0209, 0545]

LASYKAR. Originally denoting a militia or home guard, this term referred in the Revolution to well-organized irregular armed units which supported the Republic but resisted incorporation into the army (q.v.) Most lasykar opposed negotiation with the Dutch, preferring a policy of armed struggle. See also BADAN PERJUANGAN; DIPLOMASI AND PERJUANGAN. [0656]

LATAH, sociopsychological condition occurring amongst Javanese which leads them to utter obscene words or phrases or to imitate the words or actions of others. See also AMUK. [1015, 1167]

LAW. The early legal systems of Indonesia are difficult to reconstruct since these were amongst the first institutions affected by the successive waves of Indian, Muslim, and European juridical thinking. Codified *adat* (q.v.) law represents an attempt by Dutch scholars to record the traditional legal thinking of the archipelago, but this attempt was affected inevitably by Dutch political conceptions. As far as is known, crimes were often held to be as much against the spiritual order as against human victims, and during trials the veracity of witnesses was tested by ordeal. The idea of civil actions between private individuals was not well developed. Punishment commonly included monetary fines, enslavement, torture, and death (reserved for treason, lèse-majesté, murder, and theft), but rarely imprisonment or beating. Islamic law, introduced in some regions from C.13, greatly clarified commercial and personal law and added whipping and amputation to the catalogue of acceptable punishments.

When the Dutch East Indies Company (q.v.) arrived in Indonesia in C.17, it had little interest in territorial jurisdiction except as far as was necessary for its commercial purposes, and it therefore left non-Europeans as far as possible under the authority of their traditional rulers. Within VOC territories, European law applied to all. Law for VOC possessions was codified first under Governor-General van Diemen (q.v.) in 1650, when Joan Maetsuyker compiled the Bataviaasche Statuten; these remained the basis of European law in the colony until 1848 (see also DUTCH IN INDONESIA; NETHERLANDS, Constitutional relationship with Indonesia). Courts to administer Dutch law were established in Batavia in 1629 and Maluku in 1651. In 1747, however, as it acquired more territory (see MATARAM), the Company decided to retain native law for its indigenous subjects outside the cities and established *inlandsche rechtsbanken* or *landraden* to apply native law on the northern coast of Java. Chinese and other non-indigenous minorities were subject to the same courts, though legal issues within each community were often left to Dutch-appointed community chiefs (see CHINESE IN INDONESIA).

In C.19, with the introduction of direct Dutch rule, this pluralistic system was formalized with the specification of legal racial categories for Dutch subjects in the Indies (see RACE). In 1824, *adat* (q.v.) law was declared applicable to all natives (including those in the cities). In 1848, with the adoption of a new Dutch constitution, the Bataviaasche Statuten were abolished and a large part of metropolitan Dutch law was declared applicable to Europeans in the colony. From 1919 sections of this law (excluding family law) were also applied to foreign Orientals though they continued to be administered through native courts. Not until late C.19, however, was a major program to codify adat carried out. At the close of the colonial period, the legal system was divided into native ('*inheemse*') and government jurisdictions, which coincided generally though not always with the distinction between directly-ruled territories and *zelfbesturen* (q.v.). Native rulers, aristocrats, and their families were not subject to civil legal action except with permission of the governor-general. In 1918, the various branches of criminal law in the colony were united in a new criminal code, the *Wetboek van Strafwet* (now *Kitab Undang-undang Hukum Pidana*, KUHP), but this was never actually implemented for Indonesians and in 1941 it was supplemented by a separate criminal code for natives, the *Herziene Inlandsch Reglement* (HIR, Revised Native Regulations). Islamic courts (*priesterraden*) were established on Java and Madura in 1882 to administer Muslim marriage and family law.

The 1945, 1949 and 1950 Constitutions of the Indonesian Republic all validated Dutch colonial law in so far as it did not conflict with other provisions of the constitution. Especially during Guided Democracy (q.v.), this created some legal uncertainty, as many laws of the colonial era could be regarded as in conflict with principles of social justice. Law is now administered in a three-tier system, cases passing from the Pengadilan Negeri through the Pengadilan Tinggi (appeal court) to the Mahkamah Agung (Supreme Court). A new procedural code for criminal law, the *Kitab Undang-undang Hukum Acara Pidana* (KUHAP) was adopted on 31 December 1981, but many practical aspects of these regulations remain to be determined. See also LEGAL AID; SUBVERSION; YAP THIAM HIEN. [0366, 0483, 0870–0891]

LEGAL AID services began in Indonesia with the formation of informal consultation bureaus run by law students in Jakarta in 1967. A full Legal Aid Bureau, the Lembaga Bantuan Hukum (LBH) was formed in 1971 by the legal association PERADIN (Persatuan Advokat Indonesia, Indonesian Advocates Union) with financial assistance from the Jakarta governor Ali Sadikin (q.v.). Since then over 100 legal aid organizations have sprung up, with varying degrees of affiliation to the government and other organizations. They have taken an especially active role in siding with the poor in land and labor (qq.v.) disputes. See also LAW. [0885]

LEIMENA, Johannes (1905–77), medical doctor and one of the founders of PARKINDO (q.v.) in 1945. As minister of health in several early cabinets, he usefully represented the Protestant minority in government, and became a politically colorless deputy prime minister in Sukarno's first non-parliamentary *kabinet kerja* in 1957. He resigned from PARKINDO in 1959 but remained deputy prime minister along with Chaerul Saleh and Subandrio (qq.v.) in 1963 after the death of Juanda (q.v.). He had, however, little influence on policy under Guided Democracy (q.v.) and was permitted to retire in peace after 1966. [0634]

LEMBAGA KEBUDAYAAN RAKYAT (LEKRA, Institute of People's Culture), formed August 1950 as affiliate of the PKI (q.v.) in cultural affairs. Its secretary-general was Yubar Ayub. It was formed initially to oppose the activities of the Dutch-sponsored STICUSA (Stichting voor Culturele Samenwerking, Institute for Cultural Cooperation), which was finally disbanded in 1956. Its focus shifted in the mid 50s to resisting American cultural influence, especially in film (q.v.).

In 1956, it adopted the doctrine of socialist realism, arguing that art should reflect social realities and promote social progress rather than simply exploring the human personality. In particular, it promoted the idea of 'People-ness' (*kerakyatan*) in art and urged artists to move downwards (*turun ke bawah*) to draw inspiration from the mass of the people. LEKRA was rather more successful in recruiting in the visual arts than in literature; well-known painters such as Affandi, Henk Ngantung (qq.v.), and Hendra Gunawan applied LEKRA ideas to their work with success, whereas relatively few major writers (Pramudya Ananta Tur, q.v., being an outstanding exception) were active within the organization. LEKRA consistently argued that artists should receive state support and became itself a major patron of the arts during Guided Democracy. In 1963 it claimed 200 branches and 100,000 members. After 1962 it began a series of sharp attacks on those it regarded as opponents of *kerakyatan,* notably Hamka and H.B. Jassin (qq.v.) which created lasting animosities in the literary world. During this period on the other hand its own work faced increasing restriction and censorship by the military and it was banned along with other PKI affiliates after the installation of the New Order. See also CULTURE, Debate on the role of. [0150, 0796, 0822]

LEMBATA (Lomblen). See SOLOR ARCHIPELAGO.

LESSER SUNDAS (Nusatenggara). See BALI; FLORES; KOMODO; LOMBOK; ROTI; SAVU; SOLOR ARCHIPELAGO; SUMBA; SUMBAWA; TIMOR.

LIBERAL POLICY, term generally applied to the colonial policy in force from 1870 to 1900, though signs of economic liberalism emerged as early as 1853 when some renting of land to Europeans was permitted. In 1870, the Cultivation System (q.v.) was formally abolished (though many of its features remained in force) and private Western businesses were admitted to the colony. In contrast with the state-directed exploitation of the Cultivation System, the Liberal Policy was a time of extensive investment by large companies, especially in the rubber and tobacco plantations of East Sumatra (q.v.), the sugar and tea (qq.v.) plantations of Java, and the oil (q.v.) wells of Kalimantan. See also AGRARIAN LAW OF 1870. [0507, 0584]

LIEM SIOE LIONG (Sudono Salim), born in 1916 in Fujian in southern China, arrived in Java in 1936. He established a business supplying cloves (q.v.) to kretek (q.v.) factories in Kudus before the war and during the Revolution was apparently an important supplier to the Republican army in Central Java. In the 1950s he was involved in various business dealings with Suharto (q.v.), then commander of the Diponegoro Division, and began to diversify into manufacturing and banking. When the Permesta (q.v.) rebellion cut off clove supplies from Minahasa, he pioneered imports from Madagascar and Zanzibar. Under the New Order he emerged as a major business partner of members of the presidential family and was allocated monopolies and licences which enabled his group to expand into trade, manufacture, property, finance, and logging. He has also been involved in many joint ventures with foreign investors as well as partnerships with local state and private enterprises.

LIGA DEMOKRASI (Democratic League), coalition formed by the PSI, Masyumi, IPKI (qq.v.), and others in 1960 to oppose Sukarno's dissolution of the DPR (q.v.) in March. It was hampered by the complicity of Masyumi and PSI in the PRRI (q.v.) uprising and it disappeared when both were banned in August 1960.

LIMBURG STIRUM, J.P. Graaf van (1873–1948), governor-general (1916–21), closely associated with the Ethical Policy. In November 1918, with political upheavals in the Netherlands suggesting an imminent socialist revolution there, van Limburg Stirum promised constitutional revisions to give a greater say to Indonesians in the running of the colony. These 'November promises' (*November beloften*) were not fulfilled and came to be seen by nationalists as a sign of Dutch unreliability, though a government inquiry completed in 1920 did lead to constitutional changes in 1922. See also NETHERLANDS, Constitutional relationship with Indonesia. [0569]

LINGGAJATI AGREEMENT, initialled by the Netherlands and the Republic of Indonesia on 12 November 1946 and signed on 25 May 1947, as a settlement to the Indonesian-Dutch dispute. It provided for an independent federal republic of Indonesia, consisting of three states (*negara*) (see FEDERALISM). The agreement was the result of a strong personal rapprochement between the leaders of the two delegations Sutan Syahrir (q.v.) and the former Dutch Prime Minister Willem Schermerhorn (1894–1977) and was immensely unpopular in both countries. Sukarno and Hatta stacked the Republican parliament (KNIP, q.v.) to have it ratified and the Dutch parliament ratified it only after adding unilaterally a number of additional interpretations and conditions. The agreement broke down formally over the Dutch refusal to allow Republican participation in decision making for the Dutch-controlled territories and over continued breaches of the ceasefire by Republican troops. See also POLICE ACTIONS; RENVILLE AGREEMENT. [0563, 0656, 0767]

LINSCHOTEN, Jan Huygen van (1563–1611). As secretary to the archbishop of Portuguese Goa (1583–89), he travelled much in the Indian Ocean region, later publishing two books describing what he had seen. His 1596 *Itinerario naer Oost ofte Portugaels Indien* (*Itinerary to the East or Portuguese Indies*) was read widely in Western Europe and stimulated formation of both the Dutch East Indies Company and the English East India Company (qq.v.). He argued especially that poor Portuguese relations with Asian peoples gave other European countries an opportunity to compete in the markets there, and identified Java (q.v.) as a suitable base for Dutch operations. See also DUTCH EAST INDIES COMPANY. [0056]

LITERACY. See EDUCATION; WOMEN; WRITING SYSTEMS.

LOMBLEN (Lembata). See SOLOR ARCHIPELAGO.

LOMBOK. The indigenous Sasak people of Lombok came under Muslim Javanese influence in C.16, but from early C.17 Muslim Makassar and Bima (qq.v.) fought the Hindu Balinese kingdom of Karangasem for control of the island. Balinese power grew from 1677 and by 1740 Karangasem controlled the whole island. Many Balinese settled in the west and by early C.19 four independent Balinese kingdoms had emerged there, based partly on rice exports to China, Singapore, and Australia (qq.v.). The kingdom of Mataram emerged as dominant power in 1838 but faced continual resistance and occasional rebellion from the Sasaks in the east. The raja accepted Dutch sovereignty in 1843, but in late C.19 the Dutch sought closer control to suppress opium trading and slavery (q.v.). A major Sasak rebellion in 1891 was supported by the Dutch in 1894. After heavy fighting, Mataram was destroyed and the defeated court committed ritual suicide (*puputan*). See also NAGARAKRTAGAMA. [0075, 0416, 0567]

LONTAR (*Borassus flabellifer,* Arecaceae), from Sanskrit *ron tal,* leaf of the *tala* tree, probably introduced from India, but now well established especially in eastern Indonesia. Palm leaves were used for writing on Bali from C.7, though earliest use was probably of *Corypha* leaves rather than lontar. The fragile nature of palm leaves, especially in the tropics, is a major reason for the tiny proportion of traditional literature preserved in the archipelago. Lontar was gradually displaced by paper (q.v.) from ca C.17. See also ROTI. [0378, 0483, 0938, 1011]

LUBIS, Mochtar (b. 1922), journalist and novelist, founder of the newspaper *Indonesia Raya* (1949–74) and author of various novels, including *Jalan tak ada ujung,* (*Road with no end,* 1952) and *Senja di Jakarta* (*Twilight in Jakarta,* 1957). He has been a prominent part of the liberal opposition to various aspects of both Guided Democracy and the New Order (qq.v.) and was jailed by both governments. [0171, 0172, 0860]

LUBIS, Zulkifli (b. 1923) trained as an intelligence officer for the Japanese-sponsored PETA (q.v.) and during the Revolution led successive Republican intelligence organizations, notably the Polisi Militer Khusus (Special Military Police) and the Field Preparation. In October 1952 he opposed army officers (including A.H. Nasution, q.v.) who organized demonstrations urging Sukarno to dissolve parliament. As acting army chief of staff, he led a boycott of the installation ceremony of his successor, Bambang Sugeng (1913–77) in 1955 and after stepping down in 1956 allegedly staged two unsuccessful coup attempts in October and November before going into hiding, from which he emerged as a military commander of the PRRI (q.v.) rebellion. Jailed in 1961 after the rebellion failed, he was released in 1966. [0634, 0651, 0663]

LUWU, Bugis state, the earliest in southern Sulawesi (q.v.), which emerged in C.9 at the head of the gulf of Bone. Little is known of its early history, but it may have been based partly on trade in nickel (q.v.) from the interior. From C.15 it began to lose influence to states such as Wajo' and Boné. It was converted to Islam (q.v.) in C.17. [0433]

M

MADAGASCAR, Historical links with. Extensive Austronesian migration to Madagascar took place from C.5, continuing in sporadic waves until the C.12 or even C.15. The specific ethnicity of the migrants, who were probably pirates or traders or both and who probably travelled via Ceylon or South India, is uncertain. 94% of the basic vocabulary in modern Malagasy is of Indonesian origin and is closest to the languages of the Batak and the Manyaan Dayak (qq.v.). The Austronesians brought with them a number of Asian plants, including probably rice, yam, and banana (qq.v.) and created on Madagascar a hybrid Indonesian-African culture. Cultural and technological influences include rice cultivation in irrigated terraces, outrigger canoes, double funerals and the use of megaliths (q.v.) in ancestor worship. Hinduistic cultural influence from Indonesia, including an established aristocracy, is strongest amongst Imerina in central Madagascar. Approximately one-third of the genetic composition of contemporary Madagascar population is Austronesian. See also AFRICA, Historical links with; MIGRATIONS. [0397, 0764]

MADIUN AFFAIR, uprising by sections of the PKI (q.v.) in Java in September and October 1948. After the Dutch First 'Police Action' (q.v.) the Republican enclave in east and central Java faced an economic crisis which forced the government of Hatta (q.v.) to dismiss large numbers of government employees and to demobilize significant parts of the armed forces. Prime targets for demobilization were those associated with the leftist former prime minister, Amir Syarifuddin (q.v.), and politics in the Republic polarized increasingly between left and right as the austerity program bit deeper. It may not have been the intention of PKI leaders to stage a rebellion at this time, but when tensions reached the point of armed clashes and the Hatta government treated the left as rebels, PKI leaders in Madiun declared a communist government. Party leaders including Musso and Amir, then sided with the rebels, accusing the Hatta government of having betrayed the ideals of the Revolution. Full-scale civil war followed, in which Muslim-Communist antagonisms led to a number of massacres on both sides. Within a month, the rising was suppressed especially by the West Javanese troops of the Siliwangi (q.v.) Division. Musso was killed, while Amir was arrested, only to be killed by government forces during the Dutch Second 'Police Action.' The Affair made a lasting impression on Indonesian politics: the PKI was accused not only of gratuitous brutality in its massacres of Muslims but of stabbing the Republic in the back as it defended national independence against the Dutch; the party in turn accused Hatta of cynically provoking the Affair so as to have an excuse to remove the proponents of armed revolution and to come to a compromise with the Dutch. See also DIPLOMASI AND PERJUANGAN. [0630, 0662, 0749]

MADURA, island off the northeast coast of Java, generally united with it for statistical purposes. Dry, relatively infertile, and suffering regularly from famine, it was ruled by Majapahit (q.v.) until 1466, when a revolt under Kyai Demung founded Sumenep (Bangkalan) as an independent state. Islam was established in early C.16 (ca 1528) and the three sultanates of Sumenep, Pamekasan, and Madura became trading powers, though the island was best known for salt (q.v.) production and military forces. Sultan Agung of Mataram (q.v.) conquered Madura in 1623, installing the Cakraningrat dynasty as his vassals. In 1671, however, the Madurese prince Trunojoyo (q.v.) rebelled, conquered the island, captured the court of Amangkurat I of Mataram, and was only beaten back from the mainland after the intervention of VOC (q.v.) troops. During this time, many Madurese settled in eastern Java. The Company was able to conquer the eastern part of the island in 1705 and the Mataram ruler ceded the remainder in 1740, though not until 1745 was Dutch control firmly in place, the Company placing restrictions on the rulers' foreign relations and demanding tribute in the form of cash, cotton, coconut oil, and troops. Madurese *barisan* (formed 1831) were an important element in the colonial armed forces until early C.20 (see NATIVE TROOPS). In C.19, although the Cakraningrats remained the dominant family, their status was steadily eroded as they lost taxation rights; in 1813 Raffles (q.v.) introduced a government salt monopoly, which was largely farmed out to wealthy Chinese entrepreneurs (see PACHT). In 1885 the Dutch introduced direct rule, the sultan being demoted to the rank of bupati (q.v.). A later member of the family was employed by the Dutch to head the Negara Madura, formed on 21 January 1948 as part of the proposed postwar Indonesian federation (see FEDERALISM). [0006, 0519, 0526, 0702, 0917, 1051]

'MAHABHARATA,' epic poem originally from India, the earliest known Old Javanese text dating from the late C.10. Episodes (*lakon*) are widely performed in wayang (q.v.) kulit, golek and wong, and are often presented as allegories of contemporary events. The story tells of the prolonged struggle between the five Pandawas (sons of Pandu) and 100 Kurawas (sons of Dhrarashta), which culminated in the destruction of almost all the characters in a final cataclysmic battle, the Bharatayudha. See also RAMAYANA. [0116]

MAHKAMAH MILITER LUAR BIASA (MAHMILLUB, Extraordinary Military Tribunal), established by

President Sukarno on 24 December 1963 to try those deemed by the president to be a threat to the security of the Indonesian state and people but used primarily after 1965 to try those accused of involvement in the GESTA-PU (q.v.) coup of 1965. The trials began on 13 February 1966 with the surviving PKI leader Nyono and went on to include Subandrio (q.v.), the air force (q.v.) chief Omar Dhani and the coup leader Untung. Sukarno (q.v.) was not brought to trial, but evidence presented, especially at the trial of Jusuf Muda Dalam, appeared to implicate his regime in corruption and abuse of power. A total of 894 people were tried up to March 1978, most being sentenced to death or to prison terms of twenty or more years. Many of the accused were defended by Yap Thiam Hien (q.v.). See also TAHANAN POLITIK. [0669, 0686]

MAIZE (*Zea mays* Poaceae) probably reached northeastern Indonesia in early C.16 aboard Spanish ships and became an important food crop in eastern Indonesia, especially in areas too dry for wet rice (q.v.) cultivation. It spread extensively on Java from late C.18 when the availability of suitable land for rice cultivation diminished. Raffles (q.v.) reported it as Java's second staple crop after rice. By 1930 accounted for 30% of grain consumption on the island. It is now the staple food for more than 18 million people in Indonesia. [0210, 0245, 0246, 0271, 0938]

MAJAPAHIT, kingdom in East Java, generally regarded as the high point of Hindu-Javanese culture, though relatively little is known of it. After the overthrow of King Kertanegara of Singosari (q.v.) by rebels from Kediri, Java was abruptly invaded in 1292–93 by a Mongol army seeking revenge for Kertanegara's expulsion of Mongol envoys in 1289. Unaware of the details of Javanese politics, they were persuaded by Kertanegara's son

Wijaya to help him overthrow the Kediri prince Jayakatwang. With Kediri defeated, Wijaya then turned on the Mongols and drove them out. He moved his capital to Trowulan, established the kingdom of Majapahit, and took the name Kertarajasa Jayavardhana (d.1309).

Majapahit experienced a golden age under the rule of Hayam Wuruk (Rajasanagara, r. 1350–89) and his prime minister, Gajah Mada. Agricultural production was the basis of the state, but Majapahit also seems to have traded food especially to Maluku, and the king was probably its major trader in his own right. State religion was Sivaitic Hinduism (q.v.) in which the Buddha was also worshipped. Majapahit society was extensively described by the court poet Prapanca in the 'Nagarakrtagama' (q.v.), which also includes a list of supposed dependencies covering the whole archipelago, including parts of New Guinea, as well as the Malay peninsula, the southern Philippines, and perhaps northern Australia. This list has sometimes been used to give the idea of an archipelago-wide state a respectable, noncolonial antiquity (see NATIONALISM; SUCCESSION), and even to imply vague Indonesian claims on surrounding territories, but most scholars now believe that Majapahit's influence outside East and Central Java was limited to coastal areas of Kalimantan and Sumatra and parts of Maluku and Nusatenggara though a military expedition to Bali (q.v.) in 1343 is said to have established Old Javanese culture there. Majapahit apparently declined after Hayam Wuruk's death and was wracked by civil war and rebellion through much of C.15. Either it or a Hindu successor state was conquered by the coastal Muslim state of Demak (q.v.) in ca 1527. See also PAJANG. [0384, 0412, 0414, 0476]

MAJELIS ISLAM A'LAA INDONESIA (MIAI, Supreme Islamic Council of Indonesia), federation of Muslim organizations, founded in September 1937 by K. Mansur, Ahmad Dahlan and Abdul Wahab for the discussion of religious matters. At the 1938 All Islam Congress, delegates from the Partai Sarekat Islam Indonesia and the Partai Islam Indonesia (qq.v.) pushed the organization to take a stand on political issues, and in 1942 a conference of Muslim leaders under Japanese auspices agreed to recognize it as a central coordinating body for Muslim affairs. The Japanese in the event, declined to deal with the MIAI, creating instead the Masyumi (q.v.). [0608]

MAJELIS PERMUSYAWARATAN RAKYAT (MPR, People's Deliberative Assembly), Indonesia's supreme representative body, which meets once in five years, following the national elections, to elect the president, to hear his report on the conduct of government during the preceding five years and to ratify the Broad Outlines of State Policy (*Garis Besar Haluan Negara,* GBHN) which state the broad aims and principles of government policy for the next five years. It is also empowered to amend the constitution (q.v.), though in 1966 declared that the preamble to the constitution, containing the Pancasila, was inalterable. The 1945 Constitution provided for the MPR but it was not assembled until 1959, when Sukarno (q.v.) added presidential nominees (94 from the provinces and 200 from the functional groups) to the existing 281-member house of representatives to create a 575-member MPR-Sementara (MPRS, Provisional MPR). This MPRS met in 1959, 1963, and 1965 under Sukarno, in 1966 to ratify the transfer of power to Suharto, in 1967 to appoint Suharto acting president and in 1968 to elect him full president.

Under regulations passed in November 1969, a full MPR (no longer provisional) was constituted in 1971 with 920 members, comprising all 460 members of the largely elected Dewan Perwakilan Rakyat (q.v.), together with 207 presidential nominees, 121 nominees from elected parties, 130 provincial representatives, and two nominees from parties unsuccessful in the DPR elections. In 1987 membership was increased to 1,000. See also KOMITE NASIONAL INDONESIA PUSAT. [0890]

MAKASSAR (Gowa, Goa), kingdom in south Sulawesi which grew after ca 1530 from the ports of Gowa and Tallo. Reorganized from a loose federation to a centrally governed state by Karaëng (king) Tumapa'risi in early C.16, partly with the assistance of Malay refugees from the fall of Melaka (q.v.), it dominated the west coast of southern Sulawesi by the end of the century. With the decline of the rice trade from Java, Karaëng Matoaya (q.v.), ruler of Tallo and prime minister of Makassar, expanded local rice production for trade to Maluku (q.v.) in exchange for nutmeg and cloves (qq.v.). In 1605, Makassar converted to Islam and began a series of campaigns to control the region, conquering its main rival, Bone (q.v.), in a campaign 1608–11. Overseas expansion followed, with operations against Sumbawa (1617), Buru, Seram, Banten (qq.v.), and eastern Kalimantan, though in all cases it ruled through vassals rather than directly. It may have been these campaigns which dispersed the Bajau (q.v.) from the region. From early in C.17, Makassar became a major base for Portuguese, British, Danish, and Asian traders attempting to thwart the Dutch spice monopoly in Maluku and came under corresponding pressure from the Dutch to grant them a monopoly. In 1666, Cornelis Speelman launched a major expedition against Sultan Hasanuddin (1653–69), who was defeated in 1667 by the Dutch and Bugis (see ARUNG PALAKKA) forces. Under the treaty of Bungaya (1667) Makassar was reduced to little more than the port of Gowa. A rebellion by Hasanuddin in 1668–69 was suppressed.

After a period of decline in C.18, the city emerged in C.19 as a major trade center in eastern Indonesia and the capital city successively of the *gouvernement* of the Grote Oost (see DECENTRALIZATION), the Japanese naval administration in eastern Indonesia, and the Negara Indonesia Timur (q.v.). Local support for the Indonesian Republic was suppressed first by Australian troops and then, in a brutal fashion, by Dutch forces under R.P.P. Westerling (q.v.). In 1971 the city's name was changed to Ujung Pandang. [0433, 0477, 0480, 0481, 0537, 0643, 0645, 1165]

MALACCA. See MELAKA.

MALARI (*Malapetaka 15 Januari,* Disaster of 15 January), student demonstrations in Jakarta on 15–16 January 1974, seen as the first major political challenge to the New Order (q.v.). A visit by the Japanese prime minister Kakuei Tanaka was the occasion for the demonstrations and Japanese cars were amongst the targets of the demonstrators, but the growing strength of foreign companies in general, the increasing wealth of military bureaucrats and their Chinese business partners (*cukong,* q.v.), and the general corruption and extravagance of the government were the principal complaints. Student demands were summarized, like the 1966 KAMI (q.v.) demands, as *Tritura* (*Tri Tuntutan Rakyat,* Three Demands of the People), namely the dissolution of the presidential staff or ASPRI (Asisten Presiden Republik Indonesia), lower prices, and an end to corruption. The play *Mastodon and Condor* by Rendra (q.v.) played some role in focusing discontent, but the demonstrations were also a vehicle for intraregime rivalries between General Sumitro, head of KOPKAMTIB (q.v.), and General Ali Murtopo of the Operasi Khusus (q.v.). A student, Hariman Siregar and a lecturer, Syahrir, both of Universitas Indonesia, were later tried and sentenced under the Anti-Subversion Law for inciting the riots. See also SUBVERSION.

Malari led to important changes in New Order policy. Sumitro was dismissed, six newspapers (*Abadi, Harian KAMI, Indonesia Raya, Mahasiswa Indonesia, Nusantara,* and *Pedoman*) were closed and Daud Yusuf was appointed education minister with the task of depoliticizing the universities. On the other hand, economic policies were altered to encourage participation by indigenous entrepreneurs in the economy by closing some areas to foreign investment (q.v.) and by insisting that all future foreign investments be joint ventures. [0670, 0680, 0687, 0871]

MALARIA, a fever disease caused by the protozoan parasite *Plasmodium,* has been one of the blights of life in Indonesia since early times and may have been one of the factors limiting state-formation and the growth of complex societies in the region. *Cinchona* (q.v.) bark was recognized from late C.18 as offering relief and sometimes cure and its extensive cultivation on Java helped to make the tropics habitable. The connection between the disease and the bites of various species of the mosquito *Anopheles* was discovered only in 1898, and from 1924 a Central Malaria Bureau of the colonial government began eradication programs, both by water management and by use of insecticides. Extensive spraying with DDT began in 1951. See also HEALTH. [0981]

MALAY PENINSULA, Historical links with. Although attached to the Southeast Asian mainland by the isthmus of Kra, the Malay peninsula belonged historically to the island world of the Indonesian archipelago just as much as neighboring Sumatra. The indigenous Malay population of the peninsula was ethnically identical to the Malays of the eastern coast of Sumatra and the Riau archipelago and states along the straits of Melaka traditionally sought control of both sides of the waterway, regardless of which shore they happened to be on (see SRIVIJAYA; JAMBI; ACEH; MELAKA; RIAU). Buddhism and later Islam (qq.v.) reached both sides of the strait at about the same time, and with comparable impact, though the peninsula was much later in developing major kingdoms than was Sumatra. The cultural and political influence of Siam (q.v.), on the other hand, was not significantly felt beyond the northern and eastern parts of the peninsula.

The Anglo-Dutch Treaty of 1824 (q.v.) separated the peninsula from the archipelago politically, but economic ties remained strong. Penang, founded in 1786, became the major port for produce from East Sumatra (q.v.), first pepper and later rubber (qq.v.), and Singapore (q.v.) became a major entrepôt for much of the western archipelago. During C.19 and 20 there has been extensive migration from Sumatra and Java to the peninsula; Minangkabau (q.v.) communities are especially strong in Negeri Sembilan. Sumatra and the peninsula were united under the Japanese 25th army from 1942 to 1943, and in the period immediately after the Japanese surrender, an organization called Kesatuan Raayat Indonesia Semenanjung (KRIS, Union of Indonesian People of the Peninsula) under Ibrahim Yaakob briefly campaigned for the inclusion of Malaya in the new Indonesian Republic. During the Revolution, Singapore and Penang were major centers for the smuggling of weapons to the nationalists and for the legal and clandestine sale of Indonesian produce. In the 1950s, the Federation of Malaya provided some support to the PRRI (q.v.) rebellion in Sumatra. For further details, see the forthcoming *Historical Dictionary of Malaysia*. See also MALAYSIA, Relations with. [0731, 1140]

MALAYSIA (term). See INDONESIA; MALESIA.

MALAYSIA, Relations with. After World War II, the British in Malaya began to move gradually to grant greater autonomy to their Southeast Asian possessions (the Malay Peninsula and Singapore, Sarawak, Brunei and North Borneo, or Sabah; for further details see the forthcoming *Historical Dictionary of Malaysia*). In 1961 these moves crystalized in plans to create a federal state of Malaysia incorporating all British territories. Indonesia was unhappy about this proposal for several reasons: Britain was to retain her naval base in Singapore, the Malay sultans were to retain a powerful political role, people in northern Borneo seemed hostile to the federation, and Indonesia, although the largest power in the region, had not been consulted on the plan. Sukarno (q.v.) announced in January 1963 that the Malaysia proposal was unacceptable. After Brunei pulled out of the proposal and Britain offered to seek popular approval of the federation in Sabah and Sarawak, relations briefly warmed (see MAPHILINDO), but they cooled abruptly in September when Britain announced the federation would be formed regardless of opinion in the Borneo states. Indonesia then announced a Confrontation (q.v.) of Malaysia which ended only on 11 August 1966. In 1970, a 'Friendship Treaty' regulated the complex marine border between the two counties, dividing the Melaka Strait along a median line while acknowledging Malaysian traditional fishing rights and a general right of free passage in the South China Sea between East and West Malaysia, though this leaves unresolved a dispute over the ownership of two islands off the eastern coast of Borneo near the Sabah-Kalimantan border. Since the 1970s, the Malaysian government has informally permitted the migration of significant numbers of Indonesian Muslims to Malaysia to increase the 'indigenous' ('*bumiputera*') proportion of the population. Malaysia became the first country to recognize Indonesia's Archipelagic Concept (q.v.) in February 1982. In December 1987, Indonesia and Malaysia signed an agreement to cooperate in the marketing of palm oil, rubber, and other agricultural products. Both countries are members of ASEAN (q.v.). See also ARCHIPELAGIC CONCEPT; MALAY PENINSULA, Historical links with; MELAKA; SINGAPORE.

MALESIA, Latin-Italian term for the Malay world, first popularized by Odo Beccari (1843–1920) in his three-volume natural history work *Malesia* (1877). Up until 1962, the term Malaysia was more common, but the imminent creation of the state of Malaysia (q.v., 1963) demanded a change in usage, and the term Malesia was adopted for the botanical region encompassing insular Southeast Asia, peninsular Malaysia, and New Guinea, including the Bismarck Archipelago. See also INDONESIA; WALLACE'S LINE.

MALIK, Adam (1917–84), journalist and nationalist politician, one of the early leaders of the Antara (q.v.) news agency before World War II and an employee of the Japanese news agency Domei during the Japanese occupation. During the Revolution, Malik was close to Tan Malaka (q.v.) and in 1948 joined the Murba (q.v.) party. Although a strong supporter of the general structure of Guided Democracy, he opposed the rising strength of the PKI (q.v.), helping to form the anticommunist Badan Pendukung Sukarnoisme (q.v) in 1964. After the GESTAPU (q.v.) coup, he became minister of foreign affairs (1966–77) in a symbolic New Order triumvirate with Suharto and Hamengkubuwono IX (qq.v.). He served as vice-president (q.v.) 1977–82. [0676, 0686, 0697, 0706]

MALUKU, the large archipelago lying between Sulawesi, Irian and Timor (qq.v.), consisting especially of the islands of Ambon, Aru, Banda, Buru, Halmahera, Seram, Tanimbar, Ternate, Tidore (qq.v.), Sula, Kai, and Wetar. The area around Ambon formerly known as the South Moluccas (see REPUBLIK MALUKU SELATAN) is now known as central Maluku. The region is ethnically and culturally diverse, showing both Malay and Papuan influences (see also MIGRATIONS; WALLACE'S LINE). It has been economically significant since early times for its spices (cloves, nutmeg, qq.v.). In C.14, it seems to have been dominated by the Javanese kingdom of Majapahit (q.v.), while in C.16 the sultanates of Ternate and Tidore ruled many of the islands. The Portuguese signed an alliance with Ternate in 1511 and for much of the following century and a half, the Portuguese, Spanish (qq.v.), and Dutch competed with each other and with local powers for control (see also DUTCH EAST INDIES COMPANY; HONGI RAIDS). Extensive Christianization took place in the region. Since C.19 the region has been something of an economic backwater. [0051, 0058, 0453, 1009, 1010]

MANADO. See MINAHASA.

MANDAR, region on the western coast of south Sulawesi, traditionally divided into several small communities which sometimes coalesced, especially for warfare, into one or two confederations. In early C.17 it came under the domination of Makassar (q.v.). [0433]

MANGKUBUMI (?–1792), prince of Mataram (q.v.) who rebelled against Pakubuwono II in 1742 and again in 1745, especially as a result of Pakubuwono's 1743 decision to lease the north coast of Java to the VOC. He had himself declared king on Pakubuwono's death in 1749, taking the title Sultan and the name Hamengkubuwono (I) in 1755. After a protracted war with the VOC and its protégés in Mataram, he agreed in the Treaty of Giyanti (q.v.) to accept half the kingdom together with 10,000 reals as his share of proceeds from the VOC lease on the north coast. He established his court in Yogyakarta (q.v.) and was founder of the present dynasty. See also HAMENGKUBUWONO IX.

MANGKUNEGARAN. Minor court in Surakarta (q.v.), established in 1757 by the partition of the Sunanate. The court's armed forces, the Legiun Mangkunegaran, were reorganized by Daendels (q.v.), making them one of the few significant indigenous military forces on Java in the late colonial period (see NATIVE TROOPS). Mangkunegoro II (1796–1835) and IV (r.1853–81) established an extensive sugar and tobacco plantation sector in the Mangkunegaran lands. In 1946 the Mangkunegaran was formally abolished, along with the Surakarta court, after it failed to support the Republic unequivocally, but its informal position has improved in recent years due to its family connection with Tien Suharto, wife of the president. [0516]

MANIFESTO KEBUDAYAAN (MANIKEBU, Cultural Manifesto), was issued in October 1963 by a group of writers, intellectuals, and artists, including H.B. Jassin (q.v.), Gunawan Muhamad, and Wiratmo Sukito, as an affirmation of the values of 'universal humanism' and a rejection of the idea, promoted by LEKRA (q.v.), that artistic quality was better judged by social criteria than by self-referencing esthetic notions. After extensive debate, the manifesto was banned by Sukarno on 8 May 1964. See also CULTURE, Debate on the role of. [0116, 0154]

MANIFESTO POLITIK. 1. Statement issued by Republican leaders on 1 November 1945, promising *inter alia* that the Indonesian Republic would respect the property rights of foreign investors. The government hoped in this way to win international approval, but the policy aroused strong domestic opposition. See also DIPLO-

MASI AND PERJUANGAN; PERSATUAN PERJUANGAN. [0628, 0859]

2. (MANIPOL) The ideology of Guided Democracy (q.v.) as set out in Sukarno's independence day speech on 17 August 1959 and adopted by the DPA (q.v.) as the Broad Outlines of State Policy (GBHN) in September 1959. In it Sukarno called for social justice, a return to the spirit of the Revolution (q.v.), and a 'retooling' of state organs. In 1960 MANIPOL was elaborated with the addition of the formula—USDEK (*Undang-undang '45,* 1945 Constitution; *Sosialisme a la Indonesia,* Indonesian socialism; *Demokrasi Terpimpin,* Guided Democracy; *Ekonomi Terpimpin,* Guided Economy (q.v.); and *Kepribadian Indonesia,* Indonesian Identity). The precise meaning of each of these terms remained vague, but MANIPOL soon became associated as a slogan with the left in Indonesian politics and it was formally repudiated by the MPR-S (q.v.) in 1967. [0705, 0854]

MAPHILINDO, rubric for a series of meetings and conferences of leaders of Malaya, the Philippines (q.v.) and Indonesia in May-August 1963 and by extension for a proposed confederation of the three states. Indonesia, however, had already announced its disapproval of the formation of Malaysia (q.v.) and the Maphilindo idea disappeared with the full launching of Confrontation (q.v.) in September 1963, though it provided some basis for the later formation of ASEAN (q.v.). [0742]

MARDIJKERS, Portuguese-speaking descendants of freed slaves, who formed a separate, large social category in C.17 Batavia (q.v.). See also DEPOK; SLAVERY. [0493, 0495]

MARÉCHAUSSÉE. The failure of conventional military tactics in the war in Aceh (q.v.) led the colonial authorities in 1890 to form small military units of mixed race to operate as counterguerrilla or commando forces largely independent of the tactical command of KNIL (q.v.) officers. These units, familiar with the countryside and each other, and small enough to move unobtrusively, were a qualified success and in early C.20 were used in other areas as a kind of militarized police force. See also POLICE.

MARHAEN, term adopted by Sukarno (probably from a Sundanese word for a small farmer) to denote the large numbers of Indonesians, especially peasants, who, although poverty-stricken and oppressed by colonial capitalism, were nonetheless owners of some of the means of production (*e.g.*, a small plot of land or a few tools) and were thus not proletarians. In Sukarno's early usage, the term encompassed most Indonesians; later it was restricted to poorer sections of society. See also CLASS ANALYSIS; MARXISM. [0705, 0849]

MARIJUANA. See CANNABIS.

MARRIAGE, Political significance of. Amongst aristocracies in early Indonesia, marriage seems to have been, as it was in Europe, a tool for allying families and kingdoms. On the one hand, rulers typically had many wives, drawn from the families of vassals and allies and the status of those wives was often a measure of the vassals' and allies' status (see KIDUNG SUNDA). On the other hand, women were in some respects at least the locus of power and rulers gained their legitimacy in part by virtue of the women they married. Thus, Ken Angrok (q.v.) married his predecessor's widow and the Sultans of Yogyakarta (q.v.) symbolically marry the Queen of the South Seas, Nyai Loro Kidul, when they ascend the throne. The queens of Aceh (q.v.) were more or less prevented from marrying in order to prevent them from allying formally with any of the internal forces in the state. In a later time, Sukarno's marriage to a Japanese former nightclub hostess, Nemoto Naoko (Ratna Dewi Sari) led to suggestions that he was too close to Japan. The political value of marriage tended to mean that royal sons and daughters were married at or soon after puberty, but in the rest of society, later marriages (at age 15–21) seem to have been more common and monogamy was the general rule, though divorce by either side was easy and frequent. A bride price was commonly paid, but went to the bride herself, rather than her family.

The arrival of Islam (q.v.) transformed the character of marriage, though the extent to which Islamic marriage law was followed varied widely. Where Muslim influence was strongest, daughters in particular married earlier, arranged marriages became more common, and women lost the right to initiate divorce. In European society, formal marriage between Europeans and Indonesians was always strongly discouraged and sometimes prohibited, but concubinage was common. A *nyai* or concubine was sometimes little more than a sexual slave, but many became powerful partners of their European husbands and some were strong traders and managers in their own right. The status of children from these unions varied: if the father formally acknowledged them they had European status, if not they took that of the mother. When interracial marriages were permitted, the wife took the legal status of her husband (see RACE). Taylor has shown that in C.17 and 18 Batavia, political alliances between senior and junior VOC (q.v.) officials were often cemented by marriages between junior officials and the Eurasian daughters of their seniors.

In C.20, the Dutch allowed Muslim marriages to be conducted and registered by Muslim officials of the Department of Religious Affairs and this system was retained by the Republic. In 1973, however, the government prepared a draft marriage law which would have enforced monogamy, required state registration of all marriages, and permitted cross-religion marriages, which are anathema to Islam. The draft law led to fierce opposition by the PPP and Muslim groups and heated debate in parliament, and the law was eventually amended to permit polygamy, remove the registration requirement, and prevent cross-religion marriages. See also PROSTITUTION; WOMEN AND MEN. [0182, 0440, 0483, 0493, 0881, 1086]

MARXISM. Although the Partai Komunis Indonesia (q.v.) adhered in general to Marxism-Leninism, it developed Marxist theory in a number of distinctive ways. Pointing to the enormous social and cultural diversity in Indonesia, it argued that the historical stages identified by Marx were telescoped in Indonesia into a single, comprehensive struggle against capitalist imperialism of which most Indonesians were victims. The party accordingly downplayed open class struggle (though this was less the case after 1963), arguing that the primary enemies of the Indonesian people were foreign. The clear influence of elements from Marxism on nationalist leaders such as Sukarno and Hatta (qq.v.) assisted this analysis. From this followed the theory of the Dual Nature of the State, which asserted that although Indonesian society was 'semicolonial' and 'semifeudal' the independent Indonesian state after 1949 was at least partly 'pro-people' and that the party's struggle should thus be to maximize the pro-people element and not to overthrow the state as such. The party, accordingly, has never had a well-formulated program for armed rebellion, one reason perhaps for its poor performance when it has been led along that road. Party philosophy instead emphasized the promotion of socialist ways of thinking, and put a high priority on establishing the hegemony of Marxist ideas in philosophy and the arts. See also LEMBAGA

KEBUDAYAAN RAKYAT. [0571, 0843, 0848, 0849, 0855, 0864]

MASS ORGANIZATIONS (*organisasi massa, ormas*), term referring to organizations with mass memberships, generally organized around social categories such as students, women, workers, etc., and commonly associated with political parties, though parties themselves are formally also ormas. Ormas emerged on a massive scale during the Indonesian Revolution and parties typically recruited much of their support through affiliated ormas rather than by appealing directly to the public. Thus the peasant organization BTI (q.v.) with a claimed membership of 12 million was a major pillar of the PKI and one of the main strategies of the army in resisting the rise of the left was the coordination of mass organizations, first in the *badan kerja sama* (q.v.) and later in Golkar (q.v.). Under the New Order the government has sought to deprive potential opposition groups of access to the political base represented by the ormas, both by direct intervention in individual ormas and in 1985 by passing a Law on Mass Organizations which required them to accept the Pancasila as their sole basic principle (see AZAS TUNGGAL and PANCASILA), restricted their access to foreign funds, and gave legal grounds for closer government control. Since the passing of this law, a clearer distinction has emerged between ormas and *orsos* (*organisasi sosial,* social organizations), which are constructed as foundations without public membership and are thus free of some of the formal restrictions placed on ormas. [0777]

MASSACRES OF 1965–66. The suppression of the ostensibly left-wing GESTAPU (q.v.) coup of 30 September 1965 was followed not only by the banning of the PKI (q.v.) and affiliated organizations but by an extensive massacre of people associated with the left. The killings, which began in October 1965 and continued for six months, were most extensive in East and Central Java, Bali and North Sumatra, but few regions were left untouched. No reliable figures exist on the number of people killed. The first official figure was 78,000 and other estimates seldom exceed one million; most scholars today accept a figure somewhere between 200,000 and 500,000.

In part the killings were a planned operation by the army to remove the PKI as a political force. In Central Java in particular, units of the RPKAD (q.v.) engaged in systematic slaughter of Communists in several areas. Elsewhere, the initiative seems to have come from local people: longstanding social tensions aligned with political antagonisms created deep hatreds between groups so that the killings, when they came, were not directed simply at destroying Communist leaders but at extirpating whole communities. In East Java, where such antagonism was strongest, *santri* (q.v.) communities, represented by the NU youth group Ansor (q.v.), waged a sustained campaign of destruction against their *abangan* (q.v.) neighbors; in Bali, the conflict was partly one between the followers of different rajas. In both cases, most of the killers believed that they were forestalling a comparable massacre of conservatives planned by the PKI. Another important stimulus to the killing was the fact that many people who had made accommodation with the left-wing trends of Guided Democracy (q.v.) felt a need to demonstrate their anticommunist credentials clearly by promoting the destruction of the left. Some observers initially described the killings as a kind of massive running amuck (see AMUK), but this seems an inadequate explanation for the systematic character of the murders.

Indonesians remain reluctant on the whole to talk about the massacres, but the general memory of this time continues to play an important role in the political legitimacy of the New Order (q.v.), which stresses the extent to which the killings were conducted by ordinary citizens and attributes them to the tensions created by the free operation of political parties under Guided Democracy and earlier periods. [0642, 0649, 0832]

MASYUMI (Majelis Syuro Muslimin Indonesia, Consultative Council of Indonesian Muslims), Muslim political organization formed initially under Japanese sponsorship in October 1943 as a single coordinating body for Islamic affairs on Java, bypassing the MIAI (q.v.). It was headed by the conservative rural ulama K.H. Hasyim Asyari (1871–1947) and his son K.H. Wahid Hasyim (1914–53) of the NU (q.v.) and was loosely affiliated with the Japanese-sponsored Hizbullah (q.v.) militia. In 1945 it transformed itself into a political party with the twin aims of independence and an Islamic foundation for the Indonesian Republic. Numerous Hizbullah (q.v.) armed units claimed general affiliation with Masyumi, especially in the early Revolution when the party strongly opposed the government's negotiation with the Dutch, but many left in disgust in 1948 when the party backed the negotiating policy of the Hatta (q.v.) government, some joining Kartosuwiryo in the Darul Islam movement (q.v.). The Partai Sarekat Islam Indonesia (q.v.) left Masyumi in 1947 and the Nahdatul Ulama (q.v.) followed in 1952, leaving the party dominated by the modernist 'religious socialist' stream represented by Mohamad Natsir, Mohamad Rum, Sukiman Wiryosanjoyo, and others. In the early 1950s, the party was dominant in successive cabinets but its acceptability in coalition politics was damaged by its ambivalent attitude towards the Darul Islam and by its increasing identification with the Outer Islands (q.v.), as opposed to Java. It had a severe shock in the 1955 elections when, after expecting something close to a majority, it received only 20.9% of the vote. Excluded from power by the cabinet of Ali Sastroamijoyo (q.v.) and then by the transition of Guided Democracy (q.v.), Masyumi leaders took part in the unsuccessful 1958 PRRI (q.v.) rebellion, for which the party was banned in 1960. After the installation of the New Order (q.v.), former Masyumi leaders hoped that the party might be allowed to re-form, and the PARMUSI (q.v.) was initially intended as a direct successor to Masyumi. The military authorities, however, banned former Masyumi leaders from executive positions in the new party. See also MUHAMMADIYAH. [0608, 0634, 0647, 1111]

MATARAM, name of two states on Java (q.v.). 1. Early state, brought to prominence by the Hindu ruler Pu Sanjaya (732-ca 760), who is generally credited with establishing Hindu notions of god-kingship on Java (see HINDUISM; INDIA, Historical links with). He erected a *lingga* (phallic monument) on the Dieng plateau, Javanese center for the worship of Siva, and claimed a special personal relationship with Hindu gods and with his ancestors. His successors built the temple of Prambanan (q.v.) and struggled for power in central Java with the Sailendras (q.v.). In early C.10, King Sindok shifted his capital to East Java for reasons still unclear.

2. The sultanate of Mataram emerged in the 1570s under Kyai Gede Pamanahan (d. ca 1584) in the vicinity of modern Surakarta. It began major expansion under his son and heir Panembahan Senapati Inalaga (r. 1584–1601), who defeated Pajang (q.v.) and pushed his control to the northern coast and into the Madiun valley. Senapati fought Surabaya (q.v.) and established his *kraton* (q.v.) at Kuta Gede, near modern Yogyakarta. His successor Panembahan Seda-ing Krapyak (ca 1601–13) allowed the Dutch East Indies Company (q.v., VOC) a trading post at Japara (q.v.) on the north coast. Sultan Agung (q.v.), the greatest of Mataram's rulers,

defeated Madura (q.v.) in 1624 and Surabaya (1625), thus establishing hegemony over most of central and eastern Java. In 1628 and 1629 he tried unsuccessfully to drive the Dutch from Batavia (q.v.). In 1651 he banned Javanese from trading abroad, thus destroying the basis of the Pasisir (q.v.) states. The latter part of his reign was occupied with campaigns against rebellious vassals in Giri (1636) and Balambangan (1636–40) (q.v.).

Agung's son and successor Sunan Amangkurat (Mangkurat) I (r.1646–77) lost control of the north coast and faced a major uprising by the Madurese Trunojoyo (q.v.). After Amangkurat was driven from his own court by Trunojoyo, the VOC intervened on Mataram's behalf to defeat Trunojoyo (1678–79) and establish Amangkurat's son Amangkurat II (r.1677–1703) on the throne, with his court at Kartasura. The following decades were a time of cultural flowering but political disorder. In the First War of Javanese Succession (1704–08), Amangkurat II was deposed by his uncle Pakubuwono I, who ceded Cirebon, Priangan (qq.v.) and half of Madura to the VOC. A Second War of Succession broke out on Pakubuwono's death in 1719, lasting until 1723, when Amangkurat IV was installed on the throne with VOC help. In 1740, the revolt of the Chinese in Batavia (q.v.) spread along Java's north coast and was joined by Pakubuwono II. In a series of complicated maneuvers, however, he attempted to deal with the Dutch, was deposed by his followers, and was restored to power by the Dutch in 1743, establishing his court at Surakarta (Solo) and ceding the entire north coast of Java and all territories east of Pasuruan to the VOC. A Third War of Succession broke out in 1746, when the king's brother Mangkubumi (q.v.) revolted. Pakubuwono II meanwhile ceded the remains of his kingdom to the VOC and promptly died in 1749. Mangkubumi was declared sultan by his followers in 1749, taking the name Hamengkubuwono while the

Dutch installed Pakubuwono's son as Pakubuwono III. The rebellion ended with the partition of Mataram into distinct kingdoms of Yogyakarta and Surakarta under the Treaty of Giyanti (q.v.). For a list of the rulers of Mataram, see the Appendix.

Mataram was also the name of a kingdom on Lombok (q.v.). [0474, 0486, 0487]

MATOAYA, Karaëng (ca 1573–1636), a prince of the royal family of Tallo in South Sulawesi, he became chief minister under King Tunipasulu and headed a coup by the nobility which overthrew the king after he had tried to reduce noble privileges. He continued as chief minister and was architect of the alliance with Bugis states which became the basis of the powerful Makassar (q.v.) state. As the campaigns of Sultan Agung (q.v.) devastated the north coast of Java, Matoaya turned Makassar into a major free port for trade from Maluku, which the Dutch were then trying to monopolize. He also presided over the peaceful conversion of Makassar to Islam (q.v.). To defend Makassar against the expected Dutch attack, Matoaya also sponsored the development of firearms manufacture. See also PATTINGALLOANG.

MAUBERE, term adopted by Fretilin (q.v.) for the indigenous people of East Timor (q.v.). [0898]

MAX HAVELAAR, semiautobiographical novel by Eduard Douwes Dekker (q.v.), writing under the pseudonym Multatuli ('I have suffered much'), published in 1860 and describing his experiences as *assistent-resident* in Lebak in Banten (q.v.) in mid C.19. The central character, an idealistic young colonial official, attempts to redress wrongs inflicted on local people by the indigenous aristocracy but discovers that the colonial authorities have no interest in the welfare of their Indonesian subjects and is himself eventually dismissed for his pains. The novel, often compared in spirit to *Uncle Tom's Cabin,* played some role in mobilizing Dutch public opinion against the Cultivation System (q.v.) and is considered a classic of Dutch colonial literature. It was filmed in a joint Dutch-Indonesian venture in 1976, but the result was banned in Indonesia from 1977 to 1988 on the grounds that it showed that people 'were exploited not by the Dutch but by the local aristocracy.' [0173, 0523]

MEDAN. See DELI; EAST SUMATRA.

MEDICINE. See HEALTH.

MEGALITHS. Prehistorians once identified a 'megalithic' stage in the development of Indonesian culture, based on widespread signs of reverence for large stones (megaliths). Prehistorians today, however, are increasingly skeptical towards this view, arguing that there is insufficient knowledge of the ancient use of megaliths, little evidence that their use had a common origin, and no certainty that they were a central feature of the cultures involved; it may simply be that they survived other more important cultural features simply because they were stone. Megalithic traditions survive today in Nias, Sumba, and parts of Kalimantan (qq.v.), and some observers have attributed the easy acceptance of Hinduism and Buddhism (qq.v.) to a blending of megalith worship with reverence for the lingga of Siva and the stupa of Buddhism. [0373, 0390, 0420]

MELAKA (Malacca), port city on the peninsular coast of the Melaka Strait, founded in 1402 by Parameswara, a prince of Palembang (q.v.). In the tradition of Srivijaya (q.v.), with which it claimed a dynastic connection, and Jambi (q.v.), Melaka attracted traders by virtue of its strategic position, its servicing facilities and its regularized taxation (q.v.), becoming the most powerful state on the strait in C.15. It competed with Siam for control of the Malay peninsula and established outposts in Sumatra, especially in Siak (q.v.). From 1400 to 1430 it received several visits from the Chinese Admiral Zheng He (q.v.) and worked closely with the Ming rulers of China (see CHINA, Historical links with) to suppress piracy (q.v.) and to keep trade flowing smoothly. Its commercial orientation later turned westward and it became a major entrepôt for the flow of goods from the archipelago to India and the West. It also moved into pepper production and trade for the Indian market and in 1436 adopted Islam (q.v.).

Melaka's wealth, described in glowing terms by Tomé Pires (q.v.), continued to come principally from its entrepôt role and made it in many respects a model for later sultanates in the region. Wealth also made it a prime target for the Portuguese (q.v.), who captured it in 1511 with a force of 1,200 men and 18 ships (see also UPAS). Much of Melaka's trade then went to Aceh and Banten (qq.v.) and the city was attacked repeatedly by Aceh and by Riau (q.v.), where descendants of the Melaka sultans had reestablished their kingdom. Melaka fell to a combined Dutch-Riau force in 1641, but under Dutch rule the city declined further as the VOC (q.v.) directed trade as much as possible to Batavia (q.v.). British forces seized Melaka in 1795 during the Napoleonic Wars but it was restored to the Dutch in 1818. The Anglo-Dutch Treaty of 1824 (q.v.) placed it definitively under British rule as part of a general tidying up of colonial borders in the region. For further information see the forthcoming *Historical Dictionary of Malaysia.* [0058, 0430, 0446, 0473, 0488]

MELANESIAN BROTHERHOOD, catch-phrase used in Indonesian government circles for alleged Melanesian (especially Papua New Guinea, q.v.) irredentism in

Irian (q.v.). There is no evidence for the existence of such an organization, but from time to time political figures in PNG and Vanuatu have shown an especial concern for alleged Indonesian misrule in Irian on the basis of a Melanesian identity shared with the Papuans of Irian. [0912]

MELAYU. See JAMBI.

MENADO. See MINAHASA.

MENTAWAI, archipelago off the west coast of Sumatra. The indigenous inhabitants cultivate taro, yams, and sago and raise pigs and fowl (qq.v.). Their society shows many supposedly primitive features, such as little social differentiation between men and women, an absence of political leaders (though a category of traditional healers, or *kerei,* exists), and a belief that all things have a soul. The main island of the group, Siberut, is also the habitat of four endemic primate species.

MERANTAU (from *rantau,* regions around). Temporary migration by males to other regions to earn money, especially in trade, is a common feature of many Indonesian societies (see ACEH; BAWEAN; GAYO; MINANGKABAU). It generally reflects and reinforces a social structure in which the domestic influence of women (q.v.) is strong. [1028]

MERAUKE. See IRIAN; SABANG TO MERAUKE, From; SUCCESSION.

'MERDEKA!' ('Freedom!'), common greeting during the Revolution (q.v.).

MESTIZO CULTURES. See DEPOK; INDO-EUROPEANS; MARDIJKERS; PERANAKAN.

METALWORKING. Indonesia's neolithic societies first gained access to metal in the form of bronze objects introduced from mainland Southeast Asia in C.3 to 2 B.C. (see GAMELAN). The casting of bronze by the lost wax method, however, was quickly developed for both weapons and musical instruments. The working of bronze is known from mainland Southeast Asia from 2000 B.C., and most bronze used in the archipelago was probably imported, since the local deposits of tin in Bangka and Belitung (qq.v.) were not known before 1709 (see also GAMELAN). Iron (q.v.) working is known from C.10. The Javanese and Balinese kris, a long dagger, generally sinuous in shape, was traditionally made using alternating fine layers of iron and paler nickelous iron from Sulawesi, the result forming a distinctive striated pattern on the blade. After 1749, the nickelous iron used in many kris was obtained from a meteor which fell near Prambanan in Central Java. The resulting blend was said to symbolize a fusion of heaven and earth. Master smiths (*mpu*) were said to forge krisses on their knees using the heat of their fists. The fiery transformation of ore into metal and of metal into fine shapes was seen widely, perhaps under the influence of Tantrism, as analogous to the transformation of the soul after death. See also COPPER; GOLD; TIN. [0109, 0483, 1059]

'MIDDLE WAY' FOR THE ARMED FORCES, doctrine articulated in November 1958 by A.H. Nasution (q.v.) in response to the declaration of martial law in 1957 (though the term 'middle way' was coined by the lawyer Jokosutono). He argued that the armed forces should not be a 'dead tool' of the government of the day, nor should they seize power from it. Rather they should follow a 'middle way' of responsible involvement in political decision making. This doctrine was the basis of the army's partnership with Sukarno in Guided Democracy (q.v.) but has since been superseded by the doctrine of *dwifungsi* (q.v.). [0663, 0669, 0709]

MIGRATIONS. Prehistorians once identified successive waves of so-called proto- and deutero-Malays said to have entered the archipelago from mainland southeast Asia via the Malay peninsula, but it now seems that the inhabitants of western Indonesia are descended from Austronesians who emerged first in what is now Taiwan and who moved southwards from 4000 B.C. through the Philippines and into Sulawesi (q.v.) before turning west and east to establish themselves in much of the archipelago by 3000 to 2000 B.C., partly displacing and partly absorbing the established Austromelanesian peoples. Others went on to reach Madagascar (q.v.), Easter Island, and Hawaii by 1000 A.D. They brought with them the bow and arrow, canoes with outriggers, pottery, and timber and thatched houses, as well as pigs, fowl, rice, and millet (qq.v.). The Austronesian migration was followed by a series of smaller migrations of Mongoloid peoples from the Asian mainland, especially and most recently Chinese (q.v.), who assimilated into and contributed culturally to Austronesian societies rather than displacing them. The distinction formerly made between proto- and deutero-Malays is now believed to reflect differing degrees of Austromelanesian and Mongoloid influence. See also LANGUAGES; PREHISTORY. [0390]

MILITARY BUSINESS OPERATIONS. During the Indonesian revolution, most armed units established so-called *badan ekonomi* (economic organizations) to help fund military operations, and such outfits have remained in place under various names. Initially most were involved in bringing plantation produce to markets outside Indonesia, notably Singapore, but they have now moved into a wide range of commercial, construction, and other fields. They number some hundreds and include PT Tri Usaha Bakti, formerly headed by Sujono Humardani (1919–86), the Yayasan Dharma Putra, associated with KOSTRAD (q.v.), and the Propelat group, associated with the former Siliwangi (q.v.) Division. In 1970, it was estimated that such companies provided ca 50% of armed forces income. A second avenue of military involvement in business is through state enterprises (q.v.), both those seized from the Dutch in 1958, which were placed immediately under military administration, and those set up since, such as the Badan Urusan Logistik (q.v.). In 1974, active duty officers were forbidden to engage directly in business, but this regulation has been enforced only sporadically. See also CUKONG. [0280, 0287, 0316, 0669]

MILK. See CATTLE.

MILLET (*Setaria italica* Poaceae) was cultivated in Taiwan by the Austronesian ancestors of the modern Indonesians (see MIGRATIONS), but with its need for a pronounced dry season it apparently did not survive the journey through the moist tropics of the Philippines and Sulawesi. It was later re-introduced from China and is believed to have been a staple crop on Java before the spread of rice (q.v.) cultivation. It is still a minor crop in the drier regions of the eastern archipelago. [0365, 0411, 0938]

MINAHASA, region at the end of Sulawesi's northern peninsula, often including the neighboring Sangir and Talaud islands. The early inhabitants of the region have left little trace but for impressive sandstone sarcophagi (*waruga*), but they seem to have been culturally similar to the inland tribes of the southern Philippines. The major political unit was the *walak*, a territorially-based clan or clan-group, and the name Minahasa is said to refer to an alliance of such groups against the neighboring kingdom of Bolaäng-Mongondouw. They cultivated rice in labor cooperatives (*mapalus*) and raised pigs and fowl (qq.v.); from C.17 maize (q.v.) became a major crop. The Spanish established settlements at Kema and Manado (Menado) ca 1560 and Catholic missionaries were active during the next century. The Spanish, Portuguese, and Dutch competed for control of the coastal regions in C.17, the Dutch becoming dominant from 1679, when they signed an alliance with Minahasa chiefs. Catholic converts in the region were then unilaterally declared to be Calvinist. The region came under British rule 1801–16 and a major uprising took place in Tondano in 1807–09. Missionary activity by the Nederlandsch Zendelingsgenootschap (see PROTESTANTISM) began in 1824 and the region was largely converted by late C.19. An independent regional church, the Gereja Masehi Injil Minahasa was formed in 1934.

Under the Treaty of 1679, the Minahasa chiefs agreed to supply a number of products (gold, fibers) to the VOC. Coffee (q.v.) was introduced in 1797 and became a government monopoly in 1822, labor being obtained by corvée. Forced cultivation of cacao, nutmeg (qq.v.), and manila hemp followed. Labor conscription ended in 1893, but coffee remained a government monopoly until 1899. Under Dutch rule, the walak were initially preserved as the units of administration, though their number was steadily diminished, from 27 in 1824 to six in 1940. In 1877, following the Agrarian Law of 1870 (q.v.) on Java, the colonial government declared all 'waste' land to be its property. This caused great debate over the status of the region, whether allied or subject to the Netherlands Indies. In 1881 the *majoor,* or walak heads, became salaried government officials. In early C.20 coconut cultivation for copra became a major industry largely conducted by smallholder producers, who frequently, however, became seriously indebted to Chinese middlemen. A Copra Contracten Ordonnantie in 1939 attempted to regulate copra contracts in favor of producers, but had no time to have effect.

From early times, a militia had been necessary in the colony for protection against pirates from the southern Philippines (q.v.), and from early C.19 Minahasa became a major recruitment area for the colonial army or KNIL (q.v.). The presence of missionary schools led to a relatively high level of education and of fluency in Dutch in the region. Government education also expanded in the 1880s, and many people left the region to find employment elsewhere, especially as teachers and in other government services, so that along with the Ambonese, 'Menadonese' (the colonial era term for Minahasa Christians) gained a reputation as indigenous agents of Dutch rule. A Perserikatan Minahassa (Minahasa Association) was established in 1910 by G.S.S.J. Ratulangi (1890–1949), but it argued for promotion of trade and industry in the region rather than for independence. In the latter part of the revolutionary period a Minahasa organization, the Komite Ketatanegaraan Minahasa (Minahasa Constitutional Committee), argued against the region's inclusion in independent Indonesia and some groups called for incorporation in the Netherlands as the 'Twelfth Province'. In the 1950s, the region became a major center of smuggling, and an unsuccessful attempt by the central government in 1956 to close the port of Manado was amongst causes of the Permesta (q.v.) revolt. [0021, 0075, 0312, 1033]

MINANGKABAU, ethnic group in West Sumatra, now strongly Muslim but with powerful matrilineal traditions. The Hindu-Buddhist king Adityavarman (r. ca 1356–75) threw off the loose control of Javanese Majapahit (q.v.) in 1347, but the Minangkabau were traditionally organized not in kingdoms but into largely autonomous villages (*nagari*), themselves federations of kinship groups. The Minangkabau region is traditionally known as Alam Minangkabau (the land of the Minangkabau) rather than by a state name. Two broad customary law traditions existed: Kota Piliang in the Tanah Datar region and Bodi Caniago in Agam and Limapuluh Kota. Gold mines in the Tanah Datar area were the principal economic base of Minangkabau communities and up to C.17 the area was the main gold-producer on the archipelago. A VOC post was established on the coast under the Treaty of Painan (1663).

Islam (q.v.) reached the region in C.16, spreading first through Islamic schools (*surau*). Dobbin argues that economic change in late C.18 stimulated dramatic growth of Islam. Gold production declined, production of cinnamon, coffee, gambier, and salt expanded and Minangkabau men became increasingly involved in long-distance trade with the outside world. Islam offered not only a means for creating a trading diaspora, whose members helped each other with credit and commercial information, but also provided a platform for a political challenge to the old order. This challenge took the form of the so-called Paderis, a radical modernist Muslim movement which fought the adat (q.v.) chiefs for authority. The Paderi War lasted from 1803 to 1837 and included raids by Paderis far north into the country of the Bataks (q.v.). The Dutch used the hostilities as an excuse to become involved in Minangkabau politics, joining the traditional leaders against the Muslim forces. They succeeded in defeating the Paderi forces in 1837 but at the cost of entrenching Islam as the religion of Minangkabau.

Under Dutch rule, West Sumatra became a major coffee (q.v.) producing area, at first under Dutch monopoly control. With the relaxation of the monopoly and forced cultivation in early C.20, the Minangkabau moved extensively into private production of coffee, copra, and rubber. Anticolonial uprisings took place in 1908 and 1927 (see also PARTAI KOMUNIS INDONESIA) and many Minangkabau (Hatta, Syahrir, Yamin, qq.v.) were active in the nationalist movement. Strongly loyal to the Indonesian Republic during the Revolution, West Sumatra was the main center of the 1958 PRRI rebellion (q.v.). [0451, 0513, 0645, 0873, 0992, 1026, 1028, 1050]

MINDERE WELVAARTS ONDERZOEK (Diminishing Welfare, or better Diminished Prosperity, Inquiry). Under the Ethical Policy (q.v.), the Netherlands government assumed greater responsibility for the welfare of the indigenous inhabitants of the Indies. In order to provide a factual basis for policy changes, the colonial government in 1902 commissioned an investigation into the causes of poverty on Java and Madura (qq.v.). Research began in July 1904 and was completed within a year, though it was a decade before all sections of the report were published. The report seems to have had little effect on government policy, partly because of this delay and partly because it portrayed a complex situation with no simple solutions. Its detailed information on income, indebtedness, methods of agriculture, etc., have made it a major resource for researchers on early C.20 Java and Madura. [0222]

MINISTRY OF COLONIES. See COLONIES, Ministry of; NETHERLANDS, Constitutional relationship with Indonesia.

MISSIONARY ACTIVITY. See CATHOLICISM; PROTESTANTISM.

'MOJOKUTO' PROJECT, multidisciplinary research project into modern Javanese society, sponsored by the

Massachusetts Institute of Technology and focusing especially on Pare, East Java, dubbed 'Mojokuto' ('Middle-town'). Major figures in this project were Clifford Geertz (q.v.), Robert Jay, Donald Fagg, and Alice Dewey.

MOLUCCAS. See MALUKU.

MONEY. See CURRENCY.

MONGOL INVASION. See CHINA, Historical links with; MAJAPAHIT.

MONOLOYALITAS (Monoloyalty), exclusive loyalty to the state and government demanded of all state employees, especially in elections (q.v.). First articulated in 1970, monoloyalitas was intended to prevent the bureaucracy from being an arena for competing interests and to guarantee the bureaucratic base of the New Order. See CENTER FOR STRATEGIC AND INTERNATIONAL STUDIES; FLOATING MASS; KORPS PEGAWAI REPUBLIK INDONESIA. [0680]

MOOK, Hubertus Johannes van (1894–1965), Indies-born colonial official and politician. Van Mook studied Indology at Leiden University where he was strongly influenced by the 'Ethical' ideas of van Vollenhoven (q.v.) and others and returned to the Indies where he held increasingly senior administrative posts, holding the posts of director of economic affairs in 1937–41, lieutenant governor-general in 1941–42 and 1944–48, and minister of colonies in 1941–45. Unusually for colonial civil services, he was also involved in politics, as leader of the *De Stuw* group (q.v.) and from 1931 member of the Volksraad (q.v.). He was an advocate of increased autonomy for the Indies and the gradual elimination of racial distinctions.

He headed the colonial government-in-exile in Australia (q.v.) during World War II and returned to Indonesia in October 1945 as head of the NICA (q.v.) and later of the restored colonial government, though he was never promoted to governor-general. His hope that the Indonesian-Dutch conflict could be resolved by dealing reasonably with 'moderate' nationalists such as Syahrir (q.v.) was frustrated by the metropolitan Dutch insistence on restoring Dutch authority and on limiting concessions to nationalism, but his own insistence that the Dutch retain a tutelary role during an extended transition to independence was unacceptable to a great many Indonesian nationalists (see DIPLOMACY AND PERJUANGAN). By 1948 his unpopular role in the development of federalism (q.v.) and in the launching of the first 'Police Action' (q.v.) had made him a liability in Dutch negotiations with the Republic and he was dismissed on 25 October 1948. See also SUCCESSION. [0767]

MUFAKAT. See MUSYAWARAH.

MUHAMMADIYAH ('followers of Muhammad'), Muslim organization founded in 1912 by Kyai Haji Ahmad Dahlan (1868–1933), a mosque official in Yogyakarta (q.v.) to promote the modernist Islamic thought developed by Muhammad Abduh and Rashid Rida in Cairo. Modernists believed that the condition of Muslims under colonial rule and other despotism was in part a consequence of their own straying from the basic principles of the religion and their aim was thus, as they saw it, to cleanse and revitalize Islam by discarding tradition and ritual and returning to the central texts, *i.e.,* the Qur'an and the Hadiths. These views brought them into direct conflict with Islamic traditionalists who stressed the importance of studying the full body of Islamic texts in order to understand the Qur'an correctly (see NAHDATUL ULAMA). The modernists stressed the strict observance of the five pillars of Islam (the confession of faith, prayer five times a day, fasting during Ramadan, paying religious tax or *zakat,* and making the *haj* [q.v.] if possible). They also advocated the use of head-covering by women and the segregation of the sexes in public.

Muhammadiyah's main aims were to spread adherence to Islam and to promote the religious understanding of believers. It emphasized social welfare, including education, and under the Dutch did not become directly involved in politics. In 1945 it advocated an Islamic state for Indonesia and joined Masyumi (q.v.) which soon came to be dominated by modernist ideas. It survived the banning of Masyumi in 1960 and continues to be a major Muslim cultural and educational institution. See also ISLAM IN INDONESIA. [0577, 0608, 1117, 1136, 1138]

MUIS, Abdul (1890–1959), journalist and politician, educated as a protégé of J.H. Abendanon (1852–1925) under the Association Principle (q.v.), but best known for his novel *Salah Asuhan* (*A Wrong Upbringing,* 1928) which describes the difficulties faced by European-educated Indonesians in fitting into their own society. [0711]

MULTATULI. See DOUWES DEKKER, Eduard; *MAX HAVELAAR.*

MURBA (Partai Murba, Proletarian Party), founded in October 1948 by followers of Tan Malaka (q.v.) who had joined the Hatta government in crushing the PKI in the Madiun Affair (q.v.). Tan Malaka was made patron of the party, and though he took no role in its organization, his connection led the PKI misleadingly to label it 'Trotskyist.' The party strongly opposed negotiations with the Dutch, but was unable to win a political base beyond a few lasykar (q.v.) units and in the 1955 elections won only 0.5% of the vote. It strongly supported Guided Democracy, and several party members (*e.g.,* Adam Malik, q.v.) and associates (*e.g.,* Chaerul Saleh, q.v.) obtained powerful positions under Sukarno. For a time it was cultivated by the Soviet Union (q.v.) as an alternative to the PKI (q.v.), but in January 1965 the PKI persuaded Sukarno to have it banned. It reemerged under the New Order, but won no seats in the 1971 elections and was merged in 1973 into the PDI (q.v.). See also PERSATUAN PERJUANGAN. [0634]

MUSIC. The long tradition of cultural hybridization especially in Indonesian port cities has also been reflected in musical history. Although traditional gamelan (q.v.) music on Java has been relatively resistant to Western influence, a form of creole music called kroncong (q.v.) developed in C.16 and 17 and gradually spread throughout the archipelago. In C.20, something of an independent jazz tradition began to develop in the clubs of Batavia and records were produced locally from the 1920s. Music was at first relatively free of the debate over the role of culture (q.v.) and even Indonesia's national anthem, *Indonesia Raya* (q.v.), composed in 1928, shows no distinctly Indonesian motifs. In the 1950s, however, Muslim and nationalist groups increasingly opposed the spread of Western pop and rock music, arguing that it was corrupting and inconsistent with Indonesian identity. Although suppression of Western music was never entirely successful, later decades saw the growth of strong national (*pop Indonesia*) and regional (*pop daerah*) traditions, often bearing a loose resemblance in style and content to country-and-western music (see also BIMBO; DANGDUT). A thriving domestic cassette market exists for all these forms of music. See also COPYRIGHT. [0115, 0121, 0126–0128, 0131, 0135, 0140, 0145]

MUSYAWARAH, discussion of issues, often at exhaustive length, by all involved in order to reach a consensus (*mufakat*). Many nationalists, especially Sukarno (q.v.) argued that *musyawarah* was the basis of traditional village democracy in Indonesia and that it should be used in place of a Western-style system of decision making by votes. See also GOTONG ROYONG.

MYSTICISM. See KEBATINAN.

N

NAGARAKRTAGAMA (also known in many other spellings, incl. *Negarakertagama*), lengthy panegyric poem in Old Javanese, composed by Prapanca, poet to the C.14 court of Hayam Wuruk, king of Majapahit (q.v.). The poem praises the king while providing a detailed description of the life and social structure of Majapahit. A lontar (q.v.) leaf manuscript of the 'Nagarakrtagama' was captured by Dutch troops on Lombok (q.v.) in 1894; further copies were found on Bali in 1978. [0365, 0414]

NAHDATUL ULAMA (NU, 'Revival of the Religious Scholars), founded in Surabaya in 1926 by K.H. Hasyim Asyari (1871–1947) to resist the rise of modernism in Indonesian Islam which, in emphasizing direct recourse to the Qur'an and Hadiths largely dispensed with the learning of religious scholars, or *ulama* (see MUHAMMADIYAH). The organization quickly developed a strong following in East Java and south Kalimantan and was also active in founding schools and cooperatives. It joined Muhammadiyah, however, in the MIAI (q.v.) in

1937 to promote Islamic unity, and in 1943 was given a prominent role by the Japanese in the Masyumi (q.v.). Masyumi became a political party in 1945, but was dominated by modernists, and in 1952 NU seceded under Wahid Hasyim (q.v.). Led by K.H. Idham Chalid (b. 1917) after Wahid Hasyim's death, NU's political priorities were always strictly religious and it was willing to trade its support on what it saw as peripheral issues for other parties' support on religious matters. NU was represented in all cabinets from 1955 to 1971 (generally holding the Ministry of Religion) and Idham Chalid became a deputy prime minister in Sukarno's first *kabinet karya* in 1957. It ferociously opposed government policy on matters of public morality, such as state-sponsored gambling, and more recently the marriage (q.v.) law, and under its supervision the Ministry of Religion grew to become the largest government department. It surprised most observers by coming third in the 1955 elections (q.v.), but it shared little of Masyumi's unhappiness at the end of parliamentary rule in the 1950s. In this it clearly had the support of its own constituency, which was based in the *santri* (q.v.) communities of East Java and especially in the *pesantren* (q.v.). It was a willing partner in Sukarno's Guided Democracy (q.v.), representing the 'A' (for *agama* or religion) in Nasakom (q.v.), but its rural landowning supporters were strongly opposed to the PKI's land reform (q.v.) activities in the countryside and it became one of the pillars of the so-called New Order (q.v.) coalition. It soon, however, grew unhappy with the New Order's failure to favor Islam and has since proved to be the most resilient of the old political parties, largely preserving its vote in the 1971 elections and forming a major electoral pillar of the PPP (q.v.) from 1973. Its influence within the PPP, however, was always far less than its numerical following warranted and in 1984 it formally left the party in order to concentrate on its educational and social goals. See also ANSOR; ISLAM. [0634, 0828, 1121]

NAMES, Personal. Reference to Indonesian personal names often causes considerable difficulty to Westerners, the classic gaffe being the 'Achmad' sometimes (but now rarely) added to Sukarno's name to give it an impression of completeness. Many Indonesians, particularly on Java, have only one name, though there is an increasing tendency for people to follow the priyayi (q.v.) custom of giving their children multiple names, which now show some tendency to become fixed surnames. When an individual possesses two or more names, there is not necessarily any firm rule as to which should be used. Ali Sastroamijoyo (q.v.) was generally 'Ali,' Ahmad Yani (q.v.) was always 'Yani.' Although the 1973 government regulation on spelling is applied strictly to historical figures (Tjokroaminoto, for instance, being spelled Cokroaminoto), many contemporary Indonesians retain or have adopted Dutch-style spelling for sentimental, idiosyncratic, or prestige reasons. Nor is the division between names firmly fixed: the former Vice-President Adam Malik (q.v.) was once commonly known as Adammalik, while a name such as Suriakartalegawa may also be given as Suria Karta Legawa. A further complication is the use of titles (q.v.) as proper names. Amongst the Bataks and the people of the Minahasa (qq.v.), surnames in the Western sense are common, while some Chinese Indonesians used traditional Chinese surnames. Changes of name, however, are not uncommon when an individual wishes to mark some important change in his or her life; Suwardi Surianingrat (q.v.) changed his name to Ki Hajar Dewantoro as he became more deeply involved in Taman Siswa, while the Indo-European E.F.E. Douwes Dekker became Setiabudi to symbolize his political allegiance to Indonesia. Many Chinese Indonesians, for convenience and/or conviction, have adopted quasi-Indonesian names which they use as surnames, Liem, for example, becoming Salim. Amongst other ethnic groups, however, the appropriate name for address or reference is often not clear, and one must be guided by common usage rather than firm rules. On the spelling of names in this volume, see the Guide to Use.

NASAKOM (*Nasionalisme* [Nationalism], *Agama* [Religion], *Komunisme* [Communism]), political doctrine formulated by Sukarno (q.v.) as a counter to the ideological and religious diversity of the nationalist movement before World War II, though he did not coin the term *Nasakom* until the late 1950s. Sukarno argued that Religious belief, Communism and Nationalism were not fundamentally incompatible ideologies but aspects of a concern for spirituality, social justice, and national self-respect which all Indonesians shared. His refusal to accept the division between these ideologies contributed to his success as a uniting national leader.

In installing Guided Democracy (q.v.) in 1957–59, Sukarno renewed his stress on the fundamental unity of the various ideological streams within Indonesia, and Nasakom became the grounds for including the PKI (q.v.) in a broad range of government institutions from 1960 and in the cabinet from 1962. Opinions differ on whether 'Nasakomization' meant the 'domestication' of the PKI within the state or whether it was a step in the direction of a Communist takeover, but in the latter years of Guided Democracy, Nasakom was closely associated with the left in general; the right appealed rather to the principle of Pancasila (q.v.), which emphasized belief in God and made no reference to Communism. After the victory of the right and the banning of the PKI in 1965, Sukarno tried briefly to revive Nasakom as *Nasasos,* with *sosialisme* in place of Communism. See also MARXISM. [0705, 0854, 0867]

NASUTION, Abdul Haris (b. 1918), military commander and strategist. Trained before World War II at the Dutch military academy at Bandung, Nasution emerged rapidly during the Indonesian Revolution as one of the Republic's most capable military commanders, heading the West Java Siliwangi Division (q.v.) from 1946 and the Java Command from 1948. After initially favoring a Western-style frontal strategy, he developed a range of guerrilla tactics which contributed to the Dutch withdrawal in 1949 (see DIPLOMASI AND PERJUANGAN). As army (q.v.) chief of staff in 1949–52 and 1955–62 and minister of defence in 1956–66, he played a major role in strengthening internal military discipline. On 17 October 1952 after politicians associated with regional military leaders attempted to end his reforms, he backed public demonstrations in Jakarta calling for the dismissal of parliament and was suspended from his post for indiscipline, but was reinstated in 1955. He made energetic but largely unsuccessful attempts to combat corruption (q.v.) in the army. In 1957 he proposed declaring martial law in order to defuse military rebellions in the outer islands and his alliance with Sukarno was instrumental in establishing Guided Democracy (q.v.). He formulated a theory of limited military involvement in politics, known as the 'Middle Way' (q.v.) thesis, but in practice intervened heavily in politics, restricting opposition political activity and sponsoring the Badan Kerja Sama (q.v.). His power as army chief of staff was amongst the factors leading Sukarno to lean towards the PKI (q.v.) to counterbalance army influence. In June 1962, Sukarno maneuvered him into the relatively powerless post of armed forces (q.v.) chief of staff, but he remained powerful as defence minister.

In 1965 Nasution narrowly escaped being killed in the GESTAPU (q.v.) coup attempt of 30 September but, apparently for personal reasons, took a back seat to

General Suharto (q.v.) in suppressing the affair. He played a relatively small role in the construction of a political format for the New Order and was relegated to the post of Speaker of the MPR (q.v.). Since the 1970s, however, he has became increasingly critical of what he has described as corruption and maladministration under the New Order and was a signatory of the Petition of Fifty (q.v.) in 1980. [0652, 0663, 0675, 0709]

NATIONALISM. Although a number of early opponents of Dutch rule in the archipelago, such as Diponegoro (q.v.), have been mythographically promoted as national heroes, most historians agree that the emergence of Indonesian nationalism coincides with what nationalist historians themselves call the *kebangkitan nasional,* or national awakening of early C.20. The distinctive feature of this awakening was that it drew on Western thinking and took account of the socioeconomic changes brought about by colonialism to argue for an end to colonialism without a simple return to the precolonial order. Indonesian nationalism was never united by a single ideology or by a single organization, but its members shared a strong sense of participation in a movement (pergerakan) which was historically bound to win.

In comparison with the Philippines and British India, where fully-fledged movements were campaigning for independence before the turn of the century, nationalism was rather late to develop in Indonesia. This was probably a result of the limited range of educational facilities available in the Netherlands Indies until C.20, which meant that Indonesians had little access to the formerly European ideas which initially inspired movements elsewhere (see EDUCATION). The emergence of nationalism indeed coincides with the rise of a modern Indonesian elite, trained for employment in company and government offices under the Liberal and

Ethical Policies (qq.v.) or as professionals (physicians, lawyers, engineers etc.). The fact that this nationalism was *Indonesian* and not more regionally based owed much to colonial administrative and education policies. Although the Netherlands Indies was in some senses a patchwork of distinct administrations and legal systems (see LAW; NETHERLANDS, Constitutional relationship with Indonesia; ZELFBESTUREN), the palace of the governor-general in Batavia remained the unequivocal seat of power in the colony and the principal focus of nationalist action. Members of the new Indonesian elite, too, found that the borders of the colony, rather than regional boundaries or those of the Dutch empire as a whole, defined their career possibilities. Dutch writers since 1949 have sometimes argued with satisfaction that Dutch policies 'created a nation' in Indonesia, but throughout the colonial period Dutch authorities took some pains to deny this, arguing that the Indies were ethnically, socially, and culturally diverse and that the nationalist movement's assertion of an Indonesian identity was a self-serving bid for power by a small elite.

The pergerakan included some hundreds of organizations, but it has been customary to identify the following main lines of development. Budi Utomo (q.v., founded 1908), with its emphasis on progress, represented a first awakening of proto-nationalist consciousness, though its focus was Javanese rather than Indonesian. The Indische Partij (q.v.), dominated by Indo-Europeans, was the first to demand full independence for the Indies, but aimed otherwise to preserve many of the structures of colonial society. Sarekat Islam (q.v.) was the first mass party but faced insuperable problems of working out both a common political program and a plan of action and soon lost ground to the better organized and more purposeful PKI (q.v.). The PKI, however, was suppressed by the Dutch after its unsuccessful rebellions in 1926–27 and the center of the nationalist stage was taken by the so-called secular or radical nationalists, who emphasized a common Indonesian identity, irrespective of religion, race, or class. PNI, Pendidikan Nasional Indonesia and PARTINDO (qq.v.) and leaders such as Sukarno, Hatta, and Syahrir (qq.v.) were only briefly able to operate before a final decade of Dutch repression restricted political freedom to relatively moderate cooperative parties, notably PARINDRA and GERINDO (qq.v.). Only during the Japanese occupation (q.v.) were the radical nationalists able to resume leadership of the pergerakan. Some scholars, however, have argued that this general view is misleading because it gives the eventual victors (the radical nationalists) a more central role than they in fact played, and that more 'moderate' and regional organizations such as the Pakempalan Kawula Ngayogyakarta and Paguyuban Pasundan (qq.v.) and conservative figures such as Ahmad Djajadiningrat (q.v.) and Noto Suroto need to be given more emphasis.

From the start, all nationalist groups acknowledged that they faced an enormous obstacle in the form of the colonial state, especially the political police (Politiek Inlichtingen Dienst, q.v.) and the strategy for overcoming this was a major topic of debate. The PKI unsuccessfully ventured armed rebellion in 1926–27, but for most nationalists the issue was how much to cooperate with the colonial government in quasi-representative institutions such as the Volksraad (q.v.). Those favoring cooperation ('Co') hoped that this would ameliorate the conditions of Indonesians under colonialism and would lead eventually to responsible government. Those rejecting it ('Non-Co') argued that the Volksraad was no more than window-dressing and that progress could only be made by withdrawing cooperation from the colonial government so that it would eventually cease to operate. The nationalists were also divided on whether to expect support from abroad. Members of the PKI looked to the

Comintern for aid. Some Muslims hoped for assistance from the Muslim world, while others looked to Japan (q.v.), especially after the Russo-Japanese War. In the late 1930s, on the other hand, the Left was keen to cooperate with the colonial authorities against Japanese fascism, and towards the close of the Japanese occupation, younger nationalists were anxious that Japanese plans for a puppet state in Indonesia should not lead to independence being achieved as a 'gift' of any other country. This view developed during the Revolution into a preference for military action to defeat the Dutch rather than negotiation towards a compromise settlement (see DIPLOMASI AND PERJUANGAN).

During the Revolution, the Dutch endeavored to promote and recognize regional identities in a federal system (see FEDERALISM), but only in Ambon (q.v.) did a serious separatist movement emerge at this time. The Dutch retained control, however, of West New Guinea or Irian (q.v.) and encouraged hopes for independence amongst the Papuans which have survived the territory's transfer to Indonesian rule in 1963. These hopes, together with insensitive and at times brutal actions by Indonesian forces, form the ideological underpinning of the Organisasi Papua Merdeka (q.v.) or Free Papua Movement. [0341, 0365, 0384, 0543, 0545, 0560, 0561, 0571, 0576, 0577, 0582, 0584, 0585, 0591, 0610, 0695, 0858]

NATIONALIZATION. Under the Liberal Policy (q.v.), the colonial government promoted foreign investment and resorted to nationalization only of German and Italian firms after the occupation of the Netherlands in 1940. During the Japanese occupation, firms belonging to Allied subjects were appropriated, and handed in some cases to government bodies as a source of finance and in other cases to existing Japanese firms (see SUGAR). At the start of the Revolution, most such firms came into the hands of their workers, though the Republican government was publicly committed to handing all but a small number of essential industries, such as the railways and public utilities, back to their foreign owners (see DIPLOMASI AND PERJUANGAN).

In December 1957 workers and trade unions throughout Indonesia took over the offices of Dutch firms in the name of worker control. Within a few weeks control was put in the hands of the armed forces (see MILITARY BUSINESS OPERATIONS) and the seizures were ratified by parliament. Two hundred forty-six enterprises were taken over, accounting for 90% of the country's plantation output and 60% of foreign trade. British and American property was nationalized in 1963–65, but much of it was returned after 1966. Strong guarantees were also given at this time against further nationalization. See also FOREIGN INVESTMENT; INDONESIANIZATION; MANIFESTO POLITIK; STATE ENTERPRISES. [0223, 0228]

NATIVE STATES. See ZELFBESTUREN.

NATIVE TROOPS. Alongside the colonial army (see KONINKLIJK NEDERLANDSCH INDISCH LEGER), the Dutch retained a number of auxiliary units more or less descended from the armies of defeated or subordinated indigenous rulers. Some of these, such as the Legiun Mangkunegaran (see MANGKUNEGARAN) remained under the command of the *zelfbesturen* (q.v.), while others such as the *prajurits* of Java and the *barisans* on Madura operated as a kind of auxiliary police force under the command of the Dutch civilian government, though the barisans also took part in military expeditions to other islands. During World War I many Indonesians agitated for the establishment of a native militia to aid in the defence of the colony. The Dutch, however, rejected this for security reasons. In the latter part of the Indonesian Revolution, the Dutch established several quasiauxiliary units. Hare Majesteits Ongeregelde Troepen (Her Majesty's Irregular Troops) consisted of former lasykar (q.v.) recruited to the Dutch cause. In West Java especially, *ondernemingswachten* (plantation guards) recruited many Indonesians, while Veiligheidsbataljons in North Sumatra and West Java and the Barisan Cakra in Madura were intended partly to maintain law and order, partly as military backing for the federal states (see FEDERALISM). See also MARÉCHAUSSÉE; POLICE.

NATSIR, Muhammad (b. 1908), modernist Muslim leader associated before the war with the Persatuan Islam (q.v.), in which he argued that only Islam could form a correct basis for Indonesian nationality. In November 1945, along with other modernists he gained control of the Masyumi (q.v.) and in September 1950 headed the first cabinet of the unitary Indonesian Republic. His pro-Western government emphasized national reconstruction and enjoyed the benefits of the Korean War boom, but fell in April 1951, partly over its continuing financial austerity program under finance minister Syafruddin Prawiranegara (q.v.). In 1980, Natsir signed the Petition of Fifty (q.v.). [0634]

NAVY. Whereas the colonial army (KNIL, q.v.) was institutionally distinct from the metropolitan army, the naval forces in colonial Indonesia were formally part of the Dutch navy placed at the operational disposal of the governor-general, an arrangement which led to continued disputes over the appropriate division of costs between the two governments. Colonial security policy placed more emphasis on the maintenance of order within the colony than on defence from external attack, and especially after the construction of the Singapore (q.v.) naval base in 1921–38 the colonial government tended to rely on the naval protection of Britain (q.v.). The Dutch fleet in the east was largely destroyed in 1942 in the Battle of the Java Sea (q.v.).

In 1945 former members of the Kaigun Heiho (naval auxiliaries) formed by the Japanese occupation forces founded the Angkatan Laut Republik Indonesia (ALRI, Navy of the Indonesian Republic), which was, however, mainly a commercial operation, trading plantation produce to Singapore and elsewhere; after 1949 the high capital costs of maintaining a navy and the demands of internal security kept the navy small, though it received some equipment from the Soviet Union (q.v.) after 1960. [0496, 0663]

NEDERLANDSCHE HANDEL MAATSCHAPPIJ (NHM, Netherlands Trading Company, also known as the Factorij). Founded 29 March 1825 by King Willem I on the advice of Muntinghe as a quasiofficial trading corporation, the NHM acted initially as agent for the sale of government produce acquired under the Cultivation System (q.v.), earning enormous profits. Multatuli's novel *Max Havelaar* was subtitled 'The coffee auctions of the Netherlands Trading Company.' The NHM was also responsible for supplying produce, especially textiles, to Dutch industry and from 1827 to 1833 had a monopoly of opium (q.v.) sales in Dutch territory. After losing government preference in 1872, the firm moved increasingly into the financing of plantations and thence into general banking which became its major activity in the C.20. In 1964 the NHM merged with the Twentse Bank to form the Algemene Bank Nederland.

NEGARA INDONESIA TIMUR (state of East Indonesia), federal state formed on 24 December 1946 after the Malino Conference of July that year, encompassing Sulawesi, Maluku and Nusatenggara as a model of Dutch post-colonial plans for Indonesia. Makassar (q.v.) was its capital. From March 1947, semi-autonomous regions (*daerah*) were formed within the NIT itself. Although conservative, its leaders were sufficiently aware of nationalist strength to seek good relations with the Republic, and it was NIT's insistence after the second Dutch 'Police Action' that the Republic be included in negotiations on the country's future which ended Dutch hopes of using federalism (q.v.) to destroy the Republic. In April 1950 the Minahasa (q.v.) daerah seceded from NIT and merged with the Indonesian Republic, and it was followed by the remaining daerah, except South Sulawesi. In May 1950 the NIT *walinegara* (head of state), Tjokorde Gde Rake Sukawati, agreed to dissolve the state on 17 August 1950. The arbitrary actions by Republican troops sent from Java to take control, however, aroused resentment which contributed to the revolt of Kahar Muzakkar (q.v.). See also REPUBLIK MALUKU SELATAN. [0563, 0656]

NEGARA KALIMANTAN TIMUR. See PONTIANAK.

NEGARA SUMATERA SELATAN. See PALEMBANG.

NEGARA SUMATERA TIMUR. See EAST SUMATRA.

NEKOLIM (Neo-Kolonialis, Kolonialis dan Imperialis, Neocolonialists, Colonialists, and Imperialists), term coined by Ahmad Yani (q.v.) but popularized by Sukarno to describe what he saw as the major international enemies of the Indonesian people and reflecting his understanding that formal independence did not necessarily mean an end to imperialist control. Sukarno amplified the concept in 1960 by contrasting the progressive NEFO (new emerging forces) with the reactionary ODEFO (old established forces), and he sought to make this idea a rallying point for progressive countries, holding a Games of the New Emerging Forces (GANEFO) in

November 1963 and in attempting to convene a Conference of the New Emerging Forces (CONEFO) in 1965. See also FOREIGN POLICY. [0705, 0854]

NETHERLANDS, Constitutional relationship with Indonesia. From shortly after the first Dutch trading expeditions to the archipelago, Dutch power in the region was represented almost exclusively by the Dutch East Indies Company (q.v.) or VOC under a charter from the Netherlands States General. On rare occasions, the Dutch government itself despatched one or more commissioners-general (q.v.) to the East to act on its behalf, but for the most part it left the Company with untrammeled freedom of action in the region. The Company's possessions, however, were not thought of as strictly sovereign, since they derived neither from older ideas of divine appointment nor from newer ideas of popular assent. In practice, moreover, under the racially-based legal order (see RACE) in VOC territories, the Company exercised much less than full sovereign power. Even in 1795, when the Batavian Republic (q.v.) took over the assets of the VOC, it seems to have regarded them as primarily commercial, rather than territorial and sovereign, though by that time the Company was already the dominant power on Java. This state of affairs, it needs to be pointed out, was in part a convenient fiction which enabled the Company to carry out commercial and administrative activities not foreseen by those who originally drew up its charter.

From 1795 to 1815, the constitutional relationship remained confused and often vague. Until 1800, the States General ruled formally through the VOC. When the Company's charter lapsed in 1800, the colony came under direct rule, but the Napoleonic Wars and later British occupation of Java made this of little significance. A Ministry of Colonies (q.v.) was formed in

1806, though it was often united with other departments, especially that of the navy (q.v.), until 1842. From 1815 to 1848, the Ministry of Colonies, and thus the colony itself, was directly under the authority of the Dutch king, who used his position and shareholding in the NHM (q.v.) to make a considerable personal fortune. In the late 1820s the post of commissioner-general (q.v.), as representative of the Dutch government, was first united with that of governor-general, as agent of the Ministry of Colonies, and then abandoned.

In C.20, the Netherlands Indies gradually developed as a state distinct from the Netherlands. In 1903 the colonial treasury was separated from that of the Netherlands, and in 1913 the colonial government received the right to contract public loans. The colonial government established quasidiplomatic representation in Arabia (in connection with Muslim pilgrimage, see HAJ). Governors-General van Heutsz (1904–09), Idenburg (1909–16), and van Limburg Stirum (1916–21) increasingly defended what they saw as Indies interests (which were not necessarily the interests of the indigenous population) against those of the metropolis. The establishment of the Volksraad (q.v.) in 1918 gave a quasidemocratic weight to those Indies government actions which it supported. In 1922, the colony became formally a *rijksdeel* on a notionally equal footing with the Netherlands in the Dutch constitution, though remaining under the Ministry of Colonies. On 27 November 1949 the Netherlands government transferred sovereignty over the Netherlands Indies (excluding West New Guinea) to the Republik Indonesia Serikat (q.v.) which was linked to the Kingdom of the Netherlands in a Netherlands-Indonesian Union under the Dutch Crown. See also NETHERLANDS INDIES, Expansion of; NETHERLANDS, Relations with; SUCCESSION. [0005, 0601, 0656]

NETHERLANDS, Relations with. Indonesian-Dutch relations began in 1949 with a legacy of mistrust stemming from the experience of colonialism and the Revolution, from the unpopular Netherlands-Indonesian Union (see also INTERNATIONAL DEBT), and from what was seen as Dutch support for the Republik Maluku Selatan (q.v.) and other dissidents. Dutch unwillingness to contemplate a transfer of West New Guinea (Irian, q.v.) to the Republic at or after the transfer of sovereignty in 1949, however, became the major stumbling-block in relations during the following years, especially after the Netherlands categorically refused to transfer the territory in 1952 and began plans to bring it to separate independence. Indonesia attempted to pressure the Netherlands on the issue by cooling relations: negotiations on the dissolution of the Union began in 1954, though the two sides were unable to agree on how to achieve this and the Union was finally dissolved unilaterally by Indonesia on 8 May 1956. The inherited debt was repudiated on 4 August of the same year. In October 1957 the government coordinated an anti-Dutch boycott which was followed by the nationalization of Dutch firms in December. Indonesia finally cut all links on 17 August 1960, but relations were restored in March 1963, after the Dutch finally surrendered Irian (q.v.). Cordiality returned to the relationship only after the New Order came to power in 1965–66. Indonesia asked the Netherlands to chair the Inter-Governmental Group on Indonesia (q.v.), while the Netherlands is Indonesia's largest trading partner in Europe. Indonesia has seen the Netherlands as a useful counterweight to the United States and Japan (qq.v) in international affairs, but has been irritated by Dutch complaints over human rights abuses in Indonesia. In 1988, ca 100,000 Dutch tourists visited Indonesia. See also NATIONALIZATION [0634, 0744, 0765, 0767]

NETHERLANDS INDIES, Expansion of. Although Indonesian nationalists and Western historians alike were inclined to speak of '350 years of Dutch colonial rule,' the growth of Dutch power in the archipelago was gradual and uneven. The Dutch East Indies Company (q.v.), or VOC, established influence first by means of treaties with indigenous rulers. The earliest of these treaties typically gave the VOC a monopoly of trading rights in certain commodities (*e.g.,* cloves, nutmeg, qq.v.) and the right to build trading posts. Coming from a Europe which had only recently emerged from the complex hierarchy of medieval feudal relationships, the VOC did not see its activities as formally diminishing the sovereignty of indigenous states. In successive years, however, both the character of new treaties and the interpretation of old ones changed to give the Dutch what increasingly amounted to sovereign powers. In 1825, at the end of the disruption caused by the abolition of the VOC and the Napoleonic Wars (see BATAVIAN REPUBLIC), Dutch authority extended over Java, West Sumatra (Minangkabau, q.v.), Palembang, Bangka, Belitung, Banjarmasin, Pontianak, Makassar, the Minahasa, and much of Maluku (qq.v.); in addition, the Dutch held nominal authority over Lampung and Riau (qq.v.). The independent regions thus still included Aceh, East Sumatra (including the Batak regions of the interior), Siak, Kutai and the interior of Kalimantan, the remainder of Sulawesi, Bali, Lombok, Irian (qq.v.), and many regions of Maluku and Nusatenggara. The situation, however, was rather confused, with the Netherlands asserting a general sphere of influence over the entire archipelago yet formally acknowledging the independence of 'native states in amity with the Netherlands government,' a term or phrase which only disappeared in 1915 (see ZELFBESTUREN). From mid C.19 and especially after 1870, the colonial state began to fill out the territorial boundaries of modern Indonesia by conquering or incorporating these independent states. Increasingly, the colonial government preferred to demand *verklaringen* (declarations) of submission from indigenous rulers, rather than signing formal treaties with them. The sultan of Deli (q.v.) made such a declaration in 1862, a model formula for declarations was prepared in 1875, and in 1898 the so-called Korte Verklaring was adopted as a relatively standardized acknowledgement by indigenous rulers that they accepted the general suzerainty of the Netherlands Indies, agreed to follow instructions from the governor-general, and agreed to have no relations with foreign powers. Dutch sovereignty was effectively established over the entire archipelago (with the possible exception of the interior of Irian) by 1911. See also NETHERLANDS, Constitutional relationship with Indonesia. [0005, 0375, 0441, 0482, 0522, 0528, 0529, 0535, 0538, 0693]

NETHERLANDS INDIES CIVIL ADMINISTRATION (NICA), militarized Dutch colonial administrative corps attached to the advancing Allied forces during World War II to take over the government of areas liberated from the Japanese prior to the formal restoration of civil government. The prospect of a return to colonial rule aroused such hostility amongst Indonesians that the term was soon dropped officially, but NICA remained a derogatory shorthand word for the postwar Dutch administration until the end of the Revolution. See also MOOK, H.J. van. [0767]

NEW EMERGING FORCES. See NEKOLIM.

NEW GUINEA, WEST, see IRIAN; NEW GUINEA, EAST, see PAPUA NEW GUINEA.

NEW ORDER (*Orde Baru, Orba*), general term for the political system in force since the accession of Suharto (q.v.) to power in 1966 (see SUPERSEMAR), though it was first used to refer to the so-called 'New Order coalition' of army, students, intellectuals, and Muslims opposed to Sukarno and the PKI (qq.v.). The term soon came to imply a sharp contrast with the so-called Old Order (*Orde Lama, Orla*) of Sukarno, especially in government policies. The New Order abandoned Indonesia's Confrontation (q.v.) with Malaysia, as well as the Jakarta-Peking axis (see FOREIGN POLICY), opened the country to foreign investment, suppressed the PKI (q.v.), purged both state and society of left-wing influence (see MASSACRES OF 1965–66), and abandoned the rhetoric of popular democracy. Indonesia became strongly anticommunist (especially anti-Chinese) in its foreign policy, promoted economic stabilization based on political stability, and emphasized the suppression of allegedly particularist interests in the cause of development.

Many authors have suggested, however, that the contrast between the Old and New Orders may not be as sharp as first appeared. They point in particular to the continuing strong role of the military, to continued political repression and to the patrimonial, neomonarchical styles of both Sukarno and Suharto. See also POLITICAL CULTURE. [0666–0689, 0781–0785]

NEWS AGENCIES. The Algemene Nieuws en Telegraaf Agentschap (ANETA, General News and Telegraph Agency), founded by D.W. Berretty (1890–1934) was the first news agency in the Indies, but it was followed quickly by a number of small Dutch and Indonesian firms, including the Borneo Pers en Nieuws Agentschap (1926) and the Indonesische Pers Agentschap (INPERA) in 1936. Complaints that ANETA was neglecting local news led to the establishment of Antara (q.v.) in 1937. ANETA closed 1940–46 and changed its name in 1954 to Persbiro Indonesia. In 1963 it was merged into Antara. See also NEWSPAPERS. [0342, 0347, 0354]

NEWSPAPERS. From 1615, governor-general J.P. Coen (q.v.) sent news from the Indies to Europe in a handwritten circular later called *Memorie der Nouvelles,* but the first true newspaper produced for sale to the public, the *Bataviase Nouvelles,* appeared only in 1745 and was banned in 1746 on order of the VOC (q.v.). From 1810 the colonial government published the *Bataviasche Koloniale Courant,* which became the *Java Government Gazette* during the British interregnum, and resumed publication as the *Bataviasche Courant* in 1816 and the *Javasche Courant* in 1828. Independent newspapers (apart from advertisement bulletins) began publishing after 1848, the *Java-Bode* (Batavia) appearing in 1852 and *De Locomotief* (Semarang) in 1863. The earliest indigenous newspapers were the Javanese language *Bromartani* (1855) and the Malay *Soerat Chabar Melajoe,* and from the 1870s the number of newspapers in most regions grew dramatically. The nationalist press began with Abdul Rivai's *Bintang Hindia* in West Sumatra (1902), with the *Medan Prijaji* of Tirtoadisuryo appearing in Bandung in 1906. There was also a lively Chinese language press, including *Sin Po* (1910). During the Japanese occupation, publication was restricted to government papers, notably *Jawa Shinbun,* but press publishing blossomed again during the Revolution and the early 1950s; a national survey in 1954 recorded 105 dailies, though many of these were closer in style to political pamphlets than to conventional newspapers. During the 1950s and early 1960s, the PKI (q.v.) newspaper *Harian Rakjat* had the largest circulation, followed by *Pedoman* (PSI, q.v.), *Suluh Indonesia* (PNI, q.v.), and *Abadi* (Masyumi, q.v.), with *Indonesia*

Raya under Mochtar Lubis (q.v.) a major investigatory paper. From the mid 50s, however, and especially after the declaration of martial law in 1957, increasing restrictions were placed on the press, causing circulation and numbers to drop. Between 1962 and 1974, many papers were banned for allegedly supporting the Badan Pendukung Sukarnoisme, GESTAPU or Malari (qq.v.). From July 1978 the government began a program known as *koran masuk desa* (newspapers enter the village) under which free copies of the armed forces newspapers *Angkatan Bersenjata* and *Berita Yudha* were distributed to villages throughout the country, but these were replaced in December 1979 by a new series of 27 weekly newspapers and magazines published by the government especially for distribution to the villages. In 1980 all newspapers were restricted to 12 pages in length. See also CENSORSHIP; JOURNALISM; NEWS AGENCIES. [0341, 0347, 0354, 0356, 0358]

NGANTUNG, Henk (b.1921), painter especially noted for his landscapes and portraits of becak drivers and other people. He was elected to parliament on the PKI ticket in 1955 and was appointed by Sukarno to represent artists on the Dewan Nasional (q.v.) in 1957. In 1961 he became vice mayor of Jakarta and was city governor 1964–65. He was chairperson of the Central Committee of LEKRA (q.v.). [0116]

NIAS, island off the west coast of Sumatra, known especially for what was once seen as its surviving megalithic culture (q.v.), associated with ancestor worship, though this has receded greatly since the start of missionary activity in late C.19. Precolonial society was strictly divided into three classes: aristocrats, farmers, and slaves. [0093, 1049]

NICKEL was formerly obtained both from meteorites and from mines in central Sulawesi (see LUWU). A large mine was opened at Soroako in southeast Sulawesi by the Canadian firm International Nickel in 1978. The state mining firm Aneka Tambang has been mining nickel on Pulau Gebe off Halmahera (q.v.) since 1978. See also METALWORKING. [0328]

NUSANTARA, used in the Nagarakrtagama (q.v.) for the Outer Islands (q.v.) as distinct from Java, but revived in early C.20 as poetic name for the Indonesian archipelago. See ARCHIPELAGIC CONCEPT; INDONESIA.

NUSATENGGARA (Lesser Sundas), the chain of islands stretching east from Java, *viz.,* Bali, Lombok, Sumbawa, Komodo, Sumba, Sawu, Flores, Roti, Timor, and the Solor archipelago (qq.v.).

NUTMEG (*pala*), nut of *Myristica fragrans* (Myristicaceae), native of Maluku and far western New Guinea, and cultivated from early times on Banda (q.v.). Highly prized as a spice, the nuts were traded to China, India, and Europe from C.6. Like cloves (q.v.) they were a major target of Portuguese (q.v.) expansion in the region. After the Dutch seized Maluku in early C.17, they extirpated wild and cultivated trees from all places they could find them except Banda in order to keep a close control of the trade and to drive up prices (see DUTCH EAST INDIES COMPANY; HONGI RAIDS). In 1769 the French successfully smuggled plants to Mauritius, from where they spread to Singapore, Penang, and Grenada (West Indies), breaking the Dutch monopoly. Extensive cultivation began in Minahasa (q.v.) in 1840, but declined after plantations were struck by disease in 1873. [0459, 0751, 0938]

NYAI LORO KIDUL. See MARRIAGE, Political significance of.

O

OEI TIONG HAM (1886–1924), the wealthiest Chinese businessowner in prewar Indonesia. He began as holder of an opium (q.v.) farm or *pacht* (q.v.) from the colonial government, but after the Opiumregie was founded diversified into sugar, banking, real estate, and general trading. His empire was managed after his death by his sons, but was nationalized in 1961 and now trades as PN Rajawali. See CHINESE IN INDONESIA. [0287]

OIL seeped naturally from the ground in northern Sumatra in early times and was collected for use as medicine, for fuel, for caulking boats, and as an incendiary, especially in naval warfare. The commercial search for oil began in 1866, after the development of drilling techniques in the U.S., and the first sales of oil, extracted by the Dortsche Petroleum Maatschappij from wells near Surabaya, took place in 1889. Exploratory drilling began in Sumatra in 1883 in Langkat, where oil was found at 100 m depth. From 1890 the wells at Langkat and from 1892 the refinery at Pangkalan Brandan became the center of the oil interests of the Koninklijke Nederlandsche Maatschappij tot Exploitatie van Petroleumbronnen in Nederlandsch-Indië (generally known as the 'Koninklijke', q.v.). Another company, later called Shell Oil, began drilling in Kutai (q.v.) in East Kalimantan in 1891. After an oil boom in the last decade of C.19, which saw dozens of companies rise and fall, the Koninklijke and Shell merged in 1907 to form the Bataafsche Petroleum Maatschappij (BPM). Although the BPM dominated the Indonesian oil industry from that time, and launched a number of joint ventures with the colonial government (see also STATE ENTERPRISES), a significant part of the production was in the hands of the Nederlandsche Koloniale Petroleum Maatschappij, a subsidiary of the American Standard Oil Co.

Although production began on Java, those fields were soon overshadowed by those of Sumatra, producing a light grade of oil, and those of East Kalimantan, even more important, which produced a heavy grade suitable in some cases for direct use as ships' fuel. The Netherlands Indies fields were especially important to Japan, and it was an embargo on oil supplies from the colony to Japan which, amongst other things, prompted the Japanese to invade the region in 1941–42. The wells of East Kalimantan were a major target, though considerable damage was done to them by Dutch scorched earth tactics before the Dutch arrival. They were also amongst the first areas seized by the Allies on their return to the archipelago in 1945.

Oil from Cepu in Java was an important source of fuel for the Indonesian Republic during the Revolution and the south Sumatra fields were contested by the Republic and the Dutch. The American companies Stanvac and Caltex as well as Japanese firms took important shares of postwar production, but all foreign companies were under pressure to distribute a larger share of the profits to Indonesia. Indonesia joined OPEC in 1962 and foreign companies increasingly operated as production-sharing agents of the three state oil firms, all under army control: Permina, headed by Ibnu Sutowo and based in the south Sumatra fields; Permigan (formerly Nglogo Oil Mining) in Central Java and eastern Indonesia, controlled by the army's Diponegoro Division; and Pertamin (formerly Permindo), formerly a BPM-government joint venture. Oil was a major, though insufficient, source of state income under the Guided Economy (q.v.).

Production-sharing agreements continued and expanded under the New Order. The state companies merged in 1968 to form Pertamina (q.v.), which rose on a wave of enormous profits until its debt crisis in 1975. Oil provided 19.7% of state revenue (Rp66.5 million) in

1969/70. The dramatic increase in oil prices in 1973 boosted this proportion to 48.4% (Rp957.2 million) in 1974/75, providing a major cushion for development expenditure. In 1977 the United States replaced Japan as Indonesia's largest customer. The decline of oil prices in 1982 and 1986 imposed severe budget restrictions and raised questions about the long-term viability of the New Order government which has, however, survived.

Liquefied natural gas has been exported from Aceh and East Kalimantan since 1971 and Indonesia is now one of the world's largest exporters, with exports valued at U.S.$10,100 million in 1991. [0211, 0310, 0318, 0326, 0735]

OIL PALM (*Elaeis guineensis,* Arecaceae). Originally from Africa, the oil palm first appeared in Indonesia as an ornamental tree in 1848. The first commercial plantation was established on Java in 1859, but oil palm did not become a major crop until the laying out of extensive estates in East Sumatra (q.v.) from 1911. [0231, 0245, 0246, 0938]

OLD ORDER. See NEW ORDER.

ONTVOOGDING. See DECENTRALIZATION; ZELFBESTUREN.

OPERASI KHUSUS (OPSUS, special operations), organization established within KOSTRAD (q.v.) in ca 1963 by Ali Murtopo (1924–84), an intelligence officer and member of Suharto's inner circle, and Sujono Humardani (1919–86), and used initially to establish covert contacts with the Malaysian government during Confrontation (q.v.). OPSUS later helped to ensure pro-government votes in the 1969 'Act of Free Choice' in Irian (q.v.) and in general elections in 1971 and after. It apparently played an important role in the restructuring of political parties after 1971 and was officially disbanded in 1974, partly in response to the Malari (q.v.) Affair.

OPIUM (*Papaver somniferum* Papaveraceae) was widely cultivated in India (q.v.) from C.15 and extensive export to Indonesia began soon after. Opium had some use in Tantric religious rituals but its main use was recreational. From about 1670 the Dutch East Indies Company (q.v.) dominated the trade to Indonesia and sale on Java was subject to a loosely-enforced Company monopoly, for the sake of which production in the archipelago was banned. Various methods were used to market opium. Initially it was sold directly by the VOC, but Company rights were transferred in 1745 to an Opium Society consisting of private traders; this society was replaced in 1794 by a state Opium Directorate which Daendels (q.v.) replaced in turn with a system of farms or *pachten* (q.v.). Raffles (q.v.) attempted to restrict sales, partly for humanitarian reasons, partly because of extensive smuggling, but was overruled by the British authorities in Bengal. Control of opium sales was given to the NHM (q.v.) from 1827 to 1833, when the farms were restored. In 1894 after a prolonged humanitarian campaign in the Netherlands, the farm system was replaced once more by a state monopoly, the Opiumregie, which imported raw opium, refined it in Batavia, and sold it to registered addicts through a network of government shops. Sales continued on a smaller scale during the Japanese occupation, and the Indonesian Republic earned important foreign exchange during the National Revolution by selling the remaining Opiumregie stocks within Indonesia and abroad. The Regie was abolished in 1950.

Proceeds, direct or indirect, from opium sales were a significant part of state revenues, especially during C.19.

Opium addiction helped to keep laborers pliant and subservient through both clinical dependence and debt. Opium farms were generally in the hands of Chinese entrepreneurs who maintained private security forces to enforce their regional monopolies. During C.19 the vast majority of addicts were Javanese, but in C.20 a strong campaign by both nationalists and Ethical Policy (q.v.)-minded colonial officials dramatically reduced consumption and by 1942 most users were Chinese. [0531]

ORANGUTAN (*Pongo pygmaeus,* formerly known as *Simia satyrus*) large ape occurring widely in Kalimantan and less commonly in Sumatra. It first drew attention as a possible 'missing link' in the Darwinian evolution of humankind. Hunting on behalf of wildlife collectors is a serious threat to its existence. See also CONSERVATION, Nature. [0495]

ORGANISASI MASSA. See MASS ORGANIZATIONS.

ORGANISASI PAPUA MERDEKA (OPM, Free Papua Movement) was founded in 1965 in the Central Highlands of Irian (q.v.) to oppose Indonesian rule. It drew its support initially from members of the Dutch-sponsored former Papuan Volunteer Corps and from the coastal Arfak people, but now, under the influence of Indonesian policies in the interior such as transmigration (q.v.), it has wide, though uneven, support throughout the province, especially in the Baliem valley, along the border with Papua New Guinea (q.v.) and in the Carstensz Mountains. Its armed forces, the Pasukan Pembebasan Nasional, have been augmented regularly by the desertion of Papuan troops from the Indonesian army, but remain poorly armed and trained. In 1971 Seth Rumkorem declared a Republic of West Papua and the movement now claims to control about one-quarter of Irian, though most authorities are skeptical about this claim. Indonesian authorities sometimes suggest that the OPM makes extensive use of sanctuaries in Papua New Guinea, but PNG has been particularly careful to restrict its activities. The OPM continues to be racked by factionalism, which is partly tribal and partly ideological, and its leaders Rumkorem, Jakob Prai and more recently, James Nyaro, have gone into exile. Its greatest weakness remains its lack of an international sponsor. See also MELANESIAN BROTHERHOOD. [0899, 0908, 0914]

OTOKRITIK (Self Criticism), document said to be the work of the Politburo member Sudisman and containing a post-1965 evaluation by the PKI (q.v.) of the philosophies and strategies of the Aidit years. The document rejected much of the innovative Marxism (q.v.) of the party, especially the doctrine of the Dual Nature of the State, and called for armed revolution in the countryside, based on a worker-peasant alliance under the leadership of the proletariat (see CLASS ANALYSIS). This document may have underpinned the PKI's unsuccessful and brief guerrilla campaign in the Blitar area of East Java, but some authorities see it as probably emanating from Beijing. [0826, 0843]

OTTOMAN EMPIRE. See TURKEY, Historical links with.

OUDHEIDKUNDIGE DIENST. See ARCHEOLOGY.

OUTER ISLANDS, term equivalent to the Dutch *buitengewesten,* outer regions, and sometimes considered slightly pejorative, for the Indonesian islands other than Java, Madura, and occasionally Bali (qq.v.). In general, these 'outer' regions are less densely populated, lack extensive wet-rice fields, and are in some cases rich in natural resources. Shifts in the focus of economic activity can be seen in the fact that the Outer Islands accounted for only 10% of Indonesian exports in 1890, but 70% in 1940. The term also contains a sense of political distance from the center. The term is a convenient one but carries little analytical weight. See also NUSANTARA. [0239]

P

PACHT (revenue farm, pl. *pachten*), one of the most common sources of state revenue before C.20. The state typically sold or granted rights over a particular sector of the economy to a private entrepreneur, who was then at liberty to extract what he could from it and to enforce his rights with his own private police force. Pachten were commonly granted for the running of toll houses, pawnshops and gambling (qq.v.) dens, the sale of opium and salt (qq.v.), the collection of land, market and poll tax, the management of forests, and the harvesting of produce such as birds' nests, pearls (qq.v.), trepang, and sponges. In late C.19 and early C.20. the colonial government replaced many of these farms with state monopolies. See also TAXATION.

PADANG, coastal town in West Sumatra. Under Acehnese control, it became a major entrepôt for the pepper (q.v.) trade in C.17 and was seized by the Dutch East India Company (q.v.) in 1664. The British seized it in 1793 but restored it in 1819 to the Dutch. It became a major center for the export of coffee in late C.19. See also MINANGKABAU.

PADERI WAR. See MINANGKABAU.

PAGUYUBAN PASUNDAN, Sundanese cultural association founded in 1914 initially to promote Sundanese cultural identity, though it later founded schools and took part in local councils. Under Oto Iskandardinata (1897–1946?), it became the largest mass organization in West Java, but never promoted Sundanese separatism. Like the Pakempalan Kawula Ngayogyakarta (q.v.), it was part of a movement for the support of regional culture within the broader nationalist *pergerakan*. The prewar popularity of the Paguyuban Pasundan, however, was a factor encouraging the Dutch to create the federal state of Pasundan (q.v.) in 1948. See also NATIONALISM; SUNDA. [0262]

PAJAJARAN, the last Hindu kingdom in West Java, founded in 1344 at Pakuan (near modern Bogor). Although primarily an agrarian kingdom, it traded pepper (q.v.) and other produce through Sunda Kalapa, near modern Jakarta (q.v.), until that was lost to Banten (q.v.) in 1527. Banten captured the capital and slaughtered the royal family in the 1570s.

PAJANG, central Javanese successor state to Majapahit (q.v.), based probably near modern Surakarta (q.v.). It was defeated by Mataram (q.v.) in 1587–88.

PAK ('father'), term of affectionate but deferential address. See BAPAK.

PAKEMPALAN KAWULA NGAYOGYAKARTA (PKN, Yogyakarta People's Party) was founded in June 1930 by Pangeran Sosrodiningrat, whom many of his followers saw as a new Ratu Adil or Just Prince (see JOYOBOYO). With 250,000 members, it was the largest political organization in prewar Indonesia, but it worked mainly on local issues, especially forming cooperatives and preserving the powers of Yogyakarta's traditional rulers. See also NATIONALISM; YOGYAKARTA. [0580]

PAKUALAMAN, minor court established in Yogyakarta (q.v.) in 1812 under the sponsorship of Raffles (q.v.), with separate apanage rights from the Yogyakarta sultanate.

PALAPA, Indonesia's domestic satellite communications system, named for a vow by Gajah Mada (q.v.), prime minister of Majapahit (q.v.), to abstain from *palapa* (perhaps a fruit, a spice or possibly sex) until the kingdom was united. Initially planned in REPELITA (q.v.) II, it was finally commissioned in August 1976. See also TELEGRAPH. [0350, 0353]

PALEMBANG, city and state on the Musi river in south Sumatra. Probably capital of the kingdom of Srivijaya (q.v.), Palembang lost its importance after the Chola raids of 1025 and fell into the hands of the Chinese pirate Liang Danming (see PIRACY; ZHENG HE). A new sultanate of Palembang became a major exporter of pepper (q.v.) in C.16, but declined and fell subject to Riau (q.v.) after the Dutch first concluded a contract giving them a monopoly in the city in 1642 and then sacked it in 1659. Palembang reemerged in C.18 after the discovery of tin (q.v.) on Bangka and Belitung (qq.v.) in 1709 and from 1722 monopoly contracts for tin mining provided the sultanate's most important source of income. In 1812–16, however, Raffles (q.v.) forced Sultan Ahmad Najamuddin to cede the tin-rich islands as reparations for the massacre of the Dutch garrison in Palembang by the sultan's brother and predecessor Mahmud Badaruddin in 1811, an act which Raffles himself had encouraged. In a series of military and political maneuvers, the Dutch gradually tightened their control, annexing the sultanate in 1823. Sultan Taha launched an unsuccessful revolt in 1858 and the Dutch did not subdue the upland Rejang and Pasamah areas until the 1860s. In C.20 the area became a major producer of rubber and oil (qq.v.) and during the early Revolution trade in rubber to Singapore was a major source of Republican finance. Much of the area was occupied in the first 'Police Action' (q.v.) in 1947, and on 18 December 1948 the Dutch established a Negara Sumatra Selatan (NSS) under Abdul Malik based in Palembang (see FEDERALISM). The NSS was abolished on 9 March 1950. South Sumatra was the economic base of two of the early New Order's most important 'financial generals', Ibnu Sutowo and Ratu Alamsyah Perwiranegara. See also OIL. [0469, 0470, 0541]

PALM SUGAR. See AREN.

PAMONG PRAJA ('guardians of the realm'), formerly *pangreh praja* ('rulers of the realm'), the civil service on Java conceived as an institution dating from pre-colonial times. See INLANDSCH BESTUUR; BUPATI.

PANATARAN, court temple complex of Majapahit (q.v.) in East Java, built mainly in C.14. Reliefs on the walls and balustrades use distinctive wayang (q.v.) motifs. One panel depicts a cassowary, suggesting early contact between Majapahit and Irian (q.v.). [0116]

PANCASILA. The five principles of state ideology, as follows: 1. *Ketuhanan yang maha esa,* belief in one supreme God; 2. *Kemanusiaan yang adil dan beradab,* just and civilized humanitarianism; 3. *Persatuan Indonesia,* Indonesian unity; 4. *Kerakyatan yang dipimpin oleh hikmat kebijaksanaan dalam permusyawaratan/perwakilan,* popular sovereignty governed by wise policies arrived at through deliberation and representation; 5. *Keadilan sosial bagi seluruh rakyat Indonesia,* social justice for the entire Indonesian people.

The Pancasila was formulated by Sukarno (q.v.) on 1

June 1945 in a speech to the committee drafting Indonesia's 1945 constitution and was incorporated into the preamble of that constitution and its 1949 and 1950 successors. The general character of the *silas* allows widely varying interpretations of the Pancasila's content. Early Western observers saw it as a promising synthesis of Western democracy, Islam, Marxism and indigenous village democratic ideas, while it was initially embraced most enthusiastically in Indonesia by those wishing to avert the creation of an Islamic state; during the 1950s, and especially in the sessions of the Constituent Assembly (q.v.), secularists and members of other religions put forward the notion of a state based on the Pancasila as a preferable alternative to a state based on a single religion. Under Guided Democracy, on the other hand, conservative groups stressed the religious content of the Pancasila, in the form of the first principle, in order to distinguish it from ideas of the PKI (q.v.) and from leftist concepts of Sukarno, such as Nasakom (q.v.). After 1965, with the PKI vanquished, the Pancasila became once more a tool to resist an Islamic state.

From the start, the political system under the New Order was frequently referred as 'Pancasila Democracy', but it was not until about 1974 that New Order figures attempted to give content to the Pancasila by formulating the Pedoman Penghayatan dan Pengamalan Pancasila (P4, Guide to Realizing and Experiencing the Pancasila). Since this time the Pancasila has been the formal ideological basis for government policy as expressed in the GBHN and for an increasingly broad range of social relationships; labor relations are supposedly conducted, for instance, under the principles of *hubungan industri Pancasila* (see LABOR UNIONS). In 1978 an intensive program to educate civil servants in the Pancasila was begun, and Pendidikan Moral Pancasila (PMP, Pancasila Moral Education) became a part of educational curricula at all levels. In 1985, all noncommercial, nongovernment organizations were required by law to adopt the Pancasila as their sole guiding principle (*azas tunggal*) as a presumed guarantee of future political orthodoxy and harmony (see PETITION OF FIFTY; WHITE PAPER).

The Pancasila is officially not an ideology but a deep-rooted national philosophy articulated from time to time by the country's leaders (though in 1981 some figures close to the government suggested that Sukarno had not been the author of the 1945 text). It underpins a corporatist, authoritarian state system; in particular, silas 2–5 are held to preclude politics based on class or other adversarial social divisions. Even the elaboration of the Pancasila provided in P4, however, is less than detailed about the political program which flows from the Pancasila and there has been a strong tendency for the government to reserve to itself the right to decide what the specific content of the Pancasila may be. See also CONSTITUTIONS; GARUDA; ISLAMIC STATE, Demands for; KEPERCAYAAN; PETITION OF FIFTY. [0219, 0367, 0563, 0689, 0705, 0810, 0844, 0850, 0854, 0857]

PANGESTU (Paguyuban Ngèsti Tunggal, Association for Striving towards Harmony with God), Javanese mystical organization, founded in 1949 by R. Sunarto Mertowardoyo (1899–1965). With over 20,000 members, it is one of the largest of the kebatinan (q.v.) groups. [0663]

PANGLIMA, military commander, originally referring to senior *uleëbalang* (regional chiefs) in Aceh (q.v.), but adopted by the Republican army (q.v.) in 1945 as its senior appointment. Initially used for any division or military region (KODAM) commander it is now restricted to the ABRI (q.v.) commander.

PANGREH PRAJA. See PAMONG PRAJA.

PANITIA PERSIAPAN KEMERDEKAAN INDONESIA. See BADAN PENYELIDIK USAHA PERSIAPAN KEMERDEKAAN INDONESIA.

PANJI STORIES, cycle of stories derived from East Java and based on the adventures of Prince Panji in search of his bride, a princess of Daha (Kediri, q.v.), who disappeared mysteriously on their wedding night. [0116]

PANTUN, Malay verse form in four lines rhyming a-b-a-b. Typically the first couplet contains a cryptic allusion to the second, which may take the form of a proverb or message.

PAPER was produced on Java from at least 1200, using the inner bark of the paper mulberry *Broussonetia papyrifera* (Moraceae). It was probably a development from earlier felted cloth (q.v.) under the influence of Chinese paper technology and was used mainly for painting and wrapping, *lontar* (q.v.) leaves being the preferred writing surface. Lontar, however, was not suited to the writing of Arabic curves and dots, and the use of paper grew from C.14 with the spread of Islam. In C.17 paper was an important item of trade for the European companies and the VOC (q.v.) established a paper mill in Batavia. See also WRITING SYSTEMS. [0323]

PAPUA NEW GUINEA (PNG), Relations with. Since PNG became independent in 1975, relations have been dominated by Indonesian fears on the one hand that PNG may be a base for OPM (q.v.) separatists in Irian (q.v.), and by PNG fears that Indonesia may at some time attempt to take it over. PNG formally denies sanctuary to the OPM, though controlling the 750 km poorly-marked border is difficult and there is much popular sympathy for the OPM in PNG. Indonesian policies aimed at diluting the Melanesian character of Irian and heavy-handed operations against the OPM sent a flood of refugees across the border from Indonesia to PNG in the early 1980s, with a peak in 1984, and PNG confidence in Indonesian intentions diminished when Indonesian armed forces crossed the border without permission on a number of occasions. It was also discovered in 1983 that the Indonesian-built Trans-Irian Highway was being built on PNG territory for part of its length. In October 1986 the two countries signed a Treaty of Mutual Respect, Friendship and Cooperation which provided, amongst other things, that neither side would allow its territory to be used for purposes hostile to the other. [0738, 0913]

PARARATON (*Book of Kings*), Javanese text dated 1613, telling stories of Ken Angrok (q.v.) and Raden Wijaya (see MAJAPAHIT). The manuscript was discovered on Bali in late C.19. [0124]

PARLIAMENTS. See CHUO SANGI-IN; DEWAN PERWAKILAN RAKYAT; KOMITE NASIONAL INDONESIA PUSAT; MAJELIS PERMUSYAWARATAN RAKYAT; VOLKSRAAD.

PARTAI BURUH INDONESIA (PBI, Indonesian Labor Party), Marxist party established in Kediri in November 1945 by S.K. Trimurti, Setiajit, and Sakirman. It was a member of the Sayap Kiri (q.v.) and merged with the PKI (q.v.) in September 1948. The party reappeared after the Madiun Affair (q.v.) but rejoined the PKI in February 1951. A short-lived splinter Partai Buruh was formed in December 1949 by members opposed to the Madiun rising. [0656, 0749]

PARTAI DEMOKRASI INDONESIA (PDI, Indonesian Democratic Party), formed January 1973 by a government-enforced merger of the PNI, Partai Katolik, PARKINDO, Murba, and IPKI (qq.v.). As the largest component, the PNI formed the new party's core, but with the new government policy of 'monoloyalitas' (q.v.) the party lost much of the bureaucratic vote and was reduced to a narrow 'natural' constituency, especially amongst the Christian community. Government intervention, too, supporting the conservative faction of Mohammad Isnaeni and Sunawar Sukowati against that of the more progressive Usep Ranuwijaya and Sanusi Harjadinata, weakened the party's internal organization. The party's poor performance in the 1977 and 1982 elections raised the prospect that it might disappear entirely, leaving the Muslim PPP as the only opposition party. Since the late 1970s, therefore, the PDI has received discreet assistance from the authorities in the form of direct financial grants and aid in the preparation of election materials and the conduct of campaigns. The party showed a substantial recovery in 1987, overtaking the PPP (q.v.) as second party in the Jakarta region.

From its inception, the PDI has tried to stake a political position on the left hand of what is permitted in Indonesian politics, arguing against corruption and for better social services and a more even distribution of wealth. Sections of the party have also sought to present it as the heir to the ideas of Sukarno (q.v.) and his portrait has been prominent at PDI rallies, though the government has sought to restrict the extent to which the former president's name can be used. [0680, 0821]

PARTAI INDONESIA (PARTINDO) 1. Party founded in 1931 by Mr R.M. Sartono to replace the recently dissolved Partai Nasional Indonesia (q.v.). After attempting to unite PARTINDO with the Pendidikan

Nasional Indonesia (q.v.), Sukarno (q.v.) joined it in 1932 and it soon swelled to a claimed 20,000 members. The party pressed for independence by means of mass action but this attracted Dutch repression; the 1934 party congress was forbidden and the party decided to dissolve in November 1936. [0561, 0563]

(2) A small left-wing party which seceded from the PNI (q.v.) in July 1958, partly to back the policies of Sukarno (q.v.). Its existence was used to justify the appointment to more left wingers to official posts alongside the PKI, to which it became increasingly close. It was banned in 1966. [0364]

PARTAI INDONESIA RAYA (PARINDRA, Greater Indonesia Party), formed as a merger of Budi Utomo and the Persatuan Bangsa Indonesia (qq.v.) in December 1935 and led by Sutomo, M.H. Thamrin, Susanto Tirtoprojo, and Sukarjo Wiryopranoto. More conservative than GERINDO (q.v.), it was willing to cooperate with the Dutch and was instrumental in forming the moderate nationalist coalition GAPI (q.v.). It claimed 10,000 members in 1940. In 1938 it founded a commercial company, the Pertanian Bumi Putera, to initiate party-controlled agricultural and industrial enterprises. PARINDRA was hopeful that Japanese pressure on the Indies would lead to reforms and Thamrin was detained in February 1941 on suspicion of 'treasonous' dealing with Japan. The party was banned, like all others, during the Japanese occupation, but reemerged in November 1949 under R.P. Suroso, who sat in several cabinets until the party disappeared in the 1955 elections. [0543, 0719]

PARTAI KATOLIK (Catholic Party). The earliest political association of Indonesian Catholics was the Pakempalan Politik Katolik Jawi (Political Association of Javanese Catholics), founded in February 1923 and headed from

1925 by Ignatius Joseph Kasimo (1900–1987). The PPKJ was represented in the Volksraad (q.v.) from 1924 and in the nationalist federations PPPKI and GAPI (qq.v.). It changed its name several times, becoming the Persatuan Politik Katolik Indonesia (PPKI, Political Union of Indonesian Catholics) in 1930, the Persatuan Katolik Republik Indonesia (PKRI) in December 1945 and the Partai Katolik in August 1950, still led by Kasimo. With a small but solid constituency in Flores (q.v.) and Central Java, it was present in all parliaments from 1945 until it was merged into the PDI (q.v.) in 1973. [0634, 0834]

PARTAI KOMUNIS INDONESIA (PKI, Indonesian Communist Party), founded on 23 May 1920 as successor to the Indische Sociaal-Democratische Vereeniging (q.v.) and initially named Perserikatan Komunis di Hindia (Communist Association of the Indies). The PKI was the first communist party in Asia outside the borders of former Tsarist Russia and joined the Comintern in December 1920. Its leaders initially followed a 'bloc within' strategy, joining the Sarekat Islam (q.v.) and attempting to shift it to the left, but this led to bitter disputes within SI and in October 1921 PKI members were effectively expelled. The party then campaigned vigorously in its own right amongst Indonesia's small proletariat and via so-called Sarekat Merah (Red Unions) in the countryside. Encouraged by the party's popularity and alarmed by the effectiveness of the colonial security forces in dismantling the party apparatus (including the exile [q.v.] of Tan Malaka [q.v.] in 1922 and Semaun in 1923), the leaders Musso (1897–1948) and Alimin (1889–1964) planned an uprising, but were strongly opposed by Tan Malaka. Intended as an Indonesia-wide affair, the rising fizzled out in rebellions in Banten (q.v.) in November 1926 and West Sumatra (see MINANGKABAU) in January 1927. The party was banned and alleged leaders of the rebellions were exiled to Boven Digul (q.v.). Thereafter Dutch repression kept the party small and underground, though it developed a remarkable resilience which enabled it to survive, recruit, and campaign despite Dutch, and later Japanese, repression.

The party partially reemerged in November 1945, though it continued to work also through front parties, the Partai Buruh Indonesia and the Partai Sosialis, with which it made up the Sayap Kiri (qq.v.). The party argued initially that the national revolution should be safeguarded by making concessions to Western economic interests (see DIPLOMASI AND PERJUANGAN), but in early 1948 after the fall of the government of Amir Syarifuddin (q.v.) and the return of Musso from protracted exile in the Soviet Union, the party took a radical turn, arguing in *A new road for the Indonesian Republic* for socioeconomic reform as a condition for achieving independence. The Sayap Kiri parties then federated first into the Front Demokrasi Rakyat (q.v) and then into an expanded PKI. After the party's suppression for its part in the abortive Madiun Affair (q.v.), it resumed the strategy of divided parties under leadership of Tan Ling Djie (1904–1965/66), but in 1951 strategy changed dramatically under a new party leadership of Dipa Nusantara Aidit (1923–65), M.H. Lukman (1920–65), Nyoto (1925–65), and Sudisman (1920–68).

The new leaders emphasized the party's commitment to the legal political process and marked out a strong nationalist position, rejecting the continuing ties with the Netherlands and the privileges given to Western business. The lack of a large proletariat and of a clear poor peasant class was a strategic difficulty, but the party emphasized attitude rather than class origin and it pursued a mass education program through party schools, training courses, and a university, the Aliarcham Academy, using recruits to build up an organization second only to the army (q.v.) in purpose and discipline, though its strength was heavily concentrated amongst abangan (q.v.) Javanese. This effort was rewarded when the party came in fourth with 16.4% of the vote in the 1955 elections (q.v.). The growth of PKI support and influence was amongst the reasons for the PRRI (q.v.) rebellion and army commanders in many regions, remembering the party's role in the Madiun Affair, put restrictions on its activities. Certain of increasing its vote at future elections, the party was at first unhappy with Sukarno's proposals for a Guided Democracy (q.v.). Facing full-scale suppression by the army, however, if it did not accede, the PKI became an enthusiastic supporter of the president, offering him the popular backing which he needed to balance the growing power of the army. In return the party received considerable freedom to operate on Java, building its membership to perhaps 3 million by 1965; affiliated organizations such as the BTI (q.v.) accounted for many millions more. Through its cultural affiliate, LEKRA (q.v.), it attempted to establish Marxist discourse as orthodoxy in cultural affairs. And under the principles of Nasakom (q.v.) it was given increasing say in legislative and other official bodies. It was never, however, given important executive functions and Hindley has argued that the party, for all its apparent strength, was in fact 'domesticated'—implicated in a regime which failed to implement social reforms and which was losing control of the economy, but denied access to the levers of power. When the party attempted, moreover, a program of direct action (*aksi sepihak*) in rural Java to implement land reform (q.v.) laws in late 1963 it was swiftly curbed. The party remained generally aloof from the Sino-Soviet split, but in the mid 60s swung somewhat to China, following Indonesian foreign policy (q.v.). Opinions are still deeply divided on whether and to what extent the party was involved in the GESTAPU (q.v.) coup of 1965, but the outcome of the affair was fatal to the party. Within weeks the army had begun to detain PKI cadres and to oversee the killing of party members and supporters (see MASSACRES OF 1965–66). The party was formally banned 12 March 1966. Surviving members attempted to begin guerrilla resistance in Blitar (East Java) and in West Kalimantan (see PONTIANAK) and a PKI analysis of its mistakes, called *Otokritik* (q.v.), was prepared, but these movements were crushed by 1968, leaving the party represented primarily by scattered exile communities, most prominent being the so-called PKI Delegation in China led by Jusuf Ajitorop. In recent years, the Indonesian government has shown continuing concern over the alleged continued existence of PKI elements in Indonesian society, and a number of acts of sabotage have been attributed unconvincingly to the party. See also CLASS ANALYSIS; MARXISM. [0571, 0586, 0603, 0619, 0634, 0656, 0662, 0703, 0788, 0798, 0819, 0820, 0822–0824, 0853, 0864]

PARTAI KRISTEN INDONESIA (PARKINDO, Indonesian Christian Party), Protestant party based in Minahasa, Ambon (q.v.) and the Batak regions of Sumatra, formed November 1945. From the 1950s it was led by Johannes Leimena (q.v.), who enjoyed a close relationship with Sukarno and became a long-term deputy prime minister under Guided Democracy. In 1973, the party was merged into the PDI (q.v.). See also PROTESTANTISM. [0634, 0834]

PARTAI MURBA. See MURBA.

PARTAI MUSLIMIN INDONESIA (PARMUSI, Indonesian Muslims' Party). The banning of Masyumi (q.v.) in 1960 left the modernist Muslim stream largely unrepresented in Indonesian party politics, though former

Masyumi members were active in the so-called New Order coalition which helped to bring down Sukarno (q.v.). PARMUSI was created on 20 February 1968 as a legal successor to Masyumi, but the military government, wary of Muslim power, excluded former Masyumi members from leadership positions. Jaelani (Johnny) Naro, an associate of Ali Murtopo (see CENTRE FOR STRATEGIC AND INTERNATIONAL STUDIES) emerged as a major progovernment power broker and with party leaders Jarnawi Hadikusumah and Mintareja removed the Jakarta Charter (q.v.) from the party's platform. After a poor election performance in 1971, PARMUSI was merged into the PPP (q.v.) in 1973. [0833]

PARTAI NASIONAL INDONESIA (PNI, Indonesian Nationalist Party). (1) Nationalist party founded by Sukarno (q.v.) and members of the Algemene Studieclub (q.v.) on 4 July 1927 with the name Perserikatan Nasional Indonesia (Indonesian Nationalist Union) and becoming Partai Nasional Indonesia in May 1928. It aimed from the start at full independence and sought to represent Indonesians of all religious, ethnic, and class groups, though its support was strongest amongst the middle class and the *abangan* (q.v.) peasantry. It refused to seek membership of the Volksraad (q.v.) and instead aimed to build a mass following, claiming 10,000 members by 1929. Though smaller than Sarekat Islam (q.v.) had been, it alarmed the colonial government, which arrested and jailed Sukarno and his colleagues in December 1929. The remnants of the party formally dissolved in April 1931. [0561, 0563, 0695]

(2) The name PNI-Baru (New PNI) was given to the nationalist organization Pendidikan Nasional Indonesia (q.v.).

(3) On 21 August 1945, immediately after the declaration of independence, Sukarno and Hatta (qq.v.) an-

nounced the formation of a single state party, generally called PNI-Staatspartij (State Party). It was based on the cadre of the Jawa Hokokai (q.v.) and was intended to mobilize popular support for the Revolution. Internal divisions and hostility to its Japanese origins, however, made it unworkable and it was dissolved on 31 August 1945, though some branches survived to join the PNI (4). [0563, 0628]

(4) Formed in 1945 after the collapse of the PNI-Staatspartij, the PNI inherited the name of Sukarno's prewar party but not Sukarno's leadership. During the Revolution, it became a broadly-based party drawing support especially from the administrative elite and from the abangan peasantry on Java and containing a wide range of ideological viewpoints. Its leaders included conservative exponents of peace, order, and good administration, populist nationalists distrustful of the outside world and committed to improving welfare without promoting social conflict, and left-wing reformers willing to bring about radical social change. It summed up these views as Marhaenism or 'proletarian nationalism' (see MARHAEN). The party took a radical, often anti-Western view on international affairs and opposed liberalism and individualism domestically. Under the prime ministership of Ali Sastroamijoyo (q.v.), it became even more strongly entrenched in the state bureaucracy and by a narrow margin won the largest vote in the 1955 elections (q.v.). Already, however, the party had begun to lose peasant support as PKI activity in rural areas developed, and some leaders approved of Sukarno's Guided Democracy as a means to stop communist growth. During the early 1960s, with Ali as chairman and Surachman (?–1968) as secretary, the party increasingly shifted to the left, and in 1964 it adopted the *Deklarasi Marhaenis,* which maintained that Marhaenism was Marxism (q.v.) adapted to Indonesian conditions. After the GESTAPU (q.v.) affair of

1965, the PNI was heavily purged of its left wing and in April 1970 the Semarang party boss, Hadisubeno Sosrowerdoyo (1912–71), formerly associated with the business activities of President Suharto, was imposed as party chairman. More than other surviving parties, the PNI suffered from the establishment of Golkar (q.v.) as a state party, for it was precisely the PNI's bureaucratic base which Golkar seized. After a poor performance in the 1971 election, PNI was merged into PDI (q.v.) in 1973. [0563, 0628, 0634, 0825, 0830]

PARTAI PERSATUAN PEMBANGUNAN (PPP, Unity Development Party), formed on 5 January 1973 as a forced merger of the four legal Muslim parties, PARMUSI, PERTI, Nahdatul Ulama and Partai Sarekat Islam Indonesia (qq.v.), together with the non-party Himpunan Mahasiswa Islam, though all the constituent elements continued to retain their separate identities. The party was not permitted to have an Islamic name but until 1986 was allowed to use the Ka'abah (a sacred rock in Mecca) as its party symbol. The party is not permitted to advocate an Islamic state, but has generally been pro-Muslim in international affairs, opposed to foreign cultural influences in Indonesia, and in favor of extending religious education. In 1973, it was instrumental in having a Marriage Bill significantly amended to bring it closer to Islamic law (see MARRIAGE, Political significance of). In 1977, PPP members of the MPR (q.v.) walked out over government plans to give official recognition to belief (*kepercayaan*) alongside religion. The party suffered a major blow in 1984, when the NU, which had been its most successful component in maintaining electoral support, left in order to concentrate its efforts on religious renewal. See also KEBATINAN. [0680]

PARTAI REPUBLIK INDONESIA (PARI, Indonesian Republican Party). See TAN MALAKA.

PARTAI SAREKAT ISLAM INDONESIA (PSII, Party of the Indonesian Islamic Union) was formed in 1923 by H.U.S. Tjokroaminoto (q.v.) and H.A. Salim to formalize the political status of the Sarekat Islam (q.v.). Shorn of SI's left-wing components, the party was conservative and pan-Islamic, and soon shrank further with the secession of the Nahdatul Ulama (q.v.). After the death of Tjokroaminoto, the party came into the hands of Abikusno Tjokrosuyoso and S.M. Kartosuwiryo (q.v.). Salim and Mohammad Rum were expelled, and the party took a hard-line noncooperative attitude toward the colonial government at a time when other parties had begun to soften under pressure of Dutch repression. Kartosuwiryo himself was expelled in 1940 and formed a 'PSII Kedua' (Second PSII) in Malangbong which later became part of the political base of the Darul Islam (q.v.). PSII activity was banned by the Dutch in 1940 under State of War and Siege regulations, but it re-emerged in 1947 under Aruji Kartawinata and the brothers Anwar and Harsono Tjokroaminoto. Never large, it campaigned incessantly for an Islamic state, but was a supporter of Sukarno's Guided Democracy. In 1973 it was forced to join the Partai Persatuan Pembangunan (q.v.). [0634, 1111]

PARTAI SOSIALIS (Socialist Party), formed in December 1945 as merger of the Partai Rakyat Sosialis (PARAS, Socialist People's Party) of Amir Syarifuddin (q.v.) and the Partai Sosialis Indonesia (PARSI, Indonesian Socialist Party) of Sutan Syahrir (q.v.). It formed the basis of the successive governments of Syahrir and Amir, but from early 1947 increasingly factionalized between the two leaders and effectively split when Amir deposed Syahrir in June 1947, though a formal division did not take place until February 1948, when Syahrir formed the PSI (q.v.). See also SAYAP KIRI. [0563, 0656, 0704]

PARTAI SOSIALIS INDONESIA (PSI, Indonesian Socialist Party). In November 1945 Sutan Syahrir (q.v.) formed a political party of this name (but abbreviated PARSI) which soon merged with Amir Syarifuddin's PARAS to form the Partai Sosialis (q.v.). A second party, called PSI, emerged from the Partai Sosialis in February 1948, again associated with Syahrir. It had a generally Fabian socialist program, emphasizing economic planning, modernization and social welfare, but accepted the need for continued foreign capital investment in Indonesia and the political consequences of that. Sumitro Joyohadikusumo (q.v.) was a prominent member of the party in the 1950s and influenced its emphasis on regional development programs, small-scale industry, and cooperatives. Popular amongst intellectuals, in some sections of the officer corps and amongst some minorities, the PSI never developed a significant mass base and won only five seats in the 1955 elections. After Sumitro's participation in the PRRI (q.v.) uprising, the party was banned in 1960. Under the New Order, however, Sumitro and a number of other PSI figures regained important policy influence, to the extent of being seen at times as a malign secretive influence, being accused for instance of involvement in the Malari (q.v.) Affair. [0634]

PARTICULIERE LANDERIJEN, private estates, especially on the northern coastal plain of West Java, given or sold by the VOC (q.v.) from 1630 to its servants and supporters. Owners held not only freehold title to the land but quasifeudal rights over its inhabitants, including compulsory labor services (*herendiensten,* q.v.), a portion of all crops, and a wide range of incidental taxes. In some texts these rights are described as 'sovereign' and the landlords likened to the semiautonomous native rulers or *zelfbesturen* (q.v.). It was on these estates that commercial sugar (q.v.) cultivation was first introduced, but by C.19 rice (q.v.) for Batavia (q.v.) was the main crop. By C.20, some of the estates, such as the British-owned Pamanukan- & Tjiasemlanden (P & T Lands), had developed into efficient commercial operations with well-trained staff; other estates remained depressed backwaters. Such estates remained outside the colonial government's provision of education, health, and other social services under the Ethical Policy (q.v.), and became a byword for agricultural misery. Literacy rates were very low, morbidity was high, and bandit gangs were powerful. From 1912 the colonial government began the repurchase of estates, which were then incorporated into the administrative structure of the rest of Java. Repurchases stopped during the Depression, but in 1935 the government established a semiofficial company, the Javase Particuliere Landerijen Maatschappij, to acquire and administer estates, using the proceeds both for further purchases and to bring social services and infrastructure to a level where the estates could be turned over to the government without placing extra strain on the treasury. Under the Japanese the remaining estates were nationalized, but the landlords were generally retained as administrators. Estate workers and bandits took control of the estates during the Revolution, but former owners were restored with freehold title, but without feudal rights, after the Dutch seized West Java in 1947. The last of the foreign-owned estates was nationalized in 1958. [0495, 1154]

PARTIES, Political. The formation of political parties in the Netherlands Indies was first permitted in 1918, though several parties, such as Budi Utomo (q.v.), had existed effectively earlier as nominally cultural associations. The Indische Partij (q.v.) was banned in 1912 and in later years individual parties were often banned or restricted from time to time (see NATIONALISM). The Japanese dissolved all party organizations for the duration of their occupation, and the independent Republic of Indonesia briefly considered permitting only a single all-encompassing national party (PNI-Staatspartij, q.v.). Parties, however, quickly emerged after the Declaration of Independence and the multi-party system was officially authorized by Decree 'X' of 16 October 1945. Twenty-seven parties won seats in the 1955 parliamentary elections.

From 1956 feeling arose increasingly that the parties were too strong in defending their sectional interests and too weak in considering the national interest. In 1956 Sukarno urged the parties to 'bury themselves' and Guided Democracy (q.v.) was in part a system designed to diminish the access of parties to state power. Presidential Edict No 7 of 1959 required all parties to adhere to the 1945 Constitution, Pancasila and MANIPOL-USDEK (qq.v.) and sought to eliminate smaller parties by requiring all parties to have 150,000 members spread over 65 electoral districts. In 1960 Sukarno issued a decree banning parties which had taken part in rebellions against the state; this was used to ban Masyumi and the PSI (qq.v.) but not the PKI (q.v.). Further bans followed, leaving only 11 legal parties at the close of Guided Democracy. The PKI and PARTINDO (q.v.) were banned in 1966.

At the outset of the New Order, the army was determined that the open multiparty system of the 1950s should not be restored and a considerable debate opened over just what role parties should take. The parties themselves were given little opportunity to influence this debate: leading figures from before 1965 were often removed from party positions under government pressure and compliant supporters of the government were put in their places. Some army groups favored an entrenched two-party system; others suggested a 'simplification' into five groups: Islamic, Christian, nationalist, socialist-Pancasila, and functional. The 1969 Law on Political Parties banned independent candidates and denied legal status to any party with fewer than 1.2 million members, 100 branches, and 2% of the vote in the coming election. Nine parties were elected to parliament in 1971, but the government forced their representatives in parliament to form two blocs (and allowed each bloc only one formal spokesperson). In 1973 these semiformal parliamentary groupings were formalized under government pressure by a fusion of the party organizations into the Partai Persatuan Pembangunan (q.v.), comprising the four Muslim parties, and the Partai Demokrasi Indonesia (q.v.), comprising the rest. The 1975 Law on Political Parties and Golkar banned parties from maintaining permanent branches below kabupaten level, as well as removing their right to challenge Pancasila (q.v.). The government-electoral organization, Golkar (q.v.), however, was not regarded officially as a party and was exempt from these restrictions. In the 1980s, however, Golkar has taken much more the character of a party, and there have been persistent suggestions that it should become the basis of a *partai tunggal,* or sole party. [0634]

PASAI (Samudra), state in northern Sumatra (q.v.), based near modern Lhokseumawe. After converting to Islam at the end of C.13, Pasai became the major port of the Strait of Melaka, maintaining diplomatic contacts with China, India, and Siam (qq.v.). It exported pepper, oil (from seeps close to the surface), and perhaps silk (qq.v.). It was visited by Marco Polo (q.v.) in 1292 and Ibn Battuta (q.v.) in 1355 and was raided by Majapahit (q.v.) in the 1360s. In late C.15 it was increasingly eclipsed by Melaka (q.v.) and by Aceh (q.v.), which conquered it in 1524. [0402]

PASISIR (Javanese, 'coast'), the northern coast of Java (and by extension coastal regions of Sumatra and elsewhere), especially as distinguished from the kingdoms and courts of the interior. Opportunities for trade to and from Java gave rise from at least C.13 to a succession of prosperous city states along this coast—Banten, Demak, Cirebon, Surabaya (qq.v.)—which were incorporated only with difficulty, if at all, into the agrarian kingdoms of the interior. With the conversion of these cities to Islam (q.v.) from C.15, political tension between the two regions grew. The inland kingdom of Majapahit was defeated by a coalition of coastal states led by Demak, and Majapahit's successor Mataram (q.v.) only briefly controlled the Pasisir rulers, who increasingly recruited assistance from the VOC (q.v.) to resist the court, giving them a foothold in Javanese politics.

The term *pasisir* has also been applied particularly to the culture of this coastal region, suggesting an alternative Javanese cultural tradition to that of the courts of the interior. This culture is identified as Malay-speaking, internationally-minded (many rulers of pasisir states were not Javanese), commercially-oriented and culturally-eclectic. The batik (q.v.) of this region, for instance, shows considerable Chinese and European influence. [1149, 1179]

PASTEUR INSTITUTE, established in 1895 for the treatment of rabies victims and attached to the already existing Parc Vaccinogene (see SMALLPOX). The Institute began research on cholera in 1910, on bubonic plague (q.v.) in 1911 and later on typhus, staphylococcus, and other diseases. [0986]

PASUNDAN, official prewar name for the colonial province of West Java and name commonly used for the political party Paguyuban Pasundan (q.v.). On 24 April 1948, the

Dutch sponsored a federal state called Pasundan in the territories they controlled in West Java, led by the former bupati of Bandung, R.A.A.M. Wiranatakusumah in an attempt to exploit Sundanese fears of Javanese domination (see FEDERALISM). Leaders of the state toyed briefly with the idea of seeking full independence as an Islamic state on the model of Pakistan, perhaps with backing of the Darul Islam (q.v.) and also negotiated with the Dutch adventurer R.P.P. Westerling (q.v.) for armed backing. After Westerling's abortive putsch in Bandung and Jakarta in January 1950, Pasundan was discredited and it was dissolved on 9 February 1950. [0563, 0656, 0767]

PATRIMONIALISM, term coined by Max Weber to describe states in which a single ruler disposes of state wealth and power by virtue of traditional authority, rather than charisma or a regularized legal and administrative system. As an ideal type it certainly has some application to traditional Indonesia, and fits closely with the Indian-derived ideology of the *dharma-raja* or all-powerful king (see INDIA, Historical links with). Some authorities have questioned, however, whether traditional states were truly patrimonial, pointing both to elements of collegiality amongst powerful men within each kingdom (especially regional authorities such as the *bupati,* q.v.), and to supposedly democratic elements in the relationship between ruler and subject. The term neopatrimonialism has been used to describe the concentration of state authority in the hands of leaders of independent Indonesia. See also WHITE RAJAS. [0403, 0511, 0775, 1152]

PATTINGALLOANG (ca 1600–54), son of Matoaya, chief minister of Makassar and from 1639 also chief minister. Fluent in several European languages, he was a keen follower of the latest developments in geography and astronomy, and also had European works on gunnery translated into Makassarese. He maintained his father's policy of keeping Makassar an open port for all traders, but fractured the previous alliance between Bugis and Makassarese by conquering Bone (q.v.) in 1646, laying the basis for the later rebellion of Arung Palakka (q.v.).

PAWNSHOPS. The right to run pawnshops was farmed, like other state revenue sources (see PACHT), until 1903 when a government pawnshop service was created for Java and Madura. The service operated to some extent in the Outer Islands, but most of the 457 government pawnshops in the Netherlands Indies in 1931 were on Java and Madura. Annual profits were *f*6-½-to-*f*11 million.

PEAFOWL, Green (*Pavo muticus*), native of Java but now very rare there. It was formerly exported to Europe and China for decorative purposes and food. [0943]

PEANUT (*Arachis hypogaea* Leguminosae), South American plant, introduced perhaps through China by C.17 and widely cultivated for food and oil. [0245, 0246, 0938]

PEARLING was widespread in the archipelago in early times, and pearls were amongst exports to China from C.10. The coasts of Java were once known for seed pearls, used in medicine, but with the gradual exhaustion of shell beds fishing retreated to eastern Indonesia. Western companies began to move into the industry from the 1860s after the invention of the diving suit. Since early C.20, the Aru (q.v.) islands have been the industry's main center. Culturing of pearls has been done by the Marine Fisheries Research Institute in Aru and Sulawesi since 1960.

PEDIR (Pidië), Muslim state in northern Sumatra in C.15. Like Pasai (q.v.), it was an important entrepôt for pepper (q.v.). It was conquered by Aceh (q.v.) in 1524.

PEMBANGUNAN ('development'). See DEVELOPMENT IDEOLOGY.

PEMBELA TANAH AIR (PETA, Defenders of the Fatherland), military force formed by the Japanese (q.v.) in October on Java and Sumatra (where it was called Giyugun) to involve Indonesians in defence against the Allies. It consisted of 65 battalions by August 1945, with 37,000 men on Java and 20,000 on Sumatra. Battalion commanders were generally locally prominent Indonesian civilians—teachers, officials and the like—whose role was to recruit and to maintain morale rather than to command. Military leadership was mainly in the hands of company commanders and Japanese instructors. Training included use of weapons and elementary tactics, but emphasized spirit (*semangat*) and intense discipline. In February 1945, a PETA unit at Blitar revolted under command of Supriyadi (?–1945) but was crushed by Japanese forces. Between 18 and 25 August, after the Japanese surrender and before Indonesia's Declaration of Independence was widely known, the Japanese disarmed and disbanded most PETA units. Many, however, soon reassembled to form part of the basis of the Republic's army (q.v.). See also HEIHO. [0615, 0622]

PEMERINTAH REVOLUSIONER REPUBLIK INDONESIA (PRRI, Revolutionary Government of the Republic of Indonesia), a rebellion, Sumatra-based but not separatist, intended to establish a conservative national government in the face of Indonesia's swing towards Guided Democracy (q.v.). The revolt had two distinct roots: the political polarization of national politics in the late 1950s, in which a coalition of Sukarno, PNI, NU, and PKI (qq.v.), all based on Java, grew increasingly powerful at the expense of Masyumi and the Outer Islands (qq.v.); and the discontent of regional military commanders with attempts especially by Nasution (q.v.) to strengthen military discipline and to limit corruption by transferring officers from their home bases.

The revolt began on 20 December 1956, when the local army in West Sumatra took over civil government. Other units followed suit in East and South Sumatra and later Kalimantan, Sulawesi, and Maluku (see also PERMESTA). Army councils moved against corruption, arrested PKI (q.v.) members and began to repair roads in an effort to win support, while demanding a new Hatta (q.v.) government to replace the crumbling Ali Sastroamijoyo (q.v.) cabinet. On 14 March 1957 Sukarno, however, announced a 'working cabinet' under Juanda (q.v.) while declaring martial law over the whole country, thus effectively legalizing the mutinies. Meanwhile, however, a wave of political arrests in Jakarta led Muhammad Natsir, Syafruddin Prawiranegara, Sumitro Joyohadikusumo, Zulkifli Lubis (qq.v.), and others to flee to Sumatra, where they joined the mutineers in demanding on 10 February 1958 that Sukarno withdraw to a figurehead presidency, that Hatta form a cabinet, and that Nasution be dismissed. When this was rejected they declared a new national government, the PRRI, on 15 February, with Syafruddin as prime minister. On 17 February the Permesta rebels joined the PRRI. The rebels also received clandestine support from the U.S. (q.v.) and Malaya. With many mutineers reluctant to join a full-scale rebellion, the PRRI soon found its power base limited to West Sumatra and North Sulawesi and after troop landings in March 1958 both regions were largely under government control by May-June, though the rebels did not concede defeat until 1961. The rebellion enabled a far-reaching purge of the armed forces to take place and provided a basis for the banning of Masyumi and PSI (qq.v.) in 1960 on the grounds that their members had participated. [0637, 0651, 0661]

PEMUDA (youth). The notion of youth was a strong element in the national awakening of Indonesia in early C.20, but the term *pemuda* came into common political use only during the National Revolution of 1945–49, when young Indonesians spearheaded the Declaration of Independence and flocked in tens of thousands to the armed units which endeavored to defend that independence against the Dutch. Pemuda in that time came to denote, along with youth, a spirit of daring and refusal to compromise. See also DIPLOMASI AND PERJUANGAN; GENERATIONS. [0628, 0636]

PEMUDA RAKYAT (People's Youth), youth organization affiliated to the PKI (q.v.), formed in 1950 to replace the PESINDO (q.v.). It used educational and social activities to draw the interest of young people, especially in the urban and rural kampungs, but was banned along with the PKI in 1966. [0822]

PEMUDA SOSIALIS INDONESIA (PESINDO, Indonesian Socialist Youth), armed youth wing of the ruling Partai Sosialis (q.v.), founded in November 1945. PESINDO fought the Dutch and also provided quasi-military backing to the government when its policies aroused the hostility of the army and other sections of society. It became increasingly trusted and favored under Amir Syarifuddin (q.v.), who made it the core of the so-called TNI Masyarakat (People's Indonesian National Army), created to balance the power of the more conservative conventional army. In 1948 it joined the left-wing Front Demokrasi Rakyat (q.v.) and was heavily involved in fighting during the Madiun Affair (q.v.). In 1950 it became firmly affiliated to the PKI (q.v.) and changed its name to Pemuda Rakyat (q.v.). [0563, 0656]

PENDIDIKAN NASIONAL INDONESIA (PNI, Indonesian National Education, also called PNI-Baru, New PNI), nationalist party founded by Hatta and Syahrir (qq.v.) in December 1931. Both were concerned by the relative ease with which the Dutch had been able to destroy the first PNI (q.v.) by arresting its leadership, and they proposed instead to build a strong, less obtrusive party of nationalist cadres which would have the strength to resist Dutch repression. They were given, however, relatively little time to put these ideas into practice since both were arrested and exiled to Boven Digul (q.v.) in February 1934. [0561, 0563, 0713, 0847]

PENEMBAKAN MISTERIUS. See BANDITRY.

PENGHULU, formerly the title of a Minangkabau (q.v.) clan head, but used in colonial times for religious officials in state employeemnt. See RELIGION AND POLITICS. [0608]

PEPPER (*Piper nigrum* Piperaceae), properly not the fleshy hollow fruit of various *Capsicum* species ('chilli peppers', for which see CHILLI) but the small hard berries of a woody vine. Whereas the *sirih, P. betle,* leaves of which are used in the chewing of betel (q.v.) is probably native to the archipelago, true pepper was introduced from India, probably as early as 100 B.C. Commercial production was well-established on Sumatra, Kalimantan, and Java by C.14. Pedir and Pasai (qq.v.) in northern Sumatra were the earliest states to depend heavily on the pepper trade, followed in C.16 by Aceh and Banten (qq.v.). Indiscriminate clearing of forest for pepper production in this era created large areas of alang-alang (q.v.) in Sumatra and Kalimantan. At the end of C.16, Banten produced 25,000 bags of pepper a year and all male inhabitants were obliged to maintain 500 pepper plants and to deliver the produce to the sultan at a fixed price. Pepper was traded especially to the West, becoming a major target of Portuguese (q.v.) and from late C.16 Dutch commercial expansion in the archipelago. The Dutch East Indies Company (q.v.) attempted to enforce monopoly contracts in pepper ports as they had done in Maluku with cloves and nutmeg (qq.v.) but were relatively unsuccessful due to the wide distribution of the plant and the relative ease with which it can be cultivated. From C.18 the Chinese market for pepper grew while that in Europe declined. Production on Java had largely ceased by the end of C.18. Although pepper production in Bangka (q.v.) and north Sumatra increased in C.19 and Chinese immigrants became important growers, the marketing center shifted to Penang and Singapore. [0245, 0246, 0454, 0938]

PERANAKAN ('native born'), term applied to those of non-Indonesian ethnic origin born in Indonesia, and generally implying some degree of cultural adaptation to local conditions. See CHINESE IN INDONESIA.

PERCA (PERCHA), Pulau. Older name for Sumatra (q.v.). See also ANDALAS.

PERDIKAN VILLAGES. The traditional rulers of Java occasionally freed a village of the obligation to pay land tax or provide corvée labor, either as a reward for service or in exchange for the village's acceptance of the obligation to carry out some task, such as the maintenance of a school or holy place. Such villages, called *perdikan desa* were found most commonly on Madura and in

Central Java and were preserved under Dutch rule. They were commonly major centers of handicrafts, including batik (q.v.). The tax exemption of perdikan villages was abolished by the Indonesian Republic in 1946. [0294]

PERGERAKAN. See NATIONALISM.

PERHIMPUNAN INDONESIA (PI, Indonesian Association), organization of Indonesian students in the Netherlands founded in 1922, based on the Indische Vereeniging (Indies Association), founded in 1908. The PI was small, with only 38 members at its peak but its members included such later national leaders as Muhammad Hatta, Sutan Syahrir, Ali Sastroamijoyo, and Sukiman Wiryosanjoyo (qq.v.). Its major aim was to prepare Indonesian students to provide political leadership on their return from study abroad, but it also sought to inform the Dutch public on conditions in the colony. Its ideology was strongly influenced by Marxism and especially by Lenin's theory of imperialism, but many of its members, including Hatta, despaired of communism after the Comintern decision in 1927 to abandon cooperation with noncommunist nationalists, and the organization gradually split between a PKI (q.v.) wing led by Rustam Effendi and the radical nationalists led by Hatta and Syahrir, who were finally expelled in 1931. [0560]

PERIODIZATION OF INDONESIAN HISTORY. The conventional historiography of Indonesia commonly divides the country's history into three broad periods: precolonial, colonial, and independent, normally subdivided as follows—traditional societies; Hindu-Buddhist kingdoms; the arrival of Islam and the emergence of Muslim sultanates; European commercial penetration and company rule; British interregnum; Cultivation System; Liberal Policy; Ethical Policy; rise of nationalism; Japanese occupation; Revolution; parliamentary democracy; Guided Democracy; and New Order. This sequence can be criticized on a number of grounds. First, it is visible clearly only on Java, though it is possible to apply it to other regions by, for instance, omitting the Muslim period, setting the date of colonial penetration later and so forth. More important, as a system of periodization which is based on government policy and organization, it ignores deeper structures, patterns, and continuities. Van Leur and Smail, in particular, have criticized it for the prominence it gives to the European role in Indonesian history and have argued for an 'autonomous' (Smail's term) approach concentrating on the experiences of Indonesians rather than of their European rulers. Indonesian historians have often used the notion of successive generations (q.v.) in periodizing. [0384, 0386, 0387, 0403]

PERJUANGAN. See DIPLOMASI AND PERJUANGAN.

PERMESTA (Piagam Perjuangan Semesta Alam, Universal Struggle Charter), document issued by Lt. Col. H.N.V. Sumual (b. 1923) unilaterally announcing martial law in eastern Indonesia (Nusatenggara, Sulawesi, and Maluku) on 2 March 1957. The mutiny had much the same origins as the PRRI (q.v.) rebellion which it later joined. Although based in the rich Minahasa (q.v.) area and enjoying some support from the U.S. (q.v.) the rebels were defeated by government forces in June 1958. The movement finally conceded defeat in 1961. [0639]

PERMUFAKATAN PERHIMPUNAN POLITIK KEBANGSAAN INDONESIA (PPPKI, Confederation of Indonesian Political Organizations), conference of nationalist groups (especially PNI, PSII, Budi Utomo, and Paguyuban Pasundan, qq.v.) formed in Bandung in December 1927 to give a relatively united voice to the nationalist movement. Decisions were taken by exhaustive deliberations (*musyawarah*) which were intended to avoid the imposition of majority views on minorities. In April 1929, the PPPKI recognized the Perhimpunan Indonesia (q.v.) as its representative in the Netherlands. The term 'Permufakatan' in its title changed in 1930 to 'Persatuan' (Unity, Association) and the word 'Kebangsaan' (Nationality) to 'Kemerdekaan' (Freedom) in 1933. The PPPKI strongly opposed the restrictive labor regulations of the time (see COOLIE ORDINANCE) and promoted nationalist education, but its internal diversity prevented it from acting decisively. In 1933 the colonial government refused to permit its annual conference and the PPPKI withered. See also GABUNGAN POLITIK INDONESIA. [0561, 0563]

PERSATUAN BANGSA INDONESIA (PBI, Association of the Indonesian People), successor to one of the study clubs of Sutomo (q.v.), formed in 1930 to promote self-help amongst Indonesians. It was involved in the promotion of cooperatives, education, and village banks and credit unions. In 1935 it merged with Budi Utomo (q.v.) to form the Partai Indonesia Raya (q.v.). [0563, 0719]

PERSATUAN INDONESIA RAYA (PIR, Greater Indonesian Association), conservative party of civil servants and aristocrats founded in 1948. In 1953 it split over the issue of participation in the government of Ali Sastroamijoyo and two PIR, under respectively Hazairin and Wongsonegoro, competed in the 1955 elections, losing heavily. [0634]

PERSATUAN ISLAM (Islamic Union), modernist Muslim organization founded in Bandung in 1923. It opposed nationalism on the grounds that it divided Islam and because it was Western and humanist in origin. It was active in establishing Muslim schools and was strongest in West Java and West Sumatra. Its leaders included Muhammad Natsir (q.v.). In 1939 it joined the MIAI (q.v.). [0895]

PERSATUAN PERJUANGAN (PP, Struggle Union), coalition of radical nationalist organizations formed 4–5 January 1946 to oppose the Republican government's negotiations with the Dutch (see DIPLOMASI AND PERJUANGAN). Ideas of Tan Malaka (q.v.) inspired the PP and the organization was supported at first by the army commander, Sudirman (q.v.). The movement brought down the first cabinet of Syahrir (q.v.) in February 1946, but was unable to agree on a coalition to replace him, partly because Sukarno moved deftly to break its fragile consensus on what should be done. The PP then disintegrated, though some of its members were involved later in 1946 in an ambiguous confrontation with Sukarno known as the 4 July Affair, and eventually formed the core of the Murba (q.v.). [0628, 0656]

PERSATUAN TARBIYAH ISLAMIYAH (PERTI, Islamic Education Association), founded in West Sumatra in 1930 was a party of Minangkabau and Acehnese Islamic traditionalists, based in religious centers and *pesantren.* Similar in style to the NU (q.v.), it was willing to trade its support on general political issues for specific concessions to Islam, though under Guided Democracy it was sometimes considered pro-PKI; its leader H. Sirajuddin Abbas frequently visited communist countries. The party was heavily purged after 1966 and in 1973 was merged into the Partai Persatuan Pembangunan (q.v.). [0634]

PERTAMINA (Perusahaan Tambang Minyak dan Gas Bumi Nasional, National Gas and Oil Corporation), Indonesia's sole state oil (q.v.) company, responsible for managing concessions and production-sharing agreements but little involved in production itself. Oil was already an important source of discretionary funds for Suharto's government early in the New Order, but the sudden increase in oil prices in 1973 gave Pertamina under its president-director Ibnu Sutowo (b.1914) enormous wealth which was funneled along with borrowed funds into a wide range of development projects and economic ventures, including an air service, Pelita, telecommunications, real estate, and the P.T. Krakatau Steel works in Cilegon, West Java. Sutowo was close to the CSIS (q.v.) think tank which promoted import-substitution industrialization rather than comparative-advantage trading and his free-wheeling style attracted admiration from economic nationalists and condemnation from the so-called technocrats of BAPPENAS (q.v.). An investigation in 1970 criticized Pertamina sharply for loose auditing, for failure to pass on profits to the government, and for the luxurious lifestyle of senior executives.

In March 1975, Pertamina was unable to meet payment on some short-term debts and a BAPPENAS investigation under J.B. Sumarlin revealed a huge debt problem (US$10,500 million), brought about by corruption, optimism, incompetence, and waste. Sutowo was dismissed from his post in 1976, and replaced by General Piet Haryono. Pertamina's activities outside the oil business were curtailed and an austerity policy was introduced, so that the firm was solvent once more by 1978. In 1980 the Indonesian government took legal action in Singapore to try to recover allegedly corrupt income from the estate of the former Pertamina employee H. Tahir. [0320, 0680, 0797]

PESANTREN (called *surau* in Minangkabau, *dajah* in Aceh), traditional rural Islamic school, headed by a *kyai* (religious teacher). Formerly, influenced by the style of

Hindu-Buddhist *asrama,* pesantren instructed resident pupils in religious knowledge and mystical practice, emphasizing absolute submission to both Allah and the kyai. In the C.19, influenced by returning pilgrims from Mecca (see HAJ), they took on the role of more formal religious instruction, though without discarding their primarily religious orientation. In the 1920s classroom teaching and a partly secular curriculum were introduced. The first pesantren for female students was opened at Jombang (East Java) in 1924. [0702, 1069, 1113, 1116, 1129, 1139]

PETITION OF FIFTY (*Petisi Lima Puluh*). In March and April 1980, President Suharto (q.v.) made speeches implying that he was the embodiment of Pancasila (q.v.), describing it as under threat from nationalism, religion, and other ideologies, and calling on the armed forces to defend it against these challenges. The speeches aroused special alarm in two dissident groups whose members were generally associated with the establishment of the New Order (q.v.) in 1965–66, *viz.,* the Forum Studi dan Komunikasi (FOSKO), incl. H.R. Dharsono, and Lembaga Kesadaran Berkonstitusi (LKB, Institute for Constitutional Awareness), including A.H. Nasution and Ali Sadikin (qq.v.). In response, a group of fifty former generals, politicians, academics, students and others, including Nasution, Sadikin, Muhammad Natsir, and Syafruddin Prawiranegara (qq.v.), signed a petition dated 5 May 1980 expressing concern at the speeches and inviting the MPR (q.v.) to 'review' them. The government reacted strongly to this criticism, banning news coverage of the petitioners, preventing them from travelling, and depriving firms associated with them of their government contracts. [0675]

PHILIPPINES, Historical links with. The Austronesian people reached Indonesia through the Philippines (see

MIGRATIONS), and contacts between the southern islands and eastern Indonesia remained strong, especially in trade. In C.17, the Dutch and Spanish fought for influence in Mindanao, and the Dutch alliance with the Mindanao sultanate was partly responsible for its emergence as paramount power in the region. After the United States conquered the Philippines in 1898, the Americans initially saw the Netherlands Indies as offering many lessons in management of a tropical colony, and American welfare expenditure in the Philippines found echoes in the Ethical Policy (q.v.). As the Philippines progressed towards self-government, however, the Dutch grew increasingly uneasy, fearing both encouragement for Indonesian nationalism and possible southward expansion by Japan. These fears were heightened by the visit of President Manuel Quezon to Indonesia in 1934 and the later founding of a (short-lived) Pan-Malayan People's Union under Philippine leadership. During the Indonesian Revolution, Manila was an important source of supplies for the beleaguered Republic. Since 1950, Indonesia and the Philippines have combined to limit commerce and other traffic across their borders, so as to discourage links between Muslim Moro rebels in Mindanao and Sulu and radical Muslims in Indonesia, and between Christian communities in Minahasa (q.v.) and the northern Philippines. As another archipelagic nation, the Philippines has strongly supported Indonesia's Archipelagic Concept (q.v.), but is in dipute with Indonesia over jurisdiction over seas around the Indonesian island of Miangas, off Mindanao. See also MAPHILINDO. [0539, 0648, 0727, 0741]

PIAGAM JAKARTA (Jakarta Charter). See ISLAMIC STATE, Demands for.

PIG (*Sus scrofa*). Until C.20 it is difficult to distinguish accounts of the introduced domestic pig from those of indigenous warty pigs (*S. verrucosus* on Java, *S. barbatus* on Kalimantan and Sumatra, and *S. celebensis* on Sulawesi). It seems likely, however, that *S. celebensis* was the first domesticated and was taken by people to Timor and that the pigs of Irian (q.v.) are a stable hybrid of *S. celebensis* and *S. scrofa* developed between 8000 and 4000 B.C. Wild pigs were an important food source for most peoples until the arrival of Islam (q.v.), and Miles has shown that the adoption of Islam amongst Dayaks (q.v.) has had significant nutritional effects. Feral and warty pigs are widespread in the archipelago and seem to do best where human cultivation provides abundant accessible food. Since the early 1970s, the introduction of the pig tapeworm *Taenia solium* into Irian has had serious health consequences. See also TIGER. [0234, 0411, 0943, 0945, 1034]

PIRACY. A distinction between the regular depredations of the state and the irregular depredations of criminals was slower to emerge on the sea than on land in traditional Indonesia (see BANDITRY). 'Piracy,' in the form of water-borne raids against neighboring communities and the plundering of passing vessels, formed an important part of the political order in maritime societies in Indonesia (see also HONGI RAIDS). It provided an important source of income, in the form of products and slaves (see SLAVERY) and within communities established the social basis for rule by pirate chiefs. It also gave successful chiefs the means to subjugate rivals and to regularize their plunder by guaranteeing safe passage through their sphere of influence in exchange for a fixed payment. The suppression of piracy and the subjugation of rivals were thus often two sides of the same coin. Conversely, when trade declined or departed kingdoms often returned to piracy. Although this approached a system of customs collection, war vessels were often still needed to force passing merchant vessels to call at the required port. This system was adopted by the Portuguese (q.v.) on their arrival in the East.

From early C.19 Dutch and British colonial authorities worked not just to suppress slavery and unambiguously piratical activities but to prevent local rulers from collecting customs dues, in the name of free trade. Steam-powered vessels which could sail against the wind were a major factor in the European success. Occasional incidents of piracy continue to occur in the Strait of Melaka. [0435, 0494, 0598]

PIRES, Tomé (1468–ca 1539), Portuguese apothecary and author of the *Suma Oriental,* which describes his residence in Melaka (q.v.) from 1512–15. Rediscovered in 1937, this work is a major account of daily life and political and economic conditions in Southeast Asia in this period. [0058]

PLAGUE. See BUBONIC PLAGUE.

PLANNING, ECONOMIC. See GUIDED ECONOMY; RENCANA PEMBANGUNAN LIMA TAHUN.

PLURAL SOCIETY, term coined by J.S. Furnivall to characterize a society in which 'two or more elements or social orders . . . live side by side . . . without mingling in one political unit,' by which he was referring to the legal and social separation of ethnic groups in the Netherlands Indies. See DUALISM; LAW. [0555]

POENALE SANCTIE. See COOLIE ORDINANCE.

POLICE. Until C.20 police tasks in the Netherlands Indies were primarily the responsibility of local authorities. Indonesian officials commanded their own local police squads under a variety of names, the officers of Chinese communities were in charge of policing their own people, and policing functions in the European community lay largely with the civil bureaucracy itself, while all policing forces were backed ultimately by the colonial army (see KONINKLIJK NEDERLANDSCH INDISCH LEGER; NATIVE TROOPS; LAW; MARÉCHAUSSÉE). Some centralization of policing was achieved with the creation of mobile 'armed police' (gewapende politie) in 1897, but it was only after the establishment of the office of the Attorney-General (Procureur-Generaal) that central control of the police emerged. The police force nonetheless remained divided into distinct rural (veldpolitie, who absorbed the gewapende politie in 1920), urban (stadspolitie), and political (Politiek Inlichtingen Dienst, q.v.) sections.

The Japanese (1942–45) dismissed some senior staff from the Dutch period and handed political surveillance to the Kempeitai (q.v.), but otherwise preserved and strengthened the police force. During the Revolution (1945–49), the police were at first formally under control of the Internal Affairs ministry but shifted in July 1946 to the prime minister's office. Much of the police force, however, was dispersed by social revolutions, and a multitude of local police forces emerged, generally attached to regional armed forces, regular and irregular. Dual control by Internal Affairs and the prime minister was established in 1950, but in 1962 the police were formally militarized and placed under the authority of the armed forces (ABRI, q.v.) commander. See also BAKIN. [0611]

'POLICE ACTIONS' (*Politionele acties*). Military operations launched by the Netherlands Indies against the Indonesian Republic in Java and Sumatra on 21 July 1947 and 19 December 1948. They were called police actions to stress their allegedly internal character and to avoid giving the Indonesian Republic the formal recognition as belligerent implied by an act of war. The first, called Operation Product, aimed primarily at seizing plantation areas to improve the parlous financial situation of the colonial government. The resulting demarcation line was known as the van Mook line and left the Republic on Java crowded into heavily populated parts of the island's center and east and Banten. On Sumatra, the Dutch did no more than significantly expand their coastal enclaves in east, west, and south Sumatra. The second Police Action was intended to destroy the Republic, and Dutch troops entered all regions except Aceh (q.v.). Guerrilla warfare (see GERILYA), however, kept Dutch forces too thinly spread to consolidate their initial advances and international pressure brought the Dutch to negotiate once more with the Republic, leading to the Round Table Conference (q.v.). Indonesian texts generally refer to the 'police actions' as *Agresi* or *Clash* I and II. [0563, 0645]

POLITICAL CULTURE. The proposition that shared cultural values can lead to a shared attitude to politics is a plausible one, and has led many analysts, Indonesian and foreign, to argue for the existence of a distinctive Indonesian political culture. A major objection to this has traditionally been the ethnic and cultural diversity of the archipelago. The Dutch in particular saw pronounced cultural dissimilarities between the peoples of the colony and at times claimed on this basis that only their rule would preserve Indonesian unity. The argument, however, is generally not that particular values are universally held, but that they are dominant values which to a greater or lesser extent establish the terms on which people must operate politically. H. Geertz identified a 'metropolitan super-culture' (q.v.) as providing such dominant values (See also JAVANIZATION).

Indonesian political leaders have often argued that the collectivist village culture of traditional Indonesia leads to a preference for consensual politics with special attention being given to the wisdom of the elders in society (see DESA; MUSYAWARAH; SUKARNO), making Indonesia unsuited to the supposedly adversarial style of Western party politics. Under the New Order this has led to the labelling of criticism of President Suharto (q.v.) and his family as un-Indonesian (see BIMBO; SUBVERSION). Other observers, such as Mochtar Lubis (q.v.) have argued that Indonesian political culture is characterized by a feudal deference to constituted authority, while still others have seen this deferential submissiveness (*nrimo*) as typical only of Javanese society and contrasting with more dynamic and independent styles in the other islands.

Western observers have been intrigued by apparent parallels in style between both Sukarno and Suharto on the one hand and traditional Javanese kings on the other. Most of the parallels refer to elements of individual style: Sukarno's monument building (especially the *lingga*-like National Monument in Jakarta; see SEX, Political significance of), his unification of seeming irreconcilables, and his sexual encounters, Suharto's reluctance to exercise his power visibly, and both leaders' emphasis on unity, the centralization of authority, and the use of powerful words, and their avoidance of naming a successor. The principal objections to this line of argument are that it provides at best only a partial explanation of those leaders' actions and that much of the behavior involved can be explained in terms of *realpolitik* calculations. [0771–0773, 0778, 0780, 0790, 0860]

POLITICAL PARTIES. See PARTIES, POLITICAL.

POLITICAL POLICE. See BAKIN; KENPEITAI; POLITIEK INLICHTINGEN DIENST.

POLITICAL PRISONERS. See BOVEN DIGUL; EXILE; TAHANAN POLITIK.

POLITIEK INLICHTINGEN DIENST (PID, Political Intelligence Service). A clear distinction between political and conventional policing developed in the Netherlands Indies only after the rise of Indonesian nationalism (q.v.) in early C.20 and led to the formation of the PID in 1916. The PID was formally abolished in 1919 but its place was taken in 1920 by the Algemene Recherche (Criminal Investigation Division) and the term PID remained in common use until the end of Dutch rule. The political police worked both by the collection of intelligence of political organizations and by directly intervening in their activities, for instance by breaking up meetings. It was largely due to prior arrests and other preventive measures that the 1926/27 PKI (q.v.) uprisings were not more widespread. The Algemene Recherche's monthly *Politiek-Politionele Overzichten* (*Police Political Surveys*), appearing first in 1927, became the colonial government's principal source of information on the nationalist movement. The Recherche continued during the Japanese occupation under the name Tokoka, but many of its functions were taken over by the Kenpeitai (q.v.). After World War II the political intelligence functions of the Algemene Recherche were partly taken over by the Netherlands Forces Intelligence Service (NEFIS). See also BAKIN; POLICE. [0587, 0636]

POLO, Marco (1254?–1324?), Venetian traveller. On his return from China to Europe in 1292–95, Polo travelled through the Strait of Melaka, visiting Pedir and Pasai (qq.v.). His account is most often mentioned for his statement that some of the states of northern Sumatra were already Muslim, but his description is too vague to be of much use. [0067]

POLOWIJO, subsidiary crops grown on wet rice land (*sawah*) after the rice harvest, including chilli, soy beans, egg plant, maize, onions, and sugar cane. [0235, 0256]

PONTIANAK, city and state on the Kapuas river in West Kalimantan, founded in 1772 by a part-Arab pirate Syarif Abdurrahman (see PIRACY), who in 1778 accepted Dutch suzerainty in exchange for recognition as sultan and Dutch aid in establishing control of the Kapuas basin. The kingdom's source of wealth was its control of trade down the Kapuas in gold, diamonds (qq.v.), and forest products. The VOC (q.v.) withdrew its presence in 1791 but restored it in 1818, installing a resident to insure closer control of affairs. Many thousands of people, including the sultan and most of his family, were killed by the Japanese between 1942 and 1945, leaving a younger son, Hamid Algadrie, to reign as Hamid II. He was persuaded by the Dutch to head a federal state of West Borneo (Kalimantan Barat), founded on 11 May 1947 (see FEDERALISM), and became a major figure in Dutch attempts to influence the constitutional and political shape of postwar Indonesia. He was implicated in a failed coup d'etat on 23 January 1950 by R.P.P. Westerling (q.v.) and was jailed. The Negara Kalimantan Barat was dissolved on 4 April 1950. During Confrontation (q.v.) West Kalimantan was an important base for Indonesian infiltration into the Malaysian state of Sarawak, partly conducted by the ethnic Chinese Pasukan Gerilya Rakyat Serawak (PGRS, Sarawak People's Guerrilla Movement), which later became a base for guerrilla warfare by the PKI (q.v.) in 1967–69. See also KONGSI WARS. [0003, 0512, 0824]

POPULATION. Indonesia's first full census was taken in 1930 and gave the country a population of 60.7 million. Population figures before this date are based on partial surveys and guesswork with varying degrees of inspiration; they yield often widely varying results.

Demographers have given greatest attention to Java because of the island's greater density of population. Early scholars, extrapolating backwards from C.19 estimates, assumed that Java's population in early times was between one and three million. The scope of irrigation works, monument construction and political organization on the island, however, suggests perhaps a fairly steady population of around ten million from ca C.10. Raffles (q.v.) surveyed Java's population in 1815 at 4.6 million, but this is certainly an underestimate: those responsible for reporting population were already long accustomed to underreporting population in order to minimize taxation (q.v.). From 1815 to 1865, Java's population probably grew at around 1% per year, and then at around 1.2% until the end of C.19, reaching 30 million in 1900. Although Dutch authorities and many later researchers attributed this growth to Malthusian factors such as increased health (q.v.) care and the absence of war, economic changes also seem to have been important. Specifically the expansion of rice cultivation and the improvement of rice technology, together with the opening up of employment opportunities on commercial estates. Alexander has argued that the heavy labor demands made on women under the Cultivation System (q.v.) reduced the period of breast-feeding and thus also the period of post-partum infertility. From 1900 population grew at an average 1.4% per year (though there was probably little growth in the 1940s). From 1961 to 1971 the rate was about 2%. Until 1900, most of the other islands, except Bali (q.v.), were relatively sparsely populated, but population has grown dramatically in North Sumatra, Lampung, South Sulawesi, and Minahasa, especially as a result of immigration, transmigration (q.v.), and the shift to intensive agriculture.

Until about the end of C.18, population was a valuable political resource for rulers (see LABOR) and there was no question of population control as policy, though women were able to space children by prolonging breast-feeding to two-to-three years, and abortion by massage and herbs was apparently common. In early C.19, however, Raffles raised the prospect of overpopulation on Java and since then the topic has seldom been off the political agenda. Transmigration was the first solution proposed, but from the 1970s more emphasis was put on family planning (q.v.). Fertility rates have declined in the period 1967–85 from an average of 5.5 births per woman to an average of 3.3, due to the increased availability of contraceptives, awareness of the costs of educating children, and the availability of other consumption options. See also CENSUSES. [0044, 0184, 0213, 0366, 1077, 1092–1104]

PORTS. Lying mostly outside the cyclonic zone, many Indonesian ports were traditionally little more than roadsteads, ships anchoring offshore to be loaded and unloaded by lighter. Geographical location, the provision of naval protection, and the availability of supplies rather than the technical characteristics of the harbor itself were most important. The development of steam shipping and of larger draft vessels, however, led to the building of more elaborate facilities. A modern port for Batavia (q.v.) was constructed at Tanjung Priok in 1886–87; Surabaya was turned from a roadstead into a port 1917–20; new wharves were installed in Makassar (q.v.) in 1918; and Belawan, the port for Deli (q.v.) was opened in 1922. In 1954, port service facilities were transferred to Indonesian firms (see NATIONALIZATION). A major element in Indonesian port policy has been the desire to establish direct 'gateways' to the rest of the world, bypassing Singapore (q.v.). From early times, ports also formed the nuclei for the growth of cities (q.v.) and were much more important centers of urbanization than the inland settlements around the courts of Javanese rulers. See also BATAM; CORRUPTION; PASISIR; SHIPPING. [0346]

PORTUGUESE IN INDONESIA. The commercial reputation of Melaka (q.v.) led the Portuguese to establish a post there in 1509, as part of their Asia-wide string of ports and offices. Expelled by the Sultan, they returned in 1511 under Alfonso de Albuquerque (ca1459–1515) and after a prolonged struggle captured the city, going on to found settlements in Ternate, Ambon, Timor, and Tidore (qq.v.). Except for guns and clocks, Portuguese goods had little demand in Asia, and they concentrated on using their naval supremacy to tax intra-Asian trade (see PIRACY). Portuguese became a lingua franca in much of the archipelago, leaving many words in the local languages (q.v.). High tariffs in Melaka, however, drove traders to Aceh, Riau (qq.v.), and ports on Java, diminishing Portuguese revenue and leading them into a series of military and diplomatic adventures especially on the eastern coast of Sumatra, where they fought and negotiated intermittently with Aceh, Pedir, and Pasai. Illegal trade by Portuguese officials, a lack of manpower, a lack of tact in dealing with local powers (which helps to explain the spread of Islam, q.v.), and the growth of the power of the Dutch and English East Indies Companies (qq.v.) contributed to their decline. After losing Melaka in 1641, they ceased to be a major power in the region, though they retained possessions in Nusatenggara. See also CATHOLICISM; EAST TIMOR. [0442–0444]

POSTAL SERVICE. Letters are, of course, a phenomenon nearly as ancient in the archipelago as writing (q.v.) and, as a means of communication between people, were not always encouraged by rulers. From 1636 to 1701, for instance, the VOC banned all private correspondence to protect its trade secrets. The first official post office was established by Governor-General van Imhoff, 12½ cents being charged to send a letter to the Netherlands and 25 cents to receive one, though the 'poor' were exempt from these charges. Postal services were initially the responsibility of police (q.v.) officials, but from 1789 they were farmed out to private contractors (see PACHT), rates being fixed by the Company. Postmarks were used to indicate the amount to be paid by the addressee. Daendels (q.v.) restored state control of the system, and recruited forced labor to construct a post road 1000 km along the northern coast of Java from Anyer to Panarukan. Lodgings and horse stations were provided every 15 km and the road was maintained by compulsory labor services from the local population. A commission for roads and posts was installed in 1808 to insure regular services. Regulations in 1862 provided for the first postage stamps for prepayment (issued 1864) and formally made the postal service a government monopoly, though the mail contract to the Outer Islands was always let out to private tender. In 1884 the colonial government took over full running of the postal service with the establishment of PTT (Post Telegraaf Telefoon). See also GAMBLING; ROADS; SHIPPING; TELEGRAPH. [0343, 0352]

POTATO (*Solanum tuberosum* Solanaceae). Originally from the Andes region of South America, the potato reached Java, probably via Europe, in mid C.18.

POULTRY. See FOWL.

PRAMBANAN. C.9 Hindu temple in Central Java, dedicated to Durga, the consort of Siva. [[0116]

PRAMUDYA ANANTA TUR (b.1925), major Indonesian novelist. Tur's early writings from the 1940s show a terse, personal style reminiscent of Idrus (q.v.) and a cynical view of the Revolution, during which he was associated with an unsuccessful lasykar (q.v.) group and was jailed by the Dutch. He shifted left, however, in the 1950s, arguing for popular commitment in literature and becoming a major figure in the LEKRA (q.v.). He helped to formulate the doctrine of socialist realism as it applied to Indonesia in the 1960s. In 1965 he was detained and later sent to the penal island of Buru (q.v.) and was not released until late 1979. While in detention, he wrote a series of historical novels based on the emergence of Indonesian national consciousness in early C.20. These have been published in English as *This earth of mankind, Child of all nations, Footsteps* and *House of Glass* but they are banned in Indonesia itself. See also CULTURE, Debate on the role of. [0160, 0181–0183]

PRAU. See SHIPPING.

PREHISTORY. The prehistory of the archipelago is relatively little known. Remains of the hominids *Pithecanthropus modjokertoensis* and *Meganthropus palaeojavanicus* have been found in volcanic deposits on Java dated to 1.9 million years ago, while Java Man (q.v., *Homo [Pithecanthropus] erectus* and *Pithecanthropus soloensis*) lived in Central Java 1 million or more years ago. The earliest known *Homo sapiens* is Wajak Man, who lived in East Java about 40,000 years ago (though similar remains in Sarawak date from 50,000 years ago), while other *H. sapiens* remains from eastern Indonesia seem to date from about 30,000 years before the present. Wajak Man was probably an Austromelanesian (Australoid), close to the ancestors of today's Australian Aborigines, but whether *H. erectus* and the rest were the ancestors of Wajak Man is uncertain—some authorities believe the Austromelanesians migrated from the Asian mainland beween 50,000 and 100,000 years ago. They appear to have occupied most of what is now Indonesia and Australia (q.v.), but were divided 15,000 to 8,000 years ago by a 130 meter rise in sea level, which created the Indonesian archipelago and made contact with Australia vastly more difficult. It was not until 4000–2000 B.C. that the Austronesian ancestors of the modern inhabitants of western Indonesia reached the archipelago. See also CONTINENTAL DRIFT; MIGRATIONS; SUNDA SHELF. [0388, 0390, 0400, 0409, 0418, 0423]

PRESIDENT, Office of. Under Indonesia's 1945 Constitution (q.v.), the President is the head of state and of executive government and supreme commander of the armed forces. He must be *asli* (q.v.) Indonesian, more than 40 years old, believe in God, and not have been involved in subversive activities. He is officially mandatory of the MPR (q.v.) for the execution of government policy during a five-year term, though the MPR-S conferred on Sukarno the title President-for-Life in 1963 and revoked it in 1966. The president reports to the newly elected MPR at the end of his term in office and there is commonly no procedure which holds him accountable to the MPR which elected him, but he can be dismissed by the MPR at any time, as happened to Sukarno (q.v.). He appoints and dismisses ministers and cooperates with the DPR (q.v.) in the passing of legislation and the state budget, though he can also make extensive use of presidential decrees (Keputusan Presiden, KEPPRES) and government regulation (Peraturan Pemerintah, PP), which do not require legislative ratification. See also VICE-PRESIDENT. [0890]

PRIANGAN (Dutch *Preanger*), a mountainous region in southern and central West Java, extending roughly from Sukabumi to Tasikmalaya. The heartland of the Sundanese, it was the first extensive region on Java to fall under Dutch rule (in 1677) and was governed through local rulers (*regenten*) in a form of indirect rule. Under the 'Preanger-Stelsel' (Priangan system), the Dutch obliged these rulers to supervise the forced cultivation of coffee, pepper, and tea (qq.v.). See also SUNDA. [0458, 0900]

PRIBUMI ('indigene'), often abbreviated to 'Pri' and distinguished from 'Non-Pri'. Ostensibly a racial distinction between broadly Malay and Melanesian ethnic groups long settled in the archipelago and more recently arrived minorities (Chinese, Arabs, q.v.), but most commonly used to distinguish unassimilated Chinese (Non-Pri) from others. See ALI-BABA FIRMS; CHINESE IN INDONESIA.

PRIYAYI, the traditional, largely hereditary, bureaucratic aristocracy of Java. Although access to the priyayi might be by descent and/or political position, the defining feature of the class was its culture, which stressed the often pre-Islamic courtly arts of literature, music, drama, and philosophy, as well as justice and integrity in government (see GAMELAN; KEBATINAN; WAYANG). A (male) priyayi was expected to possess, it is said, a wife, a house, a horse (q.v.), a kris (q.v.), and a singing bird, representing social stability, military prowess, and esthetic sensibility. A wide range of aphorisms, many still in use, urged these values on the priyayi. *Tut wuri handayani,* for instance, the motto of the Department of Education and Culture, means 'helping unobtrusively from behind.'

Although these values were ostensibly traditional, they were encouraged amongst the priyayi by the Dutch, especially during C.19, as a means of increasing the dignity and prestige of the traditional authorities and so facilitating the system of indirect rule (see BUPATI; INLANDSCH BESTUUR). This tended to widen the apparent gap between Javanese village culture (see ABANGAN; DESA) and that of the courts. Especially since 1966, the New Order government has encouraged traditional priyayi values as a way of bolstering corporatism in the bureaucracy (see KORPS PEGAWAI REPUBLIK INDONESIA). Priyayi cultural forms, expressed especially in weddings, are now commonplace amongst village elites. See also ALIRAN; PAMONG PRAJA. [0372, 0474, 0596, 1005, 1038]

PROCLAMATION OF INDEPENDENCE (*Proklamasi*). See INDEPENDENCE, Declaration of.

PROSTITUTION is not easy to define or trace in precolonial Indonesia, though it must certainly have existed, especially in the port cities. Sexual relations seem to have been relatively easy, divorce was common, and quasicontractual liaisons seem to have been common, especially between foreign traders and indigenous women (continued today as *kawin kontrak*), or by the purchase of slave women for sexual purposes. Prostitution began to grow in C.16, perhaps because Muslims disapproved of temporary marriage, but large-scale prostitution emerged only in C.19 with the decline of concubinage amongst soldiers of the KNIL and amongst European officials and with the increase in labor mobility, which saw large numbers of indigenous men leaving their families temporarily to seek employment in the cities and on plantations. During C.19, government concern over the spread of syphilis (q.v.) led to supervision of prostitution, without, however, any attempt to improve working conditions in the industry. From 1912 the Sarekat Islam (q.v.) campaigned against prostitution, and in the 1970s Islamic groups strongly objected when the Jakarta governor, Ali Sadikin (q.v.) legalized prostitution in order both to improve conditions and to generate tax revenue. See also MAR-

RIAGE, Political significance of; WOMEN AND MEN. [0483, 1080, 1086]

PROTESTANTISM. Protestant missionary activity began in Indonesia in C.17, soon after the arrival of the Dutch East Indies Company (q.v.). From 1623 to 1633 a seminary existed in Leiden under Company sponsorship for the training of missionaries and by 1795 the indigenous Christian population of the archipelago was estimated at 70,000, much of it on Java and in Maluku. In 1820 the various Protestant churches were brought under government supervision through the Commissie tot de Zaken der Protestantsche Kerken in Nederlandsch Oost-en West-Indië (Commission on the Affairs of the Protestant Churches in the Dutch East and West Indies), also known as the Haagsche Commissie, which acted as a kind of embassy from the Dutch churches to the colonial government. In mid C.19, however, an independent Javanese Protestant community was founded in Central Java by Kiai Sadrach (1841–?). All official Protestant churches in the colony were united into a single, state-sponsored church, the 'Indische Kerk', which was disestablished only on 1 August 1935.

English methodism and German pietism prompted another wave of European missionary activity from late C.18, especially by the Nederlandsch Zendelingsgenootschap (estab. 1797). By 1906, thirty missionary societies, including many of German origin, were members of the so-called Zendingsconsulaat (Mission consulate), which coordinated mission relations with the colonial government. Most missions were given their own area for proselytization and all missions were excluded from certain areas (Bali, Lombok, Sumbawa, Flores, and large areas of Sumatra and Kalimantan). German Protestant missions were active in the Toba area of North Sumatra from 1861 and later on Nias and in southern Kalimantan. The indigenous Protestant churches conduct services in local languages and are thus administratively divided according to ethnic group, though most churches are represented in the Dewan Gereja Indonesia (DGI, Indonesian Council of Churches). Protestantism is strongest in the Batak area of Sumatra and in Maluku and Minahasa (q.v.). See also CATHOLICISM. [1106, 1114, 1120, 1123, 1145, 1151, 1165]

PROTO-MALAYS. See MIGRATIONS.

PROVINCES. Although some steps towards decentralization (q.v.) were taken under Dutch rule, the establishment of a full set of provincial governments in Indonesia was not carried out until the abolition of the last federal states (see FEDERALISM) in 1950. Provinces are the major sub-national administrative division in modern Indonesia and provincial governors, as important agents of central rule, have always been appointed by the central government, except for a brief period from 1957 to 1959 when they were elected. Under the 1974 law on regional government, however, governors are appointed from a panel of candidates chosen by a partly elected provincial assembly, the Dewan Perwakilan Rakyat Daerah Tingkat I (Level I Regional People's Representative Council), with which they co-legislate on provincial matters. The formal title of governors is thus Gubernur/Kepala Daerah (governor/regional head).

On 18 August 1945 the Indonesian Republic divided the country into eight provinces: Sumatra, Borneo (sic), West Java, Central Java, East Java, Sulawesi, Maluku, and Sunda Kecil (Lesser Sundas or Nusatenggara). This structure was overtaken by the Revolution and the formation of the federal Republik Indonesia Serikat (q.v.), but was partly recreated in 1950 with the dissolution of the RIS and the establishment of provinces in West, Central, and East Java and North, Central, and South Sumatra; the division of Sumatra had been announced by the Republic in 1948 but never implemented. Aceh (q.v.) had been briefly separated from Sumatra as a distinct province in 1949 by the emergency government of Syafruddin Prawiranegara (q.v.) but was incorporated into the new province of North Sumatra. In 1950, too, Yogyakarta (q.v.) and the Pakualaman were separated from Central Java as the Daerah Istimewa Yogyakarta (DIY, Yogyakarta Special Territory). Kalimantan, which regained provincial status in 1953, was divided into West, South, and East provinces in 1956. As part of a settlement with the rebels there, Aceh became a province once more in 1957 and a daerah istimewa in 1959. In 1956 Irian (q.v.) became an autonomous province with provisional capital at Tidore. In 1957 Maluku was restored as a province, while Central Sumatra split into Jambi, Riau, and West Sumatra, with Jambi initially including Indrapura on the west coast. Jakarta was also declared a capital territory (Daerah Khusus Ibukota, DKI) in 1957. In 1958, the provinces of Bali, Nusatenggara Barat, and Nusatenggara Timur were established in the lesser Sundas, while Central Kalimantan was removed from South Kalimantan. In 1960 provinces of North and South Sulawesi were formed; Central Sulawesi and Southeast Sulawesi separated from North and South respectively in 1964. Lampung separated from South Sumatra in 1964 and Bengkulu followed in 1967. Irian formally became a province with the 'Act of Free Choice' in 1969. Timor Timur (East Timor) was annexed and constituted as Indonesia's 27th province in 1976. Proposals currently exist to divide Irian Jaya into two or more provinces and to split Tapanuli from North Sumatra. [0563, 0903, 0909, 0910]

PURBAKALA, Dinas. See ARCHEOLOGY.

PUSAT TENAGA RAKYAT (PUTERA, Center of the People's Power), Japanese-sponsored mass organization on Java which succeeded the Tiga A Movement (q.v.) in March 1943, under the leadership of Sukarno, Hatta (qq.v.), Ki Hajar Dewantoro (see SUWARDI SURYANINGRAT), and Mas Mansur (1896–1946). Its principal task was to increase public enthusiasm for the war effort and to drive out remnants of Western cultural and political influence, and its activity was limited to little more than radio (q.v.) broadcasts and other propaganda. It operated under strict Japanese control and was given only limited access to the countryside. It nonetheless gave massive public exposure to Sukarno and Hatta and reinforced their standing as national leaders. It was replaced in January 1944 by the Jawa Hokokai (q.v.). See also JAPANESE OCCUPATION OF INDONESIA. [0563, 0606, 0613, 0615]

R

RAAD VAN INDIË (Council of the Indies), senior council for Indies affairs, generally with the task of advising the governor-general (q.v.) on matters of state. [0026, 0028, 0601]

RACE. In traditional societies, where the notion of genetic characteristics is absent, it is difficult to judge the extent of 'racial' consciousness as opposed to a simple distinction between locals and outsiders. Evidence suggests, however, that just as the traditional societies of the archipelago were rather open to cultural influences from abroad, so they were relatively accepting of those who assimilated culturally to Indonesian ways of life, the most important 'ethnic' marker being religion. In the trading cities of the coastal regions, in particular, there seems to be a long tradition of settlement and acculturation by other Asians, to the extent that it is difficult or impossible from available records to identify those who might by today's norms be called 'Chinese', 'Arab' or 'Indian'. On the other hand, expatriate communities in these ports have a long tradition of maintaining their distinct cultural identities.

The Dutch East Indies Company (q.v.) also used religion at first as its main criterion of ethnicity, regarding Christian Indonesians, in some respects at least, as Europeans for legal purposes (see LAW). Although separate native courts were established in 1747, a formal legal distinction between Europeans and others did not come into effect until 1848, when the new commercial and civil codes and codes of civil and criminal procedure were declared applicable to Europeans only. Article 109 of the 1854 Regeeringsreglement (Constitution, q.v.) formally distinguished between *Europeanen,* who were thereby equalized to Dutch citizens in the Netherlands, and *Inlanders* (natives). While this distinction enabled some special protection to be given to Indonesians, *e.g.,* in the Agrarian Law of 1870 (q.v.), it generally permitted discrimination against indigenes in conditions of employment and the provision of services. The exact criteria for racial classification were not specified, but in general legitimate children followed the race of their father and illegitimate children that of their mother. Groups which did not fall clearly into either category were allocated to one or the other, Armenians, for instance, as Europeans; wives of Europeans (from 1896) as Europeans, and Arabs (q.v.) as natives. In 1885 Chinese were made subject to European commercial law in order to simplify their dealings with European business houses and a third category, foreign Orientals (*vreemde oosterlingen*), including Arabs, gradually emerged, though it was not legally defined until the revised Constitution of 1925 (art. 163). From 1899 Japanese were classified as Europeans, and were joined by Turks in 1926, on the grounds that Turkey had adopted a European style of legal system. Movement between legal categories was also possible by means of *gelijkstelling* (alike-making), under which persons of native or foreign Oriental status could gain full legal European status if they could demonstrate that they were culturally assimilated to the European community or had special legal need for European status. In late C.19, a campaign began in Dutch circles for the abolition of racial classification as a hindrance to social development, but this was blocked by a coalition of colonial conservatives and adat (q.v.) law specialists, who argued for the sanctity of traditional ethnically-based law; steps towards legal unification were abandoned in 1928. From 1910, with the introduction of limited elections, a further legal distinction was made between Dutch citizens and Dutch subjects (*Nederlands onderdaan, niet Nederlander*). All formal racial distinctions were abolished by the Indonesian Constitution of 1945 (but see ASLI), though discimination against Indonesian citizens of foreign descent (*warganegara Indonesia keturunan asing*) continues in a number of respects. See also INDO-EUROPEANS.

RADICALE CONCENTRATIE (Radical Concentration), coalition of Indonesian and non-Indonesian progressive parties formed in the Volksraad (q.v.) in November 1918 to press for movement towards responsible government in the colony, especially after the colonial government had rejected the recommendations of the Carpentier Alting Commission on constitutional reform. The coalition fell apart as the demands of Indonesian nationalism for full independence became stronger. [0563]

RADIO. The first radio station in the Netherlands Indies was established in Sabang in 1911 for naval communications; amateur broadcasts began soon after and the first commercial station, the Bataviaasche Radio Vereeniging, began in 1925. The official Nederlandsch-Indische Radio Omroep Maatschappij (NIROM) began broadcasting in 1934. The first indigenous radio station, Perikatan Perkumpulan Radio Ketimuran (Federation of Oriental Radio Associations) was permitted in 1937, but could only broadcast on cultural and social affairs. During the Japanese occupation (q.v.), radios were used widely for propaganda in the villages, and figures such as Sukarno (q.v.) received unprecedented national coverage as a result. A national station, Radio Republik Indonesia (RRI), was founded in August 1945. [0342, 0351, 0361]

RAFFLES, Thomas Stamford (1781–1826). An official of the English East India Company (q.v.), Raffles was appointed Lieutenant-Governor of Java in 1811, after Britain's seizure of the island during the Napoleonic Wars (see BATAVIAN REPUBLIC). Hoping to persuade his superiors to retain control of the island, he attempted to restructure the Javanese economy to create a market for British manufactured goods, especially cotton, and attempted to break open the subsistence economy of the rural interior by abolishing the system of forced labor (except in Priangan) and requiring peasants to pay a land rent (q.v.) which would require them to earn money by bringing cash crops onto the market. He reduced the role of the traditional aristocracy on Java (see INLANDSCH BESTUUR), abolished the sultanates of Banten and Cirebon (qq.v.), and captured the city of Yogyakarta (q.v.) in 1812, installing a new ruler there. Many of his reforms were based on ideas already in circulation amongst Dutch opponents of VOC policy, such as van Hogendorp (q.v.). He made extensive studies of the natural history and culture of the island, publishing a *History of Java* (2 vols, 1817). In March 1816 he was removed from his post after accusations of corruption. In 1817, after Java was returned to the Dutch, Raffles was appointed British Lieutenant-Governor of Bengkulu (q.v.). He founded Singapore (q.v.) in 1819. See also BRITAIN, Historical links with. [0497, 0498, 0690, 0694]

RAFFLESIA (Rafflesiaceae), genus of parasitic plants, found in Indonesian jungles, of which one, *R. arnoldii,* produces a flower 60 cm across, the largest flower in the world. It is sometimes confused with the unrelated *Amorphophallus* (q.v.). [0938]

RAILWAYS AND TRAMWAYS. Railways were constructed, mainly on Java, from 1873 by both the state railways (Staatsspoorwegen) and eleven private companies, of which the largest was the Semarang-based Nederlandsch-Indische Spoorwegen Maatschappij. Separate small systems also existed in South, West, and North Sumatra and in Aceh. State railways accounted for 1,870 miles of track in 1942, private lines for 531 miles. There were also many Decauville lines, usually two-foot gauge, serving mines, plantations, and industrial installations. Most traffic was short-haul: freight travelled an average of 62 miles, passengers under 19 miles. The rail system fell into decline after 1931, when little new investment was made and much rolling stock and some rails were removed by the Japanese during the occupation. Under the New Order, however, the World Bank has provided aid for a national program of rehabilitation. See also ROADS; SHIPPING. [0042, 0348, 0810]

RAMAYANA. Epic story derived from India and set down in Old Javanese as the *Ramayana Kakawin* by Yogaswari, probably in C.10. Reliefs depicting the story decorate the Hindu temples of Prambanan and Panataran (qq.v.) in Java and many temples in Bali. The story is presented in *wayang kulit, wayang golek* and *wayang wong* (qq.v.) though the celebrated moonlight performances at Prambanan are a recent innovation. As with the Mahabharata (q.v.), episodes from the Ramayana are often used as allegories of contemporary events.

In the story, Prince Rama, his wife Sita, and his brother Laksamana are exiled from their father's kingdom of Ayodhya. As they wander in the forest, Sita is kidnapped by the demon King Rawana who takes her to his palace in Alengka (Ceylon). With the help of a white monkey, Hanuman, Rama discovers Sita's whereabouts and leads a monkey army to rescue her. Reunited, they return to Ayodhya and live, according to some versions, happily ever after. In other versions, however, Rama rejects Sita on suspicion that she may have been unfaithful to him during her captivity. See also MAHABHARATA. [0116, 0157]

RAMI (*Boehmeria nivea* Urticaceae), fibre plant, perhaps native to Sulawesi. It can be used to produce tough cord and extremely hard-wearing, coarse cloth. Attempts at commercial cultivation began in early C.19, but were always hampered by the difficulty of separating the fiber from the other plant materials. When this is done by hand it is a labor-intensive process, but 454 rami processes and machines patented between 1873 and 1900 were unable to make the crop commercial. During World War II both Japan and the United States developed effective processing techniques and the Japanese planted it extensively on Java as a substitute for jute (q.v.) from India. [0245, 0246, 0938]

RANIRI, Nuruddin al- (?–1666), Gujerati Muslim scholar who arrived in Aceh (q.v.) in 1637 and was appalled by what he saw as the mystical heresies being followed at the court of Sultan Iskandar Thani, especially in the writings of Hamzah Fansuri (q.v.) and Syamsuddin of Pasai. After winning over Iskandar Thani, he began to persecute the followers of Hamzah and Syamsuddin and ordered their books to be burnt. He himself, however, composed one of the classics of Malay literature, the *Bustan as-Salatin,* or *Garden of Kings,* which covered the history of Islam as well as recent scientific knowledge. He lost favor under the rule of Iskandar Thani's widow and successor Taj al-Alam and returned to India in 1644.

RASAMALA. Trees of the genus *Altingia* (esp. *A. excelsa* Hamamelidaceae), occurring widely through the archipelago, tapped for their resin or storax for trade to China from perhaps C.6. More recently they have become a major timber tree. [0936, 0938, 0948]

RATTAN (Arecaceae, *rotan*). Climbing rain forest palms of several genera harvested extensively for their strong pliant stems, and preferred to bamboo (q.v.) for pliability, durability, and appearance. Overcollection and the clearing of jungle has steadily reduced supplies and increased prices, but Indonesia still produces around 80% of the world's supply. In October 1986, export of unprocessed rattan was banned in order to encourage local processing; semiprocessed rattan was included in the ban in July 1988. [0262]

RATU ADIL. See JAVA WAR; JOYOBOYO.

REGENTS. See BUPATI.

REINWARDT, Caspar Georg Carl (1773–1854), German-born botanist, appointed in 1816 as director of agriculture, arts, and sciences in the newly-restored Netherlands Indies, where he was responsible for an expansion in medical education and was instrumental in the founding of the botanical gardens (q.v.) at Buitenzorg (Bogor). [0984, 0986, 0987]

RELIGION AND POLITICS. The division between religion and state now common in the West is of relatively recent origin and has little meaning for most of Indonesian history. While it is true to say that rulers and religous leaders have used religion for political ends, and have used politics for religious ends, the distinction is not really valid in societies where every aspect of social organization and behavior was in some respect a matter for religious concern. Religions were inevitably closely associated with the political order and with challenges to it. All the major religions of Indonesia, however, recognize at least some division of responsibility between religious and secular authorities, and the sharpening or blurring of this distinction was often driven by political motives. Traditional rulers found that successively Hinduism, Buddhism, Islam, and Christianity (qq.v.). could be used as buttresses to their rule, either as a means of acquiring allies or to reinforce the loyalty of their subjects (though both Muslims and Christians at times preferred to keep their subject peoples to different religions so that they could be governed under less demanding moral standards). Under the Dutch East Indies Company, Dutch Reformed Protestantism was the established religion and in Minahasa, for instance, people previously converted to Catholicism were arbitrarily declared to be Protestant when the region came under Dutch rule. Freedom of religion was granted in 1818, after the fall of the Company, except where it disturbed public order.

Islam, strongly offended by *kafir* (infidel) rule and with its strong emphasis on the community of Muslims, became an important focus for revolt both against traditional rulers (see ACEH and MINANGKABAU) and against the Dutch (see JAVA WAR). In late C.19, after failing to suppress Islamic radicalism, the colonial authorities adopted suggestions of C. Snouck Hurgronje (q.v.) to 'domesticate' Islam by supporting religious practice, particularly in the area of law (q.v.). A network of government religious officials (*penghulu*) was established to administer Islamic family and property law. Islam also became a vehicle for opposition to the commercial position of the Chinese (see SAREKAT ISLAM).

Independent Indonesia did not become an Islamic state (see ISLAMIC STATE, Demands for). Nor, however, is it wholly secular: not only does the state ideology, Pancasila (q.v.), set down Belief in God as a basic principle of the state but religious affairs are also administered by a Department of Religion, founded 3 January 1946, which was for many years the largest government department. The department was at first entirely Muslim and its primary goal was the promotion of Islam but its political agenda, especially since the official definition of religion was broadened in 1965, has become the promotion not just of Islam (though this still takes a major part of its budget and energies) but of religion (*agama*) in general. The spreading of religion is seen as a task of civilization and initially the department recognized only Islam and Christianity as true religions; it was not until January 1965 that a presidential decree recognized Hinduism, Buddhism, and Confucianism (qq.v.) as official religions. Since 1966, the promotion of religion has had the added purpose of 'immunizing' people against communism and only a tiny proportion of the population is now classed as *belum beragama* (not yet having a religion), though this was achieved partly by allowing animist peoples such as the Dayaks and Toraja (qq.v.) to have their beliefs classified as Hindu. In 1969, President Suharto confirmed the legal right of people to change religions and in the 1960s and early 1970s, there was substantial conversion from Islam to

Christianity and Hinduism in parts of Java. In 1978, however, the Department of Religion issued regulations forbidding proselytization amongst followers of recognized religions and limited the extent to which local religious organizations could receive support from abroad. In 1982, the official percentages of religious adherence were Muslim 88%, Protestant 5.8%, Catholic 2.9%, Hindu 2.0%, and Buddhist 0.9%, but an alternative unofficial estimate gives the figures Islam 77%, Protestantism 11%, Catholicism 4%, Hinduism 3%, Buddhism and Confucianism 0.4%, and Kebatinan (q.v.) 17% (some overlap with other categories). [0813, 1063, 1123]

RENCANA PEMBANGUNAN LIMA TAHUN (REPELITA, Five-Year Development Plan), official title of successive economic plans under the New Order (q.v.). REPELITA I ran from 1969 to 1974 and stressed rehabilitation of the economy after the Guided Economy (q.v.) of Sukarno, increased rice (q.v.) production and the improvement of infrastructure; REPELITA II (1974–79) stressed raising living standards by increasing availability of food, clothing, housing etc; REPELITA III (1979–84) aimed to expand employment by extensive public sector investment and to promote more equitable distribution of income (though it was vague on the latter point) and its aims, dependent on heavy capital inflow, had to be curtailed sharply after the fall in oil (q.v.) prices; and REPELITA IV (1984–89) stressed agriculture and industry. Although the initial inclinations of the New Order's economic policy makers in the Badan Perencanaan Pembangunan Nasional (q.v.), or BAPPENAS, were for economic liberalism, the unrestricted operation of market forces was neither politically acceptable nor economically desirable and successive economic plans have aimed especially at import-substitution industrialization, particularly in fertilizer, cement, and textiles, as well as at the improvement of infrastructure. [0233, 0280]

RENDRA, Willibrordus S. (b.1935), poet and dramatist. Admired initially for his lucid, straightforward use of language in poetry, Rendra is increasingly known for his drama, in which he attempted to adapt the techniques of Western experimental drama to Indonesian conditions and styles. His best known work is *The struggle of the Naga tribe* (1975). See also MALARI. [0177]

RENVILLE AGREEMENT, signed on 17–19 January 1948 aboard the USS *Renville,* anchored in Jakarta Bay, between representatives of the Indonesian Republic and the Netherlands Indies and providing, like the Linggajati Agreement (q.v.), for a peaceful end to the Indonesian-Dutch conflict by merger of Republican and Dutch territories into a federal republic. Whereas the Linggajati Agreement had limited the number of component states of this federation to three, *Renville* opened the possibility for people in Dutch-occupied territories to opt by plebiscite for separate *negara* (federal state) status (see FEDERALISM). On the basis of these states, but excluding the Republic of Indonesia, the Dutch proceeded to establish a Provisional Federal Government (Voorlopige Federale Regering) in 1948. In December 1948 Dutch forces launched a second 'Police Action' (q.v.) to bring Republican territory (but not the Republic) into the federation. See also SUCCESSION. [0563, 0656]

REPUBLIK INDONESIA SERIKAT (RIS, Republic of the United States of Indonesia, also RUSI), formed on 27 December 1949 as a consequence of the Round Table Conference (q.v.). The RIS was a member of the Netherlands Indonesian Union (*Unie*), along with the Kingdom of the Netherlands and guaranteed to consult the Netherlands on matters of common interest such as international debt and foreign investment (qq.v.). It was governed under a prime ministerial system with a bicameral legislature consisting of popular assembly (Dewan Perwakilan Rakyat, q.v.) and a Senate, with two representatives from each of the states (*negara*) and territories (*daerah*) making up the federation. Figurehead president of the federation, elected 16 December 1949, was Sukarno (q.v.). In its fullest form, the federation consisted of 7 *negara*—the Republik Indonesia, founded 17 August 1945; Negara Indonesia Timur (q.v.), formed 24 December 1946, dissolved 17 August 1950; Madura (q.v.), 21 January 1948–9 March 1950; Pasundan (q.v.), 24 April 1948–9 February 1950; Sumatra Timur, 25 December 1947/16 February 1948–17 August 1950, see EAST SUMATRA; Sumatra Selatan, 18 December 1948–9 March 1950, see PALEMBANG; Jawa Timur (East Java), 26 November 1948–9 March 1950—and nine other territories of varying statuses: Banjar; Bangka; Billiton; Riau; Dayak Besar (all called *neo-landschappen,* denoting that they had formerly been directly ruled territories); the capital territory of Jakarta (q.v.); and Kalimantan Barat; Kalimantan Timur; and Kalimantan Tenggara (all federations of *landschappen,* or former *zelfbesturen,* q.v.). Jawa Tengah, Padang in West Sumatra and Pulau Weh (Sabang) off Aceh had indefinite status and were not counted amongst the federation's members and were not represented in the RIS Senate. The Republik Indonesia, with borders as at the signing of the Renville Agreement (q.v.) held one-third of the seats in the federal parliament, but in fact dominated the federation from the start, with the remaining negara having, with two or three exceptions, little popular support or administrative strength. With the exception of the Republik Indonesia, the federal states were dissolved in the course of 1950, and the RIS was dissolved into the Republik Indonesia on 17

August 1950. See also FEDERALISM; SUCCESSION. [0563, 0634, 0656, 0916]

REPUBLIK MALUKU SELATAN (RMS, Republic of the South Moluccas), proclaimed on 25 April 1950 by Christian Ambonese led by NIT (q.v.) Justice Minister C.R.S. Soumokil and dissatisfied with the incorporation of the Negara Indonesia Timur (q.v.) in the Republik Indonesia Serikat (q.v.). Fighting took place on Ambon and Buru (qq.v.) from July to November 1950 and continued on Seram (q.v.) until 1956, though Soumokil was not captured until 1963. Moluccan exiles in the Netherlands have continued to campaign for the RMS, but their energy has been diminished by recent agreements permitting the exiles to return to Indonesia without risk. See also KONINKLIJK NEDERLANDSCH INDISCH LEGER. [0506, 0897, 0907]

RESIMEN PARA KOMANDO ANGKATAN DARAT (RPKAD, Army Paracommando Regiment), was formed in 1956 as part of the army command's effort to reduce the power of regional commanders by creating a mobile strike force under the direct authority of the center. Under Col. Sarwo Edhie (1927–1989) the RPKAD played a major role in the massacres of 1965–66 (q.v.) in Central Java. Under the names KOPASSANDHA (Komando Pasukan Sandi Yudha, Secret Warfare Unit Command) and KOPASSUS (Komando Pasukan Khusus, Special Unit Command), it later played a major role in the suppression of dissent in Irian and East Timor (qq.v.) and in the so-called 'mysterious killings' of 1982–83. See also ARMY; BANDITRY. [0663, 0669]

RETOOLING. See MANIFESTO POLITIK.

REVENUE FARMS. See PACHT.

REVOLUTION. The years 1945–49 are commonly referred to as the 'Revolution' (*Revolusi*), reflecting both the usage of the time and the perception that the violent change from colonial rule to independence was indeed revolutionary. Especially during Guided Democracy, Sukarno (qq.v.) maintained that the Revolution had not been completed in 1949 with the formal transfer of sovereignty by the Dutch and that not only did the province of Irian (q.v.) have to be recovered but Indonesia's social, political, and economic order had to be transformed. Under the New Order (q.v.), the rhetoric of continuing revolution was soon dropped and the period 1945–49 came increasingly to be referred to as the War of Independence (*perang kemerdekaan*), partly to emphasize the role of the army (q.v.) in securing independence and partly to avoid the suggestion that revolutions might be desirable events. At the same time, Western scholars observing continuities between the colonial period and independent, especially New Order, Indonesia, have often argued that the extent of the transformation in 1945–49 was insufficient to justify the term 'revolution.' [0628, 0656]

RHINOCEROS. Both the one-horned Javan rhinoceros (*Rhinoceros sondaicus*) and the two-horned Sumatran rhinoceros (*Dicerorhinus sumatrensis*), once common, have been hunted close to extinction. The Javan rhino is now restricted to Ujung Kulon (q.v.), the Sumatran to small pockets in southern Sumatra and Burma. Most parts of the animal were used medicinally, bezoar stones (q.v.) being most highly prized. Poachers today usually take only the horn. Many roads (q.v.) on Java are said to follow ancient rhino tracks through dense jungle. [0943, 0945]

RIAU (Rhio), sultanate established on Bintan island, south of Singapore, by Sultan Mahmud I of Melaka (q.v.)

after the fall of his capital to the Portuguese in 1511. It controlled a fluctuating territory in the Riau archipelago, on the coast of Sumatra and on the Malay peninsula, and derived its income as an entrepôt. The capital shifted frequently between the Riau archipelago and Johor on the peninsular mainland, and in 1641 the kingdom joined the Dutch in expelling the Portuguese from Melaka. After the assassination of Sultan Mahmud II (r. 1685–99), Riau was riven by a prolonged civil war. The *bendahara* (chief minister) of the kingdom, Abdul Jalil Riayat Syah (d.1721), seized the throne and with the help of his able younger brother Tun Mahmud, attempted to concentrate trade at Riau. He quickly faced rebellions in Palembang (q.v.) and Perak and amongst the Bajau (q.v.) and he was eventually deposed in 1718 and later murdered (see SIAK). Bugis (q.v.) mercenaries then gained control of the hereditary office of *Yang di Pertuan Muda,* loosely analogous to the position of Shogun in Tokugawa Japan, and effectively dominated the state until it was occupied by the Dutch in 1784. The last independent ruler, Mahmud Riayat Syah III (r. 1761–1812) attempted to play off Bugis, Malay, Dutch, and British interests but was unable to end the internal chaos. In 1819 the British obtained the island of Singapore (q.v.), in the heart of the kingdom, and the Anglo-Dutch Treaty of 1824 (q.v.) definitively divided the former territory of Riau between the two colonial powers. [0434, 0494, 0520, 0722]

RICE (*Oryza sativa* Poaceae). Wild rice occurs naturally in mainland Southeast Asia and it was cultivated there perhaps as early as 6000 B.C. It appears, however, to have entered the archipelago much later, the earliest known cultivation being at Ulu Leang in Sulawesi around 3500 B.C., probably because the early varieties were highly sensitive to climatic change (see MIGRATIONS). It was probably a staple food of Srivijaya (q.v.)

but does not appear on the reliefs of Borobudur (q.v.), suggesting that other staples, perhaps including millet, were in use. Rice was certainly well established by the mid C.13, but even as late as C.19 had not reached its current status of preferred food for most of the people of the archipelago. In late C.18 and early C.19, the colonial government sponsored a major expansion of wet rice agriculture, with the expansion of irrigation and the clearing of land and in 1905 began a sustained program to breed improved varieties. Increasing rice production was also a major aim of the Japanese occupation government in World War II.

It was initially hoped that production would increase with independence, and Java actually exported rice to India in 1946, but in the 1950s and 1960s production failed to keep pace with population growth and imports increased, despite the introduction of new varieties developed in the Philippines by the International Rice Research Institute. Promotion of rice production became a major program of the New Order (q.v.) and self-sufficiency by 1973 was an aim of the first Five-Year Plan (REPELITA, q.v.). The Green Revolution (q.v.) in fact achieved a 47% production increase in five years, but self-sufficiency was not attained until 1982. See also AGRICULTURAL INVOLUTION. [0037, 0213, 0230, 0234, 0236, 0238, 0241, 0245–0247, 0251, 0255, 0256, 0260, 0266, 0268, 0365, 0411]

ROADS have naturally played a relatively small role in long-distance communication in the archipelago; even within islands geographical barriers such as forests, mountains, and swamps tended to make water-borne communication far more important than overland links. The first road to run the length of Java was laid by Daendels (q.v.) in early C.19, and the colonial authorities began a trans-Sumatra road in C.20. Responsibility for roads was one of the tasks devolved to the provinces in 1931 (see DECENTRALIZATION), but by the end of the colonial era Indonesia was still relatively underprovided with asphalted roads. Between 1939 and 1959, the length of asphalted roads decreased by about 20%, due to lack of investment, while the number of vehicles on those roads doubled. Plans for the Trans-Sumatra Highway were revived in the early 1960s, but extensive roadbuilding did not resume until after 1966, when the World Bank assisted in a number of highway rehabilitation projects. The Trans-Sumatra and Trans-Sulawesi Highways are now completed (though some sections need major upgrading) and highways across Kalimantan and Irian are under construction. The fact that Indonesia drives on the left hand side of the road (unlike the Netherlands) is attributed (perhaps apocryphally) to Raffles (q.v.). See also RAILWAYS; RHINOCEROS. [0042, 0810]

RŌMUSHA (Japanese, 'laborer'), forced laborers drafted from October 1943 by the Japanese occupation authorities especially on Java for work on defence and other projects both on the island and in many parts of Southeast Asia. Perhaps 200,000-to-500,000 such laborers were taken to work in appalling conditions with high death rates. Only 70,000 are known to have survived and many were left stranded in various parts of the region by the end of World War II. The social dislocation caused by the removal of rōmusha from Javanese society contributed both to the hatred of officials involved in recruiting and to the sense of crisis at the end of the war. The role of Sukarno (q.v.) in recruiting was regarded by some as constituting a war crime. See also JAPANESE OCCUPATION OF INDONESIA; LABOR. [0607, 0609, 0611, 0615, 0617, 0623]

RONGGOWARSITO, Raden Ngabei (1802–73), court poet of Surakarta (q.v.) and author of the *Paramayoga* and the *Pustakaraja Purwa* which describe a mythical history of Java from the time of Adam to the year 730 AJ (see CALENDARS). He is generally regarded as the last of the great Javanese court poets. [0486]

ROSELLA (*Hibiscus sabdariffa* Malvaceae). Probably African in origin, the rosella was originally introduced for its sour, edible fruit but has been cultivated extensively since the 1920s for sacking. The Japanese planted it extensively on Java during World War II as a substitute for jute (q.v.) from India. [0245, 0246, 0938]

ROTI, island near Timor (q.v.) whose people are noted especially for their extensive use of the lontar (q.v.) palm for food and manufacture. The VOC (q.v.) signed a treaty with local rulers in 1662 in order to obtain a supply base and a possible refuge in its operations in the region. Extensive conversion to Christianity took place in C.18, and during C.19 the Dutch encouraged Christian Rotinese to settle around Kupang on Timor to create a buffer zone against the Timorese. Rotinese also moved extensively into administrative posts. [0022, 1011]

ROUND TABLE CONFERENCE. Following the Rum-van Roijen Agreement of 7 May 1949 in which the Dutch and the Indonesian Republic agreed to work towards a settlement on the basis of the Renville Agreement (q.v.), a Round Table Conference took place in The Hague from 23 August to 2 November 1949 to prepare a formal transfer of sovereignty to a fully independent Indonesia, draft a constitution for the new state, and prepare an agreement of Union between the new state and the Netherlands. The Conference was attended by delegates of the Republik Indonesia, of the Bijeenkomst voor Federale Overleg (Federal Consultative Meeting), consisting of representatives of the various negara and daerah (see FEDERALISM), and of the Dutch, with a number of minority representatives attending as 'advisors' to the Dutch delegation. The Conference did not agree on the issue of Indonesia's international debt (q.v.), which was sent to arbitration, or on Dutch retention of West New Guinea (Irian, q.v.), which was omitted from the final settlement. See also REPUBLIK INDONESIA SERIKAT. [0563, 0656]

RUBBER (*Hevea brasiliensis* Euphorbiaceae). Of Brazilian origin, rubber was not cultivated in Indonesia until the 1880s, when plantation production began in East Sumatra (q.v.). Production began to expand dramatically in C.20, and the plantations were joined by numerous smallholders, especially in central and southern Sumatra. Oversupply during the Depression led to an international production agreement which the colonial government implemented very much at the expense of smallholders, but the industry survived to become a major economic pillar for the Republic in Sumatra during the National Revolution. The cutting off of rubber by the Japanese occupation led to the development of synthetic rubber in the United States, but this did not have a serious impact on rubber markets until 1960. In 1980, Indonesia signed a further international rubber agreement intended to stabilize prices. Since the outbreak of AIDS, the rubber industry has benefited considerably from the increased demand for rubber gloves and condoms. On 1 January 1989 Indonesia banned the export of some categories of raw rubber to promote domestic processing. [0231, 0233, 0245, 0246, 0582, 0735, 0938]

RUKUN TETANGGA (lit. neighborhood basis or foundation), administrative division below village level, formed initially during the Japanese occupation as *tonari-gumi* and reestablished in 1954, they are especially important for social control and the marshalling of popular participation in government projects. [0615, 0786, 0815]

RUMPHIUS (Georg Everhard Rumpf, ?1628–1702), born in Germany (q.v.), recruited by the VOC (q.v.) and in 1653 posted to Ambon (q.v.), pioneered botanical investigation of the archipelago with his posthumously published *Herbarium Amboinense* (6 v., 1741–1750), much of which he completed after he fell blind in 1670. He also devised for the Ambonese an improved method of processing sago (q.v.). See also UPAS. [0983]

S

SABANG TO MERAUKE, From. The symbolic dimensions of the Indonesian Republic. Sabang is a port town on Pulo Weh off the northern tip of Sumatra, Merauke is in the far southeastern corner of Irian. Used during the Revolution as a simple affirmation of national unity, the phrase later became an assertion especially of Indonesia's rejection of Dutch control of Irian (q.v.), or West New Guinea.

SABILILLAH ('Way of God'), auxiliary wing of the Hizbullah (q.v.), but often forming front line units in its own right. Many units joined the Darul Islam (q.v.) in 1948. [0608, 0615, 0632]

SADIKIN, Ali (b.1927), Marines commander, appointed by Sukarno as governor of Jakarta (q.v.) in April 1966, after a brief period as Minister of Sea Communications in early 1965. Sadikin's energetic rule transformed the face of the city: infrastructure such as highways was built and commercial construction was encouraged. His ruthlessness towards those who stood in the way of a showcase city (becak [q.v.] drivers, kampung dwellers, etc.) was somewhat balanced by his efforts to provide services such as public transport, electricity, and recreation which much of the population could use. His legalization of prostitution (q.v.) and use of lotteries as a source of city revenues—29% of total city revenue in 1968, see GAMBLING—aroused hostility in Islamic circles, but he retired in 1977, one of the most popular figures in the New Order and his association with the dissident groups who produced the Petition of Fifty (q.v.) has been a major source of political concern to the government. See also LEGAL AID. [0495, 0675]

SAFFLOWER (*Carthamus tinctorius* Asteraceae). Originally from the Middle East but introduced early into Indonesia, safflower was grown widely in drier regions for its oil and dye. Safflower products were traded from East Java in C.17 and from Bali, Sulawesi and Sumbawa (qq.v.) in C.19. [0245, 0246, 0938]

SAGO (*Metroxylon rumphii* and *M. sagu* and other palms, Arecaceae), palm trees found widely in swamps, especially in eastern Indonesia, where flour prepared from the pith of the trunk is a staple food. Wild and domestic varieties are indistinguishable and sago was seldom an object of trade, being mainly consumed by its producers. Only in early C.19 was sago briefly in commercial demand for use in sizing cotton, until displaced by maize (q.v.) starch. [0265]

SAILENDRA, a powerful family of Buddhist rulers who arose in Central Java (q.v.) in mid C.8 and adopted the title *maharaja* (see INDIA, Historical links with). Their court became a major center of Buddhist scholarship and they were responsible for the construction of Borobudur (q.v.). Although they almost certainly ruled through a diffuse system of alliances and vassalages, they promoted a largely Indian doctrine of divine kingship. Through intermarriage, Sailendras also came to rule Srivijaya (q.v.) in late C.9 after they had been displaced on Java.

SALEH, Chaerul. See CHAERUL SALEH.

SALEH, Raden (Raden Saleh Bustaman, 1814–80). After showing interest in Western culture, especially painting, Raden Saleh was sponsored by Governor-General van der Capellan to study art in the Netherlands. He came under the influence of Delacroix and lived in Europe for 20 years, becoming royal painter at the Dutch court. On his return to Java, he was in some demand as a painter of landscapes and portraits. He is recognized as the first Indonesian to paint in a nontraditional way, but had little influence on later artistic developments. [0116, 0672]

SALT. As an essential for life, salt was manufactured from sea water from very early times along the coasts of Indonesia, and from mineral sources in a few inland regions; in Grobogan in Central Java, salty mud volcanoes are tapped, while the Dani (q.v.) in Irian extract it by soaking palm and banana leaves in saltwater seeps, drying and burning them. The southern coastal regions of Madura (q.v.) and north coast of East Java, however, have long been the main areas of salt production, with local rulers traditionally farming out *pachten* (q.v.) to Chinese businessmen. In 1813 Raffles (q.v.) established a government monopoly on salt production and sale, though the operation was still run through pachten. In 1904 the trade in salt was placed under a government production and selling agency, the Zout-Regie, whose operations were combined with those of the state opium (q.v.) monopoly. The salt monopoly was abolished in 1957, state salt works becoming a formal state enterprise (q.v.) in 1960. [0519]

SAMA RASA SAMA RATA (lit. 'same feeling, same level'), term coined by Mas Marco Kartodikromo (q.v.) in 1918 to express the egalitarian element in nationalist thought. It was modern socialist in its inspiration but reflected traditional ideas of a 'golden age' of justice and prosperity. See also JOYOBOYO. [0592]

SAMIN MOVEMENT, peasant movement founded around 1890 by Surontiko Samin (d.1914) in the Blora area of Central Java. Saminists attracted Dutch attention by refusing to pay taxes, but their beliefs were broader, encompassing egalitarianism, individual ownership of land, and a 'religion of Adam' which apparently predated Hindu and Muslim influence on Java (see ASLI). Samin was exiled in 1907 but the movement survived until at least the 1960s. [0363]

SANDALWOOD (*Santalum album,* Santalaceae, *cendana*), small parasitic, evergreen tree, probably native to Indonesia, cultivated for its aromatic heartwood and root, which are most fragrant in trees growing in dry, rocky soils. Sandalwood occurs extensively from East Java to Timor and was exported to China and India for incense, medicines, perfumery, and cosmetics. [0751, 0938]

SANGIË OR SANGIR ISLANDS. See MINAHASA.

SANTRI, term originally referring to a student of any religion (hence pesantren, q.v.) but now commonly used, after Geertz, for one of the broad sociocultural groupings or aliran (q.v.) of modern Java, *viz.,* the so-called pious or orthodox Muslims, also called *putihan* or white ones, whose religion contains relatively fewer or no influences from the pre-Muslim traditions of Java. Like the expression 'Outer Islands' (q.v.), the term is immensely useful for general discussion but has serious flaws when used for detailed analysis, largely because the term has been taken from Geertz's East Java context and applied to many different cases where Muslims of different degrees of orthodoxy face each other. See also ISLAM. [1005, 1018]

SAREKAT ISLAM (SI, Islamic Association) founded in 1909 as Sarekat Dagang Islam (Islamic Traders' Association) by Kyai Samanhudi (1868-?), a batik (q.v.) manufacturer and merchant from Surakarta, along with R.M. Tirtoadisuryo and Haji Umar Said Tjokroaminoto (q.v.), both priyayi (q.v.) involved in the batik trade. The initial aim of the association was to combat Chinese penetration of the batik industry, and SDI sponsored cooperatives amongst indigenous traders and organized boycotts of the Chinese. On 10 September 1912 the SDI took the name Sarekat Islam and adopted a broader political program challenging the colonial government, while continuing its promotion of cooperatives and publishing the nationalist newspaper *Oetoesan Hindia* (*Indies Courier*).

SI's expression of discontent with the colonial order won it wide popular support, and in 1919 it claimed a membership of 2,000,000, though its practical following was always far smaller. Its program, however, was confused. It aimed at the promotion of Islam and of commercial spirit amongst Indonesians, but it was also influenced by the anticapitalism of the ISDV (q.v.), many of whose members, including Semaun, also joined SI. At its first national congress in June 1916, SI promised cooperation with the colonial government for the good of the country, and in 1918 SI leaders accepted seats in the Volksraad (q.v.), but already in 1917 the party had condemned 'sinful' (*i.e.*, exploitative and foreign) capitalism and in 1919 a secret branch within the SI, called the Afdeling B (Section B) was implicated in subversive activities in West Java. Arrests and surveillance by the colonial authorities followed and much of SI's following fell away.

Although relatively conservative urban traders initially dominated SI, more radical Muslim kyai from the villages together with members of the ISDV and later the PKI (q.v.) had gradually gained more influence, sharpening the contrast between SI's Islamic and Marxist wings. At the Surabaya congress in October 1921, Abdul Muis (q.v.) and Agus Salim forced a break with the PKI by insisting that SI members could belong to no other party. PKI leaders left the central SI in 1922 and local branches divided into 'Red' and 'White' SI according to their allegiances, the Red branches later calling themselves Sarekat Rakyat (People's Unions) and affiliating with the PKI. This infighting further damaged SI's support and by 1923 when Tjokroaminoto transformed the SI rump into the Partai Sarekat Islam Indonesia (q.v.) it was only a minor political force. [0563, 0566, 0578, 0592]

SAREKAT RAKYAT. See SAREKAT ISLAM.

SASAKS. See LOMBOK.

SAVU (Sawu), small island in Nusatenggara. As on Roti (q.v.) the economy was based on tapping lontar (q.v.) palms. The Dutch signed a treaty with local rulers in 1756. Savunese were extensively recruited by the VOC (q.v.) as soldiers, and Savunese Christian migrants formed much of the elite in Sumba (q.v.) and Dutch Timor in C.19 and 20. The island was devastated by smallpox (q.v.) in 1869. [1011, 1151]

SAWAH. Wet rice field. See RICE.

SAWITO KARTOWIBOWO (b.1932) prepared a series of documents in 1976, some of which were signed by such eminent figures as Hatta, Hamka (qq.v.), Cardinal Darmojuwono, and T.B. Simatupang, criticizing alleged failures in national development under the New Order and calling on Suharto (q.v.) to resign and to hand power to Hatta. Though Sawito had no institutional base and no prospect of success, his challenge was unexpected and unwelcome. The affair was described as a 'constitutional coup' by government spokesmen and in 1978 Sawito was convicted of subversion (q.v.). [0668]

SAYAP KIRI (Left Wing), semiformal coalition of left-wing parties, the Partai Sosialis, the Partai Buruh and the PKI (qq.v.), formed in December 1946 and strengthened partly by the presence of secret PKI members in the first two parties. The Sayap Kiri formed the basis of the Syahrir and Amir Syarifuddin (qq.v.) cabinets and pursued a policy of negotiating with the Dutch while building up the Republic's armed forces. Under Syarifuddin, special favor was given to semiregular forces such as the PESINDO (q.v.). In opposition from January 1948, the parties turned sharply against all negotiations and coalesced in February into the Front Demokrasi Rakyat (q.v.). See also DIPLOMASI AND PERJUANGAN. [0563, 0656]

SCANDINAVIA, Historical links with. The Danish East India Company traded to Java in C.17, maintaining posts at Japara and Banten (qq.v.) and in the same period a great many Scandinavians served as officials and soldiers with the Dutch East Indies Company (q.v.). The great Swedish botanist Carl Linné (Linnaeus, 1701–78) worked with Indies plants in Leiden in 1735–37 and was the first to persuade a banana (q.v.) to fruit in northern Europe. A number of his students, notably Pehr Osbeck (1725–1805), Carl Peter Thunberg (1743–1832), and Clas Fredrick Hornstedt made important botanical collections on Java, in some cases with the cooperation of the Swedish East India Company. See also LANGE, M.J. [0744]

SCOUTING. The Nederlandsch-Indische Padvinders Vereeniging (Netherlands Indies Scouting Association) was formed in 1917 as a multiracial nonpolitical organization along the lines of Baden Powell's organization. Later, however, exclusively Indonesian scouting organizations, the Kepanduan Bangsa Indonesia and Persatuan Pandu Islam were formed, especially on Sumatra, as an adjunct to the nationalist movement. Many political organizations had affiliated scouting groups, which numbered 76 by 1960. In 1961, Sukarno (q.v.) forced all scouting groups to merge into the Pramuka (Praja Muda Karana). In 1978 Pramuka had a membership of 7 million.

SCRIPTS. See WRITING SYSTEMS.

SEINENDAN, semimilitary youth corps established by the Japanese occupation (q.v.) authorities on Java on 29 April 1943 to mobilize young men aged 14–25 for the war effort, especially in urban areas. Its duties included patrol and guard duties and many Seinendan units later became the basis for badan perjuangan (q.v.). See also KEIBODAN. [0615, 0617, 0656]

SEMAR, one of the clowns (*punakawan*) of traditional Javanese *wayang* (q.v.). Foolish and ugly, he is also immensely wise and powerful, representing in some views the strength of the common people. Though he appears in the Indian-origin Mahabharata (q.v.), he appears to be an indigenous tradition and is sometimes identified with President Suharto (q.v.). See also SUPERSEMAR. [0116, 0680, 0772]

SENTRAL ORGANISASI BURUH SELURUH INDONESIA (SOBSI, All-Indonesia Federation of Labor

Organizations), founded November 1946 and for much of the Revolution the only such coordinating body for labor unions (q.v.). Though never formally affiliated with the PKI (q.v.), it was influenced by the party from its foundation and was a part of the broad communist front from 1950, when Nyono Prawiro became president. Although a federation of unions, including SARBUPRI (plantation workers), SBG (sugar industry workers), and SARBUKSI (forest workers), it regarded members of its constituent unions as direct SOBSI members. It was estimated to control 50–60% of organized labor, but was shadowed in every field by noncommunist unions such as those affiliated with SOKSI (q.v.), which made the organization of strike activity difficult. SOBSI was banned in 1966. [0338, 0822]

SENTRAL ORGANISASI KARYAWAN SELURUH INDONESIA (SOKSI, All-Indonesia Federation of Employee Organizations), trade union federation which grew out of the Badan Kerja Sama (q.v.) and worked as a rival to SOBSI (q.v.) especially on army-controlled plantations. By 1963 it had 146 member organizations, claimed 7-½ million members and was one of the core organizations of Golkar (q.v.). In 1973 it was absorbed into the FBSI (q.v.). See also KARYAWAN; LABOR UNIONS. [0338, 0686]

SERAM (Ceram), island in central Maluku (q.v.). The original inhabitants, generally called Alfurs (q.v.), were slash-and-burn agriculturalists, sago (q.v.) being a major source of food, but from C.17 were drawn into limited trade with the Dutch and other Europeans. Coastal communities began to convert to Christianity and Islam in this period. The island was drawn into the Dutch sphere of influence by its proximity to Ambon (q.v.) but until C.19 Dutch involvement was limited to periodic hongi (q.v.) patrols. After independence, the jungles of Seram became a last refuge for guerrillas of the RMS (q.v.). [0019, 0512]

SERDANG, sultanate in East Sumatra (q.v.), purchased by the Dutch from Siak (q.v.) in 1884. [0528]

SERUNAI (Arabic *zurna,* also known as *saronen* and *slompret*), the traditional oboe of the archipelago, usually employing a mouthplate or pirouette and blown using circular breathing. It spread to Indonesia from the Middle East in C.14–15 and was used to add a melody line to gamelan (q.v.) on Java as well as taking a major part in the traditional ensembles of Sumatra. Its use has now declined. See also MUSIC. [0122]

SETIABUDI. See INDISCHE PARTIJ.

SEX, Political significance of. Until the arrival of Islam, sexual prowess was commonly an attribute of political power, both because rulers could seize or otherwise acquire sexual partners (see MARRIAGE, Political significance of) and because local understanding of Tantric doctrines intimately linked intercourse with the release of energy. The *lingga,* or phallic monument, was an important token of rulership. Prolific sexual activity could be both a sign of abundant power and a wasteful dissipation of power, and the downfall of kingdoms was held to be associated with a rise in licentiousness. Islam and Christianity regarded sexual promiscuity as morally wrong, rather than a waste of energy, though the burden of chastity was placed more heavily on women (q.v.) than on men, encouraging the rise of professional prostitution (q.v.) on the one hand and varying degrees of seclusion of 'respectable' women on the other.

Only in C.20, however, did sexual scandal in the contemporary sense emerge. Colonial society in Batavia (q.v.) was shaken by revelations of homosexuality in the 1930s, and during Guided Democracy (q.v.) Sukarno's sexual activity was widely deplored by strict Christians and Muslims. Some Western observers argued that Sukarno was simply behaving as a pre-Muslim ruler and described the tall national monument (Monas) in central Jakarta as a *lingga*. Accusations of gross licentiousness among members of the left-wing women's organization GERWANI (q.v.) were used in 1965–66 to help discredit the PKI (q.v.), while under the New Order rumors of marital infidelity amongst members of the ruling elite are taken by some as a sign of moral exhaustion. [0483] See also PALAPA.

SHAHBANDAR, senior official, often of foreign descent, in charge of port and trade affairs in traditional states of the archipelago. See also PORTS. [0434, 0478]

'SHARED POVERTY,' term coined by Clifford Geertz to describe what he saw as social arrangements which discouraged the formation of capital and the development of commercial elites in Javanese villages by having the wealthy provide income-earning opportunities to the poor. According to Clifford Geertz (q.v.), 'under the pressure of increasing numbers and limited resources, Javanese village society did not bifurcate, as did that of so-many other "underdeveloped" nations, into a group of large landlords and a group of oppressed near serfs. Rather it maintained a comparatively high degree of social and economic homogeneity by dividing the economic pie into a steadily increasing number of minute pieces, a process to which I have referred elsewhere as "shared poverty"' (1963, p.97). A characteristic institution of shared poverty is the open harvest, in which all can participate and receive a part of what they gather.

Debate on shared poverty, which forms an integral

part of Geertz's idea of agricultural involution (q.v.), has focused on the extent and significance of social differentiation in rural Java. Extensive landholdings are absent, but there is a sharp contrast between landed peasants (especially village officials) and others (see LAND). The practices Geertz identifies as promoting shared poverty, moreover, seem to be under constant challenge by wealthier farmers attempting to increase their share of village wealth. See also CLASS ANALYSIS; DESA. [0229, 0244]

SHELL, ROYAL DUTCH. See 'KONINKLIJKE'; OIL.

SHIPPING. From early times until C.17, there was a large indigenous shipping industry in the Indonesian archipelago. Vessels of up to 500 tonnes were built of teak (q.v.) and sailed the trade routes of the region. The term 'junk', later used for Chinese vessels, derives from the Javanese *jong*. After C.17, the size of locally-built vessels, generally called *prau* (*perahu*), declined to 100 tonnes or less.

In 1825, a steam ship called the *van der Capellan* was built in Surabaya (q.v.) to provide a regular government-funded postal service (q.v.) from Java to other islands, but in 1864–65 the mail contract was awarded to a private British-owned firm, the Netherlands Indies Steam Navigation Co. The NISN had a virtual monopoly of interisland shipping until 1890, when it lost the mail contract to the Dutch-owned Koninklijk Paketvaart Maatschappij (q.v) or KPM. With the opening of the Suez canal in 1869, regular steam ship services to the Netherlands were provided by the Stoomvaart Maatschappij Nederland from 1870.

In C.20, interisland shipping was dominated by the KPM, though there was some scope for small operators (the so-called 'mosquito fleet'), to run feeder services to the major KPM lines. In 1935, the KPM founded the

Celebes Kustvaart Maatschappij to meet competition from these feeder services. Under the 1936 Shipping Law, only East Sumatra (q.v.) was opened to foreign carriers, and was serviced primarily by firms from Singapore (q.v.) and Penang.

Interisland shipping declined dramatically during World War II with Japanese requisition of ships and destruction of vessels by Allied submarines. From early 1947 the Dutch navy blockaded Republican regions to prevent the export of produce allegedly originating from Dutch-owned plantations. At independence, control of interisland shipping was a major item on the Republic's economic agenda, and plans were laid for a state shipping enterprise which would exclude the KPM. The Central Shipowning Authority (Pemilikan Pusat Kapal-Kapal, PEPUSKA) was formed on 6 September 1950 to take over government-owned feeder services and to purchase vessels for lease to indigenous competitors of the KPM (see INDONESIANIZATION). On 28 April 1952, Pelayaran Nasional Indonesia (PELNI, Indonesian National Shipping Company) took over the assets of PEPUSKA and soon began to run vessels in direct competition with the KPM. By 1956, PELNI carried about 25% of total interisland tonnage, though an important part of this was government cargoes.

The seizure of KPM assets on 3 December 1957, officially ratified on 10 December, removed important competition for PELNI, but commercial shipping declined on the whole during Guided Democracy as plantation production diminished, infrastructure deteriorated, and trading operations came increasingly into the hands of military business operations (q.v.). By March 1963, one-third of the commercial interisland fleet was said to be in the hands of the armed forces, both for military purposes and for the military trading operations. Rehabilitation of interisland shipping, especially of ports (q.v.), was a priority in the New Order's first Five-Year Plan. In 1984, the government banned ship purchases from abroad in order to encourage the local ship-building; the local industry, however, was unable to meet demand and the ban was partially lifted in 1988. [0344–0346, 0349]

SIAK (Siak Sri Indrapura, not to be confused with Indrapura, q.v.), kingdom in Sumatra founded by Raja Kecil, a Minangkabau who revolted against Sultan Abdul Jalil Riayat Syah of Riau (q.v.), partly on the grounds that Abdul Jalil's succession was illegal, partly because of Abdul Jalil's attempts to draw trade from the Sumatra coast to Riau. Kecil deposed Abdul Jalil and killed the Sultan's brother Tun Mahmud in 1718, but was driven back to Sumatra by Bugis forces. In C.18, however, Siak became a powerful regional state on the east coast of Sumatra, controlling the sultanate of Deli, Langkat, and Serdang (qq.v.). The Dutch signed a political contract with the Sultan in 1858, on the strength of which they seized control of these northern dependencies. The last Sultan, Ismail, was forced to abdicate in 1864.

SIAM, Historical links with. Extensive trading contact between Siam and Indonesia began in C.13 with the export of Thai ceramics (q.v.), and for the next four centuries Siam was part of the general trading world of the archipelago, exporting rice, tin, iron, sugar, and cloth. In C.17, the kingdom of Ayudhya extended its influence far down the Malay peninsula and onto the east coast of Sumatra, establishing a tributary relationship with some local kingdoms which was expressed in the sending of a *bunga mas,* or golden flower, to the Thai ruler. See also SOUTH EAST ASIA LEAGUE. [0563, 0656, 0663]

SILIWANGI, reputed first king of Pajajaran (q.v.). His name was later applied to the West Java division of the

Indonesian army (q.v.), formed in May 1946. Shaped by its first commander, A.H. Nasution (q.v.), the Siliwangi was the most Westernized and conventional division of the army during the War of Independence. It was unable to prevent the Dutch from overrunning much of West Java in the first 'Police Action' in 1947 and after the signing of the Renville Agreement (q.v.) 22,000 Siliwangi troops retreated from guerrilla strongholds in West Java to Republican Central Java, where they became a major pillar of the Hatta (q.v.) government and took part in the suppression of the Madiun Affair (q.v.). [0663]

SILK was produced in Wajo' (q.v.) in south Sulawesi and northern Sumatra (see PASAI) from perhaps C.13 and was for a time exported to India. Production declined, however, in C.17 with the growing export of fine silk from China. The Dutch attempted to establish the cultivation of silk on Java after 1700, but without success. In 1934, Japanese entrepreneurs established a small industry in Minahasa (q.v.), exporting cocoons to Japan for processing. Since the 1960s production has revived in Soppeng (South Sulawesi). [0028, 0454]

SINGAPORE, port city on an island at the southern tip of the Malay Peninsula, part of the kingdom of Riau (q.v.) until C.19. In 1819 Raffles (q.v.) founded a British settlement there. Exempt from customs duties (state revenues came largely from a lucrative opium monopoly) and protected from piracy by the British navy, Singapore grew rapidly as a major trade center for the archipelago, facing little competition from the Dutch, whose attentions were focused on Java and the Cultivation System (qq.v.). From the 1880s the Dutch, concerned over the concentration of trade on Singapore introduced a variety of measures (*e.g.*, preferential tariffs) to encourage direct shipments to Europe. Singapore's influence was reduced, though it remained, along with Penang, the principal port for Sumatra.

From 1921, the British naval base in Singapore became a central element in Dutch defence policy in the Indies, and the fall of Singapore to Japanese forces in February 1942 made the loss of the Netherlands Indies inevitable. During the Indonesian Revolution, trade in plantation products and opium to Singapore was a major source of finance for the Republic, especially on Sumatra. From 1950 however, Indonesian governments sought once more to direct trade away from Singapore. See also BATAM; PORTS; SHIPPING.

SINGOSARI, kingdom in eastern Java founded in 1222 by Ken Angrok (q.v.). It marked the end of the division of Java which followed the rule of Airlangga (q.v.) and the start of period of rich cultural development on Java, especially the closer blending of Hindu-Buddhism and local folk religion. The last ruler of Singosari, Kertanegara (1268–92), annexed Bali and Madura (qq.v.) and sought to expand his rule to parts of Kalimantan and Sumatra (see JAMBI). After envoys from Kublai Khan demanded that Singosari accept closer Chinese suzerainty, Kertanegara expelled them from the kingdom in 1289. In 1292, while the Singosari army was on its way to Sumatra on a military expedition, Kertanegara was deposed and killed by Prince Jayakatwang of Kediri (q.v.). See also CHINA, Historical links with; MAJAPAHIT.

SISAL, fibrous plants of the genus *Agave* (Agavaceae), Mexican in origin, introduced probably in C.17 but commercially cultivated only after the development of industrial processing machinery in late C.19. [0245, 0246, 0938]

SISINGAMANGARAJA, a Batak (q.v.) divine king who appeared probably in C.16 and was said to be reincarnated in a line of kings, all of the same name, down to Sisingamangaraja XII, who was expelled by the Dutch from the Batak country in 1883 and later killed. The role of these kings is not altogether clear, but their function seems to have been more spiritual than directly political; they were guardians of the relationship between the Batak realm and the outside world, expressed in terms of symbolic vassalship to Aceh (q.v.). In 1825, however, Muslim Minangkabau overran southern Tapanuli, and Sisingamangaraja X emerged as a leader of the armed resistance, though he was killed in the struggle. As Dutch power in the region grew Sisingamangaraja XI and XII became focuses of anticolonial resistance, especially duuring the so-called Batak War of 1872.

SITTI NURBAYA (1922), by Marah Rusli (1889–1968), the first original novel in the Indonesian language (q.v.). It describes a conflict between tradition and modernity in Minangkabau (q.v.) society.

SLAVERY. Although definitions are contentious, most societies of the archipelago recognized slavery in the form of hereditary transferable ownership of human beings. Labor (q.v.) was a scarce commodity and slaves were both a means to and a store of wealth, though they were used mainly in domestic and commercial service, other forms of bondage such as corvée being more important for agriculture and the construction of monuments (see HERENDIENSTEN). 'Free' labor, in the sense of independent manual workers available for hire for a day or longer seem to have been virtually unknown: casual labor was obtained by renting slaves from their owners. People entered the status of slavery generally as a result either of indebtedness or of capture in warfare, though servitude could also be inherited or imposed by courts. Tribal people such as those of Nias, Sumba, Maluku, Irian (qq.v.), and upland Sumatra were most commonly victims of slave trading, though Java was a major slave exporter in 1500 and Bali (q.v.) was an important source to C.19. This shift in the source of slaves was caused partly by Islam's ban on Muslims holding other Muslims as slaves. Slavery incurred certain advantages, such as exemption from corvée duties for rulers and it was not unknown for people to sell themselves into bondage, though slaves employed in small-scale manufacture and mining often lived in appalling conditions. Movement out of slavery was sometimes possible by redemption, manumission, or simply gradual assimilation to the status of free servant.

The Dutch East Indies Company (q.v.) was a major trader in slaves, which it employed for general laboring tasks and in agriculture. In 1673 half the population of Batavia (q.v.) was said to be slave and an elaborate set of rules formally governed their working conditions. The colonial government banned trade in slaves on Java in 1818, but did not announce until 1854 that slavery would be abolished in the directly-ruled territories by 1860, and did not issue an ordinance to this effect until 1 July 1863. A continuing obstacle to effective abolition, however, was the existence, especially in south Sulawesi, of debt slavery, a blurred form of servitude difficult to regulate, and full-scale slave trading continued in parts of eastern Indonesia until at least 1910. See also BUTON; COOLIE ORDINANCE. [0335, 0524, 0539, 0483]

SMALLPOX, a major disease in Indonesia, repeatedly introduced through the centuries by trading contacts with the Eurasian land mass. Severe epidemics swept Ternate in 1558, Ambon in 1564, Sumatra in 1780–83, Savu (q.v.) in 1869, and Java, Kalimantan, and Sumatra in 1918–24. In 1815, shortly after the development of vaccination, the Netherlands Indies government sent a surgeon to Martinique in the West Indies with a number of slave children. One of these children was inoculated there with the vaccine and the surgeon carried out successive inoculations of the other children during the voyage, so that the vaccine reached Java live. A similar technique was initially used to spread the vaccine through the colony, until the development of air-dried vaccine. Colonial officials estimated that 25% of the population of Java was vaccinated by 1835. Production of vaccine from cattle (q.v.) began in 1884 at a Parc Vaccinogene which merged in 1895 with the Pasteur Institute (q.v.). Although never compulsory, vaccination was a condition of entry to lower schools. In 1968, the World Health Organization launched a mass vaccination program in Indonesia. The last recorded case of the disease in the archipelago was in 1972. See also POPULATION. [0483, 0979]

SNOUCK HURGRONJE, Christiaan (1857–1936), from 1891 adviser to the colonial government on Aceh (q.v.) and from 1889 adviser on Islamic and indigenous affairs. He brought lasting change to colonial policy on Islam, arguing that Islam was not inherently opposed to colonial rule and that the bitter opposition of many Muslims to the Dutch could be assuaged if instead of opposing all manifestations of Islam the colonial government protected and promoted religious observance while suppressing only Islamic political movements. His advice led to the establishment of an extended network of state-employed religious officials. He believed that support for Islam should be paired with a vigorous introduction of Western secular culture to the Indonesian elite (the Association Principle, q.v.) in order to create a modern elite which would share with the Dutch the task of ruling the colony. He also advocated abolition of the separate European and native hierarchies within the Binnenlandsch Bestuur (q.v.). His advice that the colonial authorities should cultivate the traditional aristocracy (*uleëbalang*) in the war in Aceh (q.v.) also contributed to the eventual Dutch victory there. After his departure from Indonesia he continued to influence colonial policy as professor of Indology at Leiden University (1907–27), where he played a major role in training colonial civil servants. See also ETHICAL POLICY; RELIGION AND POLITICS. [0500, 0852, 0892]

SOLO. See SURAKARTA.

SOLOR ARCHIPELAGO consists of the islands of Solor, Adonara, and Lomblen (Lembata), at the eastern end of Nusa Tenggara. They were listed in the Nagarakrtagama (q.v.) as a dependency of Majapahit (q.v.) but by C.16 were under the influence of Ternate (q.v.). They became a shelter for European ships en route to Timor for beeswax and sandalwood (q.v.) and the Portuguese (q.v.) established a fortress on Solor in 1566. A strong political division developed between the Catholic Demonara (Demong) communities who generally supported the Portuguese and the Muslim Puji, who supported the Dutch, though neither group ever formed a single state in its own right. The Portuguese largely abandoned the islands in 1653 but only in 1859 were the islands handed definitively to the Dutch as part of a general tidying of colonial boundaries in the region (see also TIMOR). Effective Dutch rule through the Rajas of Adonara and Larantuka was established only in late C.19. [0375, 0436]

SOURSOP (*Annona muricata* Annonaceae, *sirsak*). Like the sweetsop or *srikaya* (*A. squamosa*), soursop was introduced to Indonesia by the Spanish from the West Indies, probably before C.17.

SOUTH EAST ASIA LEAGUE, the first initiative for regional cooperation between the independent states of

Southeast Asia, was founded in Bangkok in 1947 and brought together representatives of Burma, Indonesia, Siam (q.v., Thailand), and Vietnam (q.v.). Its aim was to promote the decolonization of Southeast Asia (and in Siam's case to resist British encroachment on its sovereignty). It seems to have been an initiative especially of the Siamese Prime Minister Pridi Panomyong and disappeared after his fall and that of Amir Syarifuddin (q.v.). See also FOREIGN POLICY.

SOVIET UNION, Relations with. Suspicious of Republican leaders' cooperation with the Japanese and more interested in European affairs, the Soviet Union paid little attention to the Indonesian Republic in its first years. Only after Amir Syarifuddin (q.v.) became prime minister did relations become closer and in January 1948 an Indonesian envoy, Suripno, negotiated a consular treaty with the USSR which was, however, repudiated by the incoming Hatta (q.v.) government, anxious not to appear to be aligned with Communists. Relations cooled more sharply when the USSR endorsed the PKI (q.v.) in the Madiun Affair (q.v.) and diplomatic relations were not established until 1953. The USSR backed Indonesia over the Irian (q.v.) dispute and from 1956 became a major arms supplier to Indonesia; after 1960, Indonesia was the largest non-communist recipient of Soviet bloc military aid. Relations cooled again, however, with the Soviet-U.S. detente and as Indonesia's Nekolim (q.v.) doctrine drew it closer to China. The PKI's swing towards China and the fact that Indonesia owed ca US$1,000 million (later rescheduled) muted Soviet criticism of the suppression of the left after 1965, while Indonesia cultivated ties to preserve the appearance of nonalignment in its foreign policy. Since 1975, Indonesia has, however, been increasingly critical of the Soviet naval presence in the region and was also hostile to the invasion of Afghanistan. Since the early

1980s, however, Indonesia has shared with the Soviet Union a desire not to see the Chinese-led backed Khmer Rouge displace the Vietnamese-backed Hun Sen government in Cambodia. Steadily improving relations culminated in an economic protocol between the two countries signed on 29 October 1985 and a visit by President Suharto to Moscow in September 1989 and a relaxation of Indonesian restrictions on Soviet trade and visits. On 11 January 1990 a Soviet state enterprise signed an agreement with Liem Sioe Liong (q.v.) to establish a palm oil processing plant near Moscow. See also INTERNATIONAL DEBT; MURBA. [0749]

SOYA BEAN (*Glycine max* Fabaceae, *kedele*), seed crop probably from northeast Asia, which reached Indonesia via India. It is a major polowijo (q.v.) crop and is used to prepare a number of important foods. *Tahu* (bean curd) is made by grinding the beans and heating them in water to precipitate casein which is then pressed into cakes; *tempe* is made by inoculating parboiled beans with the fungus *Aspergillus oryzae; kecap* (soy sauce) is made by inoculating boiled beans with *Aspergillus,* submerging the fermented mass in brine, exposing it to sunlight and adding flavors such as aren (q.v.) sugar, anise, and ginger. Contamination of soya beans with aflatoxins (from *A. flavus*) is a major cause of stomach cancer in Indonesia.

SPAIN, Historical links with. Although Magellan's fleet sailed through the Indonesian archipelago in 1521, it was not until after the union of the Spanish and Portuguese crowns in 1580 that the Spanish began to move south seriously from their base in the Philippines (q.v.). Between 1582 and 1603 they sent a series of largely unsuccessful expeditions against Ternate (q.v.) but in C.17 Spanish attention soon shifted back north to the Philippines. Many useful plants of American origin reached Indonesia on Spanish ships. See AMERICAS, Historical links with. [0741]

SPELLING. See INDONESIAN LANGUAGE.

SRIVIJAYA, Buddhist kingdom centered in southern Sumatra, probably on the modern city of Palembang (q.v.) and dominating the Strait of Melaka from C.7 to early C.11. In its day the most powerful state in the archipelago, Srivijaya's position was derived from its role as entrepôt for gold (q.v.) and forest products such as benzoin (q.v.) from the region; from its role as staging post in trade between China (q.v.) and eastern Indonesia on the one hand and India (q.v.) and the West on the other; and from its naval control of the Strait. It transformed the haphazard piracy (q.v.) of earlier eras into more regular taxation of trade, which greatly smoothed commerce in the region. Relatively little is known of Srivijaya's internal political structure; the grandiloquent assertions of divine authority made by its rulers are not plausible as reflections of reality (see SAILENDRAS). Srivijaya seems likely to have been a carefully managed system of alliances with coastal chiefs and upland tribes rather than a centralized bureaucratic state. Although fabulously wealthy by accounts of the time, Srivijaya has left few material remains: in the absence of easily obtainable building stone, most of its construction seems to have been in wood and has not survived. The precise nature of Srivijaya's relationship with China is also unclear. The Chinese regarded it as tributary and its prosperity was closely tied to that of the ports of southern China, but whether Srivijaya acknowledged the relationship as tributary is unknown. Srivijaya maintained important cultural links with India, especially with the Buddhist monastery at Nalanda in Bihar and was itself a major center of Buddhist learning (see BUDDHISM). Srivijava invaded Java in 992 but its power was abruptly smashed in 1027 by a raid from the South Indian Chola dynasty. The empire's capital moved to Jambi (q.v.) but it was overshadowed by the rise of independent kingdoms in northern Sumatra and on the Malay peninsula (see PASAI). The inability of any state to revive Srivijaya's hegemony may relate to the rise of Chinese 'private' as opposed to tributary trade. See also STATE-FORMATION; TRADE, Inter-regional. [0394, 0406, 0429, 0432]

STAATSPARTIJ. See PARTAI NASIONAL INDONESIA.

STATE ENTERPRISES. Since the arrival of the Dutch East Indies Company (q.v.) in the archipelago, there has been an intimate connection between the state and business enterprise. The company itself was an enterprise with an attached state, rather than the reverse, while the early years of Crown rule, especially the Cultivation System (q.v.), were largely an example of the direct commercial activity of the colonial state. Private firms such as the NHM (q.v.) benefited greatly from close cooperation with the colonial government but were not true state enterprises.

Distinct state enterprises first emerged in C.20. In 1921, the colonial government launched the Nederlandsch-Indische Aardolie Maatschappij, a joint venture with the BPM to drill for oil (q.v.) in Jambi. The idea that some separation should be made between the state and its commercial ventures was only given legal expression in 1927, with the Indische Bedrijvenwet (Indies Enterprises Law), which allowed the government to separate commercial enterprises from the state budget. This was then applied to the opium (q.v.) factory; the pawnshops (q.v.); the government quinine and tea (qq.v.) industries; the harbors of Belawan, Makassar, and Emmahaven; the posts and telegraph service (see POSTAL SERVICE; TELEGRAPH); the Bangka tin (q.v.) industry; the military grasslands; and the reproduction section of the topographical service.

Under the Japanese, some existing enterprises were handed over to Japanese commercial interests (see SUGAR CANE), but many were placed under government departments as a source of direct finance. This system remained in place in practice during the Indonesian Revolution, when plantations in particular came under the control of local armed units. The Republican government set up a number of centralized state corporations, including the Badan Textiel Negara and the Badan Industri Negara, but these suffered from a critical shortage of capital and were often unable to take charge of the factories they nominally controlled as these were in the hands of the workers or of lasykar (q.v.) or army groups. More successful was the semi-governmental Banking and Trading Corporation (BTC) of Sumitro Joyohadikusumo (q.v.), which traded produce to Singapore and the United States.

After 1950, successive governments were determined to establish a significant publicly owned sector in the economy. Railways and the Java Bank were nationalized and the Bank Industri Negara helped finance new state corporations in the fields of shipping (q.v.), air services (see GARUDA), textile, cement, glass, automobile, and hardboard manufacture. In 1956, a state trading corporation USINDO was formed to handle the export of goods from these factories. With the nationalization (q.v.) of Dutch enterprises in December 1957, the state sector expanded dramatically. In April 1958, nationalized Dutch trading firms were reorganized into six new state trading corporations with a joint monopoly on the import of many commodities, including rice and textiles. 55% of profits from these firms were due to the state, but proceeds were generally disappointing due to corruption and deterioration of infrastructure. A central authority, the Badan Pimpinan Umum, was placed in charge of state enterprises in 1960.

Under the New Order this extensive state presence in the economy was preserved, despite IGGI (q.v.) preferences for private ownership, partly because of a lack of domestic capital to take them over, and partly because they were an important source of income and a useful tool for state intervention in the economy. The largest state enterprises currently are Pertamina (q.v.); the tin firm PN Timah; PN Aneka Tambang, which conducts general mining operations; and Perhutani (formerly Inhutani), the state forestry corporation. Public utilities, of course, are also state enterprises, as are the largest banks and two major manufacturing firms, PT Krakatau Steel and the fertilizer producer PT Pusri. See also INDONESIANIZATION. [0257, 0314]

STATE-FORMATION. The boundary between tribal and other 'primitive' political formations on the one hand and states on the other is an arbitrary one, but most scholars regard true states as having emerged in the archipelago only as part of the adoption and transformation of Indian, and later Islamic and Western, political ideas. Thus the earliest states in the western archipelago ('Ho-lo-tan', 'Kan-t'o-li' and Kutai, qq.v.) were culturally Indian in at least some respects and were probably stimulated at least in part by the emergence of trade between Indonesia and India (q.v.) around C.1 or 2.

Information on these early states allows us to say that they consisted of court bureaucracies which rested on carefully constructed networks of alliances with regional powerholders (see also BUPATI), but the relative strength of court and 'feudal' lords is hard to judge, even apart from the fact that it must have varied significantly over time. The longevity of a state such as Srivijaya and the internal organization required by the Javanese states which constructed Borobudur and Prambanan (qq.v.)

suggest a significant degree of institutionalization, but other evidence suggests highly personalized rule, and the distinction between king, vassal, and bandit leader seems to have been a fluid one (see BANDITRY; PIRACY). In contrast, the strong bureaucratic structure of the Dutch East Indies Company (VOC) gave it an organizational coherence and resilience which enabled it ultimately to subdue the entire archipelago. See also SUCCESSION. [0416, 0667]

STATISTICS. The Centraal Kantoor voor de Statistiek was established in 1924 and its work has been continued since independence by the Biro Pusat Statistik (BPS, Central Bureau of Statistics). See also CENSUSES.

STRIKES. See LABOR UNIONS.

STUW, De (*The Push*), political journal published from 1930 by the Association for the Furtherance of the Social and Political Development of the Netherlands Indies, usually called the *Stuw*-group. Most of its members were government officials or academics, and most had been influenced by Snouck Hurgronje (q.v.) at Leiden University. Their association was primarily a study and discussion group, though it argued generally for the creation of an Indies commonwealth (see SUCCESSION). The group was largely disbanded by 1933, partly because it appeared to be damaging the careers of its younger members in the conservative political climate of the day. Several of its members, however, gained influential positions in the postwar colonial administration, notably van Mook (q.v.) as Lieutenant Governor-General, and J.H.A. Logemann and J.A. Jonkman as Minister for Colonies (q.v.). They had little success, however, in pushing the Dutch government towards greater concessions to Indonesian nationalism and their often paternalistic ideas on cultural and economic development antagonized Indonesian nationalists. [0569, 0767]

SUBANDRIO (b.1910). As a young intellectual with medical training, Subandrio was posted abroad to promote the Republic during the Indonesian revolution. After serving in London (1947–54) and Moscow (1954–56), he returned to Indonesia, joined the PNI (q.v.) in 1957 and in the same year became foreign minister in Sukarno's first *kabinet karya*. He held the post until 1966 and was one of the architects of the leftist foreign policy of Guided Democracy (q.v.), including Confrontation (q.v.) with Malaysia. On becoming deputy prime minister in 1959, he resigned from the PNI to project a more national image. A skilled political manipulator, he was seen by many as typifying the byzantine politics of Guided Democracy and was amongst the first government figures targeted by conservative forces after 1965. He was arrested in March 1966, tried by the MAHMILLUB (q.v.) in October, and convicted of participation in the GESTAPU (q.v.) coup. Although sentenced to death, he remains in detention in Jakarta.

SUBVERSION. Both colonial and independent governments in Indonesia have been deeply and constantly concerned about alleged problems of subversion. The VOC feared collusion between inhabitants of Batavia and enemies outside and periodically executed those suspected of treason. In 1916 the colonial government founded the Politiek Inlichtingen Dienst (q.v.) or Political Intelligence Service, whose place was taken under the Japanese by the Kenpeitai and more recently by the Badan Koordinasi Intelijen Negara (qq.v.) or BAKIN.

These police organs have been backed by a series of laws on subversion, beginning with the so-called *haatzaai-artikelen* of 1914, based on the penal code of British India, which banned the 'sowing of hatred' of the government or of any group of Indonesian inhabitants; by irony one of the first prosecutions under these articles was of the editor of a colonial military journal which published an essay critical of the quality of Javanese soldiers. These articles were used recently to convict the dissident H.R. Dharsono (see WHITE PAPER). Lèse majesté regulations of the colonial era have also been retained by independent Indonesia (with substitution of president and vice-president for queen and governor-general) and were used against the authors of the 1978 'White Book' (q.v.). Finally, the 1963 Law on Subversion, which bans both the arousing of 'hostility, disturbances or anxiety among the population or broad sections of society' and the undermining of Pancasila or the GBHN (qq.v.), was used against Sawito Kartowibowo (q.v.) and against the alleged plotters behind the Malari (q.v.) riots. See also MAHKAMAH MILITER LUAR BIASA. [0581, 0856]

SUCCESSION. The idea that the colony of the Netherlands Indies should be succeeded by some sort of independent state emerged in early C.20. Proponents initially envisaged gradual decolonization, perhaps via an increase in the powers of the Volksraad (q.v.), towards a commonwealth arrangement along British lines, with Indonesia being essentially self-governing but deferring to the Netherlands on matters of common interest (see *STUW, De*). The idea of full independence became a part of the platform of the nationalist movement in the 1920s, though the exact mechanism of succession was not spelled out. Nationalists did not agree at first on whether the colony should gain independence as a whole or in a number of ethnically-based states (see NATIONALISM), but there was never any suggestion that sovereignty might somehow revert to the traditional rulers of the archipelago. By the 1920s there was general agreement that the successor state should encompass the entire Netherlands Indies.

Succession by Japanese military rule was sanctioned in international law by the formal surrender of Dutch forces on 9 March 1942, but was called into question by the establishment of a Netherlands Indies government-in-exile in Australia under van Mook (q.v.) and the fact that the Dutch still held the town of Merauke in the southeastern corner of West New Guinea (see IRIAN). On 6 December 1942 (7 December in Indonesia because of time differences), Queen Wilhelmina promised a postwar conference to revise Holland's constitutional relationship with the colonies (including Surinam and the Netherlands Antilles).

Japan divided the former Netherlands Indies into three zones. East Indonesia, under naval rule was intended for direct incorporation into the Japanese empire as a colony (analogous to its Pacific Nanyo territories), while the status of Java, under the 16th army and Sumatra, united with Malaya under the 25th army, was left undecided. In September 1944, the Japanese Prime Minister Koiso announced plans to set up a nominally independent Republic of Indonesia covering the entire former Dutch colony, but these had not been carried out by the time Japan surrendered on 15 August 1945. See BADAN PENYELIDIK USAHA PERSIAPAN KEMERDEKAAN INDONESIA.

The Indonesian Republic, declared on 17 August 1945, based its claim to succession on the right of national self-determination, on the argument that Dutch sovereignty had ceased with the Dutch loss of the colony in 1942 and on the initially slender international recognition it received from other countries (see DIPLOMASI AND PERJUANGAN). The Linggajati Agreement of November 1946 and the Renville Agreement of January 1948 (qq.v.) gave the Republic vague 'de facto' recognition by the Dutch, but this was withdrawn in the 'police actions' (q.v.) of July 1947 and December 1948. The

Republic received full recognition from Egypt and Syria in 1947.

Under van Mook (q.v.), the postwar Netherlands Indies government recognized the inevitable end of colonialism but sought to push the colony's successor state in the direction of a multiracial paternalistic meritocracy. In the latter part of the Revolution, this took the form of a federation (see FEDERALISM). On 9 March 1948, the colonial government was renamed the Provisional Federal Government (VFR, Voorlopige Federale Regeering) and the term Netherlands Indies was replaced in the Dutch constitution by Indonesië. On 3 November the post of governor-general (q.v.) was replaced with that of High Commissioner of the Crown. On 27 December 1949 sovereignty over the Netherlands Indies was transferred to the Republik Indonesia Serikat (q.v., Federal Republic of Indonesia, usually translated as Republic of the United States of Indonesia). West New Guinea (see IRIAN), however, was retained by the Dutch, partly on grounds of the ethnic dissimilarity between the Papuans and other Indonesians, partly on the grounds that Dutch sovereignty over the territory was stronger by virtue of the permanent Dutch presence in Merauke. West New Guinea (Irian, q.v.) was handed by the Dutch in 1962 to United Nations administration, which in turn handed it to Indonesia in 1963. The incorporation of the territory into Indonesia was ratified by an 'Act of Free Choice' in 1969.

The declaration of East Timor's independence by Fretilin (q.v.) in November 1975 was intended as an act of national self-determination, but was rejected by Portugal as the former colonial power and by Indonesia. Indonesia has argued since then that East Timor was *terra nullius,* i.e., unoccupied territory in international law, after the Portuguese administration abandoned the colony in 1975, that the colony was ethnically and geographically a part of Indonesia (a position difficult to reconcile with the inclusion of Irian) and that the provincial assembly which voted in 1976 for amalgamation with Indonesia constituted an act of self-determination.

SUDIRMAN (?1915–50), former school teacher and PETA (q.v.) battalion commander, elected army (q.v.) commander in Yogyakarta on 12 November 1945. He emphasized the value of martial and national spirit over hierarchy and formal organization in defeating the Dutch and was initially sympathetic to the radical nationalism of Tan Malaka (q.v.), though he stopped short of supporting him against the Syahrir (q.v.) government. Although his charisma made him a focal point of army loyalty, he was gradually edged out of direct command by a group of Western-trained officers including A.H. Nasution (q.v.). In December 1948, however, after the Republican cabinet was captured in the second Dutch 'Police Action' (q.v.), Sudirman, though dying of tuberculosis, led Republican forces in a guerrilla struggle against the Dutch in the Javanese countryside. In July 1949, he reluctantly submitted to the Republican government which had been restored to Yogyakarta, but died soon afterwards. See also DIPLOMASI AND PERJUANGAN.

SUGAR CANE (*Saccharum officinarum* Poaceae) is probably native to Indonesia and was first domesticated there, but improved techniques for cultivating and processing it were developed in India. Chinese visitors reported it from Java in 400 A.D., but other sources of sugar (aren, honey, lontar, qq.v.) were more important. Under sponsorship of the Dutch East Indies Company, Chinese settlers on Java produced the first commercial sugar cane in the countryside around Batavia in C.17 for export to Europe and Japan. Of 150 mills on the island in 1710, all but four were Chinese-owned, though production declined later in C.18 because of the loss of external markets, political disturbances on Java, and lack of firewood. Sugar production was an important part of the Cultivation System (q.v.). Sugar grown under government monopoly was delivered to private sugar mills, often owned by European entrepreneurs who, though they had to deliver the processed sugar at fixed prices to the Nederlandsch Handel Maatschappij (q.v.) or NHM, made enormous profits. In the first half of C.19, sugar was by far the dominant export of the colony, accounting for 77.4% of the total value of exports in 1840. Private companies established sugar plantations in the Vorstenlanden (q.v.) in this period.

In 1870 the government decided to hand over sugar production to private enterprise, though the government monopoly was not formally abolished until 1891. Sugar cane requires much the same kind of agricultural conditions as rice (and three times the volume of water) as well as a seasonal labor force, and most sugar plantations were therefore established in areas already under indigenous rice cultivation. Under a variety of exploitative relationships, the sugar growers generally gained access to their choice of land and to abundant water while leaving a portion of the rice economy intact to tide their labor force over seasonal dips in labor demand. A world crisis in 1883 drove many smaller companies out of production, but set the stage for massive capital investment, especially by the NHM, which turned the Java sugar industry into the world's most efficient, though its share of the colony's exports never recovered. The industry fared badly in the Depression (q.v.) of the 1930s and its share of the value of exports sank to around 7% by 1938.

During the Japanese occupation, the sugar plantations and mills of Java were handed over to Japanese sugar firms in proportion to their share of Japanese production. Since the combined production of Java, the

Philippines, and Taiwan was far more than the needs of the Japanese empire, production on Java was steadily reduced. During the Indonesian Revolution, the preferential laws which had given sugar plantations access to village lands were abolished, and the industry was never able to recover the access to cheap land and labor (qq.v.) which had previously underpinned its success. Postwar policies of keeping sugar prices low contributed to underinvestment and generally low yields, exacerbated by primitive technology and use of low-yielding plant varieties. In 1971 BULOG (q.v.) took over distribution and price support, and in 1972, the government launched an intensified smallholder cane program, which included reductions in tax and an improved marketing system. In 1975 plans were announced to phase out the renting of land for large sugar plantations, but despite some progress, the industry remains inefficient, absorbing 20% of total agricultural credits for only 3% of the total value of agricultural output. [0230, 0232, 0255, 0261, 0440, 0509]

SUHARTO (b. 8 June 1921), second president of Indonesia. Suharto joined the KNIL (q.v.) in 1940 and rose to the rank of sergeant before the Japanese invasion. After demobilization, he joined first the police and then the Pembela Tanah Air (q.v.) in 1943 and the Republican army (q.v.) in Central Java in 1945. During the Dutch occupation of Yogyakarta (1948–49), he commanded a 'general attack' (*serangan umum*) in which Indonesian forces briefly occupied the city before being driven back by the Dutch. In 1956 he became commander of the army's Diponegoro division but was dismissed in October 1959 for putting illegal levies on commercial activities in Central Java. Posted to SESKOAD, the army's staff college, in Bandung, he was involved peripherally in the development of the army's doctrine of dwifungsi (q.v.) before being appointed in 1961 as commander of the army's strategic reserve (KOSTRAD, q.v.). In 1962 he was placed in command of the Mandala campaign to recover Irian (q.v.), but was present in Jakarta as KOSTRAD commander at the time of the GESTAPU (q.v.) coup in 1965. His troops were instrumental in suppressing the coup and with his appointment as commander of KOPKAMTIB (q.v.) on 10 October 1965 he set about dismantling Guided Democracy (q.v.) and installing the regime which soon became known as the New Order (q.v.). The Supersemar (q.v.) order of 11 March 1966 enabled him to suppress the PKI (q.v.) and to purge the government bureaucracy. He was sworn in as Acting President in March 1967 and in March 1968 he was elected by the MPRS (q.v.) as President for a five-year term but he called general elections for 1971 and was reelected by the new MPR in 1972. He has been reelected in 1973, 1978, 1983, and 1989.

Suharto initially appeared to many observers to be a quiet and efficient military manager, using a consensual style and drawing heavily on the economic skills of BAPPENAS (q.v.) staff and on political managers such as Ali Murtopo of the CSIS (q.v.). In the mid and late 1970s, his presence retreated somewhat from the national stage as rivalry between competing generals in Suharto's inner circle not only broke into public view but was expressed obliquely in the Malari (q.v.) Affair. An attitude of *mumpungisme* (get what you can while you can) seemed to be the order of the day and observers began to refer to the leadership as a junta and to speculate that Suharto was no more than a figurehead for concealed and more powerful figures. With the drop in oil revenues and a more austere economic regime in the 1980s, however, Suharto has seemed much more clearly in control, removing apparently powerful subordinates, directly determining much government policy, and promoting Pancasila (q.v.) as the state ideology.

Several members of Suharto's immediate family, including his three sons Tommy (Hutomo), Sigit, and Bambang, have prospered enormously under his rule. See also JOYOHADIKUSUMO, Sumitro; POLITICAL CULTURE; SUBVERSION. [0657, 0666, 0679, 0698, 0712]

SUKADANA, kingdom in southwest Kalimantan, reportedly founded by exiles from Majapahit (q.v.). Its economy was based on the export of Kalimantan diamonds (q.v.) and of iron (q.v.) from Karimata. It was conquered by Mataram (q.v.) in 1622.

SUKARNO (6 June 1901—21 June 1970), often affectionately called Bung (q.v.) Karno, nationalist leader and Indonesia's first president. Sukarno became involved in the nationalist movement early as a protégé of H.U.S. Tjokroaminoto (q.v.) and after studying engineering at the Bandung Institute of Technology helped to found an Algemene Studieclub (General Study Club) in Bandung in 1926. In 1927 he founded the Partai Nasional Indonesia which expanded dramatically under the influence of his oratory. He was jailed in December 1929 and on his release joined the PARTINDO, to which he also drew an enthusiastic mass following. Arrested again in 1933, he apparently offered to abstain from politics if he were pardoned, but was exiled nonetheless to Flores and then to Bengkulu. He returned to Jakarta shortly after the Japanese invasion and agreed to cooperate with the occupation authorities. In exchange for exhorting the Indonesian people to support the war effort, he received extensive public exposure and an opportunity to broadcast lightly-concealed nationalist messages to the public. He was later criticized for his role in recruiting *rōmusha* (q.v.) laborers for the Japanese and for his vitriolic attacks on the Western allies. His speech formulating the Pancasila (q.v.) was made to a meeting of the independence preparatory body BPUPKI (q.v.) in June

1945. In August 1945, he was the only nationalist leader of truly national standing and was chosen president on the 18th. During the Revolution he played a key role in keeping the revolutionary movement relatively united; although his rhetoric generally stressed the value of unremitting armed struggle, he consistently backed the negotiating governments of Syahrir and Amir Syarifuddin (qq.v.). He allowed himself to be captured by the Dutch in Yogyakarta during the second 'Police Action' (q.v.), suggesting later that this was for reasons of strategy and publicity. His action, however, was seen as desertion by many, including sections of the army and embarrassment may have been one reason for his relatively low profile during the early period of parliamentary democracy in the 1950s. He soon became increasingly dissatisfied, however, with party politics, and in 1957 called for a system of 'Guided Democracy' to replace what he saw as the tyranny of the majority in a conventional parliamentary system. He took an active hand in forming governments after the fall of the second Ali Sastroamijoyo cabinet in 1957 and in 1959, with army (q.v.) backing, took over the prime ministership and instituted his system of Guided Democracy. Once in power, however, Sukarno proved to be less than competent at day-to-day administration, concentrating on symbolic projects such as the recovery of Irian (q.v.), Confrontation with Malaysia (q.v.), and the formulation of a national ideology called Nasakom to reconcile the conflicting nationalist, religious, and communist political parties. His self-assurance seemed to increase and in 1963 he had himself declared President-for-Life. Politically, however, he was increasingly forced to balance the army and the PKI (q.v.) in an uneasy triangular relationship. His role in the GESTAPU (q.v.) coup of September 1965 remains unclear. It seems improbable that he had any hand in plotting it, but he was at least somewhat implicated after the event by his apparent composure in the face of the coup. The crushing of the GESTAPU by Suharto (q.v.) overthrew the balance of power of the late Guided Democracy, enabling Suharto gradually to push Sukarno aside until he obtained full executive authority under the Supersemar (q.v.) order of March 1966. Sukarno was stripped of his presidency on 12 March 1967 and was confined under house arrest until he died. See also MAHMILLUB; NEKOLIM.

Scholars continue to argue over the nature of Sukarno's ideology. He was strongly influenced by Marxism, and especially the Leninist theory of imperialism; one of his theoretical coinages was the notion of the Marhaen, a category of poor Indonesians who were oppressed by capitalism and imperialism, but were not proletarians since they owned, in the form of a little land and a few tools, some of the means of production. But he was also a pious *abangan* (q.v.) Muslim and a strong nationalist. He argued that there was no contradiction between these three beliefs and the core of his thinking was an attempt to synthesize them for Indonesian use. Pancasila and Nasakom (qq.v.), though they came to have opposing political connotations, were both attempts at ideological syncretism. This blending of ideologies makes it difficult to judge how much social change Sukarno wished to introduce; his rhetoric was always that of radical change, but his practice was often less so.

After his death Sukarno was buried in the East Java town of Blitar, initially in a humble grave which has since been made a substantial mausoleum. His memory has been used especially by the PDI (q.v.) which claims to be his heir in its concern for the less well off. Since Sukarno's death various attempts have been made to downplay his role in national development; in 1980/81, in particular, it was alleged that he was not the author of the Pancasila, while in 1987 rumors circulated of vast sums he had corruptly secured which were held in foreign bank accounts. [0581, 0628, 0685, 0695, 0700, 0705, 0716, 0867–0869]

SUKIMAN WIRYOSANJOYO (1896–), member of the Perhimpunan Indonesia (q.v.) and later leader of the Partai Sarekat Islam Indonesia (q.v.) until he left in 1933 to form the Partai Islam Indonesia (q.v.). He was one of the modernist leaders who took control of Masyumi (q.v.) in 1945 and he served as prime minister from April 1951 to February 1952. His term in office was marked by hostility to the army (q.v.): pro-army leaders were excluded and lasykar (q.v.) captured by the army after the Revolution were released. Sukiman also attempted to suppress the PKI, arresting perhaps 15,000 party members in August 1951. Pro-Western in its foreign policy, the cabinet fell after it signed a secret aid agreement with the U.S. (q.v.) committing Indonesia to help defend the 'free world.' [0634]

SULAWESI (Celebes), island in the Greater Sundas. The origin of the name is uncertain: Sulawesi may derive from *sula besi,* 'island of iron', while Celebes may come from the Portuguese Punta des Celebres, Cape of the Infamous. The island's distinctive shape with four arms separated by broad gulfs has led it to be compared variously to a spider, an orchid, a giraffe, a starfish, and a drunken letter K. Only the southern arm, around Makassar (q.v.) and the northern arm around Minahasa (q.v.) are volcanic and these fertile areas are the most heavily populated parts of the island, which currently has a population of around 9 million.

Bronze Buddha images dating from C.4–5 have been found in southern Sulawesi, suggesting first Hindu influences at about the same time as on Java, Sumatra and Kalimantan (qq.v.), but no major early kingdoms developed there. Four ethnic groups dominate this region: the Makassarese in the far south, the Bugis (q.v.) further north, the Luwunese still further north, and the Mandar to the northwest. The kingdom of Luwu (q.v.) or La Galigo emerged on the southern peninsula in C.9 and the Bugis kingdoms of Boné, Wajo' (qq.v.) and Soppeng and the Makassarese kingdom of Gowa (Goa) arose in C.13 amongst a scattering of perhaps fifty small states, variously Hindu and animist. Gowa and its sister port Tallo accepted Islam in 1605 and, now commonly known as Makassar (q.v.), soon became influential beyond the peninsula in Kalimantan and Sumbawa (qq.v.). In 1660, however, Makassar was captured by the Dutch, in alliance with Arung Palakka (q.v.) of Boné.

The rest of the island meanwhile remained largely under small tribes, most notably the Toraja (q.v.) of the central mountains, though the kingdom of Bolaäng Mongondouw on the northern peninsula flourished briefly until it was subjected by the Maluku kingdom of Ternate (q.v.), which also dominated the Gulf of Tomini (see GORONTALO). The entire island was claimed by the Dutch in 1846 and was ruled loosely by the governor of *Celebes en Onderhoorigheden* (Sulawesi and dependencies), but Dutch control in the interior was not felt until late C.19.

After the Japanese occupation, the island was reoccupied by Australian troops, who were instrumental in suppressing the initial attempt by local nationalists to join the Indonesian Republic. Thereafter, Sulawesi was a lynchpin in Dutch plans for federalism (q.v.) in Indonesia and Makassar was the capital of the short-lived Negara Indonesia Timur (q.v.). After the dissolution of the NIT in 1950, Sulawesi was the site of rebellions against the central authorities by both the Darul Islam and the PERMESTA (qq.v.). Under the New Order, nickel (q.v.) mining has expanded on the southeastern peninsula and parts of the island have been an important destination for Balinese transmigration (q.v.) settlements. [0117, 0433, 0975, 1155]

SUMATRA (Sumatera, from Samudra, former name of the kingdom of Pasai, q.v.), the westernmost of Indonesia's main islands, divided geographically into a mountainous spine, the Bukit Barisan, in the west and an area of flat lowland, often swampy, in the east. The rugged terrain of the Bukit Barisan has made overland travel difficult, and a number of distinct peoples—the Gayo, Batak, Minangkabau (qq.v.), Rejang and Lebang—developed in the relatively isolated valleys of the interior. The coastal regions of the east and south were dominated by Malays (q.v.) and were tied politically, culturally, and economically to the Malay peninsula (q.v.) until the hardening of colonial and national borders. In the north the Acehnese came under Muslim influence in early times (see ACEH; ANGLO-DUTCH TREATY).

The earliest major kingdoms on Sumatra (Jambi, Srivijaya, qq.v.) arose initially as river-based controllers of the Strait of Melaka (see also PIRACY), vital to the India-China trade, but they also depended on alliance with peoples and rulers in the interior who supplied forest and mining products such as camphor, pepper, and gold (qq.v.) for trade. Later kingdoms (Pasai, Pedir, Aceh, qq.v.), for the most part Muslim, depended more on this entrepôt role, and Aceh was probably the most successful in bringing regions of the interior under its control.

European domination of the trade routes from C.18 left new coastal states (Palembang, Deli, Riau qq.v.) relatively weak, but European powers did not attempt to extend significant control over territory until early C.19. After the return of Java to the Dutch in 1816, Raffles (q.v.) attempted to build the British colony in Bengkulu (q.v.) into a major base and the Dutch became involved soon after in the politics of Minangkabau (q.v.) through the Paderi War. The British ceded Bengkulu and other possessions in Sumatra to the Dutch in the Treaty of London of 1824. Aceh was not fully conquered until 1903. The introduction of plantation crops to East Sumatra (q.v.) by private Dutch companies—the first tobacco (q.v.) in 1864, rubber and oil palms (qq.v.) in early C.20—together with the discovery of oil (q.v.) dramatically changed the economy of the island, making it the richest export area of the Netherlands Indies and later of Indonesia. The social character of East Sumatra changed drastically with the introduction of many Javanese and Chinese indentured laborers. Since independence, southern Sumatra has been a major destination for settlers under the transmigration (q.v.) program.

Sumatrans—Hatta, Syahrir, Yamin (qq.v.) and others—took a major part in the rise of Indonesian nationalism (q.v.) in C.20 and although the island was administratively united with Malaya under the 25th army during part of the Japanese occupation, local nationalists enthusiastically declared for the Republic in 1945. Fierce social revolutions broke out against aristocratic associates of the Dutch in Aceh and East Sumatra. In the latter part of the Revolution, the Dutch attempted to establish federal states in East and South Sumatra, but these were abolished in 1950. A revolt broke out in Aceh from 1953 to 1957. Dissatisfaction over Jakarta's allocation of income earned by Sumatra's exports was amongst the reasons for the 1957 PRRI (q.v.) revolt. [0048, 0058, 0090, 0206, 0470, 0570, 0976, 1134]

SUMBA, island in Nusa Tenggara. Abundant sandalwood (q.v.) trees on the coast attracted European attention in C.17 and the area was repeatedly raided for slaves. The Dutch obtained treaty rights in 1756 and instituted direct rule in 1866, but the island was relatively neglected and relatively little conversion to Christianity took place. The raising of horses (q.v.) for export began in the 1840s and the island is also known for its production of ikat cloth (q.v.). See also SAVU. [0524, 1011, 1151]

SUMBAWA, mountainous island in Nusa Tenggara, commonly divided into two kingdoms, Bima (q.v.) in the east and Sumbawa in the west. The island was a major exporter of sandalwood and later horses (qq.v.) but was devastated in 1815 by the eruption of Mount Tambora (q.v.), in which 50,000 people were reportedly killed.

SUNDA. Though hard to define precisely, Sunda refers generally to the western third of the island of Java (q.v.), dominated by the Sundanese people, though much of the northern coast is now not Sundanese (see BANTEN; BETAWI; CIREBON). One of the earliest historical states in the archipelago, Tarumanegara (q.v.) was centered near modern Bogor and the region was apparently dominated by Srivijaya (q.v.) in late C.7, but little else is known of the region until the emergence of Hindu Pajajaran (q.v.) in C.14. Islam (q.v.) reached Banten and Cirebon in C.16 and the conversion of the interior began soon after the fall of Pajajaran in 1579. Less influenced by Hindu-Buddhist traditions than the rest of Java, the Sundanese became increasingly strongly Muslim and the region was one of the centers of the Darul Islam (q.v.) rebellion. See also PASUNDAN; PRIANGAN. [0900]

SUNDA KALAPA. See BANTEN; PAJAJARAN.

SUNDA SHELF, a large southern extension of the Asian continental land mass carrying the islands of Sumatra, Kalimantan and Java. During twenty successive periods of glaciation over the last 2 million years, and most recently ca 50,000-ca 15,000 years ago, the entire shelf has been exposed. East Sumatra and West Kalimantan were then drained by the great Sunda River, flowing into the South China Sea north of Sarawak, while Java and South Kalimantan were drained by another major river flowing into what is now the Flores Sea. There were glaciers on Mt. Leuser in Sumatra at this time, and the climate seems to have been drier, but it is difficult to reconstruct the area's prehistory since most areas of possible human habitation have been flooded. See also PREHISTORY; CONTINENTAL DRIFT. [0388, 0976]

SUPERSEMAR (Surat Perintah Sebelas Maret, Executive Order of 11 March 1966), was signed reluctantly by Sukarno (q.v.), ordering General Suharto (q.v.) 'to take all necessary steps to guarantee security and calm and the stability of the running of the government and the course of the Revolution' and thus transferring full executive authority of Suharto. See also SEMAR. [0669]

SURABAYA, port city at a mouth of the Brantas river in East Java founded, according to official accounts, in 1293, when Raden Wijaya drove out the Mongols to become ruler of Majapahit (q.v.). It became an important port in C.15 under Raden Rahmat or Sunan Ngampel, but was first subject to Demak (q.v.), then briefly independent, and finally in 1625 conquered by Mataram (q.v.). It was seized by the VOC (q.v.) in 1743. Daendels (q.v.) established a naval base there. Under Dutch rule, Surabaya became the largest city in the Indies (until the early C.20) as well as the principal commercial center for eastern Indonesia and headquarters of the Dutch navy in Asia. As in Batavia (q.v.) a mixed immigrant population blended to form a distinct urban ethnic group, the *arek Suroboyo*. The city was incorporated as a municipality in 1906. It was heavily bombed by the Allies during World War II and was the scene of heavy fighting between Indonesian nationalist forces and British Indian troops in November 1945. 11 November is celebrated as Heroes' Day in its honor. [0636]

SURAKARTA (Solo), Javanese court city founded in 1743 by Sunan Pakubuwono II (r.1726–49) of Mataram (q.v.). After the Treaty of Giyanti (1755) which divided Mataram, the rump of the old kingdom became the Sunanate (*Kasunanan*) of Surakarta, remaining a relatively prosperous center of trade, agriculture, and batik (q.v.) manufacture. As in Yogyakarta (q.v.), political impotence generated a cultural florescence, Solo producing a style said to be gentler and less martial than Yogyakarta's. The Sunanate was abolished by the Indonesian Republic in 1946, after the Sunan had failed to join it unequivocally against the Dutch. See also MANGKUNEGARAN. [0485, 0568, 1167]

SURAPATI (?–1706), former Balinese slave in Batavia (q.v.) who escaped to the surrounding countryside to lead a bandit gang. In 1683 he surrendered to the Dutch and joined VOC forces, but in 1684 attacked the Company again and fled to Kartasura, capital of Mataram (q.v.), where he successfully ambushed a VOC unit sent to capture him. He then fled to Pasuruan in East Java and established an independent kingdom, defeating a Mataram army in 1690 and pushing his domains east to Madiun in 1694. Surapati was finally killed in joint campaigns by the VOC, Mataram, and Madura (q.v.) in 1706, but his descendants continued to rule the region until mid C.18. See also BALAMBANGAN. [0466]

SURAU. See PESANTREN.

SURINAM, Javanese in. Towards the end of C.19, Dutch concern over the growth of population in Java and a desire to limit the number of contract laborers from British India on plantations in the Dutch South American colony of Surinam, led to the recruitment of Javanese for work there. Between 1891 and 1939, 32,976 Javanese entered the colony, usually on five-year contracts. Some 7,684 of these were repatriated before World War II and ca 1,000 in 1954, the remainder settling in the colony. In 1962, the Javanese population was 43,000. [1055]

SUTARJO PETITION, presented to the Volksraad (q.v.) in July 1936 by Sutarjo Kartohadikusumo, a career bureaucrat, rather than a member of the nationalism movement. The Petition asked for a conference to prepare dominion status for Indonesia after ten years, along the Philippine Commonwealth model. Many nationalists believed the Petition asked for too little, but the colonial authorities' failure to act on its proposals after it had been passed by the Volksraad became a symbol of Dutch political intransigence. [0544]

SUTOMO, Dr (1888–1938), physician, founder of several 'study clubs' intended to spread nationalist awareness amongst young intellectuals, cofounder of the protonationalist Budi Utomo (q.v.) and later head of PARINDRA (q.v.). He argued especially that adherence to Islam was incompatible with nationalism. See also ALGEMENE STUDIECLUB; NATIONALISM. [0384, 0719]

SUWARDI SURYANINGRAT, R.M. (1889–1959), early nationalist and leader of the Indische Partij (q.v.). His article 'If I were to be a Dutchman' ('Als ik eens Nederlander was', 1913) was a classic turning of the arguments of European liberalism against colonialism.

Exiled to Holland 1913–19, he became interested in educational philosophy and in 1922, taking the name Ki Hajar Dewantoro, founded the Taman Siswa (q.v.) school system. In 1943, he briefly joined the leadership of the Japanese-sponsored mass organization PUTERA, but soon withdrew to concentrate on educational matters. He remained close to Sukarno, and his ideas on the governance of Taman Siswa schools were one of the elements contributing to the philosophy of Guided Democracy (q.v.). See also NATIONALISM. [0591, 0594]

SWEET POTATO (*Ipomoea batatas* Convolvulaceae) was introduced from South America by C.17. It has gradually replaced the yam (q.v.) in much cultivation, especially in Irian (q.v.), since it is quicker to grow and prepare, though it stores much less well.

SYAFRUDDIN PRAWIRANEGARA (1911–1989) studied law in Jakarta before working in the colonial, Japanese and Republican Departments of Finance and for a time as Republican finance minister. He was a prominent member of the modernist wing of the Masyumi (q.v.). In December 1948, after the Second 'Police Action' (q.v.), he became prime minister of the Emergency Government of the Indonesian Republic (Pemerintah Darurat Republik Indonesia, PDRI) in Sumatra. He was finance minister again in the Hatta and Natsir governments, and introduced a system of multiple exchange rates for the rupiah (see CURRENCY). As governor of the Bank of Indonesia 1951–58 he was a strong opponent of the Benteng Policy (q.v.) on the grounds that most Indonesians were in the agricultural sector and were not ready for accelerated industrialization. In 1958 he became prime minister of the rebel PRRI (q.v.) government in Sumatra; he returned to Jakarta under an amnesty in 1961 but was jailed until the

New Order. Initially a supporter of the New Order, he grew unhappy with its policies and in 1980 signed the Petition of Fifty (q.v.). [0563, 0634]

SYAHRIR, Sutan (1909–66) studied in the Netherlands where he joined the Perhimpunan Indonesia. On his return to Indonesia in December 1931, he joined Hatta (q.v.) to found the Pendidikan Nasional Indonesia (q.v.) or PNI-Baru, which aimed at building up a nationalist cadre in preparation for a prolonged independence struggle. Arrested in 1934, he was removed first to Boven Digul (q.v.) and in 1936 to Banda (q.v.). He was returned to Java shortly before the Japanese invasion in 1942. Unlike other nationalist leaders, he refused to cooperate with the Japanese, building instead a network of young intellectuals which became the basis for the later PSI (q.v.). After the Declaration of Independence in 1945, he campaigned strongly against the preservation of occupation-era institutions, such as the PETA and the PNI-Staatspartij (qq.v.), within the Republic. Operating through the Working Committee of the KNIP (q.v.), he was able to convert the Republic's nascent political system to the principle of parliamentary accountability and on 14 November 1945 became first prime minister, with Amir Syarifuddin (q.v.) as his deputy. His strong espousal of diplomatic means for dealing with the Dutch, however, soon made him unpopular and he was strongly opposed by Tan Malaka and the Persatuan Perjuangan (qq.v.). His cabinets fell three times over the issue and on 27 June 1946 he was briefly arrested by opposition troops. Displaced by Amir in June 1947, he went abroad to argue the Republic's case at the UN (q.v.) but returned to be captured by the Dutch in the second 'Police Action' (q.v.). He led the PSI throughout the 1950s, and presided over its disastrous performance in the 1955 elections. He was arrested in 1962 but was permitted to leave for medical treatment in Switzerland in 1965. See also DIPLOMASI AND PERJUANGAN. [0563, 0656, 0865, 0866, 0704]

SYPHILIS was probably restricted to the Americas (q.v.) until 1492, though there is evidence for some sort of venereal disease in Indonesia early in C.14. The fact that syphilis apparently did not cause an immediate epidemic when it arrived in C.16 suggests the earlier presence of some related disease, perhaps yaws. Nonetheless, the disease was widespread by early C.19, and Raffles (q.v.) established a hospital for sufferers in Yogyakarta in 1811. From 1852 regular medical checks for syphilis were required of prostitutes in all parts of Java, but since this proved costly and the connection with prostitution (q.v.) was unclear, the tests were abandoned in 1911. See also HEALTH. [0483]

T

TAHANAN POLITIK (TAPOL, political prisoners), term generally applied to the persons detained after October 1965 on suspicion of complicity in the GESTAPU (q.v.) coup attempt of 1965, though the criterion was association with the PKI (q.v.) rather than activities on the evening in question. 'A' category prisoners, often major figures, were brought to trial, 'B', generally lesser figures, were detained without trial, about 10,000 being shipped after 1969 to Buru (q.v.) and 'C' category, about 550,000 persons, were detained only briefly. According to official figures, at least 1.5 million people were detained. Most 'B' *tapol* were released by late 1979. All former *tapol,* however, are noted as such on their identity cards and are barred from a number of political and social activities. See also MAHKAMAH MILITER LUAR BIASA. [0677]

TAMAN SISWA (Garden of Pupils), school system founded in Yogyakarta in 1922 by Ki Hajar Dewantoro (Suwardi Suryaningrat, q.v.), under influence of the ideas of Tagore and Montessori. Though receiving no government subsidy, the system rapidly expanded to 166 schools in 1932, teaching from primary to teachers' training level. Taman Siswa schools aimed at sound development of personality and freedom of the individual within a broad national, rather than international, colonial or Islamic, culture. Although explicitly nonpolitical in curriculum, the schools played a major role in developing self-confidence and skills amongst young Indonesians. See also EDUCATION; NATIONALISM. [0600, 1066, 1067, 1072]

TAMBORA, volcano on the island of Sumbawa (q.v.) which erupted in April 1815 in the most massive explosion in recent human history, substantially exceeding that of Krakatau (q.v.). Perhaps 50,000 people were killed, the kingdoms of Tambora and Papegat on Sumbawa were destroyed, the rain of ash caused crop failure and famine on Bali, Lombok, and neighboring islands, and ash in the atmosphere made 1816 a 'year without summer' in Europe. See also VOLCANOES.

TAN MALAKA (Sutan Ibrahim gelar Datuk Tan Malaka, 1897–1949), Indonesian revolutionary and Marxist theorist, born in West Sumatra and educated there and in the Netherlands (1913–19). On his return to Indonesia, he became involved in labor union and later PKI (qq.v.) activity, becoming party chairman in December 1921. After backing a pawnshop workers' strike, he was exiled in March 1922 to Holland, where he stood for parliament on the Dutch Communist Party ticket before going to Moscow to join the staff of Comintern. He argued strongly for an alliance of communism with nationalism and Pan-Islam, and in 1923 was appointed Comintern agent for Southeast Asia, with headquarters in Canton. From exile, he opposed the PKI's decision to abandon its alliance with Sarekat Islam (q.v.) and to launch a premature revolution. After the uprisings of 1926–27 failed the party accused him of sabotage. The inaccurate description of him as 'Trotskyist' dates from this time.

On 1 June 1927 he founded Partai Republik Indonesia (PARI) in Bangkok; although little trace now remains of it, it seems to have spread as a secretive underground party in many parts of Indonesia during the next decade, though Tan Malaka himself remained abroad until 1942. On the outbreak of the Revolution in 1945, he favored mass mobilization on a platform of revolutionary change, in contrast to the more cautious leaders of the Republic (see DIPLOMASI AND PERJUANGAN) and became the central figure in the radical Persatuan Perjuangan (q.v.). Accused of trying to overthrow the state, he was jailed from March 1946 until September 1948, when the Hatta (q.v.) government released him in order to strengthen the anti-PKI forces. He remained, however, an implacable critic of negotiation with the Dutch and in November 1948 became 'promoter' of the new Murba (q.v.) party. He continued campaigning against the Republican government after the second 'Police Action' (q.v.) and was captured and shot by Republican troops in February 1949. [0628, 0708, 0710]

TANAH BENGKOK (*ambtsvelden*), land allocated to officials in lieu of salary. The allocation of *bengkok* lands was abolished by Fransen van de Putte in 1867 except at village level, where it remained common in Central and East Java. The strong hold of officials on these lands became a recurrent source of social tension, especially during the late 1940s and early 1960s. See also LAND REFORM.

TANAH MERAH. See BOVEN DIGUL.

TANIMBAR (Timor Laut) islands, an archipelago of ca 70, mostly low, limestone, and coral islands, with coastal villages engaged in fishing and warfare. In 1646 the VOC (q.v.) signed a monopoly treaty with some village chiefs for the trade in slaves, turtleshell, shark fins, ambergris, beeswax (q.v.), and sapanwood and briefly established forts in the archipelago which they had abandoned by the end of the century. The Dutch showed little interest in the islands in C.18 or C.19, but in 1912 a military expedition was sent to subdue them. Extensive conversions to Catholicism and Protestantism (q.v.) then took place. [0062]

TANJUNG PRIOK. See JAKARTA; PORTS; WHITE PAPER.

TAPANULI. See BATAKS.

TARO (*Colocasia esculenta* and other species, Araceae), root crop native to Indonesia, perhaps first domesticated by ancestors of the Melanesians of Irian (q.v.), giving them the demographic strength to resist Austronesian expansion after 2000 B.C. (see MIGRATIONS). It grows rapidly, is easily harvested and keeps well, and was a major crop in eastern Indonesia until about 1500 when it began to be displaced by rice (q.v.). It remains an important crop in Irian. [0234, 0390, 0938]

TARUMANEGARA, early state in West Java, based in the vicinity of modern Bogor. Its existence is known only from four Sanskrit inscriptions from around 450 A.D. which record King Purnavarman as presiding over canal construction, one of the earliest records of water management in Southeast Asia. See also 'HO-LO-TAN'; KUTAI; SUNDA.

TAXATION has been an important measure of state power throughout Indonesian history. Early rulers in the archipelago obtained significant income through personal trade, plunder (see PIRACY), and direct control of production and by means of control of labor and land (qq.v.), but the development of a state apparatus for regularized revenue collection was a gradual phenomenon. There appear to have been two key elements in this process. One was the emergence of an appanage system, under which rulers allocated particular regions or blocs of population to 'vassals' in exchange for a guarantee of military and political support, a broadly feudal system. The other was the emergence of tax farms (see PACHT). The forced delivery system of the Dutch East Indies Company in West Java (see PRIANGAN) was an attempt at the direct taxation of peasants with indigenous rulers as collection agents. This system was intensified with the institution of land rent and the Cultivation System (qq.v.). Export and import duties was an important part of state revenue after the abolition of the VOC, while property tax was introduced in 1890. A company tax was first levied in 1907, and an income tax in 1908 (it was made uniform for all races in 1920). In 1908 a poll tax (*hoofdgeld,* capitation) was levied in North and West Sumatra as substitute for land rent. The poll tax levied on Java and Madura as a substitue for herendiensten (q.v.) was abolished in 1927. After independence, export and company taxes remained the central pillar of state revenues and in 1980/81 60% of all government revenue came from tax on oil companies. Less than 1% of the population was subject to income tax. Since 1983, a series of measures including the introduction of VAT (1984) and reform of the income tax laws have attempted to broaden the tax base of the state. See also GAMBLING; PERDIKAN VILLAGES; TOBACCO. [0035, 0288, 0290, 0291, 0296]

TEA (*Camellia sinensis* Theaceae). Chinese in origin, tea was first grown in Indonesia at the instigation of Governor-General Camphuys in 1690. Extensive cultivation began in 1825 and was continued under the Cultivation System, though never with much profit and the government monopoly on production was lifted in 1865. After 1870 there was a massive expansion of private tea plantations in mountainous areas of West Java and later in North Sumatra. The industry suffered badly in the Depression (q.v.), especially because of the British Imperial Preference scheme, but by 1940 a total of 213,000 ha was under tea production, about one-third of it by smallholders, and tea was the Indies' second export earner after rubber. Extensive clearing of plantations during the Japanese occupation greatly reduced the planted areas (now 125,000 ha) and the industry was further hampered by the Darul Islam (q.v.) rebellion in West Java. Dutch plantations were nationalized in 1957 and a combination of disease, lack of investment and replanting, and poor agricultural practices has meant that Indonesian tea tends to be of lesser quality than fine Indian and Ceylon teas though it has high production volume and commands ca 8% of the world market. In the 1970s commercially bottled sweet tea (*teh botol*) gained an important share of the soft drink market. [0231, 0243, 0245, 0246, 0454, 0938]

TEAK (*Tectona grandis* Verbenaceae), introduced from India, probably ca C.10. Teak forests along the northern coast of Java became a major source of income for the VOC (q.v.). Prized for its hard wood and resistance to worms and ants, teak was used for the construction of ships in precolonial times and was extensively grown by the Netherlands Indies forestry service in Central and East Java. [0936]

TELEGRAPH. The first telegraph lines in Indonesia were laid in 1857 between Batavia and Buitenzorg and were briefly restricted to government use. An undersea cable between Batavia and Singapore (q.v.) was laid in 1859 and the first lines on Sumatra in 1866. A link with Australia (q.v.) was established via Banyuwangi in 1871. In 1905 the German-Dutch Telegraph Co. of Cologne completed a cable link to Yap in the German Pacific territories, linking the colony with Europe via Siberia and the U.S., a line independent of British colonies and British firms. In 1905 the colonial government purchased a cable ship to establish undersea connections throughout the archipelago. See also PALAPA. [0342]

TELEVISION. The national broadcaster Televisi Republik Indonesia (TVRI) began operations in 1964. During the 1980s, under an information ministry program called *televisi masuk desa* (television enters the village), sets have been provided to virtually all villages throughout the country, creating a major information conduit from the central government. The fact that people now assemble to watch television from dusk until bedtime rather than gathering to listen to stories and admonitions from community elders seems likely to be a major hindrance to the passing on of local traditions, though it is too early to say how significant this will be. Commercial advertisements were banned from television in 1981. In 1987, there were an estimated 6 million television sets throughout the country. Indonesia's first commercial televison station, Rajawali Citra Televisi Indonesia, began operation in March 1988. See also PALAPA; RADIO. [0342]

TENGGER. See ASLI; HINDUISM.

TERNATE, kingdom in northern Maluku which rose in C.13 on the basis of trade in cloves (q.v.). It converted to Islam (q.v.) in C.15 and under the warlike Sultan Baabullah (r. 1570–83) dominated much of the surrounding region, including northern and eastern Sulawesi, Banda, and the coasts of Irian (qq.v.). The Portuguese, who established a fort there in 1522, were expelled in 1574, and the island was briefly conquered by Spanish forces in 1606. The Dutch competed with Ternate for control of the clove trade, fighting a fierce war (1652–58) before Ternate finally accepted VOC suzerainty in 1667. See also TIDORE. [0020]

THAILAND, Relations with. See SIAM, Historical links with.

TIDORE, kingdom in northern Maluku, geographically close and rival to Ternate (q.v.), and like it based on the clove (q.v.) trade. It had major trading and raiding links with Halmahera and Irian (qq.v.) (and for this reason was chosen in 1956 as provisional capital of the province of Irian Barat, then still held by the Dutch). The Portuguese (q.v.) established a fort there in 1578, and the Spanish (q.v.), then united with the Portuguese, made it a center of their operations in the region in early C.17. The island was captured by the Dutch in 1654. [0020]

TIGA A (Triple A) Movement, initially a slogan, 'Japan the Light of Asia, Japan the Leader of Asia, Japan the Protector of Asia', sponsored by the Japanese on their arrival in Java in March 1942 and drawing on widespread enthusiasm for Japan's role in ending Dutch colonialism. By April 1942 the slogan had ostensibly become an organization, apparently for the mobilization of Indonesians in the war effort. It appears, however, that the organization had little substance and certainly little participation from senior Indonesian or Japanese figures. It was superseded by PUTERA (q.v.) in March 1943 but had long been of no significance. [0615]

TIGA DAERAH (Three Regions) AFFAIR. From October to December 1945, a social revolution broke out in Brebes, Tegal, and Pemalang, the so-called 'three regions' of Pekalongan residency, in which the local elite were killed or driven out and a coalition of local PKI (q.v.) members, radical Muslims, and gangsters (*lenggaong*) established a revolutionary government. The revolutionaries were nominally loyal to the Indonesian Republic but the Republic's leaders saw them as dangerous and embarrassing (see DIPLOMASI AND PERJUANGAN) and the army suppressed the movement in December 1945. [0645, 0648]

TIGER (*Panthera tigris*), the largest predatory animal in western Indonesia, preying mainly on pig (q.v.) and deer. As the number of pigs increased with the spread of cultivation, so apparently did those of the tiger, becoming a major danger to human and animal life until the C.19 when the clearing of forest began to remove its habitat. A bounty was offered on carcasses in many regions until 1897. Separate subspecies occurred on Sumatra, Java, and Bali. The Balinese subspecies was probably extinct before World War II; the Javanese was reduced to perhaps four individuals in 1989. Leopards (sometimes called panthers), also found on Java, appear to account for many reported tiger sightings. The Sumatra tiger is still relatively common and is a danger to humans in some regions. See also WALLACE'S LINE. [0943, 0945, 1057]

TIME. During the Japanese occupation the whole of Indonesia, like the rest of the Japanese empire, was placed on

Tokyo time, GMT plus 9 hours. Western Indonesian time (*waktu Indonesia Barat,* WIB) now covers the islands of Java and Sumatra; Central Indonesian time covers Kalimantan, Sulawesi, Maluku, and Nusatenggara (though Bali has sometimes been placed on WIB); and Eastern Indonesian time covers Irian. See also CALENDARS.

TIMOR, island at the eastern end of Nusa Tenggara, which is mountainous, arid and now seriously deforested. The indigenous population were of mixed Austronesian-Melanesian ancestry and included the Atoni in the west and the Belu in the center. Traders visited the island for sandalwood (q.v.) from C.7, and Portuguese arrived for the same reason in 1520. Portugal's regional center was on Solor (q.v.), but coastal Timor came to be dominated by the Topasses, or 'black Portuguese,' mestizo descendants of Dutch and Portuguese settlers and Solorese who also dominated eastern Flores (q.v.). In C.17 Makassarese influence led to the conversion of some regions to Islam (q.v.). A Dutch settlement was founded at Kupang in 1653 and a Portuguese post at Dili in 1769, but it was not until 1839 that negotiations began to sort out a colonial division of territory on the island. A treaty was signed in 1859 but only in 1914 was the border finally fixed and colonial rule firmly established in the interior on either side of the border. See also EAST TIMOR; ROTI. [0022, 0444, 0969, 1011, 1042, 1052]

TIMOR GAP. See ARCHIPELAGIC CONCEPT.

TIMOR LAUT. See TANIMBAR.

TIN. Rich alluvial tin (cassiterite) deposits are found in Indonesia on the islands of Bangka and Belitung (qq.v.), geologically an extension of the Malay peninsula, which was a major early source of tin for the production of bronze (see COPPER). Small amounts of tin were exported to China from C.13. Large-scale extraction was begun on Bangka in 1710 by the Sultan of Palembang (q.v.). Mining was undertaken by Chinese, organized in *kongsi* (q.v.), who contracted with the Sultan to pay for the right to extract tin from defined areas. This system was taken over by the Dutch in 1823, the government supplying advances of rice, oil, and money and contracting to buy tin at a price fixed in advance according to the expected productivity of the soil. Mechanization of the mining began in early C.20 and in 1927 the so-called Bangka Tinwinning was established as a state enterprise (q.v.) of the colonial government; after World War II, operations were taken over by a private firm, the Gemeenschappelijke Mijnbouw Billiton, which was nationalized in 1953. Mining began on Belitung in 1850 and by 1860 was in the hands of a private company, the Billiton-Maatschappij. Actual extraction of the tin, however, was done by Chinese kongsi. Large-scale offshore mining using dredges began in 1966. [0399]

TITLES. A wide variety of titles, hereditary and conferred, were used by the traditional aristocracies of the archipelago and many of these were preserved by the Dutch as part of their policy of retaining native rulers as agents of colonial rule. During and immediately after the Revolution, many titles fell out of use, but they seem now to be being revived. The Javanese lower aristocratic title *Raden* (abbreviated R.), and its female equivalent *Raden Ajeng* (R.A.) are commonly used today as are the Minangkabau *Sutan* (St.), the Malay *Datuk* and *Pangeran* and the Bugis *Karaëng* and *Arung*.

Many elite Indonesians have academic titles which derive from the Dutch or Netherlands Indies education (q.v.) system. Mr (*meester in de rechten*) was the primary law degree but has now been replaced by SH (*sarjana hukum*), placed after the holder's name. Drs (*doctorandus,* now SS or *sarjana sastra*) is sometimes misleadingly described as denoting completion of all requirements for a doctorate but the dissertation. Rather, it is conferred upon one who has completed the standard undergraduate course in arts and economics, and since it requires a short thesis (*scriptie*) it is perhaps most closely equivalent to a Master's degree. Ir (*ingenieur*) was the primary degree for graduates in engineering, agriculture, and similar technical fields. Dr was the standard title of the holder of a medical degree, but was commonly spelled *dokter* or dr to distinguish it from the thesis-based doctorates. See also NAMES. [0453]

TJIK DI TIRO, Teungku (1836–91) Acehnese ulama (religious teacher). He joined guerrilla resistance to the Dutch in Aceh (q.v.) in 1878 and soon emerged as principal leader of the ulama, touring the countryside to preach holy war. His example helped to establish the ulama firmly as the symbols of opposition to colonialism, unlike secular war leaders (uleëbalang) such as Teuku Umar (q.v.). [0528]

TJIPTO MANGUNKUSUMO (1886–1943). Physician and one of the founders of Budi Utomo (q.v.) in May 1908. Unlike his colleagues, he was strongly critical of the feudalism and conservatism of traditional Javanese culture, and tried to move Budi Utomo away from exclusively focusing on Java and on the priyayi (q.v.). He advocated especially the elimination of the Javanese language whose levels of address, he argued, preserved social inequalities. Dissatisfied with Budi Utomo, he left in October 1909 and in 1911 helped to found the radical multiracial Indische Partij (q.v.). He was expelled from the Indies 1913–14 but on his return was appointed to the first Volksraad (q.v.) as a representative of Insulinde (q.v.). He was sent into exile (q.v.) to Banda in

1927–41, accused of complicity in the 1926/27 PKI uprisings.

TJOKROAMINOTO, Haji Umar Said (1882–1934), trained as a government official but left to work in various jobs before becoming Surabaya leader of the Sarekat Dagang Islam. A charismatic figure, he soon emerged as a national leader and was chosen to head Sarekat Islam (q.v.) when it took its new shortened name in September 1912. Many peasants believed him to be the Ratu Adil or Just Prince of Javanese mythology, and he was reputed (incorrectly) to have been born as Krakatau (q.v.) erupted. Under his leadership, SI won a huge following, claiming ca 2 million, but it became increasingly divided between Marxists of the ISDV (q.v.) and radical Muslim scholars, whom Tjokroaminoto tried to balance in an uneasy compromise. He also sought to avoid provoking Dutch repression and accepted appointment to the first Volksraad (q.v.). He became less sympathetic to the Marxists after they criticized him in 1920, but was in jail for alleged perjury over the Afdeling B Affair when they were expelled. In February 1923 he formed the remains of SI into the Partai Sarekat Islam, but this too lost much support with the founding of the Nahdatul Ulama (q.v.) in 1926.

TOBACCO (*Nicotiana tabacum* Solanaceae) was one of the first New World plants to reach the archipelago, being reported from the court of Mataram on Java in 1601. The chewing of betel (q.v.) and the smoking of opium and probably cannabis (qq.v.) were then already known in the archipelago, and tobacco spread only gradually as a drug of addiction, often being used in conjunction with betel and/or opium. From 1830 to 1864, tobacco was grown widely on Java under the Cultivation System (q.v.). Later in the century, the Vorstenlanden (qq.v.) and West Kalimantan became major areas of Western-owned plantation tobacco, while there was extensive smallholder cultivation on Java especially in Kedu and Banyumas. The main area of production, however, was East Sumatra (q.v.), where J. Nienhuys established the first plantation in 1863/4. Indonesian cigarette consumption today is dominated by kretek (q.v.), cigarettes in which the tobacco is mixed with cloves (q.v.). The importance of tobacco excise to state income and of cigarettes as *penghibur rakyat* (comforters of the people) has led the government to discourage the emergence of an antismoking campaign. [0938]

TONARIGUMI. See RUKUN TETANGGA.

TORAJA, ethnic group in the mountains of central Sulawesi. The region was divided into numerous small communities subject to periodic slaving and plundering raids by coastal kingdoms such as Luwu (q.v.), though in C.17 most joined a temporary alliance against Bugis (q.v.) invasion. Coffee was introduced as a major crop in the 1870s and increased revenue from coffee exports seems to have enabled a few chiefs, such as Pong Tiku of Pangala, to establish themselves as regional warlords in the final decades of C.19. The Dutch conquered the region in 1905–06 as part of their general consolidation of power in the archipelago, but their administrative reorganization and demands for taxes and corvée labor sparked a major rebellion in 1917. Christianity has since spread to 80% of the population, Islam to 10%. In the 1980s traditional Toraja religion has been recognized, under the name Aluk, as a sect of Hinduism (q.v.). [0076, 0100, 0548, 1037, 1059, 1110]

TOTOK, colonial era term for anyone recently arrived in the Indies or, more generally and in contrast to *peranakan* (q.v.), to unacculturated immigrant communities. See also CHINESE IN INDONESIA.

TOURISM. Organized tourism, with fixed timetables and itineraries and prepayment for services, began only after travel permit requirements were abolished for Europeans on Java and Madura in 1902, detailed tourist guides being published soon after and ever since. In general, prewar tourism showed visitors natural phenomena (including landscapes), antiquities, and colonial architecture; whereas postwar tourism emphasized indigenous culture and food. In 1987 1.05 million foreign tourists visited Indonesia, Bali (q.v.) being the favored destination. [0100, 1161, 1164]

TOWNS. See CITIES.

TRADE, Interregional. The exchange of goods between individuals and groups is as old in the Indonesian archipelago as anywhere in the world, but it was not until improvements in shipping technology around the beginning of the Christian era that the region became part of the great maritime trade route which extended from southern China to the eastern Mediterranean. The route was in fact a complex of trade route in which most commodities traveled only part of the total distance and typically passed repeatedly from one trader to another at the entrepôt ports which dotted the coastline. Until C.10, commerce in Indonesian waters was primarily in Indonesian hands, and Southeast Asians controlled most of the shipping north to China (see CHINA, Historical links with). Indian merchants, on the other hand, dominated trade in the Bay of Bengal, though the absence of Indian vocabulary derived from trade in Indonesian languages suggests that they did not penetrate far. The rhythm of this trade was seasonal, following the changing pattern of the monsoons.

The principal goods of this trade are fairly well known. Cotton cloth from India and silk and porcelain from China were major imports, while the archipelago exported a more varied range of spices, minerals, and forest products (see ALOEWOOD; CINNAMON; GOLD; LAKAWOOD; TIN). The organization of the trade is less well understood. It has commonly been suggested that most traders were 'pedlars' operating as individuals with small capital, and carrying small quantities of relatively high-value goods between entrepôts. There is a good deal of evidence, however, that local rulers were involved not only in taxing and plundering trade (see PIRACY), but also in large scale commercial enterprises.

It is fairly clear that the arrival of Portuguese (q.v.) in Indonesia in C.16 brought little change to the pattern of trade. The Portuguese strength lay primarily in their naval power and their consequent ability to seize ports such as Melaka (q.v.) and to extract customs duties from passing merchants. The European trading companies, however, have generally been seen as a major organizational innovation, partly because their capital reserves enabled them to outlast local competitors in difficult markets and partly because their bureaucratic structures made them less dependent on the will and ability of single individuals. The Dutch East Indies Company (q.v.), however, also relied to a considerable extent on armed force to hold its dominant position in the trade of the archipelago. The rise of the European trading companies changed the balance of political power in the archipelago, thereby impoverishing the former merchant princes of the coastal states and strengthening the hand of the feudal elites of the interior. [0396, 0403, 0412, 0426, 0429, 0430, 0435, 0449, 0451, 0452, 0473, 0492]

TRADE UNIONS. See LABOR UNIONS.

TRANSMIGRATION, the government policy of shifting people from the heavily populated inner islands of

Indonesia (Java, Madura, Bali, Lombok, qq.v.) to the ostensibly underpopulated outer islands. The program began in 1902 as part of the Ethical Policy (q.v.), and by 1931 36,000 people were living in the first transmigration settlement in Lampung (q.v.). After independence, transmigration was often seen as a panacea for the problems of rural Java and extravagant plans were drafted in 1952 for using it to reduce the population of Java (then over 50 million) to 31 million by 1987. Sukarno (q.v.) announced an annual resettlement target of 1.5 million in 1964, and Suharto (q.v.) raised this to 2 million in 1966. In fact, however, no more than 340,000 people were shifted from Java to Sumatra in the years 1950 to 1965. Between 1969 and 1982, about 1-½ million people were moved, during which time the population of Java-Madura rose by about 17 million.

The program became a major undertaking of the New Order and was given legislative basis in the 1972 Law on Transmigration. It received financial and technical support from the World Bank (q.v.) but has proven very expensive, at its peak in the mid 1980s costing $7,000 per family moved and consuming 6% of the national budget. Officially there is no compulsion on people to take part, but those displaced by development projects or natural disasters are often heavily pressured to join. Until 1985, former political prisoners (see TAHANAN POLITIK) were encouraged to take part but they have since been banned.

The initial rationale for transmigration was the relief of population pressure on Java, but government statements now emphasize that the benefits of transmigration will fall to those who take part rather than those who stay behind. A further goal, less publicly stated, has been the transmission of Javanese agricultural techniques and culture to other regions both for economic development and for national integration. Settlements of Javanese and Balinese in outer regions are seen as a useful obstacle to potential local secessionist movements. Transmigration, however, has in some cases increased local tensions, especially where transmigrants have been settled on land which local people believe to be theirs; the national government has generally been unwilling, for instance, to recognize the land rights of shifting cultivators and hunting communities. There was some killing of transmigrants in Sulawesi during the Permesta (q.v.) rebellion and more recently of transmigrants in Irian (q.v.). In the 1980s, criticism of the environmental consequences of transmigration has also increased. See also JAVANIZATION; POPULATION. [0211, 0793, 0795, 0799, 0810]

TRAVEL. To protect its trading monopoly, the VOC banned from its possessions all Europeans not in its service. After the fall of the Company, various more liberal regulations were introduced, but under the Cultivation System (q.v.) the old restrictions were largely restored before being lifted in stages between 1861 and 1911 (on Java and Madura; 1916 in the outer islands) when Europeans became free to trade and reside anywhere in the archipelago, subject only to the exorbitante rechten (see EXILE) of the governors-general (see also TOURISM). Formal restrictions on the travel of Indonesians began only in 1816, with the introduction of a pass system intended to keep the labor force in place. Passes were abolished in 1863 and liberalization of travel regulations continued, a pace or two behind that for Europeans, until 1914 (on Java; 1918 in the outer islands), when travel and residence throughout the archipelago was virtually unrestricted. Chinese and other 'foreign Orientals' (see RACE) were regulated separately but in a similar way to Indonesians, being subject to pass laws from 1816 to 1863 and being required from 1835 to 1919 to live in so-called *wijken* (districts) or Chinatowns. Current regulations require

Indonesians to obtain a *surat jalan* for long or interprovincial journeys. In November 1982 a so-called fiscal fee was introduced to discourage overseas travel by Indonesians. In 1989 Indonesia announced it would abolish the requirement that citizens leaving the country obtain an exit permit. See also HAJ; MARCO POLO; J.H. VAN LINSCHOTEN; ROADS; SHIPPING; TOMÉ PIRES. [0874, 0890]

TREKKERS. Dutch residents of the Indies intending to return to the Netherlands at the end of their term of service, in contrast to the *blijvers* who intended to remain in the colony on retirement. See also DUTCH IN INDONESIA

TRIBUTE SYSTEM. See CHINA, Historical links with.

TRUNOJOYO, Raden (ca 1649–80), a prince of Madura (q.v.). He conspired with the crown prince of Mataram (q.v.) against King Amangkurat I (q.v.), who had had Trunojoyo's father killed, and, after seizing Madura in 1671 and, attacking Java, declared himself king in 1675. He defeated Mataram in 1677, capturing the court and sending the king into exile. His former coconspirator the crown prince, however, as Amangkurat II, obtained help from the VOC (q.v.) and defeated the rebels in 1679. Trunojoyo was executed in 1680. [0371, 0456]

TUAK. See ALCOHOL.

TURKEY, Historical links with. After the capture of Constantinople in 1453, the Ottoman Turkish empire was the preeminent military power and cultural center in the Islamic world and a natural focus of attention amongst the newly Islamizing peoples in the Indonesian archipelago, especially as a potential ally against the Portuguese. A Turkish diplomat, Seh Ibrahim, helped to mediate the Treaty of Giyanti (q.v.) in 1755. Aceh (q.v) is said to have accepted Ottoman suzerainty in C.16 and Sultan Ibrahim renewed the submission in 1850; his successors appealed to the Ottomans for help in 1869, just prior to the Aceh War. Turkey's abolition of the Caliphate in 1924 helped to crystallize division within the Sarekat Islam over the place of Islam: many modernists saw the reforms of Kemal Atatürk as a model for what might be achieved in an independent Indonesia; traditionalists saw them as an example of dangerous secularism, and this concern contributed to the founding of the Nahdatul Ulama (q.v.) in 1926. [0759, 1140]

TURMERIC. Spice prepared from the ends of the root fibers of *Curcuma domestica* (Zingiberaceae), valued both for its bright yellow color and its flavor. Originally exported from Southeast Asia to China and India, it soon came to be cultivated in both places. [0751, 0938]

TURTLE. The shell of the Hawksbill Turtle (*Eretmochelys imbricata*) has been exported from Indonesia to China for at least two millennia. Turtle eggs are a source of food for some communities in eastern Indonesia. [0943]

U

UJUNG KULON, peninsula on the southwestern corner of Java, the sole remaining habitat of Javan rhinoceros (q.v.). A nature reserve was declared in 1921, a game reserve in 1937, and a national park, including the volcanic island of Krakatau (q.v.), in 1980. See also CONSERVATION. [0943]

UJUNG PANDANG. See MAKASSAR.

ULAMA, Muslim teachers and religious leaders. See ISLAM; NAHDATUL ULAMA.

UMAR, Teuku (1854–99), Acehnese war leader (*uleëbalang*) and opportunist. In the prolonged Aceh War, he sided alternately with the Dutch (1883–84, 1893–96) and the Acehnese (1873–83, 1884–93, 1896–99). While Umar's own motives seem to have been mainly personal ambition, his career typified the ambivalence of the uleëbalang towards the colonial authorities on the one hand and the ulama (religious teachers) on the other and was a forerunner of the uleëbalang-Dutch coalition which uneasily ruled Aceh in the first part of C.20. See also ACEH. [0528]

UNIÃO DEMOCRÁTICA TIMORENSE (UDT, Timorese Democratic Union), founded on 11 May 1974 as the party of the East Timor (q.v.) establishment and first party after the Lisbon coup. It was dominated by mixed-race Portuguese-Timorese from the small commercial, administrative, and agricultural elites, as well as traditional chiefs (*liurai*) and more or less inherited the membership of the Acção Nacional Populár (q.v.). Its program called for general political liberalization and movement to self-government under Portuguese tutelage. From January to May 1975 it was in coalition with Fretilin (q.v.), but after staging an unsuccessful coup on 11 August joined APODETI (q.v.) in seeking integration with Indonesia. After incorporation, the UDT leader Francisco Lopez da Cruz became deputy governor, but the party ceased to exist in early 1976. [0905]

UNIÃO NACIONAL. See ACÇÃO NACIONAL POPULÁR.

UNITED KINGDOM, Relations with. See BRITAIN, Historical links with.

UNITED NATIONS. The United Nations took from the start an active interest in decolonization and was drawn into the Indonesian-Dutch dispute in July 1947, when India and Australia (qq.v.) raised the Dutch first 'Police Action' (q.v.) in the Security Council. The UN responded in October 1947 by appointing a so-called Good Offices Commission, consisting of Australia, Belgium, and the U.S. (q.v.) to facilitate a settlement. This Commission presided over the Renville Agreement (q.v.) of January 1948. At the beginning of 1949, after the second 'Police Action,' the Security Council demanded the full transfer of sovereignty to Indonesia by mid 1950.

Indonesia joined the UN on 26–29 September 1950 and was able to use U.S. good offices again in the early 1960s in the transfer of Irian (q.v.) from Dutch rule, but on 2 January 1965 indignantly left the UN when Malaysia became a temporary member of the Security Council (see CONFRONTATION). Indonesia then tried to organize an alternative UN in the form of a Conference of the New Emerging Forces (CONEFO), but this had made little headway by the time Sukarno (q.v.) lost power. Indonesia rejoined the UN in September 1966.

In November 1975, Portugal formally requested UN help in solving its East Timor (q.v.) problem, and on 12 December the General Assembly passed a motion calling on Indonesia to withdraw. On 22 December 1975 and 22 April 1976, the Security Council condemned the Indonesian invasion of East Timor and instructed Indonesia to withdraw; such instructions are binding under the UN charter, but have been ignored by Indonesia, as were annual motions of condemnation passed by the General Assembly 1975–82. [0563, 0742, 0763]

UNITED STATES, Historical links with. Traders from Britain's American colonies were present in Indonesian ports well before the revolution of 1776, and the American scientist Horsfield (q.v.) conducted important research on Java in early C.19, but U.S. interest in Indonesia did not become substantial until the middle of C.19, when U.S. missionary groups began conversion in Sumatra and growing U.S. industrialization stimulated trade. In the 1860s the U.S. exported oil to Indonesia, but from 1871 American companies, especially Socony, took an important role in oil exploration in the archipelago. U.S. investment in East Sumatra rubber (q.v.) was important and the U.S. became a major market for Indies spices, coffee, tobacco and, after 1905, oil (qq.v.). The Acehnese unsuccessfully requested U.S. help against the Dutch in 1873. [0720, 0735]

UNITED STATES, Relations with. Indonesian nationalists were aware from at least 1944 that the United States was a major power in the Western Pacific and the first actions of the Indonesian Republic were designed in part to win U.S. support for the independence struggle. Republican leaders explicitly compared their Declaration of Independence to that of the U.S. and further guaranteed the position of U.S. commercial interests in the archipelago. During the Revolution, Sumitro Joyohadikusumo (q.v.) on behalf of the Indonesian government made extensive efforts to involve the U.S. on the side of Indonesia by making commercial agreements with U.S. firms more generous than the Dutch were ever likely to concede. The U.S., however, remained generally lukewarm towards the Republic, particularly since it needed to keep the Netherlands amenable to participation in the North Atlantic Treaty Organization, and aimed primarily but unsuccessfully at a settlement acceptable to both sides. After the defeat of the PKI at Madiun (q.v.) in 1948, however, U.S. official opinion swung strongly behind the Hatta (q.v.) government as a likely bastion against communism in Southeast Asia, and after the Second 'Police Action' (q.v.), U.S. pressure forced the Dutch to make a rapid transfer of sovereignty to the Republic (see also UNITED NATIONS).

The U.S. cultivated Indonesian governments in the 1950s as potential noncommunist allies in Asia, but the idea of direct alliance with the U.S. was unpopular in Indonesia and in 1952 the Sukiman (q.v.) government fell over its acceptance of U.S. military aid. U.S. unease with Indonesia's leftward swing under Ali Sastroamijoyo (q.v.) and then under Guided Democracy led it to give clandestine military support to the PRRI-Permesta rebellion in 1958, which was exposed with the shooting down of an American B-25 pilot, Alan Pope, over Ambon on 18 May. Relations improved in the early 1960s, when the U.S. pressed the Netherlands to abandon its claim to Irian (q.v.), but deteriorated rapidly from 1962. An economic stabilization program offered by the U.S. under IMF supervision was rejected by Sukarno because of Confrontation (q.v.) with Malaysia. Contact continued, however, with the Indonesian army (q.v.) via training and supplies (by 1965 half the officers corps had received some U.S. training).

The U.S. was delighted with the accession to power of General Suharto (q.v.) in 1965–66, though the extent to which it played a role in his success is unclear; Suharto certainly knew that the U.S. would support the removal of Sukarno and the banning of the PKI, and the CIA seems to have played a propaganda role in ensuring that the ambiguous GESTAPU (q.v.) coup of 30 September 1965 was seen unequivocally by the general public in Indonesia as a communist plot. Since the consolidation of the New Order, relations have been stable. Indonesia remains officially nonaligned and committed to the removal of great power influence from the region, but in practice has aligned itself fairly closely with the United States, agreeing, for instance, to send troops to Vietnam (q.v.) as part of the International Commission of Control and Supervision in 1972. It is also widely held that Indonesia invaded East Timor in December 1975 in the belief that action had been approved by President Ford. The United States' subsequent unwillingness to accept Indonesia's annexation of the territory without demur strained relations, and from this time U.S. concern over Indonesia's human rights record and the question of copyright (q.v.) protection caused further difficulties. President Suharto annoyed the U.S. in 1988 with calls for a nuclear weapons free zone in Southeast Asia. In May 1989 a visit by Vice-President Quayle was greeted with demonstrations against the role allegedly played by U.S.-based transnational corporations in environmental destruction, especially in Irian (q.v.). [0735, 0738, 0747, 0758, 0766]

UPAS (*Antiaris toxicaria* Urticaceae, *ipoh*), tree which produces a highly poisonous sap, formerly smeared, sometimes in conjunction with locally produced strychnine, on darts (q.v.) and arrows for hunting and on swords and daggers for warfare. It was extensively used in the defence of Melaka (q.v.) against the Portuguese in 1511. The tree became the subject of a widespread scientific myth initiated by Rumphius (q.v.), which held that its fumes would rapidly kill any living thing, plant, or animal within a radius of several meters or more. The legend probably derived originally from efforts by producers of the poison to discourage closer investigation of its origins. [0936, 0938, 0983]

URBANIZATION. See CITIES.

V

VADERLANDSE CLUB, conservative association of Europeans in the Netherlands Indies founded in 1929 to promote Dutch interests in the colony and to resist Indonesian nationalism and the expansion of indigenous education. It had 9,000 members in 1930. Though sometimes vocal, it had little influence on government policy. See also DUTCH IN INDONESIA. [0552]

VANILLA (*Vanilla planifolia* Orchidaceae) plants reached Java from Central America in 1819 and flowered in 1825. A small vanilla plantation sector developed on Java in 1845, after the need for artificial pollination was realized. [0938]

VEREENIGDE OOST-INDISCHE COMPAGNIE. See DUTCH EAST INDIES COMPANY.

VICE-PRESIDENT. The post of vice-president has no formal responsibilities except to support and, if necessary, to replace the president. Mohammad Hatta (q.v.), elected vice-president in 1945 under the first constitution (q.v.), was prime minister 1948–50 by virtue of his national standing rather than his vice-presidency. He was reappointed vice-president by Sukarno in October 1950 under the provisional constitution, but resigned in 1956, after which the post remained vacant until 1973. Hamengkubuwono IX (q.v.) was vice-president from 1973 to 1978, Adam Malik (q.v.) from 1978 to 1983, Umar Wirahadikusumah (b.1924) from 1983 to 1988, and Sudharmono (b.1927) from 1988. [0890]

VIETNAM, Historical links and relations with. Strong Chinese influence in Vietnam tended to limit its role in Southeast Asia in early times, though Vietnam was a major exporter of ceramics (q.v.) to Indonesia in C.15. Thereafter the rise of European power in the region strengthened the mutual isolation. In 1947 Vietnam and Indonesia cooperated briefly in the South East Asia League (q.v.) but made no attempt otherwise to coordinate their national struggles. Sukarno recognized the DRV (Democratic Republic of Vietnam) and accepted an NLF mission in Jakarta. At U.S. request, Indonesian troops were posted in South Vietnam as part of the International Commission of Control and Supervision under the Paris Accord of 1972.

In 1977, following Vietnam's reunification in 1975, refugees from Vietnam began to arrive in large numbers in Indonesia's Natuna archipelago, and to 1981 the Indonesian camp on Pulau Galang received over 65,000 refugees for processing and transit to third countries; there was domestic concern over the high proportion of Vietnamese Chinese among the refugees and none were accepted for permanent settlement. Indonesia joined the ASEAN (q.v.) condemnation of Vietnam's 1979 invasion of Cambodia, upholding the seating of 'Democratic Kampuchea' in the United Nations (q.v.), but has consistently sought compromise over the issue, believing that Vietnam has no hegemonist ambitions beyond Indochina and that Vietnam's isolation dangerously increases the scope for great power (especially Chinese) intervention in the region. In March 1989 an Indonesian private bank, Summa Bank, announced plans to join the Saigon Industrial and Commercial Bank in the Indovina Bank, communist Vietnam's first such banking venture. See also SOVIET UNION, Relations with. [0728, 0737, 0745]

VILLAGES. See DESA.

VOLCANOES. Located at the junction of three tectonic plates (see CONTINENTAL DRIFT), Indonesia is volcanically active, 829 active volcanoes being found widely scattered in eastern Indonesia and along the spines of Sumatra and Java. Ejecta of low pH are responsible in Java, Bali, and other places for exceptionally fertile soil; ejecta of high pH in Sumatra and elsewhere are less productive. The greatest eruption in recent history was that of Tambora (q.v.) on Sumbawa in 1815. This, however, is dwarfed by an eruption 75,000 years ago in North Sumatra which created the valley now partly filled by Lake Toba, when an estimated 1500–2000 km of material was ejected, leaving a caldera 100 km long. The eruption of Krakatau (q.v.) in the Sunda Strait in 1883 is better known and recorded. Kelud in East Java has also been particularly destructive, less because of the force of its periodic eruptions (1752, 1771, 1811, 1848, 1864, 1901, 1919) than because water trapped in its crater is flung out to create dangerous mud avalanches. In 1963 Gunung Agung on Bali erupted with much devastation and loss of life. Sulphur collection has been an important local industry on several volcanoes and a number of volcanoes have been harnessed for steam power (Kamojan, near Garut, since 1926, Salak more recently). A Vulkanologisch Dienst (Vulcanological Service) was established by the colonial government in 1920. [0911, 0960, 0964, 0968]

VOLKSLECTUUR, Comite or Kantoor voor de. See BALAI PUSTAKA.

VOLKSRAAD (People's Council), representative body of the Netherlands Indies, established in 1916 and assembled in 1918 with 39 members, approximately half elected and half appointed. Membership was on an ethnic basis, with initially 15 indigenes, 23 Europeans and 'foreign orientals' (see RACE), and a chairperson appointed by the Crown. In 1931 membership was expanded to 60 (30 indigenes, of whom 20 were elected, 25 Europeans [15 elected] and 5 others [3 elected]). Elected indigenous representatives were chosen for a four-year term by indigenous members of the local and kabupaten councils as a single electorate. Initially the Volksraad had only advisory power, though as its members had parliamentary immunity it provided a platform for those nationalists who accepted election (see

NATIONALISM). From 1931 the Volksraad approved the annual budget of the Netherlands Indies and appointed a College van Gedelegeerden (Chamber of Delegates) to examine and approve ordinances of the colonial government. While all government ordinances required its approval, rejected ordinances could come into force in any case as general government regulations (*algemene maatregelen van bestuur*). See also CHUO SANGI-IN. [0563, 0601]

VOLLENHOVEN, Cornelis van (1874–1933), professor of law at Leiden University, 1901–33 and foremost proponent of *adat* (q.v.) or traditional Indonesian law. He strongly resisted moves for a single set of legal codes for the colony and was mainly responsible for the codification of adat in successive *Adatrechtbundels*. See also LAW. [0877]

VOORLOPIGE FEDERALE REGEERING. See SUCCESSION.

VORSTENLANDEN, the princely states of Central Java, that is, the Sultanate of Yogyakarta (q.v.), the Kasunanan (Sunanate) of Surakarta (q.v.) and the lesser Pakualaman and Mangkunegaran (q.v.). Descendants of the divided kingdom of Mataram (q.v.), these were the only indirectly ruled parts of the island in the latter colonial period and were thus exempt from many of the colonial regulations applied to other parts of the island. The Cultivation System, for instance, was not introduced in the Vorstenlanden and large privately owned plantations developed there rather earlier than elsewhere. The authority of the Vorstenland rulers was limited to Javanese within their domains. Europeans and others were the administrative and legal responsibility of Dutch Residents. See also PARTICULIERE LANDERIJEN; ZELFBESTUREN.

VREEMDE OOSTERLINGEN. See RACE.

W

WAJO', Bugis (q.v.) state in south-western Sulawesi, founded in 1471 by exiles from Luwu (q.v.). Its ruler, called the Arung Mataa, was elected by a council of forty princes. In 1737 under Arung Singkang (La Ma'dukelleng, 1700?–65) Wajo' attacked Bone (q.v.) and in 1739 headed a federation of southern Sulawesi states in a series of unsuccessful attacks on the Dutch in Makassar (q.v.). A Dutch protectorate was established in 1860/61. [0475]

WALI SONGO (Nine Saints), said to have converted Java to Islam (q.v.) in C.16. Their individual careers, which were not especially connected, are shrouded in legend, but several appear to have been non-Javanese and to have studied in Melaka. The first Muslim state on Java, Demak (q.v.), is said to have been founded by Sunan Gunungjati (d. 1570).

WALLACE'S LINE, named for Alfred Russell Wallace (1823–1913), a British scientist, with Charles Darwin author of the theory of evolution, evidence for which he obtained during research in Indonesia from 1854 to 1862. Previous scientific opinion had held that animal and plant forms were a direct response to environmental conditions, such as climate. Wallace, however, noted that although the Indonesian islands were climatically similar and geographically close, there was a dramatic difference in fauna and flora between the west, where typical Eurasiatic species such as tigers, rhinoceros (qq.v.), monkeys and oaks were found, and the east of the archipelago, where marsupials, megapodes (mound-building birds) and eucalypts were common. It is now known that the former were characteristic of the old northern super-continent of Laurasia, while the latter derive from the southern super-continent of Gondwana, though present biological distribution does not exactly reflect the geological origin of the islands (see CONTINENTAL DRIFT). The line which Wallace drew between Bali and Lombok and between Sulawesi and Kalimantan separating these two zones has been called Wallace's line. Wallace himself, however, recognized the existence of a transition zone, and it is now more common to refer to this distinct zone, covering roughly Sulawesi, Maluku and Nusatenggara, as Wallacea. See also PREHISTORY; SUNDA SHELF. [0075, 0418, 0972, 0974, 0975]

WARFARE is nowhere pleasant, but the ferocity of traditional battle in the archipelago seems to have been limited by a number of factors. First, warfare traditionally aimed at capturing people, representing a valuable labor resource, and obtaining allegiance of their rulers rather than winning territory, which was relatively abundant, and so combatants tended to be somewhat sparing of life. Second, prolonged defence of cities in a tropical climate was difficult and so retreat, which avoided confrontation, seems to have been a common strategy. Third, trickery, deception, and bluff on the part of commanders seem to have been prized, and surrogate battle by champions in single combat was a common strategy (see KERBAU). When conflict actually came to battle, running amuk (q.v.) seems to have played a major role, though the main reason for this furious charge into enemy ranks in disregard for one's own safety seems to have been to cause terror rather than destruction. And fourth, combatants seem to have attributed the outcome of warfare at least in part to supernatural factors, keeping for instance *jimat* or charms for their own personal protection and taking account of portents of the final result.

Against this somewhat optimistic picture must be set the accounts of warfare described by Europeans in C.16

and after, in which massacres and other military brutality are common. Some authors have indeed suggested that the Europeans brought an increased ruthlessness to warfare, but this is hard to specify or document. It does seem clear, though, that the initial military advantage of Europeans was slender and that it derived from their use of a standing army of professional soldiers rather than from technological superiority of weapons. Mercenary troops became common in the archipelago from C.17, but whether they were an older phenomenon is hard to tell. A major consequence of the Dutch presence, however, was the gradual disarming of the indigenous population, so that Java for instance, once known as a land of warriors gained a reputation for exceptional peace. See also AREN; ARMY; DEFENCE POLICY; KONINKLIJK NEDERLANDSCH INDISCH LEGER; WEAPONS. [0482, 0483]

WATER. The first public purification of water took place in Batavia (q.v.) in 1923. Since the 1980s bottled water has become a common drink. See also TEA.

WAWASAN NUSANTARA. See ARCHIPELAGIC CONCEPT.

WAYANG. Literally 'shadow', this term is now applied to a wide range of Javanese dramatic forms: wayang kulit (shadow puppets), wayang golek (solid wooden puppets), wayang beber (painted screens), wayang klitik (flat wooden puppets), wayang topeng (masks), and wayang wong (dance dramas). Although now named as if variants of a single art, these forms probably have different origins, wayang beber deriving perhaps from traditional story-telling and wayang wong from traditional dance, though it took its present form only in Yogyakarta in C.19. Wayang golek is said to have been invented by one of the Wali Songo (q.v.), Sunan

Kalijaga, near Yogyakarta in 1586, but was reported by Tomé Pires (q.v.) in 1515. Wayang kulit may be derived ultimately from South Indian shadow puppetry, though authorities are not agreed on this.

Wayang kulit employs flat leather shadow puppets manipulated by a *dalang* (puppeteer), who simultaneously provides all voices and cues the gamelan (q.v.). Its earliest recorded use was in C.9. In former times the audience watched the shadows of the puppets cast on a white cloth screen by an oil lamp above the dalang's head; more recently audiences have tended to shift around behind the dalang and gamelan to watch the finely painted puppets themselves. Wayang kulit generally presents episodes from the Mahabharata (q.v.), but within this framework the dalang has enormous scope for improvisation. Wayang kulit was used by the so-called Nine Saints to spread Islam (q.v.) on Java (it is said that the distorted shape of the characters was adopted to satisfy the Islamic prohibition on the representation of humans), and prewar nationalists, communists and post-independence governments have all seen it as a tool for spreading information and ideas rapidly to the rural population of Java. [0007, 0107, 0113, 0123, 0124, 0136, 0772, 0848]

WEAPONS. A number of traditional weapons have been in use in the archipelago, *viz.*, the *kris* (q.v.) on Java, Bali, and Lombok; the *klewang,* a long, generally straight bladed knife (Aceh); darts (q.v.) amongst the Dayaks and Bataks. Bows and arrows have also been common. Cannons were introduced by the Chinese, Gujeratis, and Turks in C.15. [0109, 0483]

WERENG, general name for various flying insects of the families Cicadelidae and Delphacidae (Order Hemiptera) occurring in plague proportions in Java since 1969 and transmitting major viral diseases of rice. Their spread is closely related to the Green Revolution (q.v.), under which more susceptible rice varieties were introduced. Overuse of pesticides has diminished the bird and other predator populations, and the number of crops per year has increased so that the life cycle of the wereng has never been disrupted by lack of food. The plague was checked briefly after 1976 by the introduction of new resistant rice varieties but within a decade the wereng had adapted and by 1986, wereng were said to be responsible for an annual loss of 200,000–300,000 potential tonnes of agricultural produce. In November 1986, however, with dramatic success Indonesia introduced a program of integrated pest management for rice, involving bans on the use of many pesticides and a start with rotation of crops between different rice varieties.

WEST NEW GUINEA, WEST PAPUA. See IRIAN.

WESTERLING, Raymond Paul Pierre (1919–87). Dutch commando and counterguerrilla specialist, born in Istanbul and thus known as 'The Turk.' He was posted with his Korps Speciale Troepen to South Sulawesi in late 1946 and used particularly brutal techniques in suppressing local Indonesian nationalists. The official Indonesian figure of 40,000 dead is probably inflated, but his victims certainly numbered some thousands. On 23 January 1950, having been recently demobilized from the KNIL (q.v.), he launched an unsuccessful coup in Bandung to bolster the governments of Pasundan and the RIS (qq.v.) against the Indonesian Republic, but in doing so brought about the fall of Pasundan. [0643, 0656]

WHALES AND WHALING. Both the blue whale (*Balaenoptera musculus*) and Rudolphi's whale (*B. borealis*) occur in Indonesian waters, the former very sporadically. *B. borealis* is hunted using traditional means by villagers of Lamakera (Solor) and Lamararap (Lomblen). [0998, 1160]

WHITE BOOK (*Buku Putih*), a systematic critique of New Order policies issued on 14 January 1978 by students at the Bandung Institute of Technology opposed to President Suharto's reelection. The book was banned and about 30 student leaders arrested and tried, including Heri Akhmadi, who was convicted on charges of insulting the head of state. See also SUBVERSION. [0856]

WHITE PAPER (*Lembaran Putih*). On 12 September 1984 army units in the Jakarta port of Tanjung Priok shot dead between nine and several hundred members of a crowd which, after having heard speeches from Muslim preachers, had marched on an army post to demand release of two men detained for allegedly assaulting two security officers said to have defiled a prayer house. The White Paper, drafted by Ali Sadikin (q.v.), retired Siliwangi division commander H.R. Dharsono (b.1925) and others, was one of several pamphlets which questioned the official version of the event. Following bomb explosions in Jakarta banks on 4 October, Dharsono was arrested and later tried under the colonial era 'haatzaai-artikelen' and on charges of undermining government authority (see SUBVERSION). He was sentenced to ten years jail (later reduced to seven).

WHITE RAJAS. The flexibility of allegiances and alliances which enabled the rapid rise and fall of petty states in many coastal regions of the archipelago, especially on Kalimantan (q.v.), also allowed a number of European adventurers to establish themselves as local rulers with local and traditional power bases. The Brookes of Sarawak were the best known of these, but others included Raja Wilson of Bengkalis, Baron van Overbeek of Sabah, Clunies Ross of Cocos, and Joseph Torry, Raja of Ambong. *Lord Jim* by Joseph Conrad (q.v.) is a fictionalized account of one such ruler. Governors-General of the Netherlands Indies took the indigenous title Sri Paduka yang Dipertuan Besar. See also KUTAI. [0168, 0529]

'WILD SCHOOLS'. See EDUCATION.

WILOPO (1909–81), PNI leader and prime minister from April 1952 after the fall of Sukiman (q.v.). His PNI-Masyumi coalition was plagued by the end of the Korean War boom, and its attempts to demobilize 100,000 troops led to the 17 October Affair (see ARMY). The cabinet fell in June 1953 over the use of police to remove peasant squatters from foreign-owned plantations in East Sumatra (q.v.). [0634]

WOMEN AND MEN. As elsewhere in the world, a social division of labor between men and women has been the rule throughout most of the archipelago, derived partly from religious notions of a distinction between active and productive energy. Thus, men were traditionally responsible for tasks such as metalworking (q.v.), raising animals, ploughing fields, felling trees, hunting and building, while women were assigned transplanting, harvesting, pottery, weaving, food preparation and marketing. There seems also to have been a widespread tradition of bilateral and matrilineal kinship, seen most strongly today in Minangkabau (q.v.) society, where ownership of land passes exclusively through the female line and men are frequently absent from the community on *merantau* (q.v.). This combination of conceptual dualism and female economic power seems to have led to societies in which the access of women to power, position, and education was not dramatically less than that of men, or at least was considerably greater than in

Chinese, Indian, or Islamic societies. Thus, female literacy was high (see WRITING SYSTEMS), there were many important women traders and diplomats (women were traditionally regarded as more adept in financial matters and in negotiation than men, partly because they were not bound by rigid male codes of honor) and there was even a tradition of women bodyguards in the courts of Aceh and Mataram (qq.v.). Women took part in the Java War as generals. South Sulawesi in C.14–19 and Aceh in C.17 were ruled by a succession of queens.

Hindu, Muslim, and perhaps Chinese influences have all helped to diminish the access of women to education and to positions of power and influence. All accepted polygyny and preferred some degree of seclusion of women, though their influence was felt at first most strongly in elite circles. In rural areas in particular, the role of women in market trade and in harvesting assured their continuing social significance, though changes in both areas in recent years have damaged their position (see GREEN REVOLUTION). In other sectors of the economy, women are most numerous as unskilled and semiskilled factory workers and as domestic help, and they face the common problems of low wages and sexual harassment. Participation by women in modern politics was unknown until late C.19, when the growing presence of educated European women as wives of government officials increased the social pressure on the wives of indigenous elite men to be conversant with public affairs. This consideration led, for instance, to the Western education given to Kartini (q.v.). Indonesian women first graduated in law in 1921 and in medicine in 1922 and a number of women were prominent in the nationalist movement.

The 1945 Constitution specified legal equality for men and women, but most political parties maintained affiliated women's organizations, rather than integrating women fully into their structures (see, *e.g.* GERAKAN WANITA INDONESIA). Official policy now stresses the role of women as wives and mothers, but women continue to hold a number of senior administrative posts. See also DHARMA WANITA; EDUCATION; MARRIAGE, Political significance of; RACE. [0440, 0465, 0483, 0493, 1028, 1077–1091, 1094]

WOMEN'S MOVEMENT. R.A. Kartini (q.v.) is generally credited with founding the women's movement in Indonesia by identifying and promoting specific interests of women. The earliest women's organizations were concerned mainly with the spreading of information on matters of interest to women. The first women's journal, *Putri Hindia,* began publication in 1909. From 1914, the journal *Putri Merdeka* began to argue that women's problems had a political solution, and four Indonesian women's conferences were held 1928–32, at the first of which a number of generally nationalist women's associations federated to form an organization which in 1932 took the name Perikatan Perhimpunan Istri Indonesia (Federation of Indonesian Women's Associations). The federation established scholarships for girls, opposed polygamy, prostitution (q.v.) and child marriage, and promoted scouting (q.v.) and hygiene. The organization Istri Sedar (The Conscious Woman), founded in Bandung in 1930 was particularly active in these areas and came frequently into conflict with the Muslim Aisyiyah. In 1932 Istri Sedar merged with other women's groups to become Isteri Indonesia (Indonesian Women). See also DUTCH IN INDONESIA.

WORLD BANK (International Bank for Reconstruction and Development). Indonesia joined the IBRD in April 1954, left on 17 August 1965 without having contracted loans with it, and rejoined in April 1967. The first IBRD credit to Indonesia, in September 1968, was for $5 million. Credits have continued to be primarily in the area of agriculture and communications. The IBRD is a member of IGGI (q.v.). The Bank has been a major funder of Indonesia's transmigration (q.v.) program, but in October 1986 issued a report strongly critical of aspects of the program's management, including lack of provision of facilities for transmigrants and lack of attention to the program's consequences. [0303]

WRITING SYSTEMS. The C.5 inscriptions of Kutai and Tarumanegara (qq.v.), which are the earliest written documents from the archipelago, are in southern Indian Grantha script, but by C.8 an indigenous adaptation of that script, usually called Kawi, was in use on Java for writing both Sanskrit and old Javanese. Writings, from left to right, were commonly etched onto the lontar (q.v.) leaves. Kawi was the basis for several other scripts in the archipelago, notably Balinese, Sundanese, Rejang, Batak, Lampung, and Madurese. Of the indigenous scripts in the archipelago, only that of Bugis is not based on Javanese but developed directly from Sanskrit. From C.14 Malay commonly used Jawi script, an adaptation of Arabic script for Persian.

Evidence is sparse on the level of literacy in precolonial times; Rijklof van Goens in 1648–54 believed that a majority of Javanese were literate and the same was said to be true of Bali in C.19. The 1920 census showed a literacy rate of 6.83% among Javanese men and 0.26% among women and many observers have suggested that precolonial levels could not have been much higher. Reid, however, suggests that this reflects a decline in literacy from earlier times, pointing out that literacy in the otherwise neglected region of Lampung (q.v.) was recorded at 45% and 34% for men and women respectively in the 1930 census as a result of the survival of the Lampung script for use in *manjau*, 'a courting game whereby young men and women would gather in the evenings and the youths would fling suggestive quatrains (*pantun* [q.v.]) written in the old script to the young women they fancied.' The Lampung script had about 14 characters and a few vowel markers and would have been easy to learn. Such literacy would have had immensely strong social incentive and was probably taught at home rather than in school. See also EDUCATION; PAPER; WOMEN AND MEN. [0483]

Y

YAM (*Dioscorea* spp. Dioscoreaceae), food plant with large starchy roots, which can grow to two meters in length. An important food crop of slash and burn peoples in Kalimantan and Irian (qq.v.), it is now being displaced by the sweet potato (q.v.), which is much easier to prepare. [0938]

YAMIN, Muhammad (1903–62), writer and politician from West Sumatra. He helped to formulate the Youth Pledge (q.v.) in 1928, and in the late 1920s he wrote some of the first patriotic poems in Indonesian, especially the collection *Indonesia tumpah darahku* (*Indonesia, land of my birth,* 1929). He later prepared a biography of Gajah Mada, prime minister of Majapahit (q.v.) which marks the start of a nationalist historiography. He graduated in law (q.v.) in Batavia in 1932, joined the Sukarnoist PARTINDO (q.v.) in the same year, and in 1937 became one of the founders of the antifascist GERINDO, though he left in 1939. He was a member of the Volksraad (q.v.) from 1938 to 1942. As a member of the independence preparation investigation committee (BPUPKI, q.v.) in 1945 he argued for the inclusion of the Malay peninsula (q.v.), northern Borneo, and East Timor (q.v.) in a Greater Indonesia.

During the Revolution he supported Tan Malaka's ideas of a vigorous program of struggle (see DIPLOMASI AND PERJUANGAN) and was arrested in June 1946, being released finally in August 1948. He was close to the Murba (q.v.) but did not join it and served in several cabinets in the 1950s. In 1959 Sukarno chose him as head of the National Planning Council (Dewan Perancang Nasional) and he became one of the leading ideologists of Guided Democracy (q.v.). [0384, 0456]

YANI, Ahmad (1922–65), career army officer. He commanded government troops in the suppression of the PRRI (q.v.) on Sumatra in 1958 and was chief of staff of KOTI (q.v.), the command of the liberation of Irian (q.v.) in 1961. In 1962, Sukarno (q.v.) appointed him army chief of staff in a move to limit the influence of Nasution (q.v.); both officers were anticommunist, but Yani was less puritan and closer in outlook to Sukarno, coining, for instance, the term Nekolim (q.v.). Yani strongly opposed plans to arm workers and peasants as a 'Fifth Force' (q.v.) and in 1965 was accused of joining a Council of Generals planning a coup to forestall a PKI takeover. He was killed in the GESTAPU (q.v.) coup attempt of September 1965. [0663]

YAP THIAM HIEN (1913–89). A lawyer and human rights activist, Yap was a major proponent of the strengthening of the rule of law in Indonesia. He defended Subandrio (q.v.) in the MAHMILLUB (q.v.) trials. His own arrest in 1968 was turned into a test of the New Order's commitment to due legal process and he was released after five days. He was a firm advocate of the full legal equality of Chinese Indonesians and for the dissolution of Chinese associations which help preserve a separate Chinese identity. See also CHINESE IN INDONESIA. [0891]

YOGYAKARTA (Ngayogyakarta Hadiningrat), city and sultanate in Central Java, founded after the splitting of Mataram (q.v.) in 1755. Formed after Dutch supremacy on Java was well established, Yogyakarta was never militarily powerful and was weakened by the creation of a minor court, the Pakualaman, within its territory in 1812, by territorial losses following the Java War (q.v.) of 1825–30 and by economic decline in C.19. Perhaps in compensation for this weakness, successive sultans (all called Hamengkubuwono) became patrons of Javanese culture, encouraging tradition and innovation to varying degrees.

As a princely territory (*Vorstenland*), Yogyakarta, like Surakarta (q.v.) was administratively distinct from the rest of Dutch Java. Nonetheless its people participated generally in the emergence of Indonesian nationalism (q.v.) in C.20. Yogyakarta became the seat of the Indonesian Republican government from shortly after the Declaration of Independence until the end of the Revolution in 1949, with a brief period of Dutch occupation from 18 December 1948 to 6 July 1949. Since 1946, Yogyakarta (including the Pakualaman) has been a special territory (*daerah istimewa*) of the Republic, with the late Sultan Hamengkubuwono IX (q.v.) as governor and the Pakualam as his deputy. See also VORSTENLANDEN. [0485, 0505, 0578, 0590, 1166]

YOUTH. See PEMUDA; KOMITE NASIONAL PEMUDA INDONESIA.

YOUTH PLEDGE (*Sumpah Pemuda*). At the second national Youth Congress, held in Batavia in 1928, delegates formally adopted Indonesia as the framework for the struggle against the Dutch, affirming that they were one people (*bangsa Indonesia*), with one language, Indonesian, and one homeland, Indonesia. See also 'INDONESIA RAYA'; NATIONALISM.

Z

ZELFBESTUREN ('self-governing regions'), official name for the native states within the Netherlands Indies, which numbered 282 in 1942. All were originally independent or semiindependent states with which the Dutch had concluded political contracts, either the so-called *lange politieke contracten,* long political contracts, which set out in detail an allied or subordinate relationship, or the Korte Verklaring, or short declaration, which simply acknowledged Dutch suzerainty (see NETHERLANDS INDIES, Expansion of). Within all states, the colonial government had extensive interventionary powers, including the free use of land, control of mining, and the right to appoint a ruler's successor. Until C.20, the general trend had been for the Dutch to abolish such states as it became convenient. The *Zelfbestuursregelen* (Self-governing territories regulations) of 1919 and 1927, however, set the nominally 'indirect' form of rule on a legal basis within the colonial administrative structure and under the *ontvoogding* (detutelization) measures of 1929 a number of states which had been abolished, such as the kingdoms on Bali (q.v.), were restored. The Republic's Law no. 22 of 1948 and the NIT (q.v.) Law no. 44 of 1950 retained the zelfbesturen as a level of government under the name *swapraja* or *daerah swatantra,* but in 1960 these were abolished. See also DECENTRALIZATION. [0363, 0546, 0909, 0911]

ZEVEN PROVINCIËN, Mutiny on the. On 5 February 1933, Indonesian and Dutch sailors on the Dutch naval vessel *De Zeven Provinciën* mutinied off Aceh over a 17% wage cut introduced by the government to reduce expenditure during the Depression (q.v.). Dutch aircraft bombed the ship to suppress the mutiny. Though the mutineers protested their political loyalty, the colonial government saw the rising as a product of nationalist agitation and used it to justify greater political restrictions soon after. [0549]

ZHENG HE (Cheng Ho) (1371–1435), Chinese eunuch, raised as a Muslim. In 1405, after a successful military career in northern China, he was sent by the Yongle Emperor of the Ming dynasty as leader of a major maritime expedition to Southeast Asia. The expedition consisted of 27,000 crew in over 300 vessels; its purposes remain unclear, but they probably included a desire to suppress piracy (q.v.) and to establish Chinese hegemony in the region. Zheng He successfully destroyed the fleet of a Chinese pirate based on the Sumatra coast of the Melaka Strait, near Palembang (q.v.), seems to have developed close relations with Melaka (q.v.), and followed the 1405 expedition with six others, but the expeditions seem to have had no long-term significance. See also CHINA, Historical links with. [0753]

APPENDICES

1. Governors-General of the Netherlands Indies

1609–1614 Pieter Both (?–1615)

1614–1615 Gerard Reynst (?–1615)

1616–1619 Laurens Reael (1583–1637)

1619–1623 Jan Pieterszoon Coen (1587–1629) (1)

1623–1627 Pieter de Carpentier (1588–1659)

1627–1629 Jan Pieterszoon Coen (2)

1629–1632 Jacques Specx (1588–?)

1632–1636 Hendrik Brouwer (1581–1643)

1636–1645 Anthony van Diemen (1593–1645)

1645–1650 Cornelis van der Lijn (1608?–?)

1650–1653 Carel Reyniersz (1604–53)

1653–1678 Joan Maetsuycker (1606–78)

1678–1681 Rijkloff van Goens (1619–82)

1681–1684 Cornelis Janszoon Speelman (1628–84)

1684–1691 Joannes Camphuys (1634–95)

1691–1704 Willem van Outhoorn (1635–1720)

1704–1709 Joan van Hoorn (1653–1711)

1709–1713 Abraham van Riebeeck (1653–1713)

1713–1718 Christoffel van Swoll (1663–1718)

1718–1725 Hendrick Zwaardecroon (1667–1728)

1725–1729 Mattheus de Haan (1663–1729)

1729–1732 Diederik Durven (1676–1740)

1732–1735 Dirck van Cloon (1684–1735)

1735–1737 Abraham Patras (1671–1737)

1737–1741 Adriaen Valckenier (1695–1751)

1741–1743 Johannes Thedens (1680–1748)

1743–1750 Gustaaf Willem, Baron van Imhoff (1705–50)

1750–1761 Jacob Mossel (1704–61)

1761–1775 Petrus Albertus van der Parra (1714–75)

1775–1777 Jeremias van Riemsdijk (1712–77)

1777–1780 Reynier de Klerk (1710–80)

1780–1796 Willem Arnold Alting (1724–1800)

1796–1801 Petrus Gerardus van Overstraten (1755–1801)

1801–1805 Johannes Siberg (1740–1817)

1805–1808 Albertus Henricus Wiese (1761–1810)

1808–1811 Herman Willem Daendels (1762–1818)

1811 Jan Willem Janssens (1762–1838)

English Interregnum

1811–1816 Thomas Stamford Raffles (1781–1826)

1816 John Fendall

Commissioners-General

1814–1816 C.Th. Elout (1767–1841) and A.A. Buyskes (1771–?)

Governors-General

1816–1826 Godert Alexander Gerard Philip, Baron van der Capellan (1778–1848)

1826–1830 Leonard Pierre Joseph, Burggraaf du Bus de Gisignies (1780–1849)

1830–1834 Johannes van den Bosch (1780–1839)

1834–1836 Jean Chretien Baud (1789–1859)

1836–1840 Dominique Jacques (de) Eerens (1781–1840)

1841–1844 Pieter Merkus (1787–1844)

1845–1851 Jan Jacob Rochussen (1797–1871)

1851–1856 Albertus Jacobus Duymaer van Twist (1809–87)

1856–1861 Charles Ferdinand Pahud (1803–73)

1861–1866 Ludolf Anne Jan Wilt, Baron Sloet van de Beele (1806–90)

1866–1872 Pieter Mijer (1812–81)

1872–1875 James Loudon (1824–84)

1875–1881 Johan Wilhelm van Lansberge (1830–1905)

1881–1884 Frederik ’sJacob (1822–1901)

1884–1888 Otto van Rees (1823–92)

1888–1893 Cornelis Pijnacker Hordijk (1847–1908)

1893–1899 Jhr Carel Herman Aart van der Wijck (1840–1914)

1899–1905 Willem Rooseboom (1843–1920)

1905–1909 Joannes Benedictus van Heutsz (1851–1924)

1909–1916 Alexander Willem Frederik Idenburg (1861–1935)

1916–1921 Jean Paul, Graaf van Limburg Stirum (1873–1948)

1921–1926 Dirk Fock (1858–1941)

1926–1931 Jhr Andries Cornelis Dirk de Graeff (1872–1957)

1931–1936 Jhr Bonifacius Cornelis de Jonge (1875–1958)

1936–1945 Alidius Warmoldus Lambertus Tjarda van Starkenborgh Stachouwer (in Japanese detention 1942–1945) 1888–1978

1941–1942 Hubertus Johannes van Mook, Lieutenant Governor-General (1894–1965)

1944–1948 Hubertus Johannes van Mook, Lieutenant Governor-General (1894–1965)

Japanese Military Governors of Java

March–November 1942 IMAMURA Hitoshi

November 1942– November 1944 HARADA Kumakichi

November 1944–August 1945 YAMAMOTO Moichiro

Hoge Vertegenwoordiger van de Kroon

1948–1949 Louis Joseph Maria Beel (1902–1977)

1949 Antonius Hermanus Johannes Lovink

Governors of West New Guinea

1950–1953 Simon L. van Waardenburg

1953–1958 Jan van Baal

1958–1962 Pieter J. Plateel (1911–1978)

2. Netherlands Ministers of Colonies

Based on: G.F.E. Gonggryp, *Geillustreerde encyclopedie van Nederlandsch-Indie*. (Leiden: Leidsche Uitgeversmaatschappij, 1934), and H. Daalder and C.J.M. Schuyt, eds, *Compendium voor politiek en samenleving in Nederland* (Alphen aan den Rijn: Samsom, 1986), fifth supplement, 1988, section A 0500.

Dates given below follow the British system with day, month, and year listed in that order. Also, see "Key to Parties" on page 514 for abbreviations listed below.

Zaken van Indië en van den koophandel (The Indies and trade)

Mr Paulus van der Helm (dir.gen.)	29- 7-1806–10-12-1807
Mr Jacob Jan Cambier	10-12-1807– 8- 1-1808

Marine en koloniën (Navy and colonies)

Mr Paulus van der Helm	8- 1-1808–1811

French occupation of the Netherlands

No minister

Zaken van koophandel en koloniën (Trade and colonies)

G.A.G.Ph. Baron van der Capellan (sec.v.staat)	6- 4–1814–29- 7-1814
J.C. van der Hoop (sec.v.staat, w.)	29- 7-1814–14- 9-1814
Jhr J. Goldberg (w.)	14- 9-1814–16- 9-1815
Jhr J. Goldberg (dir.gen.)	16- 9-1815–19- 9-1818

Publiek onderwijs, de nationale nijverheid en de koloniën (Public education, national industry and the colonies)

Mr A.R. Falck	19- 3-1818–30- 3-1824

Nationale nijverheid en koloniën (National industry and colonies)

Mr C.Th. Elout	30- 3-1824– 5- 4-1825

Marine en koloniën (Navy and colonies)

Mr C.Th. Elout	5- 4-1825– 6- 9-1829
Jhr J.J. Quarles van Ufford (sec.gen., w.)	6- 9-1829–29-12-1829

Waterstaat, de nationale nijverheid en koloniën (Water control, national industry and colonies)

Mr P.L.J. Servais van Gobbelschroij	29-12-1829– 4-10-1830
Jhr Mr G.G. Clufford (a.i.)	4-10-1830– 1- 1-1832

Nationale nijverheid en koloniën (National industry and colonies)

Jhr Mr G.G. Clufford (a.i.)	1- 1-1832– 1- 1-1834

Koloniën (Colonies)

Mr A. Brocx (sec.gen., w.)	1- 1-1834–30- 5-1834
J.G. van den Bosch	30- 5-1834–25-12-1839
J.Chr. Baud (a.i.)	25-12-1839–21- 7-1840

Marine en koloniën (Navy and colonies)

J.Chr. Baud	21- 7-1840–

Koloniën (Colonies)

J.Chr. Baud	1- 1-1842–

J.C. Rijk (a.i.)	25- 3-1848–21-11-1848
G.L. Baud	21-11-1848–18- 6-1849
E.B. van den Bosch	18- 6-1849– 1-11-1849
C.F. Pahud	1-11-1849–19- 4-1853
C.F. Pahud	19- 4-1853–31-12-1855
Mr P. Mijer	1- 1-1856– 1- 7-1856
Mr P. Mijer	1- 7-1856–18- 3-1858
J.J. Rochussen	18- 3-1858–23- 2-1860
J.J. Rochussen	23- 2-1860–31-12-1860
Mr J.S. Lotsy	1- 1-1861– 9- 1-1861
Jhr J.P. Cornets de Groot van Kraaijenburg	9- 1-1861–14- 3-1861
Mr J. Loudon	14- 3-1861–31- 1-1862
G.H. Uhlenbeck	31- 1-1862– 3- 1-1863
G.H. Betz (a.i.)	3- 1-1863– 2- 2-1863
I.D. Fransen van de Putte	2- 2-1863–10- 2-1866
I.D. Fransen van de Putte	10- 2-1866–30- 5-1866
Mr P. Mijer	30- 5-1866–15- 9-1866
N. Trakranen	15- 9-1866–20- 7-1867
J.J. Hasselman	20- 7-1867– 4- 6-1868
E. de Waal	4- 6-1868–16-11-1870

L.G. Brocx (a.i.)	16-11-1870– 4- 1-1871
Mr P.P. van Bosse	4- 1-1871– 6- 7-1872
I.D. Fransen van de Putte	6- 7-1872–27- 8-1874
Mr Willem Baron van Goltstein	27- 8-1874–11- 9-1876
Mr F.A. Mees	11- 9-1876– 3-11-1877
Mr P.P. van Bosse	3-11-1877–21- 2-1879
Jhr H.O. Wichers (a.i.)	21- 2-1879–12- 3-1879
O. van Rees	12- 3-1879–20- 8-1879
Mr Willem Baron van Goltstein	20- 8-1879– 1- 9-1882
Jhr Mr W.M. de Brauw	1- 9-1882–23- 2-1883
W.F. van Erp Taalman Kip (a.i.)	23- 2-1883–23- 4-1883
F.G. van Bloemen Waanders	23- 4-1883–25-11-1883
A.W.Ph. Weitzel (a.i.)	25-11-1883–27- 2-1884
Mr J.P. Sprenger van Eijk	27- 2-1884–21- 4-1888
Mr L.W.C. Keuchenius	21- 4-1888–24- 2-1890
Mr Aeneas Baron Mackay	24- 2-1890–21- 8-1891
Mr W.K. Baron van Dedem	21- 8-1891– 9- 5-1894
Mr J.H. Bergsma	9- 5-1894–27- 7-1897
J.Th. Cremer	27- 7-1897– 1- 8-1901

Jhr Mr T.A.J. van Asch van Wijck	1- 8-1901– 9- 9-1902
J. W. Bergansius (a.i.)	9- 9-1902–25- 9-1902
A.W.F. Idenburg	25- 9-1902–17- 8-1905
Mr D. Fock	17- 8-1905–12- 2-1908
Mr Th. Heemskerk	12- 2-1908–20- 5-1908
A.W.F. Idenburg	20- 5-1908–16- 8-1909
J.H. de Waal Malefijt	16- 8-1909–29- 8-1913
Mr Th.B. Pleijte	29- 8-1913– 8-12-1915
J.J. Rambonnet (w.)	8-12-1915– 9- 9-1918
A.W.F. Idenburg ARP	9- 9-1918–13-11-1919
Jhr Mr Ch.J.M. Ruys de Beerenbrouck (w.) RKSP	13- 8-1919–13-11-1919
S. de Graaf ARP	13-11-1919–18- 9-1922
S. de Graaf ARP	18- 9-1922– 4- 8-1925
H. Colijn (a.i.) ARP	4- 8-1925–26- 9-1925
Ch.J.I.M. Welter RKSP	26- 9-1925– 8- 3-1926
Dr J.C. Koningsberger Lib.	8- 3-1926–10- 8-1929
S. de Graaf ARP	10- 8-1929–26- 5-1933
Dr H. Colijn ARP	25- 5-1933–31- 7-1935
Dr H. Colijn ARP	31- 7-1935–24- 6-1937
Ch.J.I.M. Welter RKSP	24- 6-1937–25 -7-1939
C. van den Bussche Lib.	25- 7-1939–10- 8-1939

Ch.J.I.M. Welter RKSP	10- 8-1939– 3- 9-1940
Ch.J.I.M. Welter RKSP	3- 9-1940–27- 7-1941
Ch.J.I.M. Welter RKSP	27- 7-1941–17-11-1941
Dr P.S. Gerbrandy (a.i.) ARP	17-11-1941–21- 2-1942
Dr P.S. Gerbrandy ARP	21- 2-1942–21- 5-1942
Dr H.J. van Mook	21- 5-1942–23- 2-1945

Overzeese Gebiedsdelen (Overseas Territories, created 23- 2-1945)

Dr Ir J.I.J.M. Schmutzer RKSP	23- 2-1945–24- 6-1945
Dr J.H.A. Logemann (became PvdA)	24- 6-1945– 3- 7-1946
Mr J.A. Jonkman PvdA	3- 7-1946– 7- 8-1948
Mr E.M.J.A. Sassen KVP	7- 8-1948–14- 2-1949
Mr J.H. van Maarseveen (a.i.), KVP	14- 2-1949–15- 6-1949
Mr J.H. van Maarseveen KVP	15- 6-1949–24-12-1949

Uniezaken en Overzeese Rijksdelen (Union Affairs and Overseas Territories, created 24-12-1949)

Mr J.H. van Maarseveen KVP	24-12-1949–15- 3-1951
Dr W. Drees (a.i.) PvdA	15- 3-1951–30- 3-1951
Ir L.A.H. Peters KVP	30- 3-1951– 2- 9-1952

Overzeese Rijksdelen (Overseas Territories, created 7-11-1952)

Dr W.J.A. Kernkamp	CHU	2- 9-1952–18- 7-1956
Ir C. Staf (a.i.)	CHU	18- 7-1956–13-10-1956

Zaken Overzee (Affairs Overseas, created 14- 2-1957, abolished 19- 8-1959)

Ir C. Staf (a.i.)	CHU	13-10-1956–16- 2-1957
Mr G.Ph. Helders	CHU	16- 2-1957–22-12-1958
Mr G.Ph. Helders	CHU	22-12-1958–19- 5-1959
Drs H.A. Korthals	VVD	19- 5-1959–18- 8-1959

Key to parties:

ARP, Anti-Revolutionaire Partij (Anti-Revolutionary Party); **CHU,** Christelijk-Historische Unie (Christian Historical Union); **KVP,** Katholieke Volkspartij (Catholic People's Party); **Lib.,** Liberalen (Liberals); **PvdA,** Partij van de Arbeid (Labor Party); **RKSP,** Rooms-Katholieke Staatspartij, Roman Catholic State Party; **VVD,** Volkspartij voor Vrijheid en Democracy (People's Party for Freedom and Democracy).

a.i. = ad interim (provisional); dir.gen. = director-general; sec.v.staat = secretaris van staat (secretary of state); w. = waarnemend (acting)

3. Rulers of Early States[1]

i. Aceh

1496	Ali Mughayat Syah
1528	Salah ud-din ibn Ali
1537	Ala'ad-din al Kahar ibn Ali
1568	Husain
1575	Sultan Muda (a few days)
1575	Sultan Sri Alam
1576	Zainal Abidin
1577	Ala'ad-din of Perak (Mansur Syah)
1589?	Sultan Boyong
1596	Ala'ad-din Riayat Syah
1604	Ali Riayat Syah
1607	Iskandar Muda
1636	Iskandar Thani
1641	Safiyat ud-din Taj al-Alam bint Iskandar Muda (widow of Iskandar Thani)
1675	Naqiyat ud-din Nur al-Alam
1678	Zaqiyat ud-din Inayat Syah

1688	Kamalat Syah Zinat ud-din
1699	Badr al-Alam Syarif Hasyim Jamal ud-din
1702	Perkara Alam Syarif Lamtui
1703	Jamal al-Alam Badr al-Munir
1726	Jauhar al-Alam Amin ud-din (a few days)
1726	Shams al-Alam (a few days)

Bugis dynasty

1727	Ala'ad-din Ahmad Syah
1735	Ala'ad-din Johan Syah
1764	Badr ad-din Johan Syah
1765	Mahmud Syah (restored)
1769	Mahmud Syah
1773	Sulaiman Syah (Udahna Lela)
1773	Mahmud Syah (restored)
1781	Ala'ad-din Muhammad Syah
1795	Ala'ad-din Jauhar al-Alam
1823	Muhammad Syah
1838	Sulaiman
1857	Ali Ala'ad-din Mansur Syah (Ibrahim)
1870	Mahmud Syah
1874	Muhammad Daud Syah

ii. Singosari and Majapahit

1.	1222	Rajasa (Ken Angrok)
2.	1227	Anusapati, stepson of 1.
3.	1248	Tohjaya, son of 1.
4.	1248	Wisnuwardhana, son of 2.
5.	1268	Kertanegara, son of 4.
6.	1292	Jayakatwang of Kediri (usurper)
7.	1293	Kertarajasa Jayawardhana (Wijaya), nephew and son-in-law of 5.
8.	1309	Jayanegara, son of 7.
9.	1329	Tribuwana, daughter of 7.
10.	1350	Rajasanegara (Hayam Wuruk), son of 9.
11.	1389	Wikramawardhana, nephew and son-in-law of 10.
12.	1429	Suhita, daughter of 11.
13.	1447–51	Kertawijaya, son of 11.

iii. Mataram

1582	Sutawijaya Senopati
1601	Mas Jolang
1613	Cakrakusuma Ngabdurrahman, Sultan Agung
1645	Prabu Amangkurat I, Sunan Tegalwangi

1677	Amangkurat II
1703	Amangkurat III, Sunan Mas
1705	Pakubuwono, Sunan Puger
1719	Amangkurat IV
1725	Pakubuwono II
1749	Pakubuwono III

iv. Surakarta

?	Pakubuwono III (of Mataram)
1788	Pakubuwono IV
1820	Pakubuwono V
1823	Pakubuwono VI
1830	Pakubuwono VII
1858	Pakubuwono VIII
1861	Pakubuwono IX
1893	Pakubuwono X
1939	Pakubuwono XI
1944–46	Pakubuwono XII

v. Yogyakarta

1749	Hamengkubuwono I, Mangkubumi
1792	Hamengkubuwono II, Sultan Sepuh

1810	Hamengkubuwono III, Raja
1814	Hamengkubuwono IV, Seda Pesijar
1822	Hamengkubuwono V, Menol
1855	Hamengkubuwono VI, Mangkubumi
1877	Hamengkubuwono VII
1921	Hamengkubuwono VIII
1939	Hamengkubuwono IX
1989–	Hamengkubuwono X

4. Cabinets of the Republic of Indonesia[2]

Presidential Cabinet	31- 8-1945–14-11-1945
Syahrir I	14-11-1945–12- 3-1946
Syahrir II	12- 3-1946– 2-10-1946
Syahrir III	2-10-1946–27- 6-1947
Amir Syarifuddin I	3- 7-1947–11-11-1947
Amir Syarifuddin II	11-11-1947–29- 1-1948
Mohammad Hatta I (presidential cabinet)	29- 1-1948– 4- 8-1949
Emergency Cabinet	19-12-1948–13- 7-1949
Mohammad Hatta II (presidential cabinet)	4- 8-1949–20-12-1949

Susanto Tirtoprojo (Republic of Indonesia, Yogyakarta)	20-12-1949–21- 1-1950
Abdul Halim (Republic of Indonesia, Yogyakarta)	21- 1-1950– 6- 9-1950
Mohammad Hatta III (RIS)	20-12-1949– 6- 9-1950
Mohammad Natsir	6- 9-1950–27- 4-1951
Sukiman Wiryosanjoyo	27- 4-1951– 3- 4-1952
Wilopo	3- 4-1952– 1- 8-1953
Ali Sastroamijoyo I	1- 8-1953–12- 8-1955
Burhanuddin Harahap	12- 8-1955–26- 3-1956
Ali Sastroamijoyo II	26- 3-1956– 9- 4-1957
Juanda I (*Kabinet Karya*)	9- 4-1957–25- 6-1958
Juanda II	25- 6-1958– 9- 7-1959
Kabinet Kerja I (Sukarno)	9- 7-1959–18- 2-1960
Kabinet Kerja II (Sukarno)	18- 2-1960– 6- 3-1962
Kabinet Kerja III (Sukarno)	6- 3-1962–13-11-1963
Kabinet Kerja IV (Sukarno)	13-11-1963– 2- 9-1964
Kabinet Dwikora I (Sukarno)	2- 9-1964–24- 2-1966
Kabinet Dwikora II 'Cabinet of 100 Ministers'	24- 2-1966–30- 3-1966
Kabinet Dwikora III	30- 3-1966–28- 7-1966
Kabinet Ampera	28- 7-1966–10- 6-1968

Kabinet Pembangunan I (Development Cabinet)	10- 6-1968–27- 3-1973
Kabinet Pembangunan II	27- 3-1973–29- 3-1978
Kabinet Pembangunan III	29- 3-1978–19- 3-1983
Kabinet Pembangunan IV	19- 3-1983–21- 3-1988
Kabinet Pembangunan V	21- 3-1988–

5. Republic of Indonesia Office Holders

i. Presidents

Sukarno	18- 7-1945–12- 3-1967
Suharto (acting)	12- 3-1967–27- 3-1968
Suharto	27- 3-1968–

ii. Vice-Presidents

Mohammad Hatta	18- 7-1945– 1-12-1956
Hamengkubuwono IX	27- 3-1968–23- 3-1978
Adam Malik	23- 3-1978–12- 3-1983
Umar Wirahadikusumah	12- 3-1983–11- 3-1988
Sudharmono	11- 3-1988–

iii. Prime Ministers

Republik Indonesia (Republic of Indonesia, declared independent 17- 8-1945)

Sutan Syahrir (PSI)	14-11-1945–13- 3-1946
Sutan Syahrir (PSI)	13- 3-1946– 2-10-1946
Sutan Syahrir (PSI)	2-10-1946–27- 6-1947
Amir Syarifuddin (PSI)	3- 7-1947–11-11-1947
Amir Syarifuddin (PSI)	11-11-1947–29- 1-1948
Mohammad Hatta	29- 1-1948– 4- 8-1949
Mohammad Hatta	4- 8-1949–20-12-1949

Pemerintah Darurat Republik Indonesia (Emergency government of the Republic of Indonesia on Sumatra)

Syafruddin Prawiranegara (Masyumi)	19-12-1948–13- 7-1949

Republik Indonesia (Republic of Indonesia, constituent state of the Republik Indonesia Serikat)

Susanto Tirtoprojo (PNI)	20-12-1949–21- 1-1950
Abdul Halim	21- 1-1950– 6- 9-1950

Republik Indonesia Serikat (Federal Republic of Indonesia)

Mohammad Hatta	20-12-1949– 6- 9-1950

Republik Indonesia

Mohammad Natsir (Masyumi)	6- 9-1950–27- 4-1951
Sukiman Wiryosanjoyo (Masyumi)	27- 4-1951– 3- 4-1952
Wilopo (PNI)	3- 4-1952– 1- 8-1953
Ali Sastroamijoyo (PNI)	1- 8-1953–12- 8-1955
Burhanuddin Harahap (Masyumi)	12- 8-1955–26- 3-1956
Ali Sastroamijoyo (PNI)	26- 3-1956– 9- 4-1957
Juanda Kartawijaya	9- 4-1957– 9- 7-1959
Juanda Kartawijaya[3]	9- 7-1959– 7-11-1963
Sukarno	9- 7-1959–12- 3-1967
Subandrio (1st Deputy Prime Minister)	13-11-1963–18- 3-1966
Johannes Leimena (2nd Deputy PM)	13-11-1963–30- 3-1966
Chaerul Saleh (3rd Deputy PM)	13-11-1963–18- 3-1966
K.H. Idham Chalid (4th Deputy PM)	24- 2-1966–30- 3-1966
Johannes Leimena (1st Deputy PM)	30- 3-1966–28- 7-1966
K.H. Idham Chalid (2nd Deputy PM)	30- 3-1966–28- 7-1966

Ruslan Abdulgani (3rd Deputy PM)	30- 3-1966–28- 7-1966
Hamengkubuwono IX (4th Deputy PM)	30- 3-1966–28- 7-1966
Suharto (5th Deputy PM)	30- 3-1966–28- 7-1966
Adam Malik (6th Deputy PM)	30- 3-1966–28- 7-1966

iv. Foreign Ministers

Republik Indonesia

Ahmad Subarjo	31- 8-1945–14-11-1945
Sutan Syahrir (PSI)	14-11-1945–27- 6-1947
Haji Agus Salim (Masyumi)	3- 7-1947–20-12-1949

Pemerintah Darurat Republik Indonesia (Emergency government of the Republic of Indonesia on Sumatra)

A.A. Maramis (PNI)	19-12-1948–13- 7-1949

Republik Indonesia Serikat

Mohammad Hatta	20-12-1949– 6- 9-1950

Republik Indonesia

Mohammad Rum (Masyumi)	6- 9-1950–27- 4-1951
Ahmad Subarjo (Masyumi)	27- 4-1951– 3- 4-1952
Wilopo (PNI, ad interim)	3- 4-1952–29- 4-1952

Mukarto Notowidagdo (PNI)	29- 4-1952– 1- 8-1953
Sunario (PNI)	1- 8-1955–26- 3-1956
Ruslan Abdulgani (PNI)	26- 3-1956– 9- 4-1957
(non-active)	28- 1-1957–14- 3-1957
Subandrio	9- 4-1957–30- 3-1966
Adam Malik (ad interim)	30- 3-1966–28- 7-1966
Adam Malik	28- 7-1966–29- 3-1978
Mochtar Kusumaatmaja	29- 3-1978–21- 3-1988
Ali Alatas	21- 3-1988–

v. Ministers of Internal Affairs

Republik Indonesia

R.A.A. Wiranatakusumah	31- 8-1945–14-11-1945
Sutan Syahrir (PSI)	14-11-1945–12- 3-1946
Sudarsono (PSI)	12- 3-1946– 2-10-1946
Mohammad Rum (Masyumi)	2-10-1946–27- 6-1947
Wondoamiseno (PSII)	3- 7-1947–11-11-1947
Mohammad Rum (Masyumi)	11-11-1947–22- 1-1948
Sukiman Wiryosanjoyo (Masyumi, ad interim)	29- 1-1948– 4- 8-1949
Wongsonegoro (PIR)	4- 8-1949–20-12-1949

Pemerintah Darurat Republik Indonesia (Emergency government of the Republic of Indonesia on Sumatra)

Teuku Mohammad Hasan	19-12-1948–13- 7-1949

Republik Indonesia (Republic of Indonesia, constituent state of the Republik Indonesia Serikat)

Susanto Tirtoprojo (PNI)	20-12-1949–21- 1-1950
Susanto Tirtoprojo (PNI)	21- 1-1950– 6- 9-1950

Republik Indonesia Serikat

Anak Agung Gde Agung	20-12-1949– 6- 9-1950

Republik Indonesia

Assaat	6- 9-1950–27- 4-1951
Iskaq Tjokroadisuryo (PNI)	27- 4-1951– 3- 4-1952
Mohammad Rum (Masyumi)	3- 4-1952– 1- 8-1953
Hazairin (PIR)	1- 8-1953–23-10-1954
Haji Zainul Arifin (NU)	23-10-1954–19-11-1954
Sunaryo (NU)	19-11-1954–12- 8-1955
Sunaryo (NU)	12- 8-1955–19- 1-1956
R.P. Suroso (Parindra)	19- 1-1956–26- 3-1956
Sunaryo (NU)	26- 3-1956– 9- 4-1957

Sanusi Harjadinata (PNI)	9- 4-1957– 9- 7-1959
Ipik Gandamana	9- 7-1959– 6- 3-1962
Saharjo	6- 3-1962–13-11-1963
Ipik Gandamana	13-11-1963– 2- 9-1964
Sumarno	2- 9-1964–18- 3-1966
Basuki Rahmat	30- 3-1966– 9- 1-1969
Amir Machmud	23- 1-1969–28- 3-1973
Suparjo Rustam	28- 3-1973–21- 3-1988
Rudini	21- 3-1988

vi. Ministers of Defence

Republik Indonesia

Supriyadi (deceased)	6-10-1945–14-11-1945
Sulyoadikusumo (ad interim)	20-10-1945–14-11-1945
Mustopo (self-appointed)	November 1945
Hamengkubuwono IX (chosen by army but never took office)	
Amir Syarifuddin (PSI)	14-11-1945–29- 1-1948
Mohammad Hatta (ad interim)	29- 1-1948–15- 7-1948
Hamengkubuwono IX	15- 7-1948–20-12-1949

Pemerintah Darurat Republik Indonesia (Emergency government of the Republic of Indonesia on Sumatra)

Syafruddin Prawiranegara (Masyumi)	19-12-1948–13- 7-1949

Republik Indonesia Serikat

Hamengkubuwono IX	20-12-1949– 6- 9-1950

Republik Indonesia

Abdul Halim (ad interim)	6- 9-1950–17- 8-1950
Mohammad Natsir (Masyumi, ad interim)	17-12-1950–27- 4-1951
Sewaka (PIR)	9- 5-1951– 3- 4-1952
Hamengkubuwono IX	3- 4-1952– 2- 6-1953
Wilopo (PNI)	2- 6-1953– 1- 8-1953
Iwa Kusumasumantri (Persatuan Progresif)	1- 8-1953–13- 7-1955
Burhanuddin Harahap (Masyumi)	12- 8-1955–26- 3-1956
Ali Sastroamijoyo (PNI, ad interim)	26- 3-1956– 9- 4-1957
Juanda Kartawijaya	9- 4-1957– 9- 7-1959
Abdul Haris Nasution	9- 7-1959–24- 2-1966
M. Sarbini	24- 2-1966–30- 3-1966
Suharto	30- 3-1966–29- 3-1973

Maraden Panggabean	29- 3-1973–17- 4-1978
Andi Mohammad Yusuf	17- 4-1978–28- 3-1983
S. Poniman	28- 3-1983–21- 3-1988
L.B. (Benny) Murdani	21- 3-1988–

vii. Commanders of the Army

The formal title of the army's most senior commanding officer was *panglima* (1945–49); *Kepala staf* (Chief of Staff, 1949–60): *menteri/ Kepala staf* (minister/Chief of Staff, 1960–63); *menteri/panglima* (1963–67), *panglima* (1967–69); and *Kepala staf* (1969–present).

Supriyadi (deceased)	6-10-1945–14-11-1945
Urip Sumoharjo (acting chief of headquarters)	6-10-1945–18-12-1945
Sudirman (elected)	12-11-1945–18-12-1945
Sudirman (appointed)	18-12-1945–19- 1-1950
A.H. Nasution	19- 1-1950–15-12-1952
Bambang Sugeng	16-12-1952– 2- 5-1955
Zulkifli Lubis (acting)	2- 5-1955–27- 6-1955
Bambang Utoyo	10- 6-1955–24- 7-1955
Zulkifli Lubis (acting)	24- 7-1955– 7-11-1955
A.H. Nasution	7-11-1955–25- 6-1962
Ahmad Yani	25- 6-1962– 1-10-1965
Pranoto (acting)	1-10-1965–16-10-1965

Suharto	16-10-1965–29- 5-1967
Maraden Panggabean (acting)	29- 5-1967–17- 5-1968
Maraden Panggabean	17- 5-1968– 4-12-1969
Umar Wirahadikusumah	4-12-1969– 2- 4-1973
Surono Reksodimejo	2- 4-1973–10- 4-1974
Makmun Murod	10- 4-1974–26- 1-1978
Widodo	26- 1-1978–15- 4-1980
S.Poniman	15- 4-1980– 7- 3-1983
Rudini	7- 3-1983–24- 6-1986
Try Sutrisno	24- 6-1986–27- 2-1988
Edi Sudrajat	27- 2-1988–

viii. Commanders of the Armed Forces

T.B. Simatupang (Chief of Staff)	19- 1-1950–ca Aug. 1953 (post abolished)
Abdul Haris Nasution	25- 6-1962–12- 3-1967
Suharto	12- 3-1967–28- 3-1973
Maraden Panggabean	28- 3-1967–17- 4-1978
Andi Muhammad Yusuf	17- 4-1978–28- 3-1983
L.B. (Benny) Murdani	28- 3-1983–27- 2-1988
Try Sutrisno	27- 2-1988–

ix. KOPKAMTIB Commanders

Suharto	10-10-1965–19-11-1969
Maraden Panggabean	19-11-1969–27- 3-1973
Sumitro	27- 3-1973–28- 1-1974
Suharto (day-to-day command exercised by KOPKAMTIB Chief of Staff Sudomo)	28- 1-1974–17- 4-1978
Sudomo	17- 4-1974–29- 3-1983
L.B. (Benny) Murdani	29- 3-1983–22- 9-1988

6. Election Results, 1945–1987

[Not all *Totals* equal number of seats since either not all parliaments were elected or some seats remained vacant.]

I. Komite Nasional Indonesia Pusat, founded 16–17 October 1945 (200 seats)[4]

Party	**Seats**	**(%)**
PNI	45	(22.5%)
Masyumi	35	(17.5%)
Partai Sosialis	35	(17.5%)
Partai Buruh	6	(3.0%)
PKI	2	(1.0%)
PARKINDO	4	(2.0%)

Partai Katolik	2	(1.0%)
Sumatra	1	(0.5%)
Borneo	4	(2.0%)
Sulawesi	5	(2.5%)
Maluku	2	(1.0%)
Sunda Kecil	2	(1.0%)
Chinese	5	(2.5%)
Arabs	2	(1.0%)
Europeans	1	(0.5%)

II. Komite Nasional Indonesia Pusat, expanded 2 March 1947 (514 seats)[5]

Party	**Seats**
PNI	45
Masyumi	60
Partai Sosialis	35
Partai Buruh	35
PKI	35
PARKINDO	8
Partai Katolik	4

Workers	40
Peasants	40
Sumatra	50
Borneo	8
Sulawesi	10
Maluku	5
Sunda Kecil	5
Chinese	7
Arabs	3
Europeans	3

III. Dewan Perwakilan Rakyat of the Unitary Republic of Indonesia (formed 17 August 1950), 236 seats.[6]

Origins:

1. Members of RIS Dewan Perwakilan Rakyat	
(a) representing the Republic of Indonesia	50
(b) representing states and territories of the RIS other than the Republic of Indonesia and Pasundan	79
(c) representatives for Pasundan appointed by the Republic of Indonesia	19
2. Members of the RIS Senate	29
3. Members of the Working Committee of the Republic of Indonesia KNIP	46
4. Members of the Dewan Pertimbangan Agung of the Republic of Indonesia	13

Affiliation:

Party	**Seats (March 1951)**
Masyumi	49
PNI	36
PSI	17
PIR	17
PKI	13
Fraksi Demokrasi	13
PRN	10
Partai Katolik	9
PARINDRA	8
Partai Buruh	7
PARKINDO	5
PSII	5
Murba	4
Front Buruh	4
Fraksi Kedualatan Rakyat	4
Serikat Kerakyatan Indonesia	3
Golongan Tani (peasants)	2
no formal affiliation	26
Total	232

IV. Dewan Perwakilan Rakyat, elected 29 September 1955[7]

Party	No. of Valid Votes	% of Vote	Seats
PNI	8,434,653	22.3	57
Masyumi	7,902,886	20.9	57
Nahdatul Ulama	6,955,141	18.4	45
PKI	6,176,914	16.4	39
PSII	1,019,160	2.9	8
PARKINDO	1,003,325	2.6	8
Partai Katolik	770,740	2.0	6
PSI	753,191	2.0	5
IPKI	541,306	1.4	4
Perti	483,014	1.3	4
PRN	242,125	0.6	2
Partai Buruh	224,167	0.6	2
GPPS (Gerakan Pembela Pancasila)	219,985	0.6	2
PRI	206,261	0.5	2
PPPRI	200,419	0.5	2
Murba	199,588	0.5	2
BAPERKI	178,887	0.5	1

PIR-Wongsonegoro	178,481	0.5	1
GERINDA (Gerakan Indonesia)	154,792	0.4	1
Permai	149,287	0.4	1
Partai Persatuan Daya	146,054	0.4	1
PIR-Hazairin	114,644	0.3	1
PPTI	85,131	0.2	1
AKUI	81,454	0.2	1
PRD	77,919	0.2	1
PRIM (Partai Rakyat Indonesia Merdeka)	72,523	0.2	1
ACOMA (Angkatan Comunis Muda)	64,514	0.2	1
R. Sujono Prawirosudarso & Associates	53,305	0.1	1
Others	1,022,433	2.7	—
Total:	37,785,299	100.0	257

V. Constituent Assembly elections, 15 December 1955[8]

PNI	9,070,218
Masyumi	7,789,619
NU	6,989,333
PKI	6,232,512
PSII	1,059,922

PARKINDO	988,810
Partai Katolik	748,591
PSI	695,932
IPKI	544,803
PERTI	465,359
GPPS	152,892
PRN	220,652
PPPRI	179,346
Partai Buruh	332,047
Murba	248,633
PRI	134,011
PIR (Wongsonegoro)	162,420
PIR (Hazairin)	101,509
Permai	164,386
BAPERKI	160,456
Gerinda	158,976
Partai Persatuan Daya	169,222
PRIM	143,907
AKUI	84,862
ACOMA	55,844

PPTI	74,913
PRD	39,278
R. Sujono Prawirosudarso & Associates	38,356

VI. Java provincial elections, June-August 1957, results in 1955 elections in same regions in brackets.[9]

	Jakarta	West Java	Cent. Java	East Java
Masyumi	153,709	1,841,030	833,707	977,443
	(200,460)	(1,844,442)	(902,387)	(1,109,742)
PNI	124,955	1,055,801	2,400,282	1,899,782
	(152,031)	(1,541,927)	(3,019,568)	(2,257,069)
NU	104,892	597,356	1,865,568	2,999,785
	(120,667)	(673,552)	(1,772,306)	(3,370,554)
PKI	137,305	1,087,269	3,005,150	2,704,523
	(96,363)	(755,634)	(2,326,108)	(2,299,785)

VII. Dewan Perwakilan Rakyat–Gotong Royong (DPR-GR), composition by party, July 1960.[10]

PNI	44
PKI	30
Partai Katolik	5

PSII	5
PARKINDO	6
Murba	1
NU	36
PERTI	2
Army (functional group)	15
Navy	7
Air Force	7
Police	5
Workers	26
Peasants	25
Islamic teachers	24
Youth	9
Women	8
Intellectuals and teachers	5
Total	283

VIII. Second general elections, 3 July 1971[11]

Party	**Votes %**	**Seats in DPR**
Golkar	34,348,673 (62.80)	227
Nahdatul Ulama	10,213,650 (18.67)	58

PNI	3,793,266	(6.94)	20
PARMUSI	2,930,746	(5.36)	24
PSII	1,308,237	(2.39)	10
PARKINDO	733,359	(1.34)	7
Partai Katolik	603,740	(1.10)	3
PERTI	381,309	(0.70)	2
IPKI	338,403	(0.62)	—
Murba	48,126	(0.09)	—
Total	54,699,509		351

IX. Third general elections, 2 May 1977[12]

Party	**Votes**	**%**	**Seats in DPR**
PPP	18,743,491	27.78	99
Golkar	34,348,673	64.33	232
PDI	5,516,894	7.87	29

X. Fourth general elections, 4 May 1982, 364 seats[13]

Party	**Votes**	**%**	**Seats in DPR**
PPP	20,871,880	27.78	94
Golkar	48,334,724	64.34	246
PDI	5,919,702	7.88	24

XI. Fifth general elections 23 April 1987, 400 seats[14]

Party	Votes	%	Seats
PPP	13,730,456	16.04	61
Golkar	62,433,161	72.94	299
PDI	9,434,667	11.02	40

APPENDIX SOURCE NOTES

1. D. G. E. Hall, *A history of South-East Asia* 4th ed.; Anthony Reid, *The contest for North Sumatra: Atjeh, the Netherlands and Britain 1858–1898* (Kuala Lumpur: OUP, 1969).

2. Based principally on Susan Finch and Daniel S. Lev, compilers, *Republic of Indonesia Cabinets 1945–1965* (Ithaca, NY: Cornell Univ. Modern Indonesia Project, 1965).

3. Although Juanda's formal position from 9 July 1959 was that of First Minister (Menteri Pertama), rather than Prime Minister (Perdana Menteri), with Sukarno holding the posts of President and Prime Minister concurrently, he was effectively prime minister, *i.e.,* head of the cabinet, until his death on 7 November 1963.

4. George McTurnan Kahin, *Nationalism and revolution in Indonesia* (Ithaca, NY: Cornell Univ. Press, 1952), p. 201.

5. George McTurnan Kahin, *Nationalism and revolution in Indonesia* (Ithaca, NY: Cornell Univ. Press, 1952), p. 201.

6. Herbert Feith, *The decline of constitutional democracy in Indonesia* (Ithaca, NY: Cornell Univ. Press, 1962), pp. 94–95.

7. Herbert Feith, *The decline of constitutional democracy in Indonesia* (Ithaca, NY: Cornell Univ. Press, 1962), pp. 434–435.

8. Herbert Feith, *The Indonesian elections of 1955* (Ithaca, NY: Cornell Univ. Modern Indonesia Project, 1957), p. 65.

9. Daniel S. Lev, *The transition to Guided Democracy* (Ithaca, NY: Cornell Univ. Modern Indonesia Project, 1966), pp. 93–96.

10. Herbert Feith, 'The dynamics of Guided Democracy', in Ruth T.McVey, ed., *Indonesia* (New Haven, CT: HRAF, 1963), p. 345.

11. Oey Hong Lee, ed., *Indonesia after the 1971 elections* (Hull, Univ. of Hull, 1974), pp. 37–59.

12. Cees van Dijk, 'The Indonesian elections', *Review of Indonesian and Malaysian Affairs* 11 no. 2 (1977), pp. 42–43.

13. Leo Suryadinata, 'Indonesia's political system: continuity and change', *Contemporary Southeast Asia* 9 no. 4 (March 1988), p. 272.

14. *Jakarta Post* 27 April 1987.

BIBLIOGRAPHY

Introduction

This bibliography is a classified collection of major writings on Indonesia. As such, it is a selection from a much larger body of writings. Works have been selected for inclusion for various reasons. Some are classics in their fields—perhaps out-of-date now but nonetheless influential and worthy of continuing attention. Others are substantial monographs, that are important, reliable, and likely to withstand the test of time. Some items are less substantial but offer the most recent analysis or statement of a problem and are included because they usefully summarize the state of the art in their field, provide an introduction to other works, or offer up-to-date information. A few works have been included because they are the only available source on a particular topic, even if they are out-of-date and otherwise flawed. And some have been included because they are favorites of the compiler or because they round out the picture of writing on Indonesia.

Most of the works cited are in English. Before World War II, the bulk—and it was a vast bulk—of research on Indonesia was carried out in the Netherlands and generally published in Dutch. Since then, scholarship on Indonesia has diversified. The United States and the United Kingdom pioneered post-war English language writing on Indonesia, while the Netherlands continued as a major center, especially in anthropology and related disciplines. More recently scholars based in Australia, France, Germany, and Japan have made increasingly substantial contibutions to the field.

Scholarly research in Indonesia is hampered by political and economic conditions there, but Indonesians continue to produce important studies of their own society. This state of affairs, with major works being produced in Indonesian, English, Dutch, French, German, and Japanese makes a substantial linguistic demand even on specialists in the field and puts much important work beyond the general reader in any country. Since this bibliography is intended primarily for readers of English, the selection of titles is biased towards that language; I have, however, endeavored to include as far as possible major and especially interesting works in other languages.

The reader wanting a general and easy-to-read introduction to Indonesian history is probably best served by Zainu'ddin's *Short history of Indonesia* [0377], but anyone intending to go further will want to turn to the detailed and reliable narrative *History of modern Indonesia* by Ricklefs [0371] and to Legge's more analytical *Indonesia* [0368]. Both Ricklefs and Legge provide useful bibliographical essays on the field. Alongside these works, Wertheim's *Indonesian society in transition* [0376] and Hildred Geertz' chapter in Ruth McVey, ed., *Indonesia* [0369] provide sound introductions to Indonesian society and culture.

For the state of knowledge on Indonesia's bio-geography and geological history, the best places to turn are the volumes edited by Whitten *et al. The ecology of Sumatra* and *The ecology of Sulawesi* [0975, 0976]. Bellwood's *Prehistory of the Indo-Malaysian archipelago* [0390] supersedes most of the earlier research on Indonesia's prehistory. On very early civilization, the major work is Wolters' *Early Indonesian commerce* [0429], but the writings of Wheatley [0424–0426] and Mabbett [0404, 0405] are also good starting points. Much attention has been paid to the 'classical' Hindu period on Java, but we lack a synthesizing work to succeed Hall's 1968 general survey [0395] and the best specific account is still Schrieke's 'Ruler and realm in early Java' [0417]. Reid's *Southeast Asia in the Age of Commerce* [0483] pioneers the social history of the precolonial era, reconstructing the patterns of everyday life of the peoples of the region.

Debate continues on the nature of the coming of Islam to Indonesia, but Ricklefs' volume ably summarizes the state of opinion. Geertz' *Religion of Java* [1016] is a classic account of the character of Islam on Java, while Benda [0608] and Noer [0576] discuss the history of Islam under colonialism and Boland [1111] its experience after independence. The emergence of European power in Indonesia has been discussed in detail from a largely European point of view by Boxer [0441, 0443] and Vlekke [0375]. Van Leur's criticism of this approach in *Indonesian trade and society* [0403] is a landmark in the shift of historical attention from Europeans in Indonesia to Indonesians themselves. Moertono's *State and statecraft in old Java* [0274] and Ricklefs' *Jogjakarta under Sultan Mangkubumi* [0485] are major studies of one Indonesian region in an age when European power was not firmly established.

The literature on 'high' colonialism in Indonesia (the period from 1830 on Java and around 1870 in other parts of the archipelago until the Japanese invasion in 1942) is massive. Vandenbosch, *The Dutch East Indies* [0596] is an easily accessible compendium of official data on the colony. Sutherland, *The making of a bureaucratic elite* [0596] describes changes in the traditional elite of Java under colonial rule. Kartini's *Letters of the Javanese princess* [0564] contains the reflections of an Indonesian woman on the condition of her country and people. Perhaps the most extensive debate is on the nature of the Cultivation System in the early 19th century. The conventional view that it was an exploitative system with little but harmful effects on Javanese society is challenged by Elson's *Javanese peasants and the colonial sugar industry* [0509]. On the Indonesian nationalist movement, which grew partly in response to colonialism, Kahin's *Nationalism and revolution in Indonesia* [0563] is a standard work although almost all sections of the book are now superseded by more detailed monographs. Dahm's *Sukarno and the struggle for Indonesian independence* [0695] and Legge's *Sukarno* [0705] are major studies of Indonesia's foremost nationalist leader and later president.

Kanahele's unpublished thesis 'The Japanese occupation of Indonesia' [0610] is a comprehensive, though somewhat plodding account of the war years and can be read usefully in conjunction with Friend's study of the political culture of colonialism and nationalism, *The blue-eyed enemy* [0611], and Anderson's *Some aspects of Indonesian politics under the Japanese occupation* [0606], which describes the quickening pace of preparations for independence. Anderson's *Java in a time of revolution* [0628] carries the story through the first year of independence, while Reid's *Indonesian national revolution* [0656] is the standard general account of the years 1945–49.

Overshadowing all other works on the 1950s is Feith's *Decline of parliamentary democracy* [0634], though Sundhaussen has offered an alternative interpretation in his *Road to power: Indonesian military politics* [0663], which is also a useful starting point for reading on Guided Democracy. This difficult period still has no standard analysis, but also worth consulting are Lev, *The transition to Guided Democracy* [0647], Feith's chapter in McVey, *Indonesia* [0369] and Weatherbee, *Ideology in Indonesia* [0854]. Hindley [0822] and Mortimer [0827] are the best of many studies of the Indonesian Communist Party (PKI) in this period. Covering both late Guided Democracy and the New Order, including the massacres of 1965–66, is Crouch's *Army and politics in Indonesia* [0669], still the best standard work, though more popular volumes such as McDonald's *Suharto's Indonesia* [0680] offer more up-to-date information. The two most important interpretative works on the New Order are journal articles: Anderson's 'Old state, new society' [0667] and Liddle's 'Suharto's Indonesia' [0679]. For Indonesian foreign policy since 1945, the best starting point is Leifer's *Indonesia's foreign policy* [0742].

For a general introduction to Indonesian art, it is hard to beat Holt's *Art in Indonesia* [0116]. For a reliable survey of the economy, see Booth and McCawley, *The Indonesian economy during the Suharto era* [0213], but for up-to-date information, the regular economic surveys of the *Bulletin of Indonesian Economic Studies* are essential.

Keeping Up with Current Events

Following the latest developments in Indonesia from outside the country is never easy. Within the region, Indonesian radio and television broadcasts can sometimes be picked up, while the overseas broadcasts of Radio Australia and Nederland Wereld Omroep often contain reports on the country.

For those who read Indonesian, the newsmagazine *Tempo* is an invaluable source of current information; similar magazines, such as *Editor,* have also appeared from time to time. For English language reporting of current events, the *Far Eastern Economic Review* and *Asiaweek* are particularly valuable; reports on Indonesia also appear with some regularity in the *Asian Wall Street Journal,* the *Sydney Morning Herald,* the *New York Times* and the Dutch language *NRC Handelsblad*. The Clippings Agency Service, PT Enam-Enam, Jl Jambrut 2–4 (formerly Jl Kramat VIII), Jakarta Pusat, tel. 323969, provides a service under a wide variety of headings. The Department of Political Science, Research School of Social Sciences, Australian National University, publishes a microfiche collection of Australian press clippings on Indonesia. In addition, many Indonesian embassies provide a regular newsletter of current events.

There is a wide range of publications which deal competently with recent, rather than current, events in Indonesia. Most useful is *Indonesia Reports,* consisting of a digest of the Indonesian press together with feature articles on topics of current interest. The *Bulletin of Indonesian Economic Studies* publishes a useful quarterly economic survey, while *Asian Survey* publishes an annual roundup of political events in its January or February issue. The journal *Indonesia* publishes regular listings of major office-holders. *Inside Indonesia, TAPOL Bulletin* and *Indonesië: Feiten en Meningen* publish up-to-date critical material on Indonesian affairs. The *Flora Malesiana Bulletin* contains valuable information on recent developments on the environment. *Prisma* is Indonesia's foremost journal for scholarly debate on pressing issues; a selection of articles from this journal appears in English in *Prisma: the Indonesian Indicator. Indonesian Quarterly* publishes political analyses by Indonesian scholars who are close to the government.

Both PAIS (Public Affairs Information Service) and APAIS (Australian Public Affairs Information Service) provide bibliographical listing of recent articles on Indonesia. *Excerpta Indonesica* and the *Bibliography of Asian Studies* are essential tools for keeping in touch with recent academic research.

Abbreviations

BCAS, *Bulletin of Concerned Asian Scholars*
BIES, *Bulletin of Indonesian Economic Studies*
BKI, *Bijdragen tot de Taal-, Land- en Volkenkunde*
ISEAS, Institute of Southeast Asian Studies
JAS, *Journal of Asian Studies*
JSEAH, *Journal of Southeast Asian History*
JSEAS, *Journal of Southeast Asian Studies*
KITLV, Koninklijk Instituut voor Taal-, Land- en Volkenkunde
MAS, *Modern Asian Studies*
OUP, Oxford University Press
RIMA, *Review of Indonesian and Malaysian Affairs*
Univ., University

BIBLIOGRAPHY

GENERAL—Bibliographies

[0001] Boland, B.J., and I. Farjon. *Islam in Indonesia: a bibliographic survey*. Dordrecht, Netherlands: Foris, 1983.

[0002] *ASEAN: a bibliography*. Singapore: ISEAS, 1984.

[0003] Avé, Jan B., Victor T. King and Joke G.W. de Wit. *West-Kalimantan: a bibliography*. Leiden, Netherlands: KITLV, 1983.

[0004] Baal, J. van, K.W. Galis and R.M. Koentjaraningrat. *West-Irian: a bibliography*. Dordrecht, Netherlands: Foris, 1984.

[0005] Char Lan Hiang. *Southeast Asian research tools: Indonesia*. Honolulu: Univ. of Hawaii Southeast Asian Studies Program, 1979.

[0006] Coolhaas, W.Ph. *A critical survey of studies on Dutch colonial history*. The Hague: Nijhoff, 2d ed, 1980.

[0007] Farjon, I. *Madura and surrounding islands: an annotated bibliography 1860–1942*. Leiden, Netherlands: KITLV, 1980.

[0008] Groenendael, Victoria M. Clara van. *Wayang theatre in Indonesia: an annotated bibliography*. Leiden, Netherlands: KITLV, 1987.

[0009] Hicks, George L., and Geoffrey McNicoll. *The Indonesian economy 1950–1965: a bibliography*. New Haven, CT: Yale Univ. Southeast Asian Studies, 1967.

[0010] Jacobs, M., and T.J.J. de Boo. *Conservation literature on Indonesia: selected annotated bibliography*. Leiden, Netherlands: Rijksherbarium, 1982.

[0011] Jaquet, F.G.P. *Sources for the history of Asian and Oceania in the Netherlands*. 2 vols. Munich: K.G. Saur, 1982–83.

[0012] Johnson, Donald Clay. *Index to Southeast Asian journals: a guide to articles, book reviews and composite works*. 2 vols. Boston: Hall & Co, 1977–1982.

[0013] Kemp, H.C. *Annotated bibliography of bibliographies on Indonesia*. Leiden, Netherlands: KITLV, 1990.

[0014] Kennedy, Raymond. *Bibliography of Indonesian peoples and cultures*. New Haven, CT: Yale Univ. Southeast Asia Studies, 2d ed., 1962.

[0015] Koentjaraningrat. *Anthropology in Indonesia: a bibliographical review*. Leiden, Netherlands: KITLV, 1975.

[0016] Lan Hiang Char. *Southeast Asian research tools: Indonesia*. Honolulu: Univ. of Hawaii, 1979.

[0017] Langenberg, Michael van, ed., *Bibliography of Indonesian politics and the economy since 1965*. Sydney: Reseach Institute for Asia and the Pacific, 1988.

[0018] Nagelkerke, Gerard A. *The Chinese in Indonesia: a bibliography, 18th century—1981*. Leiden, Netherlands: KITLV, 1982.

[0019] Polman, Katrien. *The central Moluccas: an annotated bibliography*. Leiden, Netherlands: KITLV, 1983.

[0020] Polman, Katrien. *The north Moluccas: an annotated bibliography*. Leiden, Netherlands: KITLV, 1981.

[0021] Schouten, Mieke. *Minahasa and Bolaangmongondouw: an annotated bibliography, 1800–1942*. Leiden, Netherlands: KITLV, 1981.

[0022] Sherlock, Kevin. *A bibliography of the island of Timor, including East (formerly Portuguese) Timor, West (formerly Dutch) Timor and the island of Roti*. Canberra: Australian National Univ., 1980.

[0023] Volkman, Toby Alice. *Film on Indonesia*. New Haven, CT: Yale Univ. Southeast Asia Studies, 1985.

Reference

[0024] *Apa dan Siapa: sejumlah orang Indonesia, 1981–1982*. Jakarta: Grafiti, 1981; *1983–1984,* 1983; *1985–1986,* 1986.

[0025] Crawfurd, John. *A descriptive dictionary of the Indian islands & adjacent countries*. Kuala Lumpur, Malaysia: OUP, 1971. [Original edition, London 1856]

[0026] *Encyclopaedie van Nederlandsch-Indië*. 4 vols. and 4 suppls. The Hague and Leiden, Netherlands: Martinus Nijhoff and E.J. Brill, 1917–1939.

[0027] *Ensiklopedi Indonesia*. 7 vols. Jakarta: Ichtiar Baru-van Hoeve, 1980–84.

[0028] Gonggryp, G.F.E. *Geillustreerde encyclopedie van Nederlandsch-Indie*. Leiden, Netherlands: Leidsche Uitgeversmaatschappij, 1934.

[0029] *The Indonesian military leaders: biographical and other background data*. Jakarta: Sritua Arief, 2d ed., 1978.

[0030] *Orang Indonesia Jang Terkemoeka di Djawa*. [Jakarta]: Gunseikanbu, 2604 [*i.e.,* 1944].

[0031] Roeder, O.G.. *Who's who in Indonesia*. Jakarta: Gunung Agung, 1971. 2d ed. 1980.

[0032] Suryadinata, Leo. *Eminent Indonesian Chinese: biographical sketches*. Singapore: ISEAS, 1978.

[0033] *Who's who in Indonesian military*. Jakarta: Sritua Arief, 1977.

Statistical Abstracts

Changing economy in Indonesia, published by the Royal Tropical Institute, Amsterdam

[0034] 1. Piet Creutzberg, *Indonesia's export crops, 1816–1940,* 1975.

[0035] 2. Piet Creutzberg, *Public finance, 1816–1939,* 1976.

[0036] 3. Piet Creutzberg, *Expenditure on fixed assets,* 1977.

[0037] 4. Piet Creutzberg, *Rice prices,* 1978.

[0038] 5. Piet Creutzberg, *National income,* 1979.

[0039] 6. J.Th.M. van Laanen, *Money and banking, 1816–1940,* 1980.

[0040] 7. W. Korthals Altes, *Balance of payments, 1822–1939,* 1987.

[0041] 8. W.I.A.M. Segers, *Manufacturing industry, 1870–1942,* 1987.

[0042] 9. Gerrit J. Knaap, *Transport, 1819–1940,* 1989.

[0043] *Indisch Verslag 1939, II: Statistisch Jaaroverzicht van Nederlandsch-Indië over het Jaar 1938*. Batavia, Indonesia: Landsdrukkerij, 1939.

[0044] Netherlands Indies, Departement van Landbouw, Nijverheid en Handel. *Volkstelling 1930*. Batavia, Indonesia: Landsdrukkerij, 1933.

[0045] *Statistical pocketbook of Indonesia*. Jakarta: Biro Pusat Statistik, 1981.

[0046] *Statistik Indonesia: Statistical Yearbook of Indonesia*. Jakarta: Biro Pusat Statistik, 1986.

Travel

[0047] Allen, Jeremy, and Kal Muller. *East Kalimantan*. Singapore: Times Books, 1988.

[0048] Anderson, John. *Mission to the east coast of Sumatra in 1823*. Edinburgh: Blackwood, 1826; Kuala Lumpur: OUP, 1971.

[0049] Attenborough, David. *Zoo quest for a dragon*. London: Lutterworth, 1957. [Komodo]

[0050] Belcher, E. *Narrative of the voyage of H.M.S. Samarang, during the years 1843–1846*. 2 vols, London: Reeve, Benham & Reeve, 1848 [East Indonesia].

[0051] Bickmore, Albert S. *Travels in the East Indian archipelago*. London: Murray, 1868.

[0052] Bock, Carl. *The head-hunters of Borneo: a narrative of travel up the Mahakkam and down the Barito*. London: Sampson Low *et al.,* 1881 [reprint Singapore: OUP, 1985].

[0053] Bonneff, Marcel. *Pérégrinations javanaises: les voyages de R.M.A. Purwa Lelana: une visie de Java au XIXe siècle (c.1860–1875)*. Paris: Editions de la Maison des Recherche Scientifique, 1986.

[0054] Bontius, James. *An account of the diseases, natural-history and medicines of the East Indies*. London, 1769; reprinted as *Bontius tropische geneeskunde/Bontius on tropical medicine* (Latin and English dual text), Amsterdam: Nederlandsch Tijdschrift voor Geneeskunde, Opuscula Selecta Neerlandicorum de Arte Medica X, 1931.

[0055] Brongsma, C.D., and G.F. Venema. *To the mountains of the stars*. London: Hodder & Stoughton, 1962. [West New Guinea]

[0056] Burnell, A.C., and P.A. Tiek, eds. *The voyage of J.H. van Linschoten to the East Indies*. 2 vols. London: Hakluyt Society 1885.

[0057] Campbell, Donald Maclaine. *Java past & present: a description of the most beautiful country in the world, its ancient history, people, antiquities, and products*. 2 vols. London: Heinemann, 1915.

[0058] Coast, John. *Recruit to revolution: adventure and politics in Indonesia*. London: Christophers, 1952.

[0059] Cortesão, Armando, trans. & ed. *The Suma Oriental of Tomé Pires*. 2 vols. London: Hakluyt Society, 1944.

[0060] Deane, Shirley. *Ambon: island of spices*. London: John Murray, 1979.

[0061] Domalain, Yves. *Panjamon*. London: Rupert Hart-Davis, 1972. [Kalimantan]

[0062] Forbes, Anna. *Unbeaten tracks in islands of the Far East: experiences of a naturalist's wife in the 1880s*. Singapore: OUP, 1987 [originally published as *Insulinde,* London: Blackwood, 1887].

[0063] Foster, Sir William, ed. *The voyages of Sir James Lancaster to Brazil and the East Indies, 1591–1603*. London: Hakluyt Society, 1940.

[0064] Foster, Sir William, ed. *The voyage of Sir Henry Middleton to the Moluccas, 1604–1606*. London: Hakluyt Society, 1943.

[0065] Gibb, H.A.R., ed. & tr. *Ibn Battuta: travels in Asia and Africa, 1325–54*. London: Routledge, 1953.

[0066] Hanbury-Tenison, Robin. *A pattern of peoples: a journey among the tribes of the outer Indonesian islands*. London: Angus & Robertson, 1975.

[0067] Jack-Hinton, Colin. 'Marco Polo in South-East Asia', *JSEAH* 5 no 2 (1964): 43–103.

[0068] McPhee, Colin. *A house in Bali*. New York: John Day, 1944.

[0069] Medhurst, W.H., ed. & tr. *The Chinaman abroad, or a desultory account of the Malayan archipelago, particularly of Java, by Ong Tae-hae*. Singapore: Mission Press, 1849.

[0070] Mills, J.V. 'Notes on early Chinese voyages', *Journal of the Royal Asiatic Society* (1951): 3–24.

[0071] Mjoberg, Eric. *Forest life and adventures in the Malay archipelago*. London: Allen & Unwin, 1930.

[0072] Murray, James. *The mask of time: an Indonesian discovery*. Sydney: Ure Smith, 1970.

[0073] Scidmore, E.R. *Java: garden of the east*. New York: Century, 1912.

[0074] Valentijn, François. *Oud en nieuw Oost-Indiën*. 5 vols. Dordrecht, Netherlands & Amsterdam: van Braam & de Linden, 1724–1726.

[0075] Wallace, Alfred Russell. *The Malay archipelago*. 2 vols. London: Macmillan, 1869.

[0076] Wilcox, Harry. *White stranger: six moons in Celebes*. London: Collins, 1949. [Toraja]

[0077] Williams, Maslyn. *Five journeys from Jakarta: inside Sukarno's Indonesia*. New York: Morrow, 1965.

[0078] Wright, Arnold, and Oliver T. Breakspear, eds. *Twentieth century impressions of Netherlands India: its history, people, commerce, industries, and resources*. London: Lloyd's Greater Britain Publishing Co., 1909.

Guide Books

[0079] Black, Star, and David Stuart-Fox. *Bali*. Hong Kong: Apa, 1977.

[0080] Bruce, Ginny, Mary Covernton and Alan Samagalski. *Indonesia: a travel survival kit*. Berkeley, CA: Lonely Planet, 1986.

[0081] Dalton, Bill. *Indonesia handbook*. Chico, CA: Moon Publications, 4th ed., 1988.

[0082] Draine, Cathie, and Barbara Hall. *Culture Shock: Indonesia*. Singapore: Times Books, 1986.

[0083] Hoefer, Hans. *Java*. Hong Kong: Apa, 1978.

[0084] Huehn, Kurt G. *Hildebrand's travel guide: Indonesia*. New York: Hippocrene, 1985.

[0085] Oey, Eric, ed. *Indonesia*. Hong Kong: Apa, 1988.

CULTURE—Archeology

[0086] Gomez, Luis O., and Hiram W. Woodward. *Barabudur: history and significance of a Buddhist monument*. Berkeley, CA: Asian Humanities Press, 1981.

[0087] Krom, N.J. *Barabudur: archaeological description*. 2 vols. The Hague: Nijhoff, 1927.

[0088] Namikawa, Banri, *et al. Borobudur*. Tokyo: Heibonsha, 1971.

[0089] Stutterheim, W.F. *Studies in Indonesian archaeology*. The Hague: Nijhoff, 1956.

[0090] Suleiman, Satyawati. *Sculptures of ancient Sumatra*. Jakarta: Proyek Penelitian Purbakala, 1981.

See also: 0389, 0394, 0406, 0421.

Architecture

[0091] Atmadi, Parmono. *Some architectural design principles of temples in Java: a study through buildings projection on the reliefs of Borobodur temple*. Yogyakarta, Indonesia: Gadjah Mada Univ. Press, 1988.

[0092] Dumarçay, Jacques. *The house in South-East Asia*. Singapore: Oxford Univ. Press, 1987.

[0093] Feldman, Jerome. 'The house as world in Bawomataluo, south Nias', in E. Bruner and J. Becker eds, *Art, ritual and society in Indonesia*. Athens, OH: Ohio Univ. Papers in International Studies, 1979, 127–189.

[0094] Greig, Doreen. *The reluctant colonists: Netherlanders abroad in the 17th and 18th centuries*. Assen, Netherlands: van Gorcum, 1987.

[0095] Heuken, A. *Historical sites of Jakarta*. Jakarta: Cipta Loka Caroka, 1982.

[0096] Jessup, Helen. 'The Dutch colonial villa, Indonesia', *Mimar* 13 (1984): 35–42.

[0097] Keeler, Ward. *Symbolic dimensions of the Javanese house*. Clayton, Vic., Australia: Monash Univ. Centre of Southeast Asian Studies, 1983.

[0098] Kultermann, Udo. 'Architecture in South-East Asia, 2: Indonesia', *Mimar* 21 (1986): 45–52.

[0099] Prijotomo, Josef. *Ideas & forms of Javanese architecture*. Yogyakarta, Indonesia: Gadjah Mada Univ. Press, 1984.

[0100] Volkman, Toby Alice, and Charles Zerner. 'Tourism and architectural design in the Toraja highlands', *Mimar* 25 (Sept. 1987): 20–25.

[0101] Wijaya, Made. 'Trends in modern Balinese architecture: how fares the environment on the fabled isle?', *Prisma: the Indonesian Indicator* 39 (1986): 85–94.

See also: 1134.

Arts

[0102] Barbier, Jean Paul. *Indonesian primitive art: Indonesia, Malaysia, the Philippines*. Dallas: Dallas Museum of Art, 1984.

[0103] Becker, Judith. *Traditional music in modern Java: gamelan in a changing society*. Honolulu: Univ. of Hawaii Press, 1980.

[0104] Becker, Judith. 'Kroncong: Indonesian popular music', *Asian Music* 7 no.5 (1975): 14–19.

[0105] Bernet Kempers. *Ancient Indonesian art*. Amsterdam: van der Peet, 1959.

[0106] Bodrogi, Tibor. *Art of Indonesia*. London: Academy Editions, 1973.

[0107] Brandon, James R. *On thrones of gold: three Javanese shadow plays*. Cambridge, MA: Harvard Univ. Press, 1970.

[0108] Coomaraswamy, Ananda K. *History of Indian and Indonesian Art*. New York: Dover, 1965.

[0109] Draeger, Donn. *Weapons and fighting arts of the Indonesian archipelago*. Rutland, VT: Tuttle, 1972.

[0110] Duncombe, Brenda. *Art museums of Southeast Asia*. Sydney: Craft Council of Australia, 1988.

[0111] Elliott, Inger McCabe. *Batik: fabled cloth of Java*. Harmondsworth, England: Viking, 1985.

[0112] Frederick, William H. 'Rhoma Irama and the dangdut style: aspects of contemporary Indonesian popular culture', *Indonesia* 34 (1982): 102–130.

[0113] Groenendael, Victoria M. Clara van. *The dalang behind the wayang: the role of the Surakarta and Yogyakarta dalang in Indonesian-Javanese society*. Leiden, Netherlands: KITLV, 1985.

[0114] Hatley, Barbara. 'Indonesian ritual, Javanese drama—celebrating *tujuhbelasan*', *Indonesia* 34 (1982): 55–64.

[0115] Holt, Claire. *Art in Indonesia: continuities and change*. Ithaca, NY: Cornell Univ. Press, 1967.

[0116] Holt, Claire. *Dance quest in Celebes*. Paris: Archives Internationales de la Dance, 1939.

[0117] Hood, Mantle. 'Bronze drum' and (with others) 'Indonesia', in Stanley Sadie, ed., *The New Grove dictionary of music and musicians*. London: Macmillan, 1980.

[0118] Jones, A.M. *Africa and Indonesia: the evidence of the xylophone and other musical and cultural factors*. Leiden, Netherlands: E.J. Brill, 2d ed., 1971.

[0119] Kartiwa, Suwati. *Kain songket Indonesia/Songket weaving in Indonesia*. Jakarta: Djambatan, 1986.

[0120] Kartomi, M.J., ed. *Five essays on the Indonesian arts*. Clayton, Vic., Australia: Monash Univ., 1981.

[0121] Kartomi, Margaret. *Musical instruments of Indonesia: an introductory handbook*. Melbourne: Indonesian Arts Society, 1985.

[0122] Kartomi, Margaret J., ed. *Studies in Indonesian music*. Clayton, Vic., Australia: Monash Univ. Centre of Southeast Asian Studies, 1978.

[0123] Kats, J. *De wajang poerwa: een vorm van Javaans toneel*. Leiden, Netherlands: KITLV, 2d ed., 1984.

[0124] Keeler, Ward. *Javanese shadow plays, Javanese selves*. Princeton, NJ: Princeton Univ. Press, 1987.

[0125] Kitley, Philip. 'Batik and popular culture', *Prisma: the Indonesian Indicator* 43 (March 1987): 8–24.

[0126] Kunst, Jaap. *Hindu-Javanese musical instruments*. The Hague: Nijhoff, 2d ed., 1968.

[0127] Kunst, Jaap. *Music in Java: its history, its theory, and its technique*. The Hague: Nijhoff, 1973.

[0128] Kunst, Jaap. *Music in New Guinea: three studies*. Leiden, Netherlands: KITLV, 1967.

[0129] Langewis, Laurens, and Frits A. Wagner. *Decorative art in Indonesian textiles*. Amsterdam: van der Peet, 1964.

[0130] Lindsay, Jennifer. *Javanese gamelan*. Kuala Lumpur, Malaysia: OUP, 1979.

[0131] McPhee, Colin. *Music in Bali*. New Haven, CT: Yale Univ. Press, 1966.

[0132] Maxwell, Robin. *Southeast Asian textiles: the state of the art*. Clayton Vic., Australia, Monash Univ. Centre of Southeast Asian Studies, 1987.

[0133] Morgan, Stephanie, and Laurie Jo Sears, eds. *Aesthetic tradition and cultural transition in Java and Bali*. Madison, WI:

Univ. of Wisconsin Center for Southeast Asian Studies, 1984.

[0134] Pemberton, John. 'Musical politics in Central Java, or how not to listen to a Javanese *gamelan*', *Indonesia* 44 (1987): 16–29.

[0135] Piper, Susan, and Sawung Jabo. 'Indonesian music from the 50s to the 80s', *Prisma: the Indonesian Indicator* 43 (March 1987): 25–37.

[0136] Ras, J.J. 'The historical development of the Javanese shadow theatre', *RIMA* 10 no.2 (1976): 50–76.

[0137] Rodgers, Susan. *Power and gold: jewelry from Indonesia, Malaysia and the Philippines*. Geneva: Asia Society, 1985.

[0138] Sen, Krishna. 'Hidden from history: aspects of Indonesian cinema 1955–65', *RIMA* 19 no. 2 (1985): 1–55.

[0139] Sen, Krishna, ed. *Histories and stories: cinema in New Order Indonesia*. Clayton, Vic., Australia: Monash University, 1988.

[0140] Sutton, R. Anderson. 'Commercial cassette recordings of traditional music in Java: implications for performers and scholars', *World of Music* 27 no.3 (1985): 23–43.

[0141] Udin, S. ed. *Spectrum: essays presented to Sutan Takdir Alisyahbana on his seventieth birthday*. Jakarta: Dian Rakyat, 1978.

[0142] Veenendal, Jan. *Furniture from Indonesia, Sri Langka and India during the Dutch period*. Delft, Netherlands: Volkenkundig Museum Nusantara, 1985.

[0143] Wagner, Frits A. *Indonesia: the art of an island group*. New York: McGraw-Hill, 1959.

[0144] Willetts, William. *Ceramic art of South East Asia*. Singapore: South East Asia Ceramics Society, 1971.

[0145] Wolbers, Paul Arthur. 'Account of an *angklung caruk* July 28, 1985', *Indonesia* 43 (April 1987): 66–74.

[0146] Zoete, B. de, and W. Spies. *Dance and drama in Bali*. New York: Harper, 1939; Kuala Lumpur, Malaysia: OUP, 1982.

See also: 0008.

Literary Studies

[0147] Beekman, E.M. 'The passatist: Louis Couperus's interpretation of Dutch colonialism', *Indonesia* 37 (1984): 59–76.

[0148] Davidson, J.H.C.S., and H. Cordell, eds. *The short story in South East Asia*. London: School of Oriental and African Studies, 1982.

[0149] Foulcher, Keith. *Pujangga Baru: literature and nationalism in Indonesia, 1933–1942*. Bedford Park, South Australia: Flinders Univ. Asian Studies Monograph no 2, 1980.

[0150] Foulcher, Keith. *Social commitment in literature and the arts: the Indonesian 'Institute of People's Culture', 1950–1965*. Clayton, Vic., Australia: Monash Univ. Centre of Southeast Asian Studies, 1986.

[0151] Hill, David T. *Who's left? Indonesian literature in the early 1980s*. Clayton, Vic., Australia: Monash Univ. Centre of Southeast Asian Studies, Working Paper no 33, 1984.

[0152] Maier, Henk M.J. 'Chairil Anwar's heritage: the fear of stultification: another side of modern Indonesian literature', *Indonesia* 43 (April 1987): 1–29.

[0153] Marrison, Geoffrey E. 'Modern Balinese: a regional literature of Indonesia', *BKI* 143 no. 4 (1987): 468–498.

[0154] Mohamad, Goenawan. 'The Manikebu affair: literature and politics in the 1960s', *Prisma: the Indonesian Indicator* 46 (1989): 70–88.

[0155] Oemarjati, Boen S. *Chairil Anwar: the poet and his language*. Leiden, Netherlands: KITLV, 1972.

[0156] Raffel, Burton. *The development of modern Indonesian poetry*. Albany, NY: State Univ. of New York Press, 1967.

[0157] Robson, S.O. 'The Ramayana in early Java', *South East Asian Review* (Bihar) 5 no. 2 (1980): 5–17.

[0158] Sherry, Norman. *Conrad's eastern world*. Cambridge, England: Cambridge University Press, 1966.

[0159] Teeuw, A. 'The impact of Balai Pustaka on modern Indonesian literature', *Bulletin of the School of Oriental and African Studies* 35 no. 1 (1972): 111–127.

[0160] Teeuw, A. *Modern Indonesian literature*. 2 vols. The Hague: Nijhoff, 2d & 3d eds, 1979–1986.

[0161] Tickell, Paul. 'Subversion or escapism? the fantastic in recent Indonesian fiction', *RIMA* 20 no. 1 (1986): 50–67.

[0162] Watson, C.W. 'Observations on Dutch colonial literature', *Indonesia Circle* 38 (1985): 31–38.

See also: 0796.

Works of Literature

[0163] Achdiat K. Mihardja. *Atheis*. St Lucia, Qld., Australia: Univ. of Queensland Press, 1972.

[0164] Aveling, Harry, ed. *From Surabaya to Armageddon*. Singapore: Heinemann, 1976. [short stories]

[0165] Aveling, Harry, ed. *Contemporary Indonesian poetry*. St Lucia, Qld., Australia: Univ. of Queensland Press, 1975.

[0166] Beekman, E.M., ed. *Two tales of the East Indies: The last house in the world;* and Beb Vuyk., *The counselor, H.J. Friedericy*. Amherst, MA: Univ. of Massachusetts Press, 1983.

[0167] Breton de Nijs, E. [Rob Nieuwenhuys] *Faded portraits*. Amherst, MA: Univ. of Massachusetts Press, 1982.

[0168] Conrad, Joseph. *Lord Jim*. Edinburgh: Blackwood, 1900; Boston: Allen & Unwin, 1988.

[0169] Du Perron, E. *Country of origin*. Amherst, MA: Univ. of Massachusetts Press, 1983.

[0170] Koch, C.J. *The year of living dangerously*. Melbourne: Nelson, 1978.

[0171] Lubis, Mochtar. *A road with no end*. Translated and edited by Anthony H. Johns. London: Hutchinson, 1968.

[0172] Lubis, Mochtar. *Twilight in Jakarta*. New York: Vanguard, 1964.

[0173] Nieuwenhuys, Robert. *Mirror of the Indies*. Amherst, MA: Univ. of Massachusetts Press, 1982.

[0174] Pane, Armijn. *Shackles*. Athens, OH: Ohio University Center for International Studies, 1985.

[0175] Raffel, Burton, tr. and ed. *The complete poetry of Chairil Anwar*. Albany, NY: State Univ. of New York Press, 1970.

[0176] Ras, J.J. *Javanese literature since independence: an anthology*. Leiden, Netherlands: KITLV, 1979.

[0177] Rendra, W.S. *The struggle of the Naga tribe*. St Lucia, Qld., Australia: Univ. of Queensland Press, 1979.

[0178] Székely, Ladislao. *Tropic fever: the adventures of a planter in Sumatra*. New York: Harper, 1937 (Kuala Lumpur, Malaysia: OUP reprint, 1979).

[0179] Székely-Lulofs, Madelon. *Coolie* (1933). Kuala Lumpur, Malaysia: OUP, 1982.

[0180] Székely-Lulofs, Madelon. *Rubber* (1930). Singapore: OUP, 1987.

[0181] Toer, Pramoedya Ananta. *Child of all nations*. Ringwood, Vic., Australia: Penguin, 1984.

[0182] Toer, Pramoedya Ananta. *This earth of mankind*. Ringwood, Vic., Australia: Penguin, 1982.

[0183] Toer, Pramoedya Ananta. 'Revenge', translated by Ben Anderson, *Indonesia* 26 (October 1978): 43–62.

[0184] Tweedie, Jill. *Internal affairs*. London: Heinemann, 1986.

See also: 0523.

Languages and Linguistics

[0185] Anwar, Khaidir. *Indonesian: the development and use of a national language*. Yogyakarta, Indonesia: Gadjah Mada Univ. Press, 1980.

[0186] Cense, A.A., and E.M. Uhlenbeck. *Critical survey of studies on the languages of Borneo*. Leiden, Netherlands: KITLV, 1958.

[0187] Cense, A.A. *Makassars-Nederlands woordenboek met Nederlands-Makassars register*. Leiden, Netherlands: KITLV, 1982.

[0188] Durie, Mark. *A grammar of Acehnese on the basis of a dialect of north Aceh*. Leiden, Netherlands: KITLV, 1975.

[0189] Echols, John M. and Hassan Shadily. *An English-Indonesian dictionary*. Ithaca, NY: Cornell Univ. Press, 1975.

[0190] Echols, John M. and Hassan Shadily. *An Indonesian-English dictionary*. Ithaca, NY: Cornell Univ. Press, 1961.

[0191] Errington, J. Joseph. 'Continuity and change in Indonesian language development', *JAS* 45 no.2 (1986): 329–353.

[0192] Hoffman, John. 'A foreign investment: Indies Malay to 1901', *Indonesia* 27 (1979): 65–92.

[0193] Horne, Elinor Clark. *Javanese-English dictionary*. New Haven, CT, & London: Yale Univ. Press, 1974.

[0194] Maulana, Sugeng. *Glossary of abbreviations and acronyms used in Indonesia*. Jakarta: Ichtiar Baru/van Hoeve, 1980.

[0195] Nothofer, Bernd. *The reconstruction of proto-Malayo-Javanic*. Leiden, Netherlands: KITLV, 1975.

[0196] Pawley, Andrew. 'Austronesian languages', *Encyclopaedia Britannica*. Chicago: University Britannica, 1974.

[0197] Poerwadaminta, W.J.S. *Kamus umum Bahasa Indonesia*. Jakarta: Balai Pustaka, 1976.

[0198] Rafferty, Ellen. 'Languages of the Chinese of Java', *JAS* 44 no 1 (1984): 247–272.

[0199] Sarumpaet, J.P. *Modern usage in Bahasa Indonesia*. Melbourne: Pitman, 1980.

[0200] Schmidgall-Tellings, A.E., and Alan M. Stevens. *Contemporary Indonesian-English dictionary*. Athens, OH: Ohio Univ. Press, 1981.

[0201] Swellengrebel, J.L. *In Leideckers voetspoor: anderhalve eeuw bijbelvertaling en taalkunde in de Indonesische talen*. 2 vols. Leiden, Netherlands: KITLV, 1974–1978.

[0202] Teeuw, A. *A critical survey of studies on Malay and Bahasa Indonesia*. The Hague: Nijhoff, 1961.

[0203] Tuuk, H.N. van der. *A grammar of Toba-Batak*. Leiden, Netherlands: KITLV, 1971.

[0204] Uhlenbeck, E.M. *A critical survey of studies on the languages of Java and Madura*. The Hague: Nijhoff, 1964.

[0205] Vikør, Lars S. *Perfecting spelling: spelling discussions and reforms in Indonesia and Malaysia 1900–1972*. Dordrecht, Netherlands: Foris, 1988.

[0206] Voorhoeve, P. *Critical survey of studies on the languages of Sumatra*. Leiden, Netherlands: KITLV, 1955.

[0207] Wurm, S.A., and Shiro Hattori. *Language atlas of the Pacific area, part 2: Japan area, Taiwan (Formosa), Philippines, mainland and insular Southeast Asia*. Canberra: Australian Academy of the Humanities, 1983.

[0208] Wurm, S.A. *Papuan languages of Oceania*. Tübingen, Germany: Narr, 1982

[0209] Zoetmulder, P.J., with S.O. Robson. *Old Javanese-English dictionary*. 2 vols. The Hague: Nijhoff, 1982.

ECONOMY—General

[0210] Anrooij, F. van, *et al. Between people and statistics: essays on modern Indonesian history*. The Hague: Nijhoff, 1979.

[0211] Arndt, H.W. *The Indonesian economy: selected papers*. Singapore: Chopmen Press, 1984.

[0212] Boeke, J.H. *The evolution of the Netherlands Indies economy*. New York: Institute of Pacific Relations, 1946.

[0213] Booth, Anne, and Peter McCawley, eds. *The Indonesian economy during the Suharto era*. Kuala Lumpur, Malaysia: OUP, 1981.

[0214] Glassburner, Bruce, ed. *The economy of Indonesia: selected readings*. Ithaca, NY: Cornell Univ. Press, 1971.

[0215] Hatta, Mohammad. *The cooperative movement in Indonesia*. Ithaca, NY: Cornell Univ. Press, 1957.

[0216] Higgins, Benjamin. 'The dualistic theory of underdeveloped areas', *Economic development and cultural change* 4 (1956): 99–115.

[0217] Higgins, Benjamin, and Jean Higgins. *Indonesia: the crisis of the millstones*. Princeton, NJ: Van Nostrand, 1963.

[0218] *Indonesian economics: the concept of dualism in theory and practice*. The Hague: van Hoeve, 1966.

[0219] Liddle, R. William. 'The politics of *Ekonomi Pancasila:* some reflections on a recent debate', *BIES* 18 no 1 (1982): 96–101.

[0220] Mackie, J.A.C. 'The political economy of Guided Democracy', *Australian Outlook* 13 (1959): 285–292.

[0221] Maddison, Angus, and Gé Prince, eds. *Economic growth in Indonesia 1820–1940*. Dordrecht, Netherlands: Foris, 1989.

[0222] *Onderzoek naar de mindere welvaart der inlandsche bevolking op Java en Madoera*. 12 parts in 45 vols. Batavia, Netherlands: Kolff/Ruygrok, 1904–1911.

[0223] Paauw, Douglas S. 'From colonial to guided economy', in McVey, *Indonesia* [0369].

[0224] Palmer, Ingrid. *The Indonesian economy since 1965: a case study of political economy*. London: Frank Cass, 1978.

[0225] Papanek, Gustav F., ed. *The Indonesian economy*. New York: Praeger, 1980.

[0226] Rice, Robert. 'The origins of basic economic ideas and their impact on New Order policies', *BIES* 19 no 2 (1983): 60–82.

[0227] Sievers, Allan M. *The mystical world of Indonesia: culture and economic development in conflict*. Baltimore, MD: Johns Hopkins Univ. Press, 1974.

[0228] Sutter, John O. *Indonesianisasi: politics in a changing economy, 1940–1955*. 4v. Ithaca, NY: Cornell Univ. Southeast Asia Program, 1959.

See also: 0009, 0017, 0034–46, 0683, 0776, 0794, 0803.

Agriculture

[0229] Alexander, Jennifer, and Paul Alexander. 'Shared poverty as ideology: agrarian relationships in colonial Java', *Man* 17 no. 4 (1982): 597–619.

[0230] Alexander, Jennifer, and Paul Alexander. 'Sugar, rice and irrigation in colonial Java', *Ethnohistory* 25 (1978): 207–223.

[0231] Allen, G.C., and Audrey G. Donnithorne. *Western enterprise in Indonesia and Malaya*. London: Allen & Unwin, 1957.

[0232] Anderson, A. 'Plantation and *petani:* problems of the Javanese sugar industry', *Pacific Viewpoint* 13 (1972): 127–154.

[0233] Bauer, P.T. *The rubber industry: a study in competition and monopoly*. Cambridge, MA: Harvard Univ. Press, 1948.

[0234] Bellwood, P.S. 'Prehistoric plant and animal domestication in Austronesia' in G.de G. Sieveking, *et al.*, eds. *Problems in economic and social archaeology*. London: Duckworth, 1976.

[0235] Boomgaard, Peter. 'Forests and forestry in colonial Java, 1677–1942', in John Dargavel, Kay Dixon and Noel Semple, eds, *Changing tropical forests: historical perspectives on today's challenges in Asia, Australasia and Oceania*. Canberra: Centre for Resource and Environmental Studies, 1988.

[0236] Booth, Anne. *Agricultural development in Indonesia*. Sydney: Allen & Unwin, 1988.

[0237] Breman, Jan. *Koelies, planters and koloniale politiek: het arbeidregime op de grootlandbouw-ondernemingen aan Sumatra's Oostkust in het begin van de twintigste eeuw*. Dordrecht, Netherlands: Foris, 1987.

[0238] Chang, Te-tzu. 'The rice culture', *Philosophical Transactions of the Royal Society of London,* series B, 275 (1976): 143–157.

[0239] Clemens, A.H.P., and J.Th. Lindblad, eds. *Het belang van de buitengewesten: economische expansie en coloniale staatvorming in de buitengewesten van Nederlands-Indië*. Amsterdam: NEHA, 1989.

[0240] Collier, William A. 'Food problems, unemployment and the Green Revolution in rural Java', *Prisma: the Indonesian Indicator* 9 (1978): 38–52.

[0241] Dove, Michael R. 'The agroecological mythology of the Javanese and the political economy of Indonesia', *Indonesia* 39 (1985): 1–36.

[0242] Dove, Michael R. 'The practical reason of weeds in Indonesia: peasants vs. state views of *Imperata* and *Chromolaena*', *Human ecology* 14 no 2 (June 1986): 163–190.

[0243] Etherington, D.M. 'The Indonesian tea industry', *BIES* 10 no. 2 (1974): 83–113.

[0244] Geertz, Clifford. *Agricultural involution: the process of ecological change in Indonesia*. Berkeley, CA: Univ. of California Press, 1963.

[0245] Gorcum, K.W. van. *Oost-Indische Cultures*. Amsterdam: de Bussy, 1919.

[0246] Hall, C.J.J. van, and C. van de Koppel, eds. *De landbouw in de Indische archipel*. 3 vols (4 parts). The Hague: van Hoeve, 1946–50.

[0247] Hansen, Gary E., ed. *Agricultural and rural development in Indonesia*. Boulder CO: Westview, 1981.

[0248] Hansen, Gary E. *The politics and administration of rural development in Indonesia: the case of agriculture*. Berkeley, CA: Univ. of California, 1973.

[0249] Hart, Gillian. *Power, labor and livelihood: processes of change in rural Java*. Berkeley, CA: Univ. of California Press, 1986.

[0250] Hartog, Adel P. de. *Diffusion of milk as a new food to tropical regions: the example of Indonesia, 1880–1942*. Wageningen, Netherlands: n.p., 1986.

[0251] Hill, R.D. *Rice in Malaya: a study in historical geography*. Kuala Lumpur, Malaysia: OUP, 1977.

[0252] Huizer, Gerrit. *Peasant mobilization and land reform in Indonesia*. The Hague: Institute of Social Studies, 1972.

[0253] Hüsken, Frans. 'Landlords, sharecroppers and agricultural labourers: changing labour relations in rural Java', *Journal of Contemporary Asia* 9 (1979): 140–151.

[0254] Kano, Hiroyoshi. *Land tenure system and the desa community in nineteenth century Java*. Tokyo: Institute of Developing Economies, 1977.

[0255] Knight, G.R. 'From plantation to padi-field: the origins of the nineteenth century transformation of Java's sugar industry', *MAS* 14 no 2 (1980): 177–204.

[0256] Knight, G.R. '"The people's own cultivations": rice and second crops in Pekalongan residency, North Java, in the mid-nineteenth century', *RIMA* 19 no 1 (1985): 1–38.

[0257] Mackie, J.A.C. 'Indonesia's government estates and their masters', *Pacific Affairs* 34 no 4 (1962): 337–360.

[0258] McStocker, Robert. 'The Indonesian coffee industry', *BIES* 23 no.1 (April 1987): 40–69.

[0259] Maurer, Jean-Luc. 'Agricultural modernization and social change: the case of Java over the last fifteen years', *Masyarakat Indonesia* 11 (1984): 109–120.

[0260] Mears, Leon A. *The new rice economy of Indonesia*. Yogyakarta, Indonesia: Gadjah Mada Univ. Press, 1981.

[0261] Mubyarto. 'The sugar industry: from estate to smallholder cane production?', *BIES* 13 no 2 (1977): 29–44.

[0262] Peluso, Nancy Lee. 'Networking in the commons: a tragedy for rattan?', *Indonesia* 35 (1983): 94–108.

[0263] Pelzer, Karl. *Planter and peasant: colonial policy and the agrarian struggle in East Sumatra, 1863–1947*. The Hague: Nijhoff, 1978.

[0264] Rao, Y.S. *et al.*, eds. *Community forestry: socio-economic aspects*. Bangkok: Regional Office for Asia and the Pacific, 1985.

[0265] Ruddle, Kenneth, *et al. Palm sago: a tropical starch for marginal lands*. Honolulu: Univ. of Hawaii Press, 1978.

[0266] Setten van der Meer, N.C. van. *Sawah cultivation in ancient Java: aspects of development during the Indo-Javanese period 5th to 15th century*. Canberra: Australian National Univ. Press, 1979.

[0267] Sherman, George. '*What* green desert? the ecology of Batak grassland farming', *Indonesia* 29 (1980): 113–148.

[0268] Svensson, Thommy. *Contractions and expansions: agrarian change in Java since 1830*. Gothenburg, Sweden: Historical-Anthropological Project, Gothenburg Univ., 1985.

[0269] Taylor, Norman. *Cinchona in Java: the story of quinine*. New York: Greenberg, [1945].

[0270] Thee Kian Wie. *Plantation agriculture and export growth: an economic history of East Sumatra, 1863–1942*. Jakarta: LEKNAS-LIPI, 1977.

[0271] Timmer, C. Peter. *The corn economy of Indonesia*. Ithaca, NY: Cornell Univ. Press, 1987.

[0272] White, Benjamin. '"Agricultural involution" and its critics: twenty years after', *BCAS* 15 no 2 (1983): 18–31.

See also: 0509, 0525

Development

[0273] Anspach, Ralph. 'Indonesia', in Frank Golay *et al.*, eds, *Underdevelopment and economic nationalism in Southeast Asia*. Ithaca, NY: Cornell Univ. Press, 1969.

[0274] Barlow, Colin, and Thee Kian Wie. *The North Sumatra regional economy: growth with unbalanced development*. Singapore: ISEAS, 1988.

[0275] Dickie, Robert B., and Thomas A. Layman. *Foreign investment and government policy in the Third World: forging common interests in Indonesia*. New York: St Martin's Press, 1988.

[0276] Garnaut, Ross, and Chris Manning. *Irian Jaya: the transformation of a Melanesian economy*. Canberra: Australian National Univ. Press, 1974.

[0277] Hoadley, J. Stephen. 'The politics of development planning agencies: the evolution of Indonesia's Bappenas', *Asia Quarterly* (1978/1): 39–66.

[0278] Mortimer, Rex, ed. *Showcase state: the illusion of Indonesia's 'accelerated modernisation'*. Sydney: Angus & Robertson, 1973.

[0279] Muizenberg, Otto van den, and Willem Wolters. *Conceptualizing development: the historical sociological tradition in Dutch non-Western sociology*. Dordrecht, Netherlands/Providence, RI: Foris, 1988.

[0280] Robison, Richard. *Indonesia: the rise of capital*. Sydney: Allen & Unwin, 1986.

[0281] Schiel, Tilman. *Despotism and capitalism: a historical comparison of Europe and Indonesia*. Saarbrücken, Germany: Breitenbach, 1985.

[0282] Schmidt, Hans O. 'Foreign capital and social conflict in Indonesia 1950–1958', *Economic Development and Cultural Change* 10 (1962): 284–293.

[0283] Sjahrir. *Basic needs in Indonesia: economics, politics and public policy*. Singapore: ISEAS, 1986.

[0284] Soedjatmoko. *Economic development as a cultural problem*. Ithaca, NY: Cornell Modern Indonesia Project, 1962.

[0285] Sumantoro. *MNCs and the host country: the Indonesian case*. Singapore: ISEAS, 1984.

[0286] Thee Kian Wie. 'Industrial and foreign investment policy in Indonesia since 1967', *Southeast Asian Studies* 25 no 3 (1987): 83–96.

[0287] Yoshihara Kunio. *The rise of ersatz capitalism in South-East Asia*. Singapore: OUP, 1988.

Finance

[0288] Asher, Mukul G. and Anne Booth, *Indirect taxation in ASEAN*. Singapore: Singapore Univ. Press, 1983.

[0289] Boomgaard, Peter. 'Buitenzorg in 1805: the role of money and credit in a colonial frontier society', *MAS* 20 no. 1 (1986): 33–58.

[0290] Booth, Anne. 'The burden of taxation in colonial Indonesia in the 20th century', *JSEAS* 2 no. 1 (1980): 91–109.

[0291] Booth, Anne. 'IPEDA—Indonesia's land tax', *BIES* 10 no.1 (1974): 55–81.

[0292] Charlesworth, Harold C. *A banking system in transition: the origin, concept and growth of the Indonesian banking system*. Jakarta: New Nusantara, 1959.

[0293] Emmerson, Donald K. 'Gambling and development: the case of Jakarta's flower organization', *Asia* 27 (1972): 19–36.

[0294] Guillot, Claude. 'Le rôle historique des *perdikan* ou "villes francs": le cas de Tegalsari', *Archipel* 30 (1985): 137–162.

[0295] Mackie, J.A.C. *Problems of the Indonesian inflation*. Ithaca, NY: Cornell Univ., Southeast Asia Program, 1967.

[0296] Mansury. 'A bird's eye view of Indonesian income taxation history', *Asian-Pacific Tax and Investment Bulletin* (Singapore) 2 no. 12 (1984): 503–509.

[0297] Mevius, Johan. *Catalogue of paper money of the V.O.C., Netherlands East Indies and Indonesia from 1782–1981*. Vriezenveen, Netherlands: Mevius Numisbooks, 1981.

[0298] Nasution, Anwar. *Financial institutions and policies in Indonesia*. Singapore: ISEAS, 1983.

[0299] Niel, Robert van. 'The function of land rent under the Cultivation System in Java', *JAS* 23 no 3 (1964): 357–376.

[0300] Paauw, Douglas. *Financing economic development: the Indonesian case*. Glencoe, NY: Free Press, 1960.

[0301] Payer, Cheryl. 'The International Monetary Fund and Indonesian debt slavery' in Mark Selden, ed., *Remaking Asia: essays on the American use of power*. New York: Pantheon, 1974.

[0302] Skully, Michael. 'Commercial banking in Indonesia: an examination of its development and present structure', *Asian Survey* 22 no. 9 (1982): 874–893.

[0303] Thompson, Graeme, and Richard C. Manning. 'The World Bank in Indonesia', *BIES* 10 no 2 (1974): 56–82.

[0304] Wicks, Robert S. 'Monetary developments in Java between the ninth and sixteenth centuries: a numismatic perspective', *Indonesia* 42 (1986): 43–77.

[0305] Williams, Glen, and Mary Johnston. 'The *arisan:* a tool for economic and social development?', *Prisma: the Indonesian Indicator* 29 (1983): 66–73.

See also: 0427, 0525.

Trade

[0306] Alexander, Jennifer. *Trade, traders and trading in rural Java*. Singapore: OUP, 1987.

[0307] Buhler, Alfred. 'Patola influence in Southeast Asia', *Journal of Indian Textile History* 4 (1959): 4–46.

[0308] Chandler, Glen. *Market trade in rural Java*. Clayton, Vic., Australia: Monash Univ. Centre of Southeast Asian Studies, 1984.

[0309] Dewey, Alice. *Peasant marketing in Java*. Glencoe, NY: Free Press, 1962.

[0310] Gerretson, C. *History of the Royal Dutch*. 4 vols. Leiden, Netherlands: Brill, 1953–57.

[0311] Guy, John S. 'Commerce, power and mythology: Indian textiles in Indonesia', *Indonesia Circle* 42 (1987): 57–75.

[0312] Mai, Ulrich, and Helmut Buchholt. *Peasant pedlars and professional traders: subsistence trade in rural markets of Minahasa, Indonesia*. Singapore: ISEAS, 1988.

[0313] Miksic, John N. 'Traditional Sumatra trade', *Bulletin de l'École Française d'Extrême Orient* 74 (1985): 423–467.

[0314] Panglaykim, J. *An Indonesian experience: its state trading corporations*. Jakarta: Fakultas Ekonomi Universitas Indonesia, 1967.

[0315] Rice, Robert. 'Sumitro's role in foreign trade policy', *Indonesia* 8 (1969): 183–212.

[0316] Rieffel, A., and A.S. Wirjasaputra. 'Military enterprises', *BIES* 8 no. 2 (1972): 104–108.

See also: 0429, 0449, 0454, 0473, 0492.

Industry

[0317] Arndt, H.W. 'PPPT Krakatau Steel', *BIES* 11 no 2 (1975): 120–126.

[0318] Arndt, H.W. 'Oil and the Indonesian economy', *Southeast Asian Affairs* 1983: 136–150.

[0319] Bailey, Connor. 'The political economy of marine fisheries development in Indonesia', *Indonesia* 46 (1988): 25–38.

[0320] Bartlett, Anderson G., *et al. Pertamina: Indonesian national oil*. Jakarta: Amerasian, 1972.

[0321] Braake, Alex L. ter. *Mining in the Netherlands East Indies*. New York: Institute of Pacific Relations, 1944.

[0322] Castles, Lance. *Religion, politics and economic behaviour in Java: the Kudus cigarette industry*. New Haven, CT: Yale Univ., Southeast Asia Studies, 1967.

[0323] Guillot, Claude. 'Le *dluwang* ou papier javanais', *Archipel* 26 (1983): 105–116.

[0324] Hannig, Wolfgang. *Towards a blue revolution: socioeconomic aspects of brackishwater pond cultivation in Java*. Yogyakarta, Indonesia: Gadjah Mada Univ. Press, 1988.

[0325] Hill, Hal. *Foreign investment and industrialization in Indonesia*. Melbourne: OUP, 1988.

[0326] Hopper, Richard H. 'Petroleum in Indonesia: history, geology and economic significance', *Asia* 24 (1971–72): 36–66.

[0327] Palmer, Ingrid. *Textiles in Indonesia: problems of import substitution*. New York: Praeger, 1972.

[0328] Robinson, Kathryn May. *Stepchildren of progress: the political economy of development in an Indonesian mining town*. Albany, NY: State Univ. of New York Press, 1986.

[0329] Seavoy, Ronald E. 'Placer diamond mining in Kalimantan, Indonesia', *Indonesia* 19 (1975): 79–84.

[0330] Simandjuntuk, Edward S., *et al.* 'The rise of the *kretek* giants', *Prisma: the Indonesian Indicator* 27 (1983): 63–81.

See also: 0515, 0518.

Labor

[0331] Blussé, Leonard. 'Labour takes root: mobilisation and immobilisation of Javanese rural society under the Cultivation System', *Itinerario* 7 no 1 (1984): 77–117.

[0332] *Indonesian workers and their right to organize.* Leiden, Netherlands: INDOC, 1981 (5th update, 1986).

[0333] Leclerc, Jacques. 'An ideological problem of Indonesian trade unionism in the sixties: "karyawan" versus "buruh"', *RIMA* 6 no. 1 (1972): 76–91.

[0334] Niel, Robert van, ed. & tr. *Coolie budget commission: living conditions of plantation workers and peasants on Java in 1939–1940.* Ithaca, NY: Cornell Modern Indonesia Project, 1956.

[0335] Reid, Anthony, ed. *Slavery, bondage and dependency in Southeast Asia.* St Lucia, Qld., Australia: Univ. of Queensland Press, 1983.

[0336] Scherer, Savitri. 'Soetomo and trade unionism', *Indonesia* 24 (1977): 27–38.

[0337] Schiller, A. Arthur. 'Labor law and legislation in the Netherlands Indies', *Far Eastern Quarterly* 5 (1946): 176–188.

[0338] Tedjasukmana, Iskander. *The political character of the Indonesian trade union movement.* Ithaca, NY: Cornell Modern Indonesia Project, 1959.

[0339] Wertheim, W.F. 'Sociological aspects of inter-island migration in Indonesia', *Population Studies* 12 (1959): 184–201.

[0340] Thompson, Virginia. *Labor problems in Southeast Asia*. New Haven, CT: Yale Univ. Press, 1947.

See also: 0550, 0559.

Transport, Communications, and The Press

[0341] Adam, Ahmad. 'The vernacular press and the emergence of national consciousness in Indonesia', *Jebat* (Kuala Lumpur) 11 (1981/82): 1–16.

[0342] Aly, Bachtiar. *Geschichte und Gegenwart der Kommunikationssysteme in Indonesien*. Frankfurt am Main, Germany: Peter Lang, 1984.

[0343] Beer van Dingstee, J.H. *De ontwikkeling van het postwezen in Nederl. Oost-Indie*. Bandung, Indonesia: Nix, 1933.

[0344] Brooks, Mary R. *Fleet development and the control of shipping in Southeast Asia*. Singapore: ISEAS, 1985.

[0345] Collins, G.E.P. *East monsoon*. London: Cape, 1936.

[0346] Dick, H.W. *The Indonesian inter-island shipping industry: an analysis of competition and regulation*. Singapore: ISEAS, 1986.

[0347] Faber, G.H., von. *A short history of journalism in the Dutch East Indies*. Surabaya, Indonesia: G. Kolff, 1930.

[0348] Gotz, J.F. 'Railways in the Netherlands Indies, with special reference to the island of Java', *Bulletin of the Colonial Institute* (1939): 267–290.

[0349] Horridge, Adrian. *Outrigger canoes of Bali and Madura, Indonesia*. Honolulu: Bishop Museum Press, 1987.

[0350] Jones, Rebecca. 'Satellite communications: Indonesia's bitter fruit', *Pacific Research and World Empire Telegram* 7 no 4 (1976): 1–6.

[0351] Kurasawa, Aiko. 'Propaganda media on Java under the Japanese', *Indonesia* 44 (1987): 59–116.

[0352] Leclerc, Jacques. 'Iconologie politique du timbre-poste Indonesien (1950–1970)', *Archipel* 6 (1973): 145–183.

[0353] Munandir, Willy. 'Indonesian telecommunications development: an overview', *Telematics and informatics* 2 no.1 (1985): 79–89.

[0354] Oey Hong Lee. *Indonesian government and press during Guided Democracy*. Hull, England: Univ. of Hull, 1971.

[0355] Rimmer, Peter J. *Rikisha to rapid transit: urban public transport systems and policy in Southeast Asia*. Sydney: Pergamon Press, 1986.

[0356] Rodgers, Peter. *The domestic and foreign press in Indonesia: 'free but responsible?'*. Nathan, Qld, Australia: Griffith Univ. Centre for the Study of Australia-Asia Relations, 1982.

[0357] Sartono Kartodirdjo, ed. *The pedicab in Yogyakarta: a study of low cost transportation and poverty problems*. Yogyakarta, Indonesia: Gadjah Mada Univ. Press, 1981.

[0358] Soebagijo I.N. *Sejarah pers Indonesia*. Jakarta: Dewan Pers, 1977.

[0359] Soegijoko, Budy Tjahjati. 'The *becak*s of Java', *Habitat International* 10 no. 1/2 (1986): 155–164.

[0360] Szende, A. *From torrent to trickle: managing the flow of news in Southeast Asia*. Singapore: ISEAS, 1986.

[0361] Wild, Colin. 'Indonesia: a nation and its broadcasters', *Indonesia Circle* 43 (1987): 15–40.

HISTORY—General Histories

[0362] Aveling, Harry, ed. *The development of Indonesian society: from the coming of Islam to the present day*. St Lucia, Qld, Australia: Univ. of Queensland Press, 1979.

[0363] Benda, Harry J. *Continuity and change in Southeast Asia: collected journal articles*. New Haven, CT: Yale Univ. Southeast Asian Studies, 1972.

[0364] Dahm, Bernhard. *History of Indonesia in the twentieth century*. London: Praeger, 1971.

[0365] Fox, James J., *et al.*, eds. *Indonesia: Australian perspectives*. Canberra: Australian National Univ., 1980.

[0366] Kamerling, R.N.J., ed. *Indonesië toen en nu*. Amsterdam: Intermediair, 1980.

[0367] Kroef, Justus M. van der. *Indonesia in the modern world*. 2 vols. Bandung, Indonesia: Masa Baru, 1954–56.

[0368] Legge, J.D. *Indonesia*. Sydney: Prentice-Hall, 3d ed., 1980

[0369] McVey, Ruth T., ed. *Indonesia*. New Haven, CT: Human Relations Area Files Press, 1963.

[0370] McVey, Ruth T., ed. *Southeast Asian transitions: approaches through social history*. New Haven, CT: Yale Univ. Press, 1978.

[0371] Ricklefs, M.C. *A history of modern Indonesia*. London: Macmillan, 1981.

[0372] Sartono Kartodirdjo. *Modern Indonesia: tradition and transformation, a socio-historical perspective*. Yogyakarta, Indonesia: Gadjah Mada Univ. Press, 1984.

[0373] Soebadio, Haryati, and Carine A. du Marchie Sarvaas, eds. *Dynamics of Indonesian history*. Amsterdam: North-Holland, 1978.

[0374] Steinberg, David Joel, *et al. In search of Southeast Asia: a modern history*. Honolulu: Univ. of Hawaii Press, 2d ed., 1987.

[0375] Vlekke, Bernard H.M. *Nusantara: a history of the East Indian archipelago*. Cambridge, MA: Harvard Univ. Press, 1945.

[0376] Wertheim, W.F. *Indonesian society in transition*. The Hague: van Hoeve, 2d ed. 1959.

[0377] Zainu'ddin, Ailsa G. *A short history of Indonesia*. Stanmore, NSW, Australia: Cassell, 2d ed. 1968.

Historiography

[0378] Abidin, Andi Zainal. 'Notes on the lontara' as historical sources', *Indonesia* 12: 159–172.

[0379] Benda, Harry J. 'The structure of South-east Asian history', *JSEAH* 3 no.1 (March 1962): 106–139.

[0380] Cowan, C.D., and O.W. Wolters. *Southeast Asian history and historiography: essays presented to D.G.E. Hall*. Ithaca, NY: Cornell Univ. Press, 1976.

[0381] Hall, D.G.E. *Historians of South-East Asia*. London: Oxford Univ. Press, 1961.

[0382] Kroef, Justus M. van der. 'On the writing of Indonesian history', *Pacific Affairs,* 31 (1958): 352–371.

[0383] Levine, David. 'History and social structure in the study of contemporary Indonesia', *Indonesia* 7 (1969): 5–20.

[0384] Reid, Anthony, and David G. Marr, eds. *Perceptions of the past in Southeast Asia*. Singapore: Heinemann, 1979.

[0385] Robison, Richard. 'Culture, politics and economy in the political history of the New Order', *Indonesia* 31 (1981): 1–29.

[0386] Smail, John R.W. 'On the possibility of an autonomous history of Southeast Asia', *JSEAH* 2 (July 1961): 72–102.

[0387] Soedjatmoko *et al.,* eds. *An introduction to Indonesian historiography*. Ithaca, NY: Cornell Univ. Press, 1965.

See also: 0403, 0770.

To 1400

[0388] Allen, J., Golson, J. and Jones, R., eds. *Sunda and Sahul: prehistoric studies in Southeast Asia, Melanesia and Australia*. London: Academic Press, 1977.

[0389] Barrett Jones, Antoinette M. *Early tenth century Java from the inscriptions: a study of economic, social and administrative conditions in the first quarter of the century*. Leiden, Netherlands: KITLV, 1984.

[0390] Bellwood, Peter. *Prehistory of the Indo-Malaysian archipelago*. Sydney: Academic Press, 1985.

[0391] Bosch, F.D.K. *Selected studies in Indonesian archaeology*. Leiden, Netherlands: KITLV, 1961.

[0392] Buchari. 'Sri Maharaja Mapanji Garasakan: a new evidence on the problem of Airlangga's partition of his kingdom', *Madjalah Ilmu-Ilmu Sastra Indonesia* 4 no 1/2 (1968): 1–26.

[0393] Christie, Jan Wisseman. *Theatre states and oriental despotisms: early Southeast Asia in the eyes of the West*. Hull, England: Univ. of Hull Centre for South-East Asian Studies, 1985.

[0394] Coedès, G. *The Indianized states of Southeast Asia*. Canberra: Australian National Univ. Press, 1975.

[0395] Hall, D.G.E. *A history of South-east Asia*. London: Macmillan, 3d ed., 1968.

[0396] Hall, Kenneth R. *Maritime trade and state development in early Southeast Asia*. Honolulu: Univ. of Hawaii Press, 1985.

[0397] Hall, Kenneth R., and John K. Whitmore, eds. *Explorations in early Southeast Asian history: the origins of Southeast Asian statecraft*. Ann Arbor, MI: Center for South and Southeast Asian Studies, Univ. of Michigan, 1976

[0398] Hanna, Willard H. *Bali profile: peoples, events, circumstances 1001–1976*. New York: American Universities Field Staff, 1976.

[0399] Heekeren, H.R. van. *The bronze-iron age in Indonesia*. The Hague: Nijhoff, 1958.

[0400] Heekeren, H.R. van. *The stone age in Indonesia*. Leiden, Netherlands: KITLV, 2d ed., 1972.

[0401] Heine-Geldern, Robert von. 'Conceptions of state and kingship in Southeast Asia', *Far Eastern Quarterly* 2 (1942): 15–30; also published as a separate paper by the Cornell Univ. Southeast Asia Program, 1956.

[0402] Hill, A.H. 'Hikayat Raja-raja Pasai', *Journal of the Malaysian Branch of the Royal Asiatic Society* 33 no.2 (1960): 1–215.

[0403] Leur, J.C. van. *Indonesian trade and society*. The Hague, Netherlands and Bandung, Indonesia: van Hoeve, 1955.

[0404] Mabbett, I.W. 'Devaraja', *JSEAH* 10 (1969): 202–223.

[0405] Mabbett, I.W. 'The "Indianization" of Southeast Asia', *JSEAS* 8 no.1 (March 1977): 1–14; 8 no.2 (Sept. 1977): 143–161.

[0406] McKinnon, E. Edwards. 'Early politics in southern Sumatra: some preliminary observations based on archaeological evidence', *Indonesia* 40 (1985): 1–36.

[0407] Macknight, C.C. *Voyage to Marege'*. Melbourne: Melbourne Univ. Press, 1976.

[0408] Marr, David G., and A.C. Milner. *Southeast Asia in the 9th to the 14th centuries*. Singapore: ISEAS, 1985.

[0409] Meulen, W.J. van der. 'In search of "Ho-ling"', *Indonesia* 23 (1977): 87–111.

[0410] Meulen, W.J. van der. 'King Sañjaya and his successors', *Indonesia* 28 (1979): 17–54.

[0411] Misra, V.N., and Peter Bellwood, eds. *Recent advances in Indo-Pacific prehistory*. Leiden, Netherlands: Brill, 1985.

[0412] Naerssen, F.H. van, and R.C. de Iongh. *The economic and administrative history of early Indonesia*. Leiden, Netherlands: Brill, 1977.

[0413] Nihom, Max. 'Ruler and realm: the division of Airlangga's kingdom in the fourteenth century', *Indonesia* 42 (1986): 78–100.

[0414] Pigeaud, Th. *Java in the 14th century, a study in cultural history: the Nagara-kertagama by Rakawi Prapanca of Majapahit, 1365*. 5 vols. The Hague: Nijhoff, 1960–1963.

[0415] Ras, J.J. *Hikajat Bandjar: a study in Malay historiography*. Leiden, Netherlands: KITLV, 1968.

[0416] Reid, Anthony, and Lance Castles, eds. *Pre-colonial state systems in Southeast Asia*. Kuala Lumpur: Malaysian Branch of the Royal Asiatic Society, 1976.

[0417] Schrieke, B. 'Ruler and realm in early Java', in B. Schrieke, *Indonesian sociological studies* vol. 2. The Hague: van Hoeve, 1959.

[0418] Shutler, Richard, and Friedrich Branches. 'Problems in paradise: the Pleistocene of Java revisited', *Modern Quaternary Research in Southeast Asia* 9 (1985): 87–97, Rotterdam: Balkema, 1985.

[0419] Slamet-Velsink, Ina Erna. *Emerging hierarchies: processes of stratification and early state formation in the Indonesian archipelago: prehistory and the ethnographic present*. Leiden, Netherlands: Rijksuniversiteit, 1986.

[0420] Smith, R.B., and W. Watson, eds. *Early South East Asia: essays in archaeology, history and historical geography*. Kuala Lumpur, Malaysia: OUP, 1979.

[0421] Stutterheim, W. 'The meaning of the Hindu-Javanese candi', *Journal of the American Oriental Society* 51 (1931): 1–15.

[0422] Supomo, S. 'The Lord of the Mountains in the fourteenth century kakawin', *BKI* 128 (1972): 281–297.

[0423] Velde, Pieter van de, ed. *Prehistoric Indonesia: a reader*. Dordrecht, Netherlands: Foris, 1984.

[0424] Wheatley, Paul. *The Golden Khersonese: studies in the historical geography of the Malay peninsula before A.D. 1500*. Kuala Lumpur, Malaysia: University of Malaya Press, 1961.

[0425] Wheatley, Paul. *Nagara and commandery: origins of the Southeast Asian urban traditions*. Chicago: Univ. of Chicago Department of Geography, 1983.

[0426] Wheatley, Paul. 'Satyanrta in Suvarnadvipa: from reciprocity to redistribution in ancient Southeast Asia', in Jeremy A. Sabloff and C.C. Lamberg-Karlovsky, eds, *Ancient civilization and trade* (Albuquerque, NM: Univ. of New Mexico Press, 1975), 227–283.

[0427] Wicks, Robert Sigfrid. 'A survey of native Southeast Asian coinage circa 450–1850: documentation and typology'. Ph.D. thesis, Cornell Univ., 1983.

[0428] Wisseman, Jan. 'Early states in western Indonesia', *Indonesia Circle* 16 (1978): 16–23.

[0429] Wolters, O.W. *Early Indonesian commerce: a study of the origins of Srivijaya*. Ithaca, NY: Cornell Univ. Press, 1967.

[0430] Wolters, O.W. *The fall of Srivijaya in Malay history*. Kuala Lumpur, Malaysia: Oxford Univ. Press, 1970.

[0431] Wolters, O.W. *History, culture and region in Southeast Asian perspectives*. Singapore: ISEAS, 1982.

[0432] Wolters, O.W. 'Restudying some Chinese writings on Sriwijaya', *Indonesia* 42 (1986): 1–41.

See also: 0266.

1400–1800

[0433] Andaya, Leonard Y. *The heritage of Arung Palakka: a history of South Sulawesi (Celebes) in the seventeenth century*. The Hague: Nijhoff, 1981.

[0434] Andaya, Leonard Y. *The kingdom of Johor, 1641–1728: economic and political developments*. Kuala Lumpur: OUP, 1975.

[0435] Arasaratnam, S. 'Monopoly and free trade in Dutch-Asian commercial policy: debate and controversy within the VOC', *JSEAS* 4 no. 1 (1973): 1–15.

[0436] Barnes, R.H. 'Avarice and iniquity at the Solor fort', *BKI* 143 no 2/3 (1987): 208–236.

[0437] Bassett, D.K. 'The Amboyna massacre', *JSEAH* 1 no.2 (1960): 1–19.

[0438] Bassett, D.K. 'The English East India Company in the Far East 1623–1684', *Journal of the Royal Asiatic Society* (Apr. 1960), 32–47; (Oct. 1960): 145–157.

[0439] Bassett, D.K. 'British trade and policy in Indonesia, 1760–1772' *BKI* 120 (1964): 197–223.

[0440] Blussé, Leonard. *Strange company: Chinese settlers, mestizo women and the Dutch in VOC Batavia*. Leiden, Netherlands: KITLV, 1986.

[0441] Boxer, C.R. *The Dutch seaborne empire 1600–1800*. Harmondsworth, England: Penguin, 1973.

[0442] Boxer, C.R. *Francisco Vieira de Figueiredo: a Portuguese merchant-adventurer in South East Asia, 1624–1667*. Leiden, Netherlands: KITLV, 1967.

[0443] Boxer, C.R. *The Portuguese seaborne empire: 1415–1825*. Harmondsworth, England: Penguin, 1973.

[0444] Boxer, C.R. *The Topasses of Timor*. Amsterdam: Indisch Instituut, 1947.

[0445] Broeze, Frank, ed. *Brides of the sea: port cities of Asia from the 16th-20th centuries*. Kensington, NSW, Australia: Univ. of New South Wales Press, 1989.

[0446] Brown, C.C. *Sejarah Melayu, or Malay Annals*. Kuala Lumpur, Malaysia: OUP, 1970.

[0447] Carey, Peter. 'Waiting for the "Just King": the agrarian world of South-Central Java from Giyanti (1755) to the Java War' *MAS*.20 no.1 (1986): 59–137.

[0448] Chaudhuri, K.N. *The English East India Company: the study of an early joint-stock company 1600–1640*. London: Frank Cass, 1965.

[0449] Chaudhuri, K.N. *Trade and civilisation in the Indian Ocean: an economic history from the rise of Islam to 1750*. Cambridge, England: Cambridge Univ. Press, 1985.

[0450] Chaudhuri, K.N. *The trading world of Asia and the English East India Company 1660–1760*. Cambridge, England: Cambridge Univ. Press, 1978.

[0451] Dobbin, Christine. *Islamic revivalism in a changing economy: Central Sumatra, 1764–1847*. London: Curzon, 1983.

[0452] Drakard, Jane. 'An Indian Ocean port: sources for the earlier history of Barus', *Archipel* 37 (1989): 53–82.

[0453] Ellen, R.F. 'Conundrums about panjandrums: on the use of titles in the relations of political subordination in the Moluccas and along the Papuan coast', *Indonesia* 41 (1986): 46–62.

[0454] Glamann, Kristoff. *Dutch Asiatic trade, 1620–1740*. The Hague: Nijhoff, 1958.

[0455] Goor, J. van, ed. *Trading companies in Asia, 1600–1830*. Utrecht, Netherlands: HES, 1986.

[0456] Graaf, H.J. de, with Theodore G.Th. Pigeaud. *Islamic states in Java 1500–1700*. Leiden, Netherlands: KITLV, 1976.

[0457] Graaf, H.J. de. *De geschiedenis van Ambon en de Zuid-Molukken*. Franeker, Netherlands: T. Wever, 1977.

[0458] Haan, F. de. *Priangan: de Preanger-regentschappen onder het Nederlandsch bestuur tot 1811*. 4 vols, Batavia, Indonesia: Bataviaasch Genootschap van Kunsten en Wetenschappen, 1901–1912.

[0459] Hanna, Willard. *Indonesian Banda: colonialism and its aftermath in the nutmeg islands*. Philadelphia: Institute for the Study of Human Issues, 1978.

[0460] Hudson, Alfred. 'The Padju Epan Ma'anyan Dayak in historical perspective', *Indonesia* 4 (1967): 8–43.

[0461] Kathirithamby-Wells, J. *The British West Sumatra Presidency 1760–1785: problems of early colonial enterprise*. Kuala Lumpur, Malaysia: Penerbit Universiti Malaya, 1977.

[0462] Kathirithamby-Wells, J. 'The Inderapura sultanate: the foundations of its rise from the sixteenth to the eighteenth centuries', *Indonesia* 26 (1976): 65–84.

[0463] Kathirithamby-Wells, J. 'Royal authority and the *orang kaya* in the western archipelago, circa 1500–1800', *JSEAS* 17 no.2 (1986): 256–267.

[0464] Knaap, G.J. *Kruidnagelen en Christenen: de Verenigde Oost-Indische Compagnie en de bevolking van Ambon, 1656–1696*. Leiden, Netherlands: KITLV, 1987.

[0465] Kumar, Ann. 'Javanese court society and politics in the late eighteenth century: the record of a lady soldier', *Indonesia* 29 (1980): 1–46; 30 (1980): 67–111.

[0466] Kumar, Ann. *Surapati: man and legend*. Leiden, Netherlands: Brill, 1976.

[0467] Lapian, A.B. 'The contest for the high seas: the Celebes Seas area during the 16th and 17th centuries', *Prisma: the Indonesian Indicator* 33 (1984): 30–45.

[0468] Lombard, Denys. *Le sultanat d'Atjeh au temps d'Iskandar Muda, 1607–1636*. Paris: Ecole Français d'Extrême Orient, 1967.

[0469] MacRoberts, R.W. 'Notes on events in Palembang 1389–1511: the everlasting colony', *JMBRAS* 59 pt 1 (1986), 73–83.

[0470] Marsden, William. *The history of Sumatra*. London: the author, 1810; Kuala Lumpur, Malaysia: OUP, 1966.

[0471] Masselman, George. *The cradle of colonialism*. New Haven, CT: Yale Univ. Press, 1963.

[0472] Masinambow, E.K.M., ed. *Halmahera dan Raja Ampat sebagai kesatuan majemuk*. Jakarta: LEKNAS, 1987.

[0473] Meilinck-Roelofsz, M.A.P. *Asian trade and European influence in the Indonesian archipelago between 1500 and about 1630*. The Hague: Nijhoff, 1962.

[0474] Moertono, Soemarsaid. *State and statecraft in old Java: a study of the later Mataram period, 16th to 19th century*. Ithaca, NY: Cornell Modern Indonesia Project, 1974.

[0475] Noorduyn, J. 'Arung Singkang (1700–1765): how the victory of Wadjo' began', *Indonesia* 13 (1972): 61–68.

[0476] Noorduyn, J. 'Majapahit in the fifteenth century', *BKI* 134 no 2–3 (1978): 207–274.

[0477] Noorduyn, J. 'Makasar and the Islamization of Bima', *BKI* 143 no.2/3 (1987): 312–342.

[0478] Purbatjaraka, Purnadi. 'Shahbandars in the archipelago', *JSEAH* 2 no.2 (1961): 1–9.

[0479] Raffles, Thomas Stamford. *The history of Java.* 2 vols. London: John Murray, 1817; Kuala Lumpur, Malaysia: OUP, 1965.

[0480] Reid, Anthony. 'A great seventeenth century Indonesian family: Matoaya and Pattingalloang of Makassar', *Masyarakat Indonesia* 8 no 1 (1981): 1–28.

[0481] Reid, Anthony. 'The rise of Makassar', *RIMA* 17 no 1–2 (1983): 117–160.

[0482] Reid, Anthony. *Southeast Asia and Europe: the military balance.* Townsville, Qld., Australia: James Cook Univ., 1982.

[0483] Reid, Anthony. *Southeast Asia in the age of commerce, 1450–1680, volume one: the land below the winds.* New Haven, CT: Yale Univ. Press, 1988.

[0484] Reid, A. 'The structure of cities in Southeast Asia', *JSEAS* 11 no 2 (1980): 235–250.

[0485] Ricklefs, M.C. *Jogjakarta under Sultan Mangkubumi 1749–1792: a history of the division of Java.* London: OUP, 1974.

[0486] Ricklefs. M.C. *Modern Javanese historical tradition: a study of an original Kartasura chronicle and related materials.* London: School of Oriental and African Studies, 1978.

[0487] Robson, S.O. 'Java at the crossroads: aspects of Javanese cultural history in the fourteenth and fifteenth centuries', *BKI* 137 (1981): 259–292.

[0488] Sandhu, Kernial Singh, and Paul Wheatley, eds. *Melaka: the transformation of a Malay capital.* 2 vols. Kuala Lumpur, Malaysia: OUP, 1983.

[0489] Schoorl, Pim. 'Islam, macht en ontwikkeling in het sultanaat Buton', in L.B. Venema, ed., *Islam en macht.* Assen & Maastricht, Netherlands: van Gorcum, 1987.

[0490] Schrieke, B.J.O. *Indonesian sociological studies*. 2 vols. The Hague: van Hoeve, 1955.

[0491] Schutte, G.J. *De Nederlandse patriotten en de koloniën: een onderzoek naar hun denkbeelden en optreden, 1770–1800*. PhD, Univ. of Utrecht, Netherlands, 1974.

[0492] Steensgaard, Niels. *The Asian trade revolution of the seventeenth century: the East India Companies and the decline of the caravan trade*. Chicago: Univ. of Chicago Press, 1974.

[0493] Taylor, Jean Gelman. *The social world of Batavia: European and Eurasian in Dutch Asia*. Madison, WI: Univ. of Wisconsin Press, 1983.

[0494] Trocki, Carl A. *Prince of pirates: the Temenggongs and the development of Johor and Singapore, 1784–1885*. Singapore: Singapore Univ. Press, 1979.

See also: 0095, 0096, 0403, 0693, 0741

Nineteenth Century

[0495] Abeyasekere, Susan. *Jakarta: a history*. Singapore: Oxford Univ. Press, 1987.

[0496] Backer Dirks, F.C. *De gouvernementsmarine in het voormalige Nederlands-Indië in haar verschillende tijdsperioden geschetst, 1861–1941*. Weesp, Netherlands: De Boer Maritim, 1985.

[0497] Bastin, J.S. *The native policies of Sir Stamford Raffles in Java and Sumatra: an economic interpretation*. Oxford, England: Clarendon, 1957.

[0498] Bastin, J.S. *Raffles' ideas on the land rent system in Java and the Mackenzie land tenure system*. The Hague: Nijhoff, 1954.

[0499] Bayly, C.A., and D.H.A. Kolff, eds, *Two colonial empires: comparative essays on the history of India and Indonesia in the nineteenth century*. Dordrecht, Netherlands: Nijhoff, 1986.

[0500] Benda, Harry J. 'Christiaan Snouck Hurgronje and the foundations of Dutch Islamic policy in Indonesia', *Journal of Modern History* 30 (1958): 338–347.

[0501] Black, Ian. 'De "Lastposten": eastern Kalimantan and the Dutch in the nineteenth and early twentieth centuries', *JSEAS* 16 no 2 (1985): 281–291.

[0502] Bone, Robert C. 'The international status of West New Guinea until 1884', *JSEAH* 5 no.2 (1964): 150–183.

[0503] Breman, Jan. *The village in nineteenth century Java and the colonial state*. Rotterdam: Erasmus Univ. Comparative Asian Studies Programme, 1980.

[0504] Carey, P. 'Pangeran Dipanegara and the making of the Java War (1825–30): the end of an old order in Java'. D.Phil. thesis, Oxford Univ., 1972.

[0505] Carey, Peter. 'Yogyakarta, from sultanate to revolutionary capital of Indonesia: the politics of cultural survival', *Indonesia Circle* 39 (1986): 19–29.

[0506] Chauvel, Richard. *Nationalists, soldiers and separatists: the Ambonese islands from colonialism to revolt.* Leiden, Netherlands: KITLV, 1990.

[0507] Day, Clive. *The policy and administration of the Dutch in Java*. New York: Macmillan, 1904.

[0508] Dietrich, Stephan. 'Flores in the nineteenth century: aspects of Dutch colonialism on a non-profitable island', *Indonesia Circle* 31 (1983): 39–58.

[0509] Elson, R.E. *Javanese peasants and the colonial sugar industry: impact and change in an East Java residency*. Kuala Lumpur, Malaysia: OUP, 1984.

[0510] Fasseur, C. *Kultuurstelsel en koloniale baten: de Nederlandse exploitatie van Java, 1840–1860*. Leiden, Netherlands: Universitaire Pers Leiden, 1975.

[0511] Geertz, Clifford. *Negara: the theatre state in nineteenth century Bali*. Princeton, NJ: Princeton Univ. Press, 1980.

[0512] Goor, J. van, ed. *Imperialisme in de marge: de afronding van Nederlands-Indië*. Utrecht, Netherlands: HES, 1986.

[0513] Graves, Elizabeth E. *The Minangkabau response to Dutch colonial rule in the nineteenth century*. Ithaca, NY: Cornell Modern Indonesia Project, 1981.

[0514] Haan, F. de. *Oud Batavia: gedenkboek uitgegeven naar aanleiding van het driehonderd jarig bestaan van der stad in 1919*. 2 vols. Batavia, Netherlands: G. Kolff, 1922–23.

[0515] Heidhues, Mary Somers. *Bangka tin and Mentok pepper: Chinese settlement on an Indonesian island*. Singapore: ISEAS, 1991.

[0516] Houben, V.J.H. 'The position of the Mangkunegara within the partitioned political structure of Central Java', in C.D. Grijns and S.O. Robson, eds. *Cultural context and textual interpretation*. Dordrecht, Netherlands: Foris, 1986.

[0517] Irwin, Graham. *Nineteenth century Borneo: a study in diplomatic rivalry*. Singapore: Donald Moore, 1967.

[0518] Jackson, J.C. *The Chinese in the West Borneo goldfields: a study in cultural geography*. Hull, England: University of Hull, 1970.

[0519] Kuntowijoyo. 'Social change in an agrarian society: Madura 1850–1940', PhD thesis, Columbia Univ., 1980.

[0520] Lewis, Dianne. 'The last Malay Raja Muda of Johor', *JSEAS* 13 no 2 (1982): 221–235.

[0521] Lindblad, J. Thomas. *Between Dayak and Dutch: the economic history of Southeast Kalimantan, 1880–1942*. Dordrecht, Netherlands: Foris, 1988.

[0522] Lindblad, J.Th. 'Economic aspects of the Dutch expansion in Indonesia, 1870–1914', *MAS* 23 no 1 (1989): 1–23.

[0523] Multatuli [Eduard Douwes Dekker]. *Max Havelaar: or the coffee auctions of the Dutch Trading Company*. Amherst, MA: Univ. of Massachusetts Press., 1982.

[0524] Needham, Rodney. *Sumba and the slave trade*. Clayton, Vic., Australia: Monash Univ. Centre of Southeast Asian Studies, 1983.

[0525] Niel, Robert van. 'The function of landrent under the Cultivation System in Java', *JAS* 23 (1964): 357–375.

[0526] *Papers of the Dutch-Indonesian Historical Conference*. Leiden, Netherlands and Jakarta: Bureau Indonesian Studies, 1978.

[0527] Pearn, B.R. 'Erskine Murray's fatal venture in Borneo, 1843–44', *Indonesia* 7 (1969): 21–32.

[0528] Reid, Anthony J.S. *The contest for North Sumatra: Atjeh, the Netherlands and Britain, 1858–1898*. Kuala Lumpur, Malaysia: OUP, 1969.

[0529] Resink, G.J. *Indonesia's history between the myths: essays in legal history and historical theory*. The Hague: van Hoeve, 1968.

[0530] Rietbergen, P.J.A.N. *De eerste landvoogd Pieter Both 1568–1615: gouverneur-generaal van Nederlands-Indië (1609–1615)*. Zutphen, Netherlands: Walburg, 1987.

[0531] Rush, James R. 'Social control and influence in nineteenth century Indonesia: opium farms and the Chinese of Java', *Indonesia* 35 (1983): 53–64.

[0532] Sartono Kartodirdjo. *The peasants' revolt of Banten in 1888, its conditions, course and sequel: a case study of social movements in Indonesia*. The Hague: Martinus Nijhoff, 1966.

[0533] Schulte Nordholt, Henk. *Bali: colonial conceptions and political changes 1700–1940: from shifting hierarchies to 'fixed order'*. Rotterdam: Erasmus Univ., Comparative Asian Studies Programme, 1986.

[0534] Schulte Nordholt, Henk. 'The Mads Lange connection: a Danish trader on Bali in the middle of the nineteenth century: broker and buffer', *Indonesia* 32 (1981): 16–47.

[0535] Somer, J.M. *De korte verklaring*. Breda, Netherlands: Corona, 1934.

[0536] Stoler, Ann Laura. *Capitalism and confrontation in Sumatra's plantation belt, 1879–1979*. New Haven, CT: Yale Univ. Press, 1985.

[0537] Sutherland, Heather. 'Power and politics in South Sulawesi, 1860–1880', *RIMA* 17 no 1–2 (1983): 161–207.

[0538] Tarling, Nicholas. *Anglo-Dutch rivalry in the Malay world 1780–1824*. Cambridge, England: Cambridge Univ. Press, 1962.

[0539] Warren, James F. *The Sulu zone 1768–1898: the dynamics of external trade, slavery and ethnicity in the transformation of a Southeast Asian maritime state*. Singapore: Singapore Univ. Press, 1981.

[0540] Watson, C.W. *Kerinci: two historical studies*. Canterbury, England: Univ. of Kent, 1984.

[0541] Woelders, M.O. *Het Sultanaat Palembang, 1811–1825*. The Hague: Nijhoff, 1975.

See also: 0147, 0148, 0162, 0331, 0584, 0605, 0690, 0694, 0702.

1900–1942

[0542] Abeyasekere, Susan, ed. *From Batavia to Jakarta: Indonesia's capital 1930s to 1980s*. Clayton, Vic., Australia: Centre of Southeast Asian Studies, Monash Univ., 1985.

[0543] Abeyasekere, Susan. *One hand clapping: Indonesian nationalists and the Dutch, 1939–1942*. Clayton, Vic., Australia: Monash Univ., Centre of Southeast Asian Studies, 1976.

[0544] Abeyasekere, Susan. 'The Soetardjo petition', *Indonesia* 15 (1973): 81–108.

[0545] Anderson, Benedict. *Imagined communities: reflections on the origins and spread of nationalism*. London: Verso, 1983.

[0546] Benda, Harry J. 'The pattern of administrative reforms in the closing years of Dutch rule in Indonesia', *JAS* 25 (1966): 589–605.

[0547] Benda, Harry J. 'Peasant movements in colonial Southeast Asia', *Asian Studies* 3 (1965): 420–434.

[0548] Bigalke, Terance W. 'A social history of Tanah Toraja: 1881–1965'. Ph.D. thesis, Univ. of Wisconsin, 1981.

[0549] Boshart, Maud. *De muiterij op de Zeven Provinciën*. Amsterdam: Bakker, 1978.

[0550] Breman, Jan. *Control of land and labour in colonial Java: a case study of agrarian crisis and reform in the region of Cirebon during the first decades of the 20th century*. Leiden, Netherlands: KITLV, 1983.

[0551] Castles, Lance. 'The political life of a Sumatran residency: Tapanuli 1915–1940'. Ph.D. thesis, Yale Univ., 1973.

[0552] Drooglever, P.J. *Vaderlandse Club: totoks en de Indische politiek*. Franeker, Netherlands: T. Wever, 1980.

[0553] Emerson, Rupert. *Malaysia: a study in direct and indirect rule*. New York: Macmillan, 1937

[0554] Furnivall, J.S. *Colonial policy and practice*. Cambridge, England: Cambridge Univ. Press, 1948.

[0555] Furnivall, J.S. *Netherlands India: a study of plural economy*. Cambridge, England: Cambridge Univ. Press, 1939.

[0556] Helsdingen, W.H. van, and H. Hoogenberk. *Mission interrupted: the Dutch in the East Indies and their work in the twentieth century*. Amsterdam: Elsevier, 1945.

[0557] Hyma, Albert. *A history of the Dutch in the Far East*. Ann Arbor, MI: Wahr, rev.ed. 1953.

[0558] *India and Indonesia from the 1920s to the 1950s: the origins of planning*. Leiden, Netherlands: Centre for the History of European Expansion, 1986.

[0559] Ingleson, John. *In search of justice: workers and unions in colonial Java, 1908–1926*. Singapore: OUP, 1986.

[0560] Ingleson, John. *Perhimpunan Indonesia and the Indonesian nationalist movement, 1923–1928*. Clayton, Vic., Australia: Monash Univ. Centre of Southeast Asian Studies, 1975.

[0561] Ingleson, John. *Road to exile: the Indonesian nationalist movement 1927–1934*. Singapore: Heinemann, 1979.

[0562] Jones, Russell. 'Earl, Logan and Indonesia', *Archipel* 6 (1973): 93–118.

[0563] Kahin, George McTurnan. *Nationalism and revolution in Indonesia*. Ithaca, NY: Cornell Univ. Press, 1952.

[0564] Kartini, R.A. *Letters of a Javanese princess*. New York: Norton, 1964.

[0565] Kat Angelino, A. de. *Colonial policy*. 2 vols. The Hague: Nijhoff, 1931.

[0566] Korver, A.P.E. *Sarekat Islam 1912–1916*. Amsterdam: Univ. of Amsterdam, 1982.

[0567] Kraan, Alfons van der. *Lombok: conquest, colonization and underdevelopment, 1870–1940*. Singapore: Heinemann, 1980.

[0568] Larson, George. *Prelude to revolution: palaces and politics in Surakarta, 1912–1942*. Leiden, Netherlands: KITLV, 1987.

[0569] Locher-Scholten, Elisabeth B. *Ethiek in fragmenten: vijf studies over koloniaal denken en doen van Nederlanders in de Indonesische archipel 1877–1942*. Utrecht, Netherlands: HES, 1981.

[0570] Loeb, Edwin M. *Sumatra: its history and people*. Kuala Lumpur, Malaysia: OUP, 1972. [Original ed. Vienna: Institut für Völkerkunde der Universität Wien, 1935].

[0571] McVey, Ruth T. *The rise of Indonesian communism*. Ithaca, NY: Cornell Univ. Press, 1965.

[0572] Mansoben, Johsz R. 'Koreri movements in Biak, 1938–1943', *Prisma: the Indonesian Indicator* 22 (1981): 67–76.

[0573] Moh. Amanoe. 'The difference between Mecca and Digul', *JSEAS* 17 no 2 (1986): 268–281.

[0574] Nagazumi, Akira. *The dawn of Indonesian nationalism: the early years of the Budi Utomo, 1908–1918*. Tokyo: Institute of Developing Economies, 1972.

[0575] Nagazumi, Akira. 'The word "Indonesia" and the growth of its political connotation', *Indonesia Circle* 17 (1978): 28–34.

[0576] Niel, Robert van. *The emergence of the modern Indonesian elite*. The Hague: van Hoeve, 1960.

[0577] Noer, Deliar. *The modernist Muslim movement in Indonesia 1900–1942*. Kuala Lumpur, Malaysia: OUP, 1973.

[0578] Oates, William A. 'The Afdeeling B: an Indonesian case study', *JSEAH* 9 no.1 (1968): 107–116.

[0579] O'Malley, William Joseph. 'Indonesia in the Great Depression: a study of East Sumatra and Jogjakarta in the 1930s'. Ph.D. dissertation, Cornell Univ., 1977.

[0580] O'Malley, William J. 'The Pakempalan Kawulo Ngajogjakarta: an official report on the Jogjakarta People's Party of the 1930s', *Indonesia* 26 (1978): 111–158.

[0581] Paget, Roger K. *Indonesia accuses! Soekarno's defence oration in the political trial of 1930*. Kuala Lumpur, Malaysia: OUP, 1975.

[0582] Pelzer, Karl J. *Planter and peasant: colonial policy and the agrarian struggle in East Sumatra, 1863–1947*. Leiden, Netherlands: KITLV, 1978.

[0583] Penders, C.L.M. *Bojonegoro, 1900–1942: a study of endemic povery in North-East Java*. Singapore: Gunung Agung, 1984.

[0584] Penders, C.L.M. *Indonesia: selected documents on colonialism and nationalism, 1830–1942*. St Lucia, Qld., Australia: Univ. of Queensland Press, 1977.

[0585] Petrus Blumberger, J.Th. *De nationalistische beweging in Nederlandsch-Indië*. Haarlem, Netherlands: Tjeenk Willink, 1931; Dordrecht, Netherlands: Foris, 1987.

[0586] Poeze, Harry. 'The PKI-Muda 1936–1942', *Kabar Seberang* 13–14 (1984): 157–176.

[0587] Poeze, Harry, ed. *Politiek-politioneele overzichten van Nederlandsch-Indië. Deel I 1927–1928*. The Hague: Martinus Nijhoff, 1982; *deel II 1929–1930*. Dordrecht, Netherlands:

Foris, 1983; *deel III 1931–34*. Dordrecht, Netherlands: Foris, 1989.

[0588] Poeze, Harry. *Tan Malaka, strijder voor Indonesië's vrijheid: levensloop van 1897 tot 1945*. Leiden, Netherlands: KITLV, 1976.

[0589] Prince, G., and H. Baudet. *The Netherlands and the Indies: the battle against the crisis in the thirties*. Groningen, Netherlands: Institute of Economic Relations, 1984.

[0590] Reeve, David. *Golkar of Indonesia: an alternative to the party system*. Singapore: OUP, 1985.

[0591] Scherer, Savitri Prastiti. 'Harmony and dissonance: early nationalist thought in Java'. MA thesis, Cornell Univ., 1975.

[0592] Shiraishi, Takashi. *An age in motion: popular radicalism in Java, 1912–1926*. Ithaca, NY: Cornell Univ. Press, 1990.

[0593] Suleiman, Satyawati. 'The last days of Batavia', *Indonesia* 28 (October 1979): 55–64.

[0594] Surjomihardjo, Abdurrachman. 'An analysis of Suwardi Surjaningrat's ideals and national revolutionary action (1913–1922)', *Madjalah Ilmu-Ilmu Sastra Indonesia* 2 no. 3 (1964): 371–406.

[0595] Suryadinata, Leo. *Peranakan Chinese politics in Java, 1917–1942*. Singapore: Singapore Univ. Press, rev. ed. 1981.

[0596] Sutherland, Heather. *The making of a bureaucratic elite: the colonial transformation of the Javanese* priyayi. Singapore: Heinemann, 1979.

[0597] Sutherland, Heather. 'Pudjangga Baru: aspects of Indonesian intellectual life in the 1930s' *Indonesia* 6 (1968): 106–127.

[0598] Tarling, Nicholas. *Piracy and politics in the Malay world*. Melbourne: Cheshire, 1963.

[0599] Teitler, G. *The Dutch colonial army in transition: the militia debate, 1900–1921*. Townsville, Qld., Australia: James Cook Univ., 1981.

[0600] Tsuchiyi, Kenji. *Democracy and leadership: the rise of the Taman Siswa movement in Indonesia*. Honolulu: Univ. of Hawaii Press, 1988.

[0601] Vandenbosch, Amry. *The Dutch East Indies: its government, problems and politics*. Berkeley & Los Angeles: Univ. of California Press, 3d ed. 1942.

[0602] Veur, Paul W. van der. 'Cultural aspects of the Eurasian community in Indonesian colonial society', *Indonesia* 6 (1968): 38–53.

[0603] Williams, Michael C. *Sickle and crescent: the Communist revolt of 1926 in Banten*. Ithaca, NY: Cornell Modern Indonesia Project, 1982.

[0604] Wilson, Greta O. *Regents, reformers, and revolutionaries: Indonesian voices of colonial days: selected historical readings 1899–1949*. Honolulu: Univ. of Hawaii Press, 1978.

[0605] Zwitzer, H.L., and C.A. Heshusius. *Het KNIL, 1830–1950: een terugblik*. The Hague: Staatsuitgeverij, 1977.

See also: 0006, 0334, 0336, 0611, 0695, 0703, 0705, 0719.

World War II

[0606] Anderson, Benedict R. *Some aspects of Indonesian politics under the Japanese occupation, 1944–1945*. Ithaca, NY: Cornell Modern Indonesia Project, 1961.

[0607] Aziz, M.A. *Japan's colonialism and Indonesia*. The Hague: Nijhoff, 1955.

[0608] Benda, Harry J. *The crescent and the rising sun: Indonesian Islam under the Japanese occupation, 1942–1945*. The Hague: van Hoeve, 1958.

[0609] Benda, Harry J., *et al. Japanese military administration in Indonesia: selected documents*. New Haven, CT: Yale Univ., 1965.

[0610] Elsbree, Willard H. *Japan's role in Southeast Asian nationalist movements*. Cambridge, MA: Harvard Univ. Press, 1953.

[0611] Friend, Theodore. *The blue-eyed enemy: Japan against the West in Java and Luzon, 1942–1945*. Princeton, NJ: Princeton Univ. Press, 1988.

[0612] Gandasubrata, R.A.A.S.M. *An account of the Japanese occupation of Banjumas residency, Java, March 1942 to August 1945*. Ithaca, NY: Cornell Univ. Southeast Asia Program, 1953.

[0613] Hatta, Mohammad. *The Putera reports: problems in Indonesian-Japanese war-time cooperation*. Ithaca, NY: Cornell Modern Indonesia Project, 1971.

[0614] Jong, L. de. *Het Koninkrijk der Nederlanden in de Tweede Wereld Oorlog, deel 11: Nederlands Indië*. The Hague: Staatsuitgeverij, 1984.

[0615] Kanahele, George Sanford. 'The Japanese occupation of Indonesia: prelude to independence'. Ph.D. dissertation, Cornell Univ., 1967.

[0616] *The Kenpeitai in Java and Sumatra,* translated by Barbara Gifford Shimer and Guy Hobbs. Ithaca, NY: Cornell Modern Indonesia Project, 1986.

[0617] Kurasawa, Aiko. 'Mobilization and control: a study of social change in rural Java, 1942–1945'. Ph.D. dissertation, Cornell Univ., 1988.

[0618] Lucas, Anton., ed. *Local opposition and underground resistance to the Japanese in Java 1942–1945*. Clayton, Vic., Australia: Monash Univ., Centre of Southeast Asian Studies, 1986.

[0619] McCoy, Alfred W. *Southeast Asia under Japanese occupation*. New Haven, CT: Yale Univ. Southeast Asia Studies, 1980.

[0620] Nishijima, Shigetada, *et al.*, eds. *Japanese military administration in Indonesia*. Washington DC: Joint Publications Research Service, 1963.

[0621] Nortier, J.J. *Acties in de archipel: de intelligence-operaties van NEFIS-III in de Pacific-oorlog*. Franeker, Netherlands: Wever, 1985.

[0622] Nugroho Notosusanto. *The PETA army during the Japanese occupation of Indonesia*. Tokyo: Waseda Univ. Press, 1979.

[0623] Oosten, F.C. van. *The battle of the Java Sea*. Annapolis, MD: Naval Institute Press, 1976.

[0624] Reid, Anthony, and Oki Akira, eds. *The Japanese experience in Indonesia: selected memoirs of 1942–1945*. Athens, OH: Ohio Univ., 1986.

[0625] Remmelink, W.G.J. 'The emergence of the new situation: the Japanese army on Java after the surrender', *Kabar Seberang* 4 (July 1978): 57–74.

[0626] Salim, Leon. *Prisoners at Kota Cane*. Ithaca, NY: Cornell Modern Indonesia Project, 1986.

See also: 0563, 0628, 0685, 0696, 0704, 0705.

1945–1966

[0627] Anderson, Ben. 'How did the generals die?' *Indonesia* 43 (1987): 109–134.

[0628] Anderson, Benedict R.O'G. *Java in a time of revolution: occupation and resistance, 1944–1946*. Ithaca, NY: Cornell Univ. Press, 1972.

[0629] Anderson, Benedict R., and Ruth T. McVey. *A preliminary analysis of the October 1, 1965, coup in Indonesia*. Ithaca, NY: Cornell Modern Indonesia Project, 1971.

[0630] Anderson, David Charles. 'The military aspects of the Madiun affair', *Indonesia* 21 (1976): 1–64.

[0631] Crouch, Harold. 'Another look at the Indonesian coup', *Indonesia* 15 (1973): 1–20.

[0632] Dijk, C. van. *Rebellion under the banner of Islam: the Darul Islam in Indonesia*. The Hague: Martinus Nijhoff, 1981.

[0633] Federspiel, Howard M. 'The military and Islam in Sukarno's Indonesia', *Pacific Affairs* 46 no 3 (1973): 407–420.

[0634] Feith, Herbert. *The decline of constitutional democracy in Indonesia*. Ithaca, NY: Cornell Univ. Press, 1970.

[0635] Feith, Herbert. 'The dynamics of Guided Democracy', in McVey, *Indonesia* [0369].

[0636] Frederick, William H. *Visions and heat: the making of the Indonesian revolution*. Athens, OH: Ohio Univ. Press, 1988.

[0637] Ghoshal, Baladas. *Indonesian politics, 1955–59: the emergence of Guided Democracy*. Calcutta: K.P. Bagchi, 1982.

[0638] Hanna, Willard A. *Bung Karno's Indonesia*. New York: AUFS, 1960.

[0639] Harvey, Barbara S. *Permesta: half a rebellion*. Ithaca, NY: Cornell Modern Indonesia Project, 1977.

[0640] Hindley, Donald. 'Alirans and the fall of the Old Order', *Indonesia* 9 (1970): 23–66.

[0641] Horikoshi, Hiroko. 'The Dar ul-Islam Movement in West Java (1948–1962): an experience in the historical process', *Indonesia* 20 (October 1975): 59–86.

[0642] Hughes, John. *Indonesian upheaval*. New York: Fawcett, 1967.

[0643] Ijzereef, Willem. *De Zuid-Celebes Affaire*. Dieren, Netherlands: Bataafsche Leeuw, 1984.

[0644] Jay, Robert R. *Religion and politics in rural central Java*. New Haven, CT: Yale Univ. Southeast Asian Studies, 1963.

[0645] Kahin, Audrey R., ed. *Regional dynamics of the Indonesian Revolution: unity from diversity*. Honolulu: Univ. of Hawaii Press, 1985.

[0646] Karni, R.S. *The devious dalang: Sukarno and the so-called Untung-putsch*. The Hague: Interdoc, 1974.

[0647] Lev, Daniel S. *The transition to Guided Democracy: Indonesian politics, 1957–1959*. Ithaca, NY: Cornell Modern Indonesia Project, 1966.

[0648] Lucas, Anton. 'Social revolution in Pemalang, Central Java, 1945', *Indonesia* 24 (1977): 87–122.

[0649] Lyon, Margo L. *Bases of conflict in rural Java*. Berkeley, CA: Univ. of California Center for South and Southeast Asian Studies, 1970.

[0650] Mackie, J.A.C. 'Indonesian politics under Guided Democracy', *Australian Outlook* 15 (1961): 260–279.

[0651] Mossman, James. *Rebels in paradise*. London: Jonathan Cape, 1961.

[0652] Nasution, A.H. *Fundamentals of Guerrilla Warfare*. London: Pall Mall, 1965.

[0653] Nugroho Notosusanto and Ismail Saleh. *The coup attempt of the 'September 30 Movement' in Indonesia*. Jakarta: Pembimbing Masa, 1968.

[0654] Pelzer, Karl J. *Planters against peasants: the agrarian struggle in East Sumatra, 1947–1958*. Leiden, Netherlands: KITLV, 1982.

[0655] Reid, Anthony J.S. *The blood of the people: revolution and the end of traditional rule in northern Sumatra*. Kuala Lumpur, Malaysia: OUP, 1979.

[0656] Reid, Anthony J.S. *The Indonesian national revolution, 1945–1950*. Hawthorn, Vic., Australia: Longmans, 1974.

[0657] Robinson, Kathy. 'Living in the hutan: jungle village life under the Darul Islam', *RIMA* 17 no 1–2 (1983): 208–229.

[0658] Said, H. Mohammed. 'What was the "social revolution" of 1946 in East Sumatra?', *Indonesia* 15 (1973): 145–186.

[0659] Sjamsuddin, Nazaruddin. *The Republican revolt: a study of the Acehnese rebellion*. Singapore: ISEAS, 1985.

[0660] Smail, John R.W. *Bandung in the early revolution, 1945–1946: a study in the social history of the Indonesian revolution*. Ithaca, NY: Cornell Modern Indonesia Project, 1964.

[0661] Smail, John R.W. 'The military politics of North Sumatra: December 1956-October 1957', *Indonesia* 6 (1968): 128–187.

[0662] Soerjono. 'On Musso's Return', *Indonesia* 29 (April 1980): 59–90.

[0663] Sundhaussen, Ulf. *The road to power: Indonesian military politics 1945–1967*. Kuala Lumpur, Malaysia: OUP, 1982.

[0664] Tan, T.K., ed. *Sukarno's Guided Indonesia*. Brisbane, Australia: Jacaranda Press, 1967.

[0665] Wertheim, W.F. 'Suharto and the Untung coup: the missing link', *Journal of Contemporary Asia* 1 no. 2 (1970): 50–57.

See also: 0150, 0154, 0170–0172, 0220, 0333, 0563, 0669, 0700, 0706, 0710, 0730, 0746, 0749.

1966–Present

[0666] Anderson, B.R.O'G. 'Last days of Indonesia's Suharto?' *Southeast Asia Chronicle* 63 (1978): 2–17.

[0667] Anderson, Benedict. 'Old state, new society: Indonesia's New Order in comparative historical perspective', *JAS* 42 no 3 (1983): 477–498.

[0668] Bourchier, David. *Dynamics of dissent in Indonesia: Sawito and the phantom coup*. Ithaca, NY: Cornell Modern Indonesia Project, 1984.

[0669] Crouch, Harold. *The army and politics in Indonesia*. Ithaca, NY: Cornell Univ. Press, 1978.

[0670] Crouch, Harold. 'The 15th January affair in Indonesia', *Dyason House Papers* 1 no 1 (1974): 1–5.

[0671] Emmerson, D.K. 'Understanding the New Order: bureaucratic pluralism in Indonesia', *Asian Survey* 23 no 11 (1983): 1220–1241.

[0672] Feith, Herbert. 'Political control, class formation and legitimacy in Suharto's Indonesia', *Kabar Seberang* 2 (1977): 1–11.

[0673] Feith, Herbert. 'Suharto's search for a political format', *Indonesia* 6 (1968): 88–103.

[0674] Geertz, Clifford. 'Religious change and social order in Soeharto's Indonesia', *Asia* 27 (1972): 62–84.

[0675] Jenkins, David. *Suharto and his generals: Indonesian military politics 1975–1983*. Ithaca, NY: Cornell Modern Indonesia Project, 1984.

[0676] Kroef, Justus M. van der. *Indonesia since Sukarno*. Singapore: Asia Pacific Press, 1971.

[0677] Kroef, Justus M. van der. 'Indonesia's political prisoners', *Pacific Affairs* 49 no 4 (1979): 620–638.

[0678] Kroef, Justus M. van der. ' "Petrus": Patterns of Prophylactic Murder in Indonesia', *Asian Survey* 25 no 7 (1985): 745–59.

[0679] Liddle, R. William. 'Suharto's Indonesia: personal rule and political institutions', *Pacific Affairs* 58 no 1 (1985): 68–90.

[0680] McDonald, Hamish. *Suharto's Indonesia*. Melbourne: Fontana, 1980.

[0681] May, Brian. *The Indonesian tragedy*. London: Routledge & Kegan Paul, 1978.

[0682] Mody, Nawaz B. *Indonesia under Suharto*. New Delhi: Sterling, 1987.

[0683] Mortimer, Rex, ed. *Showcase state: the illusion of Indonesia's 'accelerated modernisation'*. Sydney: Angus and Robertson, 1973.

[0684] Oey Hong Lee, ed. *Indonesia after the 1971 elections*. London: OUP, 1974.

[0685] Oey Hong Lee. *The Sukarno controversies of 1980/81*. Hull, England: Univ. of Hull, 1982.

[0686] Polomka, Peter. *Indonesia since Sukarno*. Harmondsworth, England: Penguin, 1971.

[0687] Raillon, François. *Les étudients indonésiens et l'Orde Nouveau: politique et idéologie du* Mahasiswa Indonesia

(1866–1974). Paris: Editions de la Maison des Sciences de L'Homme, 1984.

[0688] Schulte Nordholt, N.G. *State-citizen relations in Suharto's Indonesia: kawula-gusti*. Rotterdam: Erasmus Univ., Comparative Asian Studies Programme, 1987.

[0689] Watson, C.W. *State and society in Indonesia: three papers*. Canterbury, England: Univ. of Kent, Centre of South-East Asian Studies, 1987.

See also: 0213, 0226, 0278, 0280, 0691, 0698, 0889, 0890.

Biography and Autobiography

[0690] Alatas, Syed Hussein. *Thomas Stamford Raffles 1781–1826: schemer or reformer?* Sydney: Angus & Robertson, 1971.

[0691] Ali Sastroamijoyo. *Milestones on my journey*. St Lucia, Qld., Australia: Univ. of Queensland Press, 1979.

[0692] Bachtiar, Harsja. 'Raden Saleh: aristocrat, painter and scientist', *Majalah Ilmu-ilmu Sastra Indonesia* 6 no 3 (1976): 31–79.

[0693] Boxer, C.R. 'Cornelis Speelman and the growth of Dutch power in Indonesia 1666–1684', *History Today* 8 (1958): 145–154.

[0694] Collis, Maurice. *Raffles*. London: Faber, 1966.

[0695] Dahm, Bernhard. *Sukarno and the struggle for Indonesian independence*. Ithaca, NY: Cornell Univ. Press, 1969.

[0696] Goto, Kenichi. 'The life and death of Abdul Rachman (1906–1949): one aspect of Japanese Indonesian relationships', *Indonesia* 22 (1976): 57–70.

[0697] Hanafi, A.M. 'In memoriam: Adam Malik', *Indonesia* 39 (1985): 149–157.

[0698] Hanna, Willard. 'The magical-mystery syndrome in the Indonesian mentality, part V: Pak Harto—the myth, the man and the mystery', *American Universities Field Staff Report Services, Southeast Asia Series* 15 no 9 (1967): 1–19.

[0699] Hatta, Mohammad. *Memoirs*. Singapore: Gunung Agung, 1981.

[0700] Hauswedell, Peter Christian. 'Sukarno: radical or conservative?', *Indonesia* 15 (1973): 109–144.

[0701] Koch, D.M.G. *Batig slot: figuren uit het oude Indië*. Amsterdam: De Brug-Djambatan, 1960.

[0702] Kumar, Ann. *The diary of a Javanese Muslim: religion, politics and the* pesantren, *1883–1886*. Canberra: Australian National Univ., 1985.

[0703] Leclerc, Jacques. 'Underground nationalist activities and their double (Amir Syarifuddin's relationship with Indonesian communism)', *Kabar Seberang* 17 (June 1986): 72–98.

[0704] Legge, J.D. *Intellectuals and nationalism in Indonesia: a study of the following recruited by Sutan Sjahrir in occupation Jakarta*. Ithaca, NY: Cornell Univ. Modern Indonesian Project, 1988.

[0705] Legge, J.D. *Sukarno: a political biography*. Harmondsworth, England: Penguin, 1973.

[0706] Malik, Adam. *In the service of the republic*. Singapore: Gunung Agung, 1980.

[0707] Moussay, Gérard. 'Une grande figure de l'Islam indonésien: Buya Hamka', *Archipel* 32 (1986): 87–111.

[0708] Mrazek, Rudolf. 'Tan Malaka: a political personality's structure of experience', *Indonesia* 14 (1972): 1–48.

[0709] Penders, C.L.M. and Ulf Sundhaussen. *Abdul Haris Nasution: a political biography*. St Lucia, Qld., Australia: Univ. of Queensland Press, 1985.

[0710] Poeze, Harry. *Tan Malaka, strijder voor Indonesië's onafhankelijkheid: levensloop van 1897 tot 1945*. Leiden, Netherlands: KITLV, 1976.

[0711] Queljoe, David de. *Marginal man in a colonial society: Abdoel Moeis'* Salah Asuhan. Athens OH: Ohio Univ. Center for International Studies, 1974.

[0712] Roeder, O.G. *The smiling general: President Soeharto of Indonesia*. Jakarta: Gunung Agung, 1969.

[0713] Rose, Mavis. *Indonesia free: a political biography of Mohammad Hatta*. Ithaca, NY: Cornell Modern Indonesia Project, 1967.

[0714] Simatupang, T.B. *Report from Banaran: experiences during the People's War*. Ithaca, NY: Cornell Modern Indonesia Project, 1972.

[0715] Sudarnoto. 'A biography of Ki Bagus Hadikusumo: early youth and education', *Mizan* 2 no 1 (1985): 78–94.

[0716] Sukarno. *Autobiography, as told to Cindy Adams*. Indianapolis: Bobbs-Merrill, 1965.

[0717] Taylor, Jean Stewart. 'Raden Ajeng Kartini', *Signs* 1 no 3 (1976): 639–661.

[0718] Veur, Paul W. van der. 'E.F.E. Douwes Dekker: evangelist for Indonesian political nationalism', *JAS* 17 (1958): 551–566.

[0719] Veur, Paul W. van der, ed. *Towards a glorious Indonesia: reminiscences and observations of Dr. Soetomo*. Athens, OH: Ohio Univ. Center for International Studies, 1987.

See also: 0024–0033, 0433.

International Relations

[0720] Ahmat, Sharom. 'Some problems of the Rhode Island traders in Java, 1799–1836', *JSEAH* 6 no.1 (1965): 94–106.

[0721] Anak Agung Gde Agung, Ide. *Twenty years Indonesian foreign policy, 1945–1965*. The Hague: Mouton, 1973.

[0722] Andaya, Barbara Watson. 'From Rum to Tokyo: the search for anticolonial allies by the rulers of Riau, 1899–1914', *Indonesia* 24 (1977): 123–156.

[0723] Arora, B.D. *Indian-Indonesian relations, 1961–1980*. New Delhi: Asian Educational Services, 1981.

[0724] 'The Australian-Indonesian relationship: a current assessment', special issue of *Australian Outlook* 40 no.3 (Dec. 1986): 131–181.

[0725] Baudet, H., and I.J. Brugmans, eds. *Balans van beleid: terugblik op de laatste halve eeuw van Nederlandsch-Indie*. Assen, Netherlands: van Gorcum, 1961.

[0726] Bone, Robert C. *The dynamics of the Western New Guinea (Irian Barat) problem*. Ithaca, NY: Cornell Modern Indonesia Project, 1958.

[0727] Bootsma, N.A. *Buren in de koloniale tijd: de Philippijnen onder Amerikaans bewind en de Nederlandse, Indische en Indonesische reacties daarop, 1898–1942*. Dordrecht, Netherlands: Foris, 1986.

[0728] Broinowski, Alison, ed. *Understanding ASEAN*. London: Macmillan, 1982.

[0729] Buchholz, Hans. *Law of the Sea zones in the Pacific Ocean*. Singapore: ISEAS, 1987.

[0730] Bunnell, Frederick W. 'Guided Democracy foreign policy: 1960–1965', *Indonesia* 2 (1966): 37–76.

[0731] Cheah Boon Kheng. 'The Japanese occupation of Malaysia, 1941–1945: Ibrahim Yaacob and the struggle for Indonesia Raya', *Indonesia* 28 (1979): 85–121.

[0732] Chia Lin Sien and Colin MacAndrews, eds. *Southeast Asian seas: frontiers for development*. Singapore: McGraw-Hill/ISEAS, 1981.

[0733] Eldridge, Philip. *Australia and Indonesia: the politics of aid and development since 1966*. Canberra: Australian National Univ., Development Studies Centre monograph no.18, 1979.

[0734] George, Margaret. *Australia and the Indonesian revolution*. Melbourne: Melbourne Univ. Press, 1980.

[0735] Gould, James W. *Americans in Sumatra*. The Hague: Nijhoff, 1961.

[0736] *Indonesian Quarterly* 12 no 2 (1984) and 13 no 2 (1985). Special issues on Vietnam.

[0737] *Inside the triangle: Australia, Indonesia and Papua New Guinea*. Melbourne: Australian Institute of International Affairs, 1986.

[0738] 'Japanese transnational enterprises in Indonesia', *AMPO* 12 no 4 (1980): 1–71.

[0739] Jones, Howard P. *Indonesia: the possible dream*. New York: Harcourt Brace Jovanovich, 1971.

[0740] Kahin, George McT. *The Asian-African Conference, Bandung, Indonesia*. Ithaca, NY: Cornell Univ. Press, 1956.

[0741] Laarhoven, Ruurdje. *Triumph of Moro diplomacy: the Maguindanao sultanate in the 17th century*. Quezon City, Philippines: New Day Press, 1989.

[0742] Leifer, Michael. *Indonesia's foreign policy*. London: Allen & Unwin, 1983.

[0743] Lijphart, Arend. *The trauma of decolonization: the Dutch and West New Guinea*. New Haven, CT: Yale Univ. Press, 1966.

[0744] Lind, Elisabet, and Thommy Svensson. 'Early Indonesian studies in Sweden: the Linnean tradition and the emergence of ethnography before 1900', *Archipel* 33 (1987): 57–78.

[0745] Macintyre, Andrew J. 'Interpreting Indonesian foreign policy: the case of Kampuchea, 1979–1986', *Asian Survey* 27 no 5 (1987): 515–534.

[0746] Mackie, J.A.C. *Konfrontasi: the Indonesia-Malaysia dispute, 1963–1966*. Kuala Lumpur, Malaysia: OUP, 1974.

[0747] MacMahon, Robert J. *Colonialism and cold war: the United States and the struggle for Indonesian independence, 1945–49*. Ithaca, NY: Cornell Univ. Press, 1981.

[0748] McVey, Ruth T., 'Indonesian communism and China', in Tang Tsou, ed., *China in crisis, volume 2: China's policies in Asia and America's alternatives*. Chicago: Univ. of Chicago Press, 1968.

[0749] McVey, Ruth T. *The Soviet view of the Indonesian revolution*. Ithaca, NY: Cornell Modern Indonesia Project, 1957.

[0750] Meyer, Günther. 'German interests and policy in the Netherlands East Indies and Malaya, 1870–1914', in John A.

Moses and Paul M. Kennedy, eds, *Germany in the Pacific and Far East, 1870–1914*. St Lucia, Qld., Australia: Univ. of Queensland Press, 1977.

[0751] Miller, James Innes. *The spice trade of the Roman Empire, 29 B.C. to A.D. 641*. Oxford, England: Clarendon Press, 1969.

[0752] Mozingo, David. *Chinese policy toward Indonesia, 1949–1967*. Ithaca, NY: Cornell Univ. Press, 1976.

[0753] Needham, Joseph. *Science and civilisation in China* vol. 3 and vol. 4 part III. Cambridge, England: Cambridge Univ. Press, 1959, 1971.

[0754] Nishihara, Masashi. *The Japanese and Sukarno's Indonesia: Tokyo-Jakarta relations, 1951–1961*. Honolulu: Univ. of Hawaii Press, 1976.

[0755] Otterspeer, Willem, ed. *Leiden oriental connections, 1850–1940*. Leiden, Netherlands: Brill, 1989.

[0756] Poeze, Harry A. *In het land van de overheerser I: Indonesiërs in Nederland 1600–1950*. Dordrecht, Netherlands: Foris, 1986.

[0757] Posthumus, G.A. 'The Inter-Governmental Group on Indonesia', *BIES* 8 no. 2 (1972): 55–66.

[0758] Ransome, David. 'The Berkeley Mafia and the Indonesian massacres', *Ramparts* 9 no. 4 (1970): 27–29, 40–49.

[0759] Reid, Anthony. 'Sixteenth century Turkish influence in Western Indonesia', *JSEAH* 10 no 3 (1969): 395–414.

[0760] Rix, Alan G. 'The Mitsugoro project: Japanese aid policy and Indonesia', *Pacific Affairs* 52 no 1 (1979): 43–63.

[0761] Scott, Peter Dale. 'The United States and the overthrow of Sukarno, 1965–1967', *Pacific Affairs* 58 no 2 (1985): 239–264.

[0762] *Southeast Asia and the Germans*. Tübingen, Germany: Erdmann, 1977.

[0763] Taylor, Alastair M. *Indonesian independence and the United Nations*. London: Stevens, 1960.

[0764] Verin, Pierre. *The history of civilisation in North Madagascar*. Rotterdam: Balkema, 1986.

[0765] Wal, S.L. van der, ed. *Officiële bescheiden betreffende de Nederlands-Indonesische betrekkingen 1945–1950*. 16 vols. to date. The Hague: Nijhoff, 1971–1991.

[0766] Weinstein, Franklin B. *Indonesian foreign policy and the dilemma of dependence: from Sukarno to Suharto*. Ithaca, NY: Cornell Univ. Press, 1974.

[0767] Yong Mun Cheong. *H.J. van Mook and Indonesian independence: a study of his role in Dutch-Indonesian relations, 1945–48*. The Hague: Nijhoff, 1982.

[0768] Yoshihara, Kunio. *Japanese investment in Southeast Asia*. Honolulu: Univ. of Hawaii Press, 1978.

See also: 0002, 1140.

POLITICS—General

[0769] Alisjahbana, S. Takdir. *Indonesia: cultural and social revolution*. Kuala Lumpur: Oxford Univ. Press, 1966.

[0770] Anderson, Benedict, and Audrey Kahin, eds. *Interpreting Indonesian politics: thirteen contributions to the debate, 1964–1981*. Ithaca, NY: Cornell Modern Indonesia Project, 1982.

[0771] Anderson, Benedict R. O'G. 'The languages of Indonesian politics', *Indonesia* 1 (1966): 89–116.

[0772] Anderson, Benedict R.O'G. *Mythology and the tolerance of the Javanese*. Ithaca, NY: Cornell Modern Indonesia Project, 1965.

[0773] Anderson, Benedict R. O'G. 'Notes on contemporary Indonesian political communication', *Indonesia* 16 (1973): 39–80.

[0774] Anderson, Benedict R.O'G. *et al. Religion and social ethos in Indonesia*. Clayton, Vic., Australia: Monash Univ., 1977.

[0775] Crouch, Harold. 'Patrimonialism and military rule in Indonesia', *World Politics* 31 no 4 (1979): 571–587.

[0776] Dick, Howard. 'The rise of a middle class and the changing concept of equity in Indonesia: an interpretation', *Indonesia* 39 (1985): 71–92.

[0777] Eldridge, Philip. 'The political role of community action groups in India and Indonesia: in search of a general theory', *Alternatives: a journal of social policy* 10 no.3 (1984/85): 401–434.

[0778] Emmerson, Donald K. *Indonesia's elite: political culture and cultural politics*. Ithaca, NY: Cornell Univ. Press, 1976.

[0779] Girling, J.L.S. *The bureaucratic polity in modernizing societies*. Singapore: ISEAS, 1981.

[0780] Holt, Claire, ed. *Culture and politics in Indonesia*. Ithaca, NY: Cornell Univ. Press, 1972.

[0781] Jackson, Karl D., and Lucian W. Pye, eds. *Political power and communications in Indonesia*. Berkeley, CA: Univ. of California Press, 1978.

[0782] Langenberg, Michael van. 'Analysing Indonesia's New Order state: a keywords approach', *RIMA* 20 no.2 (1986): 1–47.

[0783] Liddle, R. William. *Ethnicity, party and national integration: an Indonesian case study*. New Haven, CT: Yale Univ. Southeast Asian Studies, 1970.

[0784] Liddle, R. William. 'Evolution from above: national leadership and local development in Indonesia', *JAS* 32 no 2 (1973): 287–309.

[0785] Liddle, R. William, ed. *Political participation in modern Indonesia*. New Haven, CT: Yale Univ. Southeast Asian Studies, 1973.

[0786] Longsdon, Martha Gay. "Neighborhood organization in Jakarta', *Indonesia* 18 (1974): 37–56.

[0787] Mackie, Jamie, *et al. Contemporary Indonesia: political dimensions*. Clayton, Vic., Australia: Monash Univ., 1979.

[0788] Mortimer, Rex. 'Class, social cleavage and Indonesian communism', *Indonesia* 8 (1969): 1–20.

[0789] Smith, Theodore M. 'Corruption, tradition and change', *Indonesia* 11 (1971): 21–40.

[0790] Willner, Ann Ruth. *The neotraditional accommodation to political independence: the case of Indonesia*. Princeton, NJ: Princeton Univ. Center of International Studies, 1966.

See also: 0017

Policy Issues

[0791] Chin Kin Wah, ed. *Defence spending in Southeast Asia*. Singapore: ISEAS, 1987.

[0792] Cribb, Robert. *The politics of environmental protection in Indonesia*. Clayton, Vic., Australia: Monash Univ. Centre of Southeast Asian Studies, 1988.

[0793] *The Ecologist* 16 no 2/3 (1986). Special issue on transmigration.

[0794] Hainsworth, Geoffrey B. 'Economic growth, basic needs and environment in Indonesia: the search for harmonious development', *Southeast Asian Affairs* 1985: 152–173.

[0795] Hardjono, Joan. *Transmigration in Indonesia*. Kuala Lumpur, Malaysia: OUP, 1977.

[0796] Kroef, Justus M. van der. 'Indonesian communism's cultural offensive', *Australian Outlook* 18 no 1 (1964): 40–61.

[0797] McCawley, Peter. 'Some consequences of the Pertamina crisis in Indonesia', *JSEAS* 9 no 1 (1978): 1–27.

[0798] Mortimer, Rex. *The Indonesian Communist Party and land reform*. Clayton, Vic., Australia: Monash Univ. Papers on Southeast Asia, 1972.

[0799] Otten, Mariël. *Transmigrasi, myths and realities: Indonesian resettlement policy, 1965–1985*. Copenhagen: International Workshop for Indigenous Affairs, 1986.

[0800] Palmier, Leslie. *The control of bureaucratic corruption: case studies in Asia*. New Delhi: Allied, 1985.

[0801] Quarles van Ufford, Philip, ed. *Local leadership and programme implementation in Indonesia*. Amsterdam: Free Univ. Press, 1987.

[0802] Rustam, Kardinah Supardjo. 'Grass-root development with the P.K.K.', *Prisma: the Indonesian Indicator* 40 (1986): 77–84.

[0803] Sugiarto, Aprilani. 'The Indonesian marine environment: problems and prospects for national development', *Prisma: the Indonesian Indicator* 39 (1986): 14–26.

[0804] Sundhaussen, Ulf. *Social policy aspects in defence and security planning in Indonesia, 1947–1977*. Townsville, Qld., Australia: James Cook Univ., 1980.

Government Institutions

[0805] Carey, Peter. 'The Indonesian army and the state: problems of *Dwi Fungsi* in early nineteenth century perspective', *Indonesia Circle* 26 (1981): 51–58.

[0806] Conkling, Robert. 'Power and change in an Indonesian government office', *American Ethnologist* 11 no 2 (1984): 259–274.

[0807] 'Current data on the Indonesian military elite', regularly published in *Indonesia* (Ithaca, NY).

[0808] Edman, Peter. 'The Dewan Pertimbangan Agung 1959–1966: recollections of a member', *Kabar Seberang* 17 (June 1986): 142–150.

[0809] Lev, Daniel S. 'Origins of the Indonesian advocacy', *Indonesia* 21 (1976): 135–170.

[0810] MacAndrews, Colin, ed. *Central government and local development in Indonesia*. Singapore: OUP, 1986.

[0811] MacDougall, John A. 'Patterns of military control in the Indonesian higher central bureaucracy', *Indonesia* 33 (1982): 89–121.

[0812] McVey, Ruth T. 'The post-revolutionary transformation of the Indonesian army', *Indonesia* 11 (April 1971): 131–176; 13 (April 1972): 147–182.

[0813] Noer, Deliar. *The administration of Islam in Indonesia*. Ithaca, NY: Cornell Modern Indonesia Project, 1978.

[0814] Richards, R.A. 'The kabupaten program amd administrative reform' *Indonesia* 25 (1978): 183–198.

[0815] Sullivan, John. 'Kampung and state: the role of government in the development of urban community in Yogyakarta', *Indonesia* 41 (1986): 63–88.

[0816] Tjondronegoro, Sediono M.P. *Social organization and planned development in rural Java*. Singapore: OUP, 1984.

[0817] Warwick, Donald P. 'The effectiveness of the Indonesian civil service', *Southeast Asian Journal of Social Science* 15 no 2 (1987): 40–56.

[0818] Zacharias, Johannes Daniel. 'A lurah and his dynasty: a study of village officialdom in a village in south central Java, Indonesia'. PhD thesis, Monash Univ., Australia, 1983.

Political Parties

[0819] Brackman, Arnold. *Indonesian communism: a history*. New York: Praeger, 1963.

[0820] Dake, Antonie C.A. *In the spirit of the red banteng: Indonesian communists between Moscow and Peking*. The Hague: Mouton, 1973.

[0821] Dijk, C. van. 'Survey of major political developments in Indonesia in the second half of 1978', *RIMA* 13 no 1 (1979): 116–150.

[0822] Hindley, Donald. *The Communist Party of Indonesia 1951–1963*. Berkeley, CA: Univ. of California Press, 1966.

[0823] Kroef, Justus M. van der. *The Communist Party of Indonesia*. Vancouver: Univ. of British Columbia Press, 1965.

[0824] Kroef, Justus M. van der. 'Indonesian communism since the 1965 coup', *Pacific Affairs* 43 no 1 (1970): 34–60.

[0825] McIntyre, Angus. 'Divisions and power in the Indonesian National Party, 1965–1966', *Indonesia* 13 (1972): 183–210.

[0826] Mortimer, Rex. 'Indonesia: emigre post-mortems on the PKI', *Australian Outlook* 22 (1968): 347–359.

[0827] Mortimer, Rex. *Indonesian Communism under Sukarno: ideology and politics, 1959–1965*. Ithaca, NY: Cornell Univ. Press, 1974.

[0828] Nakamura, Mitsuo. 'The radical transformation of the Nahdatul Ulama in Indonesia: a personal account of the 26th National Congress, June 1979, Semarang', *Southeast Asian Studies* 19 no. 2 (1981): 187–204.

[0829] Nishihara, Masashi. *Golkar and the Indonesian elections of 1971*. Ithaca, NY: Cornell Modern Indonesia Project, 1972.

[0830] Rocamora, Joel Elisio. *Nationalism in search of ideology: the Indonesian National Party, 1946–1965*. Quezon City, Philippines: Univ. of the Philippines, 1975.

[0831] Tichelman, F. *Socialisme in Indonesië: de Indische Sociaal Democratische Vereeniging, 1897–1917*. Dordrecht, Netherlands: Foris, 1985.

[0832] Walkin, Jacob. 'The Muslim-Communist confrontation in East Java, 1964–1965', *Orbis* 13 no 3 (1969): 822–847.

[0833] Ward, K.E. *The foundation of the Partai Muslimin Indonesia*. Ithaca, NY: Cornell Modern Indonesia Project, 1970.

[0834] Webb, R.A.F. *Indonesian Christians and their political parties, 1923–1966: the role of Partai Kristen Indonesia and Partai Katolik*. Townsville, Qld., Australia: James Cook Univ., 1978.

Elections

[0835] Crouch, Harold. 'The army, the parties and the elections', *Indonesia* 11 (1971): 177–192.

[0836] Feith, Herbert. *The Indonesian elections of 1955*. Ithaca, NY: Cornell Univ. Modern Indonesia Project, 1957.

[0837] Liddle, R. William. 'The 1971 Indonesian elections: a view from the village', *Asia* 27 (1972): 4–18.

[0838] Pemberton, John. 'Notes on the 1982 general election in Solo', *Indonesia* 41 (1986): 1–22.

[0839] Suryadinata, Leo. *Political parties and the 1982 general election in Indonesia*. Singapore: ISEAS, 1982.

[0840] Ward, Ken. *The 1971 election in Indonesia: an East Java case study*. Clayton, Vic., Australia: Monash Univ. Centre of Southeast Asian Studies, 1974.

[0841] Wessing, Robert. 'Electing a *lurah* in West Java, Indonesia: stability and change', *Ethnology* 26 no 3 (1987): 165–178.

Political Thought

[0842] Bowen, John R. 'On the political construction of tradition: *gotong royong* in Indonesia', *JAS* 45 no 3 (1986): 545–561.

[0843] Cribb, Robert. 'The Indonesian Marxist tradition', in Colin Mackerras and Nick Knight, eds. *Marxism in Asia*. London: Croom Helm, 1985.

[0844] Gunn, Geoffrey C. 'Ideology and the concept of government in the Indonesian New Order', *Asian Survey* 19 no 8 (1979): 751–769.

[0845] Hassan, Muhammad Kamal. *Muslim intellectual responses to 'New Order' modernization in Indonesia*. Kuala Lumpur: Dewan Bahasa dan Pustaka, 1982.

[0846] Heryanto, Ariel. 'The development of "development" ', *Indonesia* 46 (1988): 1–24.

[0847] Legge, J.D. 'Daulat Ra'jat and the ideas of the Pendidikan Nasional Indonesia', *Indonesia* 32 (1981): 151–169.

[0848] McVey, Ruth T. 'The *wayang* controversy in Indonesian communism', in Mark Hobart and Robert H. Taylor, eds., *Context, meaning and power in Southeast Asia*. Ithaca, NY: Cornell Univ. Southeast Asia Program, 1986.

[0849] Mintz, Jeanne S. *Mohammed, Marx and marhaen: the roots of Indonesian socialism*. New York: Praeger, 1965.

[0850] Morfit, Michael. 'Pancasila: the Indonesian state ideology according to the New Order', *Asian Survey* 21 no 8 (1981): 838–851.

[0851] Suryadinata, Leo, ed. *Political thinking of the Indonesian Chinese, 1900–1977*. Singapore: Singapore Univ. Press, 1979.

[0852] Tiro, Tengku Hasan M. di. 'Indonesian nationalism: a Western invention to contain Islam in the Dutch East Indies', in M. Ghayasuddin, ed., *The impact of nationalism on the Muslim world*. London: Open Press, 1986.

[0853] Törnquist, Olle. *Dilemmas of Third World Communism: the destruction of the PKI in Indonesia*. London: Zed, 1984.

[0854] Weatherbee, Donald E. *Ideology in Indonesia: Sukarno's Indonesian revolution*. New Haven, CT: Yale Univ. Southeast Asian Studies, 1966.

Political Writings

[0855] Aidit, D.N. *The selected works of D.N. Aidit*. Washington, DC: Joint Publications Research Service, 1959.

[0856] Akhmadi, Heri. *Breaking the chains of oppression of the Indonesian people: defense statement at his trial on charges of insulting the head of state, Bandung, June 7–10, 1979*. Ithaca, NY: Cornell Modern Indonesia Project, 1981.

[0857] Bonneff, Marcel, *et al.*, eds. *Pantjasila: trente années de débats politiques en Indonésie*. Paris: Editions de la Maison des Sciences de l'Homme, 1980.

[0858] Federspiel, Howard M., tr. 'Islam and nationalism', *Indonesia* 24 (1977): 39–85.

[0859] Feith, Herbert, and Lance Castles, eds. *Indonesian political thinking 1945–1965*. Ithaca, NY: Cornell Univ. Press, 1970.

[0860] Lubis, Mochtar. *The Indonesian dilemma*. Singapore: Graham Brash, 1983.

[0861] Madjid, Nurcholis. 'Islam in Indonesia: challenges and opportunities', *Mizan* 1 no 3 (1984): 71–85.

[0862] Murtopo, Ali. *The acceleration and modernization of 25 years' development*. Jakarta: Centre for Strategic and International Studies, 1973.

[0863] Nugroho Notosusanto. *The national struggle and the armed forces of Indonesia*. Jakarta: Centre for Armed Forces History, 1975.

[0864] Semaoen. 'An early account of the independence movement', *Indonesia* 1 (1966): 46–75.

[0865] Sjahrir, Sutan. *Our struggle*. Ithaca, NY: Cornell Modern Indonesia Project, 1968.

[0866] Sjahrir, Sutan. *Out of exile*. New York: John Day, 1949.

[0867] Soekarno. *Nationalism, Islam and Marxism*. Ithaca, NY: Cornell Modern Indonesia Project, 1970.

[0868] Sukarno. *Towards freedom and the dignity of Man*. Jakarta: Department of Foreign Affairs, 1961.

[0869] Sukarno. *Under the banner of revolution*. Vol. 1. Jakarta: Publication Committee, 1966.

Law

[0870] *Adatrechtbundels,* 45 vols, Leiden, Netherlands: KITLV, 1910–1955.

[0871] Ball, John. *Indonesian legal history 1602–1848*. Sydney: Oughtershaw, 1982.

[0872] Benda-Beckman, Keebet von, and Fons Strijbosch, eds. *Anthropology of law in the Netherlands: essays on legal pluralism*. Dordrecht, Netherlands: Foris, 1986.

[0873] Benda-Beckman, Keebet von. *The broken stairway to consensus: village justice and state courts in Minangkabau*. Dordrecht, Netherlands: Foris, 1984.

[0874] Brokx, Wouter. *Het recht tot wonen en tot reizen in Nederlandsch-Indië*. 's-Hertogenbosch, Netherlands: Teulings, 1925.

[0875] Haar, Bernard ter. *Adat law in Indonesia*. New York: Institute of Pacific Relations, 1948.

[0876] Han Bing Siong. *An outline of the recent history of Indonesian criminal law*. Leiden, Netherlands: KITLV, 1961.

[0877] Holleman, J.F. *Van Vollenhoven on Indonesian adat law: selections from* Het adatrecht van Nederlandsch-Indië. Leiden, Netherlands: KITLV, 1981.

[0878] Hooker, M.B. *Adat law in modern Indonesia*. Kuala Lumpur, Malaysia: Oxford Univ. Press, 1978.

[0879] Hooker, M.B. *Islamic law in South-East Asia*. Singapore: Oxford Univ. Press, 1984.

[0880] *Indonesia: Muslims on trial*. London: Tapol, 1987.

[0881] Katz, J.S., and Katz, R.S. 'The new Indonesian marriage laws: a mirror of political, cultural and legal systems', *American Journal of Comparative Law* 23 no 4 (1975): 653–681.

[0882] Lev, Daniel S. 'Colonial law and the genesis of the Indonesian state', *Indonesia* 40 (1985): 57–74.

[0883] Lev, Daniel S. *Islamic courts in Indonesia: a study of the political bases of legal institutions*. Berkeley, CA: Univ. of California Press, 1972.

[0884] Lev, Daniel S. 'Judicial unification in post-colonial Indonesia', *Indonesia* 16 (1973): 1–38.

[0885] Lev, Daniel S. *Legal aid in Indonesia*. Clayton, Vic., Australia: Monash Univ. Centre of Southeast Asian Studies, 1987.

[0886] Lev, Daniel S. 'The politics of judicial development in Indonesia', *Comparative Studies in Society and History* 7 (1964–65): 173–199.

[0887] May, R.J., ed. *Goons, raskols and rebels: organized non-state violence in Asia and the Pacific*. Bathurst, NSW, Australia: Crawford House Press, forthcoming.

[0888] Onghokham. 'The jago in colonial Java, ambivalent champion of the people', *Senri Ethnological Studies* 13 (1984): 327–344.

[0889] Southwood, Julie, and Patrick Flanagan. *Indonesia: law, propaganda and terror*. London: Zed, 1983.

[0890] Thoolen, Hans, ed. *Indonesia and the rule of law: twenty years of 'New Order' government*. London: Pinter, 1987.

[0891] Ward, Kenneth E. 'Upholding the rule of law: the Yap affair', *RIMA* 2 no. 1 (1968): 1–8.

See also: 0581.

Islam and Politics

[0892] Bousquet, G-H., and J. Schacht, eds & trs. *Selected works of C. Snouck Hurgronje*. Leiden, Netherlands: Brill, 1957.

[0893] Federspiel, Howard M. *Persatuan Islam: Islamic reform in twentieth century Indonesia*. Ithaca, NY: Cornell Modern Indonesia Project, 1970.

[0894] Samson, Allan M. 'Army and Islam in Indonesia', *Pacific Affairs* 44 no 4 (1972): 545–565.

[0895] Samson, Allan M. 'Islam in Indonesian politics' *Asian Survey* 8 no. 12 (1968): 1001–1017.

See also: 0577, 0633, 0641, 0644, 0845, 0849, 0852, 0858, 0861, 0867, 0880.

Regional Studies

[0896] Bell, Ian, Herb Feith and Ron Hatley. 'The West Papuan challenge to Indonesian authority in Irian Jaya: old problems, new possibilities', *Asian Survey* 26 no 5 (1986): 539–556.

[0897] Bouman, J.C. *et al. The South Moluccas: rebellious province or occupied state*. Leiden, Netherlands: Sijthoff, 1960.

[0898] Budiardjo, Carmel, and Liem Soei Liong. *The war against East Timor*. London: Zed, 1984.

[0899] Budiardjo, Carmel, and Liem Soei Liong. *West Papua: the obliteration of a people*. London: TAPOL, 3d ed. 1988.

[0900] Doorn, Jacques van, and Willem J. Hendrix. *The emergence of a dependent economy: the consequences of the opening up of West Priangan, Java, to the process of modernization*. Rotterdam: Erasmus Univ., 1983.

[0901] *Het drama van de Asmat-Papuas*. Leiden, Netherlands: INDOC, 1982.

[0902] Dunn, James. *Timor: a people betrayed*. Milton, Qld., Australia: Jacaranda, 1983.

[0903] Hill, Hal, ed. *Unity and diversity: regional development in Indonesia since 1970*. Singapore: OUP, 1989.

[0904] Hoskins, Janet. 'The headhunter as hero: local traditions and their reinterpretation in national history', *American Anthropologist* 14 no 4 (1987): 605–622.

[0905] Jolliffe, Jill. *East Timor: nationalism & colonialism*. St Lucia, Qld., Australia: Univ. of Queensland Press, 1978.

[0906] Kohen, A., and J. Taylor. *Act of genocide: Indonesia's invasion of East Timor*. London: Tapol, 1981.

[0907] Kroef, Justus M. van der. 'Indonesia, the Netherlands and the "Republic of the South Moluccas" ', *Orbis* 6 no 1 (1972): 174–210.

[0908] Lagerberg, Kees. *West Irian and Jakarta imperialism*. London: Hurst, 1979.

[0909] Legge, J.D. *Central authority and regional autonomy in Indonesia: a study of local administration 1950–1960*. Ithaca, NY: Cornell Univ. Press, 1961.

[0910] Maryanov, Gerald S. *Decentralization in Indonesia as a political problem*. Ithaca, NY: Cornell Modern Indonesia Project, 1958.

[0911] Mathews, A. *The night of Purnama*. London: Cape, 1965.

[0912] May, R.J., ed. *Between two nations: the Indonesia-Papua New Guinea border and West Papua nationalism*. Bathurst, NSW, Australia: Robert Brown, 1986.

[0913] Nicol, Bill. *Timor: the stillborn nation*. Melbourne: Visa, 1978.

[0914] Osborne, Robin. *Indonesia's secret war: the guerrilla struggle in Irian Jaya*. Sydney: Allen & Unwin, 1985.

[0915] Robinson, Geoffrey. 'State, society and political conflict in Bali, 1945–1946', *Indonesia* 45 (1988): 1–48.

[0916] Schiller, Arthur A. *The formation of federal Indonesia, 1945–1949*. The Hague: van Hoeve, 1955.

[0917] Touwen-Bouwsma, Elly. 'Madoera: het Sicilië van Java?" *Gids* 8–9 (1983): 654–663.

[0918] Vickers, Adrian. *Bali: a paradise created*. Ringwood, Vic., Australia: Penguin, 1989.

[0919] Webb, R.A.F. Paul. *Palms and the cross: socio-economic development in Nusatenggara, 1930–1975*. Townsville, Qld., Australia: James Cook Univ., 1986.

See also: 0003, 0004, 0007, 0019–0022, 0274, 0276.

Racial and Minority Issues

[0920] Coppel, Charles A. *Indonesian Chinese in crisis*. Kuala Lumpur, Malaysia: OUP, 1983.

[0921] 'Indonesia', in *Encyclopaedia Judaica* vol.8 (Jerusalem: Macmillan, 1971).

[0922] Kumar, Ann L. 'Islam, the Chinese, and Indonesian historiography—a review article', *JAS* 46 no 3 (1987): 603–616.

[0923] Kwee Tek Hoay. *The origins of the modern Chinese movement in Indonesia*. Ithaca, NY: Cornell Modern Indonesia Project, 1969.

[0924] Lombard, Denys, and Claudine Salmon. 'Islam et sinité', *Archipel* 30 (1985): 73–94.

[0925] Mackie, J.A.C., ed. *The Chinese in Indonesia*. Melbourne: Nelson, 1976.

[0926] Skinner, G. William. 'Change and persistence in Chinese overseas culture: a comparison of Thailand and Java', *Journal of the South Seas Society* 16 (1960): 86–100.

[0927] Somers, Mary F. *Peranakan Chinese politics in Indonesia*. Ithaca, NY: Cornell Modern Indonesia Project, 1961.

[0928] Suryadinata, Leo. *Peranakan Chinese politics in Java, 1917–42*. Singapore: ISEAS, 1976.

[0929] Suryadinata, Leo. *Pribumi Indonesians, the Chinese minority and China: a study of perceptions and policies*. Singapore: ISEAS, 2d ed., 1986.

[0930] Veur, Paul W. van der. 'Eurasians of Indonesia: castaways of colonialism', *Pacific Affairs* 27 (1954): 124–137.

[0931] Veur, Paul W. van der. 'Race and color in colonial society', *Indonesia* (1969): 69–79.

[0932] Vuldy, Chantal. 'La communauté arabe de Pekalongan', *Archipel* 30 (1985): 95–119.

[0933] Williams, Lea E. *Overseas Chinese nationalism: the genesis of the Pan-Chinese movement in Indonesia, 1900–1916*. Glencoe, NY: Free Press, 1960.

[0934] Willmott, Donald E. *The national status of the Chinese in Indonesia, 1900–1958*. Ithaca, NY: Cornell Modern Indonesia Project, 1961.

[0935] Willmott, Donald E. *The Chinese of Semarang: a changing minority community in Indonesia*. Ithaca, NY: Cornell Univ. Press, 1960.

See also: 0851.

SCIENCE—Biology

[0936] Backer, C.A., and R.C. Bakhuizen van den Brink. *Flora of Java* [Spermatophytes only]. 3 vols. Groningen, Netherlands: Noordhof, 1963–68.

[0937] Barlow, H.S. *An introduction to the moths of South East Asia*. Kuala Lumpur, Malaysia: Malayan Nature Society, 1982.

[0938] Burkill, I.H. *A dictionary of the economic products of the Malay Peninsula*. 2 vols. Kuala Lumpur, Malaysia: Ministry of Agriculture and Cooperatives, 1966.

[0939] Carcasson, R.H. *A field guide to the coral reef fishes of the Indian and West Pacific Oceans*. London: Collins, 1977.

[0940] Fleming, W.A. *Butterflies of West Malaysia and Singapore*. Kuala Lumpur, Malaysia: Longman, 2d ed., 1983.

[0941] Habe, Tadashige. *Shells of the western Pacific in color*. Vol. 2. Osaka, Japan: Hoikusha, 1964.

[0942] Hinton, A.G. *Shells of New Guinea and the Central Indo-Pacific*. Brisbane, Australia: Jacaranda, 1977.

[0943] Hoogerwerf, A. *Udjung Kulon: the land of the last Javan rhinoceros*. Leiden, Netherlands: Brill, 1970.

[0944] Iredale, Tom. *Birds of paradise and bower birds*. Melbourne: Georgian House, 1950.

[0945] Jones, Gwilym S., and Diana P. Jones. *A bibliography of the land mammals of Southeast Asia 1699–1969*. Honolulu: Bishop Museum, 1976.

[0946] Kira, Tetsuaki. *Shells of the western Pacific in color*. Vol.1. Osaka, Japan: Hoikusha, 1962.

[0947] MacKinnon, John. *A field guide to the birds of Java and Bali*. Yogyakarta, Indonesia: Gadjah Mada Univ. Press, 1988.

[0948] Meijer, W. *Field guide to the trees of West Malesia*. Lexington KY: Univ. of Kentucky Press, 1974.

[0949] Payne, Junaidi, Charles M. Francis and Karen Phillipps, *A field guide to the mammals of Borneo*. Kota Kinabalu, Malaysia: Sabah Society and WWF Malaysia, 1985.

[0950] Reitinger, Frank F. *Common snakes of South East Asia and Hong Kong*. Hong Kong: Heinemann, 1978.

[0951] Rooij, Nelly de. *The reptiles of the Indo-Australian archipelago*. 2 vols. Leiden, Netherlands: Brill, 1915–17.

[0952] Rubeli, Ken. *Tropical rainforest in South-east Asia*. Kuala Lumpur, Malaysia: Tropical Press, 1987.

[0953] Smythies, B.E. *The birds of Borneo*. Kota Kinabalu, Malaysia: Sabah Society and Malay Nature Society, 3d ed, 1981.

[0954] Steenis, C.G.G.J. van. *The mountain flora of Java*. Leiden, Netherlands: Brill, 1972.

[0955] Tsukada, Etsuzo, ed. *Butterflies of the South East Asian islands*. 2 vols. Tokyo: Plapac, 1982.

[0956] Weber, Max, and L.F. de Beaufort. *The fishes of the Indo-Australian archipelago*. Leiden, Netherlands: Brill, 1953.

[0957] White, C.M.N., and Murray D. Bruce. *The birds of Wallacea (Sulawesi, the Moluccas & Lesser Sunda Islands, Indonesia): an annotated checklist*. London: British Ornithologists' Union, 1986. [Includes an excellent bibliography]

[0958] Whitmore, T.C. *Palms of Malaya*. Kuala Lumpur, Malaysia: OUP, rev. ed. 1977.

See also: 0010.

Geography, Geology and Ecology

[0959] Beccari, Odoardo. *Wanderings in the great forests of Borneo*. London: Constable, 1907; Singapore: OUP, 1989.

[0960] Bemmelen, R.W. van. *The geology of Indonesia*. The Hague: Government Printing Office, 1949.

[0961] Donner, Wolf. *Land use and environment in Indonesia*. Honolulu: Univ. of Hawaii Press, 1987.

[0962] Fisher, Charles A. *South-east Asia: a social, economic and political geography*. London: Methuen, 2d ed., 1966.

[0963] Fontanel, J., and A. Chentefort. *Bioclimates of the Indonesian archipelago*. Pondicherry, India: Institut Francais de Pondicherry, 1978.

[0964] Hamilton, W. *Tectonics of the Indonesian region*. Washington, DC: U.S. Govt Printing Office, 1979.

[0965] Hardjono, J. *Indonesia: land and people*. Jakarta: Gunung Agung 1971.

[0966] MacKinnon, John, and David Attenborough. *Borneo*. (World's Wild Places Series) Amsterdam: Time-Life, 1975.

[0967] Missen, G.J. *Viewpoint on Indonesia*. Melbourne: Nelson, 1972.

[0968] Neumann von Padang, M. *Catalogue of the active volcanoes of the world, including solfatara fields, Part I: Indonesia*. Naples: International Volcanological Association, 1951.

[0969] Ormeling, F.J. *The Timor problem: a geographical interpretation of an underdeveloped island*. Groningen, Netherlands: Wolters, 1956.

[0970] Simkin, Tom, and Richard S. Fiske, eds. *Krakatau, 1883: the volcanic eruption and its effects*. Washington DC: Smithsonian Institution, 1983.

[0971] Ulack, Richard, and Gyula Pauer. *Atlas of Southeast Asia*. New York: Macmillan, 1989.

[0972] Whitmore, T.C., ed. *The biogeographical evolution of the Malay archipelago*. Oxford, England: Clarendon Press, 1987.

[0973] Whitmore, T.C. *Tropical rainforests of the Far East*. Oxford, England: Clarendon Press, 2d ed., 1984.

[0974] Whitmore, T.C., ed. *Wallace's line and plate tectonics*. Oxford, England: OUP, 1981.

[0975] Whitten, Anthony J., Muslimin Mustafa, and Gregory S. Henderson. *The ecology of Sulawesi*. Yogyakarta, Indonesia: Gadjah Mada Univ. Press, 1987.

[0976] Whitten, Anthony J., S.J. Damanik, J. Anwar, and N. Hisyam. *The ecology of Sumatra*. Yogyakarta, Indonesia: Gadjah Mada Univ. Press, 1984.

[0977] Wyrtki, K. *Physical oceanography of the Southeast Asian waters*. La Jolla, CA: Scripps Institute for Oceanography, 1961.

See also: 0075, 0792.

Public Health and Medicine

[0978] Abeyasekere, Susan. 'Public health as a nationalist issue in colonial Indonesia', in David P. Chandler and M.C. Ricklefs, eds. *Nineteenth and twentieth century Indonesia: essays in honour of Professor J.D. Legge*. Clayton, Vic., Australia: Monash Univ. 1986.

[0979] Fenner, Frank. 'Smallpox in Southeast Asia', *Crossroads* 3 no 2–3 (1988): 34–48.

[0980] Mitchell, David, ed. *Indonesian medical traditions: bringing together the old and the new*. Clayton, Vic., Australia: Monash Univ. Centre of Southeast Asian Studies, 1982.

[0981] Owen, Norman G., ed. *Death and disease in Southeast Asia: explorations in social, medical and demographic history*. Singapore: OUP, 1987.

See also: 0054.

History of Science

[0982] Bastin, J.S., and D.T. Moore, 'The geological researches of Dr. Thomas Horsfield in Indonesia 1801–1819', *Bulletin of the British Museum* 10 no.3 (1982): 75–115.

[0983] Beekman, E.M. *The poison tree: selected writings of Rumphius on the natural history of the Indies*. Amherst, MA: Univ. of Massachusetts Press, 1981.

[0984] Honig, Pieter, and Frans Verdoorn, eds. *Science and scientists in the Netherlands Indies*. New York: Board for the Netherlands Indies, Surinam and Curaçao, 1945.

[0985] Kalkman, C. 'In memoriam C.G.G.J. van Steenis (1901–1986)', *Blumea* 32 no 1 (1987): 1–37.

[0986] Koninklijke Academie van Wetenschappen. *Science in the Netherlands East Indies*. Amsterdam: De Bussy, 1929.

[0987] MacLean, J. 'Carl Ludwig Blume and the Netherlands East Indies', *Janus* 66 (1979): 15–31.

[0988] Pyenson, Lewis. 'Astronomy and imperialism: J.A.C. Oudemans, the topography of the East Indies, and the rise of the Utrecht Observatory, 1850–1900', *Historia Scientarum* 26 (1984): 39–81.

[0989] Sirks, M.J. *Indisch natuuronderzoek: een beknopte geschiedenis van de beoefening der natuurwetenschappen in de Nederlandsche koloniën*. Amsterdam: Koloniaal Instituut, 1915.

[0990] Steenis-Krusemann, M.J. van. *Malaysian plant collectors and collections, being a cyclopaedia of botanical exploration in Malaysia*. Jakarta: Noordhof, 1950. [Updated regularly in the *Flora Malesiana Bulletin*.]

[0991] The, Lian, and Paul W. van der Veur. *The Verhandelingen van het Bataviaasch Genootschap: an annotated content analysis*. Athens, OH: Ohio Univ. Center for International Studies, 1973.

SOCIETY—Anthropology

[0992] Abdullah, Taufik. 'Adat and Islam: an examination of conflict in Minangkabau', *Indonesia* 2 (1966): 1–24.

[0993] Alfian. 'The ulama in Acehnese society: a preliminary observation', *Southeast Asian Journal of Social Science* 3 no.1 (1975): 27–41.

[0994] Baal, J. van. *Dema: description and analysis of Marind-anim culture (South New Guinea)*. Leiden, Netherlands: KITLV, 1966.

[0995] *Bali: studies in life, thought, and ritual*. Leiden, Netherlands: KITLV, 2d ed. 1984.

[0996] *Bali: further studies in life, thought, and ritual*. The Hague: van Hoeve, 1969.

[0997] Barnes, R.H. *Kedang: a study of the collective thought of an eastern Indonesian people*. Oxford, England: Clarendon, 1974.

[0998] Barnes, R.H. 'Lamalerap: a whaling village in eastern Indonesia', *Indonesia* 17 (1974): 137–160.

[0999] Belo, Jane. *Trance in Bali*. New York: Columbia Univ. Press, 1960.

[1000] Benda, Harry J., and Lance Castles. 'The Samin movement', *BKI* 125 no.2 (1969): 207–231.

[1001] Birkelbach, Aubrey W. Jr.. 'The subak association', *Indonesia* 16 (1973): 153–169.

[1002] Boelaars, J.H.M.C. *Head-hunters about themselves: an ethnographic report from Irian Jaya, Indonesia*. Leiden, Netherlands: KITLV, 1981.

[1003] Boon, James A. *The anthropological romance of Bali 1597–1972: dynamic perspectives in marriage and caste, politics and religion*. Cambridge, England: Cambridge Univ. Press, 1977.

[1004] Covarrubias, Miguel. *Island of Bali*. London: Cassell, 1937.

[1005] Cruikshank, Robert B. 'Abangan, santri and priyayi: a critique', *JSEAS* 3 no 1 (1972): 39–43.

[1006] Dove, Michael R., ed. *The real and imagined role of culture in development: case studies from Indonesia*. Honolulu: Univ. of Hawaii Press, 1988.

[1007] Dove, Michael Roger. *Swidden agriculture in Indonesia: the subsistence strategies of the Kalimantan Kantu'*. Berlin: Mouton, 1985.

[1008] DuBois, Cora. *The people of Alor: a social psychological study of an east Indian island*. Minneapolis: Univ. of Minnesota Press, 1944.

[1009] Ellen, R.F. 'The centre on the periphery: Moluccan culture in an Indonesian state', *Indonesia Circle* 31 (1983): 3–15.

[1010] Fox, James J., ed. *The flow of life: essays on eastern Indonesia*. Cambridge, MA: Harvard Univ. Press, 1980.

[1011] Fox, James J. *Harvest of the palm: ecological change in eastern Indonesia*. Cambridge, MA: Harvard Univ. Press, 1977.

[1012] Fox, James J., ed. *To speak in pairs: essays on the ritual languages of eastern Indonesia*. Cambridge, England: Cambridge Univ. Press, 1988.

[1013] Geertz, Clifford. 'Deep play: notes on the Balinese cockfight', in C. Geertz, *The interpretation of cultures*. New York: Basic Books, 1973.

[1014] Geertz, Clifford. *Peddlers and princes: social change and economic modernization in two Indonesian towns*. Chicago: Univ. of Chicago Press, 1963.

[1015] Geertz, Clifford. *The religion of Java*. Chicago: Univ. of Chicago Press, 1976.

[1016] Geertz, Clifford. 'Person, time and conduct in Bali: an essay in cultural analysis', in C. Geertz, *The interpretation of cultures*. New York: Basic Books, 1973.

[1017] Geertz, Hildred. 'Indonesian cultures and communities' in Ruth T. McVey, *Indonesia* [0369].

[1018] Geertz, Hildred. *The Javanese family: a study of kinship and socialization*. Glencoe, NY: Free Press, 1961.

[1019] Geertz, Hildred. 'Latah in Java: a theoretical paradox', *Indonesia* 5 (1968): 93–104.

[1020] Gerbrands, A.A., ed. *The Asmat of New Guinea: the journal of Michael Clark Rockefeller*. New York: Museum of Primitive Art, 1967.

[1021] Hatley, Ron, ed. *Other Javas: away from the kraton*. Clayton, Vic., Australia: Monash Univ., 1984.

[1022] Hefner, Robert W. *Hindu Javanese: Tengger tradition and Islam*. Princeton, NJ: Princeton Univ. Press, 1985.

[1023] Held, G.J. *The Papuas of Waropen*. Leiden, Netherlands: KITLV, 1957.

[1024] Hicks, David. *Tetum ghosts and kin: fieldwork in an Indonesian community*. Palo Alto, CA: Mayfield, 1976.

[1025] Josselin de Jong, J.P. de, ed. *Structural anthropology in the Netherlands: a reader*. The Hague: Nijhoff, 1977.

[1026] Kahn, Joel S. *Minangkabau social formations: Indonesian peasants and the world-economy*. Cambridge, England: Cambridge Univ. Press, 1985.

[1027] Kamma, Freerk. *Koreri: messianic movements in the Biak-Numfor culture area.* Leiden, Netherlands: KITLV, 1972.

[1028] Kato, Tsuyoshi. *Matriliny and migration: evolving Minangkabau traditions in Indonesia.* Ithaca, NY: Cornell Univ. Press, 1982.

[1029] Kipp, Rita Smith, and Richard D. Kipp, eds. *Beyond Samosir: recent studies of the Batak peoples of Sumatra.* Athens, OH: Ohio Univ. Center for International Studies, 1983.

[1030] Koentjaraningrat. *Javanese culture.* Singapore: OUP, 1985.

[1031] Lansing, Stephen J. *The three worlds of Bali.* New York: Praeger, 1983.

[1032] Lee Khoon Choy. *Indonesia between myth and reality.* Singapore: Federal Publications, 1979.

[1033] Lunstrom-Burghoorn, Wil. *Minahasan civilization: a tradition of change.* Göteborg, Sweden: Acta Universitatis Gothoburgensis, 1981.

[1034] Miles, Douglas. *Cutlass and crescent moon: a case study of social and political change in outer Indonesia.* Sydney: Centre for Asian Studies, Univ. of Sydney, 1976.

[1035] Mulder, Niels. *Mysticism and everyday life in contemporary Indonesia: cultural persistence and change.* Singapore: Singapore Univ. Press, 2d ed., 1980.

[1036] Murdock, George P., ed. *Social structure on Southeast Asia.* Chicago: Quadrangle, 1966.

[1037] Nooy-Palm, Hetty. *The Sa'dan Toradja: a study of their social life and religion.* 2 vols. Leiden, Netherlands: KITLV, 1979–1986.

[1038] Palmer, Leslie H. *Social status and power in Java*. London: Athlone, 1960.

[1039] Peacock, James L. 'The third stream: Weber, Parsons, Geertz', *Journal of the Anthropological Society of Oxford* 12 (1981): 122–129.

[1040] Quinn, George. 'The Javanese science of burglary', *RIMA* 9 no.1 (1975): 33–54.

[1041] Schiel, Tilman. *Processes of civilisation and paganisation: the 'traditional' society of Java as a result of colonial 'modernisation'*. Bielefeld, Germany: Univ. of Bielefeld, 1985.

[1042] Schulte Nordholt, H.G. *The political system of the Atoni of Timor*. Leiden, Netherlands: KITLV, 1971.

[1043] Siegel, James T. *The rope of God*. Berkeley, CA: Univ. of California Press, 1969.

[1044] Shiraishi, Saya. 'Silakan masuk. Silakan duduk: reflections in a sitting room in Java', *Indonesia* 41 (1986): 86–130.

[1045] Singarimbun, Masri. *Kinship, descent and alliance among the Karo Batak*. Berkeley, CA: Univ. of California Press, 1975.

[1046] Skinner, G.William, ed. *Local, ethnic and national loyalties in village Indonesia: a symposium*. New Haven, CT: Yale Univ., Southeast Asia Studies, 1959.

[1047] Snouck Hurgronje, C. *The Acehnese*. 2 vols. Leiden, Netherlands: Brill, 1906.

[1048] Sopher, David E. *The sea nomads*. Singapore: National Museum, 1965.

[1049] Suzuki, Peter. *The religious system and culture of Nias, Indonesia*. The Hague: Excelsior, 1959.

[1050] Thomas, Lynn L., and Franz von Benda-Beckmann, eds. *Change and continuity in Minangkabau: local, regional and historical perspecives on West Sumatra*. Athens, OH: Ohio Univ. Center for International Studies, 1985.

[1051] Touwen-Bousma, C. *Staat, Islam en locale leiders in West Madura, Indonesië*. Kampen, Netherlands: Mondiss, 1988.

[1052] Traube, Elizabeth G. *Cosmology and social life: ritual exchange among the Mambai of East Timor*. Chicago: Univ. of Chicago Press, 1986.

[1053] Verheijen, Jilis A.J. *Komodo: het eiland, het volk en de taal*. Leiden, Netherlands: KITLV, 1975.

[1054] Vredenbregt, Jacob. 'Baweanese', in Richard V. Weekes, ed., *Muslim peoples: a world ethnographic survey*. Westport, CT: Greenwood Press, 2d ed. 1984.

[1055] Waal Malefijt, Annemarie de. *The Javanese of Surinam: segment of a plural society*. Assen, Netherlands: van Gorcum, 1963.

[1056] Wertheim, W.F. *East-West parallels: sociological approaches to modern Asia*. The Hague: van Hoeve, 1964.

[1057] Wessing, Robert. *The soul of ambiguity: the tiger in Southeast Asia*. DeKalb, IL: Northern Illinois Univ., 1986.

[1058] Wouden, F.A.E. van. *Types of social structure in Eastern Indonesia*. Leiden, Netherlands: KITLV, 1968.

[1059] Zerner, Charles. 'Signs of the spirits, signature of the earth: iron forging in Tana Toraja', *Indonesia* 31 (1981): 89–112.

[1060] Zurbuchen, Mary Sabina. *The language of Balinese shadow theater*. Princeton, NJ: Princeton Univ. Press, 1987.

See also: 0014, 0015.

Education

[1061] Abdullah, Taufik. *Schools and politics: the Kaum Muda movements in West Sumatra, 1927–1933*. Ithaca NY: Cornell Univ. Modern Indonesia Project, 1971.

[1062] Hutagaol, Said. 'The development of higher education in Indonesia, 1920–1979'. Ph.D. thesis, Univ. of Pittsburgh, 1985.

[1063] Jones, Gavin W. 'Religion and education in Indonesia', *Indonesia* 22 (1976): 19–56.

[1064] Kartini, R.A. 'Educate the Javanese' (tr. and ed. Jean Taylor), *Indonesia* 17 (1974): 83–98.

[1065] Kroeskamp, H. *Early schoolmasters in a developing country: a history of experiments in 19th century Indonesia*. Assen, Netherlands: van Gorcum, 1974.

[1066] Lee Kam Hing. 'The Taman Siswa in post-war Indonesia', *Indonesia* 25 (1978): 41–59.

[1067] McVey, Ruth T. 'Taman Siswa and the Indonesian national awakening', *Indonesia* 4 (1967): 128–149.

[1068] Orr, Kenneth, M.M. Billach, and Budi Lazarusli. 'Education for this life or for the life to come: observations on the Javanese village madrasah', *Indonesia* 23 (1977): 129–156.

[1069] Raharjo, M. Dawam. 'The life of *santri* youth: a view from the pesantren window at Pabelan', *Sojourn* 1 no.1 (1986): 32–56.

[1070] Suryadinata, Leo. 'Indonesian Chinese education: past and present', *Indonesia* 14 (1972): 49–72.

[1071] Taylor, Jean. 'Education, colonialism, and feminism: an Indonesian case study', in Philip G. Altbach and Gail P.

Kelly, eds. *Education and the colonial experience*. New Brunswick, NJ: Transaction Books, 1984.

[1072] Tsuchiya, Kenji. *Democracy and leadership: the rise of the Taman Siswa movement in Indonesia*. Honolulu: Univ. of Hawaii Press, 1987.

[1073] Veur, Paul W. van der. *Education and social change in colonial Indonesia*. Athens, OH: Ohio Univ. Center for International Studies, 1969.

[1074] Wal, S.L. van der. *Some information on education in Indonesia up to 1942*. The Hague: NUFFIC, 1961.

[1075] Ward, Kenneth E. 'Tertiary education in Indonesia: some aspects and problems', *RIMA* 1 no 3 (1967): 1–14.

[1076] Watson, C.W. 'Higher education in Indonesia', *Indonesia Circle* 41 (Nov. 1986): 39–44.

Women

[1077] Boomgaard, Peter. 'Female labour and population growth on 19th century Java', *RIMA* 15 no 2 (1981): 1–31.

[1078] Brown, Colin. 'Sukarno on the role of women in the nationalist movement', *RIMA* 15 no 1 (1981): 68–92.

[1079] Doran, Christine. 'Women and Indonesian nationalism', *Kabar Seberang* 17 (June 1986): 20–30.

[1080] Ingleson, John. 'Prostitution in colonial Java', in David P. Chandler and M.C. Ricklefs, eds. *Nineteenth and twentieth century Indonesia: essays in honour of Professor J.D. Legge*. Clayton, Vic., Australia: Monash Univ. 1986.

[1081] Jones, Gavin W., ed. *Women in the urban and industrial workforce: Southeast and East Asia*. Canberra: Australian National Univ., 1984.

[1082] Kraan, Alfons van der. 'Human sacrifice in Bali: sources, notes and commentary', *Indonesia* 40 (1985): 89–121.

[1083] Locher-Scholten, Elsbeth, and Anke Niehof, eds. *Indonesian women in focus: past and present notions*. Dordrecht, Netherlands: Foris, 1987.

[1084] Manderson, Lenore, ed. *Women's work and women's roles: economics and everyday life in Indonesia, Malaysia and Singapore*. Canberra: National Centre for Development Studies, 1983.

[1085] Mather, Celia E. 'Industrialization in the Tangerang regency of West Java: women workers and the Islamic patriarchy', *BCAS* 15 no 2 (1983): 2–17.

[1086] Ming, Hanneke. 'Barracks-concubinage in the Indies, 1887–1920', *Indonesia* 35 (1983): 65–93.

[1087] Poedjosudarmo, Gloria. 'The position of women in Java', *Indonesia Circle* 32 (1983): 3–9.

[1088] Raharjo, Yulfita, and Valerie Hull, eds. *Women in the urban and industrial workforce: Southeast and East Asia*. Canberra: National Centre for Development Studies, 1984.

[1089] Reijs, Jeske, *et al.*, eds. *Vrouwen in de Nederlandse koloniën*. Nijmegen, Netherlands: Sun, 1986.

[1090] Vreede-de Stuers, Cora. *The Indonesian woman: struggles and achievements*. The Hague: Mouton, 1960.

[1091] Zainu'ddin, Ailsa Tomson, *et al. Kartini centenary: Indonesian women then and now*. Clayton, Vic., Australia: Monash Univ. Centre of Southeast Asian Studies, 1980.

See also: 0440, 0493.

Population

[1092] Adicondro, George. 'Transmigration in Irian Jaya: issues, targets and alternative approaches', *Prisma: the Indonesian Indicator* 41 (1986): 67–82.

[1093] Alexander, Paul. 'Labor expropriation and fertility: population growth in nineteeth century Java', in W. Penn Handwerker, ed., *Culture and reproduction: an anthropological critique of demographic transition theory*. Boulder, CO: Westview, 1986.

[1094] Arce, Wilfredo F., and Gabriel Alvarez, eds. *Population change in Southeast Asia*. Singapore: ISEAS, 1983.

[1095] Arndt, H.W. 'Transmigration: achievements, problems, prospects', *BIES* 19 no 3 (1983): 50–73.

[1096] Boomgaard, Peter. *Children of the colonial state: population growth and economic development in Java, 1795–1880*. Amsterdam: CASA, 1989.

[1097] Hugo, Graeme J., *et al. The demographic dimension in Indonesian development*. Singapore: OUP, 1987.

[1098] McNicoll, Geoffrey, and Masri Singarimbun. *Fertility decline in Indonesia: analysis and interpretation*. Yogyakarta, Indonesia: Gadjah Mada Univ. Press, 1986.

[1099] Peper, Bram. 'Population growth in Java in the 19th century: a new interpretation', *Population Studies* 24 (1970): 71–84.

[1100] Suparlan, Parsudi, and Hananto Sigit. *Culture and fertility: the case of Indonesia*. Singapore: ISEAS, 1980.

[1101] Swasono, Sri-Edi, and Masri Singarimbun, eds. *Sepuluh windhu transmigrasi di Indonesia, 1905–1985*. Jakarta: Universitas Indonesia Press, 1985.

[1102] Tan, Mely G., and Budi Soeradji. *Ethnicity and fertility in Indonesia*. Singapore: ISEAS, 1986.

[1103] White, Benjamin. 'Demand for labour and population growth in colonial Java', *Human Ecology* 1 (1973): 217–236.

[1104] Widjojo Nitisastro. *Population trends in Indonesia*. Ithaca, NY: Cornell Univ. Press, 1970.

See also: 0795, 0799.

Religion

[1105] Abdullah, Taufik, and Sharon Siddique, eds. *Islam and society in Southeast Asia*. Singapore: ISEAS, 1986.

[1106] Akkeren, Philip van. *Sri and Christ: a study of the indigenous church in East Java*. London: Lutterworth, 1970.

[1107] Anshari, E. Saifuddin. *The Jakarta Charter 1945: the struggle for an Islamic constitution in Indonesia*. Kuala Lumpur, Malaysia: Muslim Youth Movement of Malaysia, 1979.

[1108] Bartels, Dieter. 'Guarding the invisible mountain: intervillage alliances, religious syncretism and ethnicity among Ambonese Christians and Moslems in the Moluccas'. PhD thesis, Cornell Univ., 1977.

[1109] Bastiaens, J., *et al.* 'Jesus as guru: a christology in the context of Java (Indonesia)', *Exchange* 13 no 39 (1984): 33–54.

[1110] Bigalke, Terance. 'Government and mission in the Torajan world of Makale Rantepao', *Indonesia* 38 (1984): 84–112.

[1111] Boland, B.J. *The struggle of Islam in modern Indonesia*. Leiden, Netherlands: KITLV, 1971.

[1112] Brown, Iem. 'Contemporary Indonesian Buddhism and monotheism', *JSEAS* 18 no.1 (March 1987): 108–117.

[1113] Castles, Lance. 'Notes on the Islamic school at Gontor', *Indonesia* 1 (1966): 30–45.

[1114] Cooley, Frank L. *Indonesia: church and society*. New York: Friendship, 1968.

[1115] Coppel, Charles A. 'The origins of Confucianism as an organized religion in Java, 1900–1923', *JSEAS* 12 no 1 (1981): 179–195.

[1116] Dhofier, Zamakhsyari. 'The pesantren tradition: a study of the role of the kyai in the maintenance of the traditional ideology of Islam in Java'. Ph.D. thesis, Australian National Univ., 1980.

[1117] Federspiel, Howard M. 'The Muhammadijah: a study of an orthodox Islamic movement', *Indonesia* 10 (1970): 57–80.

[1118] Federspiel, Howard M. 'The political and social language of Indonesian Muslims: the case of *Al-Muslimun', Indonesia* 38 (1984): 55–73.

[1119] Geertz, Clifford. *Islam observed: religious development in Morocco and Indonesia*. Chicago: Univ. of Chicago Press, 1968.

[1120] Haire, James. *The character and theological structure of the church in Halmahera, Indonesia, 1941–1979*. Frankfurt am Main, Germany: Peter D. Lang, 1981.

[1121] Hefner, Robert W. 'Islamizing Java? Religion and politics in rural East Java', *JAS* 46 no.3 (Aug. 1987): 533–554.

[1122] Hooykaas, C. *Agama Tirtha: five studies in Hindu Balinese religion*. Amsterdam: North Holland Publishing Co, 1964.

[1123] Howell, Julia D. 'Indonesia: searching for consensus' in Carlo Calderola, ed., *Religions and societies: Asia and the Middle East*. Berlin: Mouton, 1982.

[1124] Ibrahim, Ahmad, *et al.* , compilers. *Readings on Islam in Southeast Asia*. Singapore: ISEAS, 1985.

[1125] Israeli, Raphael, and Anthony H. Johns, eds. *Islam in Asia vol. 2 : Southeast and East Asia*. Boulder, CO: Westview, 1984.

[1126] Johns, A.H. 'Sufism as a category in Indonesian literature and history', *Journal of Southeast Asian History* 2 no.2 (1961): 10–23.

[1127] Jones, Sidney. 'The contraction and expansion of the "umat" and the role of the Nahdatul Ulama', *Indonesia* 38 (1984): 1–20.

[1128] Jones, Sidney R. 'It can't happen here: a post-Khomeini look at Indonesian Islam', *Asian Survey* 20 no 3 (1980): 311–323.

[1129] Jones, Sidney. 'The Javanese *pesantren:* between elite and peasantry' in Charles F. Keyes, ed., *Reshaping local worlds: formal education and cultural change in rural Southeast Asia*. New Haven, CT: Yale Univ. Southeast Asian Studies, 1989.

[1130] Kipp, Rita Smith, and Susan Rodgers, eds. *Indonesian religions in transition*. Tucson, AZ: Univ. of Arizona Press, 1987.

[1131] Kroef, Justus M. van der. 'Javanese messianic expectations: their origin and cultural context', *Comparative Studies in Society and History* 1 no.4 (1959): 299–323.

[1132] McVey, Ruth T. 'Islam explained: review article', *Pacific Affairs* 54 no 2 (1981): 260–287.

[1133] Majid, Nurkholish. 'The progress of Islam and the reformation process', *Mizan* 2 no.1 (1985): 61–66.

[1134] Maxwell, John, ed. *The Malay-Islamic world of Sumatra: studies in politics and culture*. Clayton, Vic., Australia: Monash Univ. Centre of Southeast Asian Studies, 1982.

[1135] Mulder, Niels. 'Aliran kebatinan as an expression of the Javanese world-view', *JSEAS* 1 no 2 (1970): 105–114.

[1136] Nakamura, Mitsuo. *The crescent arises over the banyan tree: a study of the Muhammadiyah movement in a central Javanese town*. Yogyakarta, Indonesia: Gadjah Mada Univ. Press, 1983.

[1137] Nieuwenhuijze, C.A.O. van. *Aspects of Islam in post-colonial Indonesia: five essays*. The Hague: van Hoeve, 1958.

[1138] Peacock, James L. *Purifying the faith: the Muhammadiyah movement in Indonesian Islam*. Menlo Park, CA: Benjamin/Cummings, 1978.

[1139] Rahardjo, M.Dawam. 'The kyai, the pesantren, and the village: a preliminary sketch', *Prisma: the Indonesian Indicator* 1 (1975): 32–43.

[1140] Reid, Anthony J.S. 'Nineteenth century Pan-Islam in Indonesia and Malaysia', *JAS* 26 no 2 (1967): 267–283.

[1141] Ricklefs, M.C. 'Six centuries of Islamization on Java' in Nehemia Levitzion, ed., *Conversion to Islam*. New York: Holmes and Meier, 1979.

[1142] Roff, W.R. 'Islam obscured? some reflections on studies of Islam and society in Southeast Asia', *Archipel* 29 (1985): 7–34.

[1143] Saidi, Ridwan. 'The organizations of young Muslim intellectuals, past and present', *Mizan* 2 no. 1 (1985): 30–48.

[1144] Schärer, Hans. *Ngaju religion: conception of God among a South Borneo people*. The Hague: Nijhoff, 1963.

[1145] Siregar, Susan Rodgers. *Adat, Islam, and Christianity in a Batak homeland*. Athens, OH: Ohio Univ., 1981.

[1146] Stange, Paul. '"Legitimate" mysticism in Indonesia', *RIMA* 20 no 2 (1986): 76–117.

[1147] Suryadinata, Leo. 'Confucianism in Indonesia: past and present', *Southeast Asia: an International Quarterly* 3 no 3 (1974): 881–901.

[1148] Tanja, Victor Immanuel. *Himpunan Mahasiswa Islam: sejarah dan kedudukannya di tengah gerakan-gerakan Muslim pembaharu di Indonesia*. Jakarta: Sinar Harapan, 1982.

[1149] Vickers, Adrian. 'Hinduism and Islam in Indonesia: Bali and the pasisir world', *Indonesia* 44 (1987): 30–58.

[1150] Vredenbregt, Jacob. 'The haddj: some of its features and functions in Indonesia', *BKI* 118 (1962): 91–154.

[1151] Webb, R.A.F. Paul. *The church in the Sandalwood Isles*. Townsville, Qld., Australia: James Cook Univ., 1980.

See also: 0001, 0500, 0707, 0774, 0813, 0828, 0834, 0845, 0849, 0858, 0861, 0867, 0992, 0993, 1005, 1016.

Sociology

[1152] Bakker, J.I. 'Patrimonialism, involution, and the agrarian question in Java: a Weberian analysis of class relations and servile labour' in John Gledhill, Barbara Bender and M.T. Larsen, eds., *State and society*. London: Unwin Hyman, 1988.

[1153] Burger, D.H. *Structural changes in Javanese society: the supra-village sphere*. Ithaca, NY: Cornell Univ. Southeast Asia Program, 1956.

[1154] Castles, Lance. 'The ethnic profile of Djakarta', *Indonesia* 1 (April 1967): 153–204.

[1155] Charras, Muriel. *De la forêt maléfique à l'herbe divine: la transmigration en Indonésie: les Balinais à Sulawesi*. Paris: Editions de la Maison des Sciences de l'Homme, 1982.

[1156] Davis, Gloria, ed. *What is modern Indonesian culture?*. Athens, OH: Ohio Univ., 1979.

[1157] Geertz, Clifford. 'The Javanese kiyai: the changing role of a cultural broker', *Comparative Studies in Society and History* 2 (1960): 228–250.

[1158] Jellinek, Lea, Chris Manning and Gavin Jones. *The life of the poor in Indonesian cities*. Clayton, Vic., Australia: Monash Univ. Centre of Southeast Asian Studies, 1978.

[1159] Kato, Tsuyoshi. 'Different field, similar locusts: adat communities and the Village Law of 1979 in Indonesia', *Indonesia* 47 (1989): 89–114.

[1160] Koentjaraningrat, R.M. ed. *Villages in Indonesia*. Ithaca, NY: Cornell Univ. Press, 1967.

[1161] McKean, Philip F. 'Toward theoretical analysis of tourism: economic dualism and cultural involution in Bali', in Valene L. Smith ed., *Hosts and guests: the anthropology of tourism*. Philadelphia: Univ. of Pennsylvania Press, 1977: 93–107.

[1162] Milone, Pauline Dublin. *Urban areas of Indonesia*. Berkeley, CA: Univ. of California, 1966.

[1163] Nas, Peter J.M., ed. *The Indonesian city: studies in urban development and planning*. Leiden, Netherlands: KITLV, 1986.

[1164] Noronha, Raymond. 'Paradise reviewed: tourism in Bali', in Emanuel de Kadt, ed., *Tourism: passport to development?* New York: OUP, 1979.

[1165] Schefold, R., J.W. Schoorl, and J. Tennekes, eds. *Man, meaning and history*. The Hague: Nijhoff, 1980.

[1166] Selo Soemardjan. *Social changes in Jogjakarta*. Ithaca, NY: Cornell Univ. Press, 1962.

[1167] Siegel, James T. *Solo in the New Order: language and hierarchy in an Indonesian city*. Princeton, NJ: Princeton Univ. Press, 1987.

[1168] Skinner, G. William, ed. *Local, ethnic, and national loyalties in village Indonesia*. New Haven, CT: Yale Univ. Southeast Asia Studies, 1959.

[1169] Spores, John C. *Running amok: an historical inquiry*. Athens, OH: Swallow Press, 1988.

[1170] Suparlan, Parsudi. 'The gelandangan of Jakarta: politics among the poorest people in the capital of Indonesia', *Indonesia* 18 (October 1974): 41–53.

[1171] Vuldy, Chantal. *Pekalongan: batik et Islam dans une ville du nord de Java*. Paris: Archipel, 1988.

[1172] Yeung, C.M., and C.P. Lo, eds. *Changing Southeast Asian cities*. Singapore: OUP, 1976.

JOURNALS

Archipel, Bureau 732, EHESS, 54 Bd Raspail, 75270 Paris, France.

ASEAN Economic Bulletin, Institute of Southeast Asian Studies, Heng Mui Keng Terrace, Pasir Panjang, Singapore 0511.

Asian Music. Society for Asian Music, Hagop Kevorkian Center, New York Univ., 50 Washington Sq. South, New York, NY 10012, United States.

Asian Perspectives (archeology): Univ. of Hawaii Press, 2840 Kolowalu St, Honolulu HI 96822, United States.

Asian Survey, Univ. of California Press, Berkeley, CA 94720, USA

Asiaweek, 22 Westlands Road, Hong Kong.

Bijdragen tot de Taal-, Land- en Volkenkunde (Contributions to Linguistics, Geography and Anthropology): major anthropological journal, many articles in English, KITLV, Postbus 9515, 2300 RA Leiden, Netherlands.

Borneo Research Bulletin, Department of Anthropology, College of William and Mary, Williamsburg, VA 23185, USA.

Bulletin of Indonesian Economic Studies, Research School of Pacific Studies, Australian National Univ., GPO Box 4 Canberra Act 2601, Australia.

Contemporary Southeast Asia, Institute of Southeast Asian Studies, Heng Mui Keng Terrace, Pasir Panjang, Singapore 0511.

Crossroads: an interdisciplinary journal of Southeast Asian studies, Center for Southeast Asian Studies, Northern Illinois Univ., DeKalb, IL 60115, USA.

Editor, Kotak Pos 2864, Jakarta 10001, Indonesia.

Ekonomi dan Keuangan Indonesia, Lembaga Penyelidikan Ekonomi dan Masyarakat, Fakultas Ekonomi, Universitas Indonesia, Kotak Pos 295, Jakarta 10001, Indonesia.

Environesia, WALHI—the Indonesian Environmental Forum, Jl Penjernihan 1, Kompleks Keuangan no 15, Pejompongan, Jakarta 10210, Indonesia

Far Eastern Economic Review, GPO Box 160, Hong Kong.

Flora Malesiana Bulletin, Rijksherbarium, Postbus 9514, 2300 RA Leiden, Netherlands.

Indische Letteren, c/o Reggie Baay, Praam 27, 2377 BW Oude Wetering, Netherlands.

Indonesia, Southeast Asia Program, Cornell Univ., Ithaca NY 14853, United States.

Indonesia: an analysis of economic and political trends, Economist Intelligence Unit, 40 Duke Street, London, W1A 1DW, United Kingdom.

Indonesia Circle, School of Oriental and African Studies, Univ. of London, Malet St, London WC1E 7HP, United Kingdom.

Indonesia: Feiten en Meningen, Postbus 4098, 1009 AB Amsterdam, Netherlands.

Indonesia Letter, PO Box 33477, Sheungwan, Hong Kong; PO Box 54149, Los Angeles, CA 90054, USA.

Indonesia Reports, Indonesia Mirror, 7538 Newberry Lane, Lanham-Seabrook, MD 20706, USA.

Indonesian Quarterly, CSIS, Jl Tanah Abang III/27, Jakarta Pusat, Indonesia.

Inside Indonesia, PO Box 190, Northcote, Vic. 3070, Australia.

Irian: Bulletin of Irian Jaya, PO Box 54, Jayapura, Irian Jaya, Indonesia.

Itinerario, Department of History, Univ. of Leiden, Postbus 9515, 2300 RA Leiden, Netherlands.

Jambatan, p/a Reyer Anlostraat 5A, 1054 KT Amsterdam, Netherlands.

Journal of Asian History. D-6200 Weisbaden 1, Postfach 2929. Germany. (Available in microform through University Microfilms International, 300 N. Zeeb Rd., Ann Arbor, MI 48106, USA.)

Journal of Asian Studies, AAS, 1 Lane Hall, Univ. of Michigan, Ann Arbor, MI 48109, USA.

Journal of the Malaysian Branch of the Royal Asiatic Society, 130M Jalan Thamby Abdullah, Brickfields, 50470 Kuala Lumpur, Malaysia.

Journal of Southeast Asian Studies (succeeds *Journal of Southeast Asian History*), Singapore Univ. Press, Yusof Ishak House, Kent Ridge, Singapore 0511.

Kabar Seberang, Centre for Southeast Asian Studies, James Cook Univ. of North Queensland, Townsville, Q. 4811, Australia.

Masyarakat Indonesia, Biro Pemasyarakatan IPTEK, LIPI, Widya Graha, Jl Jend. Gatot Subroto 10, Jakarta, Indonesia.

Mensenrechten in Indonesie, INDOC, Postbus 11250, 2301 EG Leiden, Netherlands.

Modern Asian Studies, Cambridge Univ. Press, Edinburgh Building, Shaftsbury Rd, Cambridge CB2 2RU, United Kingdom.

Modern Quaternary Research in Southeast Asia, A.A. Balkema, Vijverweg 8, 3062 JP, Rotterdam, The Netherlands.

Pacific Affairs, Univ. of British Columbia, Vancouver, B.C. V6T 1W5, Canada.

Prisma (Indonesian language) and *Prisma: the Indonesian Indicator* (English language): LP3ES, Jl S. Parman 81, Jakarta 11420, Indonesia.

Review of Indonesian and Malayan Affairs, Department of Indonesian and Malayan Studies, Univ. of Sydney, Sydney NSW 2006, Australia.

Sojourn, Social Issues in Southeast Asia, Institute of Southeast Asian Studies, Heng Mui Keng Terrace, Pasir Panjang, Singapore 0511.

Southeast Asian Affairs, Institute of Southeast Asian Studies, Heng Mui Keng Terrace. Pasir Panjang, Singapore 0511.

Southeast Asian Studies, Center for Southeast Asian Studies, Kyoto Univ., 46 Shimoadachi-cho, Yoshida, Sakyo-ku, Kyoto 606, Japan.

Tapol: the Indonesian human rights campaign, 111 Northwood Rd, Thornton Heath, Surrey CR4 8HW, United Kingdom.

Tempo, Kotak Pos 4223, Jakarta 10001, Indonesia.

Tenggara: the journal of Southeast Asian literature, Yayasan Penataran Ilmu, Tingkat 3, Wisma Mirama, Jl Wisma Putra, 50460 Kuala Lumpur, Malaysia.

West Papua Observer, Postbus 51251, 1007 EG Amsterdam, Netherlands.

ABOUT THE AUTHOR

ROBERT CRIBB teaches the modern history of Southeast Asia in the Department of History at the University of Queensland in Brisbane, Australia. He completed his Ph.D. at the School of Oriental and African Studies in London and has since held research fellowships at the Australian National University in Canberra and the Netherlands Institute for Advanced Study in Wassenaar. He has also taught Indonesian politics and history at Brisbane's Griffith University.

Dr. Cribb's study of the Jakarta underworld during Indonesia's War of Independence against the Dutch recently appeared as *Gangsters and Revolutionaries: the Jakarta People's Militia and the Indonesian Revolution, 1945–1949* (Allen & Unwin, 1991). He is also editor of *The Indonesian Killings of 1965–1966: Studies from Java and Bali* (Monash University, 1990) and author of *The Politics of Environmental Protection in Indonesia* (Monash University, 1988). He keeps in close touch with contemporary political developments in Indonesia and is currently researching the history of environmental protection in Indonesia.